FREDERIC HARRISON

FREDERIC HARRISON

The Vocations of a Positivist

MARTHA S. VOGELER

CLARENDON PRESS · OXFORD
1984

Oxford University Press, Walton Street, Oxford OX2 6DP

London New York Toronto
Delhi Bombay Calcutta Madras Karachi
Kuala Lumpur Singapore Hong Kong Tokyo
Nairobi Dar es Salaam Cape Town
Melbourne Auckland

and associated companies in
Beirut Berlin Ibadan Mexico City Nicosia

Oxford is a trade mark of Oxford University Press

British Library Cataloguing in Publication Data

Vogeler, Martha S.
Frederic Harrison.
1. Harrison, Frederic
I. Title
146'.4'0924 B105.P6
ISBN 0–19–824733–8

Library of Congress Cataloging in Publication Data
Vogeler, Martha S.
Frederic Harrison.
Bibliography: p.
Includes index.
1. Harrison, Frederic, 1831–1923. 2. Philosophers—
England—Biography. I. Title
B1646.H24V64 1984 192 [B] 83–25203
ISBN 0–19–824733–8

Set by South End Typographics, Pondicherry
Printed in Great Britain
at the University Press, Oxford
by David Stanford
Printer to the University

To Frances and Reginald Frederic Pitt Harrison

ACKNOWLEDGEMENTS

My intellectual debts for this biography begin at Columbia University, where Jerome H. Buckley, Jacques Barzun, and Lionel Trilling sponsored my Ph.D. dissertation on Frederic Harrison's first fifty years. A full-scale biography was possible only when two large collections of correspondence became available: letters to Harrison from contemporaries and both sides of his correspondence with John Morley, which together comprise the bulk of the Harrison Collection at the British Library of Political and Economic Science, London School of Economics; and some 1,200 letters to his wife. For the extended loan of these family papers, a free hand in using them, and years of encouragement, hospitality, and friendship, I am immensely grateful to Harrison's grandson, Reginald F. P. Harrison, and his wife Frances. Another grandson, the late R. Austin Harrison, and his wife Margaret have been generously helpful.

Others whose assistance I especially value are the late Gerald Beesly, Anthony Brundage, Paulo E. de Berrêdo Carneiro, the late Marcella Carver, the Revd Alphonse Chapeau, H. Corra, Pierre Coustillas, David Crackanthorpe, Lady Darwin, the late H. G. Dixey, Shiela Sokolov Grant, Sir William Haley, Charles S. Harmon, Mary Harmon, the late Walter E. Houghton, C. C. Kohler, Mary Lago, Jacqueline Latham, Gordon Lawrence, J. G. Links, Mary Lutyens, Priscilla Metcalf, Frank Miles, A. R. Mills, Winifred Myers, the late Emil Oberholzer, Christopher Ricks, William H. Sahud, the late J. J. Salmon, Mary Salmon, John Geoffrey Sharps, Gillian Sutherland, Charles and Rita Swallow, the late Sir Charles Tennyson, A. F. Thompson, Gillian Tindall, the late Helen Gill Viljoen, the Earl of Wemyss and March, Christie Wilbur, and C. J. Wright. The librarians of California State University, Fullerton, especially Ernest W. Toy, Jr., Nancy Hunter, and Mary Jane Bragg, know how much I owe them. My most encompassing debt is to my husband, Albert R. Vogeler.

Grants from the American Philosophical Society, the American Council of Learned Societies, and California State University, Fullerton, have helped to support my research.

I wish to express my thanks to the librarians and archivists of the following institutions and firms: Aberdeen University; Algemeen Rijksarchief, the Hague; Alpine Club; Archives de France; Balliol

College; Bath Municipal Libraries; Baylor University; Bibliothèque Historique de la ville de Paris; Bibliothèque Nationale; Bishopsgate Institute; Bodleian Library; Boston Public Library; British Library; Brown University; Bundesarchiv, Koblenz; Cambridge University Library; Carl H. Pforzheimer Library; Chicago Public Library; Christ Church College; City of Lincoln Libraries; Colby College; Clifton College; Columbia University; Co-operative Union, Holyoake House, Manchester; Cornell University; Coventry Libraries; Dickinson College; Dorset County Museum; Dr Williams's Library; Duke University; Fawcett Library; Fitzwilliam Museum; Folger Shakespeare Library; Gennadius Library, American School of Classical Studies, Athens; Greater London Record Office; Guildhall Library; Hampshire Record Office; Harvard University Library; Henry E. Huntington Library; Hertfordshire County Record Office; Honnold Library, the Claremont Colleges; Hoover Institute, Stanford University; House of Lords Record Office; Imperial College of Science and Technology; India Office Library; Indiana University; International Institute of Social History, Amsterdam; John Murray, publishers; the John Rylands Library; the Johns Hopkins University; Kings College School; Knox College; Leiden University; Library of Congress; London Library; McMaster University; Magdalen College; La Maison d'Auguste Comte, Paris; Manchester Public Libraries; Mills College; Mitchell Library, Sydney, Australia; National Army Museum; National Library of Ireland; National Library of Scotland; National Library of Wales; National Portrait Gallery; Newcastle-upon-Tyne City Libraries; New York Public Library; New York University; Oxford Union; Oxford University Press; Pierpont Morgan Library; Pusey House Library; Princeton University; Royal Historical Society; Royal Institution; Ruskin Galleries, Bembridge School; St. Paul's School; South African Public Library; St. Deiniol's Library; *The Times*, London; Trinity College, Cambridge; University of Bristol; University of California, Los Angeles; University of Edinburgh; University of Illinois at Urbana-Champaign; University of Keele; University of Leeds; University of Liverpool; University of London; University of Manchester; University of Newcastle-upon-Tyne; University of North Carolina, Chapel Hill; University of Sheffield; University of Stellenbosch; University of Strathclyde; University of Texas, Austin; University of Virginia; University of Wisconsin, Madison; Victoria and Albert Museum; Wadham College; Watts Gallery, Compton, Surrey; West Sussex Record Office; Working Men's College; Yale University; York University.

Permission to cite or quote from unpublished material has been obtained from the Hon. David Lytton-Cobbold, Jonathan G. Ouvry, Viscount Knebworth, the Society of Authors on behalf of The Estate of Bernard Shaw, the Trustees of the Hardy Collection, Dorset County Museum, and Yale University Library. To these and other holders of the copyrights of materials used in this study I am greatly indebted.

CONTENTS

LIST OF ILLUSTRATIONS

Between pp. 142–3 and 270–1

ABBREVIATIONS

AH	Austin Frederic Harrison
AO	*Alumni Oxonienses: The Members of the University of Oxford 1715–1886* (1891)
Arnold, *CPW*	*The Complete Prose Works of Matthew Arnold*, ed. R. H. Super, 11 vols. (1960–77)
Berg	Henry W. and Albert A. Berg Collection, New York Public Library
BH	Bernard Oliver Harrison
BL	British Library
BLL	The Brotherton Collection, Brotherton Library, University of Leeds
Bod	Bodleian Library, Oxford
CPL	Carl H. Pforzheimer Library
CR	*Contemporary Review*
CU	Columbia University
CUL	Cambridge University Library
DNB	*Dictionary of National Biography*
EBH	Ethel Bertha Harrison (also Ethelbertha)
ER	*English Review*
ESB	Edward Spencer Beesly
FC	Family Collection
FH	Frederic Harrison
GG	George Gissing
GH	Godfrey Denis Harrison
GL	Godfrey Lushington
HC	Harrison Collection, British Library of Political and Economic Science, London School of Economics and Political Science
HCRO	Hertfordshire County Record Office
HEH	Henry E. Huntington Library
Hirst	F. W. Hirst, ed., *Early Life and Letters of John Morley*, 2 vols. (1927)
HU	Houghton Library, Harvard University
IOL	India Office Library
JHB	John Henry Bridges
JM	John Morley
JRL	John Rylands Library
LCC	London County Council Archives

LSE   British Library of Political and Economic Science, London School of Economics and Political Science
MAC   La Maison d'Auguste Comte
Mill, *CW*   John Stuart Mill, *Collected Works of John Stuart Mill*, 27 vols. (1963–   )
NAR   *North American Review*
NC   *Nineteenth Century*
NYPL   New York Public Library
PMG   *Pall Mall Gazette*
Polity   Auguste Comte, *System of Positive Polity*, trans. J. H. Bridges, *et al.*, 4 vols. (1875–7, rpt. n.d.)
PR   *Positivist Review*
RC   Richard Congreve
RC, *EPSR*   Richard Congreve, *Essays, Political, Social, Religious*, 3 vols. (1874, 1892, and 1900)
RH   René Christopher Harrison
RHS   Royal Historical Society
RO   *Revue Occidentale*
UC   University College, London
ULL   University of London Library, Senate House
UT   University of Texas, Austin
VL   Vernon Lushington
WG   *Westminster Gazette*
WR   *Westminster Review*
WSRO   West Sussex Record Office
YUL   Yale University Library

Books by Frederic Harrison with abbreviations where used and editions cited

AMB   *Among My Books* (London: Macmillan, 1912)
                     Annals of an Old Manor House (London: Macmillan, 1893/ abridged 1899)
AM   *Autobiographic Memoirs* 2 vols. (London: Macmillan, 1911)
                     Chatham (London: Macmillan, 1905)
CB   *The Choice of Books, and other Literary Pieces* (London: Macmillan, 1886)
CL   *The Creed of a Layman: Apologia Pro Fide Mea* (New York: Macmillan, 1907)

DS	*De Senectute: More Last Words* (New York: D. Appleton, 1923)
	George Washington and other American Addresses (New York: Macmillan, 1901)
GP	*The German Peril: Forecasts 1864–1914, Realities 1915, Hopes 191–* (London: T. Fisher Unwin, 1915)
JR	*John Ruskin* (London: Macmillan, 1902)
	On Jurisprudence and the Conflict of Laws (Oxford: Clarendon Press, 1919)
MH	*The Meaning of History and other Historical Pieces* (London, Macmillan, 1894), incorporating *The Meaning of History: Two Lectures* (1862)
MT	*Memories and Thoughts: Men-Books-Cities-Art* (New York: Macmillan, 1906)
MAJ	*My Alpine Jubilee, 1851–1907* (London: Smith Elder, 1908)
NSP	*National and Social Problems* (London: Macmillan, 1908)
	Nicephorus: A Tragedy of New Rome (London: Chapman and Hall, 1906)
NV	*Novissima Verba: Last Words, 1920* (New York: Henry Holt, 1921)
OSc	*Obiter Scripta, 1918* (London: Chapman and Hall, 1919)
OC	*Oliver Cromwell* (London: Macmillan, 1888)
OS	*On Society* (London: Macmillan, 1918)
OP	*Order and Progress* (London: Longmans, 1875; rpt. Hassocks: Harvester, 1975)
PCS	*The Philosophy of Common Sense* (London: Macmillan, 1907)
PER	*The Positive Evolution of Religion: Its Moral and Social Reaction* (New York: G. P. Putnam's, 1913)
RI	*Realities and Ideals: Social, Political, Literary, and Artistic* (London: Macmillan, 1908)
SEVL	*Studies in Early Victorian Literature* (London, New York: Edward Arnold, 1895)
TRM	*Tennyson, Ruskin, Mill and other Literary Estimates* (London: Macmillan, 1899)
	Theophano: The Crusade of the Tenth Century. A Romantic Monograph (London: Chapman and Hall, 1904)
	William the Silent (London: Macmillan, 1897)

THE VOCATIONS OF
A POSITIVIST

One summer morning in Paris in 1855 a twenty-three-year-old Oxford graduate, slim, ruddy-cheeked, and energetic, wound his way up the dim staircase of an unprepossessing house on the Left Bank, number 10 Rue Monsieur-le-Prince. He was keeping an appointment for which he had come anxiously prepared with a letter of introduction from his former tutor. Admitted to a suite of modest rooms, he confronted a short, dark, intense man of genius who dreamed of reshaping the advanced thought of Europe. In the next few hours, young Frederic Harrison sat enthralled by Auguste Comte's eloquent and methodical discourse, his mind flooded with inspiration. The impact of his interview, the only personal contact with the philosopher he would ever have, lasted a long lifetime. It did not make him a Positivist, but it confirmed in his mind the authentic greatness of the author he had already been reading at Oxford and would thereafter study in the growing conviction that he offered a new intellectual and social dispensation for the Western World.

Harrison found in Comte's works not only formulations for criticizing a social order from which he had become alienated, but also principles for its regeneration. Comte called not for revolution, which would have affronted Harrison's middle-class distaste for violence, but for a programme of 'Order and Progress'. Positivism, moreover, informed Harrison's youthful scholarly interests; history, politics, law, and science were all illuminated by Comte's insights and perspectives. Explaining Comte's teachings stimulated his own natural didacticism, and defending them exercised his forensic impulses. Eventually, as a leader of Comte's English followers, he found the gratification that authority and influence can bring. Though he never entertained conventional ambitions of an intellectual of his class—a berth at the University, preferment in the Church, success at the Bar, or prominence in politics—he found comparable fulfilment in directing an organization that encompassed educational, religious, and political aims. Once committed to Positivism, he let nothing undermine his identification with it; no argument was sufficiently cogent, no ridicule sufficiently devastating, no indifference sufficiently discouraging to shake him loose. Yet he shrank from any imputation of eccentric zealotry.

When *Vanity Fair* depicted him as the Apostle of Positivism, he complained that the 'cartoon business' was 'plainly exhausted' if it seemed necessary to 'drag in ... quiet Sunday teachers'.

Any just estimate of Harrison must avoid both the cartoonist's condescension and the purposeful misrepresentation of self in Harrison's response to it. He could excite denigration, but also puzzlement, respect, admiration, and devotion. To see him in the great variety of his public controversies and causes is to recognize both the continuities and the contradictions of his life. He emerges as a quintessential Englishman of robust common sense who yet earnestly promoted the idiosyncratic philosophy of an obsessive French systematizer. Essentially secular and pragmatic in his cast of mind, he embraced Comte's Religion of Humanity, with its inverted Catholicism and rigid shibboleths. He preached Comte's system as true, universal, and inevitable, but could muster only a few hundred followers and was alienated from many fellow believers by embarrassing factionalism. Notorious as a free-thinker, iconoclast, and critic of the Established Church, he was never an atheist, frequently a church-goer, eventually a church-founder. Though a model of personal propriety, he joined the circle of George Eliot and George Henry Lewes and befriended George Gissing. An inveterate traveller and student of cultures, he was also a pertinacious Francophile, an unforgiving Germanophobe, an old-fashioned Little-Englander. Both radicals and reactionaries claimed him; he was ahead of his time and behind it in more ways and with more reasons than most others who have opposed the status quo.

The son of a wealthy London stockbroker whose oldest friend was Richard Bethell, later Lord Westbury and Chancellor of England, Harrison had the social connections, habits of study, intelligence, and energy required for success at the Bar. Instead of striving for it, he practised law in a desultory way, devoting most of his time to causes and controversies. Yet he eventually became a legal examiner and professor of jurisprudence. More important in his own judgement was his use of his knowledge of the law to further the struggle of the trade unions for legal standing. Arguing their claims in print and as a member of a Royal Commission in the 1860s established his reputation as a formidable radical polemicist. One of his earliest articles had already gained him instant notoriety in the religious world by making *Essays and Reviews* a *cause célèbre*. His reputation as a man of advanced causes and trenchant rhetoric grew rapidly after that. He became known as John Stuart Mill's associate in the campaign to prosecute Governor Eyre; as Matthew Arnold's sparring partner in the debate over Culture and its role in politics; as an intimate of John Morley's when he was making the *Fortnightly Review* the leading radical journal of the 1870s; as an apologist for the Paris Commune and ardent advocate of Parliamentary reform, Church disestablishment, local government for London, Irish Home Rule, and secular and popular education; as a prominent anti-imperialist, pro-Boer, and free trader. Yet with almost equal vehemence he allied himself with conservatives opposing women's suffrage and warning about the German menace.

What the public could only guess, but his friends had cause to know, was that Harrison had an almost preternatural vitality and a fiery temper. Away from home he usually mastered his nervous energy, though his conversation was peppered with explosions of judgement. At home he was first up and last abed; he would toss about in his chair, rub his hands in agitation, and ominously rattle a newspaper that carried an uncongenial story. To his sons he could be a martinet, but more often he was jolly, whimsical, solicitous, tamed by his own intense affections and calmed by his serene and lovely wife. Some things he could not abide—careless penmanship, tobacco smoke, blood sports. Mozart soothed him, Bach disturbed him, Wagner outraged him. He was highly organized, scrupulous about details, punctual and proper to a fault, and intolerant of those who fell below the mark. In one way, however, he was singularly restrained emotionally. He seems to have had no serious affair of the heart until, as he neared forty, he chose his first cousin, twenty years younger, as his wife. In the happiness of their long marriage, which saw the birth of four sons and a daughter, he found the emotional support that had earlier come from his parents.

For the re-creation of a life so serious in aspirations and so varied in accomplishments and associations, the notion of vocation has seemed the right interpretive principle. Like Fichte, whose essay on *The Vocation of Man* helped inspire Carlyle's doctrine of work, and through it the ethic of an age, Harrison learned early that questioning the foundations of existence yielded only frustration. He therefore decided to commit himself to social utility rather than to anxious questing for religious certainty. Comte's Positivism, which ruled out metaphysical problems, ideally suited his need to be done with introspection and to become, in his own words, a 'witness and narrator' of social ills. 'Vocation' involves this idea of a calling—work done in response to some imperative and seen under the aspect of eternity. It was, of course, a characteristically Victorian notion. Harrison's life, like Newman's, or Ruskin's, or Gladstone's, was inspired by an irrepressible urge to teach truths that could in some sense save men. If he lacked their genius, he was no less sincere or certain of his calling than they. He was fortunate that the Positivist maxim, 'Live for Others', was accompanied by the admonition to keep the realms of the spiritual and the temporal distinct. Having cast himself, as an intellectual, in the role of teacher, he was exempt from tedious day to day contact with the working class. In the Positivist community he could be sure of respectful attention, but when he carried Comte's teaching to the general public he had to minimize its more bizarre features. Yet he persevered with the toughness of the practised polemicist and the assurance of the convinced ideologue. When his early optimism about the movement's prospects faded, he proved too proud and perhaps too dependent upon the satisfactions of leadership to concede publicly any loss of confidence. Moreover, he realized that as a Positivist he had a distinguishing identity that lent interest to all his utterances.

'Vocation' has further meanings. It implies an ideal of work that allows suitable expression of talent and personality. Positivism gave Harrison's energies form, his altruism a rationale; it satisfied his need for system and kept before him a vision of an ordered, peaceful industrial society. His gradual intellectual and emotional integration of Positivism with his own proclivities and circumstances is the great fact of his first fifty years. 'Vocation' also connotes social role and status. Harrison moved with ease in society, accepting the advantages of his position, cultivating tastes appropriate to a man of substance and learning. Nothing in his family life and friendships set him apart from his class. He led a small sect, but there were many of these in his London, enough of them with leaders of his own kind to make his Positivist mission part of the broad pattern of Victorian religious life. His religious vocation was in fact far less in conflict with the values and habits of his society than might be assumed.

'Vocation' has yet another significance: a source of livelihood and therefore of security. The great work of Harrison's life produced no income, nor did he imagine that it should. His father's generosity largely maintained his comfortable way of life. But as he passed fifty he began to accept payment for his periodical writings and then his books, something he had scorned earlier because of Comte's injunction against commercial journalism. As he passed sixty he turned for new subjects to his rich memory, characterizing and assessing famous men and women he had known, among them Tennyson, Ruskin, Mill, Arnold, Spencer, George Eliot, Francis Newman, and Leslie Stephen. As he passed seventy, having already published historical studies, he developed a passion for Byzantine research and threw himself into the political controversies of the Edwardian years with undiminished vigour. He had long since become a professional writer. His eighties saw the publication of his autobiography and a flood of articles prompted by the World War and its aftermath. His heartiness and healthiness became legendary in his old age. He was correcting the proofs of his thirtieth book on the eve of his death in 1923, at the age of ninety-one.

One of the features of the Religion of Humanity Harrison most valued was the doctrine of Subjective Immortality, the survival of the worthy dead in 'minds made better by their presence', as George Eliot expressed it in her Positivist poem, 'The Choir Invisible'. It is deeply ironic that Harrison, so eloquent a preacher of Subjective Immortality, has not been assured of his own. His career in its fulness is now largely unremembered. He is perhaps the most important Victorian personality lacking a modern critical biography. Reasons for his past neglect are not hard to find. The multitude of his activities and associations obscured his image. He outlived the issues and hopes that motivated his public life, outlived his reputation, outlived the contemporaries who might have memorialized him, and when he died the reaction to earnest Victorianism was in full swing. He produced no masterpiece and left no disciples. He seemed a prophet of what had become, even in his own lifetime, an irrelevant philosophy and a failed religion. These circumstances give the story of his labours an undeniable pathos. But they no longer justify neglect; indeed, they invite inquiry. The modern scholar is challenged to explain the paradoxes and find the connections in his densely textured career. The re-creation of his life in its entirety, which has only now become possible, reveals him as one of the most ubiquitous, lively, and sympathetic personalities of the Victorian and Edwardian scene; and it allows the movements of thought, the public issues, and the great men and women of his era to be viewed in new perspectives.

1

The Early Years

1831–1855

A LONDON CHILD

Frederic Harrison's earliest memories were of rural scenes near Muswell when it was a quiet village on the grassy slopes north of London.[1] But just as early he was aware of the great metropolis. From the lawn in front of the family cottage he could see the distant smoke, the steeples, and the dome of St. Paul's—the mysterious city world to which his father travelled daily by four-horse coach. London was to be his home for sixty years, but he would never fail to spend several months of every year in the country, whether in England or on the Continent. And to these sojourns he would give credit for his prolonged good health.

Harrison's ruddy cheeks, erect carriage, and vigorous movements, his downright manner and simple tastes in food, suggested that he was more akin to his yeoman forebears than he ever actually felt. The Harrisons traced their lineage back to Leicestershire farmers as early as Elizabethan times. About 1770 his grandfather, John Harrison, left the prosperous family farm near Leicester (now the Stocking Farm housing estate) and became a London builder and contractor. He built Bryanston Square, and, for his family, a house in Berkeley Street overlooking Devonshire House gardens. Harrison Street, which he laid out north of Coram's Fields, off Gray's Inn Road, still carries his name. In 1814 he retired to Leicestershire and died in the bosom of his family, leaving the Berkeley Street house occupied by one of his sons. On visits there Frederic received his earliest impressions of town life. In 1847 the house was sold to Louis Napoleon, who was to dominate his impressions of another great city in later years.

Frederic's father, Frederick Harrison, was born on 23 September 1799, the builder's sixth son by his second wife, Anna Maria, née Gatehouse, of Welsh descent. As a youth he studied architecture, intending to follow his brothers into their father's business, but at seventeen he entered the London stockbroking firm of Robert and William Hichens. There in due course he prospered. On 23 October,

1829, when his income had already reached £600, he married Jane Brice, age twenty-one, the daughter of Belfast Protestants living in London. She had had a good education by conventional standards, for her father, a granite merchant who had died of cholera, had provided well for his widow and daughter. From their house in Euston Square they sallied out to concerts and exhibitions, and to civic functions too, for Mrs Brice's brother, John Johnson, was an alderman in the City of London.

The first two years of married life Frederick and Jane Harrison spent under Mrs Brice's roof. There, in November 1830 they had a son whom they named Frederic (without the 'k' to distinguish him from his father) Robert (after Robert Hichens). He died at four months. Then, on 18 October 1831 another son was born and also named Frederic. Though given no middle name, he inherited the deceased infant's silver christening mug monogrammed 'F. R. H.', and when old enough to understand, was told the circumstances that accounted for the initials. With a gift for seeing the best side of situations, which he would retain through life, he decided that being the eldest living child but not the first-born had distinct advantages: he had the undivided solicitude that parents customarily lavish on a first child, but not the physical delicacy he thought common to the first born. Certainly he thrived, and on 29 December was carried past the stately columns of St. Pancras Church, a new Greek revival structure off Euston Road, to be baptized. Both his godfathers were prosperous businessmen with community interests. Robert Hichens, his father's partner, was a devoted churchman, and Sir John Cowan, a wine merchant in Mrs Brice's circle, would be Lord Mayor of London at the time of Queen Victoria's coronation.

While Frederic was still in arms the family moved from Euston Square to Muswell Hill, probably to avoid a new cholera epidemic. At two-year intervals his four brothers were born there: Lawrence in 1833; Charles in 1835; Robert Hichens Camden in 1837; and William Sidney in 1839. Mr Harrison's income and household expenses continued to rise and there were eventually several servants, including two nursemaids, as well as holidays in Brighton and, in 1839, at the fashionable new resort of Ramsgate. But in 1840 Mr Harrison's business affairs were so temporarily imperilled by a forgery case that his servants' wages were cut from £100 to £43 for the year, expenditures on entertainment were similarly reduced, and Nurse Naylor, Frederic's favourite, was kept on only because she insisted upon deferring her wages till the Harrisons' fortunes improved. A kind of family heroine, she probably contributed to the characteristically Victorian paternalistic attitude that her eldest charge later took in dealing with both servants and women.

Jane and Frederick Harrison were advocates of Isaac Taylor's philosophy of education,[2] according to which nature is the best schoolroom and simple ideas of morality and prudence are inculcated early, without routine learning such as schools then fostered. Frederic and his brothers gathered flowers in the meadows near their house—but Frederic, at least, did not develop any scientific interest in them or the butterflies they harboured—and were taken on walks to Hornsey village for a glimpse of a more bustling life. For quieter times they frequented the Hornsey churchyard or Highgate Cemetery and 'imbibed ... a lively and perfectly healthy love of a cemetery, as a tranquil retreat dedicated to memory and to peace'.[3] Death, in his philosophy, would have no terrors.

But the Muswell idyll was not without its intimations of danger. There was one lane the boys were forbidden to enter because of the savage bull kept there by a grandfather of Cecil Rhodes, a circumstance on which Harrison, always fiercely anti-imperialistic, later commented: 'So early did the great Empire-builder's ancestor inspire me with fear.'[4] Another troubled memory was of the well that gave Muswell its name. It had been part of a Benedictine farm and the site of a shrine to Our Lady of Muswell. Its pellucid waters were reputed to have cured some ailment of a Scottish king, but all young Frederic knew was that locally it was believed haunted by spirits; of which sort he could not discover: 'No one knew, and I looked into its depths in vain. Nothing ever came out.' He was, alas, hardly prepared for a visitation. In Taylor's view, and hence in his parents', stories about fairies or other supernatural creatures harmed young minds, and Frederic and his brothers were given sterner fare. To this deprivation he later half-humorously attributed that 'prosaic insensibility to the mystical with which I am so often and so justly charged'.[5]

When the schoolroom was indoors, Mrs Harrison supervised lessons in French, Latin, and history until Frederic's tenth year, and he was given the works usually offered carefully educated children: Macaulay's *Lays of Ancient Rome*, Wilberforce's *Agathos*, Homer in English, *Robinson Crusoe*, *The Pilgrim's Progress*. Especially memorable were the Peter Parley books by that grim New Englander Samuel Griswold Goodrich, who believed that stories like 'Puss in Boots' and 'Little Red Riding Hood' were 'full of lies' and so designed his texts to be relentlessly factual and dogmatic, to educate, not amuse.[6] One, beginning with the division of the world into land and water and sketching a history of civilization, may have played a part in preparing Harrison to accept in later years Comte's scheme of history as an orderly progression of events. And some of the events of man's past became fixed vividly in the young boy's mind by the woodcuts in the *Penny Magazine*, published by the Society for the Diffusion of Useful Knowledge and obtained by his parents from an itinerant salesman. The pictures of famous events and works of art and architecture so entranced Frederic that he tried making his own copies, an exercise that disclosed no artistic talent but gave him by the age of ten a well-stocked mind: 'I firmly believed in Leonidas and Miltiades, in Romulus and Remus, ... Julius Caesar landing in Britain, and Alfred's cakes—and in a sense I believe in them still' wrote the critic of dry-as-dust historical research years later.[7]

Mr Harrison not only encouraged his sons' interest in art but also spent part of his own leisure time drawing up plans for buildings and discussing architecture with his brothers. And though Ruskin's enthusiasm for Turner was as yet unknown to them, everyone in the family agreed on the painter's greatness. When Frederic had a tooth pulled in London, seeing a new Turner at the Royal Academy exhibition was 'ample consolation'.[8] Mr Harrison carefully planned visits to London museums, libraries, and historical sites for the boys, foreshadowing efforts of both Frederic and Charles to show others the value of such cultural pilgrimages. But in all this, one art form was neglected. Despite her own fine singing voice and musical education, Mrs Harrison allowed the boys to believe music was not 'manly', and Frederic's indifference to it continued until his adolescence. After that, however, he attended concerts and operas regularly and took as much pride in having heard the greatest musicians and singers of his time as in having known some of its greatest statesmen and authors.

Frederic's most eventful day as a child was 28 June 1838, Queen Victoria's Coronation. Just under seven, he was left with Lawrence in the grandstand facing Westminster Abbey. His mother and Mrs Brice had seats in the Abbey, and his father circulated in the crowd, sometimes returning to take the boys out into it. On one such foray a gigantic Lifeguardsman stooped over to speak to Frederic. His head full of Peter Parley tales of British heroes, the boy was awestruck, and this image of embodied national might, along with the rest of the day's impressive spectacles, gave him an enduring sense of belonging to a great country. The consternation he had expressed upon learning that its new monarch was to be a young girl vanished; never, even in the republicanism of his young manhood, would his personal devotion to his Queen be in question.

Though certain that the pastoral pleasures of childhood, heightened by occasional city excitements, had made him in the main happy as a boy, he confessed also to some childhood despondency.[9] Religious terrors, he thought, could not have been to blame, for his parents were 'simply Christian'—that is, not fanatical. But he remembered, too, being accused by his nurse of having committed an unforgivable sin in saying 'damn', and, when older, of having enough belief in a powerful deity to pray for special dispensations—an examination prize or a good cricket score. This seems a common enough pattern of servants' superstitions counteracting parents' enlightenment. After all, Isaac Taylor's pedagogic principles, which were extremely Evangelical, had left their mark; he had gone so far in one work as to posit specific duties in the afterlife. Though Harrison failed to remark on this, he did judge Taylor's scheme of home education faulty because it left children 'the prey of idleness or chance'. And he thought he had spent too much time with adults, thus developing an excessive sensitivity to criticism. He once invoked his 'Irish gift for feeling humiliation' to explain his vulnerability. He also suggested that physical causes common to adolescence accounted for his 'early self-consciousness', adding that 'there is much that has to be thought out yet as to the intense mental suffering which so many children endure.'[10] But he had little interest in psychology, and his philosophy precluded paying much attention to it, so the matter remained for him about as mysterious as the spirits in the Muswell waters.

Whatever episodes of obscure unhappiness marred Harrison's early youth, in outward circumstances he considered his life ideal. In his tenth year the family returned to London, to a house built by Mr Harrison in Oxford Square. It then bordered open country, and was also close enough to the Knightsbridge Horse Guards barracks to make riding lessons feasible; to Lord's, where Harrison developed a life-long passion for cricket; and to the Thames for boating and the Serpentine for skating. Since their parents often entertained, the boys came to enjoy musical evenings and dancing. In place of gardening, a diversion at Muswell, Mr Harrison now took his wife out on the river, a pastime they had pursued together before their marriage. And they renewed their friendship with Richard Bethell, who had often accompanied them boating before his marriage. The son of a Bristol surgeon who had attended the Brices, he had always been driven by intense ambition. When in his fourteenth year his family's finances deteriorated, he had obtained a Wadham College Scholarship at Oxford. After taking his BA at eighteen and his MA at twenty, he was called to the Bar in 1823, when he was only twenty-three. Mr Harrison's brother Charles, a solicitor in Bedford Row, gave him his first brief, and he did so well that the year before the Harrisons returned to London he took silk. His wit was celebrated but, in Harrison's view at least, it lacked malice most of the time, and was only 'the spontaneous ebullition of keen insight, mastery of phrase, and disdain of criticism'. Yet the model of professional success he obviously presented—he became Lord Westbury and was Lord Chancellor—was not one young Harrison sought to emulate.[11].

It was Bethell who advised the Harrisons to send Fred—as he was known in the family—to Joseph King's day school in St. John's Wood, where two of Bethell's own sons studied, as well as a son of Macready, then at the height of his acting fame; of Thomas Landseer, an engraver who popularized the animal paintings of his famous brother Edwin; and of Richard James Lane, the Arabic and Egyptian authority. Unlike Bethell's, the reputations of these men impressed Fred, who was already developing a great admiration for achievement in the arts. And in his tenth year he sought certain successes of his own. Latin and Greek, which he now started, were sources of delight, for Mr King, versed in the new German philology, taught both by using great literature, giving the root form of nouns and verbs as they appeared, and explaining case, tense, and something of a word's development. He cited rules only to untangle difficult constructions, and then verbally, without a grammar. By the age of twelve, Fred had read Homer and Herodotus, Virgil and Livy, Caesar and Ovid, and was familiar with Xenophon, Euripides, and Euclid in parts. So vivid did some works seem that he tried illustrating them. For a storm scene in the *Aeneid* he drew ships bobbing on waves from which Neptune emerged as from a trapdoor. Like his art, Fred's verse was uninspired—'The air was mild, the sky serene,/ The waters gently foam,/ No dark or threatening cloud was seen,/ When Paul set sail for Rome'—but his prose translations were better. In his class of six or eight he was usually first. More important, he was finding in prose composition pleasure he would later compare to the 'solace which a dog has in gnawing a bone'.[12]

Largely because his English prose was so good, Fred was placed with boys of more than his age when, at eleven, he entered King's College School as a day boy in the summer term of 1843.[13] Opened in the month of his birth, the school was a junior department of King's College in Somerset House, the Strand, established to offset the 'godless' University College of the Benthamites in Gower Street. Mr Harrison's devout business partner, Robert Hichens, had contributed £60 to the school, and in consequence was able to nominate Fred, thus saving his father part of the fees. The School prepared boys to move not only up to the college (literally—the School was in the basement), but to Oxford or Cambridge, to a profession like the law or medicine that did not then require a university education, or into business. The last option was taken by Lawrence and Charles Harrison, who entered in 1846 and 1848. The reputation of the school was excellent, due in great part to its Headmaster, the Revd J. R. Major, who in his thirty-five-year tenure was responsible for nearly one hundred boys in the *DNB*. Not all were scholars, of course, and Harrison recalled Major as 'curiously inattentive' and deficient in philology, a judgement that may owe something to Bethell, who occasionally made Fred recite and was probably censorious of pupil and teacher alike. But for the rest of his life Harrison enjoyed reading the classics so long as he had an English translation at hand for the hard parts, and he liked rendering favourite authors into his own prose. (In 1902 his version of a speech by Pericles in Thucydides circulated among friends and came to the notice of Samuel Butler, who pronounced it 'too often clumsy, stilted, Johnsonian, and affected', but gave up after an hour spent trying to do better himself.) If Harrison did not acquire impeccable scholarly habits at King's, he at least learned how to excel in examinations. The year before he left, he was third in the school's top form and won honourable mention in the school's scholarship competition. In the 1848 term, in which he departed, he won a First Class Scholarship and the English Essay Prize. When, years later, he deplored the emphasis on examinations in education, it was not a case of the grapes being sour.[14]

Precocity has a way of causing trouble, as Fred learned. He was set apart by the boys, excluded from their rougher games and dubbed 'Fan'. Had he known that his mentor, Bethell, had been called 'Miss Fanny' at Oxford because of his precision of speech and pedantry, he might have borne his trial more gracefully.[15] As it was he sought desperately to appear manly by making the most of his stocky frame and energy, but his clear complexion and rosy cheeks were against him. 'Fan' he remained until the intercession of his first real friend, Charles Cookson.[16] He already had a knowledge of world events, ideas, and literature that surpassed even Fred's. Related to Wordsworth, Cookson naturally defended the Laureate in their debates, which often included another friend, James Rolfe. Fred, fairly ignorant about modern writers, espoused Pope and Dryden and, when politics came to the fore, the Tory convictions of his parents.

Cookson, Rolfe, and Harrison were among those who planned a school magazine that was nipped in the bud by the Principal of King's College, Dr Richard Jelf, who may have feared that the boys' interest in religion was likely to lead to controversy. Among probable contributors was Martin Irving, later Professor of Classics and English at Melbourne University and the son of the Carlyles' friend who had founded the Catholic Apostolic Church; the future lawyer Alfred Bailey; the future *Times* sub-editor William Stebbing; one of the era's true polymaths, Frederick Gard Fleay; and, from King's College, Charles Henry Pearson, the future historian and social theorist.

One who could not be counted among Fred's close friends, though they shared a bench for a time, was Henry Parry Liddon, who would become canon of St. Paul's and famous for his eloquence. Looking back, Harrison called him a 'priest among boys' because of his indifference to almost everything but theology and a manner that Harrison considered condescending.[17] More congenial by far were Irving, though he was his closest academic rival, and Cookson, a Tractarian like Liddon, but one interested more in ritual than theology. He took Fred to St. Margaret's Church in Margaret Street, a centre of what would later be termed Ritualism, until Mr Harrison, who disliked all excess in religion, put a stop to Fred's visits.[18]

And wise he was, from his standpoint, for Fred had a distinct predilection for ritual. He had pitied his Quaker neighbours at Muswell Hill because their meeting house was not visited by Archbishop Howley, whom Fred once saw preach in rochet and short wig. And in France, where the family spent summers from 1846 to 1848, Fred came to love the magnificent services of the great cathedrals, a welcome contrast to the stark Presbyterian offices that in Scotland left him 'chilled to the bone'.[19] But religious ideas, theology, and Bible study held little interest, though Mr Hichens did what he could to encourage Fred by sending him books and inveighing against Dissenters. His confirmation was performed by no less a personage than Bishop Blomfield; but it was not a significant experience for the boy. Only when he was fifteen did religious ideas, apart from ritual, begin to interest him. Then he was struck by the antithesis in Paley's *Evidences of Christianity* between the Christian ideal of duty and the classical ideal of fame. His own childhood conception of the heroic came to seem 'narrow, unworthy, and puerile'; the image of the gigantic Lifeguardsman at the Coronation faded, and was replaced by that of Paley's world-renouncing Christian—a change he later thought rendered him 'through life a desultory and rather inefficient bystander in the great world of action', with 'the desire of fame, power, or place ... an object of indifference and even of contempt'.[20]

Whatever the long-range effects of Christian teachings on Harrison were, they do not seem to have made his social conscience more sensitive. It is true that before leaving King's he wrote a letter to the *Daily News*—his first publication—condemning a city regulation that forced discharged hospital patients to deliver a written expression of gratitude to the officer who had signed their admission papers. In it he asked 'how high shall we value a charity which dictates its own reward, and enforces it with an ungenerous threat ...?' This perception of humbug was worthy of Dickens, who had helped to found the paper.[21] Yet in recalling his youth Harrison says little about having noticed the social inequities and terrible miseries that must have been forced upon his attention in London, especially in the infamous streets near the Strand, beyond remarking that the chimney sweeps had filled him with 'wonder, pity, and horror'. Nor, apparently, was his social conscience much stirred during those summers in France. The first was spent in Boulogne, even then a fashionable watering place, another on a large estate at Caen owned by the family of a Mrs Lawrence, a client of his father's after whom his second son was named. What impressed Fred there was not so much the poverty and ignorance of the peasants, which would trouble him later as a danger to republican France, but the self-imposed frugality of his wealthy hosts. But he did not ponder long over it, being absorbed in French history. On a trip to Bayeux he studied the great tapestry, and, meeting a master from King's by chance, caught his enthusiasm for Norman architecture.

Since it was the past, not the future of England and France that interested young Fred at this time, the European revolutions of 1848 and the Chartist demonstration in London produced in him only schoolboy responses; he noted that Louis Philippe's flight fell on the anniversary of the Tarquins' expulsion from Rome, and on 10 April he and his friends amused themselves by betting on the likelihood of bloodshed in the streets of London and by encouraging the gentlemen who were patrolling their neighbourhood in top hats to assist the constabulary. That June he travelled by train to Oxford to sit for a Wadham College scholarship at Bethell's suggestion, and though the morning newspapers reported the insurrection in Paris, it was his own fate, not that of working men across the Channel, that preoccupied him.

By coming third in the examination, Harrison gained the scholarship, but being only seventeen he did not matriculate until the following April and did not go up to Oxford until the autumn after that, in 1849. Meanwhile, ranking second at King's, he did little regular work. By then cricket was a passion, and he had begun playing with friends at Lord's. There they studied such famous bowlers as F. W. Lillywhite, who occasionally gave his young admirers a ball or two. Public recitations filled some of his time. He played Brutus to Cookson's Cassius in Shakespeare's *Julius Caesar* for the second straight year (Bethell's son Richard had played Cassius the previous year) and he delivered Joan of Arc's lines from Schiller's *Maid of Orleans*, having struggled over verses of his own about 'Heaven's own bride' who 'bowed beneath the steel—and smiled—and died'. He would never excel at either poetry or oratory, and he soon abandoned the former altogether; but politics and religion between them turned him into a competent if not outstanding speaker. During his last months at King's, reading and experimenting in prose composition occupied much of his time and, like the recitations and acting, were good preparation for what lay ahead.

Fred left those basement classrooms in the Strand with memories that mellowed as he aged. He turned up frequently at Old Boy gatherings thereafter and in 1883 gave a measure of his school loyalty when he learned from a former classmate, Thomas J. Dymes, that he and his wife and eight children were almost destitute and in debt. Though he had not laid eyes on Dymes for over thirty years, Harrison collected some £200 from Old Boys who remembered the stout, pasty-faced fellow, and turned the money over to another, later friend of Dymes. This was Charles Lutwidge Dodgson, who, during their few meetings, impressed Harrison by his 'quaint oddities and generosities'.[22]

AN OXFORD RADICAL

After spending the summer holidays of 1849 with his family in the Scottish Highlands, Harrison entered Wadham College, thus becoming the first of the London Harrisons to embark on a university education. Sidney would follow in 1858, and his other brothers had cultural interests, but it was Fred whom the family acknowledged as its intellectual. The scholarships attested to that. They pleased his father not only as a sign of his promise but also because they paid a good portion of his expenses at the university. The King's scholarship covered £82 of the £404 Mr Harrison recorded in his 'Memorandum of College Expenses', covering Fred's first three years at Oxford. At the outset there was furniture at £25, books at £20, wine at £3, a 'Sunday outfit' at £3/6, and £41 for fees.

Fred's pleasure in establishing himself at the university was marred by the discovery that the dons were too busy with their own affairs to pay much attention to his, and the students appeared either bookish or silly, or preoccupied with games and gossip and caring little about the London world of theatre, music, and art in which he had begun to feel at home. A letter filled with complaints brought Mr Harrison's sympathetic explanation: the transition from the familiar realm of family and school, in which he had been 'looked up to, respected, and loved', into a strange society had been sudden. A 'shock to the whole nervous system' was inevitable, considering his 'sensibilities'. Moreover, at

King's he had not recently followed a regular course of study; perhaps he was finding it hard to concentrate. But he possessed 'a mind of keen observation, great reflection, [and was] fond of speculative deduction and thoughtful abstraction ... '. Overwork without enough diversion might also be contributing to his misery. His mother, of this opinion, recommended no more than one hour of reading at a time.[23]

The lack of external pressure was probably partly responsible for Fred's initial sense of dislocation. At this unreformed Oxford, attendance at lectures was uncommon, and the first of the two examinations he would take for his degree would not come round for more than a year, and then they would cover the work of the schools—classical languages and literature. Those hoping for a First Class usually engaged tutors to help them cram as the examination drew near, but Fred gained the idea that at Wadham it was a matter of indifference how many men won honours. His competitiveness, encouraged at King's, seemed to have no place, and he was temporarily at a loss to know how to direct his energies. His freedom gave him a chance to cultivate new friendships, two of which would help to banish his disquietude and wed him to Wadham as nothing else could. Both of Fred's closest Wadham friends had grown up in rural Evangelical parsonages without much acquaintance with the cultural or business life of London, which he had seen at close hand. They had friends of their own, of course, and loving families watching their development, just as he had; but for all three, their coming together, the gradual co-mingling of their thoughts and aspirations, would subordinate all past ties to the promise of the future.

The first to share his confidences was Edward Spencer Beesly. Born 23 January 1831, the eldest son of the Revd James Beesly, of Feckenham, Worcestershire, he had prepared for the University in his father's rectory. Tall and willowy, with sandy hair, fair skin, and penetrating blue eyes, he presented a marked contrast to Fred's stocky frame and dark hair and eyes. His rather gentle manner, too, seemed at first altogether unlike Fred's excitable ways, but Beesly would prove as capable of moral indignation and of audacious denunciations of what he disapproved of as the outspoken Fred. Interested like him in history and more politically aware, Beesly made a fine sounding board.[24]

The other friend was John Henry Bridges, born 11 October 1832. His father, the Revd Charles Bridges, Vicar of Old Newton, Suffolk, was known in Church circles for his commentary on Psalm 119, and for having had something to do with George Borrow's mission to Spain (though after it he was said to complain that Borrow's account contained too much on donkeys and not enough on Bibles). Among Bridges's relatives were Elizabeth Fry, the prison reformer, and Edward Gibbon Wakefield, the emigration publicist. The influence of his family's religion had been reinforced for Bridges by six years at Rugby. There he had worked hard enough to gain a Wadham College Scholarship and was known as one of the 'really literary and really philosophical minds in the sixth form'. Slight of build with fair hair and bushy brows, he was the most serious and most religious of the three Wadham friends. But he had a 'boisterous laugh', which Fred, impressed though he was by Bridges's elevated conversation, was relieved at times to hear.[25]

Though Harrison, Beesly, and Bridges thought of themselves as the Three Musketeers, in time they accommodated another Wadham man, George Earlam Thorley, who would remain at the college and ultimately become Warden.[26] The four welcomed the name 'Mumbo Jumbo' given them by others, apparently because it was thought they held secret rites. Actually, the cold duck they regularly and somewhat ostentatiously ordered for Sunday breakfast, thus arousing suspicions, was initially only their response to the prohibition against hot dishes on Sunday handed down by the Sabbatarian Warden of their college, the Revd Benjamin Symons, known, because of his size, as Big Ben. At these gatherings, and on their long walks, the friends would scrutinize every passing event and idea without restraint. They were conscious of a desire to impart a higher moral tone to their College and to improve their own minds. Fred, for one, was capable of considerable self-denial in the service of this double mission. With the announcement of the funeral plans for the Duke of Wellington, drawn up by the Duke himself and calling for the most elaborate procession ever seen in London, in November 1852, the Warden, out of fears for his students' safety, decreed that only those with a friend in London could attend. Most students produced the requisite connection, but Fred declined to apply for the privilege, though his parents had obtained a seat for him in St. Paul's. He told Beesly he could not 'coach up the necessary enthusiasm' for a man who 'had all an Englishman's weakness, and, though he lies unburied, I must say, his faults'.[27]

In Fred's eyes the Duke's outstanding fault was to belong to the military. The Mumbo had imbibed the pacifism of Cobden, Bright, and Victor Hugo. Fred opposed Britain's entry into the Crimean War in 1854 and was 'scandalised' by Tennyson's *Maud*, which seemed to welcome it.[28] Not only the Lifeguardsman but even Carlyle's version of the hero, once cherished, had become suspect. 'For my part', Fred informed Beesly after reading Carlyle's *History of the French Revolution*,

I would rather see a few thousand men each consciously feeling himself part of a whole, governing themselves however faultily, than a very millennium in which a whole world was on its knees superstitiously listening to the words of one, be he a quintessence of virtue and wisdom.[29]

With France governed by the Emperor Napoleon III, Fred was hard put to reconcile his love of that country with his growing liberalism. Burke provided the way: 'It is true', Harrison lectured Beesly, 'that liberty is a mockery in France, but those other two, Equality and Fraternity are not a mockery, but living realities, those two without which liberty loses half its sweetness, and with which servitude loses half its pain.'[30] The conflict between authoritarianism and freedom would never be entirely settled in his mind, and his desire to see France in the best possible light would continue to tax his ingenuity. His youthful Francophilia did not always sit well with Beesly. When during the Oxford years he intimated that the French might profit from some Anglo-Saxon notions of tolerance, Fred replied that actions were less important than the ideals behind them, and in theirs the French were unmatched. 'In a word, I cannot but think that the people of Paris in some measure realise that great ideal of a civilised community which Pericles gives in his funeral oration.'[31] Beesly, in time, would agree. But even before then, having decided that their 'great French dispute' had reached 'a pitch which throws that of Fox and Burke into the shade', Fred declared that since 'Mumbo can think no wrong', he and Beesly must have been merely misunderstanding each other, not truly differing.[32] The rationale would help to maintain their friendship for six decades.

Conversation and correspondence so modified Harrison's opinions that he later recalled having entered Oxford 'with the remnants of boyish Toryism and orthodoxy still holding on' and leaving it 'a Republican, a democrat, and a Free-thinker'.[33] No one did more to work this change in him than Richard Congreve, who became his tutor in the autumn of 1852. Acknowledged to be one of the most impressive men at the University, he had studied at Rugby under Dr Thomas Arnold, who recognized his abilities. At Wadham he took First Class Honours, and in 1843 his MA. After teaching at Rugby he returned to Wadham in 1848, when he was thirty, and with A. P. Stanley began disseminating the liberal, anti-dogmatic ideas of history and religion of their famous mentor. A steady gaze, set lips, and a Roman nose gave Congreve an imposing appearance. His powers of work were, at least in those years, extraordinary, and his interest in students unusual.[34]

Yet Fred soon saw that restlessness and hostility towards colleagues were absorbing much of Congreve's strength. 'I wish you were all drowned', he once heard Congreve mutter as he left the Common Room. Such irascibility seemed a woeful flaw in so gifted a man. It kept Harrison from feeling close to him as a student, and it would disastrously affect their subsequent relations. But there was no denying Congreve's cosmopolitanism, which Harrison could not resist during the Oxford years. Unlike many Fellows, who seldom left the University except to go on reading parties, Congreve had travelled on the Continent and was immersed in French literature and thought. He might lack imagination, but he had a grasp of history and modern politics equal to that of the best men at Oxford. And they included Benjamin Jowett, a young Balliol tutor already turning out prize men, and Mark Pattison, whose failure to gain the Rectorship of Lincoln College in 1851 exemplified to Harrison the intriguing at the University he so despised. Jowett conceived of Oxford as a place to prepare men for leadership; Pattison saw it as a place for furthering knowledge. To Congreve, social and political reforms seemed the necessary goals of education. Of these perspectives—not mutually exclusive, of course—Fred found Congreve's the most congenial, but also a cause for some alarm. He felt 'more and more puzzled at the ferocity of these world-wide philanthropists, these men who "love all who come behind them and before" ' but had little sympathy for their immediate contemporaries.[35]

Yet it was Harrison's ultimate belief that Congreve did him more good than any other teacher he had at Oxford. His Latin tutor, the eminent scholar John Conington, seemed 'rather a dry pedant, with a mania for neat phrases'.[36] His logic tutor, Henry Wall, was merely 'a sharp hack'.[37] And a French tutor proved memorable chiefly for having given him a pass to the Great Exhibition, where the 'appalling vulgarity' left him 'groaning over the misdirected labour'.[38] But he was sufficiently caught up in the tutorial system to advise his father about teachers for his younger brothers, still at school; when Robert's academic future seemed cloudy, Fred urged seeking the 'deliberate opinion' of the boy's tutor on the ground that 'it is well to know as accurately as possible the capabilities of children, though generally best to act as if we were quite uncertain of our knowledge.'[39]

Despite his negative view of individual dons, Harrison would later judge his Oxford education 'as good a mental training as possible', largely, it would seem, because in his day men concentrated on Aristotle, Plato, and the classical historians. Modern history, which the Oxford Commission Report brought in, was, in his judgement, potentially valuable but in the event produced undesirable specialization. Science he deemed even worse in this respect, and deplored its increasing role at Oxford after his day.[40]

Far more important than the influence of any don or course of study at Oxford on Harrison's later life was the change in his perception of religion. His own accounts of his religious evolution are somewhat confused, and no doubt the stages were not clearly marked. On the one hand he later asserted that men in his day gained the conviction that 'education means something more than collecting a number of known facts, that, in a word, *religion* is a reality which counts, and that it is all-important what that religion is to be.' On the other hand he discovered that for him it would be impossible to continue with the old religion. He attended chapel daily and twice on Sundays, for that was mandated by the Warden, and he spent long periods of time discussing the sermon of the week with his friends preparatory to writing the obligatory summary of it. The process proved destructive to certainty, and enhanced the solidarity of the Mumbo. Together the friends observed, in Harrison's words, that since each week brought a different man into the pulpit, 'The creed—"necessary if we are to be saved"—of one Sunday' became 'the heresy of the next'.[41]

So arduous was the task of reconciling divergent views that Harrison came to prefer the chapel in the evening, when its impact was almost exclusively aesthetic, at least to him. And this love of ritual did not go unobserved. Because of his association with Cookson, now at Oriel, and others of Puseyite leanings, Harrison found himself numbered among the 'black sheep' by the Evangelical Symons, who a decade earlier had harried Newman, and as Vice-Chancellor of the University had prosecuted W. G. Ward. But far from feeling 'any qualm or anxiety or conscience' because of his state of religious unrest, Fred could write to Beesly about being in a 'state of gestation' and unsure how long 'the birth' would take. Meanwhile, he coolly deflected his mother's anxiety by telling her of being 'surprised and shocked' at friends who were defending 'that most pernicious doctrine of the *development* of Christianity, i.e., that the Apostles' Gospel was intended to be modified by us'. And he lamented that 'many of fine spirit, good aims, bright intellect are turning all that is exalted even in their moral nature to build a system, pure, and beautiful, but *unchristian*.' His friends, he speculated, had been drawn into unorthodoxy in reaction to their strict Evangelical upbringing, which he contrasted to his own, from which he had learned 'conviction without bigotry, piety without fanaticism, true Faith, not without reason'.[42]

Though there was probably more strategy than sincerity in that letter, Harrison was indeed one of those who believed himself to have been led away from Christianity less by arguments about theological difficulties than by appeals to moral teachings. He no doubt lost his orthodox convictions some time before he made his new position clear to his parents, for how could he formulate for them what seemed so unclear to himself? Looking back, he said his hold on orthodoxy had been 'completely shaken' by works like W. R. Greg's *Creed of Christendom*, which appeared in 1851, David Strauss's *Leben Jesu*, which he read in George Eliot's translation, and Francis Newman's *Phases of Faith*, published during Harrison's first year at Oxford. But he also remembered the role of such 'devout and noble spirits' as Frederick Robertson, Theodore Parker, Tennyson, Browning, the followers of Dr Arnold and Coleridge, and his new distaste for the Catholicism of John Henry Newman and the Anglo-Catholicism of Pusey, as well as his abhorrence of the Philistine Protestantism of Symons. Even F. D. Maurice, whose sermons at Lincoln's Inn he heard a few years after Maurice's dismissal in the early 1850s from King's College for trying to make the doctrines of Eternal Punishment and the Atonement more morally palatable, figured in Harrison's accounts of his own religious history. Though Maurice impressed him as 'a good dear creature', his penchant for 'parading every moral objection to the Orthodox Bible and scheme of salvation', and then insisting that 'we must take it all down for the sake of the beauty of Christ's mission, etc.' undercut any personal influence Maurice might have had because of his good intentions and fearlessness. Harrison summed up his teaching as 'Credo quia impossible', and rejected it.[43]

His own resting place after orthodoxy was Theism, a kind of fuzzy speculation about some providential power. But it was more than a mere dilution of Christianity; it derived in part from the writings of Giuseppi Mazzini, a name often on the lips of his tutor in Italian, Aurelio Saffi, who with Mazzini, had been one of the short-lived triumvirate in Rome in 1849. Brought to Oxford after its demise by sympathetic Englishmen, Saffi lectured in a 'moth-eaten voice' (according to Carlyle) and transmitted to many of Harrison's generation his own passion for Dante, Italian nationalism, and Mazzini's notion of a divine 'collective humanity' that imposed moral obligations.[44]

Another, quite different agent dissolving his orthodoxy was John Stuart Mill's *System of Logic*. Used as a text at Oxford, its anti-intuitionism and call for verification of hypotheses did much to create the secularism to which Fred increasingly responded. He welcomed its rational empiricism also as an antidote to German metaphysical thought. It had so beguiled one of his tutors that he set topics in logic on subjects Fred, with his relentlessly prosaic mind, could not understand—on 'being', for example, and 'consciousness', 'noumena', and 'the absolute'. Such exercises, he thought, 'settle nothing in the end'.

And when Beesly admitted to a similar philosophical quandary, he asked him why he did not 'take refuge in Mill and his sources?' and added: 'I am gradually being absorbed into that system.'[45]

The key word here is 'sources'. Mill's method of reasoning about social problems owed much to Auguste Comte, whom Mill valued not only because Comte had seen that no *a priori* theory of progress was tenable, but because he had offered in its place his Law of the Three Stages. According to it, man's thinking about nature had begun in a Theological Stage, in which he attributed all phenomena to supernatural agents (ultimately, with monotheism, to one agent); had progressed to a Metaphysical Stage, in which abstract forces or principles were understood as the causes of phenomena; and, in the most advanced thinkers, was in the Positive Stage, in which the search after absolutes is abandoned as futile, and man devotes himself to the study of the invariable relations existing among phenomena—in short, to the formulation of scientific laws. In his six-volume *Cours de philosophie positive*, published between 1830 and 1842, Comte constructed a hierarchy of the physical sciences according to the progress each had made towards the Third Stage: mathematics, the essential discipline, came first; then came astronomy, which had provided the first true laws about the world, laws that were the most general, simple, and independent of those of the other sciences; then physics, which taught the value of experimentation; chemistry, which produced the art of nomenclature; biology, which embodied the comparative method; and social physics, in which social phenomena were studied according to the integrated methods of the other sciences beneath it in the hierarchy. This final 'science' he named 'sociologie' and said would be the last to reach the Positive Stage. And he promised in time to add as as seventh 'science', ethics.[46]

It is important to recognize how many respected theorists of Harrison's youth had ideas parallel to Comte's, for to conceive of Harrison choosing to follow a foreign philosopher who was entirely at odds with English thought would be to underestimate his intellectual conservatism. Comte attracted him initially because he knew him at second hand through the work of contemporaries he respected, Mill foremost. There was also Mazzini's idea of a collective humanity that would govern all intellectual and political enterprises (so similar to Comte's belief that all intellectual progress should be in the service of mankind, which he, too, presented as an abstraction, 'Humanité'); Bentham's prediction that the future history of moral science would parallel the recent inspiring record of the natural sciences; Francis Newman's view of Christianity as a late but not a final stage of man's religious development; Macaulay's reliance on science to improve man's lot on earth (the essay on Bacon); and Carlyle's denunciation of metaphysics and demand for a new industrial order in which humane values would replace the selfish ones that had so long dominated the commercial and intellectual life of the West. This latter idea, of an industrial order resting on moral values—ultimately of medieval origin—Comte had appropriated from his early mentor Henri Saint-Simon, whose influence on Mazzini and Carlyle had also been profound.[47] Even W. G. Ward's book, *The Ideal of a Christian Church*, notorious at Wadham since Symons's persecution of the author, cited approvingly the warning of a 'French political writer'—clearly Comte—that the modern tendency to separate private interest from public welfare had produced an immoral society.[48]

Harrison first learned of Comte's early theories from a summary of them by his not uncritical disciple, Émile Littré, in a volume given to Harrison by Cookson. It is tempting to see Cookson's act having immediate benefits, as had his rescue of Harrison from schoolboy bullies. But Harrison himself made no such claim.[49] Indeed, he was probably quite as influenced by George Henry Lewes's *Biographical History of Philosophy*, popular at Oxford since its publication in 1845–6. Under Mill's influence, Lewes had studied and even visited Comte, and in his book did Positivism the inestimable service of placing it in the mainstream of English empiricism. Furthermore, though he sketched Comte's ideas only briefly, Lewes declared that all metaphysical speculation was worthless (thus he undercut most of the thinkers he had discussed before Comte) because 'the positive method is the only method adapted to human capacity'.[50] Fred embodied this thesis in an essay for Congreve, but declined, when asked, to say precisely what he meant. He later recalled that he had been thinking only of 'the philosophy of Bacon, Hume, Mill, and Comte in a general sense—the philosophy of experience and logic'.[51]

Only after reading an account of Comte in an old *Edinburgh Review* did Fred realize—and immediately announce to the Mumbo—that the Frenchman's teachings lay behind Congreve's. And so they did. Congreve had met Comte in Paris in 1849, begun a correspondence, and from him obtained copies of his later works, then difficult to purchase in England. Just as Mill had underplayed the anti-Christian implications in Positivism in order not to jeopardize the reception of his *Logic*, Congreve, who was in Holy Orders, felt obliged because of those implications to refrain from direct references to Comte. His restraint might account for some of the abrasiveness in his manner that so troubled Harrison.[52]

As Congreve's discontent with Oxford mounted, Harrison's identification with its traditions grew. In debates at the Oxford Union he and his set sought to 'madden the Conservatives by their unemotional Radicalism'.[53] He played cricket for his college's eleven and filled many afternoons boating and taking long walks. In 1851 he made the first of many trips to Switzerland, travelling with Lawrence and glimpsing the Alps initially from the same vantage-point as had Ruskin, at Schaffhausen. And like Ruskin he delighted in the horse-drawn carriages that took roads through areas rail travellers of later years would never see. [54] Such diversions in and out of term-time, along with the inadequacy of his school preparation in Greek and Latin and his faith in 'luck and "native cheek" ', explain why he received only a Second Class in his first important examination, in 1852. A summer in Kingston-on-Thames and a visit with Mrs Brice in Paris helped to restore his spirits.[55]

Convinced that 'the last cram is everything', Fred worked so hard in the next few months that he developed a distaste for the examination system that coloured all his later views on education. He would never forget his Wadham friend Robert Henry Codrington, who, as the examination drew near, announced that as he sat studying a squirrel would perch on his Greek lexicon. Diagnosing 'brain fever', Harrison implored the young man to seek medical advice. Sir Henry Acland, Regius Professor of Medicine, persuaded Codrington to suspend study for a time; and he went on to attain eminence as a missionary and a scholar.[56] Fred, though suffering from no such strain himself, complained in the spring of 1853 of feeling 'dispirited'. He was hoping to find a niche at Oxford, at least temporarily, and a Fellowship at Wadham required at least a Second Class degree. Letters home contained enough of his apprehension to bring his ever-solicitous father on a visit, after which Fred declared that, 'though not very cheerful', he was 'quite collected and resigned'.[57] The examination he took that spring, the first affected by the Oxford Commission, contained unexpected changes in format, but he thought the topics set showed the 'good sense' of his examiners: J. M. Wilson, Mark Pattison, and Benjamin Jowett. They did not count blunders and gave 'credit for thought, good sense, and general grasp of ... subjects'.[58] When the class list appeared, the faithful Cookson dispatched a telegram to the anxious family at Oxford Square: 'Fredericus Harrison, first class— thank God'.[59] Another friend fired a pistol from a college window in jubilation at Fred's triumph, and Big Ben reluctantly bestowed on him a set of Milton.[60]

Ignoring his ineligibility for Honours (he had exceeded the maximum terms of residence), Fred read for the new Modern History School examination in November, and did well enough to bring high praise from his examiners and an 'Honorary' Fourth Class. That quite satisfied him, but not his father,[61] and Fred had to console himself for this unusual lack of paternal indulgence by making a second excursion with Lawrence. This time they went down the Rhone to Marseilles, then by steamer to the small fishing village of Cannes, by coach to Nice, by *vettura* to Genoa, by steamer again to Leghorn, and by train to Florence, where at the home of Isa Blagden, known to their parents, her friend Robert Browning told them which churches and frescoes to see.[62]

Back at Oxford at the end of 1853, Fred felt uncomfortably pressed to choose a vocation. His father, with exasperating logic, warned that 'decision, in any action of life, is highly necessary to the attainment of its object.'[63] His mother expected him to become a clergyman, and it is possible that his uncle Charles tried to expedite her ambitions. In the spring of 1854 he sought to obtain from the First Lord of the Treasury the right to name the next incumbent of fashionable St. Mark's Church in St. John's Wood in exchange for releasing the incumbent from a mortgage worth £3,250, purchased by Charles when the church was built. The request was denied. (In the same year Charles presided over the founding of the Great Northern London Cemetery—and put that same vicar on his Board of Directors.)[64] Such trafficking in religious partronage must have offended Fred. He had already expressed his dismay at the arranged marriage of Charles Harrison's daughter to the much older son of a duke, Lord Amelius Beauclerk, for 'plebeian money', and thereafter seems to have had nothing to do with that side of the family.[65] Meanwhile, his father and Richard Bethell, in his avuncular way, were convincing him that law was the right profession. It would, Fred conceded, offer 'a fair means of support in return for a fair day's work (without absolutely sacrificing all other pursuits or throwing oneself into the race for success)'.[66] The old, Paley-tinged dislike of worldly ambition coloured his thoughts still, though the evidences of Christianity had come to look meagre. When asked by his father what had become of his ambition, Fred protested:

I am ambitious and confident enough to think that I have within me something, now confused and weak, which with cultivation might become stronger and clearer, by means of which many or some few might be benefited or aided. I feel that there are many things defacing the earth which would be removed if men knew more of them and which need a witness and narrator ... [67]

To add to the disquiet caused at home by his uncertain dedication to the law and his vague references to some social mission, Fred requested permission to remain at the University after taking his degree. Mr Harrison reluctantly consented. The situation became complicated in March 1854, however, when Congreve suddenly announced that he was resigning Holy Orders, his Tutorship, and his Fellowship, and departing for London, where he hoped finally to be free to advance Positivism openly. He wished Harrison and Thorley to assume his tutoring responsibilities until Bridges, whom he most favoured, could succeed him, in about two years. Fred saw in the plan the chance to defer becoming 'completely absorbed' in law, which he would begin to study in his vacations, meanwhile starting to keep his terms at Lincoln's Inn.[68] But after consulting Bethell, Mr Harrison issued an ultimatum: 'either decide *now* for *clerical* and *scholastic* pursuits for *life* or for secular ones; *if* for *the latter, accepting* the *present proposal* is a *fatal thing.*' Bethell went further. More time at Oxford would 'rather unfit than qualify' him for the study of law, which required an 'elastic' mind, which he had already. As for his reforming aspirations, no occupation except in the Church offered 'a wider field of usefulness than the law'.[69]

Though admitting the 'extreme awkwardness of taking a man's opinion and then not acting upon it', Fred resisted the counsel from London and accepted Congreve's tutoring responsibilities. By July he had obtained a Fellowship.[70] The following year proved to be among the most enjoyable of his whole life, and, in his view, among the most useful. As an undergraduate he had occupied 'quiet, gentlemanly' rooms decorated with statues of Apollo and Niobe from home,[71] but his new quarters, on the first floor, at the west end of the front of the College, were larger, with an oriel window framing a lovely view. He did not 'particularly enjoy' tutoring,[72] but it left time for his own study and for the discussions to which he had become addicted. Besides the Mumbo, there was the Essay Society, nicknamed the 'Mutual Improvement Society', whose founding members included G. C. Brodrick, W. H. Fremantle. G. J. Goschen, A. G. Butler, and Fred's school friend, Charles Pearson.[73] At the Oxford Union Fred had by now boldly opposed Church Rates and England's foreign policy ('unworthy of a free people'), endorsed John Bright ('enlightened and patriotic'), and pronounced the Pre-Raphaelites capable of offering 'hopes for a revival of art' but also possessed of 'some deplorable delusions'.[74]

Besides delivering such weighty judgements, Fred served the Union as Librarian for three terms, preceded by Beesly and followed by Bridges. In office they could stoke the fires they set in debate. Fred, for example, proposed for acquisition Harriet Martineau's new translation of Comte's *Cours de philosophie positive*, and Beesly added

Lewes's *Comte's Philosophy of the Sciences* and Francis Newman's *Phases of Faith*.[75] By now the three friends—but not Thorley—were commonly identified with Congreve and hence with Positivism. So, too, was another member of the Union, Godfrey Lushington, who like Bridges was from Rugby, and who would soon bring his twin brother Vernon, from Cambridge, into their circle.[76] The Union's members included a number of men who resisted the appeal of Positivism but not of friendship with Fred: Albert O. Rutson, Mountstuart E. Grant Duff, and, from the Essay Society, Goschen, Butler, and Pearson.

During this period Harrison also grew closer to eminent Oxford men senior to him whom he had met through Congreve but who were not sympathetic to Comte—A. P. Stanley, Goldwin Smith, and Francis Jeune—and to his own examiners, Pattison and Jowett. All active university reformers, these men had goals Harrison did not entirely share. Smith and Pattison, for example, wished to promote science and specialized study, which conflicted with Comte's valuing of science primarily for its methodology and his distrust of research for its own sake. But their desire to release the colleges from clerical control accorded well with Comte's view of Christianity as an outmoded religion. Fred, in his extreme way, praised as 'masterly' Henry Halford Vaughan's pamphlet on reducing Church influence at Oxford, especially its criticism of Pusey (a 'putrid corpse') and the 'drivelling plan' of the entrenched conservatives (the 'old creatures').[77]

In the summer of 1855 Harrison, on the strength of his friendship with Congreve, secured an interview with Comte in Paris. The philosopher, then fifty-six and with only two more years to live, had just completed what would be his final large work, *Système de positive politique*, and was eager for disciples, especially in England, the nation he placed only after France among the five he deemed destined to form the Western Republic. He therefore welcomed Harrison cordially to his modest rooms at 10 Rue Monsieur-le-Prince, near Odéon, on the Left Bank. A short, intense figure with a large head and penetrating black eyes, he searched the youthful face before him for evidence of agreement, discoursing methodically in French 'with extreme volubility, precision, and brilliance' in answer to questions about his system set at his own request by his young visitor. Upon learning that Harrison still called himself a Christian, or at least a theist, he explained that he did not expect followers to abandon theistic ideas altogether, though he believed that their study of science would lead to that. He spoke, Harrison later recalled, 'entirely as a philosopher—much as J. S. Mill would speak—not at all as a priest'.[78]

At the time of their meeting Harrison probably knew little of Comte's life—of his bitter academic feuds and loss of friends and positions, or of his pathetic idealization of an ordinary woman, Clotilde de Vaux, after her death, and in spite of her refusal to accept him as a lover. Nor could he ever bring himself to see Comte in his last years as most others saw him: an eccentric recluse, a dogmatic visionary working out in a synthetic religion of obsessive formalism his own prejudices and frustrations. Rather, in that morning's talk, Harrison found inspiration for a lifetime. Therefore, forgetting his characterization of Comte as a philosopher only, Harrison, with somewhat unusual rhetorical excess, wrote in another passage that he had 'been suffered to know in the flesh' that 'mighty spirit' who 'made me feel the beauty of the new faith which he lived and died to teach mankind'.[79] 'Altogether', he concluded, 'I must say that no interview of my whole life was so interesting and instructive, and no man I have ever seen, unless it were Mazzini, was so impressive as a powerful personality and genius.'[80]

2

Neo-Positivism

1855–1861

NEW STUDIES

Harrison left Oxford feeling free at last of 'all that sneaking annotation of the book of life which worries the plain understanding so in colleges and schools'.[1] For his holidays he planned to tour Tuscany disguised as a painter, but reports of cholera in Italy forced him to settle for a more conventional ramble through Austria and Germany with Lawrence and Charles. He found Nuremberg 'a wonderful fossil' and Munich a 'city of royal caprice', but Berlin and Dresden offered little except for the galleries, and in Vienna there was a 'garrison' atmosphere.[2] His distaste for German as opposed to French and Italian culture was fixed for a lifetime; on his frequent visits to the Continent during the next half-century he would spend but three days on German soil.

Back in London by the end of November, he entered the law chambers of Joshua Williams, a conveyancer at Lincoln's Inn who for £ 105 taught conscientiously in the precise, graceful language that gave his legal texts their distinction. Harrison appreciated his verbal brilliance but decided that though lawyers might seem no worse than their fellows, they fostered a corrupt system. He took to addressing fellow students as 'expert thieves'.[3] In 1857, however, he found six months' relief studying Roman law as a private pupil of Henry Maine, Regius Professor of Civil Law at Cambridge, then lecturing in Middle Temple Hall. It was not easy overcoming Mr Harrison's contention that the history and theory Maine was introducing into legal studies would be of little practical use,[4] and in the end Harrison believed his association with Maine had 'hardened' his 'habitual indifference' to legal practice. But Maine had also encouraged in him a 'keen interest in Jurisprudence on its scientific side' and increased his already formed determination to study history and law side by side 'and so read the latter aright'.[5] A bonus was the circle of brilliant young men to whom Maine introduced him—James Fitzjames Stephen, Vernon Harcourt, and George Venables—all, like Maine, eking out legal fees by writing anonymously for the *Saturday Review*.[6] But lacking their motivation, Harrison did not seek similar employment. The anonymity and slashing style of the 'Saturday Reviler' so offended him that he composed a mock prospectus for the journal promising as writers well-educated gentlemen free from 'the insidious affectation of "principle" '.[7]

To study equity law Harrison went from Williams to John Wickens, then Junior Counsel to the Treasury. As the date early in 1858 set for his call to the Bar approached, he obtained Mr Harrison's permission to stay for a time with Wickens even after that event, having learned that Wickens had thought he was getting a more experienced man than Harrison turned out to be. Besides wishing to prove himself, Harrison probably did not feel able to handle briefs independently, and in any case he was enjoying his conversations on 'books and general anecdotes of life' with Wickens as they walked home in the same direction each evening.[8]

The clear-sighted Mr Harrison suggested about this time that Oxford had weakened Fred's tolerance for 'the dry drudgery of legal work'. But he had not become idle. When he finally took his own chambers by the end of 1858, at number 7 New Square, Lincoln's Inn, he could get through a mortgage, a will, and an equity suit in court, though his heart was not in it. At Comte's suggestion he was poring over texts of the physical sciences, and also attending lectures by Richard Owen, Thomas Huxley, and John Tyndall, and visiting natural history museums. He even engaged as a tutor Edward Liveing, a medical student.[9] They concentrated on the brain and sense organs because Comte, who dismissed psychology as a discipline, explained human behaviour by reference to three faculties of the brain: the affective, speculative, and active. The affective were the strongest ('We tire of thinking, and even of acting; we never tire of loving') and were of two kinds, the personal and the social, promoting, respectively, egoism and altruism (Comte's term). Man's duty was to subordinate the former to the latter, to 'Live for others'. But it was also to 'Think in order to act'.[10] Harrison's thinking about science was never more than perfunctory, but he acquired enough information in these years to justify in his own mind Comte's claim for the applicability of scientific methodology to social thought.

Comte's stress on the biological organism's *milieu* (another of his coinages) gave Harrison an 'open mind' about *The Origin of Species*.[11] Still, Darwin's emphasis on competition in the evolutionary process was less attractive to him than Comte's on co-operation. Comte's lack of evidence for his theories did not trouble Harrison, who once defined the 'Positivist minimum of science' as 'a flea bite … in a sense an enlightened ignorance'.[12] He believed his own study of science had saved him from 'a pedantic specialism' and from 'attempting to settle ultimate principles by vague hypotheses and so-called intuitions'.[13] But he was not very interested in 'why men and animals were so created'.[14] He also regretted Bridges's study of science, attributing to it his Third Class at Oxford in 1854; in their 'narrow pedantry' the examiners had not rewarded his 'wide reading'.[15]

Harrison himself was more eager to see Bridges excel in historical than scientific studies. Therefore, since Bridges decided to compete for the Arnold Essay Prize in 1856, when the topic set was 'European Jews in the Middle Ages', Harrison turned over to him the notes and books he had already collected for an essay of his own under the guidance of a leading Hebrew scholar known to Sir Isaac Goldsmid, the financier, a friend of the Harrisons. Happy to be free of competition, which he disliked, and of the scholarship, which he was finding onerous, Harrison rejoiced when Bridges gained the prize and, soon afterwards, an Oriel Fellowship.[16] He was less pleased by Bridges's decision to study medicine. Comte required such an education for the Positivist priesthood, but Bridges was thinking far less of that than of his desire to practise medicine. Yet he was sufficiently drawn to Positivism as a system at this time to accompany Congreve to Paris for the comme-moration service held for Comte by Positivists three weeks after his death from cancer at the age of fifty-nine on 7 September 1857.[17]

Upon learning of the death, Harrison told Beesly of experiencing 'a singular number of feelings', but the one he dwelt on in his letter was his hope that Congreve and Bridges would no longer believe a Positivist Church possible. Though Harrison deplored the 'horror and scorn' Comte's religious ideas had aroused, he confessed: 'The more I am drawn to his philosophy as a whole, the more unsatisfactory I find his religion and his church.'[18] His own study was increasingly in history. To Beesly, then teaching history at Marlborough College, in Wiltshire, he proposed founding a school of historians to provide England with an account of its past that was free of the bias of existing texts.[19] That such a reading would reflect ideas from both Carlyle and Comte seems likely. Harrison pronounced Bridges too 'serene' about Positivism, and seems to have thought Vernon Lushington's series on Carlyle in the *Oxford and Cambridge Magazine* in 1856 'visionary',[20] but he was himself clearly under the spell of the romantic medievalism common to Comte and Carlyle. When Millais exhibited *Sir Isumbras at the Ford* in 1857, Harrison construed the autumnal scene and great age of the knight as signifying the end of an era, and the knight's concern for the children he is ferrying across the river on his horse as representing the turning of 'generous strength' from war to humane deeds under the inspiration of 'thought of holy maid and holy church', which in the picture are suggested by the nuns on the distant river bank.[21]

Congreve, who had already reached the shore of Positivism, was pronounced a 'Positiviste complet' by Comte at their last meeting, which occurred after Congreve had left Oxford and married his cousin, Maria Bury (no celibate priesthood for Positivists). Then the Congreves settled down in obscure rooms in South Fields, Wandsworth.[22] Harrison called infrequently, out of a sense of duty, and learned with dismay of Congreve's occasional lecturing. 'The world's history from Adam to '56 is the least portion he deigns to take at once', Harrison said of his former mentor's now thoroughly Comtean approach to history; Comte's system could clearly 'paralyse the minds of its best followers'.[23] He had joined Thorley in helping Congreve prepare a new edition of Aristotle's *Politics* in 1854,[24] but spoke critically of Congreve's more obviously Positivist publications: a pamphlet in 1856 calling for Britain's return of Gibraltar to Spain, and another in 1857, a response to the Mutiny, demanding total British withdrawal from India. Both essays illustrated Comte's principle of the subordination of politics to morality. To Harrison, however, the first essay also revealed the 'fatal petrifaction' of its author's mind,[25] the second his arrogance—that of a man atop a post shouting: 'Gentlemen: I am an atheist, and I strongly advise you to cut your throats.'[26]

Misguided as Congreve's political propaganda seemed to Harrison, still worse was his translation in 1858 of Comte's *Catéchisme positiviste*, the thirteen 'systematic conversations' between a woman and a Positivist priest about the Religion of Humanity. Harrison complained to Beesly about the detail: 'If he [Comte] had said only there that is my sketch, work it out, I should have been a Positivist out and out, for it never appears to me incompatible with theism.'[27] The parodic nature of Comte's ritual, however, precluded such easy acceptance. His nine 'social sacraments' were Presentation (like baptism), Initiation (at the age of fourteen), Admission (at the age of twenty-one), Destination (at the age of twenty-eight), Marriage, Maturity (at the age of forty-two), Retirement, Transformation (at death), and Incorporation (seven years after death). Women were excluded from Admission, Destination, Maturity and Retirement, since these sacraments concern men's working life. Woman's role as moral teacher and inspirer was seen in private prayer, which was to be directed to man's three 'guardian angels', mother, wife, and daughter (with substitutes allowable if necessary). The object of public worship, Humanity, or the *Grande Être*, was depicted in terms suspiciously like those Comte used for Clotilde de Vaux. Harrison likened her influence to Beatrice on Dante;

but Comte had produced a polity, not a poem. It was for an earthly paradise ruled over by thirty bankers, whose vocation fitted them for the task by removing them from the labour of the masses they would direct. Even the son of a London stockbroker might balk at that.

But Harrison did not go so far as Fitzjames Stephen, who considered Comte mad.[28] Schooled in Plato and acquainted with Hegel, Harrison could appreciate Comte's use of the abstraction 'Humanity' to inspire altruism in man's life (his 'objective existence') and to represent the corporate body man joins in death (his 'subjective existence'). Comte's idea of men venerating women as morally superior coincided with an attitude that Harrison, like most Victorians, took for granted.[29] And his own love of High Church practices prepared him to see the point of Comte's religious ritual, even while regretting the rigidity with which Comte presented it. Moreover, features of Comte's religion derived from the rationalist practices of the French Revolution, an event which Harrison had learned to value from Carlyle as well as from Comte: Comte's calendar, with four-week months and a thirteen-month year, originated in republican calendars used in Paris during and after the Revolution; and the names Comte gave his months and days honoured great historical figures, as did much of the Revolution's iconography. The 'Positivist Library', a normative list of some 150 authors and 270 titles, had obvious educational value. Not surprising, then, was Harrison's assertion that his own 'attachment' to France was 'positively religious', and was being strengthened by Positivism. But he felt no 'need now of a separate Church—of a few half-prepared, half-trained, half-hearted enthusiasts ... No! Positivism as yet can be only *Education* ... A John the Baptist may be needed to prepare. We are not yet ready for a Christ.'[30]

Harrison's education in religion for a time consisted of systematically visiting London chapels and churches. F. D. Maurice at Lincoln's Inn Chapel, as well as more orthodox divines, confirmed his earlier disillusionment with the creeds. Of course, the personal appeal of the men he heard varied; Maurice's sweetness and humility contrasted with Charles Spurgeon's 'gloriously coarse' ways. When Mrs Harrison complained that by wanting to hear Spurgeon Fred showed a 'morbid craving for excitement', he described the great Baptist as 'remarkable', his extravagances suited to his audiences and obtrusive only when compared to the 'starched pulpit' of the Established Church.[31] Congreve, she had come to believe, was 'not a Christian man', but Fred pointed out that Congreve's religion was not his and said they never discussed the matter. But he also confessed that her views were not his either. She saw the Church 'through the bright medium of ... affection and duties'; he had to look into the wide facts.... Do I not see it as a selfish sect—pressing on other Christians—keeping them from its schools and colleges—grasping its own wealth? Do I not see year after year more complete estrangement from the poor? ... A church must teach—bind—regulate. *I must find one that will.*³²

Harrison may have concentrated on the weakness of the Church as an institution in order to divert his mother's attention from the weakness of his own allegiance to its doctrine. He had not yet openly criticized either its teaching or pastoral work, but had channelled his anticlericalism into university reform agitation. The Act of 1854 had left religious tests as requirements for the MA, for voting in Convocation, and for most fellowships, and had set up a Commission to formulate principles to guide the colleges' reform of their statutes. In London Harrison helped to co-ordinate efforts by C. S. Roundell, Charles Bowen, James Bryce, Lyulph Stanley, Albert Rutson, and other former Oxford friends, with those of reformers within the University like Goldwin Smith, Mark Pattison, and Benjamin Jowett.³³ Harrison's own proposals for Wadham included drastically diminishing the Warden's power and liberalizing fellowships, innovations others wanted too but which seem to have increased the personal animus against him. He reported to Beesly after one Oxford visit: 'The Warden shrieked about infidels, atheists, backbiters ... coming down from London to disturb the harmony of a happy family.... The row's begun.'³⁴

Before that row was finished, Harrison had undertaken to teach in an institution requiring no religious tests, the Working Men's College, founded in 1854 by Maurice to bridge the gap between London working men and the educated. The role of teacher as Maurice conceived it was comparable to that of the philosopher who in Comte's scheme would enlighten the proletariat and thus prepare for the Positivist era. Teaching at the College was an early stage in Harrison's apprenticeship as a Positivist leader. Maurice, for his part, welcomed idealistic young graduates like Harrison and did not inquire into their religious attitudes. And at first Harrison's seemed hardly to matter; nor did Maurice's trouble Harrison at first. Christian Socialism, he assured Beesly, meant 'only that men and teachers are working well and pleasantly and sometimes make vague remarks about Mammon worship'. Harrison taught both Latin and history—the French Revolution, Napoleonic Wars, the rise of modern Italy and France, the growth of British industry. 'Pitching into the Pope' or the Constitution could be amusing; taking a group of students to Switzerland, where Harrison knew how to travel inexpensively, proved enjoyable; and there was satisfaction in entertaining them at his parents' eighteenth-century summer residence

with its wooded landscapes, at Eden Park, near Beckenham, Kent.
Moreover, it was exhilarating to have some of London's most talented
men as colleagues: barristers like Tom Hughes, author of *Tom Brown's
Schooldays*, John Malcolm Ludlow, a Francophile like himself,
Frederick James Furnivall, the philologist, and M. E. Grant Duff and
Fitzjames Stephen, who wrote for the *Saturday Review*; Oxford friends
like Pearson, Cookson, and Godfrey Lushington; and the Pre-
Raphaelites, Edward Burne-Jones, Thomas Woolner, and Dante
Gabriel and William Rossetti, as well as two of the Brotherhood's
admirers, John Ruskin and Vernon Lushington.[35]

In the glow of such fellowship even Maurice appeared at first to be 'a
rare and splendid man' who, 'if it were not for the trail of the old
university slime over him and his friends, would do great things'.[36] But
that trail became obstructive when Harrison proposed teaching history
by historical epochs, with themes related to those in other courses
when possible. Thus, when a history class studied Roman Britain, a
grammar class might take up the influence of Latin on English. Such a
scheme he argued would overcome much student discontent stemming
from 'unsatisfactory because undirected efforts'.[37] Maurice thought
otherwise. He hated system, and behind Harrison's suggestion detected
the ideas of Comte, which Maurice thought offered a 'mere science
millennium'. He also feared Positivist impieties, and had already quashed
Furnivall's attempt to teach Mill's essay *On Liberty* and to introduce
Sunday excursions and dancing. With Harrison he employed the
strategy that had always brought Furnivall into line: he threatened to
resign if not upheld by the school council. Inevitably, it was not he but
Harrison who departed.[38]

ITALY: A NEW NATION

Politics as much as science and the study of religion and history
propelled Harrison towards Positivism in the 1850s. Opposing the
Crimean War and the British in India (though never with Congreve's
intransigence) gave him the experience of defending minority views, if
only to friends. It also gave him a hero, John Bright. Yet when the
Radical Quaker returned to Parliament in 1857 Harrison expressed
only qualified satisfaction; growing 'out of the position of English
radicals', he was growing into Comte's 'harmonious system'.[39] Comte
had depicted war as a corollary of 'theologism' but acceptable as a
defensive strategy during the Transitional Stage; in the Positivist era it
would be eliminated and the energies that had supported it diverted
into industry.[40] Britain was only in the Transitional Stage. Therefore

the refusal of radicals like Bright to support nationalist struggles for independence on the Continent was regrettable to Harrison. But how far Britain should go in backing foreign patriots he did not make clear, and he often wrote as if threats alone against repressive regimes would suffice. When in 1859 Napoleon III and Cavour conspired to free Lombardy and Venetia from Austrian rule, and the British government supported the status quo, Harrison's liberal sympathies were augmented by his long-standing literary interest in Italy. He had begun his study of Dante under Saffi at Oxford, and continued it in London under another Italian exile close to Mazzini, Frederico Campanella. By chanting sonorous verses from the *Divina Commedia* before retiring, Harrison led his grandmother, whose room adjoined his, to fear he had been 'perverted' to Rome and was praying in Latin. In fact, he had interleaved the text with sheets of his criticisms of Dante's religion and was longing to see the end of the Pope's temporal power.[41] Yet he did not think Mazzini's work towards that end beneficial; from the 'conspirator's dark chamber ... not altogether healthy or pleasant' were issuing ideas about humanity and duty reminiscent of Comte's, but also instructions to revolutionaries abroad that Harrison could not reconcile with Comte's injunction to 'Live Openly' and 'Destroy Only What You Replace.'[42] Neither Mazzini nor Saffi trusted Napoleon III's adoption of the Italian cause in 1859, but Harrison thought the Emperor's pamphlet on the subject 'masterly' and told Beesly that if only England had such a statesman the nation could, with France, 'now certainly (without war) advance the Italian question to a point from which it never could recede'.[43]

He was therefore not among the Volunteers enrolled by Hughes and Furnivall in 1859 to learn military techniques that might be needed to repel the French in a possible invasion. On the contrary, when Napoleon III sent troops into Italy in April, Harrison sought an expression of support for him, appealing first to Bright, without success, then to the editor of the *Daily News*, who endorsed his plan for a committee to flood London and provincial newspapers with articles advocating 'hearty sympathy with the Italian people' and (in deference to mounting Francophobia) 'respectful watchfulness' of the French.[44] He also gained support from two members of the Friends of Italy, Francis Newman, whose *Crimes of the House of Hapsburg* Harrison had read at Oxford, and George Jacob Holyoake, the Secularist, who in turn brought in Francis Pulszky, the exiled Hungarian nationalist. Pulszky's correspondence with Louis Kossuth, then in Italy raising an army for the French, provided useful information.[45] Co-ordinating the efforts of such notorious radicals was heady work, and Harrison's prose became contentious. Tennyson, in his poem on the Volunteers, 'Riflemen, Form!' had asked: 'How can a despot feel with the free?' Harrison now replied: 'A despot can make men free—as Louis XVI secured American independence.'[46] Beesly, for once more soberly pedagogic, urged men taking to the platform to use maps to illustrate the military operations and to sketch the historical events that had led to them.[47]

Hardly had the London campaign begun than the French abruptly halted operations in Italy. In July Napoleon made peace with the Austrians at Villafranca. The terms seemed to assure Victor Emanuel control of Lombardy, but left Venetia to Austria and restored the reactionary regimes of Modena and Tuscany. Cavour resigned in dismay, and Guiseppi Garibaldi, the famous soldier he had called into action, was in a quandary. Though 'prostrated' himself, Harrison resolved to 'put the best face on matters' and in the *Daily News* congratulated the Emperor's supporters: 'You saw that it was in his interest to do the good he professed, and … beyond his power to do the evil which was imputed.'[48] Matthew Arnold attributed Napoleon's withdrawal to pressure from the French clergy, who feared a secular Italy, and Francis Newman blamed it on Prussia's threat to intervene.[49]

Unsure himself, and unable to rest without knowing the results of the peace, Harrison set out for Italy on 26 August, assured by friends that Lord Palmerston and Lord John Russell, Prime Minister and Foreign Secretary of the new Liberal Government, approved, and carrying introductions to Italian leaders from Francis Newman, Holyoake, and others. He promised to send letters to the *Daily News*, *Morning Post*, and *Westminster Review* office, but declined offers to have his expenses paid. His reward would be seeing history in the making.[50]

The patterns were not always clear. Crossing the Alps at Mont Cenis Harrison noticed how fit the homecoming French soldiers appeared; why had they not been allowed to do more? At Turin he secured introductions from Cavour's associate, Count Mamiani, and Baron Poerio, the Neapolitan whom Gladstone's intervention had freed from King Bomba's prison in 1851. Cavour's Florentine representative, Senator Matteucci, offered to introduce him to Cavour himself, but upon learning of the despairing statesman's preference for privacy, Harrison, more the gentleman than the journalist, sacrificed the opportunity, to his later 'utter and perpetual sorrow'. Sailing from Genoa to Leghorn he met volunteers jabbering enthusiastically about joining up with Garibaldi in the Romagna (where Harrison later saw him in his red shirt); in Modena he talked with Luigi Farini, acting Governor; and in Florence he met the 'Iron Baron' Ricasoli and others in the Provisional Government there. Since everyone expected Piedmont to annex central Italy, Harrison too became sanguine and took time to indulge his cultural interests. He attended a soirée in Florence given by the city's intellectual leader, Fiovan Pietro Viussiux, and in Ravenna went on a pilgrimage to Dante's tomb with the aged Count Cappi, who had known Byron and his efforts in behalf of the Carbonari and who now asked of this latest visiting Englishman, so obviously a friend of Italy, 'E vuoto?'—and now, nothing?[51]

Harrison gave highly optimistic answers to this question in the letters he sent home for publication. He reported that 'offences against public authority' had entirely ceased—'the very robbers had vanished'—and traced this remarkable state of affairs to the people's resolute desire for unification and to their strong municipal governments, which he called a legacy of ancient Rome. But he did not suggest how the conflicting claims of national and local authorities were to be reconciled. Nor did he mention Comte's belief that Italy's 'political decomposition' was nearer its 'normal state' than unification would be, since in the Positivist era all large nations would be broken up. Rather he dwelt on the rejoicing in Florence over liberation from the north; the 'honesty and honour' of King Victor Emanuel; the financial wizardry of the Marquis Pepoli in Bologna; and the swift justice rendered by 'dictator' Farini in Parma when an agent of the old regime was discovered in a railway car—he was immediately decapitated and Harrison later saw the head atop a column in the Piazza.[52] Reaching home on his twenty-eighth birthday, he reiterated his praises of the new order in three more letters in the *Daily News* and had the satisfaction of seeing himself referred to in an editorial as 'an eminent personage'.[53]

Harrison followed Garibaldi's 'wonderful and brilliant' expedition of the One Thousand closely in the newspapers, and had letters from new acquaintances in Italy to augment the journalists' reports of the diplomacy that brought central Italy into Victor Emanuel's kingdom. Yet when he finally published an essay on Italy for the *Westminster Review* in January 1861, it treated the founding of the modern Italian state mainly as an illustration of Comte's central motto: 'Order and Progress'. Cavour represents the party of order—of the monarchy and constitutionalism; Garibaldi the party of progress—of revolutionary action. Each has historical analogues. Cavour's are Cromwell, William the Silent, and Danton—all men who surmounted 'the rules of prudence, legality, and moderation'—and Garibaldi's are the Maid of Orleans and the French Republicans of '93. But Cavour alone overcame the drawbacks attendant upon his virtues, his 'legality' stopping short of 'formalism' and his appetite for power being modified by public opinion. Garibaldi, with the illusions of revolutionaries, showed more character than intellect, and it was well that he chose to retire, like Cincinnatus, to private life, a model of 'social duty'.[54] Such rhetoric became embarrassing when Cavour wrote to Harrison acknowledging this work of his 'masterly pen'. Had Cavour actually read it? wondered Harrison. Becoming 'more and more disgusted' with political journalism, he resolved not to fall 'deeper into the literary groove'.[55] He therefore held his pen when Garibaldi attacked Cavour in the Chamber, when shortly afterwards Cavour died, and when Garibaldi suffered a humiliating defeat at Aspromonte. To Beesly, however, Harrison confessed that he thought Italy in a 'fatal situation—in which conservatives have no heart—and revolutionaries no sense'. Here was a new gloss on 'Order and Progress'.[56]

'NEO-CHRISTIANITY'

Though he predicted 'Promethean suffering' for Garibaldi's 'great spirit' because it was infected by the 'revolutionary virus',[57] Harrison's own radicalism had been sufficient to ensure his welcome in the circle of writers for the *Westminster Review*. Bridges introduced him to the editor, John Chapman, sometime in 1859 when, upon returning from medical studies in Paris to continue his work at St. George's Hospital in London, Bridges lodged in the Albion Street house that was home to Chapman and his family and a congenial gathering place for his friends.[58] Not a university man himself, Chapman was always on the lookout for well-educated contributors. Earlier in the decade he had happily turned over editorial responsibilities for a time to Marian Evans, the future George Eliot, who left his employ shortly before she began her life with George Henry Lewes in 1854. The Positivism of Bridges, Harrison, and Beesly (also in Chapman's circle) was no drawback; the *Westminster* had for years been thought of as the work of a 'Comtist coterie'. Chapman's publishing firm had accepted Harriet Martineau's translation of the *Philosophie positive* and Congreve's of the *Catéchisme* when most other firms would have rejected them on religious grounds.[59] Among members of Chapman's set Francis Newman, Professor of Latin at University College, probably had political and religious views closest to Harrison's. Herbert Spencer, embarked on a great philosophic synthesis rivaling Comte's, was perhaps the most impressive to him. There was also R. W. Mackay, author of yet another evolutionary study, *The Progress of the Intellect*,[60] and W. M. W. Call, an ex-clergyman who had reluctantly abandoned a translation of the *Philosophie positive* when he learned of Harriet Martineau's. His review of Congreve's *Catéchisme* was sympathetic enough for Congreve to include him on the list of eight persons to receive his circular on the commemoration of Comte's death held in Paris in 1858—a list that did not contain the names of Beesly or Harrison.[61]

Beesly was able to join the *Westminster* set because in 1859 he left Marlborough College, to Harrison's relief, to become Principal of University Hall, a Unitarian residence for University College. Beesly, like Arthur Hugh Clough earlier in the post, was not expected to conduct prayers, but it was understood that he would not proselytize for Positivism either. One of the hall's founders, the benevolent eighty-four-year-old Henry Crabbe Robinson, considered Beesly genial, if a bit inflexible in his unorthodoxy, and may have said a useful word to the right person when Beesly sought the Professorship of History at the College.[62] Harrison did his part by getting his father to speak to Sir Francis Goldsmid, a member of the Council of University College and son of a founder, Sir Isaac Goldsmid, his financier friend. Beesly gained the post and would hold it for over thirty years, for most of that time acting also as Professor of Latin at Bedford College.[63]

But no sooner had Beesly come within an easy walk of Harrison's chambers than Bridges decided to leave London for Melbourne, New South Wales. First, on 7 February 1860, he married his cousin, Susan Torlesse, the daughter of an Evangelical vicar in Stoke-by-Nayland, Suffolk, near the parsonage in which he had been brought up. She shared his religious views, and at the village wedding Harrison sensed the hostility towards them of both their families, a major reason they had decided to act on the teachings of their relative, Edward Gibbon Wakefield. When the Revd Mr Bridges warned at the wedding breakfast that godlessness 'leadeth to destruction', Harrison, as best man, found it hard to muster up the customary nuptial jollity.[64] In reality he was sorely anxious about his friend's departure. It seemed the dissolution of Mumbo, which he had come to think of as indispensable, an almost mystical body. He, Beesly, and Thorley presented Bridges with a ring like one they would also wear, engraved with the words 'propter te' chosen by Harrison from a passage in the *Imitation of Christ* that Comte had used in an invocation to Clotilde de Vaux in the *Politique positive*: 'I will love you more than myself, and will not love myself except for you.' But Harrison insisted that their use of the words signified only 'attachment to Mumbo' and allowed for 'any interpretation'.[65]

He was less indulgent towards the interpretation of Positivist and of

Christian texts offered by others. When Congreve publicly inaugurated the Religion of Humanity in England on 8 January 1859 with a sermon in his Wandsworth rooms linking Time and Space and Humanity in a 'Trinity of our religion', Harrison thought the attempt premature.[66] But he was not prepared to break openly with his old tutor.[67] It was different when seven Anglicans, six in Holy Orders, published *Essays and Reviews* early the next year in an effort to modify Church teachings to accommodate biblical scholarship and science. Harrison made a name for himself among Chapman's writers and, indeed, in a far wider circle, by reviewing the work in the *Westminster*. No more sensational entry into the 'higher journalism' could be imagined—and no more revealing disclosure of his own convoluted religious attitudes.

Harrison's interest in *Essays and Reviews* stemmed in great measure from its origins at Oxford, where five of the seven contributors had been educated: Jowett and Pattison, his examiners; Henry Bristow Wilson, whose heterodox Bampton lectures he had found 'masterly'; Baden Powell, Savilian Professor of Geometry and like Pattison and Jowett a prominent University reformer; and Frederick Temple, Headmaster of Rugby. The others were Charles W. Goodwin, a Cambridge Egyptologist whose brother, Bishop Harvey Goodwin, Harrison knew slightly; and Dr Rowland Williams, Vice-Principal and Professor of Hebrew at St. David's College, Wales. Harrison's attention may have been directed to the volume by the *Westminster*'s brief notice of it in July, 1860, five months after its publication, calling four of the essays negative in their treatment of received ideas—Williams's for his sympathetic review of Baron von Bunsen's biblical criticism, Baden Powell's for his scepticism about miracles, Goodwin's on the incompatibility of modern geology and the Mosaic cosmology, and Jowett's on judging biblical texts by general literary criteria. It found essentially constructive the essays by Temple, on non-Christian as well as Christian sources of civilization, by Pattison, on religious thought in England in the eighteenth century, and by Wilson, urging religious tolerance to create a national church.[68] During the summer Harrison visited Oxford and learned from William Lambert Newman, a Fellow of Balliol and protégé of Jowett's, that Jowett was dissatisfied with the book's quiet reception and wished its 'real character and aim' more widely known. Accepting the charge, Harrison obtained Chapman's commission for an essay and waited for his summer holiday to write it.[69]

Harrison probably did not know that the *Westminster*'s account of *Essays and Reviews* was in fact written by one of the authors, Wilson, who, like Pattison, had been contributing to Chapman's journal for some time. As reviewer Wilson had quoted from a passage in the book's preface asserting that though the seven had composed their essays independently, their common purpose was 'to illustrate the advantages ... from a free handling ... of subjects peculiarly liable to suffer by the repetition of conventional language and from traditional methods of treatment'. Harrison desired to do justice to that aim, which he respected, but also to accomplish several purposes of his own, not all, however, originating with him. Here he was, supposedly enjoying his summer holiday, and instead, he complained to Beesly, struggling to write an essay that would please Chapman, and somehow express the 'deference' he felt for Jowett and Pattison ('Who am I to criticise them?') as well as his sense of how 'pitiful' he felt them to be. The required anonymity of his essay seemed partly to blame for his uneasiness; he had taken over from Congreve Comte's express condemnation of all unsigned publications. Composing his letters on Italy he had felt the same frustration. Such journalism was 'twice cursed. It curseth him that writes and him that reads.' Finally, at the appropriately named Eden Park, under the apprehensive eye of his mother, he ate the journalistic apple and wrote 'furiously, neither pausing nor correcting, at the rate of five or six pages of print *per diem*'.[70]

Harrison's best, his most controversial essays, seem to have been written this way: after long brooding over some grievance, and initial anxiety about the consequences, he would overcome the subconscious resistance and finish in a burst of creativity, enabled by his school and university training to write clear and vigorous prose with great efficiency and requiring little emendation. The resistance to be overcome in this instance was manifold. He knew his father would deplore his participation in religious controversy and his mother find new cause to worry about his spiritual well-being. And what would Jowett and Pattison think? Did not *they* deserve at least that respect for 'thought, good sense, and general grasp of their subjects' which they had given *him* on his examination? What really drove his pen, he later asserted, was his sense of 'how hollow was the ground on which the book rested, and how many minds were being drawn into this shallow compromise instead of fairly seeking for sure truth'.[71]

He entitled his essay 'Neo-Christianity' to convey at the outset the impression that what the Essayists were saying was new—which he knew to be true for the majority of Anglicans, but not for the *Westminster*'s readers—and that they were all saying the same thing—which he knew was denied in the Preface; although he insisted that joint publication implied joint responsibility. And his aim was to push the Essayists' conclusions to their logical limits, to show that 'the moment one cardinal dogma is surrendered as uncertain or even provisional, the whole intellectual framework gives way.... Creeds, like Caesar's wife, cannot even bear to be suspected.' By identifying the authors as 'representatives of our ecclesiastical foundations' he sought to suggest that their words carried weight in the Church, even while he stressed how unacceptable their ideas would be to most church-goers. That the book had raised no immediate outcry he took to mean that it had been 'studied, pondered, and approved' at the universities, though his purpose was to expose the split in the educated clergy over how it should be received. Temple he singled out for adopting from Comte 'without acknowledgement and possibly unconsciously' a comparison of the evolution of mankind with the growth of a colossal man, an idea that was in fact a commonplace, and of misusing the idea by virtually identifying mankind's history with that of the West, thereby neglecting Confucius, Muhammad, and Buddha, figures to whom Comte gave at least lip-service. Even more obviously designed to make a new religion seem imperative was his warning against 'denouncing bibliolatry in order to encourage bibliology'. In the end he granted that honour was due the Essayists for their courage in stating their conclusions, but he insisted that what was needed was 'strength, not merely to face the world, but face one's own conclusions.... Religion, to regain the world, must not only be not contrary to science but it must be in entire and close harmony with science.... Not only must it have a place beside philosophy, morals, and politics; but it must guide and elevate all these.'[72]

Compared to Congreve's open preaching of Comte's system, Harrison's allusions to it were so tenuous as to constitute little more than what could be termed 'Neo-Positivism'. Even so, he may have feared he had gone too far. He waited for Chapman to come down to Eden Park to read, approve, and take away his text. He then set off for his first holiday in the Lake District, where he remained until after the essay appeared. His letters were unusually filled with complaints. At Lowood Inn on Windermere a Lancastrian's burr offended him, as did friendly overtures of a 'young Manchester bagman' wishing to join him on walks. The fells seemed Lilliputian after the Alps, and a head cold and rain further lowered his spirits. He was 'wretched' at Bolton Abbey, though in a 'Byronic' mood that enabled him to enjoy his misery, and at Fountains and Rievaulx he mused of past times 'when men could live whole lives of unbroken repose, beauty, and devotion'. England's ruins reinforced Comte's romantic medievalism. At Rybourne, near Halifax, he stayed with Bridges's friends, George and Georgina Hadwen, a wealthy mill-owning family, from whom he learned that Bridges's parents looked upon their son's exile with a kind of relief. Shocked at such intolerance, Fred wrote his mother: 'It is impossible that you could ever come to look on me as they do on him even if I shared, which I do not, his opinions.'[73]

Just where Harrison did stand became a subject of discussion upon his return home, for 'Neo-Christianity' was by then known to be his work. Chapman forwarded two letters of congratulation, one from Huxley, expressing 'the entire sympathy and concurrence of a few active men of science'; the other from John Tyndall, exclaiming: 'Won't it open the eyes of these Oxford men!'[74] Other *Westminster* writers added their praise. The response from Oxford was different. Samuel Wilberforce, Bishop of Oxford, was the first to show that his eyes had been opened. In the *Quarterly Review* he quoted Harrison to support his own contention that the Essayists had deceived themselves in trying to retain Christianity's 'subjective powers' without its 'objective truths', and he advised those in clerical office to resign.[75] For Harrison there was little gratification in being named as an ally by the man who the previous June had goaded Huxley at the famous British Association meeting at Oxford. Harrison was even more dismayed when A. P. Stanley attempted to rescue the Essayists in the April *Edinburgh Review* by 'bitterly' attributing much of the weight of Wilberforce's attack on them to the '*Westminster* manifesto'. To Stanley it presented 'the mixture of Paganism and Catholicism in which the followers of M. Comte have found a refuge'. He accused the author, whom he did not name, of 'retaining a certain amount of religious sentiment' but not belief in divine revelation.[76]

Harrison lost no time in remonstrating with Stanley, assuring him that Chapman had shortened his article and hence misrepresented its meaning.[77] Yet in Harrison's two printed accounts of Chapman's visit to Eden Park he makes no mention of any distorting of his text, saying only that Chapman was delighted with it, especially the title, but finding it too long, cut twenty pages, which Harrison himself burned. And in a diary entry in 1863 he said of the published article: 'I retract nothing…. As to the base notions attributed to me, their authors themselves regret them.' This leaves unclear the grounds for his critics' regret, but it is in keeping with Harrison's statement in 1907, when, reprinting the essay, he denied that it had been 'ill-timed, unjust, or overstated'.[78] Whatever Stanley came to believe about Harrison's intentions being thwarted, and for whatever reasons he came to believe it (no letter from Harrison to Stanley survives) he did not remove all reference to the Positivism of 'Neo-Christianity's' author when he reprinted his own essay. Yet in a letter to Harrison about the episode he speaks as if Harrison had denied that he was a fully-committed

Positivist. Stanley apologizes for having caused him 'unnecessary pain', expresses chagrin at having 'misunderstood' his essay, and reports that upon learning from Jowett that Harrison's Fellowship was in danger he had 'lost no time' in talking to the right people and could assure Harrison that 'nothing is intended to be done.' He even asks to be allowed to intercede again if Harrison's Fellowship seemed vulnerable.[79]

After Stanley's article appeared, Jowett, somewhat more sternly than he, wrote to Harrison to point out that no one holding a fellowship should jeopardize it by injudicious pronouncements. And he was strongly against the author of 'Neo-Christianity' (Harrison is never named) doing anything to vindicate his position; instead he should make 'energetic and persevering efforts to alter it ... '.[80] Only in a second letter, a reply to one from Harrison that does not survive, does Jowett mention Positivism openly, and then it is to express his satisfaction at learning that Harrison is 'not a Positivist' and to note that he once studied Comte and found him 'much more of a metaphysical and speculative thinker ... than is commonly supposed'. Jowett agreed with something Harrison had written about the need for 'great religious changes' and also agreed that religion had to be 'much more based on fact'. But it could not exclude 'the hope of a future life, or communion with God, or the sanctifying and elevating influence of the N[ew] T[estament]'. Assuming, or pretending to assume, that Harrison's article had misrepresented his own views, Jowett appealed to both martyrdom and self-interest: 'Everyone who takes part in any political and religious movement must count to be misrepresented, and sometimes the best way out is by silence ...'. Harrison could not be 'too cautious'. Jowett ended by declaring that Stanley would be 'grieved at driving you out of your Fellowship' for Stanley's 'strong language' had stemmed from his belief 'that you wanted to drive us out'.[81]

If that had not been Harrison's aim, what was? He himself later noted with surprise that all of the Essayists known to him personally remained on good terms with him, Wilson and Goodwin even telling him he had 'served the cause'.[82] The move against his retaining his Fellowship came to nothing. Nor did he volunteer his resignation, having discovered when conducting a survey, in connection with the agitation to remove religious tests, that the undergraduates held 'curiously different views' about what signing the Thirty-Nine Articles actually implied, and no one thought he 'literally engages his belief in each position'.[83] This would not be the last sociological inquiry that served to justify the predisposition of the surveyor.

What made Harrison's escape from retaliation so remarkable was that all the Essayists (except Baden Powell, who died in 1860) suffered harassment. The most seriously troubled were Williams and Wilson, tried in the Court of Arches on thirty-two charges. Harrison later said he gave 'time, money, and every assistance' to their defence, which in Williams's case was conducted by Fitzjames Stephen, an especially relentless critic of Comte and brother to the literary critic Leslie Stephen, who resigned his Cambridge tutorship on religious grounds just about this time. Harrison also joined with others to 'resist' the 'odious persecution' of Jowett, which included his humiliating trial for heresy at Oxford, and a mere token salary as Regius Professor of Greek. And so far did Harrison seem to identify himself with the oppressed liberals in the Church that he attended the trials of Williams and Wilson; and when a crusty Anglican clergyman greeted him affably, he even declared that the Church 'must have good life in it yet'.[84] The trial was of special interest to him because presiding over the Court of Arches was Dr Stephen Lushington, father of the twins and a friend of Jowett's. At the age of eighty, he was nearing the end of a distinguished career in which in his piety he had managed to find time to write hymns for children.[85] He ruled that both the defendants were guilty of denying divine inspiration of the Bible and Wilson also of denying the doctrine of eternal damnation.[86]

The appeal of Williams and Wilson to the Judicial Committee of the Privy Council in 1864 was equally fascinating, and more gratifying, to Harrison. Presiding was the Lord Chancellor, Lord Westbury, his old friend Richard Bethell. The four lay judges and Bishop Tait of London, with the two Archbishops dissenting, acquitted the appellants of having taught anything inconsistent with Church formularies, a verdict that led Harrison's witty friend at the Bar, Edward Henry Pember, to compose in his presence the now often-quoted epitaph for Lord Westbury. In the version authenticated by Harrison he is said to have 'closed a long and successful life by dismissing Hell with costs, and thus he deprived the religious world of its last hope of Eternal Damnation'.[87] Actually, of course, Lord Westbury's career did not end with the decision—he may later have wished it had—and his ruling did not affect the beliefs of most Anglicans. Their position was far better illustrated by the 137,000 Church members who sent thanks to the Archbishops dissenting from the majority, by the 11,960 clergymen who signed an Oxford Declaration attesting their belief 'without reservation' in scriptures and eternal punishment, and by the Bishops who voted in Convocation to condemn *Essays and Reviews*.[88] Harrison was as scornful of these evidences of fundamentalism in the Church as was Westbury, but whereas the Lord Chancellor vented his spleen by assailing 'Soapy Sam' in the Lords, Harrison kept his eye on the Church as a whole and judged that what it had 'won in Liberty it has lost in Honesty', for 'the Creeds became a matter of open opinion.' There was now no gainsaying Comte's epithet for the Established Church: 'l'hypocrisie Anglicane'.[89]

Comte's judgement of Anglicanism took on new meaning in March, 1861, when a letter from Bridges told of the death of his wife only months after their arrival in Melbourne. He was sending the body home for burial and asked Harrison to arrange the interment if his own ship did not arrive in time. Recalling the image of a gravestone worked in a bookmark he had noticed among the wedding gifts of the dead woman, Harrison condemned the religious morbidity of her family which had apparently influenced her to request burial near them. 'Human nature over the grave asks some awful questions', he commented to Bridges's friend Mrs Hadwen: 'Let each mind answer them for the present as it can best and can find most right.' He at least was ready to find solace in what Comte called 'subjective immortality': 'This we know, that all that is well done lives after us, that the life, the action of each never dies, but goes on for ever, living and bringing good to perfection bound up for ever in the life of our race.'[90]

Another cause of his sadness about this time was the realization that 'Neo-Christianity' had plunged his mother into 'deep shock and grief'. Until the 'dark cloud' dissipated, as in some months it did, he confided his speculations about human providence and prayer to his diary and to Mrs Hadwen, who under Bridges's influence had become sympathetic towards Positivism. Some said the demise of the old creeds produced despair, but he had 'no doubt that the world is very good and going to good'. Yet he took Jowett's advice and not only refrained from defending his position in public but also urged Mrs Hadwen to say nothing about hers. He, in any case, felt no desire to do so. When Bishop Colenso's book on the mathematical inconsistencies of the Pentateuch provoked the next Church controversy, in 1862, Harrison marvelled that the work's 'stale difficulties and wrangling spirit' could interest anyone; 'pulling the Bible narrative to pieces' held no attraction for him, since he regarded it as only one of many records of man's religious history.[91] Nor did he take the bait when Maurice and his friends issued *Tracts for Priests and People* as a reply to *Essays and Reviews*, though Ludlow in one essay denounced Comte for worshipping Clotilde de Vaux's dessicated arms (curious misinformation) and Maurice blew hot and cold about the 'Oxford man'—Harrison is not named—who usefully revealed challenges to the Church but in a 'defiant and contemptuous' manner and without understanding the issues.[92] But by this time Harrison had resigned from Maurice's staff at the Working Men's College and felt no need to notice this new trace of the 'Oxford slime'.

THE NEW HISTORY

Though relieved by Harrison's resignation, Maurice, like the Essayists, showed no hostility towards him. When Harrison asked help for an old school friend who had abandoned Holy Orders because of religious doubts, Maurice replied cordially, even holding himself and other Churchmen responsible for such cases because of their readiness to 'murder the truth which the other perceives'.[93] Such forbearance might have caused Harrison to regret his departure from the Working Men's College if the students had not disappointed him. He had started teaching convinced of his unfitness to instruct them, and never entirely lost his admiration of their 'strong, horny hands', but he soon came to see the men as 'mere parasites of the middle classes' desiring to learn 'passable English' in order to rise in the world.[94]

The Cleveland Hall in nearby Fitzroy Square seemed less restrictive when in 1861 he was introduced there as a lecturer in history by the radical publishers Edward Truelove and George Jacob Holyoake. Both men were sympathetic to Positivism; indeed, Holyoake had been larding his lectures and publications with Comte's formulas to provide the ethical content indicated by the term 'secularist' he used for himself as opposed to 'atheist'. Lacking self-confidence, he had lost the leadership of the secularist movement to the more brash and militant Charles Bradlaugh, who signed his works 'Iconoclast'. Holyoake was always deferential to Harrison, hoping perhaps to enlist his talents for his own purposes. Harrison, for his part, had already learned the value of such a well-connected radical during the campaign to aid the Italian nationalists. But lecturing at Cleveland Hall proved a 'very repulsive task'. The men lacked the rudimentary knowledge to appreciate the historical theory he sought to convey in the hope of influencing their politics.[95] 'Pedantic erudition', he told them, should not be their goal. They could rely on a few carefully selected texts and visits to museums, galleries, and historical sites, studying always cultural achievements and benefactors, not failures or villains. Above all they should grasp the 'connection of history'—its pattern of cause and effect—to prepare for the 'complete and balanced system of life' that the 'rich harvest of science' and material improvements would bring.[96]

Unsatisfied though he was with his lectures, Harrison published them in 1862 as *The Meaning of History*. His first book, it was ignored by major periodicals but served to launch the journalistic career of

James Thomson. Writing for the first time as 'B. V.' (in Bradlaugh's *National Reformer*), he judged that what was apparently new in the book was untrue, and what was true was only platitudinous. Though not yet known as 'the Laureate of Pessimism', he was especially hard on Harrison's advice about overlooking the wicked and unsuccessful in history. If Harrison saw the review, which is doubtful, he might have regretted having paid £ 120 for the book's publication.[97]

Some time in 1863, Harrison left Cleveland Hall, disappointed because he had attracted few listeners and created so little enthusiasm for either the rational republicanism of the French Revolution or the idealized Catholicism of the Middle Ages, individually or in the combination offered by Comte.[98] But in the same year he was able to call attention to both sides of Positivist thought in reviews for *The Reader*, a new journal dominated first by the Christian Socialists and then by Mill and some of the secularists of the *Westminster* set. In an early issue Harrison praised a study of the French Revolution that depicted it as having still-unfolding consequences, a major tenet of Comte's, and also a biography of St. Bernard of Clairvaux that replaced the image of the theologian with that of the moralist, an interpretation quite compatible with Comte's, who had included him in his Calendar.[99] Harrison meant his review to encourage the already marked Positivism of the biographer, James Cotter Morison, a barrister of Lincoln's Inn just his own age who had followed him at Oxford by several years. Like Harrison, he had independent means, his father having concocted Morison's Pills (to Carlyle a convenient symbol for any social panacea) and founded the British College of Health (to Matthew Arnold the epitome of 'the grand name without the grand thing').[100] Harrison also promoted Positivism in *The Reader* by welcoming in its pages Bridges's translation of Comte's *Discours sur l'ensemble* (*The General View of Positivism*), the first section of *Système de politique positive*, begun by Bridges on his sad return voyage from Australia. The review conceded that the work would offend many, but declared that it was not meant 'to be so much studied as worked out—not to be known, but to live by, not to believe, but to feel'.[101]

Harrison did not himself altogether avoid the philosophical issues thrown up by Comte. As a former student of Maine's he was able to read the manuscript of *Ancient Law*, the important book that grew out of Maine's lectures, and write one of its earliest reviews. It appeared in the *Westminster*, in April 1861, during the controversy over *Essays and Reviews*. Like many of the Essayists, Maine dealt with the idea of progress, and Harrison called the book a 'really scientific' work, finding its account of the three 'instrumentalities' by which society's changing needs are met in the law—'legal fictions, equity, and legislation'—parallel to the three stages discernible 'in so many other objects of inquiry'—the religious, metaphysical, and scientific.[102]

Despite this special pleading, Harrison's review pleased Maine.[103] But the Positivist view of history it pointed to had already drawn fire from the Regius Professors of Modern History at both Oxford and Cambridge. At Oxford, Congreve's old friend Goldwin Smith rejected the idea of a science of history and dismissed Comte's Law of the Three Stages as unverifiable and misguided in its elevation of intellectual over moral progress.[104] At Cambridge, Maurice's Christian Socialist colleague Charles Kingsley pointed out that the conception of law in human affairs was not new—man had long spoken of moral law—but the idea of law advanced in 'Neo-Christianity' was inadequate because it did not allow for free will.[105] Both Kingsley and Smith read history as a record of moral effort under God's Providence and thought their position threatened by Buckle, Mill, Comte, and others who wanted to apply the techniques of science to social thought.[106] Beesly, replying to Kingsley in the April *Westminster*, waxed so wrathful over the novelist's failure to distinguish between descriptive and prescriptive law that Harrison, still anxious about the reception of 'Neo-Christianity', asked indignantly: 'How shall I appear when it is known to be by a hand so close to mine ... ?'[107] Yet he conceded in the same letter that a draft of his own reply to Smith had seemed 'angry' to Charles Bowen, a barrister friend from the Oxford Essay Society, and that at Bowen's urging he had deleted the 'vituperative parts', treating Smith in the end only with 'a sort of good-natured contempt'.

But like 'Neo-Christianity', Harrison's article, published in the *Westminster* exactly a year after that essay, conveyed contempt far more clearly than good nature. Once again he sought to pull his opponent further in the direction of his own philosophy than the opponent wished to go. He quoted Smith's lectures to demonstrate that by assuming that like causes yield like results, Smith himself relied on what others called law. But, following Mill, Harrison also conceded that 'tendencies' might be a better word than 'law' for an observed uniformity in the operation of free will, which, agreeing with both Kingsley and Smith, he thought required by common sense. The subject, however, he believed need not concern the historian. His task was to provide historical data. It was the sociologist who constructed the laws of society. In thus drastically constricting the historian's role, pushing the problem of free will back a stage but not meeting its issues, and ignoring the other difficulties associated with calling history a study based on scientific methods, Harrison was merely following Comte.

But rather than pursue the questions raised by Smith, he devoted much of his essay to Smith's epigrammatical style, deeming it inappropriate, though actually admiring it enormously.[108] 'What a wit the beggar has', he exclaimed to Beesly.[109] And attempting to demolish him as a stylist led Harrison to formulate epigrams of his own. Smith, for example, was the 'Voltaire of the orthodox'. When Smith objected in the *Daily News* that Harrison (whom he identified only as the author of 'Neo-Christianity') had misrepresented him,[110] Harrison, also in that paper, again dwelt more on Smith's rhetorical strategies than his arguments, and declined altogether to follow up Smith's subsequently published letters.[111] It was no good 'wrangling' with a man as useful as Smith was to University reform, Harrison avowed.[112] His silence is perhaps better explained by his distaste for philosophic abstractions. It was as keen as his dislike of 'pulling the Bible to pieces', which similarly prevented him from replying to the critics of 'Neo-Christianity'. Moreover, his mother was dismayed by this latest sign of alienation from Oxford and Anglicanism, and Bridges, now practising medicine among the poor in Bradford, where Harrison visited him after dispatching his reply to Smith, chided him for wasting time on controversy when social problems needed attention.[113] In contrast to Congreve's insistence on the letter of Comte's teaching, and his disdain for all who would not accept it, Harrison was imbibing the spirit. He welcomed the chance to ally himself with reformers of many persuasions. They were not, as Congreve in his rigidity declared, merely 'blind castaways',

but are wise, tender, and true. Positivism—if it is the religion of duty—is surely not to be preached as a new and strange doctrine, to be learnt painfully like a new speech. It is here! It is come! The earth is full of it. The time is ripe. And the best of the world are all unconscious disciples and apostles of it.[114]

3

Alliances with the Working Class
1861–1870

Among Comte's 'unconscious disciples' Harrison would certainly have included the Christian Socialists. Four members of Maurice's staff—Hughes, Ludlow, R. B. Litchfield, and Godfrey Lushington (a conscious disciple by this time)—contributed to a special report on trade unions and strikes for the National Association for the Promotion of Social Science in 1860 that contained the kind of factual information Harrison thought needed for the new sociology. Speaking on the Industrial Revolution at the Working Men's College in that year, Harrison said that only by comparing prices and wages in recent decades could one hope to determine how far down the social scale the benefits of technological advances had penetrated. And though on his trip north later that year he noted the contrast between the 'obvious comfort, intelligence, health, and cheerfulness' of the 'best workmen', and the 'penury, brutality, and suffering' of others (whose 'blood and vice' were 'on the hands of the employer'), he thought it futile to speculate further without 'long reflection and investigation'. Gaining 'personal familiarity with the men themselves' became his second goal in a list he made in his diary about this time. Clarifying his religious views came first. He already knew that religion had to do with 'the good of mankind'. So his third goal followed from his first two: promoting working-class education—and his own as well. An alliance with the Christian Socialists enabled him to further all these aims.[1]

A major strike in the London building trades provided the opportunity. It had begun in 1859, when the unions were denied their request for a nine-hour day in place of the ten-hour day and Saturday half-holiday. Congreve, taking his thesis from Comte (though it coincided with what all friends of labour were saying), supported the men on the ground that they needed the extra time for 'moral and mental cultivation'. Lacking Marx's belief that capitalism inevitably exploited workers and the system was doomed, he did not attack it generally, but only advised the men to obtain 'competent counsellors'.[2] His medical studies, undertaken to fulfil Comte's requirements for the Positivist priesthood, precluded his acting further just then. But early in 1861, when the strike entered a new phase as the workers resisted the imposition of an hourly pay system, Harrison and Beesly thought labour's side of the struggle deserved airing. To investigate the issues they therefore joined with the same four members of Maurice's staff who had written for the NAPSS volume, and two barristers, Thomas Randle Bennett and Richard Holt Hutton.

It took weeks to arrive at a consensus. The employers proved as inaccessible to the committee as they had been to the union leaders, who now welcomed the committee's intervention. When the issues in the various disputes became clear—more than one building firm and several unions were involved—Harrison, for one, was irate. He saw the masters exhibiting 'deliberate selfishness, chicanery, and meanness' and the men 'united, intelligent, resolute, and moderate'. A strike meeting in the Surrey Theatre proved to be as full of pathos as any melodrama staged there. Writing with full heart, he drafted so bitter a letter for his colleagues to sign that Ludlow, who had learned the virtues of moderation in advocating industrial co-operatives, insisted on revising it. Harrison became almost as angry at him as he had been at Alfred Mault and Edward Lucas, two of the more aggressive builders. But Ludlow's judgement prevailed, and the two long letters published over the committee's names in *The Times*, *Daily News*, and *Spectator* were models of judicious argument. They pointed out that the hourly pay system would diminish employment in bad weather and slack periods; and since there would be no overtime pay, employers would be tempted to increase working hours. Skilled workers would be reduced to the status of casual labourers.[3]

Telling Beesly about his quarrel with Ludlow, Harrison conceded that the Christian Socialists' long service to labour had earned them the right to dominate the committee. But once its letters appeared he looked elsewhere for further support. He published two more on his own, initialled, and got Chapman to call the first to Mill's attention. Great was his annoyance when he learned from Chapman that the author of *Principles of Political Economy* believed hourly pay might be useful in improving workmanship! The comment seemed irrelevant, evidence of the harm that could stem from 'purely academic and doctrinaire opinions'.[4] Far worse, of course, was the average middle-class Briton's opinion of unions, fed as it was by press accounts of labour's rapacity and the inexorable economic 'laws' that doomed its aspirations. The *Spectator*, before Hutton became its editor about this time, had spoken of the normal work day as set by nature, from sunup until sundown. And so hostile to strikes was *The Times* that Harrison found reading its back files 'like coming upon the traces of some old crime'.[5]

The work of the committee was obviously not enough. Even before it helped obtain a compromise settlement in most of the affected firms—hourly pay at a rate that gave the men their old earnings for a ten-hour day, and an approximation of the Saturday half-holiday—Harrison described the stone-masons' part in the struggle at the 1862 meeting of the NAPSS. His paper provided the pretext for others to advance hackneyed arguments about the uselessness of unions and iniquities of strikes, with the attack led by William Newmarch, whom Marx would dub the 'Pharisee of political economy'. Yet almost as dismaying to Harrison was the interest of many delegates in the problems of working women. From the Positivists' perspective, the less said the better about a social reality that conflicted with their teachings about man's 'guardian angels'.[6]

Offsetting the utopian element in Harrison's approach to industrial society was his very practical assistance to the 'new model' unions that developed in the early 1860s. In these societies, largely patterned on the Amalgamated Society of Engineers, insurance benefits and strike funds were controlled by a central London office—in the engineers' union by William Allan, in the stonemasons' by Henry Broadhurst, and in the carpenters' (whose early history Beesly recounted in glowing terms for the *Westminster Review* after the builders' strike) by W. R. Cremer until 1862 and then by Robert Applegarth. With other officials of the larger unions, these labour leaders formed a London Trades Council, to which Harrison and Beesly became unofficial advisers.[7]

But Harrison was not content only to respond to appeals for advice; he actively sought out information about working-class conditions. On his trip north in 1861 he carried introductions from Holyoake, an authority on the co-operatives that flourished there, and from Francis Newman, whose work on political economy he had read at Oxford. Bridges provided other introductions and served as guide. Much they saw was encouraging: the model co-operative at Rochdale; the mill at Burley owned by the Liberal MP and Quaker, W. E. Forster; a workers' performance of *Coriolanus* in Staleybridge to which he was taken by the fiery old ex-Chartist preacher Joseph Rayner Stephens; and a mechanics' institute at Huddersfield. A clergyman Bridges knew spoke so earnestly about his parish duties that he made the Church seem still useful. Of the employers they saw, two especially impressed Harrison: Bridges's friend George Hadwen, the Halifax mill-owner Harrison had met the previous year; and William D. Hertz, a Bradford yarn merchant married to a promoter of working men's education who in later years would be a popular London hostess, Fanny Hertz. Both she and Georgina Hadwen would encourage Harrison's attachment to Positivism and help to convince him that there were generous souls who shared his social ideals. But nothing could efface the 'grimy vault' that troubled his thoughts long after he had returned from the north to the pastoral beauty of Eden Park.[8]

Convinced that his darker conclusions about industrial life merited circulation beyond family and friends, Harrison embodied them in a talk to the Working Men's College and sent a copy to Mrs Gaskell, whose novels had dealt with some of the places he covered. Her reply to him was cordial, but to Godfrey Lushington she complained of his failure to recognize the problems created by the poor Irish flooding into the north.[9] Soon there was a conspicuous source of distress in Lancashire, the 'cotton famine' caused by the blockade of American Southern ports in the Civil War. To investigate charges brought by Bridges and Rayner Stephens, among others, that relief funds for the unemployed were being mismanaged, Harrison, accompanied this time by Godfrey Lushington, returned to the area.[10] Before leaving London he joined other radicals in St. James's Hall to show support for President Lincoln and the Union. Bright's assertion on that occasion, that there was a new rapport between manufacturers and workers because of their common endorsement of the Union's cause, may have dissuaded Harrison and Lushington from publishing anything embarrassing to the relief officials they later interviewed, many of them factory owners.[11] In any case, the account that appeared with their joint signatures in *The Times* exonerated the administrators of most of the charges, though it also insisted that since all charity caused 'moral starvation', public works were desperately needed to provide temporary employment.[12] Reviewing the Central Relief Committee's report, Harrison in the *Westminster* noted, too, that while legislation for such a work programme was already under consideration, 'Government we all know ... never does anything till it is forced.' As for the role of the social investigator in forcing such action, he had mixed feelings. He sympathized with those who denounced the relief system, but also believed that by provoking criticism from such skilled polemicists as Charles Kingsley they had perhaps damaged their cause. Such a crisis required 'nerves like a surgeon's'; 'to do any good, one must not go mad.' And he saw, too, that writing on controversial issues was like 'standing in the pillory to be pelted'. There was something to be said for Comte's vision of a world without newspapers, with placards alone to keep the public informed.[13]

But paradoxically, trying to help usher in a social order on Positivist lines led Harrison deeper into journalism. One paper in which he wrote regularly on working-class matters in the 1860s was the *Bee-Hive*, a weekly founded in the wake of the builders' strike by a young carpenter, George Potter, one of its co-ordinators. At first Harrison was favourably impressed by Potter's energy and efficiency but he soon came to distrust his recalcitrance with employers and his 'catch-penny' journalism. Yet there was no denying the value of his paper as a 'free platform which one can mount without giving any pledge'. Harrison and Beesly, another regular contributor, were careful not to abuse their privilege by obtruding their Positivist theories.[14]

Harrison also managed to stay on good terms with the London Trades Council, many of whose members feared that the strikes Potter sometimes casually recommended would jeopardize their treasuries. Harrison's stand on the issue was somewhere between these extremes. Thus, in 1865 he was one of a committee of barristers who, after investigating accusations against Potter brought by George Odger, exonerated Potter of the more damaging ones, which included his alleged usurpation of the London Trades Council's prerogatives by convening labour leaders to gain their backing for striking North Staffordshire iron workers who had rejected an arbitration proposal.[15] The same industrial conflict provided Harrison with the subject of an article in the first issue of the *Fortnightly Review* in May of that year. But 'The Iron-Masters' Trade Union' offered a more sophisticated and more revolutionary rationale for strikes than had the impulsive, prag-matic Potter. Harrison argued that strikes were necessary to find out whether in any given industrial conflict the supply of labour exceeded or fell short of the demand, information that in his judgement was crucial to the fair determination of wages. The conventional argument, that wages fluctuated with prices, seemed to him specious, since a decrease in the price of a product could create a new demand for it that would in the end require more labour and allow an increase in wages from the increased profits. He did not entirely repudiate the orthodox economists' notion of laws of competition fixing wages up to the limit allowed by a 'wages fund'—the mythic sum total of money available for wages in any industry—but he insisted that profits were far more subject to fluctuation than had been usually supposed. An employer would have to open his books to the public to convince anyone that raising wages would cause his ruin. Whether or not Harrison was here consciously applying Comte's maxim 'Live Openly' is not certain. But there is no denying the Positivism of his further contention: that strikes were inevitable in an economy where social justice had not yet been attained, whereas the lockout was an industrial *coup d'état* exhibiting 'in the natural heads of society, a wanton contempt for every social duty'.[16]

By writing for both the *Bee-Hive* and the *Fortnightly*, Harrison made sure that his critique of the industrial order reached both the working and middle classes. Without much effort he could have increased his influence on the former, since Potter invited him to the paper's staff parties and even wished to give him editorial duties. But regular journalism had no appeal, and Potter's soirées proved tedious. The comic songs, recitations, and speeches by men whose tastes and education were far different from his own were a portent of what closer association with the staff would entail.[17] Moreover, Potter showed no interest in Positivism. Nor did the owners of the *Commonwealth*, another working-class weekly for which Harrison and Beesly wrote, and which Harrison was invited to edit. Explaining why he had not accepted the offer, Harrison told Beesly that the time might come when trade union priorities and Positivist goals conflicted; and, he asked, 'on political and social things, can we go in for less than Comte pure and simple?'[18] The *Fortnightly* made going in for Comte easy. Harrison was one of the group that had planned the periodical under the editorship of George Henry Lewes. His *Leader* articles on Comte in the early 1850s and his collection of a subsidy for the philosopher were probably what led Harrison to declare himself at the time ready to overlook Lewes's 'private enormities'—an allusion, apparently, to Lewes's liasion with the future George Eliot.[19]

Harrison first met the novelist on New Year's Day in 1860, when she and Lewes and he were guests of the Congreves in Wandsworth.[20] The Leweses (as they called themselves, though they were not married, for Lewes already had a wife) and the Congreves had become friends the previous year, after Mrs Congreve, hearing of their presence in the South Fields neighbourhood of Wandsworth, recalled her childhood acquaintance with Mary Ann Evans in Coventry and initiated a reunion. The Congreves rejoiced in her company and tolerated Lewes's; his high spirits and reputation as a bohemian were uncongenial to them.[21] They soon introduced Bridges to her, and then Harrison. Both were aware of their good fortune in meeting this newly risen star in the London literary firmament, but neither young man hesitated to cross her on matters concerning cherished convictions. Bridges expressed regret that she had written to *The Times* defending her choice of anonymity in publishing *Adam Bede*,[22] and Harrison, at their New Year's Day meeting, dared to challenge her assertion that military pomp seemed to have become more conspicuous than it had once been, a speculation at odds with Comte's belief that industrialization spelt the decline of warfare. It was a trivial matter, but Harrison remembered it, and also how deferentially she had behaved towards him, though he was only a twenty-eight-year-old barrister unknown to the general public, and she forty, with years of editing and writing behind her and a promising future in fiction.

It was not their common friendship with the Congreves nor the interest they shared in Comte that transformed Harrison's acquaintance with George Eliot into something more like friendship (the closeness of their relationship should not be exaggerated). Rather it was Harrison's essays on industrial topics that called him to her attention in the mid-1860s. Invited by Lewes to contribute to the *Fortnightly*'s first issue on any topic 'short of direct attacks on Christianity', Harrison told Beesly, who had received a similar invitation, that they should advance Positivist principles.[23] With this in mind Harrison developed his justification of strikes and theory of employers' responsibility for labour's welfare. Though the essay's excessive length led Lewes to set it in small type, Harrison had still more to say. Hoping to discredit once and for all the 'cruel jargon' of the orthodox political economists, he therefore went to Eden Park that spring to produce a companion piece. At first the writing went no easier than had the early stages of 'Neo-Christianity'. Perhaps he again mistrusted his ability to confute the ideas of well-known theorists; perhaps he doubted that anything he could write would go beyond what others had said. In any case, eventually ideas came to him so rapidly that he could hardly fit them all into his text, and upon finishing declared to Beesly that he had either 'written arrant stuff or proved pol. ec. to be all a mistake'.[24]

'The Limits of Political Economy' in fact falls between these extremes. It played a part in undermining the economic theories being used to discredit unions and strikes and, like his first essay, on the iron-workers, and a later reply to an ironmaster, it helped to dissociate Adam Smith from the orthodox economists who liked to cite *The Wealth of Nations*. Whereas they drew from it the idea of industry benefiting from a free economy, he pointed to Smith's insistence upon the social context of economic activity, and his concern for proper distribution as well as efficient production.[25] Besides claiming Smith as a source of his arguments, as had Comte, Harrison claimed Mill, a bolder move since Mill was just then retracting part of his earlier praise of Comte.[26] Of Comte's more embarrassing notions—his Festival of Machinery, for instance—Harrison said nothing. Rather, he stressed that Comte, like Smith, emphasized the interrelatedness of all social phenomena. Harrison's purpose was to resist divorcing economic from other realities, to deny independent status to the laws of economics just as he had already denied such status to the laws of history. Thus he sought to bring another side of human behaviour under the rubric of Sociology.

And though he would later assert that Comte alone lay behind his critique of orthodox political economy,[27] Harrison's initial difficulty in formulating his position may have come from his awareness that much of what he was thinking was similar to what Carlyle and Ruskin had already so dramatically written. Carlyle he did not yet know personally; but while still at the Working Men's College he had been introduced to Ruskin by F. J. Furnivall and invited to call at Denmark Hill, the house in south London to which, after his marriage had failed, Ruskin had returned to resume life with his wealthy parents.[28] His growing radicalism irked his father, who on one occasion when Harrison was their guest at dinner cried out: 'John! John! What nonsense you're talking!' He later sought Harrison's help in 'setting John straight' about the 'accepted authorities' on economics, which Harrison saw would be about as easy as getting John to 'accept the authorities of Chinese Mandarins'. Besides, Harrison sympathized with his new friend's struggle to maintain independence in the face of overwhelming parental solicitude and conservative views. And perhaps more to the point, he hoped to interest Ruskin in Comte. Suspecting as much, Ruskin insisted that he could read nothing taxing. When Harrison asked his opinion of Plato's *Republic*, thinking thus to suggest a comparison of it and Comte's polity, Ruskin countered by asking what indeed Plato had said—a query that to his fellow Oxonian seemed as 'wild as if he had asked me what was said about sin in the Pentateuch'. But once aware of Ruskin's 'Socratic ironeia', Harrison heroically sought not to take offence, no matter how sorely vexed. Ruskin, always wayward and allusive, once lamented that Harrison had failed to help him 'to beat at least this into people's heads—that very different consequences are likely to result from making a cannon ball—or a pudding'.[29]

Unlike Ruskin, Harrison did not dwell on the unhappy alliance of industrial and military technology, because to do so would have exposed the error of Comte's optimism about the inevitable disappearance of war among advanced nations. But when condemning employers' inhumane practices, Harrison could command a Ruskinian rhetoric. Thus, when an ironmaster responding to his first *Fortnightly* essay asked why employers should not be able to purchase fifty shillings' worth of puddling (a mixing process) in the same manner as he purchased fifty shillings' worth of pig iron, Harrison answered: because the 'human machine' lost its value when not purchased, being liable to the 'fatal defect of dying'. Similarly, in denying that all transactions could be ruled solely by economic values, Harrison declared that trying to buy 1,000 pounds' worth of wife would raise questions, and that one did not 'go to a physician or a lawyer or a priest and haggle about a fee'. But, unlike Ruskin, he also weighted his text with statistics from trade union records to show that strikes often succeeded, lockouts often failed, and unions offered benefits apart from their effect on wages.[30] All this made Ruskin 'heartily glad', though he reiterated his own more radical thesis: there could be no useful discussion of political economy 'so long as wealth is an undefined term'.[31]

If the utopian strain in Harrison's thought never quite matched Ruskin's, neither did it Comte's. Both Ruskin and Comte conceived of labour as service to humanity that no mere wage could recompense. In the face of such idealism, what did differentials in pay matter? In *Unto this Last* Ruskin dismissed the subject as unworthy. And like Comte he set no limit to profits but stressed the vital and potentially benevolent role of capital. Harrison at least provided some criteria for dealing with these and other thorny issues. He even risked alienating his working-class friends by entitling his reply to the ironmaster 'The Good and Evil of Trade Unions', and ending it with an account of the selfishness and combativeness unions fostered by dividing artisans according to skills and by doing little or nothing for the unskilled. But he considered these points only in passing, as evidence of 'a want of a higher moral spirit in all engaged in industry alike'.

He was equally even-handed about co-operatives. Christian Socialists, trade union leaders, university radicals, secularists, and some political economists, including Mill, regarded them as milestones on the road to a more just society. Harrison, too, appreciated their utility, but he pointed also to their failure to reach the poorest, who could no more afford shares in them than unskilled workers could afford union dues. And he noted that because most co-operatives were retail stores, not manufacturing enterprises, they left unchanged the relation between capital and labour. He called the principle behind them 'bastard communism', and, never an exponent of class mobility, he deplored the opportunity they gave some working men to become administrators. Like Comte he wished society to 'abandon all useless and irritating discussion as to the origin and distribution of wealth, and proceed at once to establish the moral rules which should regulate it as a social function'.[32]

George Eliot expressed 'delight' at his essay, which may not altogether have surprised him; in the same *Fortnightly* issue Lewes had an account of Comte that, despite its 'flippancy', Harrison judged 'very good' and thought showed her influence; indeed, he called it the 'first announcement of her Positivism'.[33] He may therefore have hoped that, when he called at the Priory, their house near Regent's Park, in January 1866, in response to her invitation, the conversation would turn to Comte. When he arrived and found Beesly, Spencer, and Huxley already there, such a topic might have seemed likely. But what he later recalled of the evening was her preoccupation with her partly written novel, *Felix Holt, the Radical.* Drawing him aside she asked his help, not with the novel's social theory, which some critics have seen as Positivist-inspired, but with legal details connected with the eviction of her fictional family from its estate. He readily undertook the assignment, deciding at once that she should make the case one of settlement, not straight heirship. Advising her later how to go about it he declared that 'points of law are so little connected even remotely with the happiness of mankind that I fall with a will upon one which I hope will be'.[34] In his zeal he sketched a new plot complication, then withdrew it as a 'gross absurdity', noting humbly 'how rash it is for *critics* to presume to *construct* even a cell in an organism', a metaphor she would have appreciated. But when he offered further suggestions, she politely observed that he was calling for more coincidences in her plot than it could bear.[35]

Though modern critics have seen Positivism in *Felix Holt*, it was the purely literary merit that Harrison praised to the author, claiming to know families in which it was being read aloud like poetry, and to have read it himself '4 or 5 times'.[36] When a reviewer criticized its legal details, Harrison defensively termed the man 'an ignoramus' and persuaded his old friend and fellow barrister Alfred Bailey to defend them in the *Pall Mall Gazette*.[37] Yet for all that, he was not himself entirely satisfied with the novel, and boldly remonstrated with the author about the language the illegitimate son uses when asking his mother about her dark past; to Harrison his words seemed 'too intensely painful'.[38] George Eliot's realism would continue to trouble him, but he again contributed to it in his own way by providing legal details for *Daniel Deronda* in the summer of 1866. Then, perhaps thinking he had earned the right to tap her professional ability as she had his, he again broached the idea of her depicting what he now called the 'grand features of Comte's world'. The story, he suggested, could be set in a remote French-speaking community in Normandy or Canada—some place in which Catholicism's 'social tone' would have lingered on after an intellectual revolution had transferred the prestige of the Church to science, and a local manufacturer had moralized industry. People needed such an image of the 'healthy moral control' of society, he maintained, but only a 'miracle or a great work of art' could 'flash it onto their souls'.[39] Behind this request was Comte's notion of art as 'ideal representation of Fact', and utopias as the anticipation of fact. But George Eliot's conception of fiction was different. Utopias did not work on the emotions, she explained, and therefore she eschewed them; and 'aesthetic teaching', which she aspired to because it dealt with life in its 'highest complexity', would cease to be aesthetic if it lapsed into 'diagram'. She could promise only to keep his suggestion in mind.[40]

Though Harrison, (like others) found Positivism in her next work, *The Spanish Gypsy*, he invoked her own literary principles to question if its 'form equals the conception'. He feared that her characters were 'treason to human life'.[41] Even franker with Beesly, he called the work's mixture of narrative and drama 'one of the most unhappy conceits that ever entered human brain', and the whole, despite 'grand bits', a 'fiasco'.[42] After her death in 1880, when he could be candid in print, he said her idea of duty was far narrower than the Positivists' because she had made race rather than humanity the highest good. As for her hero, Harrison thought him rather like Congreve in his single-mindedness, and echoing Leslie Stephen, said he behaved 'like a lunatic'.[43] Such a lapse on George Eliot's part did not, however, prevent Harrison from reiterating his request for an 'idealisation of the Positivist vision of society' from her pen. This time she advised him to undertake the task himself.[44] But he, no more than she, was willing to confront the difficulties of salvaging from Comte's rigidly constructed social system those features that might seem relevant to modern-day England, and to offer them as a coherent whole. Rather, he would circle around the subject producing countless essays, lectures, and reviews touching on many aspects of Comte's scheme but without assembling his thoughts into a comprehensive whole. There is no evidence that he ever made notebook extracts from Comte's works as George Eliot did, or knew of her prodigious labours. They show her closer to Comte in work habits than was Harrison, who was better at getting up subjects in the heat of a controversy, or when given an assignment, than at the self-directed, throughly planned, and architectonically complex literary task.

Though he claimed to enjoy prose composition, and to be willing to defy conventional opinion, Harrison did not always heed the call to battle during the years when orthodox political economy was under attack. Thus he guessed rightly that an anonymous critique of his defence of unions that appeared in the *Pall Mall Gazette* in 1865 was by Fitzjames Stephen, brother of his friend Leslie Stephen, but he contended himself with restating his views so concessively that Stephen found them 'thoroughly sensible' and no more on the subject was said by either just then.[45] And when the notoriously contentious William T. Thornton, an authority on political economy and a good friend of Mill's, devoted a *Fortnightly* essay in 1868 to the Positivist theory of labour, Harrison asked Beesly, 'What does that queer beggar Thornton mean by poking at us?'—but he made no effort to find out.[46] He came closest to summarizing his position in 1870 after another of Mill's friends, J. E. Cairnes, accused Comte's English followers of not understanding political economy as a discipline. Ready by then to identify himself openly with the Positivists, Harrison replied that orthodox economists were 'stereotyping a system which we seek to transform'.[47] Yet he did not believe that aim unique to Positivism. The economist T. E. Cliffe-Leslie, for example, he thought 'right on land and a very good man all round'.[48]

In 1878 John Kells Ingram, Regius Professor of Greek at Trinity College, Dublin, named Harrison among others whose work he thought gave political economy scientific status. He made this claim in an important address to the British Society for the Advancement of Science, a distinguished group to which he deserved to belong, being regarded by some of his academic colleagues as 'the best educated man in Europe'. Later Librarian and Vice-Provost of his college, Ingram was all the time a secret Positivist, in correspondence with Congreve and acquainted with Harrison.[49] His high regard for his fellow Positivist as an economist was apparently not shared by everyone; Harrison was invited to join the prestigious Political Economy Club only in 1875, the year its centenary celebration of Adam Smith's *Wealth of Nations* prompted the criticism of the discipline as a science to which Ingram would respond. And though many years later Harrison would claim to have written the 'earliest systematic criticism' of orthodox political economy, he is not named in accounts of it by Mill, George Howell, or Henry Sidgwick.[51] As with 'Neo-Christianity' and scientific history, he was better at seeing the problems in new theories and methodology than in employing them in some constructive and systematic endeavour. It was not only his disinclination to pursue abstract studies that kept Harrison from writing more on economics during the crucial transitional years that produced the modern discipline. For almost a decade after 1867 his attention was focused not on the limits of economic theory but on the limits of trade union activity set not by theory but by the courts.

THE ROYAL COMMISSION

This new phase of Harrison's alliance with the working class aimed at nothing less than securing preferential legal status for organized labour.

He began more moderately, however. Early in January 1867 the Court of Queen's Bench ruled in the case of Hornby v. Close that the boilermakers' union could not prosecute its larcenous treasurer. By acting to restrain trade—for example, by calling strikes—the union had put itself outside the scope of the Friendly Societies Act that since its passage in 1855 had been thought to protect its funds. Harrison denounced the judgment as virtually equating union functions with 'betting and gambling, ... public nuisances and immoral considerations— things condemned and suppressed by the law'. He argued that union regulations pertaining to hours and conditions of work were analogous to the restrictions the medical and legal professions imposed on their members. And though he acknowledged that laws had to be general enough to allow for a judge's interpretaton, he complained that this latest ruling reflected only upper- and middle-class views, and ignored the 'ways of thought' of working men.[52] On 11 February he joined union leaders and radicals on the platform of the Agricultural Hall in Islington for a public meeting urging the new Parliament to produce a much-discussed working-class franchise. Beesly, who had helped make the arrangements, spoke.[53] Harrison did not, but he came with a new prestige in labour circles. Two days earlier he had been appointed to the Royal Commission which was about to begin a thorough investigation of trade union rules and activities.

Harrison's name had been recommended to the Home Secretary, Spencer Walpole, by a delegation from the London Working Men's Association after Potter had failed to get a working man appointed. Walpole said the Commission should be impartial rather than representative of classes, but when pressed he agreed to choose a middle-class man from a list submitted by Potter's delegation, and to balance that appointment with a nomination of the employers. After selecting Harrison in the former category from a list that included Beesly and Godfrey Lushington, Walpole stuck by his choice, even when reminded that Harrison was not the unions' nominee and that he had written revolutionary essays on their behalf—self-cancelling arguments when taken together.[54] Harrison, after overcoming his father's initial fear that this new responsibility would damage his law practice, became one of the Commission's most diligent members, attending thirty-nine of its forty-seven London sessions, held from 18 March 1867 to 24 July 1868. This good record would have been even better had not his law practice ironically increased just at this time. He was acting as junior counsel for the Bovill Flour Milling Company in a fight over patents, and also representing the debenture-holders of the financially embarrassed London, Chatham, and Dover Railway, then the subject of Parliamentary bills in which the Harrison family was greatly interested, having, as Harrison confided to Beesly, invested in the company 'up to the eyes'.[55] But if he would not sacrifice his own and his family's welfare on the altar of the Royal Commission, neither would he neglect the working men's. When absent from meetings he diligently read through testimony he had missed. Once he sat through a session when bronchitis made him speechless. And during the Christmas break in 1867 he took advantage of a visit to Bridges in Bradford to descend into a coal mine to see the 'whole process' sketched recently by a witness before the Commission.[56]

As the youngest and least eminent member of the Royal Commission, Harrison was fascinated—and dismayed—by the play of temperament and ideology among its members. The Chairman was Sir William Erle, retired Chief Justice of the Court of Common Pleas, where he had proved a 'dogged advocate' of orthodox economics. Accustomed to having his own way on the bench, he was 'constantly unfair'.[51] When he lost his composure, the leadership devolved upon the supremely confident and amiable Lord Elcho. He had headed a Select Committee in 1866 that recommended relaxing some but not all the punitive effects on unions of the Master and Servant Act, which in breach of contract cases provided unfairly for the fining of employers but the imprisoning of workers. During the early months of the Royal Commission Elcho piloted a bill embodying his modest reforms through the House of Commons.[58] In the Lords it was in the charge of another member of the Commission, his brother-in-law, the Earl of Lichfield, the arbitration advocate whose proposed intervention in the iron-workers' dispute Potter had ignored, thus prolonging the conflict about which Harrison had written in his first *Fortnightly* essay.[59] The 'steady good sense' and 'popular sympathies' of these two noble colleagues Harrison later contrasted to the 'tart, angry, and purely negative' contributions of Sir Arthur Roebuck, MP for Sheffield and one of those who had originally requested the Royal Commission in the hope that the publicity it would give to the lawlessness of the sawgrinders in his constituency would discredit the entire trade union movement.[60] And there were two other 'keen opponents' of unions: Sir Daniel Gooch, MP, Chairman of the Great Western Railway and a director of the company that had just laid the first transatlantic telegraph cable;[61] and William Mathews, one of the ironmasters Harrison had made the object of his obloquy in the *Fortnightly*. It was poetic justice that Mathews had been appointed to offset Harrison.[62]

Of the three experienced government officials appointed, Herman Merivale, permanent secretary to the India Office and a prolific contributor to the periodicals, proved occasionally helpful but 'independent, critical, and orthodox' in his economic views. Of two others Harrison left no impression: James Booth, former secretary to the Board of Trade, and Sir Edmund Walker Head, former Poor Law Commissioner and Governor General of Canada, who died before the Commission had completed its work. Harrison's own personal ally among the members was the 'loyal' and 'genial' Tom Hughes. But busy with his advocacy of co-operatives, arrangements for a utopian community in Tennessee, and the promotion of legislation in the Commons, Hughes proved 'very willing' to let Harrison assume the main burden of presenting labour's case.

And Harrison handled the task brilliantly. Knowing union leaders, he picked the most effective witnesses from their ranks and counselled them how to deflect attention from the more controversial practices of unions: their restrictions on apprentices and their tactics during strikes. Under his direction they stressed the unions' 'friendly' (insurance) benefits and their successful record of forestalling strikes by negotiation. Harrison was, of course, less in control when employers took the stand. The testimony of Alfred Mault, a builder he had come to know during the strike of 1861, especially vexed him, for Mault proved 'an exceeding clever fellow' who had 'got up his case perfectly'. His account of secret union rules against efficiency and machine-made bricks caused Harrison momentary anxiety about his own over-sanguine statements on union practices. 'My God! think if I should publish a formal recantation!', he wrote to Beesly. But it never came to that. Mault ultimately admitted that the larger unions were guiltless of such offences, and that employers sometimes repudiated legitimate arbitration offers.[63] James Nasmyth, self-made engineer and inventor of the steam hammer, was another formidable witness: his reckless individualism made him seem to Harrison like some 'wild beast'.[64] Also threatening was the visiting New York manufacturer Abram S. Hewitt, who regaled the Commissioners with details of American strikers' strong-armed tactics.[65] But the adverse effect of such testimony paled beside that of William Broadhead, Secretary of the Sheffield Sawgrinders' Society, whose assaults on non-union workers had dismayed friends and foes of organized labour alike. Under the immunity granted witnesses, he confessed that his union had indeed financed the outrages ascribed to it. Though 'greatly grieved', Harrison vowed not to 'cave in'.[66]

Nor did he. When at a public meeting convened by the unions to dissociate themselves from the Sheffield crimes Beesly declared that 'murder by trade unions was no better and no worse than any other murder', he was not only vilified in the press—*Punch* dubbed him 'Professor Beastly'—but faced dismissal from both University College and University Hall. Unnerved but loyal, Harrison assured him that the speech's 'tremendous effect' could not be all bad in the end. He then complained in the *Pall Mall Gazette* that an 'organized effort' was trying to bring 'social and professional ruin' to a man whose good influence on labour was unrivalled even by that of Tom Hughes, Beesly having consistently urged moral instead of material remedies for social ills—the implication being that Hughes's enthusiasm for co-operatives was somehow less worthy than the Positivists' elevating abstractions.[67] Harrison himself had not heard Beesly's speech, thinking it inappropriate as a member of the Royal Commission to attend the meeting. Instead, he had spent the evening at a dinner given by Lord Houghton for some Liberal friends, including Gladstone, and among the guests was Sir Francis Goldsmid, whose influence may have helped Beesly to obtain his University College position. Ironically, Goldsmid would soon lead the movement to oust him. Eventually, however, both the College and University Hall voted to retain him (the former's governing body taking its direction from George Grote, who had given Comte financial assistance years ealier).[68] By this time Congreve had published a pamphlet comparing the anonymity of Beesly's critics to the secrecy of the Sheffield criminals, a point Harrison thought worth calling to the attention of Fitzjames Stephen, whom he surmised was one of the anonymous journalists to whom Congreve had referred. By sending a copy of the pamphlet to this long-standing enemy of Positivism Harrison precipitated another exchange between them, but again it ended in amity.[69]

Not so easily conciliated was Tom Conolly, a rough-speaking stonemason who was monitoring the Royal Commission's sessions for the unions. Speaking on the same platform as Beesly, he had asked flippantly, apropos of Sheffield, 'What can you expect of a town that returns Mr. Roebuck?' The notoriously irascible 'tear-em-Roebuck' thereupon informed the Commission that either he or Conolly had to go. To keep the group intact, Harrison voted with the majority to dismiss the stonemason, and suffered conscience pangs later upon learning that Conolly had reminded the London Trades Council that he had been in the delegation that had put Harrison on the Commission in the first place. Then it was Beesly's turn to intercede: he assured the Council that it had 'no truer friend' than Harrison. Yet to Karl Marx, whom he had known for some years, Beesly confided that he sometimes found Harrison too 'diplomatic', too ready to 'spare the sensibilities of the middle class'.[70] Not till after the Royal Commission had wound up its interviews did the value of Harrison's diplomacy become fully evident.

It was late in the summer of 1868 before Harrison retired to Eden Park with the more than 20,000 questions and answers that comprised the evidence of the ten already published reports of the Royal Commission. Then, with what he told George Eliot was 'the most continuous kind of effort I have ever had to make', he hammered out a draft final report.[71] When the majority of his colleagues rejected it in favour of one Booth had prepared, Harrison, with the help of Hughes and occasionally of Merivale, Elcho, and Lichfield, fought it 'line by line'. But Harrison and Hughes had no intention of signing Booth's document in any form. Having succeeded in modifying it, they wrote a short dissenting statement, which, Harrison was delighted to learn, Lichfield was willing to sign. Then, since Lichfield did not agree to every argument, Harrison drew up a twenty-two page 'Detailed Statement' that he and Hughes alone signed. Together comprising the 'Minority Report', these two documents define the goals that the trade union movement would seek and largely realize within the next decade.[72]

Both the Majority and Minority Reports took the continued existence of unions as irrevocable and called for protection of their funds. But the Majority Report's conditions for such protection would virtually preclude strikes. The Minority Report, on the contrary, would overturn common law whereby combinations were unlawful and punishable as conspiracy, a view it termed a 'relic of feudalism', when the state sought to 'enforce morality'. Implied was Comte's idea that the state would gradually divest itself of spiritual functions. The Minority Report also urged repeal of the statute by which actions in even peaceable strikes could be ruled illegal because it proscribed behaviour variously termed 'intimidation', 'molestation', and 'obstruction'. And finally, with an ingenuity usually credited to Harrison, the Minority Report argued that trade unions should be given the advantages of both friendly societies and corporations without the disadvantages of either. Since acting in 'restraint of trade' was a necessary function of unions, they should not be registered merely as friendly societies in order to have their funds protected; but, since they were liable to harrassment if brought into the courts, they should also not be treated merely as corporations. Rather, they should be accorded 'bare legal recognition', and if they filed rules containing nothing criminal with the Registrar of the Friendly Societies, they should obtain the protection accorded organizations not having union functions. In Positivist terms, unions would become a recognized part of the industrial order simply by forswearing violence—which belonged in any case to the old military order—and promising to 'Live Openly'.[73]

Since the interim reports of the Royal Commission had revealed Harrison to be a persuasive advocate of trade unionism, even before the appearance of the Final Report in mid-March 1869 he was being sought after by students of the labour movement. Jules Simon, the French socialist, came for introductions to labour leaders for himself and the Comte de Paris, whose book on English unions, translated by Nassau Senior and edited by Hughes, Harrison considered essentially the work of Simon.[74] The German economist Lujo Brentano, then studying English labour, used a pre-publication copy of the Final Report given him by Harrison.[75] And Harrison may have helped James Macdonell, a brilliant young Scottish journalist who came to London in 1865 already well disposed towards Positivism, and who turned his review of the Final Report into a generous treatment of unions.[76] But the Royal Commission's evidence was also used to continue if not increase the long-standing public animus against labour. Charles Reade searched out its more lurid details for his novel *Put Yourself in His Place*, first published serially in 1869 and later dramatized as *Free Labour*—the climax of a literary tradition of denigrating organized labour that included fiction by Dickens and Mrs Gaskell.[77]

Since two Parliamentary bills to safeguard union funds had failed during the life of the Royal Commission, Harrison, who had helped to write one of them, did not wait for the Final Report to appear before embodying its principles in a new measure.[78] He wished it to be introduced into the House of Commons by Anthony J. Mundella, the Liberal who had replaced Roebuck as MP for Sheffield. A Nottingham hosiery manufacturer and arbitration advocate, Mundella had shown himself so understanding of working men's aims in testifying before the Royal Commission that Harrison thought of him as a 'regular trump' who had 'taken the demos into partnership'. But as a new MP Mundella cautiously insisted on having Harrison's bill co-sponsored by Hughes, a gratuitous identification of it with Christian Socialism. Harrison expressed his annoyance only privately, however, and took satisfaction in thinking of his own role as that of 'the Punch and Judy man pulling his puppets about behind the green baize and the children below half afraid when he speaks thr' his nose'.[79] The puppets included union leaders of whom not all were convinced that their middle-class barrister friend always knew their best interests. To secure their support, Harrison explained the bill to both factions of the London union world, Potter's and that of the great amalgamated societies, and by late June there was enough harmony to allow for the joint public meeting he proposed. Beesly seized the occasion to insist that a division of the House on the bill should be forced so that labour could identify its false Parliamentary friends. Harrison, on the platform, noted the 'sickly grin' of Samuel Morley, the Liberal MP in the chair, whom he justifiably never fully trusted, and the 'ghastly grin' of Marx, who was of course ready to doubt the good faith of all liberal employers. 'What rubbish meetings are!', Harrison concluded.[80]

The July *Fortnightly* carried Harrison's final plea for his bill, a clever argument that it would actually decrease government interference with industry by restoring to workmen only what they had once enjoyed: the legality of their societies and the security of their funds.[81] But no such appeal to *laissez-faire* principles dear to Liberals could obscure the bill's threat to the economic interests of many in the party. The Government obtained the bill's withdrawal by promising a measure of its own in the next session, and Parliament acted only to protect union funds temporarily. Harrison was one of those consulted in framing this legislation, and his 'ability, industry, patience' on behalf of the unions were praised by Hughes in a speech in the House of Commons.[82] But that was small compensation for the failure to meet labour's full demands. Harrison's regret was especially keen because this Parliament had been returned by a franchise that for the first time in history included working men, and he had played a role of some importance in bringing them into political life.

PARLIAMENTARY REFORM

Holyoake's description of the Positivists as 'political cuckoos who laid their eggs in other people's nests' aptly explains Harrison's ubiquity in reform groups of the 1860s.[83] Until 1867 there was no organized Positivist movement in England. Much the more important, therefore, were his ties with Oxford friends like James Bryce, Albert Rutson, George Otto Trevelyan, Albert Venn Dicey, and Thomas Hill Green, and Cambridge men like Leslie Stephen, Henry Fawcett, and Henry Sidgwick—all somewhat his junior. Precisely when he first met these men, to which of them he was closest, and what they thought of him are issues not easy to settle. But the goals they held in common suggest that Harrison's Positivism, such as it was in the sixties, proved no bar to congeniality.[84]

A major reform all these and many other radicals of the period desired was the removal of religious tests at both universities. Agitation that gained impetus from *Essays and Reviews* and from Stanley's move to London as Dean of Westminster Abbey in 1863 produced a bill to remove the tests at Cambridge. It was by collecting signatures at about the same time for a petition to Parliament asking for a similar measure for Oxford that Harrison had learned how little subscription to the

Thirty-Nine Articles meant to most men who signed them.[85] The next year he was among the 121 reformers from the universities, Parliament, the Bar, the clergy, and the world of religious Dissent who met in the Freemasons' tavern in London on the 10th of June to plan further strategy, a meeting that has been used by scholars to identify the 'academic radicals' of the period. It was characteristic of Harrison to attend such a gathering and also to comment later that he wondered why time and trouble were not saved by 'simply signing a declaration saying "bother the 39 Articles" '.[86] He no doubt spoke more judiciously when with four other lawyers—Mountstuart Grant Duff, Charles S. Roundell, Charles Bowen, and John G. Dodson (author of the Cambridge measure, which failed)—he met Edward Miall and John Carvell Williams, leaders of the Liberation Society, who had long been agitating for a total separation of Church and State. The demise of a bill introduced by Goschen some months later, and the very moderate nature of the relief attained by the Clerical Subscription Act of 1865, together convinced Harrison that their cause had to be subsumed under the broader banner of Parliamentary reform.[87]

Many of the would-be university reformers frequented the same discussion and dining clubs where Harrison spent his bachelor evenings; loosely organized, these groups left meagre evidence of their existence. At the Hardwicke Club, consisting of lawyers, he could debate political and economic issues with men who had a common vocabulary; and if he thought the keenest among them—Leonard Courtney, Edward Clarke, Montague Cookson, and Charles Russell—might prove too much for him, he would bring along Beesly.[88] Less intellectually taxing were the two-guinea banquets of the Cobden Club at the Star and Garter in Richmond, where the younger men were expected to listen to speeches on free trade by Liberal MPs and toast them and their principles. Mill was sometimes present, and he also dominated the Dominicans, an ironically named Sunday evening group that included Sir Charles Dilke, John Morley, Henry Fawcett, and Leslie Stephen. Harrison and Beesly talked occasionally about forming a group of their own. However, just as they also were entertaining thoughts of starting their own paper, to be named 'The Republican', but made do with the *Bee-Hive*, so in 1865 they fell in with the inclinations of others to organize the Century Club. Deciding whom to include caused Harrison no little anxiety, for he wanted just the right mix. In the end the club turned out to be, in his words, 'Liberty Hall', with the 'pure milk of Liberal doctrine' flowing in the veins of all, but with no single purpose. 'Peers, as such, were not excluded.' It may have been in this setting that he first came to know Lords Amberley and Houghton. Huxley added scientific rationalism, and Mark Pattison, John Llewelyn Davies, and William ('Hang Theology') Rogers provided liberal Anglicanism. Since the club met when Parliament was not sitting, MPs could attend. And there were journalists like Frank H. Hill, Walter Bagehot, Herbert Paul, John Macdonell, and Thomas Chenery. Their meeting place was rented and served no food, and in deference to the temperance champion, the affable Sir Wilfrid Lawson, no alcohol either, only soda-water. But pipes and cigars were allowed, and Harrison, a lifelong hater of all forms of tobacco, later marvelled that he had consented to be 'poisoned' by the smoke.[89]

The radical women Harrison came to know in these years did not always prove as congenial as their male counterparts. Mill's step-daughter, Helen Taylor, for instance, he called a 'gorgon', though 'profound', and Clementia Taylor, wife of Peter Taylor, MP for Leicester, a 'queer one'.[90] Their advocacy of women's suffrage may explain the epithets. He grew fond of Lady John Russell, whom he visited at Pembroke Lodge, Richmond, introduced there probably by her son Lord Amberley or nephew Arthur Russell, and he liked to think that she and her husband, the former Prime Minister, appreciated his 'playful radicalism', though he called their tolerance of it merely the 'homage of hypocrisy to liberalism'.[91] That the most celebrated Liberal hostess of the day, Lady Palmerston, ignored him was understandable; he in turn considered 'Old Pam' the 'most consciously a rascal of our leaders'.[92]

At the other end of the social scale were the working men's clubs and gatherings like those Potter delighted in organizing. Comte had sanctioned such activities as a provisional substitute for a church in the transitional era; the presiding spirit, he advised, should be an educated member of the spiritual power whom workers would learn to trust.[93] Since Henry Solly's Working Men's Club and Institute Union embodied such paternalism, Harrison could give it his blessing, but he was as little inclined to be active in it as in Potter's soirées.[94] The situation was ironically reversed when, largely at his father's urging, Harrison sought admission to the Reform Club in 1864 and for a time wondered if he could muster the requisite backing. The men Mr Harrison suggested as sponsors seemed to Fred much too sympathetic to the Church to welcome the author of 'Neo-Christianity'; and Goschen, whom he approached and who would have served nicely since he had become a wealthy banker and was a newly-elected MP for the City, claimed to have put his name down for the candidacy of too many men lately to wish to do so for Fred. In the end his distasteful remote relation, Lord Amelius Beauclerk, sponsored him. Relieved to have it over, Fred was determined not to be cowed by the atmosphere of gentility and conservatism. And he was so far successful that members once rebuked him and some friends when, standing at the Club's windows, they returned the salute of working men in a suffrage parade passing below on Pall Mall: seeing the Club's name the marchers had mistakenly surmised that it signified the politics of all within.[95]

At home, too, Fred's values were sometimes at odds with his family's interests. Lawrence and his father, for example, found their business 'sneezy' during the Union's blockade of Confederate cotton shipments during the American Civil War,[96] while Fred was often preoccupied with demonstrations in London expressing support for the Union cause. The loyalty to Lincoln shown by unemployed mill hands in the North of England strengthened his faith in the moral superiority of the working class, and the attempt of some in the official classes to obscure the moral issues of the war and discredit the republican ideal added to his reasons for wishing to dilute their political strength with working-class votes. Yet his 'republicanism' had a dimension alien to many radicals; when the end of the Civil War seemed near he predicted to Beesly that 'old Abe' would be elected for life by a 'grateful people' eager to escape the 'democratic dodge'.[97] In England, Parliament's neglect of the people's problems was his main argument for seeking a working-class franchise, but he was careful not to invoke any principle of political rights—according to Comte, like natural rights, a metaphysical idea.

Harrison used the *Bee-Hive* not only to sketch the social and economic discontent of the working class but also to relate its plight to Britain's foreign policy. The Government's inattention to the oppressed Poles was a case in point. Describing a large working-class audience convened to denounce Russia's treatment of Poland, he noted the scarcity of MPs on the platform and in the audience the small number of men who could vote. The implication was that the unenfranchised filling the hall possessed a superior political morality. A war allying England, France, and Austria to free Poland, he once declared, would 'lose half its burden and nearly all its incidental evil'. The language was Burke's, but the rationale Comte's. Poland was in 'the vanguard of civilised mankind', whereas Russia belonged to Asia, to 'a lower type, to semi-barbarism'.[98] Yet if it served his purpose he could appreciate the culture of Asians. When a British fleet bombarded Kagosima in retaliation for the murder of a British merchant in 1863, he condemned the wanton destruction and traced the incident to Britain's ruthless commercialism in opening up Japan, part of the 'store of accumulated injustice' a working-class electorate would have to redress.[99]

The Government's handling of Garibaldi's long-awaited London visit in April 1864 increased Harrison's impatience with the ruling classes and, incidentally, with the Italians as well. Harrison and Beesly assisted Odger, Cremer, Edmond Beales, and other working-class leaders, as well as long-standing friends of Italy like Holyoake, Peter Taylor, and William Shaen to plan a popular London reception. Fearing it might become too revolutionary, Harrison urged Beesly to 'keep Odger straight'.[100] The trouble, ironically, was to come from another quarter—the aristocracy, whose blandishments proved more dangerous in the eyes of some than the people's unprecedented demonstrations in the streets. Before Garibaldi could begin a triumphal tour of provincial cities, he announced that ill health would force his departure for the Continent. Saffi, Harrison learned, thought Garibaldi had been over-awed by the great people he had met, but Harrison had another explanation: 'like all religious enthusiasts' Garibaldi had believed he could influence figures of power. 'Poor old madman, Jesus Christ himself would have found Pam a tough one.' Gladstone, in Harrison's reading of the events, had acted in compliance with France's objections to Garibaldi's visit and made him feel obliged to leave. Harrison therefore urged Odger and the others to organize meetings and post placards expressing the people's 'shame' over this dismissal of their hero.[101]

Unfortunately for Harrison's peace of mind, his labour friends proved all too zealous; they arranged a protest rally on Primrose Hill. Believing it would not be tolerated by the police, and warned by his father that he might damage his professional standing in a confrontation with the authorities, Harrison was in no mood to attend. Positivists, he reminded Beesly, were not so ready for the revolution as Beales and Shaen, but trusted to 'moral rather than political means'.[102] In the end, however, he did attend, and even spoke at the meeting, which was, as he had predicted, dispersed. And he came to another rally in the same place two weeks later, arriving late enough, however, to remain inconspicuous, and the affair went off without interruption. Shaen reproved him for missing the procession before the speeches, but that seemed a small price to pay for keeping his name out of the papers. It was with a troubled conscience that he exclaimed to Beesly: 'These platforms and committees are beastly; let us return to our diggings.'[103]

Harrison's diggings for the next few days happened to be in Oxford. There he read with disbelief of Gladstone's vigorous claim of innocence when asked by a delegation from the City and Working Men's Garibaldi Committee if he had indeed acted for the Government to secure the General's departure. And when the next day Gladstone told a surprised

House of Commons that in his judgement every man not personally unfit or politically dangerous was 'morally entitled' to a vote, Harrison decided Gladstone was seeking to placate the class he knew he had offended. Writing to Beesly, who was preparing a pamphlet on Garibaldi's departure, Harrison urged him not to hold back from 'pitching into' Gladstone ('the more you squeeze him the more you get') for he was 'hooked to us now and can't draw back'.[104] But Beesly permitted his pamphlet to be suppressed, and Harrison couched his *Bee-Hive* complaint about Garibaldi's treatment in general terms, citing the 'false and tricky tone' men in public life were acquiring 'under the influence and example of Lord Palmerston', whose system of government was one of 'dodges tempered by dinner parties'. Gladstone had become too useful to reformers to be denigrated openly.[105]

Distressing as was the thought of an understanding between Garibaldi and Gladstone, it seemed less dangerous than Mazzini's ingrained conspiratorial ways. When Harrison contributed to a Mazzini fund in 1865 he said he did not wish his money to be used for a march on Rome, which Mazzini was known to be plotting and Harrison thought bound to fail.[106] When such a campaign was launched by Garibaldi in the summer of 1867, Harrison could only grumble about the 'silliness and boyishness' of Italians—traits he blamed on the absence in their history of a 'puritanical phase'.[107] Yet such was the spell of the General that, only a few weeks later, Harrison on a Continental holiday sought him out in Geneva (a city that had certainly had its puritanical phase), where Garibaldi was a guest of honour at an International Peace Congress. The irony of his presence could have escaped no one; but what Harrison later recalled was Garibaldi's speech advocating a religion of reason in which 'men of the élite of science and intelligence' would be the priests, and his blessing of a child presented to him by the widow of one of his fallen soldiers.[108] His defeat at Mentana soon after was especially deplorable to Harrison because it came at the hands of the French. In an unusual palinode Harrison admonished his *Bee-Hive* readers: 'Those who, like myself ... have given a partial and qualified acceptance to Napoleon as temporary dictator of the French Republic, have a duty to perform in repudiating him now.'[109]

Though he gave lip-service to the idea of British workers co-operating with their Continental counterparts, Harrison was less interested than Beesly in the International Working Men's Association, formed in 1864 to promote that end. Beesly occupied the chair at its inaugural meeting and was soon considered a friend by Marx, who rapidly took control of the organization. Beesly's account in the *Fortnightly* of its first six years treated it favourably,[110] and even before then Harrison had interrupted his holiday a second time during the summer of the Peace Congress to attend the International's annual meeting, held that year in Lausanne. But he went only as an onlooker, preferring, said the *Bee-Hive*, not to sit with the delegates. Marx himself was absent, busy in London with the imminent publication of *Das Kapital*, a work whose significance neither Harrison nor Beesly would ever acknowledge.[111]

More important to the Positivists than either the later Risorgimento or the early International was the deterioration of England's relations with France, which in their eyes was the key to European peace and progress. When Prussia invaded Schleswig and Holstein in 1864, Britain failed to act with France, as Napoleon III had suggested, though earlier British pronouncements had led Denmark to expect help. Bismarck and Franz Joseph divided up the duchies with impunity, and two years later Prussia's victory over Austria shifted the balance of power still further in Bismarck's favour. All this greatly eroded Harrison's trust in the ability of Britain's ruling classes to maintain European peace.[112]

In Jamaica as well Harrison saw events outstripping the capacity of British officials to act responsibly. Late in 1865 the colony's governor, Edward Eyre, attempted to forestall what he later said he believed would be a bloody insurrection. His actions proved intolerable to liberals in England, for, under the martial law he imposed, a prominent mulatto critic was seized, irregularly tried, and hanged; over five hundred blacks were murdered and hundreds flogged; and a thousand homes were destroyed. Siding with the protest group in England that Carlyle dismissed as 'nigger-philanthropists', Harrison told his *Bee-Hive* readers that he looked to their enfranchisement to end 'this system of cruelty and rapacity abroad'.[113] As a member of the Jamaica Committee's executive he worked under Mill's driving leadership to bring Eyre and two of his officers to trial in England. When a Royal Commission investigating the case praised Eyre's 'promptitude and vigour' while conceding that the penalties he imposed had been 'excessive', Harrison in the *Commonwealth* compared the oppressed Jamaicans to English workmen. And in the first of six passionate letters in the *Daily News* he denounced martial law as a 'system of periodical raids with fire and sword ... and a circuit of "bloody assizes," in which ruffianly subalterns play the part of judges, and a furious butcher is at once attorney-general and sheriff'.[114]

Such language struck Mr Harrison as 'calculated well enough to stir up the multitude against the government', but, he asked Fred, was it entirely 'proper, just, or decorous'? Eyre, he knew, had the backing of many 'respectable' people, including Carlyle, Dickens, Kingsley, Tennyson, Tyndall, Ruskin, and Froude. Still, he trusted Fred's judgement enough to urge him to take his comments for 'just what they are worth and no more'.[115] Since to Harrison they counted for less than his own indignation, he continued to write with undiminished fire. It was, he insisted, imperative to control the 'tiger in our race' lest violations of constitutional law 'grow into a precedent in the dark, like a poisonous fungus around its roots'.[116] His indictment of the political use of martial law was general enough to have lasting importance and cogent enough to coincide with the arguments used by Fitzjames Stephen, the Jamaica Committee's counsel, in applying in court for the arrest and trial of Eyre and his officers.[117] When the latter were exonerated, Stephen withdrew from the Committee on the ground that any further action by it would be merely vindictive. Harrison was among the unrelenting who sought a conviction of Eyre in a civil court. The attempt failed, but Harrison's perseverance earned him an expression of gratitude from Mill that he treasured.[118]

In his last letter on martial law, at the end of 1866, Harrison argued that 'lawlessness spreads fast. What is done in a colony to-day may be done in Ireland tomorrow.' The suspension of *habeas corpus* in response to Fenian violence across the Irish Sea soon produced exactly the conditions Harrison feared. All the more welcome, therefore, was Bright's call for collaboration between English and Irish leaders. Harrison allowed himself to hope that a new era was at hand, one that would bring about the 'extinction' of the Irish Church 'without oppression' and without a 'Keltic republic'—the Irish were not ready for that.[119] Since the highest priority at the moment seemed to be to obtain political rather than criminal status for Fenian prisoners, he joined others affiliated with Congreve to embody that demand in a petition. Signed 'Citizens of England', it was presented to the Commons by Bright early in May 1867. When his attempt to read it aloud in the House provoked outcries, Bright paused to commend the petition's repudiation of violence and secrecy as political strategies and observed that the eleven signers were men of good education and social standing. At a later sitting Mill, too, spoke favourably of the petition; and even Disraeli asked how, given the sponsors' social position, the House could reject the document without appearing to suppress opinions merely out of dislike of them. With this conjunction of liberal and conservative support, the petition was accepted. Harrison, too busy in court and with the Royal Commission on Trade Unions to attend either session of the House, was delighted to find that the Positivists could create such a stir. But nothing he heard about the reception of their petition improved his opinion of a Parliament still urgently needing reform.[120]

The Irish petition was not the first joint political statement of Congreve's little group of friends. In the spring of 1866 there appeared a 603-page collection of seven essays called *International Policy: Essays on the Foreign Relations of England*. Harrison took major responsibility for editing the work. Two contributors, his good friends, were not then, or ever, known as Positivists: Charles Cookson, at the War Office, and Edward Pember, the clever barrister who had composed Lord Westbury's epitaph. Both proved slow in finishing their assignments, and two other original contributors eventually withdrew: Godfrey Lushington, upon becoming engaged to Arthur Hugh Clough's sister-in-law, Anne Smith, and S. H. Reynolds, a Fellow of Brasenose brought in to replace him, who decided that Bridges's essay was too dogmatic.[121] Henry Dix Hutton, a Dublin barrister who had met and corresponded with Comte, stayed the course but vexed Harrison by his 'long-winded' letters; and even Beesly caused annoyance by being too epigrammatical.[122] But Frederick Chapman offered terms Harrison thought generous: half-profits, no financial risk, and a 'sumptuous' magenta cloth binding with the title in gold.[123] It was agreed that the preface would contain only a modest reference to Comte and the title-page one of his innocuous maxims: 'The fundamental doctrine of modern life is the subordination of Politics to Morals.'

To A. J. P. Taylor the volume has seemed significant as the first composite work to propose an ideal foreign policy for England.[124] Congreve, the most doctrinaire Comtist, argued that the West, with Britain and France in the lead, must exercise its proper role in the development of mankind by its example of unity and political morality; Beesly called for a 'loftier morality' than Christianity taught and rehearsed Britain's past diplomatic lapses; Pember deplored the nation's record in India, Bridges its exploitation of China, Cookson its entry into Japan, and Hutton its treatment of all uncivilized peoples. Harrison focused on England and France, urging closer ties in order to purge both of characteristic evils, England of her 'commercial rapacity, industrial greed, and stolid conservatism', France of her 'military ambition, revolutionary disorder, or tyranny veiled under the name of public welfare'. Perhaps suspecting that there was a flaw in his logic—for what if the alliance compounded instead of neutralized their evils?—he privately confessed that only the historical part of the essay satisfied him.[125] The volume aroused little attention. The Revd William Henry Fremantle, an Oxford friend of Harrison's, detected some unfairness to Christianity. Maurice, however, liked the book. Lyulph

Stanley, who would become a leader in the struggle for secular public education, predicted that it would make more enemies than converts. And George Eliot, perhaps groping for a tolerable appraisal in the absence of firm convictions, hoped it would 'serve as leaven'. It was with that purpose in mind that Harrison, who called it a Positivist *Essays and Reviews*, 'talked it up' at Oxford.[126]

Early in 1867 there appeared two other volumes of essays designed to state the case for a widened franchise, *Essays on Reform* and *Questions for a Reformed Parliament*. These were the work of some twenty-one writers, most, if not all, known to Harrison. To the second work he contributed a short piece roundly condemning Britain's European policies as 'pretentious nihilism' and the Government's attempt to influence the course of the American Civil War as a betrayal of popular sentiment. The only other Positivist represented was Godfrey Lushington, who wrote on trade unions. But the values expounded in both collections were compatible with those being advanced by the Positivists. Like them, these writers thought of themselves as members of an intellectual élite, and though lacking political experience, hoped to introduce a higher moral tone into political life and to demonstrate their own fitness to direct political activity.[127]

It is not surprising, then, that one of the harshest critics of these volumes was Robert Lowe, a member of an older generation of Parliamentary liberals and a leader in the opposition to franchise reform. Treating the contributors in turn, he had only a short space for discussion of Harrison's essay and employed it to express thanks that Britain's foreign policy for the past decade had not been in Harrison's hands, for Lowe counted 'six good wars' England would have had to fight if Harrison's views had prevailed.[128] The previous year Lowe had declared in the Commons that though the supporters of Gladstone's franchise measure might be 'inspired apostles of a new Religion of Humanity', they were guilty of 'the most puerile fallacy' if they thought the franchise would prove a good in itself.[129] But in fact, the Positivists had consistently made specific reforms in domestic and foreign policy, and not a general ideal, their rationale for a working-class electorate. Comte's teaching eschewed any reference to natural or political rights—a position so definite that a major financial supporter of the *Commonwealth*, Samuel Kell, had accused the Positivists of injuring the campaign for Parliamentary reform. In the ensuing controversy Harrison called himself a 'disciple' of Comte but said that was not the same as being an 'apostle'.[130] By the time Lowe published his Parliamentary speeches early in 1867, he was able better to appreciate the Positivists' stand and noted in his preface that Comte, like himself, had rejected 'sentimental, metaphysical ... and abstract arguments'.[131] Reading this, Harrison had a twinge of remorse, for he had just dispatched to the *Fortnightly* an essay carrying his major statement on the franchise issue—and Lowe was his scapegoat.[132]

Harrison's essay contested Lowe's claim that Parliament had been doing everything necessary for the people and therefore no constitutional reform was necessary. Lowe's speeches, Harrison said, had given the upper classes 'a cause', the middle classes 'food for thought', and the working classes 'indignation which had knit them into a power'. The House of Commons, from Harrison's perspective, had as its 'grand vice' its 'splendid unconsciousness that it has any vices'. Representing only the upper class and the 'least public-spirited' of the population just below it—that is, the business interests—it had reached an 'organised deadlock' that only the introduction of working-class representation could break. He entitled his essay 'Our Venetian Constitution', Disraeli's term for the weakened state of the monarchy created by the power of the eighteenth-century Whigs.[133]

Besides contesting the benign view of Parliament advanced by one of its most eloquent members, Harrison meant his essay to challenge the equally sanguine theories of government just put forth in *The English Constitution*, a series of essays in the *Fortnightly* by Walter Bagehot, editor of the *Economist* and a brother-in-law of one of the Positivists' severest critics, William Rathbone Greg. Bagehot had purported to describe how government actually worked, how its 'dignified parts'—royalty and the aristocracy—diverted the masses, who remained deferential while the 'efficient parts'—Parliament and the Cabinet—actually governed. What Bagehot celebrated, Harrison denounced as the 'shams of government'. Adopting a line from Tennyson's 'Lotos-eaters', Harrison termed the members of Parliament 'gods of Epicurus' who 'lie beside their nectar, heedless of an ancient tale of wrong'. As a corrective to such complacency he began and ended his essay with a quotation from Comte: 'The hypocrisy inherent in English Constitutionalism can never be effectually suppressed without the intervention of the people'; and 'If the English patricians can effect the requisite recasting of their system, they may yet escape passing under the yoke of the workmen.' To this he added: 'But if not—then not.'[134]

Harrison knew his literary and historical allusions suited the *Fortnightly*, though in the *Bee-Hive* they would have been inappropriate. He also knew that his references to Comte would not be out of place. When Lewes had become ill at the end of 1866, the editorial reins had passed to John Morley, then a twenty-six-year-old journalist who had a high regard for Positivism, partly derived from his Lincoln College friend, Cotter Morison. Unlike Morison's father, who had left him a small fortune, Morley's father, a Lancashire physician, had cut him off altogether when he rejected Christianity.[135] Harrison, whose relations with his father fell between these extremes, was finding in Positivism the rationale for a social conservatism that accorded well with his father's views, even while his political radicalism, equally rooted in Comte, sometimes caused Mr Harrison anxiety. Reconciling the two positions, Harrison argued in his essay that bringing working men into the political arena need not alter the way government worked as much as some people feared it would. England's 'richer classes' would retain leadership, for 'wealth, habit, tradition, skill, every form and influence which governs daily life gives to this real, but ill-defined class, a real but ill-defined supremacy.'

As descriptive sociology this was prescient. But Harrison went further. He supposed that a popular franchise would probably put only two dozen working-class MPs in the Commons, and none at all in the Cabinet. How the pressure applied by the electorate to the working-class MPs would be transferred to the government is not made clear; but that Harrison was talking about changing the balance of power in political life is certain. He knew that Disraeli was expected to insist upon 'fancy franchises'—extra votes for the wealthy and educated— and would try to redistribute Parliamentary seats to favour Conservative areas as well. Therefore Harrison took care to respond to Lowe's much-publicized argument that the working class was unfit to vote because of its 'venality', 'ignorance', 'drunkenness', and 'facility for being intimidated'. Drawing upon an assumption that Comte shared with many political theorists, Harrison asserted that the working class was not a class at all but the 'body politic', of which other classes made up the 'special organs'. Free of the 'restless egotism' found in 'all who accumulate wealth', working men possessed 'the brightest powers of sympathy, and the readiest powers of action'. Here he was thinking of their enthusiasm for such heroes as Lincoln, Garibaldi, and Kossuth, and the financial contribution one union might send to another involved in a costly strike. As for the working man's lack of culture as a reason for denying him the vote, or the educated man's possession of it as a ground for giving him an extra vote, that was 'the very silliest cant of the day'. Culture was 'a desirable quality in a critic of new books' but in politics it meant 'simply a turn for small fault-finding, love of selfish ease, and indecision in action'.[136]

Matthew Arnold's satirical response to this outburst against culture brought Harrison a lasting place in the history of Victorian literature.

Arnold, consciously seeking to ingratiate himself at Oxford University in his final lecture as Professor of Poetry in June 1867, associated Harrison not only with radicals like Bright but with the members of a 'school whose mission it is to bring into order and system that body of truth with which the earlier Liberals merely fumbled'. Harrison was a 'well-meaning' but dangerous friend of the working class, teaching 'violent indignation with the past' and 'abstract systems of renovation applied wholesale'.[137] Earlier, in his more jocular *Pall Mall Gazette* letters, he had invoked an image of Harrison as Jacobin by describing him 'in full evening costume, furbishing up a guillotine' in a London back garden.[138] Perhaps that sketch of him as traitor to his class cut too close to the bone, for Harrison never remarked on it publicly. But he could not allow himself to be derided at Oxford without responding. At Eden Park late summer he therefore sought once again to press the thesis of an antagonist to an extreme and so demonstrate its inferiority to Positivism.

Since Arnold's *Pall Mall* letters had contained much dialogue, and dialogue (as interview) was the form in which the Royal Commission's evidence was being presented, Harrison fell naturally into that mode in constructing his essay. And he quickly mastered the same kind of aggressive humour that Arnold himself used and whose history includes *Candide* and *Sartor Resartus*. Harrison makes the brash Prussian savant of Arnold's letters, Arminius von-Thunder-ten dronckh (who derived from Voltaire) and a gullible Englishman (of the sort Arnold loved to portray in order to demolish) discuss an Oxford lecture given by Culture (Arnold is never named). What the Englishman admires, Arminius deplores as 'flabby religious phrases' and 'metaphysical old bones'—suggestions of the two stages in Comte's evolutionary scheme that precede the Positivist millennium. Arminius defines 'culture' to mean ' belles lettres, and aesthetics', and presents a Comtean image of humanity as a woman in a 'raging crowd' of monsters—death, sin, and cruelty—'bearing the destiny of the race like a close-veiled babe in her arms' while Culture sits 'aloft with a pouncet-box to spare her senses aught unpleasant, holding no form of creed ...'. Yet as Arminius extracts more details of the lecture from Culture's naïve admirer, its teachings emerge as rather similar to Comte's. Both venerate the past, oppose violent reforms, extol the cultivation of human faculties, and believe in progress. Culture's greatest fault in the end is said to be that it 'had not adequately studied the great French thinker whom it travestied'.[139]

'I laughed till I cried', said Arnold about his reading of Harrison's essay, which he called 'scarcely the least vicious' of responses to his

Oxford lecture.[140] And when they met in June 1869, Harrison found he liked Arnold better 'in the flesh than in the spirit'.[141] Arnold had by then referred copiously to Harrison's 'very good-tempered and witty satire' in the essays that, with the lecture, make up *Culture and Anarchy*. And having somehow divined, or pretending to know, that he dressed meticulously, Arnold made Arminius in the *Pall Mall* series go off with Harrison, 'a much better-dressed man', in order to pursue with him 'researches concerning labour and capital'. In the reprinted version in 1871 these are said to be 'hardly ... palpitating with actuality', a curious comment in light of the circumstantial character of the Royal Commission's eleven reports.[142]

That the two men differed also on what constituted political actuality is evident in their responses to the 'Hyde Park Riots' of July 1866, when a crowd milled about for several days on public grounds from which the police had sought to exclude a Reform League demonstration. To Arnold the event symbolized the people's predilection for lawlessness; to Harrison it was a mere 'frolic' of little consequence, 'unpremeditated'. Like Arnold, he thought officials had been unwise to close the park to the Reform League when there were insufficient forces on hand to keep the people out, but he also agreed with Mill's advice to the League's leaders: that they should not try to stage another demonstration unless they were confident that a revolution would be both justified and feasible.[143]

Harrison did not always seem to know just how far he thought his working-class friends should go in their agitation for Parliamentary reform. He showed surprise but no marked disapproval upon learning that Congreve desired 'strong measures'.[144] Yet he told Howell he lacked time and money to help the League himself, and preferred to make his contribution with his pen.[145] Of the League's president, Edmond Beales, a barrister like himself, he sometimes spoke rather contemptuously. When plans for a demonstration in May 1867 were announced in spite of the Government's prohibition of a gathering, Beesly told him that Beales and his colleagues were 'panting for a row'; yet Harrison attended the demonstration, and perhaps because it went off peacefully, called it 'splendid'. The League's successful defiance of the authorities seemed to prove what he had long been asserting, that the ruling class in England did not rely on force to maintain its position, but on 'skill in working the machine', skill inadequate on this occasion but manifest when put to the test by Garibaldi's visit.[146]

Similarly ambivalent was his advice to the working class after Disraeli's Reform Bill received the Royal Assent in August 1867, adding a million voters to the electorate—far more than most radicals had hoped for. The political manœuvring that produced the Act seemed to Harrison the result not only of political cynicism but a faulty Parliamentary system, and both were circumstances that he knew would undercut effective representation by the new voters.[147] He therefore advised them to send one of their own class to Parliament if they could; if not they should send 'friendly' employers, who would know their problems. He thought MPs should be paid, but he warned against electing men who considered a Parliamentary career a mere job.[148] Privately he was far from impressed by some working-class leaders. He held Howell personally responsible for the unbusinesslike procedures of *Commonwealth*, and he called Potter and Cremer 'thieving scoundrels' when they charged him a guinea for a ticket to the Crystal Palace celebration of the franchise victory after advertising that he would be present as one of the evening's attractions. More seriously he noted that Broadhead and his accomplices were uncontrite after the Royal Commission had exposed their criminal acts.[149] Such experiences lay behind Harrison's advice to the London Trades Council meeting he addressed in March 1868; he declared then that the voters should send to Parliament 'the best men of any class' but, more to the point, they should emulate the citizens of Paris who at the dawn of the Revolution had demanded that the Assembly give them bread instead of speeches. The loaves now were the reforms for which Harrison and his radical friends had long been calling: a county franchise, equitable distribution of Parliamentary seats, honest elections, fair rates, and, above all, improved working-class education.[150]

Harrison struck a more individual note in the April *Fortnightly* when to offset Greg's 'Cassandra wails', Carlyle's 'shrieks', Arnold's 'dirge over Culture', and other alarmist pronouncements on the advance of democracy, he reiterated his theory of the working man's 'strange' deference to authority and custom. It is true that by not protesting against the Government's coercive policies in Ireland and aggression in Abyssinia, the newly-enfranchised electorate had disappointed him, but he could only hope that these were mere lapses in the superior political morality attributed to the working man by Positivist theory. In any case, he did not envisage the new electorate finding its way unguided. Melodramatically he announced that the nation would come to realize it possessed a 'philosophic class' that had 'silently worked out a root-and-branch reconstruction of existing society'.[151]

The General Election late in 1868 demonstrated that such a total reform of the political system was not on the horizon. Rutson complained to him of Liberal whips withholding a constituency from him because he lacked the money to contest it, and he was not the only 'academic liberal' so treated.[152] Moreover, Harrison learned from Conolly (once again friendly) that Liberal officials had secretly engaged Cremer to help secure the candidates they desired, often at the expense of labour men. Odger and Howell, it turned out, were similarly employed.[153] Conolly's story convinced Harrison that he and Beesly should eschew all electioneering; its practices, in any case, he found 'ludicrous'. Total strangers turned his chambers into a 'proletariat caucus' by asking him to produce working-class votes for their candidates although he insisted he had no such influence. And at least two candidates he decided to endorse publicly did not have his entire confidence. Gladstone was one. Harrison told Beesly it would be 'unpolitic' not to back him since he had 'done much to approach us on all great questions'. Sir Roundell Palmer was the other. Hoping to stand in the Liberal interest at Oxford, he was known to oppose Gladstone's commitment to disestablishing the Church in Ireland, one of the 'great questions' for the Positivists.[154]

The election results, like the campaigning, put Harrison in an ambivalent position. Many men he hoped to see returned were defeated— among them Mill, Morley, Beales, Amberley, Auberon Herbert, and Godfrey Lushington (though Comte's proscription of active politics for the 'philosophic class' would have mitigated his regret in Lushington's case). Also defeated were the only three working men who stood—Cremer, Howell, and William Newton. But such results may have troubled Harrison less than most radicals. The working class, after all, had helped to give the Liberals a great victory, and would, he assumed, continue to contribute to the pressure from without on which his hopes for further reforms largely rested.

BACHELOR, LAWYER, FRIEND

Early in the 1860s Mr Harrison moved his family from Oxford Square, first to 64 Upper Hyde Park Gardens, and then into a grander thirty-room house just north of Hyde Park, number 10 Lancaster Gate, at the corner of Craven Terrace. There, in his early thirties, Fred felt nothing like the dreariness that Lytton Strachey would experience in a similar house just down the street a quarter of a century later.[155] Since an ordinary day might take Harrison to Lincoln's Inn, the courts, University Hall, or a hotel, office, or public house to meet with fellow radicals, and in the evening to a friend's drawing room or the theatre or concert hall, he welcomed the chance to 'vegetate and brood' at home without 'rebuke or contempt'.[156] Long letters he wrote home while travelling show his interest in his brothers' careers. Lawrence, before leaving Lancaster Gate in the autumn of 1865 to marry Mary Anne Clarke, the daughter of the Revd Sir Charles Clarke, of Worlingham Hall, Suffolk, wrote to Fred to express his gratitude for help when he was in 'low spirits'.[157] Fred in his high-mindedness sometimes purported to believe: 'Happiness is humbug; it generally means inactivity.' Perhaps this only reflected his sense that, for all his activities, something was missing from his life, some emotional centre. But work could dispel loneliness, and he found a lesson in the sad end of James Winstanley, a wealthy Oxford graduate who had known Bridges in Paris and contributed to the Positivists there. In 1862, after returning to England without fixing on a vocation apart from managing his Leicestershire estate, he disappeared without a trace. Reports of a troubled mind suggested suicide as the explanation. Unsettled by the event, Harrison momentarily feared he too lacked direction, a clear goal.[158]

The best record of Harrison's inner life during the early sixties is found in his letters to Mrs Hadwen; hers do not survive. They began corresponding about the death of Susan Bridges and John's return to England. But Harrison soon introduced a more personal note by revealing his religious uncertainties and, during one of her rare London visits, by bringing her to meet his mother to enable them to talk over the 'unhappy affair' of 'Neo-Christianity'.[159] He also implied a greater intimacy by sending gifts to her children, though his genuine enthusiasm for the then popular writings left by the eight-year-old 'Pet Marjory' Fleming, published in 1863,[160] shows that he was not dissembling when he expressed interest in the young Hadwens. Still, his letters to Mrs Hadwen hint at a more than avuncular role for himself in her family: for him she had become, he wrote, 'a type of what is earnest, rational, resolute, tender, and holy', and she would be responsible if ever his life became 'worth living'. By not acknowledging his indiscreet outpourings, Mrs Hadwen led Fred in time to realize that he had no claim on her, and to confess that 'our vile human nature is such that it breaks out [and] sometimes in violent discontent will not take what is given it thankfully.' Distance and time cooled his ardour, and when she came to London to enter her son at King's College School in 1867, Fred observed quite unromantically to her that his own mother had made a similar mission almost twenty-five years before.[161] The overblown quality of these letters suggests that, whatever emotions they expressed, he was also using them to experiment in prose style. This was the period in which he built upon the already hyperbolic diction of his youth, and would consequently be warned by Arnold, through the voice of Arminius, to abandon 'Carlylese'.[162]

Believing that polite society might ostracize him at any time for something he said or wrote, Harrison seems to have taken heightened pleasure in 'all sorts of butterfly acquaintances' it offered. In spite of his youthful sneers at the Great Exhibition, the Crystal Palace in its new location at Sydenham was just the right place to bring a lady friend for edification and amusement. He and Beesly often took a box at the opera, and both became familiar enough with the stage by 1865 to damn its productions confidently when asked by Fraser Rae to contribute to *The Reader*. Fred's new dundreary whiskers were perhaps inspired by Edward Sothern's, but he decried that actor's 'vulgar' imitation of aristocratic manners and asked his readers impatiently why London had to be the only capital city in civilized Europe lacking 'a little rational enjoyment' for a 'man of taste'. The theatre was indeed at a low ebb in the sixties, but Harrison confessed later that his *Reader* critiques were 'hardly serious', merely 'burlesque satire'.[163]

Europe was not only a useful stick for beating cultural and political backsliders in England, but a region of infinite fulfilment to which Fred returned almost every summer in his last decade as a bachelor. Often travelling alone, he recounted his adventures in letters, and sometimes arranged talks to family and friends upon his return.[164] When Bridges and Beesly prepared for their first Continental tours, he provided copious advice: take *eau de cologne* and a leather drinking cup; explore the coupe bed's mechanics early in the train trip; deal sternly with porters—'Kick them if they are troublesome and say "no" to everything.'[165]

While travelling he sometimes met the unexpected with irascibility, and reached for his pen. Delayed in the Ticino Valley by floods, he fired a letter off to *The Times* denouncing the 'total want of social organisation' that kept travellers uninformed.[166] Spending two nights with guides in a cave during an ascent of the Wetterhorn led him to contemplate a paper for the Alpine Club on the 'barbarous and demoralizing' side of mountaineering. Not long after, he had another spell of anxiety when he gazed up at the north face of the Matterhorn at the spot from which four members of Edward Whymper's party had fallen 'the day the rope broke' just two months earlier, in July 1865. But, back in London, he did not write the essay; instead, he penned a guide to the disposition of his literary remains in the event of his demise.[167] Yet his response to the glories of the Alps had not always been so clouded. In a review of Alpine guidebooks for the *Westminster* in 1860 he justified mountaineering by man's need at times to feel what only high mountain reaches could offer, the sense that he is 'a marvellous atom in a marvellous world'. He stopped short of claiming to have experienced the religious ecstasy he thought Leslie Stephen had felt when climbing. And he even apologized to Beesly for the inflated and 'slipshod' rhetoric of his review, the result of an effort to simulate the spontaneity of letter writing.[168]

Among the friends to whom Fred reported his travel adventures were two pairs of middle-aged sisters living near Eden Park: Arabella and Louisa Shore, nine and seven years his senior, at Elmer's End, and their intimate friends Emily and Ellen Hall, twelve and nine years older than he, in West Wickham. Much used to Continental sojourns themselves, and all fond of reading, they appreciated learning not only what he did but what he picked up of London literary gossip. The Revd Thomas Shore, an Oxford man who supported his family by tutoring, having abandoned the Church years earlier because of religious scruples, was fond of Fred almost at once. Less receptive when the subject was Comte, Mr Shore nevertheless knew and admired Congreve personally, and had read 'Neo-Christianity' aloud to his daughters before they made Fred's acquaintance. They all saw behind Fred's 'prim and formal' manner his 'gentle, courteous ways', and though they liked all the Harrison youths, Fred was their favourite. Louisa was especially drawn to him, perhaps because she was the most literary: she had published *War Lyrics* (with Arabella) in 1855, *Hannibal*, a drama, in 1861, and was working on a study of Alfred the Great. The subject had always interested him, and he advised her to omit all romance from her text, for Alfred 'never was in love except during ... his wedding fete'. With that comment, and his equally vehement condemnation of love scenes in fiction—he was especially hard on George Eliot's Romola because she favoured a 'heartless coxcomb'— he hoped, possibly, to lower the emotional temperature around Eden Park.[169]

Meanwhile, he kept his distance from eligible women in London as well, convinced that he could not expect to find there what he sought in a wife: a woman 'entirely one with me, by birth, habits, training, beliefs, and hopes'.[170] But she was within sight all the time: his first cousin, Ethel Bertha Harrison. The only daughter of Mr Harrison's younger brother William, a wealthy West Indies merchant, and his wife Anne, she was born on 27 October 1851, and so was almost exactly twenty years younger than Fred. Like him she was somewhat shorter than average in height, and her dark eyes and abundant dark hair gave her, it was said, an Italian look. Growing up with one younger and three older brothers at Claybury, a large Georgian house on the edge of the Epping Forest near Chigwell, she had been 'hedged in with love' and was confident and happy. An ancient school nearby had provided good tutors, and by her teens she knew Latin, French, and German, was an accomplished pianist, and a seasoned European traveller.[171] So devoted was Fred to her by the late sixties that he once even ignored the Positivists' opposition to blood sports and accompanied her on one of the famous hunts in her area. Seeing him there, Anthony Trollope, who had moved to Waltham Cross nearby for the sport, shouted in his bluff way, 'What are *you* doing here?' Telling Beesly of the encounter with 'that snob ... in pink, looking like a jolly butcher on a hippopotamos', Harrison got his own back by calling Trollope's latest novel, *Can You Forgive Her?* the 'blackguard' work of a 'low brute'.[172]

In his own romantic frame of mind, Fred could hardly have been expected to appreciate Trollope's story of a young blade wooing his cousin partly because he coveted her wealth. Fred's own suit was untainted in that way. So willing had he always been to stay within his means that he worried his father by offering to give up his horse in order to save for his future household.[173] But Fred's love was prudent, as he himself admitted, in quite another way. He and Ethel, he told Kate Amberley, had 'read, studied, and conversed together, till hardly an idea or sentiment can exist which we do not share'. He was aware, too, of the 'great satisfaction of marrying into a family that is connected with one's own ... they know and are quite prepared to face all one's heresies'.[174] Congreve's marriage had been of just that sort. And so, too, would be the union of Bridges and Mrs Hadwen's daughter Mary Alice, which was planned for the first day of June 1869, when the bride would be nineteen. Congreve, overlooking the advantage of having his closest disciple marrying into a family that had long shown sympathy for Positivism, protested in his rigid way that Bridges was flouting Comte's doctrine of eternal widow[er]hood. But in the face of the united Mumbo, Congreve was forced to swallow his objections.[175]

Beesly's marriage followed Bridges's by little more than a month, and like it took place in church. At the last minute Fred decided not to attend, pleading work in the courts, but perhaps deterred by recalling the 'sniggering bridesmaids' at Bridges's wedding. Beesly, almost as cautious as Harrison and Bridges, was marrying Emily Crompton, sister of the two Positivists they had come to value in their work with trade unions: Henry, Clerk of the Assize on the North West Circuit, and Albert, a Cambridge man who had left the Bar to join the pioneering steamship firm of Alfred and Philip Holt, Liverpool Unitarians closely associated in both religion and business with Alfred and Charles Booth, the latter to become famous for his survey of London. Though Emily Beesly held the Broad Church views of her brother-in-law, the

Revd John Llewelyn Davies, she respected Positivism, and was so eager to meet her husband's colleagues that she got him to invite Fred and Ethel to University Hall before their marriage—an idea thought 'too American' by Ethel, who preferred waiting till her mother could chaperone them.[176]

The same conventional attitude towards marriage dictated Ethel's response to John Stuart Mill's *Subjection of Women*, which the author rode over from Blackheath to Eden Park to present to her and Fred, later writing to Fred that he hoped he could join 'even partially' in the movement for women's emancipation. Ethel found the relation between man and wife set forth by Mill too much like that of 'college chums' who had 'mutual affection and respect' for each other but were 'self-sufficing units apart', not, as she thought they should be, a 'union of correlatives'.[177] Fred was always quick to point out that the Positivists wanted women's education to equal that of men's. He had in fact been lecturing and examining in English history at the Working Women's College in Queen Square, founded in 1864, along with old acquaintances from Working Men's College days—Maurice, Hughes, John Llewelyn Davies, and John Chapman. Yet he disapproved on principle of women working outside the home. Similarly, though he supported the movement for women's higher education, he never became reconciled to women's colleges at Oxford. Fortunately for him, Ethel expressed no desire to take part in any efforts to widen women's sphere.[178]

The 1860s brought not only marriage but professional advancement to Harrison and his closest friends. Congreve obtained his medical degree in 1866 without intending to practise, and in 1870 moved from Wandsworth to Mecklenburgh Square, Bloomsbury. Bridges, after eking out a living in general practice in Bradford, was appointed a factory inspector for the North Riding of Yorkshire in 1869. Within a few months his Rugby friend George Goschen, then President of the Poor Law Board, named him one of the Board's medical inspectors in London, a temporary post that became permanent under the new Local Government Board in 1871. The following year the Bridges moved from London lodgings to a house in Wimbledon.[179] Meanwhile, Godfrey Lushington was made Secretary to the Royal Commission for the Digest of the Law, and at the end of 1869 became Legal Counsel to the Home Office. Vernon, his identical twin, had married in the same year, 1865, and having seen service in the Royal Navy and published on naval law, became Secretary to the Admiralty in 1869.[180]

Though Harrison spoke scornfully of Godfrey's plunge into the 'bottomless pit of office', he was pleased enough to succeed him as Secretary to the Royal Commission for the Digest of the Law at a salary of £400. The position, he hastened to note, did not make him a member of government. Moreover, he could whole-heartedly endorse all efforts to make the legal system more efficient.[181] To that end in 1863 and 1864 he had written up civil and foreign cases in the Privy Council for *New Reports*, a short-lived journal that also employed friends from Lincoln's Inn such as Montague Cookson, E. H. Pember, Horace Davey, and Leonard Courtney.[182] Though he owed his appointment in 1869 to the Royal Commission's Chairman, Lord Westbury, he did not consider it the kind of improper patronage for which his old friend had been forced to resign as Lord Chancellor four years earlier. Not only had he never approached Westbury for any preferment, but he soon found the position was no sinecure.[183] Much of his time had to be spent covering up the decline of Westbury's once-great mental powers. Other members sometimes seemed to him hardly more competent, though they were eminent in the profession: Baron Hatherley, the Lord Chancellor; Earl Cairns, former and future Lord Chancellor; Sir Roundell Palmer, former Solicitor-General and Attorney-General and another future Lord Chancellor; Henry Thring, Parliamentary Counsel; Sir Thomas Erskine May, President of the Statute Law Revision Committee; and Robert Lowe, now Chancellor of the Exchequer. Distrustful of one another, and especially of Westbury, they could not agree on the specimen digests they were empowered to prepare, and they wound up their affairs in 1871 with little accomplished. More to Harrison's liking was his appointment early in 1870 on Maine's recommendation as Examiner in Jurisprudence, Roman Law, and Constitutional History for the Council of Legal Education. The work involved co-ordinating studies in the Universities and the Inns of Court, and allowed him to further his old plan of treating law and history in a single context.[184]

By midsummer 1870 Fred and Ethel could at last fix the date of their marriage. Like the Bridges and the Beeslys they agreed to their family's desire for a church service. Chided on this, Fred could only reply that at least he had not gone to the Lords for his bride, as had Henry Crompton, who had just become engaged to Lord Romilly's daughter.[185] Announcing his plans to Morley, who had been reading law in his chambers, Fred inadvertently prompted Morley to disclose something of the embarrassing circumstances of his own civil marriage earlier that year. Morley's letter does not survive, but probably it echoed one he had sent to Crompton, calling the marriage imprudent for 'family and other clearly political reasons'. His wife, it seems, listed as 'Rose Ayling, spinster' on the marriage register, had two young children, John and Florence, whom Morley adopted as his own. Learning something of this, Harrison said he was 'content to think whatever you do is rightly done' and he would not 'seek to know more than you care to tell me'.[186]

With Morley and Beesly trusted confidants, Harrison increasingly asserted his independence from Congreve, though for a time Harrison apparently failed to recognize the full extent of their incompatibility. It was he who suggested to Beesly and other friends of Congreve's that they collect a purse to enable him to travel in Europe to regain his health after his taxing medical studies.[187] And Harrison was among the most active of those who searched out and offered to pay for the hotel room in Bouverie Street, off the Strand, in which Congreve delivered nine lectures on Positivism in May and June 1867. The presence at the first talk of some seventy-five people, including George Eliot and Lewes, Lord Houghton, G. O. Trevelyan, and Lady Amberley, was most gratifying. But when attendance fell off sharply after that, Harrison, though disappointed, did not blame the subject but Congreve's dreary delivery, which indeed struck George Eliot, for one, as 'cold'.[188] Hearing the next year that the Century Club was to vacate its rooms, Harrison suggested to Beesly that they take over the premises as a 'temple' for 'regular lectures'.[189] But 'temple' was clearly ironic. He was still resisting Congreve's efforts to make Positivism a closed sect. Of course he joined the London Positivist Society, which Congreve founded in the spring of 1867, modelled on Comte's all-male discussion group of 1848. But Harrison sometimes invited to its meetings men as different as George Howell, the one-time bricklayer turned 'respectable radical', and Charles Eliot Norton, Boston Brahmin, Harvard professor, and art historian.[190] When some interesting visitor who seemed incompatible with Congreve turned up, Harrison might invite him to meet a small group of Positivists in his chambers without Congreve. And though he invoked Comte's name in a lecture in March 1867 on 'Sundays and Holidays' in the Sunday Evenings for the People series organized by Amberley, Huxley, Mill, and others to challenge Sabbatarianism, his own comparison of the Continental Sunday, with its open museums and theatres, to the 'weary, dull, stale, and unprofitable' English Sunday, was otherwise unexceptional secular humanism.[191]

An open break between Harrison and Congreve did not occur until 1869. The occasion was Huxley's attack in the February *Fortnightly* on Positivism as 'Catholicism minus Christianity'. Harrison regretted the stridency of Congreve's reply, which failed to quell his adversary, and, weary of being baited by Huxley about Comte's scientific pretensions whenever they met at the Century Club, entered the controversy with his own *Fortnightly* essay. It conceded the difficulty of knowing what the term 'Positivism' implied, since Comte had been variously accused of being over-religious and anti-religious, authoritarian and anarchist, excessively emotional and excessively rational. Much as Lewes and Mill had done, Harrison distinguished between those who accepted Comte's religion entirely and those who did not, and by placing himself in the latter category he incurred Congreve's anger. When, in reading the manuscript before publication, Congreve demanded certain changes, Harrison refused, thereby losing, by his own account, Congreve's 'confidence' or 'even friendship'.[192]

Other friends responded to the article less harshly. George Eliot merely regretted its personal nature.[193] Ruskin declared himself unwilling to interfere with any consolation Harrison might derive from a Religion of Humanity, though he thought it must be 'one of the most microscopic "isms" which have ever become particles of coagulations for the wondering imaginations of men'.[194] In reply, Harrison referred him to a controversy he was just then having in the *Pall Mall Gazette* with Fitzjames Stephen, who, writing from India, where he had gone to replace Maine as legal member of the Viceroy's Council, had scoffed at the idea of anyone caring for humanity in the abstract. How much had Harrison suffered upon learning of the execution of 70,000 Cantonese?[195] Harrison had responded by holding up Stephen's own legal career as a praiseworthy example of the public service Positivism sought to foster.[196] Privately, however, he knew that the 'Problem of Positivism,' as he had called it in the title of his essay, remained unsolved. What Comte's system meant to him and to his friends was to become clearer during the following decade.

4

Shaping a Positivist Polity

1870–1880

Harrison regarded 1870 as his *annus mirabilis*. Before then he had been 'a supernumerary, an experiment, a youth open to employment, with no settled schemes or any permanent career'; after, he was a man with beliefs 'forged ... by slow steps' who had 'at last a wife, a home, and children', and was 'a fully franchised citizen ... who felt a clear course before him, and was conscious of being fit to run it out'. He had 'ceased to be a prey to weariness or disappointment, much less despair'.[1] These assertions, from *Autobiographic Memoirs*, are in a literary tradition that for him had several sources. Comte had spoken of a 'second life' he owed to Clotilde de Vaux, and Mill of his great debt to Harriet Taylor. But the inspiration for a 'new life' that Beatrice gave Dante may have been foremost in Harrison's mind. He dedicated the *Memoirs* to Ethel in their fortieth anniversary year and then quoted the poet's words to Virgil in praise of the *Aeneid* from the first canto of the *Divine Comedy*: 'Vagliami il lungo studio e il grande amore.' His own long study had of course been the works of Comte.

That study entered a new phase early in 1870 when two barristers in Congreve's circle, Alfred Cock[2] and Francis Otter,[3] began to search for a permanent meeting place for Congreve's circle of Positivists. Harrison thought this premature but, unwilling to be left out, agreed to share expenses and to plan lectures. Ironically, the room leased in March was at number 19 Chapel Street (now 20 Rugby Street), in a narrow, two-storey red-brick building on land owned by Rugby School, where Congreve had been groomed for quite a different career than he was now beginning. Just off Lamb's Conduit Street, the building was therefore only a short walk from the Working Men's College in Great Ormond Street that in some ways was the Positivists' model. But one of their distinctive notes was the ornamentation of the room with plaster busts of Comte at the front, and, along the sides, of the thirteen worthies for whom he had named the months of his Calendar. There were also portraits, several donated by Harrison, of heroes naming the weeks of the Calendar, and a Positivist lending library. At the entry of the building Congreve placed a marble tablet proclaiming in pale green letters (the colour of the future according to Comte) the words 'Church of Humanity', followed by several Positivist mottoes. This, Harrison complained to Beesly, was 'a trumpery attempt to label other people's things, against their avowed intentions ... We shall have winking images one day.' Enough Positivists concurred to make Congreve change 'Church' to 'School' and move the tablet inside.[4]

Two meetings were held on Sundays: in the morning, a lecture on Positivism, usually by Congreve; in the evening, a talk on moral or political issues. For years there was no Sunday ceremony, which led Samuel Butler's friend Eliza Mary Ann Savage, a visitor in 1872, to find the place more 'dismal' than a mechanics' institute. Unattractive enough herself to discourage any romantic thoughts Butler might have had, she nevertheless noted the plainness of the congregation, though she thought the lecturer that morning—probably Beesly—handsome, and the first Englishman she had heard pronounce 'Guizot' and 'Broglie' correctly.[5] As her observation suggests, the Francophilia at Chapel Street (as the centre came to be called) distinguished it among places of ethical teaching. So, of course, did its Comtism. Yet there were similarities, and seeing the success of heterodox preachers in London whom he knew—Charles Voysey at his Theistic Church, Moncure Conway at South Place Chapel, and Stopford Brooke at St. James's and later at Bedford Chapel—as well as of the secularist Holyoake and the atheist Bradlaugh, encouraged Harrison to believe that the Positivists could find a following. But Congreve, he feared, might be an obstacle. Reluctant at first to embark on the venture, Congreve soon assumed leadership. He kept track of subscriptions scrupulously, and his sincerity and erudition were exemplary; but at making converts he was inept. Harrison once went so far as to call him 'the beadle, not the Priest of Humanity'.[6]

Understandably then, Harrison felt most at ease in Chapel Street at the weekly evening meetings of the London Positivist Society, over which Beesly presided. But even he sometimes failed to give satisfaction. His control over the discussions seemed occasionally lax to Harrison, who feared that the young Indians coming from the near-by Inns of Court were less interested in Positivism than in airing their anxieties about their studies, practising their English, or arguing over British policy in their homeland. Especially tiresome was one Dadabhai Naoroji, whom in the next decade Harrison would heartily endorse as the first Indian Member of Parliament.[7] In 1870 he found him a less able spokesman for India than a twenty-eight-year-old Scotsman,

James Cruickshank Geddes, on home leave after nine years as a magistrate in the Bengal Civil Service. He had been drawn to the Positivists by Congreve's pamphlet on India, and in 1871 he and Mrs Congreve's niece, Emily Bury, who lived with the Congreves, were married in the first Positivist wedding ceremony in England. It was performed by Congreve after their civil vows.[8]

More taxing to Harrison's patience than the 'discussion forum' at Chapel Street were the analyses of papers at the Metaphysical Society. He was invited to join late in 1869, shortly after its founding. Dean Stanley had recommended to the originators—James Knowles, architect and editor, Charles Pritchard, astronomer, and the poet Tennyson— that some unorthodox thinkers be included. The membership eventually embraced most of the leading religious and social critics of the day— Huxley, Bagehot, Froude, Tyndall, Pattison, Ruskin, Greg, Maurice, Lowe, and Leslie and Fitzjames Stephen among them.[9] Harrison's conduct initially seemed as disruptive as his ideas. Arriving late at one meeting before he knew everyone, he slipped into an empty seat by a large, fierce-looking bearded man, who, irked when Harrison gave no sign of recognizing him, announced, as the others all stared, 'I am Mr. Tennyson!' The paper that evening, by James Martineau, brother of Comte's early translator but no admirer of his work, was entitled 'Is There any "Axiom of Causality"?' When his turn for comment came, Harrison said impertinently that Martineau's theory was 'as good as any other', but he 'did not want to know about Cause at all ... It was like asking if the moon was made of green cheese. Who knows—who cares?' To this the Laureate, still smarting, thundered: 'Why do you come here—what business have you amongst us?' 'I came to learn', Harrison replied coolly (by his account) 'but I don't understand a word.' With this the bard exploded: 'If I were a Comtist—no God, no soul, no future—*no right and wrong!!* I should not care to live.' Harrison, however, had the last word: 'I can assure you it is the only thing for a happy life.'[10] His first paper, given the next month, was on 'The Relativity of Knowledge', and it was aimed, he told Morley, at undercutting 'metaphysical hairsplitting, which can lead to nothing'.[11]

When possible Harrison avoided serious discussion of philosophic and religious issues altogether. He dispatched Disraeli's *Lothair*, a novel in which an English aristocrat rejects in turn Catholicism, atheism, and revolutionary politics for Anglicanism, as a mere 'romance of the peerage'. The novel's images of high life he dismissed as absurd, its prose style as ludicrous—explainable only by imagining that after long hours in Parliament the author had hastily composed his text and given it to his servants to revise.[12] Along with his own Carlylese,

Harrison produced such skilful parodies of Disraeli that Morley failed to detect where in one instance Harrison left off and the novelist began.[13] Once again he chose the dialogue form. A Land and Labour League radical as literal and serious as Harrison's Arminius denounces the novel's snobbery. Adopting much the same worldly persona as he had in the dialogue on Culture, Harrison defends the novel as a useful satire of modern English life comparable to Beaumarchais' evocation of the *ancien régime* in *Figaro*. Harrison ends by quoting Carlyle's similar interpretation of Figaro in the *French Revolution*. And Carlyle's image in *Past and Present* of a poor Irish widow proving her sisterhood with her betters by spreading typhus may also explain Harrison's calling London's cholera epidemic at just this time 'the avenging spirit of pauperism'. With Bridges supplying medical details of the danger, both Disraeli's novel and the Metaphysical Society's discussions seemed, at times, trivial.[14] Impatient to go beyond fiction and philosophy, Harrison was eager to make Chapel Street more than a forum for debate.

But he was still unwilling to consider Positivism the complete embodiment of his religious aspirations, or to break utterly with Anglicanism. That became clear in the summer of 1870, when he and Ethel planned their long-awaited marriage. Their parents were re-conciled to the twenty-year difference in their ages, and to the qualified acceptance of Comte he had recently outlined in 'The Problem of Positivism', and there was apparently no thought of a civil marriage with Congreve officiating. On 17 August, Fred and Ethel were married in the fashionable Christ Church, at the far end of Lancaster Gate from the Harrisons' house. It was a 'strictly family affair'.[15] The ceremony was performed by Fred's Oxford friend, the Revd William Henry Fremantle, Vicar of near-by St. Mary's, Bryanston Square. Though Liberal enough to have contemplated writing for *Essays and Reviews*, he was also circumspect enough to be rising in the Church: he was chaplain to the Bishop of London and lived at Fulham Palace.[16] Everyone agreed that Fred made a model bridegroom, and that Ethel, despite her youth, was wonderfully composed. But she forgot her purse at the reception, held at 10 Lancaster Gate; and when it was sent on to her she found herself addressed for the first time as 'Mrs' rather than 'Miss' Harrison.[17]

The wedding journey took them first to the Calverley Hotel in Tunbridge Wells, where Queen Victoria had spent summers as a girl. In its lovely gardens and elegant lounges they pondered the news of a 'conflict of conflicts' about to begin a hundred miles from Paris. The Franco-Prussian War, which had started two weeks earlier, was entering a crucial stage. Harrison would later claim that at its outset he had considered Napoleon III the aggressor. He was by then disillusioned with the Emperor; but he had mistrusted Bismarck even longer and predicted 'Armageddon' when the conflict began. Now, despite warnings from Ethel's mother about the 'horrid sights' that might make 'a most painful, even injurious impression on the mind of a young girl', the couple carried out the plans they had made to travel through France and Switzerland to Italy, and they had several 'glorious weeks' on Lake Como.[18]

During their stay, Napoleon III was defeated at Sedan on 2 September. Returning home through France in October, Fred and Ethel passed columns of French soldiers marching from the battle area and looking fit enough to continue the war. Why, then, had their government been abandoned by England? Harrison wondered. In London by late October he learned that the proclamation of the Republic in France had dispelled much British hostility towards France and the Prussian siege of Paris was arousing great sympathy for its citizens. Less gratifying were reports about contributions to that change in public opinion made by Congreve and Beesly. The Positivists, hardly half a year in their new centre, had allied with the extremists who urged the British government not only to recognize the new French Republic but also to take up arms in its behalf. Beesly called for some 20,000 British soldiers. Congreve expressed equally extreme views, and, to defy the press, used placards to convey them, since Comte had designated the use of such substitutes for newspapers in the Positivist era. *The Times* derisively dubbed them 'mural appeals',[19] and Harrison was dismayed. But Morley's suggestion that Britain maintain complete neutrality was even less acceptable.[20] Eager as always to strike just the right note, Harrison read everything on the war he could find. Since he and Ethel were living at Lancaster Gate until they found a house of their own, it was almost like his bachelor days, when he could withdraw from the conflict to prepare his sally. By the end of November it was ready for Morley—'Bismarckism: The Policy of Blood and Iron'. Far from taking a more moderate stand than his colleagues, the essay asserted France's claims on Britain so ardently that it moved George Eliot to tears.[21]

Readers moved to thought, however, might have detected inconsistency in it as well as passion. While calling on Britain to stop the German dismemberment of France by 'arms if necessary', Harrison said nothing about the much-discussed deficiencies in Britain's military forces. As a Positivist he could never condone conscription, which some were recommending.[22] When his article was criticized, he reverted to his more colloquial style in four *Pall Mall Gazette* letters re-creating

Arminius as a Dutch statesman. He chides those Liberals who continued to hope for a Prussian victory after the circumstance that had made it seem desirable had disappeared—the rule of Napoleon III. In his own voice Harrison deplored the expected German annexation of Alsace and Lorraine, calling the historical and ethnic rationale for it offered by Carlyle, E. A. Freeman, and Max Müller 'pedantry in its dotage'. Germany after all had until recently been only 'a wild jumble of half-civilised turbulent duchies' and the doctrine of civil rights cited by her apologists was 'the jargon of an adventurer'.[23]

Having dealt thus with the intelligentsia, he addressed the working class, first in the *Bee-Hive*,[24] then at St. James's Hall, where the Positivists, trade unions, and radicals like Bradlaugh staged a 'hotly bellicose' meeting. They also sent a petition to Gladstone calling for British intervention in the war to save France.[25] By the middle of January 1871, news of the Parisians' bitter cold and hunger brought Harrison's hatred and fear of the Germans to a new pitch. In a second *Fortnightly* essay on the war he rehearsed the stages by which the two nations had been brought face to face and demanded that England act—'with your moral force, if you please, since we are told that England has no physical force left'. To fail to act would result in what his title predicted, 'The Effacement of England', a phrase that could also stand for what he feared an unchecked Germany might bring about.[26] At a week-end party at Fryston Hall, Lord Houghton's residence in the West Riding, Harrison's desperation astounded Lady Stanley, who heard him telling the apostate French Carmelite Père Hyacinthe, fresh from his spell-binding London lectures pleading for aid to France, that he had not gone far enough: 50,000 Irishmen ought to be dispatched across the Channel, thus frustrating Germany's designs and, incidentally, solving the Fenian problem.[27] But that may have been only a modest proposal.

By trying to infuse the working class with their own militarism, the Positivists lost some of the good will they had earned by their defence of trade unions. Men as politically different as Ruskin, Mill, Marx, Lord Arthur Russell, and Viscount Amberley were all dismayed.[28] Apparently only Amberley challenged Harrison directly, and for his pains received a disquisition on the 'wanton barbarity' of Germans, the 'intensely French' sentiments of the British workman, and the danger that the governing classes in England would misread the people's sentiments and 'break down fearfully'.[29] As a member of the governing class, Amberley remained critical of the Positivists, though when his cousin Arthur Russell impugned their motives he defended them.[30]

Frenchmen predictably liked Harrison's articles better. The Duc de

Broglie, France's ambassador in London, to whom at Houghton's insistence he sent a copy of 'Bismarckism', expressed his pleasure.[31] So did two leading French historians who learned of it, Jules Michelet and François Guizot. The seventy-two-year-old Michelet wrote from Florence, where he and his second wife had gone to escape the war, their flight arranged by an acquaintance of Harrison's, Marie Souvestre, who, having closed her girls' school at Fontainebleau, also found refuge there. It was she who read Harrison's essay to Michelet. And another acquaintance of Harrison's, Browning's friend Isa Blagden, provided Michelet with Harrison's address.[32] Replying to Michelet's letter, Harrison sent a copy of his second *Fortnightly* article on the war and reiterated its claims of a 'conspiracy' in England of the wealthy and the press to ignore the people's sympathy for France. He predicted that it would not be possible to bring public opinion round in time to save Paris.[33] Michelet was gratified to find an Englishman 'si française', and praised him so warmly in his own account of the bleak situation, *La France devant l'Europe*, that though Harrison edited Isa Blagden's English translation of the book he declined to be thanked by name in Michelet's preface.[34] This was not entirely modesty. He considered her prose inadequate, and in any case doubted Michelet's contention that the rural French had been eager to continue the war. Yet he welcomed the historian's new interest in England and proudly called on him in Paris with Ethel in 1872. A sporadic correspondence continued until Michelet's death two years later, after which Harrison took charge of the widow's fund in England for an elaborate monument in Père Lachaise to Michelet's 'spotless life'.[35] Guizot, by contrast, he judged a 'severe Puritan and a rigid Conservative', and ignored his invitation to visit.[36]

Nor did Harrison heed his father's advice to 'take a leaf' from Guizot's 'calm and thoughtful' books and modify his own prose style.[37] To convey the emotion that usually underlay his articles he liked to write 'in one burst', as if speaking.[38] Yet the *Echo*'s report of the St. James's Hall meeting on the war commented that 'Mr Harrison speaks almost as badly as Mr Bradlaugh writes. Mr Bradlaugh speaks almost as well as even Mr Harrison writes.'[39] Certainly his essays, like his letters to Michelet and to others at this time, convey his sense of a civilization betrayed by a ruthless European power and the influential classes in England, and of France at once the scapegoat and potential saviour of the West. And nothing would disperse that bitterness. Years later he still wrote passionately of Gladstone's refusal to intervene as his 'gran rifiuto'.[40]

When troops of the National Government, seated in Versailles, tried to seize the Parisians' cannon, and they in turn established the Commune in March 1871, Harrison justified their move to Morley as one entirely within the rights of the people of Paris: the 'purest, most honest, direct, and intelligent part of France'. After all, they were holding out for a 'real Republic', and wisely saw that the rich had no 'right to grind out of the workman, his wife and child the uttermost farthing; to leave him naked, half-starved, ignorant, filthy'. The privileged classes—'ces bougres du bourgeois'—were 'lying, cheating, selfish, callous, calumnious brutes' who deserved whatever befell them.[41] Such views, he explained, had taken ninety minutes to 'roar out' at Chapel Street.[42] And they did not stem from Comte alone. 'It is as Carlyle said, take away the bauble of the ballot box. The 2,000,000 workmen in Paris and other great towns are the "best men" ... Legitimate government be damned! ... I fall back on force!'[43] He admitted that force was what Thiers at the head of the National Government was using against Paris. His own justification of the Commune rested not in logic but in the conviction that logic should not govern politics. Emotions should. He had already told Morley that Mill was doing much harm by teaching Englishmen to 'chop logic in politics', whereas politics, like virtue as conceived by Aristotle, was a matter of 'right feeling, trained, intelligently trained feelings I grant,—but not of syllogisms'.[44] He now saw that Carlyle's utterances contained 'much truth', though the man himself was 'a depraved old brute—only half human'.[45]

As the agony of Paris continued, Harrison depicted the Positivists as 'the True Constructive Revolutionists'. They might reach only two dozen or so 'queer half-taught young men', he told Morley, but he, for one, felt 'dangerous'. His 'instincts' were to 'side prima facie with the weak' in any case, there being always 'plenty to side with the strong'.[46] Hence his outrage when Lowe introduced a new tax on matches with 'his Latin and his jokes and his sneers to play catchpenny with the lives of starving women and children'.[47] Having decided to write on the Commune for Morley, Harrison asked if he could say the Paris workman was 'the Messiah of modern civilization', the capitalist 'Judas' will 'betray him', and the 'chief Priests and Pharisees (literateurs and journalists) will mock at him, etc. Do not you be Peter and deny your Lord.'[48] But that was too much even for an editor who spelt God without a capital letter.

The Commune's virtues in Harrison's eyes were multiple: after all, its name and red flag and dechristianization programme all derived from the Paris Commune of 1793, and it defied a government that had rejected Paris's claims to be a concentration of the nation's moral and intellectual powers. The Commune was 'the genius of France' resuming the task begun by the French Revolution. And one consequence of the Revolution was decentralization. Harrison began his article by quoting Comte's view that the population of 'normal' political states—that is, in the Positivist era—would be from one to three million; and in his text Harrison endorsed the Commune's decentralizing aims. He may not have known that the Jacobin–Blanquist majority actually aspired to legislate for all France. In any case, it was precept, not practice, he was looking to, since so many of the new government's stated aims coincided with Positivist ideas: its rejection of suffrage, of parliamentarianism, of a standing army, and of Church–State ties, especially of the Church's control of education. He noted that these aims had been formulated without help from the Positivists, and that they could not sanction the Commune's reliance on force or its 'communistic' tendencies, though they could endorse the government as the first in Europe organized by working men who believed 'not in god, nor in any man', but saw that 'capital and its holders must adapt themselves to nobler uses, or they had better cease to exist.' He offered no hope that the Commune itself would survive, but promised that its memory would, in spite of the monarchists' 'bloody vengeance'.[49]

When that vengeance came with the fall of the Commune in May, leaving 25,000 Parisians dead and much of the city in ruins, many Englishmen declared that the people deserved their fate. Harrison of course could not agree, yet when Admiral Frederick Maxse sought his support for a protest against such public sentiment, Harrison withheld it. Thiers, of the National Government, he pointed out, was forming a Republic that the English should not criticize lest a worse system take its place.[50] In July, using information he had been collecting for a history of the Commune, he wrote another essay for Morley. He may have been hoping not only to modify the largely adverse reactions to the Commune in the press but also to counteract Marx's address to the International. Marx's criticism of the Commune for failing to act aggressively against the Versailles government and the bankers rested on a more overt advocacy of militarism and anti-capitalism than a Positivist could countenance. Similarly, Marx's picture of the International's role in the uprising must have seemed exaggerated. In any case, without mentioning Marx by name, Harrison depicted a working-class movement based more on local loyalties than ideology, one that was respectful of private property and civil order. He did not, however, fail to use the event for his own purposes: drawing on eye-witness reports from Maxse, the Paris Positivists, and refugees already streaming across the Channel, he asserted that the Commune had maintained exemplary order till its last days and was even then not responsible for the violence committed by desperate and ill-used Parisians at the mercy of the Versailles soldiery. It is often said that Marx created a myth of the Commune to serve future revolutionaries. Harrison tried to create two of his own: one was of the Commune as a kind of *ad hoc* local committee leading the French people to a new order and giving new lustre to the historical role of Paris as the source of progressive ideas; the other was of Europe at the crossroads where Communism and Positivism met—'Let capital shrinking from the fires and shambles of Paris choose which of these it will have.'[51]

The assertion embodied an obvious inconsistency. He had, after all, insisted that the Commune rested on no firm philosophic grounds. Why, then, call such a choice inevitable? In any case, by so doing he did not correct the common understanding that Communism and Positivism meant about the same thing. The *Pall Mall Gazette* had already denounced the Positivists as 'Our Own Reds', a charge echoed by *Punch* ('Confound them both') and by John S. Storr, brother of a Positivist, in the *Bee-Hive*. Regarding the Positivist Society and the International as equally subversive, Sir Thomas Larcome, a Privy Councillor in Ireland, collected newspaper cuttings on them both; and Lord Salisbury, reviewing works he thought inimical to political stability, included Marx's address and Harrison's second Commune article to illustrate extreme anti-capitalist arguments. The French literary critic Hippolyte Taine, then lecturing at Oxford, called Harrison 'le plus notable Communiste d'ici'; and Henry James, like Arnold before him, would profess to be amused by the contrast between Harrison's 'highly ornate and conventional appearance' and his radicalism—his 'Comtism, communism etc.'.[52]

No doubt furthering the identification of Positivists and Communists was a paragraph in *The Times* on 1 June 1871, the same day Taine mentioned Harrison. It cites a letter of Harrison's read to a London meeting convened by the International to consider ways of preventing extradition to France of Communard refugees. Harrison's opinion was that no legal grounds for such action would be found.[53] This indeed proved to be so, but amnesty did not come till the end of the decade, and meanwhile many refugees lived in poverty. Their plight drew the Positivists into charity work that on principle they had not considered part of their mission. And equally notable, they co-operated in these efforts with a relief society founded by the International. It was governed by the exiles themselves, and eventually Harrison discovered that dissension among them was alienating 'all the better men' among their supporters, which left some thirty or so 'utterly demoralized'

refugees who were unfit for anything but 'chattering politics' and were
destined, in his judgement, to end in 'pauperism, disease, death, and
prison'.[54]

But for the 'educated and honourable' exiles Harrison and the
Positivists felt all the more responsible. At Chapel Street they offered
free classes in English and used their professional and social connections
to find employment for the men as clerks, translators, and language
teachers.[55] Ethel did her part by visiting the women and children in
their makeshift homes. Having only recently moved into their own first
house, the Harrisons opened its doors to the refugees. But even with
screening of sorts, there were embarrassing episodes. They later liked
to recall the occasion on which one of the Frenchmen disclosed in
agitation that the husband of another guest had earlier in France
condemned him to death, and Ethel immediately restored his
equanimity: 'Cela n'y fait rien dans notre salon.'[56] When the treatment
of the refugees by others was at issue, Fred could become irate.
'Pinching housewives write on scented paper for a "distressed" maid of
all work at one pound a year. Procuresses want "an inexperienced girl
of 17". Oxford men want a Communist by the next train to live with
them', he complained to Morley.[57] He was annoyed, too, when Louis
Blanc, the French socialist, and Eugene Oswald, a liberal German who
taught at the Working Men's College, asked him to sign their petition
urging Thiers not to deport the geographer Elysée Reclus to New
Caledonia; special treatment for a writer, especially when it required
deferring to the 'bloody gang of miscreants' in Paris, went against
Harrison's grain.[58] The discovery that not all Communards were honest
was also dismaying; one victim was the philanthropic physician
Humphry Sandwith, author of one of the few English defences of the
Commune outside Positivist and Communist circles.[59] The ingratitude
of some exiles, though it took longer to emerge, was equally disappointing. Camille Barrère, for example, was treated handsomely by
the Harrisons, perhaps because he claimed descent from the 'Anacreon
of the Guillotine'; posted to London in the French diplomatic service
some years later, he informed them that he could no longer be seen in
their house because of their reputation as radicals.[60]

Of course, there were gratifying experiences as well. The Communards put Harrison in touch with some 'first rate' French artisans,
men like Albert Theisz, a bronze-worker who had headed the
Commune's postal service.[61] There was a most memorable encounter
when Marx brought to Harrison's chambers the former commissary of
the Commune police, Le Moussu, to have a dispute over patent rights
to a copying machine arbitrated. In his account of the episode—the

only version, apparently—Harrison does not describe Marx but recalls the delicate good looks of the Frenchman, who boasted of having ordered the execution of the Archbishop of Paris and other hostages of the Communards in those terrible last days. Harrison recounts how hard it had been to get both men to swear the oath on the Bible with which such proceedings had to begin, and how, after they had at last fleetingly touched the book (which he, no more than they, regarded as holy), and he called for their arguments, Marx, the great dialectician, 'floundered about in utter confusion'. The judgement went to Le Moussu.[62] The problems of others led him to confess to Morley a feeling of shame when contemplating those 'starving devils whom I call citizen and address with fraternity and whose shoes in the Kingdom of Heaven I am not worthy to black'.[63] Sometimes everyone he met at London dinner tables seemed secretly in sympathy with the Commune; at other times he sensed a hostility towards it that justified in his mind 'all that the Reds in France or here cry out for'.[64] After such emotional commitment, it was hard to learn, as learn he did, that many of the refugees looked upon him as merely 'a *bourgeois* with a fad, whose help could not repay one-thousandth part of the miseries which the class to which I belonged had caused'. But he had gained 'a curious insight into the utter instability of French society'.[65] Comte's dictum, no progress without order, took on new meaning.

There were other vexations besides politics for Harrison in the spring of 1871. Ethel spent weeks with his parents in Torquay, and her loving letters were an inadequate substitute for her calming presence. Dinner invitations occasionally alleviated loneliness but could also expose a gulf between himself and others in his class: 'When we are in our own house (if we ever are) we will never waste one minute of time or thought on any human being whom we can't honestly assert to be worth knowing', he promised Ethel.[66] In writing to Morley about the Commune it was easy enough to quote Proudhon: 'La propriété, c'est la vol', to insist on 'the Abolition of the Bourgeoisie' and to want to 'damn everybody who has money in the funds'.[67] But Mr Harrison had a great deal of money in the funds, and it was this that Fred and Ethel had to look to if they were to have a house of their own. Finding a suitable one proved difficult. In March, Fred's heart was set on property Ruskin owned in Paddington, but Ruskin's lawyers proved unable to obtain a clear title.[68] Finally, number 1 Southwick Place, only a few streets from Lancaster Gate, became available and seemed right. Mr Harrison at first objected to its proximity to a public house, but gave in.

Firmer when it came to decorating, Mr Harrison caused Fred to complain to Morley: 'Here am I rampaging about the new society and industrial order, and I have had a dozen men any one of them as good as myself employed for 6 weeks in trying to hit the correct tint which I or rather my art-crazed family think indispensable.' Luxury was 'incompatible with the true faith' but it was often 'a greater interference with mental activity to force on oneself a life and an atmosphere to which one has not been brought up, than to suffer certain luxuries which might no doubt be dispensed with'. It was 'a great question' and one he wanted to 'attack'.[69] Meanwhile, Ethel, perhaps sensing his confusion, wrote playfully from Torquay that she had spied a little cottage in which they could live quietly as 'Positivists, Mohamedans, or Choctaws', troubling only 'a few old talkative rooks'. It was, she added, owned by a Mr Mallock. She could not have known that a scion of that Devonshire family was already at Oxford sharpening the satirical talent he would use against Positivism before the decade was out.[70]

Harrison, too, sometimes dreamed of plain living and high thinking in the country, especially when the Morleys settled in the spring of 1871 in Pitfield House, on the Hog's Back road, near Guildford, with a view of the South Downs that Mill on a visit called the finest he had seen in southern England. But Morley was quick to point out Harrison's unfitness for isolation, his need for the stimuli of London groups like the Positivist Society, the Metaphysical Society, the Cosmopolitan Club (to which Lord Houghton had introduced him in 1871), and the Radical Club (which grew out of the Century).[71] In time all of these but the Chapel Street meetings would prove unsatisfying: the Cosmopolitan he would not 'care about'; the Radical's dinners conflicted with family gatherings and cost more than working men could pay.[72] And his theories seemed also to make Metaphysical Society meetings uncomfortable. When Grant Duff acted 'sulky' one evening, Harrison guessed that the Positivists' outspoken views on France were to blame. There were other annoyances on that occasion. The paper, by Arthur Russell, concerned the Absolute, and to Harrison seemed a 'tissue of incredible statements'. During the purely social part of the evening he happened to praise the current exhibition of Murillo's paintings to Ruskin, who responded that Murillo was a 'vulgar mindless, low brute' admired only by 'vulgar mindless low people'.[73]

Of course, London offered all the old pleasures of theatre, concerts, and art exhibitions, now made the more pleasurable to Fred by the radiant Ethel at his side. There was nothing they could not talk about. The difference in their ages apparently added to their love. Her musical ability and literary interests impressed him especially because of her youth; and she took his side on public issues with the deference of a daughter. Their intimate life apparently proved all the more satisfying because so long imagined and desired. Their happiness was immeasurably enriched by the birth of sons at regular two-year intervals in the seventies. Despite his late start, by the time Harrison was forty-six his own family closely reproduced the one in which he had grown up; and Ethel had four sons to love in place of her four brothers. Having been carefully nurtured themselves, Fred and Ethel were devoted—in some ways excessively—to their children. They named them, with literal adherence to Comte's rule for the sex that 'has to think and act', after exemplars in the Calendar of both the spiritual and the temporal realms. Hence Bernard Oliver Harrison (born 28 November 1871) honoured St. Bernard of Clairvaux and the Great Protector; Austin Frederic (born 27 March 1873) the Church Father, or perhaps the missionary who converted Kent with Queen Ethelberta (as Ethel Bertha sometimes spelt her name), and Frederick the Great as well as the child's father and grandfather; Godfrey Denis (born 28 November 1875) the French crusader and the patron saint of Paris; and Christopher René (born 27 April 1877) two discoverers, one of a new world, the other of a philosophic method.

Again with Positivist precepts in mind, Ethel and Fred took more responsibility for the day to day care of the boys than did most parents of their class. For the first year Ethel managed without a nursemaid; and when she and Fred crossed the Channel in 1872 to see the Third Republic in its infancy, they left 'Doddy'—Bernard—with her mother. By holiday time the following October there were two 'saints', but in rooms in Ventnor on the Isle of Wight their only servant, engaged there, was a fifteen-year-old maid of all work. Harrison reported to Morley that she looked like a street Arab, flew at her meat like a zoo lion, stole food when Ethel napped, and knew only one lullaby, 'Glory! Glory! Hallelujah'—which made him speculate about 'how vast are the powers of consolation possessed by that old Jewish religion.' And consolation was needed just then. Ethel had suffered a miscarriage upon arrival, and Austin, cutting teeth, was 'troublesome as a wasp'. Sorting out legal papers from 'butcher bills, toys, poultices, and prescriptions' caused Fred to think he knew what 'the most abject penury' entailed, and 'on what a thread does happiness hang.'[74]

Comte in his infinite wisdom had found servants 'admirably adapted to be the last natural link, between ... Family and ... Society'.[75] But good links were hard to find. Fred and Ethel decided against taking on George Eliot's cook's daughter after learning that her former employer had found the girl's undergarments 'arrogantly good' and her manners with men too refined.[76] Discharging one incompetent nursemaid, who threw herself weeping on her knees beside the baby's crib in an effort to dissuade him, caused Harrison to ponder on the 'arbitrary' power of persons in his station.[77] He saw the truth in Morley's assertion that upper-class women's harsh treatment of their women servants sometimes drove them into prostitution—but not in the argument of Josephine Butler and others then fighting against the Contagious Diseases Acts, that the solution to the problem lay in better work opportunities for women.[78]

As the Harrisons' need for servants increased with their family's growth, so did their means of affording them. In 1872 Harrison was named Examiner to the new Oxford Honour School of Jurisprudence at 120 guineas a year. He thought he owed the appointment to the determination of the Attorney General, George Jessel, to obtain men not already on the University faculty; but Maine had told Bryce that Harrison was simply one of the three best men applying.[79] He was not only gratified by the post's prestige and salary but amused that the appointment had been communicated to him by Spencer Walpole, the mild-mannered Home Secretary who after the 'Hyde Park Riots' of 1866 was said to have been reduced to tears by the pugnacious president of the Reform League. Consider, Harrison asked Morley, 'poor old Walpole politely begging me to represent constitutional law in the education of our future judges and legislators. It beats him weeping with Beales.'[80] Besides this new income, Harrison by 1875 was receiving £ 250 annually for examining at the Inns of Court (where he found the Indian students on the whole more impressive than at Chapel Street).[81]

With the birth of each son Harrison's allowance from his father increased, till by 1875 it was £700 a year. Mr Harrison reasoned that Fred and Ethel should be 'on a par' with their neighbours. He gave an annual sum rather than occasional gifts because he believed a man 'should know what he has to rely upon; then he can cut his coat according to his cloth; his mind is at rest.'[82] Moreover, Mr Harrison noted, Fred's scholarship at Wadham had cut the cost of his education, and now the entire family wanted him to be able to pursue his interests without financial anxiety. And this was made easier by the fact that his brothers had '*ready made*' sources of income: Robert and Lawrence as stockbrokers in their father's 'splendid business', and Sidney and Charles as solicitors in their uncle Charles's prosperous law firm.[83] Fred was grateful, but not reconciled to financial dependency. It galled him to know that he would probably not earn £200 a year in his profession, while '150 pushing asses quite snub me and trample on me.'[84] What made it worse was his conviction that most lawyers were 'bigots in religion and party hacks in statecraft'.[85]

Harrison's Positivism precluded his attempting to enter Parliament himself, though Morley, who had tried, frequently urged him to consider doing so. Freedom to express his own ideas was too crucial to sacrifice, however. In the mid-seventies he also declined a lucrative position— one he never described—which would have prevented any further speaking out on public issues.[86] And partly for the same reason he turned down H. R. Fox-Bourne's invitation, seconded by Mill, to make the *Examiner* into a truly working-class organ.[87] He did not wish to confine himself in any case to a working-class audience and by then had almost ceased writing for its papers. Morley's reports to him of the interest such authors as Mill, Robert Lytton, and Walter Pater took in his *Fortnightly* essays were encouraging him to believe he had literary talents worth cultivating. He tried once to ease the burden of writing regularly for the *Fortnightly* by hiring a short-hand secretary, but was so disappointed with the results that he let Morley pay the cost, though he was still not accepting payment for his articles.[88] The correspondence of the two men in the seventies suggests Harrison's increasingly literary and journalistic concerns; it is filled with his complaints about misprints; contrite excuses for missed deadlines, caused often by the pains he took to amuse as well as to edify; and expressions of delight when he achieved some happy turn of phrase. Morley's own productivity in that decade was not a little daunting. Besides editing and writing for the *Fortnightly* he produced a series of volumes of collected essays and studies of Voltaire, Rousseau, and Diderot. Harrison sought to account for his own lesser output by admitting to 'idleness, indecision, and moodiness'. But Morley, with the advantage of one who had isolated himself in a succession of homes outside London, surmised that Harrison would have 'struck the highest mark of composition ... if he had not been addicted to the bar, to London, to Society, to Switzerland, and to happiness generally.'[89]

THE TEMPERING OF RADICALISM

Morley's assessment had merit but did scant justice to Harrison's ever-growing addiction to time-consuming public causes. One was the struggle for new trade union legislation to incorporate the principles of his Minority Report. The Liberal Government introduced its long-awaited bill in February 1871, but though framed by Godfrey Lushington at the Home Office, it only partly reflected what Harrison and his friends wanted. It would protect union treasuries but also make peaceful picketing a crime. Ignoring his father's plea not to jeopardize his standing with the Government by criticizing its bill publicly, Harrison joined Beesly, Henry Crompton, and Ludlow in urging its repudiation by the Trades Union Congress, now the most representative organ of the labour movement.[90] George Howell, secretary to its Parliamentary Committee, drew Beesly's fire for having helped the Liberals attain office without clear promises to labour, and in 1872 provoked criticism from all the Positivists for recommending acceptance of a compromise bill offered by the Government. Harrison detailed its defects in the *Bee-Hive* but sought to mollify Howell at the same time. He was unsuccessful, and at the next Trades Union Congress meeting, at Leeds, early in 1873, Howell managed to 'lose' Harrison's paper calling for the subordination of 'every political object' to trade union goals, even if it meant 'the break-up ... of the great Liberal party'. Annoyed by Howell's pettiness and conciliatory attitude toward the Liberals, Harrison fulminated to Morley about labour's 'lying, thieving, jealous, vain, ignorant, irritable lot of self-style leaders'.[91] But then, putting aside his bitterness and acting on his conviction that changes in public opinion had to precede changes in legislation, he chronicled recent abuses under the existing laws in three *Tracts for Trade Unionists* that the Parliamentary Committee circulated and published long letters in the *Bee-Hive* and *The Times*. He also supplied Morley with details of cases involving imprisoned strikers to use in the *Fortnightly*, and with other Positivists he obtained assistance for their families.[92]

Yet, seemingly compromising the radicalism of this campaign to show labour's vulnerability in an economy dominated by capital, Harrison commended the argument of a great railway industrialist and self-proclaimed friend of the unions, Thomas Brassey, that by adjusting pay and hours, managers of large enterprises like his could, presumably without union interference, meet both their own and their employees' needs. Pleased with what seemed to justify Comte's faith in the managerial wisdom of capitalists, Harrison even suggested his own innovation: two eight-hour shifts arranged so that one began before dawn and another in the early afternoon, thus eliminating the standard dinner break. In its remoteness from practical acceptability this was worthy of Comte's behavioural engineering.[93] And in addressing the Trades Union Congress in Sheffield in 1874 Harrison advised unions not to support any legislation affecting hours of work unless an extremely good case could be made for it.[94] Capital, this seemed to imply, had greater credibility than government in dealing with such issues. No wonder a reporter at the meeting found Harrison a tamed lion,[95] and that he himself suspected that he appeared 'mild and moderate' to the members of an employers' association who took him to visit the Hadwens after the meeting.[96]

Harrison's alienation from the Liberal Party was increased by its Education Act of 1870. Designed to provide the first government, or Board schools in England, it also provided for continued appropriation of funds to Church of England schools. This, and the efforts of the Nonconformists to introduce non-sectarian religious instruction in the new Board schools, ran counter to the Positivist teaching against state interference in education or religion. Harrison's belief that instruction paid for by the state should not go beyond the three Rs, music, and drawing, was apparently not publicly known at first, for soon after returning from his wedding journey he learned he had been nominated to stand for Westminster in the first London School Board election, to be held in November. Although at first he was willing, mainly to test the secularism of the constituency, his name does not appear in the final list of candidates. Eventually he expressed more agreement with Auberon Herbert's rejection of state aid to all education than with the National Education League's efforts to stop state aid only to Church schools.[97] Morley's enthusiasm for the League and its dynamic head, Joseph Chamberlain, the radical mayor of Birmingham, added to the differences between Morley and Harrison. After the Liberals' electoral defeat in March 1874, Chamberlain proposed a new basis for a Liberal resurgence with a dramatically-styled programme: 'Free Church, Free Land, Free Schools, and Free Labour'. This struck a more sympathetic chord with Harrison at first than with Morley, who was still focusing on education as the main political issue of the day. But Harrison feared that no demand for 'Free Schools' in Chamberlain's sense of the term could gain national support, and that 'Free Labour' would antagonize the industrial interests in the Liberal Party. In any case, the immediate legislative goals Morley and Chamberlain were contemplating interested him less than they once had. In late 1873 he had already told Morley there was 'something much higher than national education, and that is the national sense that it wants a creed'.[98]

A similar impatience with even the most worthy legislative goals because of the attractions of the long-range aims of Positivism eventually undermined Harrison's commitment to another great Liberal cause of the seventies. The disestablishment and disendowment of the Church of England, which the Liberation Society had been advocating for decades, had the support of many influential Nonconformists and always received a high priority from radicals defining the work of a reformed Parliament. It was first in Chamberlain's list of four Freedoms. A Church divorced from the State was to the Positivists an essential expression of Comte's doctrine of the separation of the temporal and the spiritual powers. Harrison had of course been gratified by

Gladstone's abolition of Church rates, disestablishment of the Church in Ireland, and removal of religious tests at the universities, all in his first ministry. In 1873 Harrison responded to the Liberation Society's call for assistance from outside its largely Nonconformist membership in planning the next stage of its campaign, and met its leader Edward Miall and his associates together with Morley, Chamberlain, and Herbert Spencer. Later, chided by Morley for a certain slackness in his commitment, Harrison took a pose of ironic wonder at his friend's zeal: Morley was the 'Pusey of the Liberationists! Keble of the Infidels, John the Apostle of the Unbelivers! Pope of the Atheists! ... Infallible sceptic!' He himself, while not 'the Hot Gospeller of Infidelities', was assuredly 'stout' and 'true'—but also 'flooded with work'.[99]

And with family matters. A few days after the birth of his third son, Godfrey Denis, on 28 November 1875, Harrison could report that the child 'already shakes his fist when he hears the Church bell'. Yet Harrison found time to attend the major Liberationist conferences in London in the seventies. More important, he undertook to lecture on disestablishment there and in Manchester, Liverpool, and Birmingham. Sometimes he spoke for two hours at a stretch, advancing closely-reasoned arguments, confident legal judgements, and supportive historical evidence with a rhetorical verve he rarely equalled. One address made a pamphlet for the Liberationists comparable to his *Tracts for Trade Unionists*; another became a *Fortnightly* article; and a third, of masterful persuasiveness, a special supplement to the *Nonconformist*.[100] With some trepidation, he even questioned the historical premisses of E. A. Freeman's defence of the Church's right to its property, which Freeman compared to that of any ordinary corporation. Harrison denounced this 'big blunder' of the 'worshipful company of Freemanikins', declaring that the question would be settled not on historical but on social grounds—an argument like that with which he had countered Freeman's support of Germany's claim to Alsace and Lorraine in 1870. Harrison had been arguing only a few years earlier against treating unions and corporations as legally the same; now he sought to justify confiscating rather than protecting property, to place the Church, like the unions, outside established legal practices and so render it vulnerable to its critics. Freeman privately called him an 'atheistical mountebank', but to Harrison's surprise did not reply.[101] Mr Harrison, who chanced to be staying in the same hotel in Palermo as the historian and had observed his withdrawn nature, considered Fred's language 'too gladiatorial'.[102] The term applies equally well to Harrison's response to an assertion of John Tulloch, Principal of St. Andrews, that an alliance between Positivists and Dissenters could benefit neither group. Why, Harrison asked, did Anglicans put up with a spokesman from the Church of Knox so animated with 'the spirit of flunkeyism'?[103]

Just as Harrison had given the unions legal advice, so he was asked by the Liberationists in the spring of 1876 to review their disendowment scheme for legal loopholes, having been chosen over Fitzjames Stephen as 'likely to take more interest in it'.[104] But though he commended it as sound, and praised it in his speeches when it was published the next year, it eventually proved so controversial and divisive in its brusque approach to expropriating Church property that it became almost a liability. By that time—the close of the seventies—he had ceased to work actively for the Liberation Society. Its Nonconformist leaders, with their unchanging sectarian perspective and obsession with one unreachable goal, were no more congenial associates in the long run than his working-class allies had been. They held back from trying to swing the 1880 election on the disestablishment issue, and Gladstone remained adamantly loyal to the Church establishment. The campaign reached a last crescendo in 1885 with Chamberlain's Radical Programme—its disestablishment plank written by Morley—but Harrison was right in thinking that time had passed the issue by and the Liberal Party leaders would never endorse separation of Church and State in England. Years later he would explain the campaign's failure rather simplistically by asserting that the struggle had narrowed down to a confrontation between Evangelical Nonconformity and the Anglican Church, and the 'effective sympathy' of the nation went to the Church. He did not fail to register strong opinions when new Church and State issues arose, but disestablishment had been replaced by more immediate and practical national concerns. Morley, who over the years would shift from one enthusiasm to another in his search for a winning Liberal cause, might have discerned the deeper reason for Harrison's defection as early as 1874. Even then, when his friend was just committing the *Fortnightly* to disestablishment, Harrison said he hoped Morley might yet turn his attention 'to founding rather than destroying churches'.[105]

While the Church and State issue in England united Harrison and Morley in a common cause for much of the seventies, the problems of Church and State in Germany sharply divided them for a few months. Bismarck had brought a series of state actions against the Catholic Church, including expulsion of the Jesuits, and culminating in May 1873 with the Falk Laws, under which the government virtually controlled clerical education and appointments. Morley was untroubled by this campaign of *Kulturkampf*, for he welcomed the reduction of

Catholic, and especially Jesuit power in Germany; but Harrison thought undermining the independence of religion threatened liberalism throughout Europe. And he was less afraid of the Church's strength in Germany. At least he assured the Ultramontane Roman Catholic Archbishop Henry Edward Manning, a new friend at the Metaphysical Society, that he opposed *Kulturkampf* with equanimity because he never imagined that the principles of the Roman Catholic Church would prevail, and thought that so long as its leaders did not employ force on their behalf they had 'the most perfect right to try what they can do'.[106] A little like his theory of strikes testing the economy, the assertion implied that in a struggle for existence, the faith best suited to society would survive. At Manning's suggestion, the two discussed the German text of the new laws, and in the cordial atmosphere that soon developed between them, Harrison ventured to ask England's leading Catholic spokesman why he was not supporting disestablishment in England as a way of gaining 'millions of new adherents' from among the Anglicans who would leave their Church once it had lost its traditional prerogatives. The realistic Manning doubted that such a windfall would be forthcoming, and said that in any case he held the principle of a State Church 'too sacred to be broken in upon'.[107]

Ironically, Harrison gained the chance to air his views on the *Kulturkampf* from Morley, who in the autumn of 1873 put the 'Public Affairs' section of the *Fortnightly* into Harrison's hands. He was content in his first essay to discuss the issue of Church and State relations in general terms, calling it a 'crucial test' of statecraft.[108] But four months later he denounced the *Kulturkampf* explicitly, arguing that 'the sole function of the State is to punish the illegal action, not to amend the vicious opinion.' This echo of Mill's *On Liberty* did not prevent Morley, Mill's disciple, from defending Bismarck's policy in an editorial comment on Harrison's article that precipitated a private acrimonious exchange—Harrison regretting that 'some of that bile those damn dissenters exude sticks to you', and Morley scoffing at Harrison's reliance on 'a nonsensical preconception picked up out of a French dreamer and system-monger'. The friendship survived the episode, thanks to the importance both attached to their occasional meetings and copious correspondence, and to Ethel's peacemaking overtures.[109]

One preconception that linked that French dreamer to British radicals like Harrison and Morley was republicanism. Shortly after coming down from Oxford, Harrison expressed his dislike of monarchy by delighting in Thackeray's satiric lectures on the four Georges, though his admiration was somewhat undercut by learning that on the evening they were to meet at the house of a common friend, Thackeray pleaded gout—and was later said to have dined with a duke.[110] Harrison's theoretical opposition to monarchy did not prevent him from applauding Bright's defence of Queen Victoria at a reform meeting in 1866 after Acton Ayrton criticized her reclusive behaviour. Harrison later recalled leaving the hall to march down Regent Street arm in arm with masons and joiners shouting 'God save the Queen!'[111] Like many Liberals, the Positivists defined republicanism broadly, as the absence of hereditary privilege, not merely the repudiation of monarchy. But with the creation of the Third Republic in France, they caught the anti-monarchical fever sweeping England. Harrison lectured on the issue at least once, to some Bermondsey leather-sellers, and promised Morley an essay raising 'the whole question of monarchy as a principle'.[112]

By the time he got round to it in the spring of 1872, however, the Prince of Wales's recent critical illness had silenced most republicans, and the House of Commons had ignominiously defeated a motion by Harrison's republican friends Auberon Herbert and Sir Charles Dilke to investigate royal finances. Harrison realized that something 'lighter and less savage' was now called for: 'really, we want a good laugh which will carry the day against this absurd revival of royalty', he told Ethel.[113] He therefore treated the monarchy as a mere 'hereditary grand master of ceremonies', and managed to be satirical about both the 'Beefeater Party', which rallied round the throne, and Republican clubs devoted to 'the encouragement of the Day after Tomorrow'. Ranking himself among 'republican conservatives', he suggested that the very existence of the monarchy was 'a conclusive argument against any wanton meddling with it'.[114] Yet he showed enough scorn of the status quo to give Morley 'the smell of burning palaces'; and one historian of the republican movement has called Harrison's essay its 'peak'.[115]

Unlike some radicals of his acquaintance with careers in politics to consider—Chamberlain, Dilke, and Joseph Cowen, for example—Harrison never disavowed his republicanism. He was part of the 'London rabble' Henry James observed in the Easter holiday of 1877 trudging through rain-swept streets behind the coffin of George Odger, who had been an eloquent working-class republican. The novelist identified Odger as a man who had nurtured a 'perverse desire to get into Parliament',[116] but Beesly, in a heartfelt eulogy at the graveside, honoured him as a 'great citizen', a title he said was 'beyond the power of Kings or an Act of Parliament to bestow'.[117]

Gravesides required solemnity; journalism did not. Harrison regretted that Beesly's younger brother, Augustus, an assistant master at Marlborough College, spoiled an attack on the game laws by 'unmannerly' prose, and that Morley was sometimes 'too crushing and withering' in dispatching his enemies.[118] So sensitive to the delights of witty political prose was Harrison that upon guessing or learning from someone in 1874 that Sir Charles Dilke was the author of the anonymously-published *jeu d'esprit* on governmental ineptitude, *The Fall of Prince Florestan*, Harrison sought to prolong the mystery and extend the satire. Addressing Dilke as 'Dear Prince', he claimed that the boating slang in the work had tipped him off, for he knew of no other university man capable of such clever prose. He urged Dilke to acknowledge his literary child because Arnold was being credited with it—which obviously irked—and when Dilke failed to do so suggested that he explain the story as Florestan's attempt to imitate Arnold, or as the work of Harrison posing an Arminius's brother to show up Arminius's Oxford circle as 'sad prigs'. Further fantasies of deriding Arnold were precluded when Lady Dilke quashed all speculation about authorship by having herself announced at an evening gathering as 'Mrs Florestan'.[119]

Like republicanism, social and legal reform wrought by political means sometimes seemed less important to Harrison than Comte's theories. Disraeli's Manchester speech on sanitation in 1872 prompted the Positivists to draw up their own programme of reforms, including an eight-hour work day, working-class housing, free education, and public transport, parks, and libraries. Two decades later Harrison sent Beatrice Webb a copy as an example of 'early municipal socialism'.[120] But it was also an example of Positivism's utopianism, because these innovations were to come about through a growing concern for Humanity. Nothing was said about political agencies to effect the changes. At Chapel Street the emphasis was usually on voluntary action. There was also more than a hint of quietism in Harrison's refusal to help prepare the defence of Odger and others faced with prosecution for defying new park regulations imposed by Acton Ayrton (who was as contemptuous of the people as of their Queen). Harrison contributed to the men's expenses but said they would have to 'take the consequences' if the court upheld the new laws. He attended an Electoral Reform Association meeting at which Dilke made the laws an argument for a wider franchise (and heard Chamberlain speak for the first time), but by arriving late he did not have to sit on the platform—a strategy he had used before.[121]

Though he disapproved of defying existing law, Harrison did not look to it to uphold morality. One reason his loss of religious faith had not subjected him to the anxieties felt by others in his state of unbelief was that he did not share their quandary over what to offer as a sanction for morality. In the Positivist scheme, desire for Humanity's approbation and fear of its disapprobation would replace orthodox notions of heaven and hell. Hence when James Fitzjames Stephen, despite his own latitudinarianism, fell back on the old principle of religious rewards and punishments in *Liberty, Equality, Fraternity* in 1873, Harrison felt obliged to submit once again to the 'yoke of composition' to refute his reasoning. But only some of it. Stephen had conceived of the book returning from India, where he had been legal member of the Viceroy's Council. The paternalism of the British regime there had impressed him, and Mill's teaching about liberty and equality came to seem misguided. On these issues Stephen's thought was utterly compatible with Positivism, Harrison told Morley; and Stephen's criticism of the 'vague St. Simonianism' in Mill's idea of fraternity was also acceptable, because, Harrison noted, Comte had constructed his 'scientific religion' precisely with a view to overcoming this inadequacy in other secular religions.[122] Indeed, it was Stephen's failure to distinguish between Comte's Religion of Humanity and its competitors that annoyed Harrison. But he was determined to 'set down naught in malice', he told Morley. When he told Stephen as much during a chance encounter, he, in his characteristically gruff manner, replied: 'Write when you have indigestion. I don't want your praise, all jovially [sic] and friendly.'[123] Now Harrison found it all the easier to write aggressively, Stephen being, in his opinion, the worst of the 'pushing asses' in the law courts. He described him to Morley 'thrusting his huge carcass up the ladder of preferment, and turning round with pants to say, "I am for God, damn your eyes".'[124] Stephen was a 'big bully and a philistine' who had to be 'utterly squelched'—finished, 'as Pascal finished the Casuists'.[125]

And like Pascal Harrison wished his prose to be lucid and devastating. But Stephen had 'flung up a whole army of problems and ideas which set one boiling all over', and it was not easy to compose 'a work of art' to be read as one reads *Faust*. Polishing an epigram could take days, and in the end the whole required at least four revisions. Even then, some uncertainties remained. Thinking of one particularly successful barb made him laugh aloud in the night, but he feared he might be too daring, that his title—'The Religion of Inhumanity'—for example, might be too 'savage'.[126] It turned out to be not his only striking inversion of a well-known phrase. Having found too little orthodoxy in Neo-Christianity to do the work of religion, Harrison now sought to show that 'Stephenism' contained too much. It revived the hell the Essayists had tried to 'dismiss with costs' and advanced instead

'Calvinism minus Christianity'. It was the belief of a man who 'thinks very poorly of the Gospel [Stephen, after all, had defended Rowland Williams before the Court of Arches] but thinks something useful can be made of the Apocalypse'. His Paradise would be filled with those who had 'elbowed their way to fortune and place', but would have no corner for the 'weak and foolish'. As usual, Harrison undermined more capably than he built. He nowhere met Stephen's assertion that the threat of punishment could deter men from evil. Referring to Stephen's Indian experience, Harrison remarked that since the English kept order there by means of 'the old tyrannies', they naturally felt 'something of the satisfaction of Providence resting from its work'. Though a lawyer himself, he opposed Stephen's application of legalistic conceptions to moral issues, preferring to view them not in the context of the real but of the ideal. And Mill's recent death conveniently provided him with the pretext for what he described to Morley as 'one of Liddon's sermons done into Comte'. It presented Humanity as an 'organic being', and Subjective Immortality as capable of inspiring good and overcoming evil. The influence of Harriet Taylor on Mill, and of Mill himself, were evidence that 'we, of all others, have a right to say, "O Death, where is thy sting? O Grave, where is thy victory?" '[127]

Though he saw that 'stuffing in promiscuous epigrams' was 'a bad plan' in writing, Harrison could do no other in confronting Stephen. He did not reply to Stephen's rejoinder in the second edition of *Liberty, Equality, Fraternity*.[128] Meanwhile, he added to his tribute to Mill in an address at Chapel Street later reprinted in a volume of memorial essays.[129] But what he chose to emphasize in the career of his friend was his introduction of Comte's thought into England. And when Morley elaborated on Mill's ideas of liberty in an important work of his own, *On Compromise*, Harrison offered guarded praise, calling the 'Subjective Synthesis' more useful.[130] In writing 'Public Affairs', too, he sometimes showed little faith in the rationalism that Mill and Morley considered essential to politics. Before the 1874 election he advised working-class voters to make a candidate's stand on the labour laws the test of his merit. That seemed rational enough. But explaining the Conservatives' victory he denied that voters were ever 'strictly logical' and told Morley that in this instance they had reacted against the 'fierce crudities of Millite radicalism'.[131] Mr Harrison rightly saw that Fred was doing little to help 'a lame dog over the stile'.[132] Whether the lame dog was the Liberal Party, Millite radicalism, trade unionism, disestablishment, republicanism, or legislation for social welfare or education, Harrison could offer only intermittent help. His eyes were too steadily fixed on a distant, all-embracing sociology.

In the spring of 1874, after six months of writing 'Public Affairs', Harrison turned it back to Morley, whose editorial note rebuking Harrison's *Kulturkampf* article still rankled. Moreover, he needed additional free time, for he was assembling his political essays into a book. 'Selling one's thoughts over twice' troubled him, but it was only a figure of speech; he had not accepted payment for periodical work. Without a published volume to his name, he believed he would never attain acceptable status as a social critic or fully know the public's response to his ideas. Morley proved most helpful, and suggested Harrison wrote a 'sort of showman's drum and trumpet prelude to the wonderful programme going on inside'.[133] In the 389-page volume Harrison produced and Longman's published early in 1875, 122 pages were new. Not all were needed; without editorial demands and adversaries' stimuli, Harrison often wrote diffusely.[134]

His title was Comte's motto, *Order and Progress*. His stated aim was to show how the two elements of the title had to be reconciled to make government more efficient. Walter Bagehot, in a recent *Fortnightly* series, had made a somewhat similar attempt to reconcile physics (Darwinian science) and politics. Harrison included his own *Fortnightly* essay on Parliamentary reform that had alluded to Bagehot on the constitution and in turn had been alluded to by Arnold in *Culture and Anarchy*. Arnold's title names two mutually exclusive ideas, not, like *Physics and Politics* and *Order and Progress*, two ideas meant to be reconciled. All three works, however, sought to find a centre of authority in social thought. Harrison's derives from the family; he dedicated the book to his father 'with a lifelong sense of the truth that the primary school of politics is the home'. Well on the way to re-creating his father's role in his own family, Harrison could hardly be expected to see its undemocratic, even oppressive side, especially since it meshed so well with Comte's paternalism. And it was Comte who enabled him to fulfil the aim of the book, to show how to reconstruct government out of the 'debris of institutions, half feudal and half democratic'. *The Polity* stressed the need for a new political organization to serve industrial society, and Harrison's image of government was the machine: the House of Commons existed to grind out statutes fed into it by a strong executive. Parliament's traditional debating function was distinctly subordinated to its legislative work; like obedient women and children, the legislators merely expedited orders from above.

Another aim of the book was to promote Positivism as a philosophy mediating between that of Mill and Carlyle, representatives here of reform and reaction respectively. Harrison's debt to Mill shines most clearly in the reprinted essay on Parliamentary reform, in which public opinion is said to be the major sanction of all government, and unearned privilege is denounced. Harrison compares Carlyle's idea of a strong executive to Comte's, preferring Comte's because it denies the executive any control over the military or economic function of government. Harrison had been drawing closer to Carlyle in recent years, though he would never equal Vernon Lushington or Cotter Morison in his admiration. To Morley he weighed Carlyle's strengths and weaknesses after visiting him in Chelsea following an invitation prompted by his first article on the Paris Commune. He found Carlyle's house, situated in 'a very dismal corner of this foul city', an edifying contrast to Tennyson's 'royal Palace', Aldworth, near Haslemere (where Fred and Ethel had been shown around by the Laureate after encountering him by chance nearby), to Thackeray's 'mansion' in Palace Green, to Dickens's 'houses and theatres', and to Browning's 'duchesses' boudoirs'. At least to Carlyle literature was 'not a trade'. His faults were quite other; he was a 'narrow Bible-ridden prejudiced savage, Scotch peasant, glorified with strong poetical gift', a man of one theme: 'God and Devil—God what I, Thomas, like, Devil what I, Thomas don't like, and often what I don't understand'.[135]

By stressing the similarities between Comte, Mill, and Carlyle, Harrison did not make his critics more favourably disposed toward his Positivism. Leslie Stephen declared that no theory contingent upon accepting Comte's religion could be useful; the *Pall Mall Gazette* thought Harrison might as well have divided the book into 'Thoughts on the Government of the Earth' and 'Thoughts on the Government of the Moon'; the *Saturday Review* scorned its 'dandified contempt for practical considerations'; the *Westminster* predicted its repudiation by both admirers and critics of the Parliamentary system; and even Mr Harrison scoffed at the notion of Comte as the 'Philosopher of Nations'.[136] There was small comfort in learning from Sir Henry Parkes in Australia that he thought the book might prove useful on that side of the globe.[137] Harrison grumbled to Morley that 'if one of us were to make remarks about the horses for the next "Derby", there would be a hollabaloo about Clotilde de Vaux, Priestcraft, monkeys, and protoplasm.'[138]

Any suggestion that Positivism was obscurantist was galling to Harrison because what he valued in Comte most was his claim to scientific rigour. Its absence in Alfred Russel Wallace's articles on spiritualism led Harrison in 1874 to remonstrate with Morley for publishing them.[139] Yet in the same year he did not feel able to refuse Lewes's request that he review his *Foundations of a Creed*, which extended the province of empirical inquiry to include psychological investigation, something Comte had excluded from his hierarchy of sciences. Without actually judging whether by introducing psychology under the rubric of physiology Lewes would be able to provide the 'foundations of a creed', Harrison could recommend the book to those awaiting 'the amalgamation of Philosophy and Religion'.[140] But he did not himself feel capable of going beyond Comte on so crucial an issue, and in any case had no more interest in discussing the subtleties of the human mind than in discussing theories of political economy, or metaphysics, or theology.

Rather than building on Comte's system, Harrison and his Positivist friends were busy in the mid-seventies trying to make that system more accessible to English readers. Inspired by Bridges's translation of the first part of volume one of the *Système de positive politique*, published in 1865 with money contributed by friends like Lewes and George Eliot as well as the Positivists themselves, the translation of the four volumes, published between 1875 and 1877, was a co-operative work. Bridges completed the first volume; Harrison the second (*Social Statics, or the Abstract Theory of Social Order*); Beesly, the Lushingtons, Mrs Hertz, and Samuel Lobb, an Anglo-Indian, the third (*Social Dynamics, or the General Theory of Social Progress*); and Congreve the fourth (*The Theory of the Future of Man*). Harrison's text presents the social theories apart from their historical evolution, and hence is relentlessly abstract. Accordingly, Harrison found the translation a terrible burden, and his prose has none of the animation of his *Fortnightly* essays. Comte had viewed Aristotle's *Politics*, which Harrison had helped Congreve to edit, as a prototype for the abstractions in *Social Statics*,[141] but in the preface to his translation of that work Harrison asserted that understanding it would require the 'dispositions and habits' of the scientist. He could only have meant the willingness to pursue an intellectual task rigorously despite tedium, for Comte had certainly not based his work on empirical study, as Aristotle had, nor sought to verify his conclusions.

Especially remote from reality was Comte's discussion of women. Destined to save man from the 'corruption' to which his life of action made him susceptible , women were at once deified and denigrated. Ethel, who volunteered to help Fred with his labours and may even have done some of the translating, silently registered her objection to this message by allowing herself to be diverted from the work by a project of her brother-in-law Charles Harrison. Inspired by the discoveries of Layard and other archaeologists, it was a catalogue of 857 photographic plates of some 5,000 artifacts in the British Museum selected by experts and put in chronological order to illustrate the history of man. The catalogue, containing Charles's introduction, was available free at the British Museum, and he had pressed a copy on Ethel.[142] With mock dismay Fred told Morley she obviously preferred it to his own 'strong course' in sociology. Indeed, she lacked the 'abject attitude of "the woman" in the immortal dialogue' [Comte's *Catechism*], which, in 'a Positivist wife who (though I say it) is a pattern, has not a little staggered me. Is the "moral providence" then infected with the accursed spirit of criticism incidental to our revolutionary anarchy?'[143]

The 'accursed spirit of criticism' was certainly discernible when *Social Statics* appeared. Mr Harrison wished it had been a book on English law, 'for the many', and not like Comte's, 'for the few'.[144] Arnold acknowledged his presentation copy by remarking that 'Comte is not a good writer of French, whereas you are a very good one of English. A thousand thanks! but yet do not spent your life and talents over Comte!'[145] Morley, having recently finished a rather unsympathetic article on Comte for the *Encyclopaedia Britannica*, and 'thoroughly sorry' Harrison had undertaken the translation at all, professed to be amazed that it left him still 'a hale man and the father of babes'. But he speculated, too, that Comte's 'papistry' had lent Harrison's own prose a 'certain ease, comprehensiveness, width of reference' causing it to resemble Newman's.[146]

Whether or not it affected his prose, Comte's 'papistry' was evident in Harrison's rapturous appreciation of Sutton Place, a Tudor manor built in 1524 near Guildford and owned continuously since then by Roman Catholics. It was there that Harrison completed his translation of *Social Statics*, and, almost as onerous, the index for all four volumes of the *Polity*. In 1874 his father had leased Sutton Place, set in a 1,000-acre park, when the terms of Eden Park rose above what he would pay. Though virtually retired from business, he still liked a residence in stockbroker country, and Sutton Place had unique charms for the son of a builder with architectural experience of his own. One of the earliest and finest examples of Tudor domestic architecture, its Gothic brick exterior was ornamented by terracotta worked by Italians brought to finish Hampton Court. Furnished by the owner, Francis Henry Salvin, an expert on falconry, the house boasted heraldic devices in stained glass windows and a suit of armour. Fred's parents and brothers added their own plunder from foreign holidays. The very desk on which he first described the place to Morley might, he speculated, be that on which the builder's son, Sir Richard Weston, had written the letters to Anne Boleyn that led to his execution with her for high treason. On Sundays one could hear echoes of the Mass being said in the east wing, a provision in the lease, but Harrison no more minded that than had the Gladstones or the Shaw-Lefevres, previous tenants. Alluding to the concealed passage in his dressing room, which resident priests had used during the years of persecution, he invited Manning (now Cardinal) to come and see the 'survival of the Tudor violences'.[147]

That some of the furnishings in Sutton Place were 'utter Wardour Street' did not trouble Harrison, for they suggested 'the march of generations, and the unity of life'.[148] To preserve and intensify this feeling of antiquity, he drew up plans for restoring the long gallery, adding a drawing room, and replacing deteriorated window mullions. This led Mr Harrison, at the age of seventy-five, to consider the irony of paying for innovations in a house he would soon be quitting for his 'final abode'. But he caught something of Fred's 'gushing enthusiasm' and spent £1,000 on the house in one year. For final specifications they called in the distinguished architect Norman Shaw, who in 1877 would design a £12,000 house in Cadogan Square for Lawrence, then Fred's only married brother. When Sutton Place was thus restored, Mr Harrison could report that it 'certainly astonished the natives'.[149]

In the seventies Fred and Ethel found holiday places apart from Eden Park and Sutton Place. They occupied Bonscale, a modest hillside farmhouse on the south shore of Lake Ullswater in 1874, and the next year returned to the Howtown Hotel, just down the road and already known to others in the family, the 'old world quiet' of that remote part of the Lake District compensating for the 'stern-bare and rather dark' countryside.[150] In 1875 they broke their journey on their way north at Cooper's Hill in Gloucestershire, where there were spectacular views and, for Fred and two of Ethel's bachelor brothers, bracing walks and rides, including a jaunt to nearby Cheltenham to lunch with Frederick W. H. Myers and Francis Newman.[151] And in 1877 and 1878 there were prolonged stays in two notable places leased to the Harrisons by their owners, both formidable ladies who had tenuous connections with the Positivists.

The first was Les Ruches, a girls' school in Fontainebleau, owned by Michelet's friend Mlle Marie Souvestre. She had been known to the Harrisons since at least the beginning of the decade, probably through the Paris Positivists. Her father, a prolific writer and Academician, Émile Souvestre, had been one of Comte's executors. But she was no disciple of anyone; in Harrison's eyes she was an 'intellectual Bedowen'. He and Ethel visited her in 1872 and 1874, and three years later rented quarters in the unoccupied school for the late summer. She helped him stay abreast of French politics, while he in turn introduced her to families who might provide pupils. Morley's sister taught at Les Ruches briefly, but he thought her fees too high to let his stepdaughter become her pupil. Other acquaintances of Harrison's whose daughters were educated by her included Joseph Chamberlain, Stuart Rendel, Charles Kegan Paul, Richard Strachey, T. H. S. Escott, and Richard Potter—though his most gifted daughter, Beatrice, deplored her 'absence of humility' and declined to be sent. Harrison admired Mlle Souvestre's intellect and 'eye for character', and smiled at her dogmatism. She dared, for example, to find fault with George Eliot's prose, and, when Ethel took her to call on the Leweses, observed critically, 'elle s'écoute quand elle parle.' In art as in literature, the school mistress 'liked what she liked', though she accused Harrison of lacking aesthetic principles.[152] She did, however, drive him and Ethel through the forest one day to Barbizon to visit the rustic studio of Jean François Millet. There Harrison explained to the aged artist that his canvases would fetch more if he left off consigning them to a single Paris dealer—advice that went unheeded by that radiantly simple spirit. Back in London, Harrison found his praise of Millet's scenes of pious peasant labour rebuffed by Ruskin, who pronounced them too gloomy. Work, he insisted, should be depicted as cheerful, and he added that the famous 'Pig-Killers' would seem tragic only to a pig.[153]

The second holiday house was Sunnyside, at Freshwater, on the Isle of Wight. Owned by the photographer Julia Margaret Cameron, it was rented by the Harrisons for the summer of 1878 while she stayed at nearby Farringford, Tennyson's house, in his absence.[154] Mrs Cameron's link to the Positivists was a curious one. Twelve years earlier one of Congreve's followers Henry Stedman Cotton, from a prominent Anglo-Indian family, as was Mrs Cameron, had fallen in love at first sight with her young parlourmaid and model, a girl known as 'Madonna Mary' because of the pose she often took in Mrs Cameron's portraits. Cotton married the girl and almost immediately departed for India and his first government post. In 1878 they were back in London on leave, but whether they revisited the scene of their courtship and met the Harrisons is unknown. What Harrison chiefly remembered about that summer was the familiarity he gained with the scenery depicted in many of Tennyson's poems.[155]

That autumn the Harrisons left Southwick Place for 38 Westbourne Terrace, a five-storey house owned by Mr Harrison that would be their last London residence. In a colonnaded row built in the 1840s to be the 'most splendid' in the metropolis with a 'superior salubrity' due to its high ground and sandy soil, its 'Palmy days', Mr Harrison conceded, were over, but the ground rent was only £55 and he predicted that Ethel could run the house on 200 guineas a year. Near Lancaster Gate and Paddington station (for Oxford trains), it had some twenty rooms, allowing for a schoolroom, a conservatory, and a 'sanctum' for Fred; and there was stabling for his horse in the mews. Mr Harrison trusted Fred and Ethel to decorate it without 'going off in a showy manner as too many do', but her father, Mr Harrison's brother William, more expansively suggested using a room off the staircase landing for statues—'Eve at the fountain or something of that sort'—and he begged for 'picture papers ... with scenery, lakes, etc.' in the nursery.[156] No longer was Fred troubled by his family's aesthetic concerns, as at the time of the Commune. Besides his Arundell Society reproductions of old masters and his beloved Piranesi scenes of Rome, there were eventually paintings by leading contemporary artists. Two were by Walter Crane; one showed an ancient traveller with staff and lantern, presented to the Harrisons by George and Rosalind Howard after Fred dubbed it 'the Positivist Pilgrim', perhaps because he knew of Crane's youthful interest in Comte; the other was Crane's portrait of Ethel in her drawing room, with Morris paper, an Oriental rug, and Chinese vases in the background. There was also a portrait of her richly gowned in velvet displaying the reserve of a Pre-Raphaelite lady, by William Blake Richmond, whose father George Richmond had done a charming chalk drawing of Mr Harrison years earlier.[157] And there was a painting of René by Huxley's daughter, Marian Collier; it depicted him in a black velvet suit with a wide white collar wearing a plumed hat and with one hand holding a riding whip, the other resting on the head of a great collie dog. When exhibited in 1882 in the Grosvenor Gallery (whose director, Comyns Carr, was a brother-in-law of Lawrence Harrison's wife) *Punch* dubbed the painting 'Hamlet Junior'.[158] To complement the aesthetic décor of the house, Ethel dressed the boys in Kate Greenaway garb and they favoured Walter Crane picture books and valentines and accepted their father's view of Burne-Jones as 'a man of brains apart from his brush'—but that may have been due to the strawberries they were served at his studio.[159]

In the midst of all this 'sweetness and light' Harrison had not forsaken the trade unions, though his interest gradually diminished. Mistrust of their powerful Trades Union Congress was one reason. At its inception it had criticized his treatment of Conolly during the Royal Commission on Trade Unions, and in 1874 it was divided over his recommendation that labour should not co-operate with a new Royal Commission that Disraeli appointed upon taking office. Harrison denounced the Commission as a 'dilatory' tactic and did not hide his anger at Alexander MacDonald, the Chairman of the TUC, and Hughes, for joining it as members.[160] Nor did he trouble to attend the

TUC's annual meeting in 1875 at Liverpool for fence-mending. As luck would have it, when the winners of a TUC essay contest he and Henry Crompton had judged were announced, it turned out that they had awarded a prize (the papers were unsigned) to a notorious critic of unions, from, of all places, Sheffield.[161]

Another reason for Harrison's diminished involvement with labour—and Beesly's too—was its success in 1875 and 1876 in obtaining the legislation they had defined as its goal: strikes were made legal and unions were permitted to register under the Friendly Societies Act without sacrificing their exemption from legal liability. Ludlow, who opposed this last provision, was Secretary of the Friendly Societies and hence instrumental in formulating the procedures it required. Neither he nor Harrison could foresee the direful eventual consequences for the labour movement. At the time, Harrison was sanguine about the measures, even praising Lowe as a 'scientific jurist' for his part in meeting labour's desires.[162] But he let Henry Crompton write the *Digest* of the new laws, and mentioned Howell's book, *The Conflicts of Capital and Labour*, which summarized the struggle to obtain them, only in passing, in an essay dealing largely with speeches by three Positivist workmen in France.[163] Ironically, the unions' triumph came in a decade of economic troubles that reduced the funds of some societies and made strikes less promising than they had seemed to Harrison in the more prosperous sixties. Comte had had nothing to say about such problems. Though Harrison wrote a pamphlet published by the TUC in 1879 to refute Lord Bramwell's endorsement of diminished production as a palliative measure, it shed little light on the issues.[164] Certainly the Positivists were disappointed by labour's indifference to causes about which they felt intensely, like justice for Ireland, anti-imperialism, and disestablishment; but the most obvious reason for their drift from the trade union movement was the death or retirement of the leaders to whom they had been closest and their replacement by men—many from outside London—who were increasingly able to dispense with middle-class advisers.[165]

While Henry Crompton continued to urge working men to concern themselves with law reform after the passage of the trade union legislation of 1875 and 1876,[166] Harrison found a new and more theoretical focus for his legal interests. In 1877 the Council of Legal Education appointed him and James Bryce Professors of Jurisprudence, International Law, and Constitutional Law. At last Mr Harrison could hope for 'important and durable' legal studies instead of the 'ephemeral' works, 'however clever', that Fred had been publishing. What Fred ultimately produced fell somewhere between those extremes: five essays, derived from his lectures, that law students used for decades (though they appeared as a book only in 1919) and that were also of sufficient general interest and readability for Morley to compare to popular works by Arnold and Maine and to publish in the *Fortnightly* in 1878 and 1879.[167]

The first two of these essays set out the merits of the two opposing schools of legal thought: the historical school, represented by Henry Maine; and the analytical school, represented by John Austin. Just as Harrison had sought to reconcile the principles of order and progress in his 1875 volume, so now he sought to justify the claims of both these schools. Maine's value was in showing how law had changed to keep pace with changing ethical perceptions, Austin's in showing how legal principles could be separated from historical and ethical contexts. The latter, said Harrison, was especially important for the practising lawyer, for he needed to know what the law actually was, not what it had been or could be. And Austin's conception of sovereignty was useful to the social theorist in challenging the doctrine of 'rights', which, Harrison noted, another philosopher—obviously Comte—had eliminated from his vocabulary altogether.[168] The third essay presented an additional ground for valuing the law as it actually was, at the expense of reformist sentiment: only existing law could be codified. The failure of the Commission on the Digest of the Law had not undermined his belief in the importance of that objective.[169]

Harrison's last two *Fortnightly* essays on jurisprudence dealt with civil cases involving laws of two or more nations. 'Intermunicipal Law', the term he proposed for such a study, never caught on, though the subject became increasingly important. As an example of what it might involve, Harrison imagined an English inheritance case complicated by a French marriage—a situation he had twice urged George Eliot to consider for her fiction. Now his purpose was to explain that, despite the differences in their legal systems, England and France had more in common with each other than with any other legal system of Europe, since both had evolved largely out of the decisions of judges and not out of theory. He was claiming a kind of empiricism for the law in the two nations that the Positivists believed were leading the West's social evolution.[170]

THE THIRD REPUBLIC

Britain's political problems in the closing months of Gladstone's first ministry seemed to Harrison 'mere shadows' compared to those of France. He dealt with both in 'Public Affairs' from October 1873 to

May 1874, and on the strength of a visit to the 'centre of civilization' in April wrote a full-scale essay for Morley on 'France After the War'. While the advent of a Conservative government in Britain, which seemed imminent by the end of 1873, would, in his words, mean mainly 'a larger infusion than usual of country squires into office, and a kindly interest in drains', in France the succession of MacMahon to the Presidency of the Republic and of the Duc de Broglie to the leadership of the Cabinet meant the repression of civil liberties that did not 'cease to be a crime because it is cynically avowed'.[171] In Germany the Catholic clergy had been subjected to repression, but in France the clergy were allied with the authorities. Neither situation was in accord with the Positivists' conception of legitimate State function.[172] Where the parliamentary system was 'palpably worked out', as in France and Spain (the republican Castelar there opposed General Serrano, 'another MacMahon'), the task was 'not to destroy the inevitable dictatorship but to convert it from being the tool of a faction, and to make it the organ of the nation'.[173]

It was one thing to advocate strengthening the executive as a means of combating 'legalised anarchy' in Britain, where there was considerable independence of religion and education, and quite another to advocate it in France, where the entrenched conservatives allied with the Church created a 'black International'.[174] Harrison therefore had to look elsewhere for promise of progress in France. As in assessing Italy's future in 1859, so now he pinned his faith on the strong individual around whom republican forces could rally, Léon Gambetta. His courageous attempt to prolong France's resistance to Prussia in 1870, and even his Italian background, must have reminded Harrison of Garibaldi, while his political conduct in opposing the conservative republicans showed a statesmanship comparable in some ways to Cavour's. After Dilke arranged an introduction, Harrison, writing to Morley, compared his latest hero to some 'rough, red, fleshy, hideous and fierce animal'; but he also used terms that suggested the ideal head of the Positivist temporal realm. Gambetta resembled

un banquier Juif—un banquier de génie bien entendu, mais un banquier, a Rothschild père, a man who foresees ... who cares for success, not for appearance ... who knows what men want, and works with the patient intensity of a financial genius ... Italian pas Français, homme d'état de Ier order, as patient as Dizzy ... no trace of the Jacobin ... exactly *the* man.[175]

What Harrison admired as pragmatism others derided as opportunism; hence in the *Fortnightly* he depicted Gambetta as an antidote to the Communards, who he had by now come to see as 'fanatics to whom metaphysical theories are of more importance than national results'. And the rural population against which the Commune had rebelled now seemed to him to be accepting republicanism because Gambetta's great respect for property and order overcame their fear of the 'Red Spectre'.[176]

Harrison's confidence in Gambetta was not shared by a leading French Positivist, Dr Jean Robinet, who by 1875 was refusing to appear on platforms with Pierre Laffitte, the head of the Positivist Society in Paris and an intimate of Edmond and Juliette Adam, in whose republican salon Gambetta starred.[177] Nor was Gambetta much admired by Cotter Morison, the Harrisons' host in Paris in 1872 and 1874. He deemed the French 'too sectarian' for stable government under any parliamentary system.[178] The truth lay between his pessimism and Harrison's optimism. In 1875 the French hammered out a constitution, and in 1876 Gambetta's party gained a majority in the Chamber of Deputies. But the next year MacMahon replaced the moderate republican Prime Minister, Jules Simon, with the reactionary Duc de Broglie; and when the deputies declined to recognize him, MacMahon dismissed the Chamber and called for new elections: the so-called 'seize mai' crisis. Harrison, who was planning his family's visit to Mlle Souvestre at Les Ruches in Fontainebleau for August and September, wrote to his old school friend William Stebbing, then acting as editor of *The Times*, offering to send the paper a weekly letter 'of a literary kind on the political condition of France, and the attitude and tone of classes, etc.'. Knowing Gambetta, Louis Blanc, Victor Hugo, and leading Republicans in Paris, he would get introductions to their acquaintances in the provinces and so extend his coverage—if paid enough to 'make it worth my while'. And to preclude interference from French authorities ordered to restrict the republicans' activities, he would not sign his letters.[179] This double offence against Comte's rule forbidding remunerative and anonymous journalism suggests how far Harrison had drifted from the influence of Congreve, who upheld both tenets strictly. It may also, perhaps, reflect the financial strain Harrison felt in providing for a growing family. Stebbing agreed to his terms, and Mr Harrison hoped that in provincial France Fred might gain the 'sort of insight, away from the crowd', that made Philip Hamerton's *Fortnightly* articles on French life 'amusing and instructive'.[180]

But unlike Hamerton (a painter who had learned to view Comte sympathetically from Mill's works and Lewes's advice),[181] Harrison sought not merely to sketch life as it was but to arouse indignation against the conservatives in office and admiration for their republican critics. In September, while still living at Les Ruches, he began by describing Thiers's funeral in Paris as an example of their extraordinary restraint. Gambetta, who had been reconciled with the moderate republicans the previous spring, the better to resist their common enemy, led the mourners, who included some three hundred former Republican deputies. The procession moved slowly past other Republicans standing along the way in perfect silence. The effect was 'inexpressibly majestic'.[182]

After escorting Ethel and the children back to London, Harrison began his second extended adventure in foreign journalism. He was eighteen years older than he had been setting out for Italy in 1859, but just as partisan. At his first election meeting, in a Paris working-class district, he even found a lesson for the English in the orderliness of the proceedings, which he maintained exceeded that of British election meetings, except on 'very favourable occasions'.[183] When he left Paris, Albert Rutson accompanied him briefly, but his 'odious French ... absurd Cook's tourist get up, his stammer ... his inquisitiveness', and his tiresome head cold all caused Harrison to shake him off.[184] Harrison's itinerary took him to Orleans, Tours, Poitiers, Bordeaux, Toulouse, Carcassonne, Avignon, and Lyons, a programme so hectic that in one twenty-six-hour period he slept only four hours and dispatched three long letters to *The Times*. Yet he managed sightseeing as well, and for every one of his eleven reports 'From an Englishman in the Provinces' there was one to 'Dearest Wife', with details about outwitting Broglie's agents by mailing his letters at night and departing early the next morning.[185] Ethel sent his published letters to Edmond Schérer at *Le Temps*, who translated them for his paper and for use by local committees, since articles from foreign journals were more likely to pass government censors than French accounts. But once Ethel received word that an order had been issued for Fred's arrest. She dispatched directly to him the letter from the Duc de Broglie he had received in 1870, thinking it might serve as a character reference if there was trouble. In fact, Harrison's closest call came when some republicans to whom he showed it momentarily thought him an *agent provocateur*.[186]

It was gratifying work. Everywhere Harrison found the republicans confident and patient, the priests grasping for temporal power, and the 'Marshalic legend, like the Napoleonic legend ... discredited'. His reports were lively, opinionated, and, as he had promised Stebbing, not competitive with 'ordinary reporting'. Back in Paris by the end of October, he found that they had been appreciated. Gambetta 'roared' his thanks, and Barthélemy St Hilaire expressed his similar sentiments 'more like an Academician'. *The Times*'s regular Paris correspondent, the clever bohemian Henry de Blowitz, who had given him introductions and now called him 'le Livingstone des provinces', paid him the supreme compliment of seeming jealous.[187] Blowitz need not have feared for his laurels: though feeling 'awfully rich' with Stebbing's cheque in his pocket, Harrison declined his proposal to stay on as a special correspondent. What if he should be sent to Armenia? he asked Ethel.[188] Just before departing for London he interviewed a political prisoner in the Conciergerie, still operating as in the days of Marie Antoinette, and depicted its 'judicial terrorism' for English readers.[189] Once home, he condemned MacMahon and his party in the *Fortnightly* as 'sickly specimens of this melancholy reversion of Humanity' and used other terms Mr Harrison regarded as 'coarse and low.'[190]

Since the elections put the republicans firmly in power, Harrison could soon be more sanguine about French affairs. After attending a trade union congress in Lyons in 1878 he assured his *Fortnightly* readers that there was no systematic socialism among French workmen.[191] Watching Gambetta preside over the Chamber of Deputies the next year proved as thrilling as seeing Sarah Bernhardt in *Mithridate* or meeting Turgenev (who was 'just like his books ... great, calm, melancholy, thoughtful, patient').[192] In the *Fortnightly* Harrison explained the reforms proposed by Gambetta's party so that they seemed hardly more daring than the familiar programme of the English radicals.[193] Yet before the year was out, Jules Ferry, Gambetta's education minister and, ironically, one of his several associates influenced by Positivist theory, announced a law to circumscribe the independence of the Catholic Church. Harrison had not sought to capitalize on Gambetta's public praise of Comte, or to link his party with Positivism directly, but now he felt betrayed. Without openly acknowledging his dismay, he merely vowed that when he and Ethel visited France in the coming months he would avoid politics altogether. They would spend their time seeing the chateaux and churches of the Loire, symbols of the aristocracy and of religion that could be appreciated entirely on aesthetic and historical grounds.[194]

EASTERN QUESTIONS

Disturbing as anti-clericalism in French and German politics was to Harrison, religious zeal in British politics came to seem worse. It delayed national education, aggravated the disestablishment controversy, and fuelled an unprecedented outcry against the Turks for actions that led to war in Eastern Europe and had unfortunate consequences in Afghanistan. When reports of the Bulgarian massacres by Turkish mercenaries became known in England in the spring of 1876, Harrison was working closely with the Liberationists on their disendowment scheme. Much of June he spent driving with Ethel in the southern countries to revive her spirits after long hours nursing her mother. And then a correspondence with Ruskin spilled over into *Fors Clavigera*, Ruskin's published series of letters to British workmen, necessitating a reply in the July *Fortnightly*.[195] Early in July Anne Harrison died, and Fred arranged the burial, which was in London's Great Northern Cemetery, founded two decades before by his uncle Charles.[196] Feeling as if he had lost a second mother, Fred took the boys, Ethel, and her grieving father to a secluded house in Fairmile Park, Cobham, for the rest of the summer. While public meetings allying Church and Chapel in outrage over the Government's apparent endorsement of Turkish misrule were being staged all over the country, Harrison was enjoying inspiring views of the South Downs in the midst of pines and deodars, content to think that 'at my gate, all access to mankind ends.'[197]

In the area he encountered two acquaintances who shared his distaste for the religious fervour of the anti-Turk campaign. At Cobham church (to 'keep up the credit' of his landlord) he saw 'Matt' Arnold worshipping 'in correct style'. Afterwards Arnold showed him over Pains Hill Cottage and spoke 'very bitterly of the progress of dissent in his fold'.[198] When the hottest days were over, the Harrisons drove to Flint Cottage on Box Hill to visit George Meredith, to whom Harrison felt free to grumble about Morley's 'too scathing' comment on Disraeli's flippancy in responding to the news of the atrocities.[199]

But formulating his own views of the vexed Eastern Question for Morley in mid-September proved difficult. Harrison could 'sympathise with the noble outburst of feeling' against the Turks, and even find much that was 'warm and satisfying' in Gladstone's sensational pamphlet on the 'Horrors', despite certain 'very hasty and doubtful things' in it. Yet autonomy for the subject peoples of the Porte, which he thought Gladstone wanted, would produce 'universal turmoil'. A statesman could save the situation 'without a crusade and without planting Russia in Constantinople', but neither Gladstone nor Disraeli was the man.[200] Early in the year Harrison had told Morley that Gladstone had brought needed 'fire and elevation' to the Adam Smith celebration at the Cobden Club, and described an amiable chat with him at a Metaphysical Society meeting, noting his 'freedom from small egotism and self-consciousness', and a certain affectation of speech he attributed to Gladstone's many years in Parliament. But in the discussion .that evening Gladstone had appeared no wiser than 'green curates', for he had suggested that the moral teachings of Christianity should be regarded as evidence of its truth. His resignation from leadership of the Liberal party after the 1874 election seemed to Harrison no loss.[201] But Disraeli, who had just become Lord Beaconsfield, was even less acceptable as a political leader; and Harrison thought both he and his ambassador in Constantinople, Austen Henry Layard (Charles Harrison's inspiration) should resign. The 'lasting charm' of Disraeli's novels had never been evident in the man on the occasions Harrison observed him at social gatherings—he seemed aloof and condescending— so Harrison let pass opportunities to make his acquaintance.[202]

In sympathy with neither of the great political rivals of the day, Harrison could only implore Morley not to 'encourage the silly Christian cry of "down with the Beastly Turk!" '[203] He wrote from Sutton Place, where he was working on the index to the *Polity*, in which Comte egregiously predicted that because the Turks lacked 'revolutionary poison' and enjoyed a 'concentration of wealth', their nation would be the second outside the West to become Positivist. The first would be Russia.[204] Yet now the Czar was threatening to invade the Ottoman Empire. Congreve put the case for maintaining the status quo against Russian designs so strongly in the October *Fortnightly* that Harrison, all the more embarrassed because Laffitte in Paris was, like Congreve, an ardent Turkophile, felt compelled to assure Morley that he knew as well as anyone that the Turks were corrupt beyond hope of reform, and that in any case Positivism did not need them for its future.[205] His sense of isolation in this stage of the crisis was heightened by a leg injury he sustained while playing lawn tennis at Sutton Place with his brother Robert's fiancée, Helen Eustace Smith. For days he could not walk, and so was unable to get to London to hear what was being said about the political situation resulting from the atrocity news. Some leaders of the agitation against the Government's inaction—Freeman, Forster, Bryce, and Humphry Sandwith—had authority to speak because of their first-hand knowledge of the Ottoman provinces, but Harrison had no special information, nor even a clear policy to enunciate. He might not have written anything on the crisis if Morley had not goaded him.[206] And even after sending in his article for the December *Fortnightly*, he confessed he lacked 'stomach for the fight' it might provoke.[207]

His title, 'Cross and Crescent,' like 'Order and Progress' the year before, was meant to suggest the necessity of reconciling opposites. Forgetting his criticism of Congreve, he urged that the Porte's political domination of its subject peoples be maintained because, for all its faults, its government 'divides them least'.[208] Thiers had used that formula to promote his conservative republic after the Franco-Prussian war, and had it not evolved in a more liberal direction? Like Congreve and Beesly, Harrison also argued that Ottoman rule was not much worse than that of European governments 'at their worst', and that other tyrannies had failed to rouse the British lion. So harsh was he with the Dissenters for stirring up the lion that Morley, who was just then busy cultivating them in the cause of disestablishment, wielded his editorial pen freely. In the end, Harrison proved somewhat more temperate than his father, who wrote: 'I simply do not think there is a pin to choose between them, but I hate an Imperial, lying Sycophant, more than a wretched Musselman.'[209]

So did Harrison, but since he thought it imperative to prevent 'that good-for-nothing Jew pledging us to fight for the integrity of the Ottoman Empire', he attended a meeting at St. James's Hall on 8 December, held to persuade Lord Salisbury to insist on Ottoman reforms when he represented Britain at the imminent Constantinople Conference. Except for Gladstone, the speakers were not MPs but Church and professional men, many known to Harrison: Canon Liddon, James Bryce, C. S. Roundell, Anthony Trollope, George Trevelyan, Lord Arthur Russell, and George Howard among them; and on the platform were friends and acquaintances like Ruskin, Pattison, Burne-Jones, W. E. H. Lecky, and Stopford Brooke. Harrison, however, went solely as a spectator, and later told Morley (who scorned the exhibition of 'mind' without power) that he had agreed with the 'politicians' but 'groaned at what I heard from the parsons'.[210] When the Czar's troops suffered defeats in the early stages of the war, which the Constantinople Conference had been powerless to prevent, Harrison did not conceal his satisfaction from Morley: 'the sole justification of those who began and those who encouraged this orgy is that it should succeed; to deluge two continents and to embitter two races under a terrible *mistake* is an infernal crime in politics.' Yet he insisted that he was not advocating 'permanence' for the Ottoman system.[211]

Nor did he condemn its partial dismemberment by the Berlin Congress in the summer of 1878. In Chapel Street discussions he even condoned Britain's acquisition of Cyprus, accepting the Government's argument that it would improve Britain's monitoring of both Russia and the Porte. Beesly, taking a more orthodox Positivist position, contended that by 'sharing in the scramble' for territory, Britain showed that moral concerns mattered less than protecting India.[212] Following Comte's maxim 'Live Openly', Beesly reported this lack of unanimity in the first of the *Occasional Papers Issued by the London Positivist Society* with the self-righteousness that maddened his critics: 'Complete agreement on concrete questions of politics and morals arising from time to time is not immediately attainable even by Positivists, although they may expect to attain it sooner and more completely than the disciples of other religions.'[213]

The Positivists were usually able to present a united front publicly because they chose to comment on issues for which Comte had provided guidance. They devoted little time to the worsening economy, since Comte was hardly useful in explaining unemployment and falling wages, even though he had been in refuting the wages-fund theory and defending unions. As for private charity, Comte, aiming at the total regeneration of society, had said little about reclaiming individuals from poverty, old age, and disease. As his critics tirelessly reiterated, 'Live for Others' was so vague and demanding as to be virtually meaningless. By far the majority of Positivist Society discussions and *Occasional Papers* concerned Britain's small wars of empire. They could be confidently denounced as morally, politically, and economically indefensible in Comte's terms.

Yet Harrison did not become one of A. J. P. Taylor's 'troublemakers' incautiously. Often he let the official Positivist pronouncement represent his stand on foreign policy. Sometimes he joined *ad hoc* committees, like the successful one headed by William Morris to appeal to Dean Stanley not to allow a memorial in Westminster Abbey to Napoleon III's nephew, the 'Prince Imperial', slain in the Zulu War with British troops in 1879. E. H. Pember, who had composed the famous epigraph on Lord Westbury, contributed some charitable lines about 'the guiltless bearer of a guilty name' to the flood of eulogistic verse. But Harrison deemed the Abbey too sacred to be associated with a Bonaparte, especially one fallen in imperial warfare.[214] Sometimes, however, he found the orthodox Positivist position too extreme. Lowe's defence of the Ashanti War in 1873 seemed more appropriate than Congreve's opposition, which, Harrison told Morley, was based on a 'hatred of commerce' and the reasoning of a 'fanatic': Congreve would 'send a polite message to the King of Ashantee, present him with a complete copy of the works of Comte, and leave the European traders to be massacred'. After Morley asked facetiously if Harrison had 'a second cousin in the palm oil line', Harrison included a warning in his next 'Public Affairs' essay against any 'holy war to teach Africans sounder morality'.[215] He did not return to imperial themes in that series until its end, but then, in May 1874, he reminded the incoming Conservative government that every extension of empire increased England's 'vulnerability'. Since Russia might realize her dream of aggrandizement through an alliance with Germany, he urged 'strict defensive' ties with the Austrians, Italians, French, and smaller European states.[216]

Given his opposition to imperial adventures, Harrison reacted somewhat belatedly to the Second and Third Afghan Wars of 1878 and 1879, but they produced in him his characteristic modes of agitation. He was of course represented in the London Positivist Society's protest against the Viceroy's demand for a British Resident in Kabul to match the Russian mission.[217] Beesly argued that the military action this would probably entail would add to India's already insupportable economic burdens. These had been discussed in pamphlets by Congreve in 1857 and James Geddes in 1871, and in two recent *Fortnightly* articles by Henry Cotton. But the Positivists were too little known in Anglo-Indian circles in London, and too generally hostile to Britain's role in India, to be invited to join the committee organized by a former Viceroy, Lord Lawrence, to urge Beaconsfield to convene Parliament for a debate on the invasion that was already under way by the fall of 1878. Nor were they able to identify themselves with Lord Lawrence's associate, Lord Northbrook, in opposing the military action. Northbrook appealed in *The Times* to the conception of international law, which to the Positivists, as to Fitzjames Stephen, who leapt to the Government's defence, had no philosophical or legal credibility.[218] It was only after the end of the Second Afghan War in May 1879, and the beginning of yet another cycle of military intervention a few months later, that Harrison and the Positivists joined forces with those outside their circle.

The Third Afghan War was set off in September by the murder of Sir Louis Cavagnari and his party in Kabul shortly after they had established the British mission there in accord with the terms that ended the second war. The Viceroy immediately dispatched a punitive expedition which soon became a full-scale invasion aimed at Kabul. To demand information about the operation Harrison and Beesly helped organize two meetings in early December. At the first Beesly presided and the speaker was Lt.–Col. Robert Osborn, an authority on Indian affairs who had just resigned from the army and was actively opposing the Viceroy's policy, especially his press restrictions.[219] At the second, with Leonard Courtney, a radical MP and Lincoln's Inn colleague of Harrison's, in the chair, the speaker was Sir Arthur Hobhouse, another Lincoln's Inn barrister and Beesly's brother-in-law; as a former legal member of the Viceroy's Council, he could warn about the probable cost of the war.[220] In size and publicity, neither meeting approached those staged in the Bulgarian agitation two years earlier.

Nevertheless, Harrison told Bryce, who had been active in that campaign, the public was 'sick of these wars' and the Liberal whips should realize the potential usefulness to the party of such pressure groups. The Positivists, having declined to speak out against the Government in the Balkan crisis, were 'as resolute as any of the Liberals ... against a policy of aggrandisement, war and empire in Africa, Asia, or anywhere else', and were especially outraged by the new Afghan war because 'it is our own government and men who are committing the crimes'.[221]

Harrison was not using 'crimes' loosely. He regarded the rewards offered by the British to Afghans who turned in countrymen resisting the invasion a breach of the ethics of 'civilized warfare', which were based on the assumption that men have a right to defend their own country. The hanging of those captured was 'lawless butchery'.[222] But pressing such accusations against one's own government and army entailed inevitable unpleasantness. Harrison did not personally know the British commanding officer in Afghanistan, General Sir Frederick Roberts, but he was on friendly terms with the one man who held a higher position: Lord Lytton, the Viceroy, whose 'Forward Policy' had precipitated both Afghan wars.

They had met through Morley—for Lytton had literary as well as diplomatic ambitions. In 1873 the Harrisons had spent an enjoyable weekend with Morley and Lytton, then on leave from his embassy post in Paris. The party was at Knebworth, the Tudor house in Hertfordshire Lytton had just inherited from his father, the novelist Edward Bulwer Lytton. Ethel charmed a letter of Dickens for her autograph collection from his biographer, John Forster, another guest, and Harrison revelled in the Gothic touches of the place, no more troubling to him because they had been lately added than would be the modern 'antiquities' of Sutton Place in later years.[223] And Harrison was prepared to overlook his host's private peccadilloes. Shortly after the visit Harrison told Morley that if Lytton, who had just lost a son, hoped to father a child again, he would have to forgo tobacco, alcohol, and French cuisine.[224] Some of his own characteristics had not escaped Lytton. In a verse epistle to Morley he asked if Morley had been talking 'treason' with

> the *Fortnightly* chiefs of the Radical garrison,
> Implacable Beesly and the high-minded Harrison?
> Whose manners are mild as his pen is audacious,
> And whose spouse is so pretty, so clever, so gracious,
> That were I in his place ('tis a figure of speech, Sir)
> I'd wish things to remain as they are.[225]

Harrison seemed ready to see things remain as they were in India when in 1876 Lytton succeeded Lord Northbrook as Viceroy. Harrison told Morley that their friend should 'leave work to the drudges' and impart to his subjects 'poetry, magnanimity, and gentleness'.[226] But Lytton was bent on overturning Northbrook's policy of 'masterly inactivity' by planting a British envoy in Kabul. When there were objections in England, he sent an apologia to Harrison distinguishing between men of action like himself and those who, doing nothing themselves, 'have the privilege of finding fault with all that has been done'.[227] Yet Lytton was not without defenders. Fitzjames Stephen endorsed his rulings on tariffs, taxes, judges, and the press in *The Times*,[228] and Sir John Strachey, Lytton's finance minister, in England on leave, persuaded Morley to defend Lytton's financial policies when H. M. Hyndman criticized them with arguments drawn from Geddes and Naoroji. Morley even promised never to let Lytton be attacked in the pages of the *Fortnightly*.[229]

But attacked in the *Fortnightly* he was, by the high-minded Harrison, in December 1879—not directly for his 'Forward policy' or for the financial burden it imposed on India, though Harrison deplored both, but for the actions of the Indian soldiers sent by Lytton to avenge the deaths of Cavagnari and his party. Harking back to Jamaica in 1866, Harrison called his essay 'Martial Law in Kabul'. Once again it was military power used against civilians that he condemned. In so doing he invoked ideas of 'natural moral law' and 'civilized warfare' at odds with his Comtean distrust of metaphysics and the teachings of Austinian jurisprudence. Yet by quoting proclamations issued by General Roberts and Lytton, as well as semi-official reports of executions, he gave his essay the stamp of a legally trained mind. And for colour he compared Roberts, a veteran of the First Afghan War and the Great Mutiny, and one of England's most popular military heroes, to Akbar.[230] When Bryce remonstrated that this denigrated the Mogul, Harrison confessed that he had snatched at the name for effect, his text having grown out of an address to the Positivists.[231] They published it as a pamphlet,[232] and the Liberal Association did the same with his *Fortnightly* essay, amended to include evidence of fifty-nine more executions in November and December.[233]

In January Harrison and Hobhouse formed an Afghan Committee to send a Memorial to the Government requesting an inquiry into the executions. Signed by seventy prominent men, including two bishops and the Duke of Westminster, it appeared in *The Times* on 3 February and was discussed in Parliament's opening session two days later. Dilke in the Commons echoed its demand and Earl Granville in the

Lords praised its 'calm and almost judicious language', but Beaconsfield airily dismissed it as without 'the slightest documentary evidence'—[234] which was precisely what the Memorial was asking for.[235] Ten days later, both houses heard read a letter from General Roberts replying to Harrison, whose article had been sent by the India Office to Lytton, who had forwarded it to Roberts in Kabul. Lytton had suggested to Roberts that he should justify his use of martial law by stressing the plight of his army 'in the heart of a hostile country', a formulation Roberts strengthened to read 'living as we are among a nation of fanatics'. His words convinced *The Times* that nothing further need be said, but Harrison had already begun collecting information for 'Martial Law in Kabul, II'.[236]

A major source was the *Pioneer Mail*, a semi-official Indian paper that was one of the few permitted to send a correspondent into Afghanistan. Hobhouse made the back issues available to Harrison, and he combed them so prudently that when the correspondent reprinted his dispatches he deleted most of those quoted by Harrison. They showed clearly that Roberts, both by precept (his proclamations) and practice (the executions), had aimed not only at retribution but also at subjugation of the Afghan people.[237] Hobhouse also relayed information from Lord Northbrook and a former military member of Lytton's Council, Sir Henry Norman, now on the Council at the India Office in London, both of whom had been denouncing Lytton's expansionist policies.[238] Blue books provided other details. So persuasive was Harrison's article that Roberts conceded privately that he understand how Harrison had come to his view of the proclamations.[239] And even Lytton, who had written to Harrison about the 'real pain' the first article caused him, now wrote to say he did not find Harrison's motives unworthy, though he thought Hobhouse's were.[240]

The source of Lytton's animus against Hobhouse is clear. Both Harrison and Morley had informed him that Hobhouse, with Morley, was to stand for the Liberals at Westminster in the General Election early in 1880.[241] Harrison's first Martial Law essay appeared the day after Gladstone's first Midlothian speech. In that historic campaign, before unprecedented crowds, Gladstone again and again decried, as Harrison and his friends had been decrying, the Government's witholding of information about the Afghan war and its immorality. His exhortation, 'remember the rights of the savage ... in the sanctity of the hill villages', had a counterpart in Harrison's bitter image of doomed Afghan soldiers to whom 'life perhaps was dear', marching 'with such quiet courage to a gallows'.[242] These appeals to conscience played their part in returning the Liberals to office in March 1880.

Lytton, who resigned when the election results were known, wrote to Harrison with something of his old cordiality before leaving India, having been assured by Harrison that he had attacked the 'system' and not Lytton nor Roberts nor the army, and that he had taken no part himself in the 'great whirlpool of the elections'.[243]

Harrison did not mention to Lytton his own disappointments in the election results. Hobhouse and Morley were both defeated, and the Liberals who were returned seemed on the whole unlikely to encourage the 'national awakening' to the dangers of empire for which he had been calling. For example, the Duke of Argyll, who was sure to be prominent in the new Cabinet, had only belatedly supported the Harrison–Hobhouse Memorial, and then had declined to use new information on the Afghan situation sent him by Harrison for a speech later in February to the House of Lords. Argyll instead chose to rehearse the past, when he had been Secretary for India under Gladstone, and thus, to the dismay of Lord Ripon (who would replace Lytton as the new Viceroy) he allowed the Conservatives to 'slip over the failure' of their policy.[244] Moreover, in 1877 Argyll had written pejoratively of Positivism in 'The Influence upon Morality of a Decline in Religious Belief', a 'Modern Symposium' in the *Nineteenth Century* to which Harrison and Fitzjames Stephen also contributed; and in a book on the Afghan crisis he had declared that if the 'clever Englishmen' espousing Comte's ideas continued to deny the British credit for having improved India by 'pure ascendancy of superior mind', they would be as useful in debates on public issues as 'dogs baying at the moon'.[245]

Not all his critics were as openly hostile as Argyll, but Harrison must have realized how offensive his articles were bound to be to friends and acquaintances who admired Lytton—for example, Sir Richard Strachey and his wife, George Eliot and Lewes, Fitzjames Stephen, Alfred Lyall, and Tennyson. There was some comfort in the praise of old adversaries like Freeman and Greg, and in the urging of Norman and others that he write still more on Afghanistan.[246] But the kind of drive that had sustained Mill's pursuit of indictments in the Eyre case was missing in Harrison in 1880. He had already told Charles Eliot Norton that he was 'wholly and finally given over to the religion of Positivism in the fullest sense'; and now to Lytton he affirmed his intention of promoting 'the Positivist belief on somewhat wider lines than it has been stated in England'.[247]

5

Shaping a Positivist Religion
1875–1901

POSITIVIST POLEMICS

Churches and creeds are all lost in the mists:
Truth must be sought with the Positivists.

Wise are their teachers beyond all comparison,
Comte, Huxley, Tyndall, Mill, Morley, and Harrison:
Who will adventure to enter the lists
With such a squadron of Positivists?[1]

Mortimer Collins's Aristophanic poem in 1870 lumped together birds of quite different feathers, and the years that followed showed that even like-feathered members of Comte's English flock did not always agree. Harrison had once declared that 'wherever two or three are gathered together, there is a trade society',[2] but he was less quick to find the features of the early Church in the Positivist movement. While even George Eliot, with all her reservations about Comte, could depict Congreve's proselytizing efforts in terms that recall those of the Apostles, Harrison in 1872 felt 'in no sense a member of any religious organization in this country or elsewhere'. 'Elsewhere', of course, referred to Paris, where he deemed the Positivists 'deficient in energy, good sense, and creative faculty'.[3] He therefore declined to contribute to their funds, as Congreve expected his associates to do, or to support their short-lived political journal, *La Politique Positive*, founded in 1872 by Eugène Sémérie, a physician with a taste for radicalism acquired during the Commune. Morley no doubt added to Harrison's apprehensions by observing that the Paris Positivists, whom he noted numbered seven, like the 'candlesticks in the Book of Revelations', had as their chief a man who spouted 'atrocious nonsense' about the Germans—this was Pierre Laffitte—and that the only 'sane talker' among them was a carpenter—Fabien Magnin. Morley, who had been introduced to the Positivist community by Cotter Morison, had kinder words for Dr Robinet, whose vast knowledge about historical Paris was a resource for him when writing his books on French thinkers.[4]

Laffitte, aged forty-seven when Chapel Street opened, had gained his role in the movement by default. No one else pressed for it; and the Master, contrary to his own teaching, had not named a successor. Like Comte a lapsed Catholic and mathematician, Laffitte had studied medicine to qualify for the Positivist priesthood, but had no sacerdotal ambitions. He preferred to promote Comte's social and philosophical doctrines by lecturing and publishing. To this end he even took Comte's widow into court to obtain permission to edit Comte's literary remains, which she rightly, but unsuccessfully, argued would damage his reputation by revealing the aberrations of his last years. The case was reported in the London *Times* just when Chapel Street opened, which no doubt added to Harrison's distrust of 10 Rue Monsieur-le-Prince, the meeting place of the Positivist Society.[5] In 1873 Laffitte showed a Comtean tendency to avert his gaze from embarrassing facts. A twenty-six-year-old French pianist, Gustav Pradeau, affiliated with Chapel Street, was discovered to be living with another man's wife; and when at the insistence of his younger colleagues Congreve appealed to Paris for a ruling, Laffitte failed to provide it. Harrison, Beesly, and others who sought Pradeau's ouster felt obliged to give way to Congreve, who argued that since the woman had borne Pradeau's child they should accept the union. The matter was dropped, but not forgotten.[6]

Despite the inadequacies of both Laffitte and Congreve, the work of Chapel Street proved irresistible to Harrison. In it, as in most things, Ethel gave him her support, entertaining and at times mothering members of the tiny community. When Mary Christie, daughter of the recently deceased barrister, Liberal MP, and diplomat William Dougal Christie, confided to her a tale of unwanted attentions pressed by another Positivist, John Overton, a middle-aged coppersmith, Ethel sought to divert his attention to one of her philanthropic projects. Overton had already published a novel of working-class life, and though he protested that he wished to die a working man like Felix Holt, he in fact hated his humble circumstances. That he considered his class responsible for Mary Christie's rejection is clear from his bitter suggestion to Ethel that he compose a 'Tale of the Early Positivists' and call it 'Final Perseverance: or, the Lady and the Pig'. Ignoring the implications, Ethel advised that 'in work lies the best cure for personal sorrow'.[7] Overton would say as much himself in a second novel, *Saul of Mitre Court* (1879), about a social prophet who discourses to working men quoting Comte, Carlyle, George Eliot, and the Chapel Street leaders.

Counselling self-renunciation put the Positivists in good company, especially when they cited one of Comte's sacred texts, the *Imitation of*

1. Frederic Harrison, September 1862, studio of Nadar, Paris

2. (*Above*) Eden Park, Beckenham, Kent.
Summer residence of Frederick Harrison
and family, 1859–1874

3. (*Right*) Frederick Harrison,
1799–1881

4. (*Below*) Sutton Place, Guildford,
Surrey. Leased by Frederick and later
Sidney Harrison, 1874–1902

5. 10 Lancaster Gate, Harrison's
London residence in the 1860s

6. 38 Westbourne Terrace,
Harrison's London residence,
1878–1902

7. Blackdown Cottage, Sussex, Harrison's country residence, 1888–1897

8. Richard Congreve, 1884

9. John Morley, 1883

10. Edward Spencer Beesly,
about 1880

11. John Henry Bridges,
about 1890

Christ, by Thomas à Kempis. The great value found in this devotional work of the fifteenth century by Victorians as diverse as George Eliot, Acton, Gladstone, Arnold, Morley, Blunt, and General Gordon was once attributed by a Positivist to its ability to make the reader forget all about the author's 'God, his Christ, his Eucharist, his Bible, and Hell, and Cross, and Heaven', so powerful was the consolation and inspiration of its message: selflessness and spiritual striving.[8] Harrison, who had selected 'propter te' (because of you) for the Mumbos' rings in 1860, had the phrase inscribed on a ring for Ethel. Her reading from the book in English, Latin, and French versions would be one of their children's earliest memories; and she would write the sketch of the author's life for the Positivists' *New Calendar of Great Men* in 1892. Meanwhile, the scholarship of other Positivists increased the work's circulation. Morley had overlooked the *Imitation* when he predicted that Comte's religion would fail because it lacked a compelling inspirational text.[9]

As their devotion to the *Imitation* suggests, the Positivists in practice occupied a middle ground between secularism and Christianity. At Chapel Street it was the educational side of Comte's work that Harrison first sought to promote: English classes for Communard refugees, instruction in the 3 Rs for people too old to benefit from the 1870 Education Act, political discussions, and courses in Comte's teachings. Of these activities he left little record; viewed from the perspective of his later Positivist leadership, they must have seemed merely an apprenticeship.

During his years at Chapel Street Harrison was serving another kind of apprenticeship at the Metaphysical Society. Having climbed the great staircase of the new Grosvenor Hotel and found a place in the private room set aside for the dinner meetings, he was in a social and intellectual atmosphere quite unlike that at Chapel Street. Instead of old friends and untutored, perhaps half-persuaded seekers after wisdom or inspiration or status or comradeship, here were some of the keenest and most famous men of the day, men accustomed to deference, self-confident, aggressive, impatient when crossed. But as his bravado with Tennyson on their first encounter suggests, Harrison was determined from the outset not to be cowed. Had he not survived two Royal Commissions, emerging from one unscathed, from the other triumphant? Invited to join early in the Society's existence, just after he had published 'The Positivist Problem', he came under no false colours. He remained active for over a decade, almost to its dissolution early in 1880, presenting altogether four papers, a number exceeded only by five of the thirty-eight members who gave papers. He also very probably made spirited comments on others' papers (discussions were not recorded), and he contributed to the three published symposia arranged by the Society's co-founder and secretary, James Knowles, after he had left the editorship of the *Contemporary Review* to found the *Nineteenth Century* in 1877. Knowles's biographer sees his editorial career emerging from this involvement in the Metaphysical Society, and the same could be said of Harrison's career as a Positivist: its baptism of fire made his subsequent proselytizing more sure.[10]

After attending only four meetings, Harrison, in July 1870, a month before his marriage, gave his first paper, on 'The Relativity of Human Knowledge', a full-scale attack on the intuitionists—though prominent among them in the Society was Sir Arthur Russell, who had sponsored his admission. Dealing with 'metaphysical quirks' plunged Harrison into waters as deep as those he had fathomed to undermine orthodox political economy and scientific history, and he felt just as apprehensive in this new intellectual venture. After appealing to Morley for reassurance, he felt more confident but no more tolerant than he had ever been of one of the Society's typical concerns: 'Not only I don't know "what will become of my immortal soul" but I have not the smallest curiosity to know—any more than to pry into the question what minute of what hour I was begotten.'[11] The next year, following Russell's account of the Absolute, Harrison contributed to a 'lively debate' by espousing the 'common sense of sensible men' to whom such a conception as the Absolute meant nothing.[12] In a later paper of his own he insisted that the philosopher's only legitimate task was to separate valid from invalid inquiries—with metaphysical questions, of course, in the latter category.[13] Having thus drastically reduced philosophy's sphere, he tried to retain religion's traditional role in maintaining morality: he could agree with the outspoken atheist and mathematician William Kingdon Clifford in repudiating traditional theology as intellectually untenable, but also with the eloquent Bishop of Peterborough, William Connor Magee, who denied that unaided reason could mediate between man and society. The religion Clifford would jettison and Magee preserve was not, of course, what Harrison advocated to validate morals; that could only be a 'human' and 'scientific' religion which 'in its own way' had 'its Revelation, its Future, its External Power, and its common Brotherhood'.[14]

To its consistent adversaries the religion of Positivism seemed too theological and suggested clerical despotism, but such arguments had long been aired. Appearing in Mill's posthumously published *Autobiography* in 1873, they had caused Comte's one-time friend to slip greatly in Harrison's esteem. In religion, as in jurisprudence and social theory, order was coming to seem more crucial than progress, establishing a new religion now more important than undermining the old. Harrison made this evident in 1875, the year *Order and Progress* and the English translation of the first two volumes of Comte's *Polity* appeared, by publishing two long essays on 'The Religious and Conservative Aspects of Positivism' in Knowles's *Contemporary Review*. When Morley, then hotly competing for just such controversial articles, complained of being disloyally abandoned, Harrison claimed that he had merely obliged Knowles with something Morley would not have wanted for the *Fortnightly*.[15] Though disingenuous, the comment shows Harrison's understanding that he was moving beyond the form of Positivism acceptable to Morley, to a system pledged to the 'useful, the demonstrable, and the human'—a partial translation of Comte's account of his own usage. But he also defended the Positivist priesthood, doctrine, worship, and discipline.[16] Only 'the pedantry of sect' could 'dare to monopolise to a special creed those precious heirlooms of our common race', the sacerdotal forms of Christianity. To this Matthew Arnold replied that, for the English at least, and the middle-aged an old among them especially, only in the Bible and Christianity could the power of religion reside: 'Habits and associations are not formed in a day.'[17] The Prophet of Culture was employing sociological wisdom overlooked by the founder of sociology and his English disciple.

It was not only the Christians' jealous claim to established usages that Harrison was attacking: the 'elastic theosophy' of modern theologians was once again his target. It was not surprising, then, that a reply came from the one contributor to *Essays and Reviews* who also happened to belong to the Metaphysical Society—Mark Pattison. By then at last Rector of Lincoln College, he had married the gifted and vivacious Emily Francis Strong, twenty-seven years his junior and now a restless and wilful young Oxford matron. Though she would later recall that Comte's *Catechism* gave her the strength to endure the 'shock to her beliefs' presented by 'an intellectual society at Oxford not animated by faith in a revealed religion', Positivism failed to reconcile her to either her morose husband or the tediousness of university life. Searching for livelier company, she occasionally included the Harrisons among her guests, and they very likely had opinions about whether the misalliance of Dorothea and Casaubon in *Middlemarch* owed anything to the Pattisons—still a debated topic. Unfortunately, Harrison disliked the novel and said nothing that has survived about its origins; but since he thought Pattison a 'cross grained old Bookworm', he may well have seen a resemblance between him and the scholar looking for the key to all mythologies—an entirely anti-Positivist enterprise.[18]

If Pattison was even more misanthropic than he had been at the time of *Essays and Reviews*, Harrison was more self-confidently aggressive. Hearing that Pattison was preparing a reply to the *Contemporary Review* articles, he urged him to abandon the 'usual jesting criticism of those ignorant of what they are speaking about, without any belief themselves'. Pattison, side-stepping the implication that he had not studied Comte nor worked out a religious position of his own, replied that he could already imagine Harrison 'devouring the mangled limbs of your victim', and, alluding to Harrison's growing reputation for controversial journalism, said he knew Harrison preferred being criticized to being ignored.[19] Both thereupon set about settling old scores. Pattison depicted Comte as destitute of poetry, humour, or literary grace, and suffering from delusions that had made him 'first impractical, then arbitrary, finally monstrous'. His notion of Humanity as a supreme being seemed most unlikely for anyone as 'solid, practical, sane, cultivated ... [and] conversant with the active life of the present' as Mr Harrison, who must have been driven into Comte's camp by a desperate need for an alternative to liberal Christianity. To this new creed, however, he had brought a 'power of statement ... hardly surpassed by any living writer and [which] should be enlisted in a worthier cause'.[20]

Acknowledging these 'handsome words', Harrison informed Pattison he was writing another essay to 'clear up' issues dividing them.[21] Published by Knowles, it took the form of a dialogue, with Pattison cast in the role Arnold had played in the essay that provided the model. Magdalen College provided the scene. A visiting London barrister, Phaedrus, known to have studied Comte, confesses to Sophisticus, an Oxford don, that after long hesitation he has come to see that 'Humanity is the most real' and 'most ennobling object of reverence', though he leaves 'hot-gospelling' to 'supernatural believers'. Learning that the Rector of Lincoln has been 'moved from his philosophic perch' to criticize Comte, he presses Sophisticus for an account of the Rector's views, which he takes to be widely held at the University—much as in 'Neo-Christianity' Harrison had pretended to believe the Essayists' views were widely held in the Church. Phaedrus has great play with a passage by Pattison about how philosophy 'defecates the idea [of God] to a pure transparency', setting it against Arnold's assertion that religion must be 'built upon ideas about which there is no puzzle'. Phaedrus, eloquent on Comte's religion, has the last word.[22] Harrison assured Pattison that nothing personal was meant by all this, and Pattison seems to have been persuaded.[23] Eight years later, in his last, lingering illness, he replied to the Harrisons' message of sympathy by expressing surprise at their having 'more than once stretched out a hand to shield me from adversaries'.[24] He may have alluded to circum-stances now lost from view, or in his need for affection, always great and intensified in his last years, estranged from his wife, he may simply have conjured up an unrealistically mellow image of Harrison.

Though Pattison chose not to continue the controversy, an even more contentious member of the Metaphysical Society could not 'get that paper of Mr Frederic Harrison's out of my head'. John Ruskin had been Slade Professor of Art at Oxford since 1870 and was not at all happy with the changes that had occurred at the University since his student days. In *Fors Clavigera* he therefore demanded in his abrupt way to know their views of progress, which he identified with evolution and the Positivists. Was he more comely than Theseus in the Elgin marbles? Had Devonshire pippins and Cheshire cheese improved over the years? Was the 'resonant bronze' of the feminist Miss Frances Power Cobbe preferable to the 'silent gold of ancient womanhood'? The 'advocates of Evolution' were 'mostly occupied with frogs and lice' and blinded to human reality. Harrison, for one, should leave Oxford traceries (alluded to for atmosphere in Harrison's dialogue) to jackdaws, since he 'couldn't know a good one from a bad one', and stick to law: as a member of 'beautifully bewigged humanity' could he explain the legal status of usury? The 'great Human Son of Holothurian Harries' was commanded to reply.[25]

He did, in both *Fors* and the *Fortnightly*, after groaning to Morley that Ruskin's 'mad kind of squeal' put his 'ear out'. He felt 'remorse in dealing with the fantastic creature as a reasonable being, and in being so contemptuous of so winning and noble a madman'. It was like 'a roadside boy hooting after Lear or Shylock ... no doubt Lear is unreasonable, and Shylock misanthropical—But Lear and Shylock are men with a tragedy—and a roadside boy is a roadside boy still.'[26] But putting aside his sense of proportion, he gave due consideration to all Ruskin's charges: he defended Comte's view of progress, noted that great art had come in decadent periods, traced his own passion for the Gothic to his youth, and observed that lawyers did not make law—they merely practised it.[27] Yet there was still enough grace in his arguments for Grant Duff to declare him 'one of *the* two or three writers of the day', and Joseph Chamberlain to assert that the essay was a better palliative for gout than colchicum.[28]

Like Pattison, Ruskin accompanied his polemics with private assurances of good will. And he admitted to needing religious consola-tion more than ever because of the recent death of Rose La Touche, the young woman he had so impossibly hoped to marry ever since her early girlhood. Hearing of the recent death of Ethel's mother, he referred to that of his parents to give point to his confession: '*Religion* with *me* means belief in the Resurrection.'[29] To this Harrison predictably replied that Positivists met death 'with utter truth and real sympathy, making the life after death a satisfying and ever present thing'.[30] Unpersuaded, Ruskin wrote scornfully of the 'Religion of Manity' and the 'entire school of modern rationalists', especially Mill, 'a mere loathsome cretin'.[31] The violence of his language was a symptom of the agitation that soon gave way to unmistakable insanity, interrupting the correspondence. In 1880, his 'brain-power' temporarily restored, Ruskin urged Harrison to consider, merely as a 'logical exercise', how the world would look 'on the hypothesis of there being a *real* God!'[32] The proposal confirmed what Harrison had hinted at in his essay by calling it 'Past and Present', and what he had said outright to Morley: 'The real thing behind Ruskin is Carlyle, and behind Carlyle is God— who still has a following and may yet give trouble.'[33]

Like the controversies with Pattison and Ruskin, Knowles's 'Modern Symposia' in 1877 and 1878 carried to the public some of the arguments Harrison had been advancing in the Metaphysical Society. He later claimed to have suggested the symposium format,[34] which indeed reflected his discontent with the completely free discussions of the Metaphysical Society. Even this new arrangement, whereby a paper was commented on in turn by contributors, each of whom saw only it and the commentaries preceding his own, with the author summing up at the end, sometimes frustrated him, so confident was he that if only he had enough time he could compel assent to his position. No one, it seemed, was willing to study Comte's system on his own.

The first symposium was on 'The Influence upon Morality of a Decline in Religious Belief', a paper by James Fitzjames Stephen. For the most part he reiterated the strictures on irreligion in *Liberty, Equality, Fraternity*. Harrison could agree with Stephen and the commentators before himself, Lord Selborne (Sir Roundell Palmer), and Dr James Martineau, who held religion necessary to morality; but he also advocated a position unacceptable to them or the remaining participants: the Dean of St. Paul's, the Duke of Argyll, W. G. Ward, R. H. Hutton, W. K. Clifford, and T. H. Huxley.[35]

The second symposium, based on a Metaphysical Society paper by Harrison on 'The Soul Before and After Death', gave him the chance to identify with 'positivist' thinkers who, he pointed out, were not confined to Comte's followers but had in common a disbelief in any soul existing independent of a body, or of an afterlife consisting of 'ceaseless psalmody'. Then, by redefining 'soul' to mean 'a consensus of human faculties', moral as well as physical, he was able to promote

Comte's idea of 'posthumous energies' constituting a kind of immortality. He identified himself with the Positivists (with a capital P) and quoted George Eliot's poem, 'O May I Join the Choir Invisible', published in 1874 and widely assumed to express Comte's doctrine of Subjective Immortality. If by invoking so eminent a name as hers Harrison hoped to forestall criticism, he had underestimated the antipathy to Comte of his fellow participants: Huxley, Hutton, Roden Noel, Lord Selborne, Canon Barry, W. R. Greg, Baldwin Brown, and W. G. Ward. Replying to them, he was especially hard on Huxley, at one end of the philosophical spectrum, who claimed too much for the physical sciences, and with the Christians at the other end, who held out an image of 'celestial glory' that was self-indulgent and unworthy of aspiring humanity.[36] Harrison's father, diffidently calling himself an 'ignoramus' in such matters, observed that humanity with its 'errors and corruption' could have no place in a future state—a belief he said was no more 'conjectural' than Fred's, but would do little harm if wrong, whereas Fred's, if unfounded, could have 'disastrous consequences'. And he had to smile at Fred desperately pointing to 'talented individuals' he thought were coming round to his view (George Eliot for one?) while ignoring the 'equally clever *hosts*' who remained hostile. He hoped this would be Fred's last controversy.[37]

Of course it was not, but his father's uneasiness may explain why Harrison did not take up the challenge to Positivism thrown down by one of the cleverest of the hostile hosts: William Hurrell Mallock. Much like Harrison in 1860, Mallock burst upon the literary scene in 1876 as a young Oxford graduate raising the alarm about the attenuation of religion among men associated with his university. *The New Republic: Culture, Faith and Philosophy in an English Country House*, his counterpart to 'Neo-Christianity', has among its satirical portraits a 'Mr Saunders', who represents that part of Harrison's philosophy compatible with Huxley, Tyndall, and Clifford—their criticism of Christianity and defence of science. But Mallock's equally unflattering portraits of Jowett, Arnold, and Pater probably amused Harrison, for he shared Mallock's disdain of their religious waffling. Mallock's second book, *The New Paul and Virginia: or Positivism on an Island*, however, undoubtedly hurt. An even more capricious Voltairean satire, it appeared first in the *Contemporary Review* in 1878 as a kind of supplement to Knowles's symposia, raising some of the same issues they raised, and in its book form contained an appendix with passages taken from works by Huxley, Tyndall, Clifford, Harriet Martineau, and Harrison (his from the Symposium on the Soul) to direct the reader to the sources of the satirized ideas. Whether its protagonist, Professor

Paul Darnley, who preaches a religion of progress, subjective immortality, and 'cosmic emotion', is meant to be Harrison is not certain. (Ironically, much of the action occurs in an idyllic cottage like the one Ethel had spied on Mallock property in Dorset soon after marrying *her* professor, but she cannot be identified with Paul's aged and ugly wife in the story.)[38] Even if Harrison did not see himself caricatured, Mallock's perverse suggestion that Positivism encouraged licentiousness and cruelty and a worship as silly as baying at the moon would explain why the book 'nearly maddened' him.[39] Mallock in his later works tiresomely argued that all 'positivism'—Comte's and mere 'cowardly agnosticism'—drained life of meaning, a view Harrison called 'unmanly' but did not contest at length until 1895. By then the arguments of both seemed shopworn and their controversy was little noticed.[40]

By revealing the Metaphysical Society's obvious inability to find 'some common ground on which theists, agnostics, and scientists could meet', Harrison's Symposium on the Soul may well have hastened the Society's decline. Its end was foreshadowed by the third symposium, which abandoned metaphysics altogether, its topic being: 'Is the Popular Judgment in Politics More Just than that of the Higher Orders?' Harrison's defence of the Paris Commune conveniently provided Sir Arthur Russell, who led off, with an illustration of what he called injudicious praise of working-class politics; but Russell's distinction between working-class participation in the electoral process on the one hand and in government on the other, was one Harrison, when his turn came, could endorse, as had Hutton and Grant Duff before him. By insisting on the political wisdom of trade union leaders as well, Harrison led Greg and Lowe, who also followed him, to reassert their old fears of democracy. Gladstone, who came last, foreshadowed his Midlothian election campaign by stressing the common man's moral superiority, a thesis that was to enable Harrison to overlook their differences in religion and become one of Gladstone's most ardent supporters—but not until the next decade.[41]

Harrison's last Metaphysical Society paper was a largely favourable review of Lewes's posthumously published *Study of Psychology*, edited by George Eliot as the fourth volume in his series, *Problems of Life and Mind*. Harrison had reviewed the first volume in 1874, welcoming its attempt to do what he was then trying to get the Metaphysical Society to do—distinguish between 'intelligible' and 'unintelligible' philosophic inquiries. He naturally approved Lewes's stress on empirical methodology, and though he could not entirely support Lewes's cautious move beyond it, he recognized Comte's importance to Lewes's work.[42] The Harrisons were among the dozen or so 'out and out rationalists' at Highgate Cemetery for Lewes's burial on 4 December 1878, Harrison having learned of the death by a chance call at the Priory the day after it occurred. In subsequent clubroom talk and two obituaries he set out Lewes's claims on posterity.[43] The *Study of Psychology*, a copy of which George Eliot sent to Harrison, argued that mind was a product not only of the biological but of the social organism. This 'first approximation' of a new psychology thus showed a way of getting beyond the materialism of Huxley, Tyndall, and others to whom Mallock had misleadingly been linking Harrison under the rubric of 'positivist'. Comte, it is true, denied that introspection could serve psychology, or even that psychology deserved a place in his hierarchy of sciences, but by admitting ethics, and leaving it un-constituted, he had opened the door for conceptions others called 'psychological'. Even more important, Comte's notion of Humanity lay behind Lewes's thesis of a 'general mind' influencing the individual, an idea advanced also by George Eliot. Harrison therefore had no trouble making his Metaphysical Society paper serve Positivist purposes and also gratify her.[44]

At the close of 1879 the Metaphysical Society began winding down. Harrison, like others, later recalled that when everyone had stated his position there was no need for further discussion. Huxley's comment, that the Society 'died of too much love', is often quoted, and Knowles's account of its 'wonderfully genial and kindly tone' parallels comments by Magee, Russell, Grant Duff, Martineau, and Henry Sidgwick.[45] Far less complimentary, Harrison remembered Manning's 'elusive in-genuity', Selborne's 'impenetrable orthodoxy', Magee's 'boisterous dogmatism', Huxley's 'dialectic skill', Fitzjames Stephen's 'sledge-hammer' logic, and the 'superior aloofness' of Tennyson that to Harrison did not conceal his inability to follow the arguments.[46] Bagehot once offended by winning general assent to his assertion that members should look upon any professed atheist as immoral until he disproved the suspicion, a comment Harrison thought Bagehot directed at him: 'Can you conceive literary drivel getting to such a pitch of indifference to all toleration?' he asked Morley.[47] But he could not conceal his own intolerance. To Morley he boasted of telling Pattison, Greg, and Manning—'worn, grey, ghosts of men'—that they were 'on the road to a madhouse',[48] and called Gladstone's comments 'silly sermons'. The agnostics, he later complained, had nothing useful to say either.[49] No wonder that as the only Comtean Positivist present he felt isolated and often angry.

Weary of defending his views to an unsympathetic Metaphysical Society, Harrison did not seek to participate in two organizations that might be said to have carried on some of its functions. He helped Shadworth Hodgson plan the Aristotelian Society, and may have initially joined, but its professional approach to philosophy could not long interest him.[50] Nor could the activities of the Society for Psychical Research in 1882. Publication of two articles on spiritualism by one member, Alfred Russel Wallace, in the *Fortnightly* had heightened his suspicions of Morley's Positivist sympathies, and though he was on friendly terms with two other members, F. W. H. Myers and Henry Sidgwick, and could admire the anti-vivisectionism of a third, R. H. Hutton, their investigations for the Society dismayed him. He would, he once said, 'sooner trust the butcher boy and newspaper boy out of the streets to investigate the tricks of some card sharpers'.[51] And of attempts to link their séances to religion he asked: 'Why must our souls be immortal because a banjo can play without hands in a dark room?'[52] In the next decade his impatience with theological hair-splitting would lead him to urge Cardinal Manning to found a group to consider the social effects of religion, limiting its members to person with a definite creed. But the list of members Harrison proposed was so dominated by 'popery' and Positivism that Manning became doubtful, and before anything could be arranged the London dock strike diverted the attention of both.[53]

Though Harrison might try to convince his father that many enlightened thinkers were veering towards Positivism in the 1870s, both were aware of works besides Mallock's criticizing or in some way rivalling Comte. The most comprehensive of these critics were Leslie Stephen and Edward Caird, nicely representing Cambridge and Oxford respectively. Stephen's *Essays on Freethinking and Plain Speaking* (1874) and review of *Order and Progress* (1875) carried further the arguments he had contributed to the Positivists' debate with Huxley in 1869.[54] Caird's essays, reprinted as *The Social Philosophy and Religion of Comte* (1883), earned Harrison's private tribute as the best 'critical' estimate of Comte, but he had to be content with its mixed judgement, the result, said Caird, of his desire to find out 'the best that Comte meant, and not the worst that his words could be taken to mean'.[55] Far less compatible at Oxford were idealists associated with Caird—F. H. Bradley, T. H. Green, William Wallace, and Bernard Bosanquet— and in James Martineau's lectures there on 'Ideal Substitutes for God' and Arnold's 'Being not ourselves that makes for righteousness' there was little to gratify a Positivist. Walter Pater's image in *Studies in the History of the Renaissance* of the Mona Lisa embodying 'all the thoughts of the world ... the idea of Humanity', and Winwood Reade's conception in *The Martyrdom of Man* of a 'glorious One' that had evolved through time and deserved man's reverence were closer to Comte's central notion; but Pater also warned against 'facile orthodoxy', naming Comte's specifically, and Reade gave more prominence to mankind's defeats than to its achievements. In any case, Harrison was less interested by now in separating the wheat from the chaff in these and other works than in planting, at last in full season, for himself.

SCHISM WITHOUT HERESY

The Positivists believed that Comte's system integrated man's 'intellectual' and 'affective' natures in the service of 'wisely ordered activity'. But at Chapel Street the reverse happened: a schism. 'Que voulez-vous dans le pays de Henri VIII?', asked Laffitte in Paris,[56] forgetting that Littré had broken with Comte's orthodox disciples and that Comte himself had created his system in revolt against his mentor Saint-Simon, a circumstance Comte generally overlooked. More irony: understanding the English schism requires insights from a subject Comte always treated disdainfully—psychology. It is unlikely that any of the persons involved understood fully his own or anyone else's motives, and they cannot be reconstructed with total confidence today; but the inconsistency and irrationality of some positions taken, and the powerful emotions disclosed in the letters, memoranda, and publications amply documenting the events, all suggest that here was no reasoned parting of friends.

The first emotion in the chain of events that led to the schism was the outrage Harrison, Beesly, and Bridges expressed openly to Congreve upon learning in 1876 that Gustav Pradeau had audaciously requested the sacrament of Presentation for the child of his adulterous union—and, even worse, that Congreve had consented to administer it.[57] Since the first Pradeau incident, in 1872, Harrison's relations with Congreve had been outwardly cordial (though he told Morley he could no longer be sure of receiving Congreve's communications to the Positivists because 'our High Priest regards me with an air of ostentatious antagonism').[58] In the spring of 1873 Harrison took over Congreve's Sunday morning lecturing to free him for a trip to France to meet Mrs Congreve, who was returning from a visit to the Geddes in India; and early the next year he had Bernard and Austin 'presented' at Chapel Street.[59] And that was no insignificant act in Harrison's eyes. In 1876 he told Congreve his administration of the sacrament to Pradeau's child would be 'very grave for our future as a body'.[60] In subsequent letters, showing open acrimony, he noted that Congreve had begun addressing him as 'Mr Harrison', and asked what a return to the formal mode implied;

and he disagreed with Congreve's decision on what exactly volume three of Comte's *Polity*, in Congreve's own translation, should contain.[61] Yet early in 1877 he allowed his third son, Godfrey Denis, to receive the sacrament of Presentation from Congreve, and spoke appreciatively to George Eliot of Congreve's reading for her poem on the Choir Invisible in his New Year's Day Address.[62]

It is sometimes said that Congreve's emphasis on religion at Chapel Street caused the schism in the English Positivist movement. Harrison's letter to George Eliot suggests otherwise, for in it he went on to report that John Llewelyn Davies had found in her poem the 'germ of a new hymnology' and to ask if she could write something specifically for the Positivists, 'either in prose or verse, for public or private use, by way of collect, hymn, or litany ... to give form to our ideas of sympathy and confidence in humanity'. Since the last two volumes of the *Polity* had recently appeared, he also pleaded for her 'full estimate' of it, explaining that the world was 'running off upon the details of Comte's ritual, and the dominant principle is being forgotten by it and overlaid by Positivists'. This suggests that he saw in her literary gifts and prestige a way of neutralizing the stigma bound to cling to any Positivist ritual. Unfortunately, she proved no more willing to provide Positivist prayers or exegesis than the Positivist utopia he had sketched for her a decade earlier. It is just possible that had she been ready to identify more openly with the Religion of Humanity, as Harrison boldly proposed, he and his colleagues might have reconciled themselves to Congreve's leadership, and that Congreve, with such a powerful name behind him, might have been more conciliatory.

Harrison's appeal to George Eliot did not exhaust his efforts to bring ritual to Chapel Street. He would later recall urging a 'tentative form of Congregational worship' on Congreve that he was 'not very keen to begin'. Congreve, on the contrary, recorded his belief that Harrison and his associates were never very serious about the Religion of Humanity.[63] It is safe to assume that Harrison, for one, would not have been long satisfied with any ritual initiated by the man whose lectures he had judged 'dry, dogmatic, and dull'. And Congreve's earliest efforts at public worship were uninspired. In 1875 he prefaced his Annual Address by invoking the name of Comte, 'wisest and noblest of teachers', his disciples, and 'our common mother, the Earth'. He introduced Sunday prayers in 1877, and in a service commemorating Comte's death on 5 September the next year called Humanity the power 'from whom we derive everything', thanked 'Holy Humanity' for her blessings, and expressed the pious hope that her servants would be worthy of them and attain 'union, unity, continuity'.[64] Well might he so pray. By then the rupture with his oldest associates was all but complete.

Congreve himself brought on the climax of the prolonged conflict by allowing Drs Sémérie, Robinet, and Audiffrent to draw him into a conspiracy in 1877 to supplant, or at least to supplement, Laffitte's leadership. On one visit to Paris in that year Congreve was surprised to find Harrison and Beesly there encouraging support for Laffitte, action inconsistent with Harrison's earlier criticism of the direction from 10 Rue Monsieur-le-Prince.[65] But just as Congreve underestimated Laffitte's staying power—for his French critics lost their nerve in the end—so he underestimated the need of his Chapel Street colleagues for an external sanction for their religious observances. Paris alone could provide it. They had all begun their religious odyssey in an episcopal Establishment and found the notion of a mere rootless sect repellent. Congreve, more completely free of his religious past, craved autonomy and authority. Therefore, in September 1877, acting on the flimsiest of promises of support from his French friends, he formally broke with Laffitte.[66] Curiously, this did not deter Harrison from allowing his youngest son, Christopher René, to receive the sacrament of Presentation from Congreve in February. Perhaps this merely shows how religious Harrison had become; like Roman Catholics he may have been distinguishing between the office and the person of the priest.[67]

In any case, Congreve soon proved less tolerant of his younger colleagues than they of him: on 1 May 1878 he summarily dissolved the Positivist Society he had called into existence eleven years before. A week later its members met, and a majority agreed to reconstitute the society, again under Beesly, but excluding Congreve; whereupon Geddes, Kaines, and Cotton left the room to signify their loyalty to their chief. The dissidents met again in September and October, but without Harrison, who was on holiday in Mrs Cameron's house on the Isle of Wight. He wrote urging a compromise with Congreve if possible, on the ground that the differences dividing them were not of doctrine but of persons.[68] The advice was similar to what Laffitte usually offered in times of conflict—and about as effective. Bridges, Beesly, and Vernon Lushington more forcefully issued statements defending Laffitte, Lushington even accusing Congreve of 'spiritual ambition'.[69] On 9 October Harrison, in what turned out to be his last communication to his former tutor, demanded an explanation for his 'deliberate disruption of the Positivist community', a letter Congreve ambiguously said threw 'light on many things'.[70] Even more revealing of Harrison's antagonism was his annotation of a defence of Congreve's stewardship circulated by Cotton later that month: Harrison judged Laffitte 'in moral character the superior to Congreve, as he is in intellectual, in heart, and in every grace of nature'; and overlooking his own initial refusal to regard Chapel Street as a church, he now asked why Congreve had delayed so long in introducing religious observances there. He did not mention Laffitte's failure to have done so in Paris.[71] Finally, early in November, the ever-procrastinating Laffitte appointed a 'Positivist Committee' of seven to administer the affairs of the dissidents, with Bridges as President and Harrison, Beesly, Morison, Vernon Lushington, and Henry Ellis as the other members. Soon known as the London Positivist Committee, or simply the Positivist Committee, it would with inevitable changes in membership and leadership, govern the affairs of the chief Positivist body in England for the next generation. Yet its first experience was humiliating: Henry Crompton, lessee of Chapel Street with his brother Albert, refused its request to exclude Congreve from the premises, and the Committee had no choice but to withdraw and seek new accommodation.[72]

The schism strained but did not entirely sever relations between the dissidents and the Cromptons, Cotton, Kaines, Geddes, and others faithful to Congreve. Some, like Kegan Paul and Mary Christie, maintained connections with both groups. But the schism ended almost thirty years of friendship between Congreve and his three Wadham pupils. Understandably, it was described in later years in very different terms by the participants. Harrison in his autobiography maintained that his own desire for some form of worship, and Congreve's reluctance to initiate it, was their only real difference of opinion, a statement that does no justice to Congreve's introduction of the sacraments, liturgical readings, and prayer, all before the schism, or to the disagreements over Pradeau and the *Polity*. Congreve spoke of his former pupils 'sliding into hostility' towards him, and in grim understatement concluded that this 'operated badly on the spread of the religion, for which in fact they were hardly genuinely in earnest ... Personally they were repellent.'[73] To Patrick Geddes, the many-sided botanist and social planner who as a student of Huxley's frequented Chapel Street in the 1870s, the split seemed due chiefly to the unwillingness of the Wadham triumvirate to prolong their pupil-teacher relation with Congreve.[74]

The suggestion is valid. Harrison's feelings toward Congreve are best understood by comparing them to his changed attitude towards his father. Mr Harrison's advanced age, infirmities, and tolerance of his son's rebelliousness all worked to dissipate the anger Fred had felt as a young man over his family's religious and vocational aspirations for him. In 1907 he told Edmund Gosse that the troubled childhood and youth depicted in *Father and Son* was far different from his own 'pedestrian, smooth, cheerful' early years, for unlike the stern tenets of the Plymouth Brethren of Gosse's parents, the real religion of his family had been 'the solid verdict of the "world"'. And though his own life had been an attempt to 'put a negative to this', the struggle had been 'steady, quiet, peaceable'. He had had his way 'without outburst, without tears, without any loss of mutual affection and even of respect and confidence towards one another'.[75] Far from telling the whole story, this account nevertheless shows the state of mind Harrison had attained by the time of the schism. Memories of past anguish had faded, the mutinous son had become the father of four sons himself, and in his need to discipline his own boys had found new understanding of his parents. Congreve, meanwhile, had grown increasingly irritable and dogmatic, slow to accommodate to what his younger colleagues thought was needed at Chapel Street. Unlike Mr Harrison, who still had two unmarried sons at home and the other three nearby, and had come to terms with all their many interests and ideas, Congreve's family at the time of the schism comprised his wife, her sister Emily Geddes, Mrs Geddes's daughters Emily and Mary (living in their own house while James Geddes was in India but in his absence looking to Congreve for guidance), the daughters of the American Positivist Henry Edger, Sophie Clotilde and Beatrice Blanche, as well as his own sister Julia on occasion. The deference of this feminine household had spoiled Congreve; unused to having to compromise at home, he was usually not prepared to do so at Chapel Street. Harrison, having attained the self-confidence of a husband, father, and widely-read controversialist, had finally found Congreve's authoritarianism intolerable and allowed himself to show his hostility.

And perhaps because he had grown up with four brothers, Harrison proved more capable of sharing responsibility and authority in the new Positivist Committee than Congreve had in his old organization, not only with Bridges and Beesly, but with the Paris group. After the schism he began contributing to a fund to support the Positivist Society at 10 Rue Monsieur-le-Prince, sent photographs of his sons, books, engravings, a bust of Descartes, and articles for the new Positivist bi-monthly publication, *La Revue Occidentale*. Laffitte became 'Mon cher Maître', and once, with Ethel, he signed a letter to him 'Vos amis fidèles et disciples dévoués'.[76] His deferential stance (which expressed in French seems exaggerated to English speakers) was made easier by Laffitte's passivity and reluctance to make challenging *ex cathedra* pronouncements. Indeed, there was a chronic problem in getting Laffitte to speak at all. His habit of leaving letters unanswered, and of being late with his annual report and financial statement infuriated Harrison in later years, as did his editorial laxness. Harrison's recourse was to address complaints to Laffitte's associates, chiefly Constant Hillemand, editor of the *Revue*, and Laffitte's aide, Charles Jeannolle. But neither Harrison nor his colleagues ever questioned the right of their French 'confrères' to oversee the promotion of Positivism in England by what Beesly at the time of the schism vaguely termed 'preaching and other ways'. To have done so would have undercut the rationale for their break with Congreve: the belief that they had adhered to a vital apostolic tradition while Congreve had seceded into sectarianism.

At first the absence of a permanent meeting place precluded long-term plans. The Positivist Committee met informally in Harrison's law chambers, Beesly's University Hall rooms (which he and his family left for their own house in Finsbury in 1880), or the offices of the London Trades Council, and for Sunday lectures they hired rooms, first in the Co-operative Institute in Castle Street in the spring of 1878, then in the Cavendish Rooms in Mortimer Street the next winter. The members took turns summarizing the *General View of Positivism* and made its reissue in Bridges' translation one of their first publications. By 1880 they could expect as many as three hundred to attend on a good Sunday. Meanwhile, Beesly regularly convened the all-male Positivist Society to discuss politics; the first of its *Positivist Comments on Public Affairs* was on the Congress of Berlin. Bridges inaugurated an annual New Year's Day Address in 1879, but because of ill health turned over the Presidency of the Positivist Committee to Harrison the next year. In his address on 1 January 1880 he pointed out that he and his colleagues were in 'earnest sympathy' with other Positivist groups in England (he was alluding to a new Positivist centre in Liverpool, not to Chapel Street, but mentioned neither by name), Ireland, France, Sweden, and in North and South America. In fact he would never care much about any of these organizations. And though he also insisted that he spoke for a 'veritable church', he made a point of its requiring of members 'no pledges, formalities, shibboleths'.[77] The *Annual Reports* of his Committee would always read like those of some purely educational or political body, so concerned were they with lecture and publication arrangements, receipts and expenditures, and social activities.

At the time of the schism Harrison's personal life was as filled with uncertainties as was the Positivist movement. His father, now past eighty and living the year round at Sutton Place, was growing weaker. Ethel's father, a lonely widower, was sometimes too depressed to leave his house in Warrington Crescent, especially after his West Indies import business suffered reverses early in 1879 and he feared meeting old friends on the street. Harrison's nephew, Cecil, Robert's eldest son, born in 1878, had a serious orthopaedic ailment, and Harrison's own boys suffered from time to time with the common but still dangerous children's diseases. Ethel, the source of most anxiety, had not entirely recovered from giving birth to four children in six years; rheumatism and gout—though she was not yet thirty—aggravated a tendency towards malaise no doctor would ever fully understand. Truly did Dr Dubuisson, the husband of Dr Robinet's daughter, observe that Comte's doctrine of resignation was 'toujours faute à prêcher, mais toujours difficile à pratiquer'.[78] Harrison's own buoyant health and spirits were taken for granted by his family, but on one lovely spring day in 1880 he seems to have experienced a 'mid-life crisis'. He was, after all, nearly fifty, and at the time away from Ethel, on whose solicitude and good sense he relied. Resting in the Wadham College room assigned to him while examining in the Law School, he suddenly thought about having first come to Oxford as a mere boy, when Ethel had not yet been born. He then tried to envisage a future time when neither of them would exist. It was an idea he could not bear to contemplate. Writing to her he compared the experience of that day to 'going into a cemetery and sitting down beside one's own grave ... I seem to be my own son looking at myself—as one who died in his teens.' This was perhaps the closest he would ever come to an existential awareness, and even then he sought to reject it by adding, 'But this is stuff'. Another time, earlier in his marriage than this, when Bernard was still a baby and Ethel's absence similarly provoked a melancholy reverie, he had written to her of the child's beauty being 'so horribly like those angel boys in the religious books who die early', and confessed: 'I never feel very much in love with the Toby [Bernard], without feeling sick at heart, as if it could not last'.[79] Having such hostages to fortune, Harrison could well credit Comte's teaching about the sacredness of family ties and their acting as motive for social sympathy. Unfortunately, he was too much the proper gentleman to refer to such personal and deeply-felt experience in his countless essays and addresses advancing the claims of the Religion of Humanity.

NEWTON HALL: SCHOOL, CHURCH, COMMUNITY

After more than two years in the wilderness of hired rooms, Harrison allowed his colleagues to persuade him to lease a free-standing hall in Fleur-de-lis Court, Fetter Lane, off Fleet Street.

Its historical associations were rich enough even for Positivists. It stood in the garden of what had been the house owned by 'Praise God Barebones' of Cromwell's Parliament. The house and garden had been purchased on the advice of Sir Isaac Newton and Sir Christopher Wren in 1710 by the Royal Society (whose first home had been, appropriately, Wadham College). The hall was built later in the century for the Society's collections, which would form the basis of the British Museum in Montague House, Bloomsbury. In 1782 the Society sold the property to the Royal Scottish Corporation. The hall, which was in the style of Wren and had excellent acoustics, served as its chapel and was let for meetings; Coleridge delivered his Shakespeare lectures there. The Barebones house next to it had burnt down shortly before the Positivists found the premises available. Because of its history and the role of science in their system, they named it Newton Hall. The neighbourhood was far from salubrious—the hall's entrance on a narrow alley was especially mean—but it, too, had historical associations. Hobbes, Dryden, Richard Baxter, and Tom Paine had lived close by, Dr Johnson not far away in Gough Square, and Wesley and Whitefield had preached in a Moravian chapel just across Fetter Lane near Clifford's Inn.[80]

Conscious of how easily he and the other dissidents had been thwarted at Chapel Street by an uncooperative lessee, Harrison made sure Newton Hall's twenty-one-year lease carried his own name; as co-signer he chose Albert Cock, a barrister on the Queen's Bench he had recently added to his Committee. And he took infinite pains over the interior arrangements. Larger than the Chapel Street room, it was some 27 feet wide and 54 feet long, with space for well over 150 chairs, a piano in the back, and an organ in the front. The Positivists painted the walls the obligatory pale green. Near the entrance, at the back, they placed a bust of Newton on a pedestal, a bookcase for their lending library of Positivist works, and, over it, a photograph of Laffitte. Above the fireplace, also in the rear, they ranged small busts of forty-eight worthies from the Calendar, and on the side walls between tall windows they mounted thirteen life-sized heads of those heroes of Humanity who name the Positivist months. At the front was a platform with lectern and bench and a table bearing a bust of Comte. Emblazoned on the front wall in large capital letters was a triptych of sacred formulas: 'Family—Humanity—Country'; 'The Foundation Order—The Principle Love—The End Progress'; 'Live for Others— Live Openly.' Behind Comte's bust Harrison hung a copy of Raphael's Sistine Madonna—but only after he decided it would not alienate the residual Protestant and atheistical prejudices of his congregation.[81]

For at least two years he had been ready for such a concrete expression of his commitment to religious Positivism, having, by early 1879, fitted out a corner of his library at Westbourne Terrace with a copy of a Holbein painting of the Virgin, busts of Comte and some of the Calendar's worthies, and pictures to represent stages of civilization— for example, a scene of Mount Olympus by Raphael suggesting polytheism. Austin would remember that at table there was a form of grace, and prayers on Sunday mornings, with a short address by his father in his 'serious, somewhat censorious voice'.[82]

For the opening of the hall, on 1 May 1881, Laffitte came from Paris and stayed three weeks at 38 Westbourne Terrace. Harrison arranged the details carefully, getting Cotter Morison to accompany Laffitte, who spoke no English, and seeing that he was entertained. The genial Grant Duff, whom Congreve had introduced to Comte, gave a dinner for the Harrisons and their guest, and Harrison took him to a meeting of the Political Economy Club. There an amused Dilke observed Harrison treating the Frenchman with all the respect an old lady of the Faubourg would show the Pope or the Comte de Chambord or both combined—until Laffitte happened to boast of France's current imperialist venture in Tunis, whereupon Harrison's 'politesse' momentarily vanished. At Newton Hall Laffitte held two 'conferences publiques', delivered several addresses, attended regular meetings of the Positivist Society, and administered two sacraments—Presentation, to the infant son of Benjamin Fossett Lock, a Chancery lawyer, and Admission, to Ellis's son-in-law. Harrison worried about whether a table used on this occasion would seem too much like an altar, and in perplexity about suitable orations begged Laffitte to compose his own. In all these activities, Laffitte's lack of English made interpreters essential. Austin, just eight, was not impressed, perhaps, he surmised later, 'because M. Laffitte spoke from a sitting posture and dwelt so frequently and with such an emphatic pause on the conjunction *et* (as Frenchmen do), which, in my opinion, was weak'.[83] William Morris, invited by Harrison to attend the festivities, declined on the ground that his French was not good enough, though he said the antiquity of Newton Hall would bring him to see it one day.[84]

Why the ordinary Londoner came on Sundays (the hour varied) during the next twenty-one years must be conjectured; though Comte coined the term 'sociologie', his disciples did not anticipate the modern discipline's opinion surveys. For the humbler members, belonging to a fellowship claiming to be the advanced guard of mankind was perhaps enough. For others, it could have been the distinguished leaders, to be seen and heard at close range. The most idealistic and religious would find inspiration in the frequent references both to Humanity's past achievements and future greatness. 'We must be cautious', Harrison warned in his inaugural address in 1881, 'very cautious, how far we allow ourselves to slide into a mere parody of what is called worship in Churches and Chapels.' Two years later he protested that at Newton Hall 'service or ritual there is none; neither priest nor acolyte', an assertion he never changed. Yet in time the Positivist sacred formulas were recited with words of inspiration and even a benediction was pronounced:

> May faith in Humanity teach us how to live!
> May hope in Humanity strengthen us in need!
> May love for Humanity fill our hearts, giving peace within us
> And with all men!

And soon, too, a trained choir was rendering words from well-known poems and songs, or compositions by Positivists, and there was hymn-singing by the congregation. Always there was the inducement to turn the mind to science or history or literature or art made intelligible to a half-educated audience. The experience would be largely passive, but so it was in most churches.[85]

Apart from the leaders of Newton Hall, only a few individuals emerge from the anonymity of those Sunday gatherings. One is William Knight, a briefless Lincoln's Inn barrister who tried both Chapel Street and Newton Hall but in his poverty, tuberculosis, and oppressive family circumstances found nothing in either place to keep him from committing suicide.[86] Letters by two other men describe an influence only somewhat more profitable: one recalled Harrison's history lectures and admonitions against tobacco—but also admitted to an attachment to the Theosophical Society; the other alluded to Positivist principles proving useful when he left Newton Hall—for Chapel Street.[87] The journalist Arthur Porritt became an admirer of Harrison's after he took pains to identify for Porritt a man he had come to the hall to interview.[88] Other journalists found their way to the hall also, seeking amusing details about its ritual or a report on his Annual Address. Harrison's sons rejoiced when some distinguished visitor turned up— Morley, Grant Duff, Wilfrid Blunt, or Thomas Hardy, for example; their parents' great work then seemed to be getting on. None was more conspicuous than the splendidly garbed Chinese diplomat, Sir Chihchen Lofengluh (who, invited to Westbourne Terrace, caused smiles by eating with his fingers and declining English tea).[89] Some Japanese students once appeared, directed to Newton Hall by the psychologist James Sully, a colleague of Beesly's, who thought their ancestor-worship might make the idea of the Great Being appealing.[90] And, of course, there were the Indians, whom Ethel, no more than her husband, considered likely converts: she noted that they always said what 'will please you to hear'.[91] Harrison was of course too sensible ever to press for allegiance from anyone. Publicly he maintained that the proper business of Positivism was not to strive for greater numbers or to add one more to the many religious sects of London; it was to 'free us from the temper of mind which creates them'.

On the whole the Positivists had to be content with the clerks, schoolteachers, housewives, and other lower-middle-class people who attended their Sunday meetings in place of the true proletariat Comte had fondly expected would form the redemptive alliance with his philosophic heirs. But whatever mingling of the classes there was seemed salutary to Overton, who had followed Harrison in the schism. 'How you get people so far apart so close together puzzles me', he once exclaimed to Ethel. He lectured a few times at Newton Hall but Harrison was no egalitarian and preferred better-educated teachers.[92] His success in securing them, and in promoting groups and activities at Newton Hall aroused the jealousy of Congreve, who ungenerously attributed it to the presence of wealthy members like Morison and the Lushingtons and did not see it as evidence of Harrison's energy and organizing talents. By 1886 Congreve was telling his wife that they had to be careful not to let Chapel Street become 'too gloomy' for the young.[93] Moreover, while Congreve was often ill and preached without enthusiasm, Harrison, according to Moncure Conway, who headed the South Place Ethical Society in Finsbury, could make 'every mind and heart one with his in sympathy' when he spoke, 'without any trick or gesture or rhetoric'.[94] And Harrison took pride in his growing powers. Describing an early lecture he told Ethel he had leapt and gambolled 'in exultation about the old poets' and feared that Bridges and others were 'scandalised'—but he added, 'I am getting the art of interesting the public.' The applause on that occasion, however, disconcerted him; 'people do not clap real sermons.'[95]

Like his speaking, Harrison's administrative duties at Newton Hall exercised abilities he had been cultivating over the years. Just as he efficiently saw to the upkeep of 38 Westbourne Terrace and to the family finances, so he supervised the maintenance of Newton Hall and its funds, for a time as treasurer. When his brother Robert donated a silver teapot and two dozen cups and saucers, Harrison added spoons. No detail was too small for him; and his colleagues were as unlikely to challenge his decisions as was Ethel in family matters. One of his satisfactions at Newton Hall was the adequacy of income without the need to resort to collections or seat charges. In 1884, a typical good year, subscriptions to the Central Fund, which was sent to Paris to maintain Comte's rooms and support his old servant and Laffitte, totalled £200; the General Fund, which derived from subscriptions as well as from lettings of Newton Hall, and was used to maintain the building and advertise its meetings, amounted to £288; and the Publishing Fund, only partially expended, with printing and distributing by the firm of Reeves and Turner, in the Strand, amounted to £23.[96]

Even before Newton Hall opened, Harrison obtained Laffitte's permission to hold a festival in 1883 honouring Muhammad at what the Positivists calculated would mark the beginning of the fourteenth century of his life, which they thought unfairly neglected by Christians. Within a month of the hall's inauguration, Bridges initiated the custom of honouring worthies from the Calendar on the anniversary of their death (in this instance it was Calderon); on 31 December 1882, the Day of All the Dead, Vernon Lushington presided at a service that also became an annual event; and on 5 September 1883 the English Positivists commemorated Comte's death in emulation of their French colleagues. All these observances were part of Positivist worship, which Harrison now considered the centre of religion. And of course there were the sacraments marking the great epochs in life, which—all but Retirement and Incorporation (in the Great Being)—Harrison from time to time administered. He later insisted that 'in this, as in every other part I had in the Newton Hall movement, I was simply obeying a call from my fellow believers'; that the forms he had devised were 'rudimentary', always made public, and invested with no magical powers; and that the term 'sacrament' derived ultimately from the Latin word for the Roman military oath of allegiance to the state and public service.[97] He was protesting perhaps too much.

The first sacrament Harrison composed and administered, Destination, in December 1881, inadvertently expressed his own dedication to his new vocation of Positivist priest as well as that of the recipient, J. Carey Hall, to his new position on the British consular staff in Japan. Comte, in explaining this sacrament, had noted that men of theory more often than men of action chose a career not selected for them by their fathers. This was both true and not true of Harrison. His work at Newton Hall did not fulfil his parents' hope that he would become an Anglican priest, yet it vindicated their willingness to let him put aside the professional and business ambitions of his brothers. Free to follow his own intellectual and cultural interests, he had arrived at his true vocation, and his family accepted his destination. He thus had the best of two worlds: theirs, one that affluence from business made comfortable, and his own, with its public recognition, religious fulfilment, and intellectual gratifications. Winters were planned around his duties at Newton Hall; summers and early autumns he was free to leave London, and usually did. But at the end of the year in which he seemed finally to have defined this way of life to accommodate his long-evolving conceptions of himself and his vocation, he fell under a shadow from which he would emerge only slowly, and then it was to feel himself suddenly among 'les ranges des vieillards'.[98]

The news that his father could not live much longer came to Harrison in the early autumn of 1881, after he and Ethel had returned from a cruise in the Mediterranean with his brother Charles on Charles's yacht. Mr Harrison had suffered a serious heart seizure at Sutton Place. He died a few weeks later, on 2 November, in the presence of his sons, and was buried in Brookwood Cemetery at nearby Woking. All this was still fresh in Harrison's thoughts when in the sacrament for Hall he equated '*every* honourable task' with 'public service'. Mr Harrison's service to the business community of London provided a legacy exceeding £213,000, twice what his brother Charles had left at his death the previous year. After some £36,000 and his real property was left to his widow, mostly in trust, and small sums given relatives, business partners, and servants, there was something over £30,000 for each of his five sons, in addition to recent gifts from him of about £10,000 to each.[99]

Harrison's new wealth hardly changed his life outwardly. He continued to serve as treasurer at Newton Hall, where the minimum subscription was 3d; but inwardly his father's death had changed his mood and his sense of himself enormously. Still in a state of despair six months afterwards, he told Morley, 'My brain seems to have had something snap inside it. I can just get on with the plain stuff; but for the slightest rise into any imaginative strain—I feel as if the pinion was broken and the wing hangs when I try to rise from the ground.'[100] To Ethel he wrote even more gloomily that hardly a day passed without his recalling his father's 'deathbed, and the hospital, and the funeral, and all the rest. I seem ... to have become a man with only a few remnants of years to live, and his strength gone; nothing done in all these 50 years, and too late to begin anything now.'[101] On the last day of 1881, the Day of All the Dead, he gathered his sons about him at Westbourne Terrace for a memorial service, to give them, he told Laffitte, 'leurs premières idées sur la théorie de mort'.[102] That theory informed his address on the same day at Newton Hall two years later, when he introduced the first performance of a cantata written for the Positivists by one of their members, Henry Holmes, Professor of

Violin at the new Royal College of Music. The text was 'O May I Join the Choir Invisible', which the Harrisons, Beesly, Bridges, and Congreve had all heard read, in part, at George Eliot's funeral in Highgate Cemetery some four months before the opening of Newton Hall and which the Positivists used regularly in their own memorial services.[103] With both father and distinguished literary friend now in the company of transfigured Humanity, Harrison found new meaning in Comte's eschatology.

The 1880s brought death to others close to Harrison. In 1881 his brother Robert's daughter died of diphtheria and was buried 'sans mot', the father being agnostic.[104] In 1884 Vernon Lushington's wife died, leaving their three daughters, all musicians (on their way to being 'she-Joachims' according to her close friend Emma Darwin) in their Kensington Square house, the father 'upheld in this great sorrow ... by the deep conviction that the Dead still bless the living'.[105] In 1889 Mrs Beesly succumbed to cancer in the Beeslys' new house in Warrington Crescent, leaving four sons (the eldest, Gerald, ill in Glasgow) and a husband who in Harrison's words bore his grief 'like a Roman general'.[106] And Ethel's health, never good, became a source of extreme anxiety in the summer of 1884. Writing to Moncure Conway, Harrison said that never before had he 'so clearly realised all that a human religion means ... how the very instruments of science, the morphia needles, and the like, seem revelations, and doctors, relations, friends, and nurses seem transfigured ministers of humanity'.[107] His mother, apropos of one of his addresses, remarked: 'How truly you say the dead are not laid to their rest but living around us more revered more loving than in life—but to me not a memory only but a full faith that we shall meet hereafter ... Surely Comptism [*sic*] is Christianity without Christ.' But she added: 'You have chosen a noble work, and ... will find the fruits of your labours in the influence you will exercise in teaching men to lead a good and holy life.'[108]

From the first, Harrison was encouraged to undertake his 'noble work' not only by his religious faith but by his experience, and that of his colleagues, in teaching. Besides the most able of the Chapel Street group that had left Congreve, there were some promising new recruits. One was Benjamin Fossett Lock, a Dorset friend of Thomas Hardy's educated at Eton, Cambridge, and Lincoln's Inn who, like Harrison, examined for the Inns of Court. Besides lecturing on the Positivists' reading list he served as their librarian and eventually joined Harrison's Committee.[109] Several men with medical or science degrees lectured in their subjects without, apparently, committing themselves to Positivism; an exponent of the innovative Tonic Solfa system of teaching music conducted singing classes and helped with the choir; and a Parisian lady taught French.[110] For lectures on education in 1882 Harrison secured Frederick Gard Fleay, a class-mate from King's College School who had earned the nickname of 'the industrious flea' at Cambridge and, after a brief immersion in Positivist theory prompted by Harrison, went on to an important career in literary and linguistic scholarship far too specialized to serve or even please the Positivists.[111] No teacher (except occasionally one in language or music) was paid at Newton Hall; nor were there fees for the students, or examinations or certificates. The Positivists' voluntary principle derived from Comte, though it prevailed, with other sources, in many comparable adult schools. Unique, however, was their practice of recalling with reverence the names in the Calendar whenever remotely relevant: a class in geometry might be asked to meditate on Euclid's gift to Humanity. It became increasingly difficult to attract students to Newton Hall's classes towards the end of the century, when the proliferation of state schools and new opportunities in higher education made its work superfluous. Educational progress, ironically, rendered obsolete the application of Comte's philosophy of progress to the classroom.

Less vulnerable to social change were the pilgrimages that six or seven times a year Newton Hall leaders conducted to places hallowed by the life or death of some worthy. Due often to Harrison's planning, these excursions were more seriously conceived and rigorously executed than most tours of the sort popular with social and religious societies of the time. In the first year they were offered, 1884, Positivist pilgrimages were made to Rolls to honour William Harvey; to Waltham Abbey, associated with King Harold; to Hampton Court to meditate on William III; to Chalfont St. Giles to see Milton's house; to Penn's grave at Jordans, where Harrison spoke at the Quaker meeting house; and to St. Albans for a tribute to Francis Bacon. The following year Harrison led a more ambitious overnight excursion to Stratford-upon-Avon, where he lodged his group in a temperance hotel. The most regularly visited place was always Westminster Abbey, whose densely-packed memorials might have been erected expressly for the Positivists, and which Dean Bradley, like Dean Stanley before him, sought to make inviting to men of all religious persuasions, or none. The most memorable and most distant expedition undertaken was a week-end in Paris in 1886, with Harrison as guide to Comte's grave in Père Lachaise; l'église St Paul, where he had worshipped, in his fashion; Clotilde de Vaux's house in Rue Payenne; and, of course, 10 Rue Monsieur-le-Prince. One of the entourage wrote rapturously of the voice that welcomed them as they reached the entrance to Comte's rooms at the top of stairs 'trodden daily by the feet of the great master': it was 'the same voice that has times out of number thrilled with its burning eloquence ... the voice of Mr Frederic Harrison, our great teacher'.[112] This account, and one in Figaro, depicted Harrison moved to tears by Laffitte's greeting, an account Harrison denied in a letter to Ethel summing up his experiences in far from sentimental terms:

I have played showman till I am hoarse and have no soles left to my feet ... We sally out a motley string of 'touristes Anglais', with every form of hat, coat, and mantle. Presently we come to an open space, and I mount on a step and begin a historical lecture—a dozen idlers gather to listen and in 5 minutes there is a crowd, and the gendarmes come to beg us to move on. They think we are the Salvation Army![113]

Like the Salvation Army, the Positivists thought Church and Chapel should not have all the good tunes. Vernon Lushington, an accomplished musician, organized the first of a series of music festivals in 1882 with a talk on Mozart illustrated by pictures and a concert. Occasionally Sir George Macfarren, the blind composer and Principal of the Royal Academy of Music, assisted with performances on Sundays till his death in 1889, and his wife, also a musician, who had obtained Newton Hall's piano from the Darwins, continued to be helpful.[114] (Henry Holmes, whose ambitious cantata on the Choir Invisible was perhaps Newton Hall's most significant musical performance, resigned from Beesly's Positivist Society in 1886 and presumably was not active at the hall when, seven years later, the discovery of his long record of philandering among his women violin students forced him to flee with his family to San Francisco.[115]) Ethel directed a ladies' choir when her health permitted, and in 1890 published *Service of Man*, her collection of the texts of hymns and anthems sung by it and by the congregation. The little square volume, its format common to the genre, illustrates the eclectic nature of Positivist teaching, for it contains works from authors as diverse as Wordsworth and Dante, Blake and Newman, Shelley and Wesley. There were also poems by acquaintances such as W. M. W. Call (known to Harrison from the *Westminster* circle), Kegan Paul (who had been converted to Roman Catholicism and helped get Ethel permission to use Newman's poem), Stopford Brooke (whose literary interests Harrison encouraged), Stanton Coit (Moncure Conway's successor at the South Place Ethical Society), and Thomas Sulman (a Chapel Street Positivist who had studied art under Ruskin at the Working Men's College). George Eliot's poem on the Choir Invisible was of course included, and its theme was exploited in many of the forty-four selections by Positivists. Ethel herself contributed twelve hymns, and if she did not reveal the 'true gift of religious poetry' credited to her by her husband, she skilfully and feelingly employed hallowed traditional metres and transmogrified Christian imagery. Successful hymns, she said, needed 'generations of feeling' behind them. Her edition of 1,000 copies was depleted by the turn of the century, having been drawn on by non-Positivists and even by Chapel Street. Vernon Lushington, who had privately published his own Positivist hymns, urged her to bring out a new edition, which eventually appeared in 1908. Both agreed that Newton Hall's hymns were often badly performed, but Ethel praised the 'generous impulse' that had always prevailed among her ladies, who came to rehearsals despite the hall's 'odious approaches', the inconvenient hour, and the onus of being identified with Positivism.[116]

The stigma of Positivism may, however, have hindered the growth of the guilds for young women and men founded at Newton Hall to serve the area. The first, organized in 1884, offered classes in French, drawing, musical drill, and literature, and discussions on sanitation and housekeeping, with eclecticism again the key: one lecture was titled 'Needles and Pins, Papers and Pens, Pots and Pans'.[117] The young men's guild was started in 1889 by Robert George Hember, a recruit from South Place,[118] Shapland Hugh Swinny, a thirty-two-year-old Cambridge man of independent means and wide interests,[119] and Francis S. Marvin, a twenty-six-year-old teacher who, with Swinny, would become a mainstay of the Positivists in the next generation.[120] Their guild held classes in debating and musical drill, and arranged cricket and football matches; occasionally there were socials with the women. The Harrisons monitored all these activities. Ethel, infinitely resourceful, cooled lemonade crocks in the family's bathtubs, pressed her sons into decorating the hall, and, in answer to Swinny's complaints that 'her' girls were flirting with 'his' boys, declared: 'It ought not to be beyond us to deal with this fact of nature.' Her husband, worried about keeping the youths from 'turning the Sacred Institutions of Humanity upside down', drew the line at boxing within the precincts of Newton Hall.[121]

A year after its creation by Laffitte, the London Positivist Committee began issuing annual reports and financial statements, recording its activities, and reprinting some of its addresses in translation in *La Revue Occidentale*. In 1893 the Committee launched a more ambitious record of its work, *The Positivist Review*, a monthly edited and financed by Beesly, who distributed it to subscribers at 6d an issue. Now a widower with his boys grown, he had just retired from University College and so had the necessary time. Bridges, who had retired from his medical inspectorship the previous year, was similarly free to contribute regularly, as did Harrison, who was by then no longer engaged in legal education. With some assistance from their colleagues and occasionally from outsiders, the old triumvirate managed to fill each twenty-four-page number with new or re-published articles and addresses accompanied by Newton Hall notices. Since much of the writing was political, the *Review* belatedly fulfilled the Mumbo's old dream of having its own organ. But the excitement Positivism had generated in the 1850s had long dissipated; and the *Review*'s narrow focus and relentless seriousness in an age of popular journalism further limited its readership. It won praise from the *Manchester Guardian* for its liberal politics and literary quality, but even Beesly conceded it was not much read outside Newton Hall.[122]

Neither, to Harrison's deep regret, was the vast compendium of biographical sketches of the 558 worthies in the Positivist Calendar which he persuaded the Positivist Committee to authorize soon after he became its President. He was beginning then to use Comte's dating system, by which every day of the year was assigned a biographical identity: thus a letter to 'Dear Wife' on 2 February 1881 is dated 'Sophocles'; and one to Morley on 19 October 1884 carries the year as well, counting from 1789: 'Diderot 96'. The *New Calendar of Great Men*, which eventually appeared in 1892, was intended to inculcate that system among Positivists and also to serve a wider educational function. Harrison later considered the volume his most important literary achievement as a Positivist. But like so much he did in the service of his creed, it placed him beyond reach of two different rewards, for it proved too academic to be popular and thus attract recruits to Positivism, and too much permeated by Positivist bias to be acclaimed without reservation in the intellectual community.[123]

POSITIVISTS AT LARGE

In his inaugural address at Newton Hall, Harrison, following Comte, audaciously contrasted St. Paul's 'religious appeal to the conscience of all men' to Christ's 'mixture of hallucination, or even of imposture, with violent anarchism'. In seeking to emulate the founder of the Church as a social institution, Harrison encountered his own troublesome Colossians and Thessalonians. Bridges feared at times that Newton Hall was too religious and its political manifestos no more useful than 'passing censure on a tornado'; and Beesly found fault with its accounting procedures.[124] But these were passing complaints. More serious was Cotter Morison's neglect of the Positivists for his literary and drinking friends, whom he entertained at Clairvaux, his Hampstead house, and on his yacht. To Ethel he seemed a 'fallen angel', but her husband worried about the unseemliness of lectures at Newton Hall by the 'boozy skipper'. And in 1888 he was aghast at the 'astounding paradox' of Morison's book, *Service of Man: An Essay towards the Religion of the Future*, which argued that man should not be saddled with the conception of moral responsibility: saints were born, not made. Morison's death shortly afterwards obliged Harrison to invoke the face-saving aspect of the doctrine of Subjective Immortality and ask the Positivists to remember their departed colleague 'as he was at his best'. To them this especially meant Morison's generosity, for he left them £500, the largest legacy the Positivists were ever to receive.[125]

Troublesome in a different way was one of the poorest of Positivists, the Russian-born William Frey. He had idealistically renounced a career in the Czar's army to undertake what proved to be an eighteen-year-long experiment in communal living in America before arriving in London with several other Russian exiles and finding his way to both Chapel Street and Newton Hall. It soon fell to Harrison to inform him that he could not sell his 'Russian Brotherhood whole grain American finger rolls', or distribute his vegetarian tracts at Newton Hall, or print its literature on the Brotherhood's press. Nor did Frey's attempts to reconcile Newton Hall with Chapel Street win any favour with Harrison. Finally, in 1888, acting as a barrister, he declined to endorse Frey's application for a visa to Russia, where Frey wished to go ostensibly on family business, but in Harrison's judgement in order to proselytize, as he had on a visit there three years before, when he had carried his brand of Positivism even to Tolstoy. Frey's death in 1889 brought members of both Positivist groups to the graveside in Highgate Cemetery. Harrison spoke, but in acknowledging Frey's abstemiousness it is doubtful that he went so far as Beesly, who in a Newton Hall address suggested that Frey's allotment of only 4d a day for food could, with modification, serve as an example to all. Ever practical, Harrison busied himself with arranging the return to America of Frey's destitute family and friends.[126]

Not all Harrison's problems could be buried, but with a cool head and firm hand he managed to deal with many of them to his satisfaction. When the treasurer and the secretary of his Committee, the improbable pair Alfred Cock and Fossett Lock, resigned their offices in 1887 in opposition to the Positivist Society's condemnation of Lord Salisbury's Irish coercion policy, Lock refused to hand over his keys and records without orders from Laffitte himself. Harrison, who had appointed Lock to the Committee and taken him on the yachting cruise with

Charles in 1881, was outraged; and he soon manœuvred the offending Lock out of office.[127] Harrison's desire to further the careers of his friends led to another problem in 1889. Soon after helping to make the men's guild successful, F. S. Marvin secured an assistant inspectorship in the Education Department, largely through Harrison's intervention, and was lost to Newton Hall for the next seven years in the provinces. When a promotion brought him back to London Harrison placed him on his Committee; and Ethel, advising him about places to live, reminded him of his proper status: 'in these days of settlements and doing good to one's poorer brethren' it was wise to remember the advantages of living 'with our equals and as much as possible with our superiors as we can bear'.[128] If Morison's self-indulgence distressed the Harrisons, so too did they repudiate martyrdom for Positivists, whether it took the form of Frey's physical trials or Marvin's social deprivations.

The Harrisons mingled comfortably enough with their 'equals' during the Newton Hall years, and occasionally with their 'superiors', never overstepping the bounds of propriety to proselytize, but not hiding their religion either. It served admirably when death came to friends or acquaintances who lacked church affiliation. Unveiling a memorial tablet to Lady John Russell in the Free Church at Richmond in 1900, Harrison, who had enjoyed gossiping with her at Pembroke Lodge in 1897, when he and his family were staying at nearby Rutland Lodge, depicted her as a Roman matron bearing 'that rare flame which we attribute to the martyrs of our sacred and secular histories—the power of inspiring those whom she impressed with the resolve to do right'.[129] At the memorial service for Fanny Hertz's husband, Harrison invoked Comte's notion of the ennobled capitalist; and when the Hertzes' son-in-law died prematurely, he offered the dead man's high standing among his fellow lawyers as assurance that he had joined the 'choir invisible'.[130] Neither man had been a Positivist. Nor was Grant Allen; at his cremation service in 1899, Harrison praised the writer's courage in his last illness and his books on science and comparative religion, but claimed to know nothing of his novels, which he privately deplored. Of Allen's philandering, so blatant that Harrison once told Morley that mothers in Haslemere refused to let their daughters accompany him on specimen hunts, he of course said nothing.[131] But then, speaking only good of the dead was a venerable tradition long before Comte affirmed the Great Being's forgiving selectivity.

While Harrison's many social connections and public activities outside Newton Hall added stature to his work there, Congreve soldiered on at Chapel Street with a diminishing reputation. He was outliving his friends, his most able followers had departed in the schism, and remaining colleagues pressed rituals upon him that increased the obloquy he had long endured for his faith.[132] His ties with Laffitte's critics dissolved, and those with Laffitte were minimal. Neither Congreve nor Harrison ever considered reconciliation. 'Gare à vous— le diable est déchaîné', Harrison once warned Laffitte when Congreve's whereabouts were unknown; and Congreve waited maliciously for Harrison to 'write himself out'.[133] But Harrison, with a certain exaggeration, proposed to Laffitte that a 'réunion des Positivistes Anglaises' could already be said to exist in so far as the two London groups were co-operating in support of a fledgling Positivist centre in North London that would contribute to Laffitte's Paris fund.[134] When the new centre, located in the Hornsey Road—of hallowed childhood memories for Harrison—instituted religious practices directed by the Chapel Street Positivist Joseph Kaines, Harrison's Committee cried 'insubordination'. It took some time to achieve a *via media*, which, however, then endured until the North London group dissolved in 1900.[135]

The progress of Positivism elsewhere pleased Harrison somewhat more. A Manchester group founded in 1884 was headed by Charles Harold Herford, at the age of thirty-one already on the way to eminence as a literary scholar. When Harrison arrived at Memorial Hall in Manchester one Sunday morning to lecture, he found an audience of 1,000 people, six times what he could expect at Newton Hall. Unfortunately, Herford departed for a professorship at Aberystwyth in 1887, and when he returned in 1900 did not seek to revive the then moribund organization.[136] Charles Gaskell Higginson, who had replaced him, was related to the Martineaus and initially impressed Harrison so favourably that he exclaimed to Laffitte, 'Voici enfin notre Bossuet trouvé.' Higginson set out to reproduce Newton Hall's functions in Manchester; but he went on to decide that he and Kaines in North London should receive a 'mandate apostolique' from Laffitte. That was too much for Harrison, who had never had such an ordination; but he suggested a compromise by which he, Higginson, and Kaines would all be given a 'general consecration'. Higginson's decision not to go to Paris ended the problem. Eventually he obtained a medical degree, which supported his claim to the Positivist priesthood, and like Bridges he practised medicine.[137] In 1900 his removal to Birmingham brought an end to the Manchester Positivist Society, but he continued to lecture in London. 'Energetic mais un peu gauche' was Harrison's judgement to Laffitte; to Ethel he mentioned a certain likeness to Malvolio.[138]

Congreve's satellites were in Birmingham, Liverpool, Leicester,

Newcastle-upon-Tyne, and three of its neighbouring towns. The Liverpool group, dating to the late seventies, was the oldest, the strongest, and the most religious of them all—really no satellite but a bright luminary in the heaven of alternative religions in England. Its presiding spirits were first Dr Thomas Carson, a physician; then Henry Crompton's brother Albert, and Sidney Style and his wife Susan. She was Fossett Lock's sister and an artist who turned her talents to Positivist worship much as Ethel had; her painting, 'Magna Est Vis Humanitatis', depicts a madonna blessing three children who signify the three races, while a setting sun behind shows the decline of the old faiths. In their Church of Humanity the Liverpool Positivists used a hymnal of chants and anthems in Italian, Latin, and English—'Ave Maria' preceded 'Ave Clotilde'—and commemorated Comte's death each year by partaking together of bread and water.[139] The Newcastle group, founded in 1880 by the even more sacerdotal Malcolm Quin, had an iron church in which Quin, gorgeously robed, presided; for his proselytizing missions he devised a portable altar. A man of little formal education, Quin was assisting Robert Spence Watson in running the National Liberal Federation at its Newcastle headquarters in 1884 when Harrison accepted a speaking engagement in that city under its auspices. *En route* from London, the ever-fastidious Harrison changed his gloves, inadvertently removing the yellow pair he had agreed to wear for identification by Quin at the station. The resulting confusion convinced Quin that he could expect little from so bourgeois a Positivist. Harrison, who was taken to see the iron church, for his part realized how brash was Quin's attempt to 'Catholicize' Positivism. Later Quin's efforts to 'Positivize' Catholicism would seem to Harrison evidence of his 'refreshing audacity', but nothing to take seriously.[140]

No such bemusement characterized Harrison's judgement of Congreve's religious evolution. Admittedly, Chapel Street's ritual was more elaborate than Newton Hall's (neither ever entailed vestments), yet Harrison often wrote as if his former mentor's development into a religious leader had no parallel in his own career. Actually the finances and programmes of the two centres were remarkably similar. Congreve, for example, drew on an annual income from subscriptions in 1888 of £303, while Harrison had £366 coming in during that year. Both centres had loosely affiliated satellites in England, and each helped support Positivists in Paris, Congreve for a time assisting Laffitte's opponents. Both sponsored social activities, though Chapel Street's were fewer. And its leadership was far weaker: Henry Cotton entered politics and therefore minimized his Positivism, and Henry Crompton was beset by illness. Congreve's own health, failing since the schism, declined markedly following surgery in 1888. After a decade of delegating responsibility at Chapel Street whenever he could, Congreve died in July 1899 at the age of eighty, aware that his mission had largely failed. Beesly sent a tender letter to the widow, but Harrison seemed able to produce only an impersonal, if strictly fair, account of Congreve's influence at Oxford for *The Wadham College Gazette*.[141] The irrepressible Quin made an unsuccessful bid to insinuate himself into the position Congreve's death left vacant ('Praise the Lord!' was Ethel's response to his rebuff), and after an interregnum during which Kaines died and Crompton retired, Alfred Haggard, an ex-Indian magistrate, took over. Harrison and he enjoyed cordial relations, but so long as Congreve's family survived there seemed no hope of a reunion between Chapel Street and Newton Hall.[142]

Harrison's most constant source of anxiety in Positivist affairs during the Newton Hall years was neither Chapel Street nor its satellites, for he paid them little heed, but Laffitte, whom he dared not ignore if he hoped to maintain the principle of his own ministry sanctioned by a higher authority. But this entailed swallowing much that offended his sense of propriety and legality. He had no trouble accepting Laffitte's appointment to the new Chair of the History of Science at the Collège de France in 1892. 'Let the Brazilian dogs howl as they please!' he said when told that those hyper-orthodox Positivists viewed Laffitte's acceptance of the honour as a capitulation to officialdom. To Harrison it seemed well deserved after Laffitte's years of successful public teaching, and besides, it brought a salary he would need in his last years as well as prestige to the Positivist movement.[143] Nor was Harrison prepared to object openly when Laffitte formed a company in his own name in 1893 to purchase the building at 10 Rue Monsieur-le-Prince together with Comte's furniture, archives, and memorabilia, even though Laffitte simultaneously suppressed as superfluous Comte's original Positivist Society, thereby alienating old Positivists like Dr Robinet. Though that corollary action seemed unwise to Harrison, he invested in the company and encouraged other English Positivists to do so. Obtaining its financial reports, to say nothing of dividends, would not be the least of his frustrations in dealing with Paris in later years.[144] Meanwhile Laffitte, despite declining health and much prodding, refused to make a decision about naming a successor until 1897, and then he chose Charles Jeannolle, an undistinguished civil servant who had been no more than his administrative assistant. Jeannolle's indifference to both the educational and the religious aspects of Positivism made Laffitte's choice anathema to the old guard in Paris; but, once again, Harrison was so relieved to have the matter settled that he did not balk at details.[145]

Providing for a successor to Laffitte had come to seem infinitely urgent to Harrison the previous year, when he had observed his old chief in both Paris and on his estate near Cadillac, in the Gironde. At the age of seventy-three Laffitte was nearly blind and pathetically awkward—in frequent danger, Harrison told Ethel, of being struck down in the city by bicycles and 'auto-cars whizzing along the streets at 20 miles an hour'. And in the country Laffitte tolerated 'shocking brutalities'. Everything in the old farmhouse he occupied was 'rotten and broken'. The chest of drawers in Harrison's room was crammed so full he had to lay his clothing on a table. Just outside was a 'decayed' veranda from which anyone could peer in, and three feet from it, in a garden overrun with weeds, was the outhouse, its door slamming back and forth revealing 'two *bancs percés*'. Within twenty feet of the house a small lumber mill belched steam and made an intolerable racket. Over the din Laffitte shouted imperialistic and pro-Russian diatribes. When taxed by Harrison how he could endorse the politics of both the Sultan of Turkey and the Czar of Russia, he barked: 'Bah! we have the same enemies!' At meals he ate 'like a hungry dog', and, accompanying Harrison part of the way on his return to Paris, he deemed it 'inutile' to bring a change of clothing for their stay overnight in Bordeaux. 'No doubt the old monks may have gone about like that—but I do not think it adds anything to a philosopher of the nineteenth century', was Harrison's judgement.[146] It was in ironic contrast to his accolade on Laffitte a few months before in *Cosmopolis* comparing him to 'some of the more attractive savants of the eighteenth century' and singling out for praise his 'indifference to form'.[147]

One act of Laffitte's earned Harrison's unqualified approval: his proposal to erect a statue of Comte in Paris on the centenary of his birth in 1898, to be paid for by public subscription. Harrison appealed to Positivists and non-Positivists alike, assuring the latter that a donation did not imply allegiance to Comte's principles. Goldwin Smith was one so persuaded, but Harrison sent doleful letters to Paris about others who dodged his net. Positivists, of course, rallied, even Sir Godfrey Lushington, who had severed his connection with Newton Hall after becoming Permanent Under-Secretary of State in 1885 (he was knighted in 1892). An elderly American whose devotion to Comte went back forty years sent his mite with a query: had Harrison ever tried introducing Positivism to 'princes and potentates'? Congreve, however, sourly opposed the scheme as too secular. He need not have worried. A larger-than-life bust (not the statue proposed) was unveiled in the Place de la Sorbonne—three years after Congreve's death and four years after Comte's centenary. Its massive pedestal was flanked on one side by a seated scholar brooding over a folio representing philosophy, and on the other side by a standing woman holding an infant and a vegetable frond symbolizing humanity's religious aspirations. Vexed by the delay and otherwise occupied, Harrison did not attend the ceremony, but sent a message. Laffitte, whose mental powers had declined markedly ('dying from the top' Ethel called it), made his last public appearance.[148] Early the next year he succumbed to the 'great anti-Positivist' (Quin's term for death), leaving behind a moribund Positivist movement that had failed Harrison's hopes but still engaged his loyalties.

6

Positivism, Politics, and Philosophy

1880–1901

With the Liberals victorious in the General Election in April 1880, Harrison lost no time in trying to radicalize Gladstone's ministry. He urged Sir Charles Dilke to demand a Cabinet post: had not Dilke carried Chelsea, an important London constitutency? He must make Gladstone and Harcourt know him as their equal in Parliament. And he must work closely with other Radicals, especially the newly-elected ones, who were 'keen to do something' because they had not been 'ground down by experience of difficulties in Parliament'. To act was urgent; the Tory had to be 'killed' and 'put in his coffin and not only put in his coffin but [its lid] screwed down, and a brass plate nailed on the top'. There should be no 'dodges about the land or the Church, etc.'. What was wanted was the redistribution of about eighty seats, a county franchise, and an eight o'clock poll. Morley must be found a seat as well; though his 'uncompromising spirit' make him incapable of providing leadership like Dilke's, the Radicals needed his 'tongue and pen and drive'.[1]

The Whiggish nature of the new Cabinet filled Harrison with 'something very like disgust', but he remained optimistic. He assured Dilke, named Under-secretary at the Foreign Office—not a Cabinet post—that the 'arrangement' pleased him more than would any other;[2] and he congratulated Chamberlain on his Cabinet appointment as President of the Board of Trade, though Chamberlain accepted it only by breaking an agreement with Dilke binding each to decline office without the other.[3] To Mundella, made Vice-President of the Committee of Council on Education, Harrison wrote warmly but with a humourous sally about Mundella's fondness for 'certain old Books', an allusion to his Christianity, which to Harrison constituted a drawback since Mundella would be presiding over public schooling.[4] Advocacy of completely secular education may have contributed to Morley's defeat, but there was consolation in his new position as editor of the *Pall Mall Gazette*. Like the *Fortnightly*, which he would still edit simultaneously, it would reliably carry the Radicals' point of view.

Soon enough both Morley and the Government proved disappointing. British troops were not immediately withdrawn from Afghanistan, and at the Battle of Maiwand in July 1880 they suffered their worst defeat in forty years. General Roberts's historic march to Kandahar then secured the safe evacuation of the country, but also—less congenial to Harrison—absolved Roberts of the stigma resulting from his conduct during the occupation of Kabul.[5] Six months later British troops suffered another bitter defeat in the Battle of Majuba Hill in the Transvaal, the Boers having taken up arms to secure the freedom Gladstone had promised and then postponed. This brief war was the subject of a Positivist manifesto in February 1881, and great was Harrison's consternation when Morley only reluctantly accepted it for publication in the *Pall Mall Gazette* and assigned it to an obscure corner. He also declined to print an open letter on the subject from Harrison to Bright unless Harrison removed some of the harshest passages, for in charging Bright with betrayal of his old anti-imperialism, Harrison had (he admitted to Ethel) employed some 'strong' language. Exasperated, Harrison published the letter in two parts in J. Passmore Edwards's *Echo*, a paper whose name proved singularly appropriate, since Harrison consciously echoed Bright's famous Crimean War speech about hearing the Angel of Death, as well as Gladstone's Midlothian admonition about the sanctity of the native homestead.[6]

The Irish, meanwhile, had been pressing their claims to political autonomy less successfully than the Afghans or Boers despite an Irish contingent in Parliament so strong it constituted a 'third party'. The Positivists had new reason to support its members, for they liked to think that the Land League's use of the boycott against evicting landlords fulfilled—unconsciously, of course—Comte's prediction that social 'excommunication' would one day replace law courts. To Harrison and Beesly, Ireland's condition was comparable to that of France on the eve of the Revolution. The Government's Coercion Bill, introduced early in 1881, aroused their wrath, for it gave authorities virtually arbitrary powers of arrest in Ireland, similar, Harrison argued, to the use of *lettres de cachet* during the *Ancien Régime*. Overriding their less aroused colleagues, he and Beesly formulated a Positivist protest while the provisions of the bill were still being debated in the House.[7] Even the Government's conciliatory Land Bill, introduced after the coercion measure, was not entirely welcome; Harrison, who studied its complexities assiduously, complained that it came too late and was too moderate to pacify the Irish, especially since many of their leaders were behind bars. But he confined these reservations to the *Revue Occidentale* and congratulated Dilke for his 'super human' efforts on the bill's behalf.[8] Since it had taken an unprecedented fifty-eight sittings of the House, he then wrote two articles for the *Nineteeth Century* on the less controversial subject of Parliamentary reform, reiterating the pleas for more small committees and shorter, more frequent sittings that he had introduced in *Order and Progress*, and noting that innovations would be more necessary when Gladstone's 'Homeric' presence was gone.[9] Similar suggestions were springing up 'like mushrooms', but the Prime Minister took the trouble to acknowledge Harrison's.[10]

One cause of Parliamentary obstruction during these months was the 'Fourth Party', composed of Randolph Churchill, John Gorst, Henry Drummond Wolff, and Arthur Balfour. Obstreperous Conservatives out to embarrass their own and the Liberal leaders, they earned little sympathy from Harrison. One evening in February 1881, when Churchill was sparing with Gladstone over the Coercion Bill, Harrison, along with Churchill's wife, the notorious Jennie, was a dinner guest of Blanche, the Countess of Airlie, whose granddaughter would one day marry the Churchills' son Winston. Harrison was on good terms with Lady Blanche's brother Lyulph Stanley, and with Ethel had spent the previous August with her sister Rosalind Howard at Naworth Castle, near Carlisle. Now he was struck by the lack of family solidarity shown by his hostess, for she expressed the hope that her brother-in-law George Howard, about to stand in the Liberal interest in a by-election, would be defeated. Her other guests were all Tories also, but it was not this so much as their upper-class ways that he dwelt on in describing the evening to Ethel, who was with his parents in Torquay. The party was made up of the '*crème de la crème suprême*', he said: the Marquess of Blandford, Randolph Churchill's elder brother, and the Marquess of Hamilton, and their wives. Blandford had asked to be invited to meet Harrison, for they shared an interest in the land question. Harrison found him 'sincerely anxious to form right views', but 'rather ignorant'. More engaging was 'Billie' Russell, the famous *Times* correspondent, who praised his letter on the Transvaal war in that day's *Echo* and told amusing stories while becoming 'caressingly drunk'. The amount of food and spirits consumed astounded Harrison, as did his hostess's invitation to the gentlemen to smoke in her drawing room after dinner. It was the ladies who interested him most. They acted impulsively, like 'spoilt children'. Jennie Churchill 'had that peculiar sparkle and southern fire of the finest American beauty. She must have been Trollope's original for the American girl who marries the Duke's son.' She arrived with a 'tame young man about the Marlboro House', and their use of a hired cab surprised him, for his mother had been urging him to buy a carriage for Ethel on the ground that all fine ladies owned their own. Jennie and her escort spent part of the evening cavorting in the hall on the pretext of looking for a Morris pattern in a new carpet. Though the doors were closed against them, their shrieks and laughter could still be heard. All the ladies wore black gowns, simple in style and perfectly fitting, which set off their jewels admirably: 'That is style indeed', he remarked. He also gave the women credit for 'ease, self-possession, alertness, real capacity for grace', but, perhaps thinking of the divorce scandal that barred Lord Blandford and Churchill and their wives from some London houses, he concluded that 'no real goodness can thrive in such a life.'[11]

Harrison's disdain for high society had been fuelled by political radicalism in his youth, and now his own solid intellectual attainments and secure family status additionally precluded any restless seeking to emulate a taskless life of pleasure. Those attainments were confirmed in 1878 by his uncontested election to the Athenaeum Club. In that Parthenon of earned eminence in Waterloo Place he had trouble keeping the waiters from calling him 'Sir Frederic'. Morley had nominated him, and eventually another scorner of titles, Herbert Spencer, proposed him for committee service. All three valued the club's library, and Morley and Harrison welcomed the chance to mingle with notable writers, artists, scientists, and politicians. The Victorian—and Positivist—theme of achievement honoured, which the club and the careers of the three friends illustrated, was one Harrison preached at home to his boys; and it lay behind his faith in the eventual success of their tutor, George Gissing.

Beginning in 1880, Harrison had a new opportunity to glimpse a world very different from that of Mayfair or the Athenaeum. On a July evening at Sutton Place he picked up a new three-decker novel, *Workers in the Dawn*, sent him by the author, then twenty-two and unknown to the public. George Gissing's accompanying letter said the book's harsh treatment of the clergy had offended the reviewers and he hoped for a judgement from someone unencumbered by 'pessimistic creeds'. Harrison's writings, he added, had led him to Comte, who had influenced his 'intellectual development'.[12] With such an introduction, Harrison put aside his belief that most contemporary fiction was not worth reading and sat up far into the night with the novel. The next morning he wrote to the author to express his admiration of its literary power and to say that he would like to meet him in London. He did not hide his objections to the book's portrayal of London low life, but he promised to recommend the work to literary friends. In a postscript he said he trusted his wife's judgement in fiction more than his own, and she had praised the book's presentation of the highest type of working man and thought it full enough to make six stories, though she also asked 'Where are the "Workers in the Dawn"?'[13]

To Harrison their absence was probably less serious than the advice the Positivist heroine gives the protagonist, long familiar with poverty, when he inherits money. She urges him not to adopt a life of philanthropy, which has ruined her health, but to recognize that he was 'born to be an artist'. It is no wonder that Harrison thought the book's 'social and moral aim' might not be 'sufficiently strong to justify the deliberate painting of so much brutality', but that did not prevent him from recommending the work to '*eight* literary friends' (in Gissing's proud words to his brother), including Kegan Paul and Morley, 'who made Arnold read it'.[14] Culture apparently could do nothing for the young man, but journalism gave him a chance. Morley commissioned him to write on socialism for the *Pall Mall Gazette*,[15] and through Beesly's recommendation Turgenev engaged him to report quarterly on British politics for a Russian journal.[16] Meanwhile, learning that Gissing supported himself by tutoring, in early December Harrison asked him to take over the lessons of nine-year-old Bernard and seven-year-old Austin. Until then Ethel, in good Positivist fashion, had been their teacher except for Latin, which Harrison taught them himself. (Godfrey and René were still in the charge of a governess.) But an undiagnosed ailment now reconciled Ethel to turning over her responsibility to her husband's new young friend while she sought to recover her strength at 'The Brambles', the 'sweetest nest' the Bridges had recently built in Wimbledon. There the childless Mary Bridges cosseted her and the good doctor monitored her symptoms and read Turgenev aloud to them evenings. At 38 Westbourne Terrace Bernard and Austin were delighted with their new tutor from the moment they first spied his slender form, handsome features, and dark wavy hair. After their father's sternness over their blotted copy books, and their mother's subdued sweetness, which made it painful to be disobedient, Gissing's youthful boisterous laughter was refreshing. When Ethel returned home later in the month, still in indifferent health, they were happy to learn that Gissing would be their permanent teacher in the new year, and he, given a generous retaining fee for the holidays, was equally satisfied.[17]

A cold kept Gissing away for a week in February 1881, making Harrison realize how dependent he had become on the young man. Ethel was in Torquay, and he busy preparing for the opening of Newton Hall a few months away, Positivist manifestos on the Transvaal and the Coercion Bill, and the second of two essays for Knowles on

'Creeds Old and New'. Teaching the boys became a troublesome distraction; being responsible for them, six servants, a horse, a dog, and the house proved more than he had bargained for; and to add to his frustrations it snowed, the roof leaked, a pipe burst, and a servant boy disgraced him by appearing in public in a shabby coat (for punishment Harrison set him Bible verses to copy). Complaining of all this to Ethel he said he feared losing his temper in the schoolroom, where the boys were as slack as the sons of George and Rosalind Howard.[18] When Gissing returned, Harrison therefore did everything he could to keep him well and content: he made him leave his slippers in the schoolroom, since wet feet were thought to have caused his cold; allowed him to begin his teaching later to permit more time in the mornings for his 'true work', writing; and, because he looked undernourished, kept him often for luncheon.[19] Even the suspicion that Gissing was proving a 'duffer at teaching' did not make Harrison any less considerate or prevent him from getting Gissing more pupils, Alfred Bailey's son, for example, and Vernon Lushington's gifted daughters.[20]

Nor was Harrison put off by the 'strange sad story' Gissing told him one morning after meeting an old school friend at 38 Westbourne Terrace. This may have been Charles Gaskell Higginson, the Manchester Positivist whose years at Owens College had overlapped Gissing's.[21] He would have known about the abrupt end of Gissing's very promising career as a student there in 1876, when he had been caught stealing money from fellow students in order to reclaim a young prostitute with whom he had fallen in love. After a month in prison at hard labour, young Gissing wandered about the United States, sometimes near starvation, before returning to London to devote himself to fiction, writing a good deal before a small inheritance enabled him to pay for the publication of *Workers in the Dawn*. Harrison not only listened to Gissing's account of these events sympathetically, but commiserated when he told of having an ailing wife whose doctor's bills and medicines he could scarcely afford.[22] This was the same girl, Marianne Helen, who five years before had ruined his college career; her maiden name, coincidentally, was Harrison. When her drunkenness and violence became so uncontrollable that a policeman advised Gissing to obtain a divorce, Harrison not only seconded the suggestion but gave Gissing the impression he would advance the money for it. Gissing in the end found divorce impossible, but he had already decided that he and his wife must live apart, and on one occasion Ethel offered to find lodgings for her.[23]

The Harrisons' response to Gissing's marital problem was, of course, at odds with their religion, but no more so than had been their acceptance of the Leweses' 'marriage'. The fact that Harrison's old friendship with George Eliot ended in the same half-year in which his new friendship with George Gissing began sheds light on both Harrison's hopes for Positivism and his literary associations. Just two months before he first heard of Gissing, Harrison had been forced to confront new evidence of her incomplete adherence to Positivism. She had sent John Cross, a close family friend twenty years her junior and the brother-in-law of the Positivist Francis Otter, to inform Harrison of their imminent marriage. She wished to ascertain the Positivists' response to the news. Harrison assured Cross, whom he already knew, that he would not dream of applying the Positivist doctrine of eternal widowhood to anyone 'aloof from our ways and our thoughts'.[24] In reality he was deeply offended, so much so that he avoided the Crosses when they returned from their European wedding trip in July. Learning on 23 December of her sudden death, he sent the grieving husband a message excusing his failure to have called on them;[25] but to Morley years later he would confess how glad he was that he had never seen her as 'Mrs Cross'.[26] When Herbert Spencer solicited his opinion as to whether Cross should seek to bury her in Westminster Abbey, Harrison advised against it on the ground that a religious service would be inappropriate.[27] Yet he attended her burial in Highgate Cemetery, which was preceded 'by a Unitarian service in the chapel conducted by Dr Thomas Sadler, who had presided over Lewes's service there two years before. Harrison rode in the fourth mourning carriage with George Howard and, ironically, two men associated with *Daniel Deronda*, the novel that to him had revealed how great was the gap between her religious aspirations and his own: Frederick Burton, whose illustrations for the novel she cherished, and Edmund Gurney, the psychic researcher whom Leslie Stephen thought provided some of Deronda's characteristics. Beesly and Congreve also attended, riding in separate carriages.[28] All the Positivists were no doubt gratified to hear 'The Choir Invisible' quoted, but they did not exaggerate her attachment to their creed when commenting on her death. Beesly in his 1881 New Year's Day Address a few days later called her only a partial adherent of their views, as did Harrison, in writing to Laffitte, but he added that her death was a 'profound loss to the movement'.[29]

All the more welcome, therefore, were the signs the young Gissing was already showing of interest in Positivism. Whereas George Eliot seems never to have disclosed, even to the Positivists, the extent of her devotion to Comte's works—for example, she copied out many passages over the years in her notebooks[30]—Gissing gave the appearance of an enthusiastic convert. By early November he had attended a meeting of

the Positivist Society at the Harrisons' house (which of course George
Eliot, as a woman, could never have done even if she had wished to),
he was recommending Comte's works to his family, and was even
dating his letters by Comte's calendar. Just before Laffitte's visit for
the inauguration of Newton Hall in May 1881, Gissing was worrying
about whether his French would allow him to converse with the director
of international Positivism.[31]

But Harrison was due for another disappointment: within a year
Gissing had become disenchanted. He expressed his new position in an
essay, 'The Hope of Pessimism', which he did not seek to publish out of
concern for offending the Harrisons, whom he still saw frequently
when he came to teach.[32] In it, in his correspondence with the Harrisons,
and in his next published novel, *The Unclassed*, in 1884, he left no
doubt about their intellectual differences. Both essay and novel argue
that the common human lot is to be unhappy and the artist alone is
justified in optimism, for he finds material for his art in mankind's
wretchedness. When Harrison repudiated the novel's 'moral
dynamite',[33] Gissing contritely offered to sever his ties with the family;
but soon afterwards he was telling Ethel of his low spirits and his
'preposterous' circumstances, a clear bid for her sympathy and the
continuation of the old relationship.[34]

Nor did Ethel fail him. She, after all, had been schooled in the
handling of misanthropic novelists of working-class life by dealing with
Overton. And Harrison could not afford to relinquish so valuable a
member of their household. When Ethel became too ill to go on a
family holiday in the Lake District in August, 1884, Harrison stayed
with her at Sutton Place and sent Gissing with the four boys and two
servants. Lodged in an old farmhouse called Bonscale, on Lake
Ullswater, known to the Harrisons from previous visits, he and his
charges climbed and rowed, and one day Gissing revelled in a solitary
walk from Patterdale to Grasmere and back.[35] When he left after a
fortnight, his place was taken by Ethel's brother Crawford, who had
just completed his Oxford degree. For their last two weeks the boys
enjoyed more organized sports at the nearby Howtown Hotel with the
three sons of Montague Cookson, brother of Charles, whose Wordsworth connections had impressed Harrison as a boy.[36] Gissing 'benefited
prodigiously' from the fortnight.[37] Ironically, he introduced Ullswater
as a setting in *Thyrza* (1887) in which an idealistic young man's lectures
to working men in a centre something like Newton Hall prove largely
futile; and he mentioned the area again in *The Private Papers on Henry
Ryecroft* (1903), about the life of ease enjoyed by a Gissingesque
character who recalls bitterly the uncongenial work of his youth—
obviously tutoring.

Back in London in September Bernard and Austin had a few more lessons from Gissing[38] and then entered St. Paul's School, an old foundation newly re-located in the Hammersmith Road. It was far better appointed than King's College School in the Strand, and a school friend of Harrison's was on the staff. The 'unsurpassed' headmaster was Frederick William Walker, well known to all the Wadham Positivists and, more crucial, to Jowett, an Old Boy of St. Paul's who smoothed the way of its best graduates to Balliol.[39] Gratified that Bernard had obtained a Foundation Scholarship, Harrison asked Gissing to consider adding Godfrey and René to his growing list of students. But Gissing declined, and predicted to his brother that he would be seeing little more of the Harrisons. 'Nor could it be otherwise', he added, 'we were so little kin. I never met more conventional people.'[40]

Yet Gissing himself was becoming more conventional, partly from associating with the Harrisons. He was 'getting to like the atmosphere of cultured families', and when Bernard wrote inviting him to dinner in 1886 he felt slighted because the invitation had not come from Ethel.[41] He could look back on his relations with the family with pleasure except, perhaps, when he recalled the actual tutoring. He had enjoyed talking literature with Harrison, and getting Ethel to play the piano for him. Sutton Place, where he had taught the boys in summers, held great delights—writing poetry in a punt on the River Wey, rambling along the lovely Surrey roads, and once joining the family for a picnic tea laid out by five servants and presided over by old Mrs Harrison. The house itself was a wonderful place to read or dream in. He conceded that it was fortunate the occupants were the Harrisons, and not some 'retired rag, bone, and bottle dealer who would have broken the stained glass windows because they kept out the light'.[42] Spending a day at the Hermitage, in Elstead, another sixteenth-century house in Surrey which the Harrisons occupied for part of 1885 and 1886, Gissing was pleased to find that, though much less grand than Sutton Place, it too was 'far beyond the reach of ruffiandom'.[43]

If most of Gissing's fictional characters existed within the reach of ruffiandom, some enjoyed the pleasures of an affluent world the Harrisons revealed to him. The heroine of *Isabel Clarendon* (1886) lives in a sixteenth-century house named Knightswell after a legendary spring reminiscent of Muswell's, about which Gissing may have heard from Harrison.[44] And Isabel's past—she was married at nineteen to a much older, wealthy Liberal barrister, the son of a stockbroker—duplicates Ethel's. Since Isabel is a widow, Gissing may have been indulging in a fantasy, for she is attracted to the hero, a Gissingesque youth, but he feels too socially inferior to welcome her advances. Gissing was not immune to Ethel's charm; indeed he even found her portrait by W. B. Richmond (painted in the manner of the 'great Florentines' according to *The Times*) the only canvas of interest at the Grosvenor Gallery in 1884.[45] But in 'The Lady of the Dedication', a short story, he may have more realistically depicted his relationship to the Harrisons, and perhaps for this reason did not publish it. The hero, a writer, lives near Tottenham Court Road, as Gissing once did, and is close to starving. He loves a nursemaid in a family much like the Harrisons, who in fact had a nursemaid for the two younger boys during Gissing's years at Westbourne Terrace. The husband in this family studies the Irish Land Bill and is preoccupied with his writing and editing, while his wife graciously manages the house and supervises the care of three young children—one of whom is named Godfrey.[46]

Whether or not Gissing really entertained fantasies about Ethel, he viewed Harrison as benevolent but not entirely congenial. He often mentioned Harrison's kindness but complained of his lack of humour, once citing his inability to appreciate the comic indecencies of *Venice Preserv'd*. Harrison, for his part, thought Gissing a 'sort of amateur Fakir of modern slum life' with a 'taste for misery' even when he could afford to live better.[47] Austin later put their incompatibility in other terms. His father 'could not understand a man who knew all about the sordid conditions of poorer London and yet had no religion. Gissing could not understand a man talking about religion who did not know all about London's sordid ugliness.'[48] The difference between them is further suggested in the way each expressed compassion for victims of mischance. When a workhouse fire killed some children on Christmas day in 1883, Gissing wrote a poem for Ethel forbidding mourning on the ground that they had escaped the 'heat and burden of noon'. When the following year contractors repairing Whitley's department store in Westbourne Grove sought to deny benefits to workmen injured on the job, Harrison and C. S. Roundell collected funds for their legal and living expenses.[49]

During the years of their closest intimacy, Gissing came to regard the reform of fiction as more important than any attempts on his part to reform society, while Harrison continued to juggle religious and political concerns. The many crises of Gladstone's second ministry were especially frustrating because as an outsider he could only speculate about their significance even though he sometimes acted as if he could influence policy. One such crisis was the Phoenix Park assassinations on 6 May 1882 of Lord Frederick Cavendish, the new Chief Secretary for Ireland, and Thomas Henry Burke, the permanent Under-Secretary.

Ethel had taken Austin to Brighton for his health, and on the first night of her absence Harrison experienced 'one of those fits of depression most people have—but I never'. The next morning, a Sunday, he heard of the Dublin murders and declared he had 'long looked for this' and 'deplored' the 'miserable prospect'. Yet at the Athenaeum everyone showed 'quiet self control', even W. E. Forster, though he might have been lying dead in Cavendish's place if he had not resigned as Irish Secretary over Parnell's release from gaol during the recent mood of conciliation. Riding in the park Harrison saw other MPs who looked unperturbed, but he heard the next day that the brokers were 'roaring like mad bulls' in the City.'[50]

It was the financial interests in the City that Harrison blamed for another political crisis in 1882. When Gladstone's government began to fear that Arabi Pasha, minister of war in the Khedive's regime in Cairo, was threatening the dual control Britain and France had set up to protect the bondholders to whom the Khedive was hopelessly in debt, a British naval unit was ordered to Alexandria. Perhaps because he did not wish to offend Laffitte, who looked more benignly upon the Egyptian adventure than did the English Positivists, Harrison acted independently of Newton Hall to revive the idea of an Anti-Aggression League he and Herbert Spencer had talked about during the 1879 Afghan War. With Morley, Hughes, Bryce, Fremantle, Sir Arthur Hobhouse, and others, including MPs, they held a public meeting on 22 February to announce their intention of opposing any British aggression and promoting Parliamentary control over foreign affairs.[51] In later speeches and published letters Harrison sounded a theme most provocatively stated by him in the *Pall Mall Gazette*, 'Money, Sir, Money, is the sole motive of this act of war', an analysis A. J. P. Taylor has called the 'first, rather crude attempt to expose the financial basis of Imperialism'.[52] Some of the League's members were less bold. Morley, for example, challenged Harrison to show why Britain should leave Egypt and the Suez Canal to foreigners. In reply, Harrison argued that Britain could justify a more active role in Cairo only if foreign intervention appeared likely; until then he would endorse Arabi's demand of 'Egypt for the Egyptians'.[53] He reaffirmed this in an open letter to the Prime Minister on 1 July, accusing him of compromising his Midlothian principles.[54] Gladstone denied the charge, but it seemed confirmed in less than a fortnight when the fleet bombarded Alexandria.[55] Later a force under General Wolseley pursued and defeated Arabi's army at Tel-el-Kebir. By then most of the League's MPs had dropped out, unwilling to embarrass the Government further, and Spencer soon decided he had ruined his health in the agitation and must retire from public life. Harrison was dismayed but not despairing; he had already found a more pertinacious ally in Wilfrid Scawen Blunt.

In many ways Blunt proved more congenial than the self-protective politicians and the valetudinarian Spencer. Nine years Harrison's junior, he was an ex-diplomat with useful connections abroad and with both parties at home. Exceptionally handsome, and capable of high spirits, he was familiar with the part of England Harrison had come to love, for he had been born and partly brought up in Petworth, Sussex, owned by Lady Leconfield, his aunt. His wife was the granddaughter of Byron, whom Harrison had called 'our greatest poet since Milton' in *The Times* a decade earlier,[56] and Blunt was a poet himself. Harrison may not have known that his new friend's amorous proclivities quite matched those of his wife's famous ancestor, but he was probably struck by the parallel of Blunt's undertaking the cause of the Egyptians just as Byron had fought for the Greeks. Blunt had been airing his opposition to the British presence in Egypt without success before meeting Harrison, and he later declared that if they had become acquainted sooner they might have changed the course of events.[57] Throughout their co-operation Harrison felt obliged to restrain Blunt lest he publish something libellous, and, when George Howard also recommended caution, Blunt made his open letter to Gladstone incisive but without personally offensive matter. Harrison followed suit with a letter of his own in July.[58] He, of course, had the Positivists to reinforce his appeal, and since they issued a manifesto declaring that under some circumstances 'fidelity to party' became a 'crime', they were pleased when Bright resigned from the Cabinet in protest over the bombardment of Alexandria. Alluding to that act of political courage, Francis Newman credited the Positivists with having 'snatched from the Quakers the garland of honour for prompt and overt protest against our Egyptian iniquity'.[59]

Yet in the midst of the crisis Harrison removed himself from the controversy by taking himself and his family (and would have taken Gissing, had he consented) to Ste Adresse, Normandy, for a late summer holiday. Sitting on the esplanade, with the tricolor fluttering gaily overhead and the flowers blooming nearby, Fred and Ethel probably looked remarkably like the couple in Monet's painting of just this scene sixteen years earlier. Harrison spent part of the holiday drafting a family history from details Ethel and he had been assembling since his father's death. He must often have thought of his father's generous hospitality and attention to the details of life, for there was much amiss in the old farmhouse Harrison had engaged. Though he had specified that 'cleanliness' and 'healthiness' were important requirements, he found that the roof over Austin's bed leaked and in the rain the room soon became flooded. When the boy cried out in alarm and his father responded fully dressed, Austin asked why he had not been asleep. 'I read, and someday I expect you will too', Harrison replied. Curious to see for himself, Austin stole downstairs one morning and found him asleep in his chair, a book on the floor beside him, and looking, for once, quite calm. With unaccustomed familiarity Austin crept closer and stroked his father's greying whiskers, 'a wholly intimate and possessive caress'.[60]

Back in London that autumn Harrison found Blunt raising funds for the legal defence of Arabi, who was to be tried in Cairo. It seemed 'a cruel thing to leave Blunt to bear it all', but Harrison saw that their situations differed. Blunt had encouraged Arabi's rebellion and so felt responsible for his plight, whereas his own efforts had been confined to admonishing the British government. Moreover, he had come to believe that Gladstone and his colleagues were 'resolved to save Arabi's life and to expel him from Egypt' and were 'using the trial to threaten the Sultan and the Khedive and the Pashas' while enjoying the idea of Blunt and his friends 'saddled with costs'. Since as a lawyer Harrison knew these could 'increase at will', he urged Blunt to act cautiously.[61] Far from taking his advice, Blunt eventually spent £3,000 of his own money on Arabi's defence, while Harrison contributed ten guineas and helped the Positivists collect another £62. When Arabi was given a sentence of death that was commuted to exile, Harrison's prediction appeared to be accurate. Blunt announced himself content and arranged to have Arabi sent to Ceylon, where, Blunt liked to think, Adam had fled after losing Paradise. The Positivists, unbeguiled by such fancies, but also less attuned than Blunt to political realities, got Bright to present a petition to Parliament calling for Arabi's complete freedom.[62]

Not only did the Positivists fail to attain their objective—Arabi went to Ceylon—but they soon realized that the British were remaining in Egypt. Instead of objecting, however, Harrison said he could condone the occupation so long as it stopped short of annexation. He even joined Blunt in opposing the suggestion that other European nations should share the Anglo-French responsibility for Egyptian affairs. No trustee should delegate his duty, Harrison declared in 1884, citing the 'sacred principles of equity law' and for good measure calling Gladstone's Cabinet more 'seriously desirous of the good of Egypt than any other Cabinet in Europe'.[63] But soon goals came to seem less important than means. The emergence of the Mahdi in the Sudan led the Government late that year to dispatch General Charles 'Chinese'

Gordon to evacuate Khartoum in an attempt to avoid military confrontation. While the fate of Gordon and the city hung in the balance, Harrison told Morley that Gladstone was a 'wonderful war horse but the Nile will drown him yet';[64] and in his New Year's Day 1885 Address to the Positivists he credited Gladstone with 'resisting the forward policy' in Egypt, but said that by showing 'weakness before powerful clamour' he had incurred responsibility for the crisis in the Sudan, for 'the cause of civilization is not served by launching amongst savages a sort of Pentateuch knight errant.' The journalists who were treating Gordon as a martyr were 'parasites of the parasites of our great Liberal statesman'.[65]

The most objectionable of these journalists in Harrison's eyes was W. T. Stead, who had made his mark denouncing the Bulgarian atrocities and then assisted Morley at the *Pall Mall Gazette*. With Morley's entry into Parliament in 1883 to fill the seat left vacant by the death of Ashton Dilke, the brother of Charles, Stead became editor. It was a change deplored by Harrison since he held Stead accountable for Morley's reluctance to oppose the Government during the Transvaal war.[66] But when the massacre of Gordon's force at Khartoum became known in England in February 1885, Harrison had to concede that even without Stead at his elbow Morley was undependable in the Radical cause. After the Conservatives moved a vote of censure on the Government's Sudan policy, he framed an amendment that exculpated Gladstone, explaining to Harrison that 'we must keep the Old Man in.'[67] A month earlier Harrison had been urging Morley and Leonard Courtney to act with the anti-imperialist Radicals and leave Gladstone, Chamberlain, Dilke, and others behind the Egyptian imbroglio to 'take care of themselves'.[68] But in calmer moments he followed Morley's lead: addressing the Peace Society in March, Harrison said he discerned in the nation 'gratifying signs' of 'good sense' that would 'forbid the further prosecution of the war'.[69]

Unlike Beesly, who initiated a public meeting to protest against continuation of the war in the Sudan,[70] Harrison was more comfortable working with party Liberals than against them. During the years in which Gladstone's Irish and African policies were so often provoking his wrath, he was always ready to forgive and forget once a crisis had passed. And he was consolidating friendships with leading Liberals in a variety of ways during these years. Early in 1882, for example, being 'absurdly interested' in the new Royal Courts of Justice, G. E. Street's Gothic castle then being completed in the Strand, he made proposals for the building's inauguration to George Shaw–Lefevre, Gladstone's first Commissioner of Public Works, and wrote an essay on the history of the courts that appeared in *The Times* on the morning of the opening by the Queen. As he noted in his essay, she declined to follow his proposal that she hear some 'formal motion' as a 'symbolic gesture' recalling the ancient Curia Regis. Still, there was pageantry enough to fulfil his expectation that it would be 'like a play', and he was proud to march in the procession with fellow members of the Inns of Court.[71]

The 'mass of learning carefully concealed' that Harrison said his essay contained was historical, not architectural. His law colleague Frederick Pollock would later comment on Harrison's 'charitable reticence' in dealing with the 'lifeless late Victorian Gothic' design of 'the most inconvenient public building in Europe'.[72] Not altogether concealed, however, was Harrison's criticism of the judicial system's anomalies. Earlier in 1882 he had devoted two *Fortnightly* essays to the 'curiosities' in the law of treason.[73] In 1885 he began serving with Fitzjames Stephen, Sir Henry Maine, Godfrey Lushington, Charles Bowen (now a judge), and Lords Bramwell, Lingen, Acton, and Coleridge on a committee appointed by the Lord Chancellor to publish historical State trials after 1820, the year at which an earlier committee had left off. (The reports, some culled from rare publications, were edited by John Macdonell, brother of James, the Scottish journalist.)[74] And when Maine died in 1888, Harrison served as his old mentor's literary executor and, with Frederick Pollock, edited Maine's lectures on international law.[75]

As his appointment to the State Trials Committee suggests, Harrison did not lose all favour in Liberal circles by criticizing the Government's Irish and imperial policies. In March 1884 Liberal officials in Leicester invited him to stand in the by-election necessitated by the death of Peter Taylor. G. J. Holyoake offered to become the candidate but was rejected, and Spencer, invited a month before Harrison, had refused the nomination. Harrison, too, declined, saying he preferred to form rather than represent public opinion. He pointed out that since Parliamentary government required party discipline, members had to vote on grounds other than conviction at times, and his own political aims would make that difficult. They were too advanced for some Liberals, too conservative for others: he would wish to resist any increase in empire, deny the state control over religion and education, and remedy Parliament's paralysis caused by its involvement in administration. At the same time he wanted Irish Home Rule, more local government, and land laws that made the owner and cultivator one. The last two goals distinguish his political individualism from that of Spencer, who had, like Harrison, told the Leicester officials that he preferred to influence opinion from outside Parliament.[76] Spencer was, of course, entirely unsuited for Parliamentary life, whereas Harrison could have been effective. And he apparently did not believe that independent views necessarily made a man unfit for political service. When Beesly over-looked Comte's proscription against spiritual leaders seeking temporal power and stood for the Liberals in Westminster in the General Election in 1885, Harrison endorsed his candidacy, partly, he said, because Beesly would be like Mill and Morley in his independence if elected (he was not).[77]

One of the political goals Harrison included in his statement to the Leicester Liberals was that hardy perennial of the Radicals, land reform. Ignoring the role of conveyancers like himself in perpetuating the old land transfer system, he asked his Oxford law students in 1880 to sit an examination paper on the social and economic objections to the land laws, which he had just denounced in the *Revue Occidentale* as 'absolument vicieux'.[78] But in 1878 he distinguished between the land system in England, where it was 'exceedingly rare' to find a landowner who 'takes all and gives nothing', and that of Ireland, where abuses justified the 'extinction of landlordism'.[79] The debate took on new urgency after Henry George brought his single tax scheme to England in the early 1880s. Receiving from George his pamphlet denouncing British radicals for being half-hearted about Irish land reform, Harrison urged Lord Bramwell, his old adversary in the Political Economy Club, to reply, and was in turn urged by Bramwell to do so himself.[80] One attempt was disconcerting. Armed with statistics, he went to the Trades Union Congress in Nottingham in 1883 to argue in a scheduled address on the history of unions that, since they had become virtually benefit societies because of the small number of strikes in the worsening economy, they should concentrate on their own economic problems and eschew larger questions. To strengthen their finances he suggested that the more affluent members should forgo their retirement benefits. This whimsical notion perhaps explains why the TUC leaders cancelled his address at a later session: the topic was land reform, one they now knew he believed should not concern them. He publicly dismissed the affront as a 'slight misunderstanding', but privately vowed to attend no more of their congresses. Before leaving Nottingham he indulged his upper-class tastes by touring two large estates that, in his view, exemplified the advantages of consolidated landed wealth. At Wollaton, an Elizabethan manor, he marvelled at the picture collection and at the underground stables and gas fittings of the estate's colliery; and at Newstead Abbey he rejoiced to find Byron's ancestral home improved beyond the poet's 'wildest dreams', though happily still possessed of its romantic 'odour of fate and ruin'.[81]

In his undelivered TUC address, published in the *Pall Mall Gazette*, Harrison called George's single tax more objectionable than Alfred Russel Wallace's land nationalization scheme, for Wallace would at least compensate the owners. Yet George's criticism of the existing system he thought had some merit.[82] He was, therefore, among those who assembled at St. James's Hall early in 1884 to welcome the American reformer as he embarked on his second mission to Great Britain.[83] Shortly afterwards, both men carried their messages on land reform to the North. In Edinburgh, five hundred people turned out to hear Harrison at the Philosophical Institute despite a storm that brought the barometer to the lowest point reached in the British Isles for 120 years. The 'boisterous and jolly' classicist John Stuart Blackie enlivened the occasion by banging his gold-headed cane on the platform, shouting 'At last I found a Radical who has common sense!' In touring the city Harrison had the best possible guide, the future urban planner Patrick Geddes. Harrison had known him at Chapel Street a decade earlier, when the brilliant twenty-year-old, discontented with the rationalism of Huxley at Imperial College, had drifted into Congreve's circle and begun his lifelong interest in Comte and sociology. Now an Edinburgh University lecturer in botany, he was applying Comtean thought to economics and would soon open a Social Union modelled on Newton Hall, to whose funds he had been contributing.[84] But Harrison recognized that the restless and versatile reformer could never be an orthodox disciple of anyone's. Nor did he expect conformity in his host in the next city to which he took his campaign against Henry George. This was Malcolm Quin, who met him at the Newcastle railway station—the occasion on which Harrison's change of gloves caused a momentary *contretemps*. Quin whisked him off to address his followers at the iron church, and later in the day Harrison delivered his scheduled talk on Henry George to a Sunday lecture society. In the chair was Robert Spence Watson, founder of the National Liberal Federation, which had been giving much attention to the land issue, and who, with Quin's assistance, had engineered Morley's ticklish nomination and election as MP for Newcastle the year before. While Harrison was invoking Positivist principles against George's brand of socialism, that same evening George was invoking Mosaic law in a Dundee pulpit as its justification.[85]

In Edinburgh Harrison had stayed in the comfortable house of a seventy-year-old industrialist with philanthropic interests, Robert Miller. 'Kindly, intelligent, and genial', he reminded Harrison of his father; and he proved paternal indeed at the end of the year. Remaining anonymous to the public, Miller gave Harrison and six trustees £1,000 with which to hold a conference on 'Industrial Remuneration' in London. The Statistical Society arranged the meetings, which were held from 28 to 30 January 1885 in Prince's Hall, Piccadilly. Harrison persuaded Dilke to act as chairman after Morley turned him down with the comment that he was more content with politics, which required less study than economics, for you had only to 'lay about you with a quarter staff'. In the *Pall Mall Gazette* Harrison explained that the conference would be free of party character, its model being the Social Science Association meetings of 1860. *The Times* wondered if anything useful could come from the diversity of opinion to be represented. The topics, too, were far-ranging: whether industrial production had benefited capital or labour more; whether there were 'remediable causes' for unemployment and low wages; and whether wider distribution of capital and land, or their management by the state, would improve community welfare. In his remarks to the delegates Dilke cited a need for the 'mental and moral development of the people', and Harrison and Beesly orchestrated that theme when their turn to speak came, Harrison calling George's appeal to the rights of man and will of God 'more fitting to a negro camp meeting than to an industrial society'. Other speakers expressed predictable views. John Burns, representing the newly-formed Social Democratic Federation, compared the Positivists' reliance on moral reform to an attempt to moralize a boa constrictor coiled around its victim. Geddes, speaking for his Social Union, declared urban housing reform a central issue. Morley, the biographer of Cobden, hailed free trade. Balfour, heir to vast Scottish estates, warned that heavy land taxes would upset credit arrangements. Wallace and Francis Newman argued for land nationalization, while Lord Bramwell opposed it with economic theory and the Revd Stewart Headlam with Christian teaching. Bernard Shaw, making his first important appearance in public for the Fabians, likened landowners to burglars.[86]

Since the Industrial Remuneration Conference has been termed noteworthy largely as an early platform for English socialists, there is irony in Harrison's having arranged it and, at its conclusion, edited the papers.[87] Alfred Russel Wallace, with whom he exchanged barbs in *The Times* over their respective presentations, eventually received £500 from the benevolent Miller to 'help the toiling millions', whereas the efficient Harrison spent so little of Miller's subvention that the remainder financed lectures in Scotland by Wallace, William Morris, Geddes, and others.[88] Meanwhile, forgetting the toiling millions momentarily, Miller sent Harrison a de luxe edition of *Modern Painters* (*Unto this Last* would have been more appropriate) and at his death in 1898 left him £100.[89].

In June 1885 the Liberals left office and the political world began preparing for a general election to be held in November. It would be the first with the greatly enlarged franchise produced by the 1884 Reform Act and the concomitant redistribution of seats. Both innovations had been high on Harrison's list of political goals. Since much other legislation he had looked for had not materialized, he welcomed *The Radical Programme*, the collection of anonymous *Fortnightly Review* articles published in July with an introduction by Joseph Chamberlain, its 'onlie begetter'. The essays' proposals for tax and land reform, stronger local government, and disestablishment all coincided with Harrison's own political goals. Immured for the summer and early autumn in Elstead, a sleepy hamlet of some ten houses that had changed little over the centuries, he now decided that the difference between land reform in Ireland and in England was not so crucial as he had been suggesting; the call for more small landowners in England, he informed Morley, was only a return to 'old principles' needed to combat 'a growing Socialism and Communism, and a land hunger in democracy which threatens to swallow up English society'.[90] *The Radical Programme* was Chamberlain's bid for leadership of the Liberal party, which Harrison, for one, was prepared to endorse, having become convinced that the ex-screw manufacturer from Birmingham was 'much more vital than that old ass of a G.O.M., who ... has never got over the secret fear of *great* people and *safe* people, in which as a promising young plutocrat of the old school he was bred up'.[91] Dilke, as Chamberlain's closest associate, seemed likely at last to take an important place in the next Liberal government. But as the summer wore on, developments in the outer world dramatically changed Harrison's relations with both men, and within a year he found himself closer to the Liberal leadership than either.

THE TEMPORAL ORDER

Nothing better illustrates Harrison's multiple perspectives on late Victorian political and social life than the divorce suit brought in August 1885 by Donald Crawford naming Sir Charles Dilke as sole co-respondent.[92] Crawford, who had been legal secretary to the Lord Advocate in Gladstone's recent government, was a Lincoln's Inn barrister and, until his marriage in 1881, the first secular Fellow of Lincoln College, Oxford, appointed during the rectorship of Mark Pattison, to whom he had been devoted. And there was a further association with Harrison. Crawford's wife, Virginia, was one of six daughters of the wealthy shipbuilder and Liberal MP for Tynemouth,

Thomas Eustace Smith, and his flamboyant and socially ambitious wife. Two of their other daughters were Helen, wife of Harrison's brother Robert, and Maye, widow of Sir Charles Dilke's brother Ashton. At the time of his suit, Crawford was planning to contest the seat for North-East Lanark in the November elections. Perhaps because of his political ambitions he had not acted sooner against his wife, whose adulteries had been the subject of anonymous letters he had been receiving for some years. It was her confession, naming Dilke as her seducer, that finally gave him grounds, and he remained fixed in his resolve to rid himself of her, though Liberal party leaders sought to dissuade him from his course. Even before the trial Dilke protested his innocence in a letter to his Chelsea constituents, and they returned him in the election that November; but in the election the following July he was defeated in the general Liberal débâcle.

The Harrisons were on visiting terms with all the persons central to the scandal but may not have known that Dilke had had illicit relations with the mother of Virginia and Helen when they were children. To Ethel, Mrs Smith seemed 'a little fond of show', but, she added, 'who is perfect?' Fred thought Mrs Smith's daughters looked and behaved like actresses. Still, there was no denying the pleasure of talking politics with the Smiths at either their Prince's Gate house, with its Pre-Raphaelite décor, or at their country place in Thames Ditton, where they claimed to have instituted the week-end house party.[93] The Crawfords had residences in both London and Edinburgh (next to Robert Miller's, Harrison learned). And the Robert Harrisons moved among various residences—a London house, a country place on the Thames, Sutton Place, and hotels abroad. The two couples shared not only affluence but a striking disparity in age: Virginia Smith was eighteen when she married Donald Crawford, then forty-four, and Helen Smith nineteen when she married Robert Harrison, then forty. Moreover, Emily Strong Pattison, to whom Dilke had been secretly engaged when the scandal broke, and whom he married in the midst of it, was twenty-seven years younger than Harrison's and Crawford's friend, the late Rector of Lincoln, whose last days had been embittered by her attachment to Dilke.

To Fred and Ethel, thriving in their own December–June marriage, these differences in years may not have seemed an adequate explanation for the discontent of the wives, which in any case could hardly justify their infidelities. The Harrisons had known the Smiths since early in their own marriage, for they were in the same London social set. Harrison registered no surprise when he described Robert's bringing Helen Smith, then eighteen, to Sutton Place to meet the family a year before their marriage in 1877. Mr Harrison found her 'pretty' and 'quite natural', and Fred had played tennis with her until he injured his leg.[94] The death of Robert and Helen's first-born child from diphtheria in 1882 was a sorrow felt by all the Harrisons.[95] That Helen apparently attempted suicide at the time may have had as much to do with guilt as with bereavement. Only a few months earlier, while Robert lay temporarily paralysed in St. George's Hospital after a fall from his horse, Helen and Virginia had entertained medical students from the hospital in rented rooms nearby. Helen was introducing her sister to the excitements of adultery quite independent of anything Dilke may have shown her. The sisters, apparently unrepentant, later shared the favours of an army officer whom Virginia probably once hoped to marry.

Fred and Ethel were in Elstead when the divorce suit was announced in early August, and it was from there that he wrote to Morley some weeks later professing to know nothing of 'this black C. W. D. business' except that 'my brother growls, mutters, and curses somebody, but whom I cannot make out … They are abroad. I wait destiny, with bowed head and will call on no god but Fate.'[96] In October, however, he must have told Morley that he believed Dilke guilty, because Chamberlain, to whom Morley conveyed the opinion, replied, 'F. Harrison's sources of information are tainted. Please tell him for me for what it is worth that I am *certain* Dilke is innocent.' Harrison thereupon conceded that he had not seen Robert or his wife since June and had 'not the smallest private knowledge or influence in the matter'.[97] The judge's decision in the divorce trial in February 1886 failed to confirm Harrison's view, but it also failed to support Dilke's claim of innocence. Fearing questions about his relations with Virginia Crawford's mother, Dilke had not taken the stand. Paradoxically, the judge granted the divorce but dismissed Mrs Crawford's evidence against Dilke. Claiming that he was the victim of a conspiracy, Dilke invoked the Queen's Proctor to have that evidence re-examined in a second trial. Held in July, this time before a jury, it let stand the divorce decree, in effect ruling that Mrs Crawford's accusations about Dilke were supportable and his denials, now made under oath, were not.

The trials must have caused the Harrisons considerable embarrassment. The testimony of Helen Harrison's butler showed that she had shielded her sister's adultery; and later investigations undertaken by Dilke in a vain attempt to prove his innocence disclosed lurid details of the sisters' joint sexual activity. He now reasserted his suspicion of a conspiracy. To some—but not to Dilke himself—Chamberlain seemed the logical inspiration for Virginia Crawford's accusation that Dilke had been her seducer, the motive being to remove Dilke as a political rival. Harrison probably did not take this view, but he thought Chamberlain implicated in an even more serious kind of subterfuge. Writing to Morley after the second trial, he recalled his own previous condemnation of Dilke and significantly added: 'It is not swinish bestiality, villany, treachery, and shamelessness ... But the unravelling of a long, elaborate, desperate conspiracy to suborn a jury and defeat justice, and poison public and private opinion—that on the part of a Privy Councillor etc—that is the social, political crime.' Chamberlain was

> very deeply tainted with that charge. He was the public, officious, violent second of his colleague, and assisted him (till within a month or two) in his infamous conspiracy. If Jo were so blind a fool as to be taken in, he never so belied his reputation for acuteness. His motive was only too obvious. He was warned to the full. In fact the Q——n ought properly to strike off the list two (not one) rt. honbles.[98]

It appears that Harrison judged Chamberlain's perfidy to have been in helping Dilke to evade justice, possibly in the belief that Dilke would eventually be ruined, leaving Chamberlain without a rival but exculpated as a seemingly loyal friend.

The Dilke trials made sensational newspaper copy, and no editor exploited them more purposefully than W. T. Stead, the notorious 'purity' crusader. As Morley's assistant on the *Pall Mall Gazette* he had appeared to Harrison to be a mere 'creature' of Chamberlain's and partly to blame for Morley's reluctance to publish the Positivist protest against the Transvaal war.[99] When Stead became editor on Morley's entry into Parliament, he gave Newton Hall considerable coverage, noting that one did not have to agree with its religion to value Harrison's political views. In 1886 he even asked Harrison to expound them for the paper.[100] Harrison declined the invitation, perhaps because it came from Holloway Gaol, where Stead was serving a three-month sentence for illegally acquiring the evidence used to expose forced prostitution of minors. His series, 'The Maiden Tribute of Modern Babylon', convinced Ethel that he had 'finally gone off his head'.[101] Stead offended the Positivists not only by denouncing vices they were too decorous to name but by lending his columns to their critics. In 1884 he had reported Canon Liddon's denigrating sermon at St. Paul's on the Religion of Humanity, and when Harrison replied, Stead tried to perpetuate the controversy between the old school friends.[102] He again showed his penchant for meddling after the Dilke trials by taking Virginia Crawford under his wing, with consequences that must have surprised the Harrisons. He gave her newspaper assignments, thus launching her in journalism, and introduced her to Cardinal Manning, who received her into the Catholic Church. She went on to a distinguished career in social work and local government.[103]

Helen, by contrast, allowed the waters of family and society to close over her. At the height of the scandal Robert commissioned the young John Singer Sargent to paint her portrait. For this full-length study she chose a bold red and white gown, but with her cropped dark hair, angular figure, and tense, vulnerable expression, she appears ill at ease in it, and defiant. When exhibited at the Royal Academy the canvas aroused considerable comment. One critic judged it would prove 'decidedly unpleasant' as a 'household companion' and hoped it was 'unjust to the lady'.[104] In depicting her as a troubled, if elegant woman, perhaps it was not. Lady Ottoline Morrell, visiting Shiplake Court, the grand Tudor house on the Thames that Robert built for his family in 1890, found to her regret that 'one had to be on one's best behaviour', which for her spoiled the enjoyment of their art collection.[105] Helen may even have followed Virginia into religious repentance in the next forty years of her life; now they lie side by side in the Catholic precinct of the cemetery founded by Harrison's uncle Charles, whose 'selling' of his young daughter to the much older Lord Amelius Beauclerk in 1852 had marked the beginning of Harrison's estrangement from that branch of the family.

Neither Dilke nor Chamberlain was subjected to the kind of punitive action Harrison in his anger had wanted, but the scandal destroyed Dilke's chances of ever holding high office, though he later regained a Parliamentary seat; and Chamberlain, untouched by the scandal, abdicated the Radical leadership and eventually left the Liberal party over the issue of Irish Home Rule. Harrison, meanwhile, was moving closer to its leadership during 1886. Gladstone's commitment to seeking some form of Irish Home Rule led Harrison to forget his old contention that Irish unrest could be allayed by land reform alone. Gladstone ceased to be that 'old ass of a G. O. M.' who had stumbled into a new imperialism, and became once more the venerable party leader, taking the place in his political pantheon once held by Dilke and Chamberlain as potential leaders, and Gambetta, whose death in 1883 had seemed a great blow to French republicanism and to some extent to Positivism.[106] But like other Liberals prepared to follow Gladstone's lead on Ireland, Harrison had no way of knowing in the winter of 1885–6 what the recent convert to the cause envisaged. Without waiting to find out, early in the new year Harrison called for maintaining the imperial union—about which Chamberlain was adamant—but also for a 'real

Irish government'. He did not say how both conditions could be met.[107]
The return of the Liberals to office in February, and Morley's surprising
appointment as Irish Secretary after only three years in Parliament,
inspired Harrison to more concrete proposals, perhaps because he
now felt that he had a friend in power. After signing himself 'your old
Comrade in Arms' when congratulating Morley, he wasted no time in
sketching an Irish bill. It provided for retaining Irish MPs in Westminster
to deal with imperial affairs and establishing a government in Dublin to
handle Irish domestic issues. The Dublin executive would at first be
named by the British, eventually by the Irish, and it would have veto
power over legislation passed in Dublin as well as authority over the
military. *The Times* thought the scheme constructive but unlikely to
satisfy the Irish.[108]

And it satisfied neither Morley nor Gladstone. Their fateful bill,
introduced in April, gave more autonomy to the Irish Parliament than
Harrison would, and excluded Irish MPs from Westminster altogether,
though the Prime Minister was open to compromise on that sensitive
issue. The defeat of the measure on its second reading by a combination
of Conservatives and disaffected Liberals—henceforth Unionists—split
the Liberal party and precipitated a bitter election in July. Characteristic
of the way he juggled Positivist and political concerns, Harrison led a
Newton Hall pilgrimage to Paris immediately after the dissolution of
Parliament in June, thus missing the early stages of election excitement.
Back at home, however, he issued a spirited pamphlet, *Mr Gladstone
or Anarchy!* which embodied his intense animus against defectors from
Gladstone's camp: 'What can it matter if Professors Tyndall and
Huxley think Mr Gladstone a villain? What has Mr Goldwin Smith got
to teach us when he comes for a summer holiday from his voluntary
exile ... we want neither chemists, colonial editors, nor popular
preachers, or actors, to teach us how to settle our great public questions.'
Chamberlain's defiance of Gladstone was treason: he had been 'trying
on the Liberal Crown before the old king has lost his vigour'.[109]

So strong was Harrison's commitment to Gladstone and Irish Home
Rule, the main election issue, that at the end of June he at last put aside
his Positivist scruples and accepted an invitation to contest the Parliamentary seat for the University of London. His expenses would be
paid by a committee of constituents opposing the Unionist views of the
incumbent, Sir John Lubbock. With the voting less than a fortnight
away, there was no thought of a real campaign, and the candidates,
being old friends, exchanged polite letters. Adopting the procedure
Beesly had used the previous year in standing for Westminster,
Harrison declined to canvass and published a single statement on

Home Rule as the great issue. His committee chairman was J. Allanson Picton, a seventy-six-year-old former Congregationalist minister who in 1884 had succeeded Peter Taylor as Radical MP for Leicester—the seat which, for different reasons, neither Harrison, nor Spencer, nor Holyoake had contested. Harrison's agent was his brother Charles, who had stood for the seat for Holborn unsuccessfully the previous year. With pledges from only 300 of the 2,577 constituents, and an opponent counting on some five hundred fellow scientists for votes, Harrison entered the lists with little hope. And he received only 28 per cent of the ballots.[110] Beesly, who was standing for Marylebone, received a slightly higher percentage, the victor there being Lord Charles Beresford, the hero of the Sudan campaign. Since both Positivists considered themselves martyrs to Home Rule, their disappointment was not for themselves but for Gladstone, whose resounding defeat appeared to be a sad end to his political leadership. 'What a collapse!' Harrison wrote to Morley, who had himself been returned; Gladstone had 'fallen like Arthur the blameless king in the last great fight with the heathen'.[111]

And like Arthur, the G. O. M. disappeared—to Hawarden—from whence he would reappear in the fulness of time. In his absence his traitorous knight Chamberlain staged the Round Table Conference, which failed to find a solution to the Irish dilemma, and a far fiercer Arthur—Balfour—emerged to preside over a policy that balanced coercion and conciliation to little effect. Supported by some former Liberals, it made for unprecedented acrimony in London society, and in the heat of the battle the Positivists relaxed another of their restrictions. They took pride in Mrs Beesly's presidency of the Women's Liberal Association of Paddington, where the Beeslys now lived, and in her stirring lyrics for 'The Wearing of the Green'.[112] Harrison urged Morley to find Beesly a Parliamentary seat, and to be 'bloody, bold, and resolute'; since Chamberlain had 'all but killed himself', and Dilke, 'the fool perjured caitiff', had disappeared from politics, Morley must assume the place at the head of the Radicals they had once held jointly.[113] For his part, Harrison kept the cause before the public with his pen, and for a few years was a familiar figure in Gladstone's social world. Like everyone in it, Harrison had his favourite G. O. M. story. It concerned Mrs Gladstone preparing to sign the guest book at Sutton Place and her husband interjecting, 'My name comes first, my dear!'[114]

One couple close to the Harrisons who were split by Home Rule were George and Rosalind Howard, he becoming a Unionist MP for East Cumberland, she (a sister of Lyulph Stanley) remaining an ardent Gladstonite. Despite their differences the Howards were still together in August 1886 when the four Harrison boys joined them and some of their eleven children at Castle Howard for several weeks. Bernard, the family's aspiring artist, was set to copying canvases by George Howard, a dedicated painter, and Austin read novels by Scott at Rosalind's behest. Godfrey and René fished and rambled over the vast estate. All the boys played cricket, and when indoors complained of the absence of newspapers and the erratic meals. 'We all fly about the room for bread, beef, peas, porridge, and etc', Austin reported to his parents. The Howard children teased each other to the point of cruelty and their mother bullied everyone, though when two hundred school-children arrived for a feast she was gracious enough. Towards the end of their stay the Harrison boys learned the purpose of their visit: to clear the way at home for the arrival of a baby sister.[115] Born on 2 September, she was named Olive in honour of the Great Protector, whose biography their father was just then writing, and would be duly presented at Newton Hall with Rosalind Howard as sponsor. Eventually, however, the Harrisons drifted out of her circle, having no sympathy with her temperance and women's suffrage work and deploring her evolution into a 'cruel witch' who alienated her husband and children by her 'pride, conceit, and temper'.[116]

The birth of his daughter in his fifty-fifth year coincided with Harrison's decision to give up his law chambers in New Square, of late little used, and devote himself more exclusively to pen and preaching. At Newton Hall he had the unenviable task of trying to make Comte's social philosophy appear a worthy competitor of the varieties of socialism emerging in the 1880s. Yet he did not undertake a thorough study of the economic issues. His foray into economics in the 1870s had left him with a distaste for theory. Moreover, the socialists did not seem to justify the effort. 'I regard Karl Marx as an iconoclast, and a fool', he later told Austin when he offered to introduce him to August Bebel.[117] The home-grown varieties of socialists seemed little better, though some claimed to have been influenced by Comte: Hyndman, who founded the Social Democratic Federation after initial meetings in 1881 in which Beesly participated; Belfort Bax, who admired Chapel Street's defence of the Paris Commune; the first Fabians, especially Sydney Olivier, who like Gissing had tutored a Positivist's son (Henry Crompton's), and Sidney Webb, who recognized similarities between Fabian and Comtean economic doctrines.[118] Harrison's strategies in dealing with socialism included conjuring up an image of Darwin, Tennyson, Carlyle, and Burne-Jones pleading in vain before a socialist board to be freed of manual labour in order to pursue their rightful work; he foresaw a national treasury emptied of funds for vital social services by administrators who lacked business acumen. Usually, however, he insisted that Positivism was itself 'moral and religious socialism'. Quoting Harcourt, 'We are all socialists now', he once explained that

we are none of us going to be frightened out of useful practical measures by the use of cant terms ... And if we find it necessary, in order to protect a weak and suffering class, that the State should interfere, the State shall interfere, professors of dismal sciences and Auberon Herberts to the contrary notwithstanding.

Such pragmatism, however, did not imply any zeal on Harrison's part to force the state to interfere. He did not participate in any of the mass protests by the unemployed, by socialists, and by others in 1885 and 1886 angry at the Government's inaction; though when the police used force the Positivists registered their usual complaint about the temporal power's interference with spiritual leaders. When coercion of the Irish was added to the protesters' grievances in 1887, he attended at least one demonstration in Hyde Park, on that occasion complimenting Blunt on the carrying power of his voice. But he kept his own for Newton Hall.[119]

The socialist who may have owed the most to Harrison was Beatrice Potter. Before she formed her famous 'partnership' with Sidney Webb in 1892, Harrison was one of her mentors. He helped to introduce her to the studies that led to her youthful 'apprenticeship' in social investigation under her uncle, Charles Booth, who had himself imbibed a good deal of Positivist theory from his relations, Albert and Henry Crompton.[120] The Potters moved in some of the same social circles in the 1870s and 1880s as the Harrisons. At the time of the Dilke scandal Beatrice wondered if her father's London house had not been where Helen Harrison had met one of her lovers.[121] A sister of Beatrice's attended Les Ruches, but Beatrice declined to follow her and had mixed feelings about Mlle Souvestre. She admired her brilliance but not her irreligion, for though Beatrice saw the age as one in which the 'emotion of self-sacrificing service' had been transferred 'from God to man', she never ceased yearning for a creed. Her father, a wealthy northern railway magnate, liked to conduct his daughters to various places of worship, including Newton Hall, where, in 1889, Beatrice observed that Harrison's address on 'living for others' seemed 'forced'. Comte's religion, she decided, was only a 'pitiful attempt by poor humanity to turn its head round and worship its tail'. She did not underestimate the influence of Comte. 'Practically we are all Positivists', she wrote, echoing the familiar assertion about socialism. But she believed that humanity needed to aspire to 'a superhuman force'.[122]

She confided these adverse views of Harrison's religion to diary entries published only after his lifetime, for no more than George Eliot or Gissing would she offend him by public criticism.

Unpublished passages in her diary show that even apart from his Positivism Harrison was somewhat uncongenial to her. He seemed 'ungenerous' in his treatment of Herbert Spencer, to whom she was devoted, and at the same time too eager to 'propitiate' more 'powerful enemies'. He was, for example, 'always telling John Morley ... to make it easy for Jo Chamberlain to come back to us'. This apparent deference would especially have annoyed her since she had painfully mixed feelings about Chamberlain, whom she had rejected as a suitor. There were further misgivings about Harrison. He did not look at her squarely when they talked.[123] He was too prone to take people at their 'market value'. As a champion of trade unions herself she could not but regret that he had abandoned serious study of their problems for other subjects. His obvious enjoyment of his comfortable circumstances offended her ascetic soul. Yet she gave him credit for not letting society's distractions rob him of a vigorous intellectual life. She once called him an 'original thinker', which is more than he ever claimed for himself. And she saw that his encouragement of young intellectuals like herself was admirable, and that his standards of thought and conduct set him above the 'ruck of clever authors, successful barristers, and minor politicians on the make'. In the end she may have felt closer to Ethel, who was, after all, nearer to her own age and, when apart from her husband, very amusing with her 'gossip about political and literary personages—phrased with motherly beneficence, but spiced with just enough denigrating wit to make the mixture thoroughly delectable'.[124]

In an essay on the London dock strike of 1889 Harrison named both Beatrice Potter and Charles Booth among the writers who had prepared the public to view favourably the militancy of the unskilled unions. Another friend, Cardinal Manning, had 'brought out the Catholic Church on its grandest side' by his skill in the negotiations; and John Burns, the socialist and a chief promoter of the strike, had become its 'keynote' by acting from 'a sense of social duty'. Among institutions creating the climate of opinion in which the strike succeeded, Harrison listed many with which he had either been associated or had endorsed: the older unions of skilled workers, the Working Men's College, Toynbee Hall, the National Association for the Promotion of Social Science, the Industrial Remuneration Conference—and Newton Hall. His assessment pointed to a harmony of efforts that made the socialists seem insignificant. Still, H. H. Champion, recently driven from the SDF because of Hyndman's dislike of organized labour, praised the essay, it was reprinted in New York by the new American Federation of Labor, and it is usually cited in modern accounts of the dock strike.[125]

Harrison made no pretence in his essay of offering first-hand information about the events. He had, even by that time, never been to the East End of London. But then, he had prepared a scheme for Irish Home Rule without ever having crossed the Irish Sea. He was becoming more a theorist and less the social investigator he had been in the 1860s. To facilitate his writing and escape the distractions of town, in 1886 he took a ten-year lease on Blackdown Cottage, a sixteenth-century house much altered over the years, situated high on the wooded southern slope of Black Down, on the Surrey–Sussex border south of Haslemere. The region was becoming studded with homes of writers, the greatest of whom lived the closest, the Laureate, at Aldworth, built for him by James Knowles on the east slope of Black Down. Like it, the Harrisons' cottage was isolated, overlooking fields and woodlands that made the situation ideal for the boys' school holidays and Olive's first rambles. Sutton Place, still occupied by Harrison's mother and Sidney, was less than an hour away by train and carriage. Much closer was Verdley Place, in adjacent Fernhurst, owned successively by two prominent Liberal lawyers, C. S. Roundell until 1889 and then Horace Davey. The latter, an ardent Home Ruler and Gladstone's Solicitor General, would become Lord Justice of Appeal in his last ministry and Baron Davey of Fernhurst. The Daveys were good friends, and there were other acquaintances nearby like Frederick Pollock, Grant Allen, the Pearsall Smiths, and Rollo Russell, whose mother Lady John Russell and sister Agatha often stayed with him. But Harrison preserved time to write, in a rustic nook carved out of the hillside behind the cottage which the family named 'Kilmainham' after the Dublin gaol in which Parnell had been imprisoned. Visitors from the outer world would be taken past this spot to the top of the 918-foot hill for a panoramic view that Tennyson had celebrated as 'Green Sussex fading into blue / With one grey glimpse of sea'. At closer range they would be shown the estates of the Dukes of Norfolk and Richmond, of the Earl of Egmont, and of Baron Leconfield. The Harrisons must surely have appreciated the irony of settling in 'one of the most conservative districts in England'.[126]

Among its best features was its proximity to London. In less than two hours from the cottage door he could be speaking at Newton Hall, conversing at the Athenaeum, or reading at the London Library. And for six years beginning in 1889 he found himself frequently at the

Haslemere station to go up to town for a new and important reason: to take part in London's first comprehensive governing body. He had long been interested in the city's past, present, and future. In 1883 he had endorsed Shaw–Lefevre's protest against billeting soldiers in the Tower of London, and in an address in 1887 to William Morris's Society for the Protection of Ancient Buildings he deplored alterations being made in Westminster Abbey for the Jubilee as another threat to the city's 'sacred' architectural heritage.[127] Like most London radicals, he was a member of F. B. Firth's London Municipal Reform League, founded in 1881, and a long-time advocate of strengthening the city's governing powers, which were divided among numerous agencies and boards until the Local Government Act of 1888 created the first London County Council. His own 'ideal London', described in a Toynbee Hall address, would contain only about a quarter of a million residents, with communal facilities for the working class and other amenities that would require a 'collective system'. The *Pall Mall Gazette* declared that such views placed him 'altogether among the socialists'.[128] It was therefore appropriate that he should become a member of the first London County Council, which was soon called socialist by its critics.

Harrison always maintained that his nomination as an LCC alderman, like his appointment to the Royal Commission on Trade Unions, came to him as a surprise. In fact, with the election of his brother Charles as a councillor for Bethnal Green, one of the city's poorest districts, the choice of Harrison as an alderman followed logically. Charles was an active member of the Liberal party, a prosperous solicitor, a director of railway and insurance companies, an indefatigable traveller, and, since 1886, married to the widowed sister of the Earl of Lanesborough. 'What are the times and seasons at which Mr Charles Harrison takes food or sleep?', once asked Lord Rosebery, who twice served the LCC as chairman. Charles had for some time been promoting his pet reform schemes: leasehold enfranchisement; partial shift of rates from the occupier of city property to the ground landlord; and the 'betterment principle', which would increase those rates when city improvements raised property values.[129] From the beginning of the LCC he set out to organize a reforming contingent, helping to divide the newly-elected members into two camps, the Progressives, of which he expected to be a leader, and the Moderates. At the first meeting, on 31 January 1889, with Sir John Lubbock as temporary chairman, Charles no doubt exerted his influence in the election of aldermen. Of the twenty seats to be filled, the Progressives elected nineteen of their nominees, and Harrison was among them.[130]

It is easy to see why he was immediately willing to serve. It was not a popularly elected position; indeed, the aldermen were intended to provide a restraint on the popularly elected councillors. The office carried considerable prestige; he could think of himself as a kind of elder statesman. Service was voluntary and non-remunerative. All these features were attractive to a Positivist. Best of all, of course, the LCC promised to fulfil a need the Positivists had already identified in a manifesto urging just such a new municipal body, for strong local government was essential to Comte's aim of breaking up Europe's traditional political units.[131] Ironically, it was not long before Harrison complained that the Progressives wanted to bring the police under LCC authority and take over certain functions better retained by the vestries and other parish bodies, for he found that he was rather less radical than many Progressives.[132] But he approved most of their proposals, even agreeing to the restriction of liquor licensing and monitoring of theatres for indecencies, two encroachments on the spiritual powers, according to Positivist theory. All these were lesser matters, after all, compared to the Progressive programme for improving life by what Harrison liked to call 'Home Rule for London'.[133]

He especially admired two of the Progressives' leaders. One was John Burns, famous as 'the man with the red flag' at the Trafalgar Square demonstration of socialists and unemployed in February 1886. His appeal for Harrison was the same as Overton's: he represented the enlightened working man. Almost thirty years Harrison's junior, bluff of manner and, like Harrison, short and stocky, Burns seems to have treated his grey-bearded, frock-coated colleague with a good-natured familiarity. He once told Ethel after an article of Harrison's had caused a stir that she had better fortify Blackdown Cottage with Austin in command, get Bernard to secure the hill, and send their manservant Caesar to justify his name by taking the local post office; and if all this failed she was to call for him.[134] The second and more decorous socialist was Sidney Webb. His attempt to 'permeate' the LCC with Fabianism even before he joined it in 1892 was quite in accord with Harrison's reforming methods. The Harrisons welcomed him as Beatrice Potter's fiancé when some in their set would not accept a man without a 'socially attractive family', and for this she was grateful. Harrison told Ethel, however, that 'Beatrice Potter is not going to marry S. Webb *because* she is becoming a socialist—But she became a socialist *because* she meant to marry S. Webb.' Making the best of things soon after this, he sent her a copy of the *Social Programme* he had helped to draw up at Chapel Street in 1872, telling her it was true 'municipal socialism'.[135]

Though Harrison did not join the LCC because he had become a socialist, he was proud to be a member of that body, which many called socialist. During its first term, ending in March 1892, he attended 133 of its 234 meetings, a good record, voting to open museums, galleries, and libraries on Sundays and some evenings; circulating a petition to free Lincoln's Inn Fields from the monopoly of his fellow lawyers; and insisting on union wages for work on LCC projects. His committee work concerned bridges and water, and he backed Charles on the important Improvements Committee and the Parliamentary Committee. As chairman of the latter, Charles steadfastly refused to forward any proposal to Parliament for action if it did not incorporate the betterment principle, or, if land purchase was involved, if it did not compensate occupiers who had invested in the property. In consequence the Parliamentary Committee accomplished very little in the LCC's first years. After the Progressives' clean sweep in 1892, Charles became vice-chairman of the LCC, and Fred was swept into the chairmanship of the Improvements Committee by the same wind. Believing, as he had told the Industrial Remuneration Conference, that no 'abstract rights of property' should prevent 'laying out our cities as health and convenience suggest', he led his committee in planning two new avenues to reduce traffic, eliminate slums, and, incidentally, provide jobs. One was through Bermondsey, where he had preached republicanism in 1871; the other, modifying an old Metropolitan Board of Works proposal, was a 100-foot wide thoroughfare connecting Holborn with the Strand. Since both schemes embodied the betterment principle, they failed to win Parliamentary approval, and Harrison concluded that real improvements in London could begin only when the national legislature revised local taxation.[136]

Frustrated by Parliament's rejection of Progressive proposals and wanting more time to write at Blackdown, in September 1893 Harrison submitted his resignation. He instructed the party whip, Dr William Job Collins, to act on it when he thought best, and in good Positivist fashion also recommended a successor, Lord Morpeth, the eldest son of the Howards, now the Earl and Countess of Carlisle. Hearing shortly afterwards that the Progressives had offered the nomination instead to C. T. Ritchie, a Unionist with protectionist views, Harrison sent Collins an angry letter. When Ritchie declined to stand, Harrison, greatly relieved, explained that he had feared the Progressives were throwing away their chance to get a useful recruit. He added that he did not share Sidney Webb's desire to 'attack, worry, and embarrass the present Liberal government at every step'; indeed, not the least of his worries was that his Parliamentary friends would blame him for having helped an enemy into office.[137] Among those friends were Sir John Lubbock and Lord Rosebery, chairmen during Harrison's time as alderman. Neither had proved entirely satisfactory. At the first council meeting Lubbock allowed the Moderates to force an adjournment that drained Progressive momentum, and he later declined committee assignments.[138] Rosebery, though he seemed 'heaven-sent' at times, was even more diffident. At Mentmore, his country seat, he was the perfect host—'What ease, what cheer, what wit, what Culture!', Harrison exclaimed on one visit[139]—but his threats of resignation jeopardized Progressive goals. When asked to take the chairmanship a second time in 1892 he disconcerted Harrison by talking for half an hour 'without saying whether he accepted it or not', and then gave only a qualified assent and retired from the room leaving his place at the table strewn with 'fragments of paper—thousands—which he had twisted in his anxiety'.[140] No true leader of men behaved like that.

Serving on the LCC fulfilled all Harrison's political aspirations, but not Charles's. He was unable to get a seat in Parliament, despite Fred urging his merits to Morley, until 1895, and then he represented Plymouth for only two years. On Christmas eve 1897 the 'hoarse guttural' voice Beatrice Webb remarked upon in her diary was stilled for ever, following a sudden seizure.[141] His body was cremated and his ashes placed in the family vault at Brookwood Cemetery, Woking, where only the previous year the five Harrison brothers had buried their mother, who had died at Sutton Place in her eighty-ninth year.

Six months before Charles's cremation, Harrison had published an essay defending this still controversial means of giving death a 'scientific' dimension. In return for a copy, he received an invitation from the leading cremation advocate, the surgeon Sir Henry Thompson, to one of his famous 'octaves', a dinner of eight courses, for eight people, at eight o'clock, at number 35 (numbers totalling 8) Wimpole Street.[142] Not all Harrison's suggested innovations in urban life were so cordially received. At Toynbee Hall he returned to the theme of an ideal London in 1898, suggesting that though 'the mind is rather repelled by the prospect of this monotonous multiplication of Queen Anne's Mansions', more large block housing would make room for 'fine avenues, parks, gardens, and boulevards', a 'millennium' that the *Spectator*, for one, thought far too 'mechanical'.[143] The same paper would later complain that his praise of the LCC was excessive, and so it must have seemed to many, for in numerous articles he depicted its aims, actions, and aspirations as those of a selfless band of dedicated souls who assumed that they were 'set there to protect the labouring poor'.[144] In his tireless efforts to enhance the LCC's prestige he collected subscriptions in 1906 for a group portrait of the first members,[145] annoyed Walter Crane by criticizing his omission of the sword of St. Paul from the design of the LCC seal,[146] and lamented the absence of headquarters architecturally worthy of the LCC's high functions.[147] When Parliament finally approved a plan for a Holborn-to-Strand avenue in 1899, he had many suggestions about the design and, to honour the origin of what would be the most important London improvement since Regent Street in 1830, he urged that it be called 'The Council Broadway'. His recommendations were ignored, but inadvertently the ceremonies opening the avenue in 1905 fell on his seventy-fourth birthday, and he was proud to attend. Appropriately, the occasion was graced by the presence of the Sovereign, for the name chosen for the avenue was 'Kingsway'.[148]

THE SPIRITUAL ORDER

Though proud of the LCC's progressive action, Harrison helped his colleagues to reject one innovation, the active participation of women. Women could vote in LCC elections, and three were on the first council, Lady Sandhurst and Jane Cobden as regular members, and Emma Cons as an alderman. When their membership was challenged, Harrison voted against the Council's petitioning Parliament to seat them, and he endorsed a court ruling that denied Lady Sandhurst the right to take her place. Counsel persuaded the other two women not to exercise their privileges as members though they continued to attend meetings. It was not until 1900 that women were empowered by law to sit on borough and city councils.[149]

Less than three months after the LCC first began harassing its women members, Lady Sandhurst presided at a meeting of the Women's Liberal Federation, formed to enable volunteers from its membership to replace hired party agents whose activities had been restricted by the Corrupt Practices Act of 1883. Though the meeting had been called to support Gladstone's Irish Home Rule scheme, and its members included women from among his Liberal friends, such as Lady Davey, Miss Mundella, and Arabella Shore, to Harrison it seemed a bad portent.[150] Even worse was the Women's Council of the Conservatives' Primrose League. Lord Salisbury, the Prime Minister, supported it and seemed about to seek the vote for propertied women in order to swell his electorate. Yet Harrison was not at first enthusiastic when asked in May 1889 to help Louise Creighton, the Church historian's wife, and Mrs Humphry Ward issue an appeal against women's suffrage in the *Nineteenth Century*, with Knowles's blessing. Such action, Harrison warned, would ironically do just what they all deplored, 'accustom women to the mechanical artifices of political agitation'.[151]

This impeccable logic may not entirely explain Harrison's hesitation. Mrs Ward was an old friend, but he had reservations about her. In the mid-eighties, when he and Ethel were at Elstead, they had brought their boys to play with her daughters at nearby Borough Farm, where she was writing *Robert Elsmere*, the novel that was to make her famous in 1888.[152] Whatever the Harrisons may have said on that or other occasions about their work as Positivists, they must have regretted *Robert Elsmere*'s appearance, for, with a condescension worthy of her uncle Matthew Arnold's treatment of Comte, the novel depicts a Comtist couple. James Wardlaw, a briefless barrister, and his dreary wife, who tends their children 'as a Positivist mother is bound to do', help out in the Unitarian centre in the East End to which the novel's hero comes after his loss of faith drives him from the Anglican ministry. Elsmere soon 'eclipses' Wardlaw, a 'man of meaner gifts', but invites the couple to dine in the hope of reconciling his wife to his new vocation. Instead, the Wardlaws outrage her, he by dwelling on his infant's 'baptism' by an eminent French Positivist (a detail Mrs Ward probably derived from the *Pall Mall Gazette*'s humorous account of baby Olive Harrison's 'presentation' by Laffitte) and his wife by asking her why she does not come to her husband's centre. She answers that she is still a churchwoman; but before the novel ends she is assisting Elsmere in the work of his 'New Brotherhood of Christ'. He holds Sunday services with lay sermons and carefully selected hymns, and conducts social and educational programmes for local artisan families. The similarity to Newton Hall is inescapable, though secularist and ethical centres shared some of these features. Moreover, everyone knew that *Robert Elsmere* was a *roman á clef*, with portraits of Pattison, Jowett, and T. H. Green, all friends from Oxford, where the author had spent her adolescence and first year of marriage, and where, probably, she had first met the Harrisons. How could her fictitious Comtists not have seemed a kind of betrayal to them? Mrs Ward ignored Harrison's advice to let Gladstone's criticism of the novel's 'religion of humanity'—Gladstone's term for Elsmere's religious haven—go unanswered. Instead she published a dialogue espousing it as 'the New Reformation'. To Harrison it must have seemed only the latest form of 'Neo-Christianity'.[153] In spite of all this, he accepted her invitation to help organize the anti-suffrage appeal. It was not the first time, nor the last, that a common cause brought him into an unlikely alliance.

The planning took place in Ethel's drawing room, a meeting she later described as free of all 'political, social, and religious bias'.[154] The phrase hardly characterizes the decision that emerged: to collect signatures for the appeal only from women who came from prominent families or were known for 'useful work' outside the home. Ethel and Mrs Beesly, who was already suffering from the cancer that would take her life within the year, set about approaching women in both these categories of the élite. Discouraging women who fitted into neither category proved troublesome, and so, too, was trying to win over some whom the committee deemed valuable supporters but who held back, like Mrs Leslie Stephen and Beatrice Potter, both of whom eventually signed, and Lucy Crompton and Lady Grant Duff, who did not. Neither did Lady Rosebery, though she and her husband so agonized over the decision that Harrison told Morley impatiently they were 'too conscientious'; 'one can't be absolutely right, and it is better to decide wrong than to spoil your dinner and your night's rest.' Because '*all* the Randolphian ladies' signed, he thought his list might be 'rather too Conservative', but he assured Morley that it '*blocks* Salisbury this year at least', and he told Mrs Ward that it laid the question 'to rest for this generation at least'.[155]

In June, when the *Nineteenth Century* published the appeal, the Harrisons were in Paris, leaving Morley to enjoy 'convalescence' at Blackdown Cottage after the 'fever' of the Parliamentary session.[156] They were home by July, when Knowles published another list of supporters of the Appeal and also, less welcome, objections to it by Mrs Millicent Fawcett, widow of Mill's associate, and Maye Dilke, widow of Ashton Dilke and one of the more serious-minded of the Eustace Smith daughters. Harrison tried to get Beatrice Potter to write a response, but she declined to jeopardize her status as an impartial social fact-gatherer any further by publicly opposing a cause endorsed by so many working-class women; besides, as a financially independent woman she felt 'wholly indifferent' to her own disenfranchisement.[157] Mrs Fawcett had noted that the anti-suffragist list contained a majority of such fortunate ladies, and that it conspicuously lacked names of ladies known for charitable works or the extension of women's opportunities, most of these being proponents of women's suffrage. The July *Fortnightly* gave some evidence of this in its list of about 2,000 suffragist women. Meanwhile, Bryce considered trying to organize the 'Antis' (as the opponents of women's suffrage came to be called), but he soon dropped the idea, perhaps because Ethel told him of her difficulties in mounting the Appeal.[158]

Harrison's first important public treatment of the suffrage issue came in a Newton Hall address in 1891 for which he probably drew not only from Comte but also from a popular text, *The Evolution of Sex*, written by Patrick Geddes and his former pupil J. Arthur Thompson.

While the Appeal had relied on vague terms like 'the disabilities of sex' and 'custom and habit resting ultimately upon physical difference, against which it is useless to contend', *The Evolution of Sex* purported to speak scientifically. It contended that men's metabolism favoured them with a 'katabolic' state of abundant and spendable energy, whereas women's 'anabolic habit' was to store up energy for their reproductive functions.[159] Citing 'sound biology', Harrison argued that women were 'subject to functional interruption absolutely incompatible with the highest forms of continuous pressure'. Moreover, the history of civilization showed the benefits of restricting women to family life, where their refinement of sympathy could freely influence husband and children. But he was concessive too. He entitled his published talk 'The Emancipation of Women' because of its stress on the need to improve education for women and relieve them from crushing factory labour, and he allowed that in 'a thousand ways' they might be usefully active in 'more or less public institutions', Newton Hall being an example.[160] When at least one hundred newspapers reported the address, he had to admit that the Positivists were not always victims of a 'conspiracy of silence'.[161] Since his views were mostly Victorian commonplaces, many of these notices were favourable, but Mrs Fawcett easily met his arguments in a devastating reply. She ended by identifying his opinions as those of a 'rich man who has never had to work for a living' and who believed that if thirty or so people in Fetter Lane left off trying to preserve the 'womanliness of women', the 'primaeval institutions of society' would be destroyed.[162]

Among the newer institutions of society that troubled Harrison in the eighties were the schools and universities. Their mission of educating and stimulating the young seemed undermined by the increasing importance of competitive examinations. As an examiner in the law he had learned to spot Jowett's prizemen by their solidly prepared performances and lack of wide interests, and he came to believe that such successful students often lacked the altruism of his own Oxford generation. As a parent and friend of parents he had seen how preparing for examinations could dishearten the young. He and Ethel approved Beesly's decision to let his youngest son Lewis escape the school grind by studying biology under the unorthodox Geddes in Edinburgh, where Lewis eventually became a distinguished surgeon—though presumably not without examinations.[163]

The Harrisons did not altogether save their own boys from the examination mill. Bernard lost his scholarship at St. Paul's in 1887 despite tutoring by Gissing, but he won a prize for art before going on to Balliol in 1888, where in only two years he announced that he wished to become a painter.[164] After obtaining advice from Burne-Jones, Millais, and other artists, the Harrisons sent him to Paris to find his way under the eye of Ethel's brother Darent, who had given up business for art some years earlier.[165] Anxious about the youth's welfare amidst bohemian temptations, Harrison asked friends to keep an eye on him: the Paris Positivists, P. G. Hamerton, the artist who claimed to have been influenced by Comte, and even his old adversary Lord Lytton, now British ambassador in Paris.[166] But Bernard soon found his own protector. He was received into the Roman Catholic Church. According to Austin, his father proved 'surprisingly sensible' and 'even spiritually interested'.[167]

Austin's escape from formal schooling came less quickly. After three years at St. Paul's, another three at Harrow, and study in Lausanne, Munich, and Berlin, he failed the Foreign Service examination. Harrison's disappointment was all the keener since he believed Austin might have passed if all his papers had been legible (Harrison took inordinate pride in his own clear hand). Moreover, he had personally asked Lord Salisbury to put Austin's name on the list of candidates.[168] In the end he had to watch his son enter upon a vocation he had himself sought unsuccessfully to avoid, journalism. In 1898 Austin took a night post on *The Times* reading European telegrams, and was soon transferred to Berlin. His father visited him there later that year, eager to observe if the German people were as efficient as reported. He discovered that, in any case, Austin was amazingly inefficient when it came to arranging transport and sight-seeing. Though he had not been on German soil since his wedding journey, Harrison planned their jaunts and, discovering acquaintances and friends of friends in the city, introduced Austin to people who might prove useful. Before leaving he met Austin's superior, whom he thought to be jealous and ignorant—and decided that upon his return to London he would deliver an ultimatum to Moberley Bell at *The Times* to raise Austin's salary.[169]

The education of the younger Harrison children proved at first less troublesome. Godfrey had three years at Clifton College and some tutoring before joining his uncles Sidney and Charles as a solicitor, in which role he became a mainstay of the family. René had five years at Clifton, then took a degree at Merton College, Oxford, in 1897, and became an architect in the firm of Thomas Graham Jackson, a Wadham man who had recently designed the Examination Schools at Oxford and restored other buildings.[170] For Olive, of course, no vocation was contemplated, and she studied under the supervision of her parents through early adolescence, an arrangement that left her socially immature.

In 1888, when all the boys were still at school, Harrison contributed to a *Nineteenth Century* symposium on examinations that showed how widely held his own views were. The series began with a protest against the existing system by F. Max Müller, E. A. Freeman, and Harrison. They were supported by four hundred names. More were solicited and a Royal Commission proposed.[171] In the following months the defenders of the system had their say, and there was also further criticism from Frederick Pollock, Francis Galton, Harvey Goodwin, and Auberon Herbert.[172] The Earl of Wemyss and March, formerly Lord Elcho, placed the case for an inquiry before the House of Lords, which rejected the appeal, thus ending the series but not the controversy.[173] Harrison's role in it shows his reservations about democratic advances; just as he thought the family required a strong husband and father, and the government a strong executive, so he wished the teacher to reign supreme in the classroom, unchecked by external examiners. Privately he conceded that the weakest side of the case against competitive examinations was the patronage common in the Civil Service they had been introduced to undercut, though his own efforts on behalf of Austin and many others show him a ready user of the Old Boy network and other avenues of influence.[174]

Consonant with his criticism of competitive examinations was Harrison's enthusiastic support for innovations in education designed to serve those outside the universities and to place less stress on examinations than they did. One such scheme was the University Extension movement, in which university men taught liberal subjects to those who might otherwise receive no formal education beyond board school. Not a paid extension lecturer himself—he was too busy with other matters and too old for the travelling it required—Harrison gave three lectures under the movement's auspices, in one applauding its Summer School at Oxford as a way of making the University 'more truly national'.[175] And in 1886 he took a year's term as president of the Social and Political Education League founded the previous decade to provide speakers on timely public issues for community organizations, a service to which he cleverly applied his version of the old knightly code, 'sagesse oblige'.[176]

Despite their preference for voluntarism in education, several Newton Hall Positivists were promoting the existing state system in a variety of ways. Marvin moved steadily ahead in the Education Department, Bridges endorsed the call for more rate-supported schools and orphanages, and in the school board election of 1894 Harrison backed candidates like Lyulph Stanley and Graham Wallas, who defended the 1870 system against the Revd J. F. Pardiggle and others seeking to undermine it by increasing State aid to voluntary schools.[177] On the larger question of whether the old local authorities or a new central agency should administer public education funds, Harrison again favoured the old system; but he had to watch its dismantling as a Parliamentary Bill allowed the new London County Council to finance technical schools, a Royal Commission headed by Bryce created a new Board of Education, and Sidney Webb, chairman of the LCC's Technical Education Board, applied liquor revenues to funds linking LCC-aided schools to the universities.[178]

Given his differences with the Webbs on education and socialism, Harrison's response to Beatrice's request for a contribution to the new library of the Fabians' London School of Political and Economic Science is understandable. He declined to send money, and, venting the frustrations of decades, demanded to know if the library would

exclude the mountains of rubbish and perverted industry that is called political science? And what is political science; and who decides what is, and what is not science? ... What does the School teach? What is its Philosophy? What is its Religion? Wnat are its Ethics? I suppose it says it has none. It accepts the Philosophy, Ethic, and Religion of say—Arthur Balfour, the Bishop of Oxford, and Sir Charles Dilke ... I don't believe there can be any economics (other than Ricardo's or Bimetallism) without religion ... Is the School of Political Science Socialism? And if so what is Socialism? And why should a man who has £1,000 give any of it to his neighbour? And what should his neighbour do, if he won't give any? These are ultimate questions which I want to have answered.

He confessed that

after thirty years of utterly vain and profitless labour to get a few fundamental problems of social life solved, or even considered—I am coming to feel that all isolated and purely departmental research is so far worse than useless that it draws off good men and women from the one paramount question—'What shall I do to be saved?' ... And thus I come in my pessimistic moods to think we had better give up education altogether, neither read nor write more—abolish schools—burn libraries, and let us start fair and try again.

He ended by returning to a subject they had recently been discussing, women's suffrage. Beatrice had apparently told him that she regretted having endorsed the Antis' Appeal in 1889, and Harrison had spoken of a 'future massacre of women' that would come when men were driven 'beyond all male patience'. He now took pains to point out that he meant the remark as a 'prophecy' not a 'threat', and he promised that should such an event occur he would try to save her.[179] Under the facetious language can be detected a bitterness that undoubtedly stemmed from her indifference to the ideals to which as a young woman he had introduced her. Even George Eliot and Gissing seem not to have disappointed him so deeply.

The LSE was not the only London institution attracting financial support the Positivists might have envied at the turn of the century. In 1899, J. Passmore Edwards gave Harrison £10 for Newton Hall while he gave the Webbs £10,000 for their new school and Mrs Ward £12,000 for her settlement house in Bloomsbury. The latter was an outgrowth of earlier centres she had founded in the area to give concrete expression to the ideas of *Robert Elsmere*. Ironically, her first venture was housed in University Hall, where Beesly had once had to make his Positivism acceptable to the Unitarians, and the man she chose for warden was Philip Henry Wicksteed, a Unitarian minister who in earlier years had fallen under Beesly's influence and to whose Little Portland Street Chapel Mrs Beesly had brought their children in the 1880s. Mrs Ward gained the support of many others known to Harrison, including Lord Carlisle, Lady John Russell, Stopford Brooke, Frances Power Cobbe, James Martineau, and Samuel Barnett. Why, Harrison must have asked, would they do nothing for Newton Hall?[180]

The most famous Victorian settlement was Toynbee Hall in Whitechapel, named for the young Oxford economic historian who introduced the term 'Industrial Revolution', and whose early death cut short a career devoted to promoting the welfare of workers. Years before, Harrison had lectured on the social revolution wrought by technology for Maurice at the Working Men's College, and his writing influenced the founder of Toynbee Hall, the Revd Samuel A. Barnett, a Wadham man thirteen years his junior. But Barnett's approach to philanthropy was not that of the Positivists: he believed in providing material relief to the poor and getting university men to live among them as a means of elevating their thoughts and manners. In 1872, when he was still using St. Jude's, his church in Whitechapel, as the centre for his social work, Barnett had visited Chapel Street and was disappointed to find that the Positivists resembled 'a lot of parsons' in their 'worship of the letter rather than the spirit of the master's books' and their 'contempt for the outside world'. But Harrison, though he had said little and seemed 'mysterious', had struck him as promising.[181] During the period between the Positivist schism and the opening of Newton Hall, Ethel assisted at one musical Sunday evening at St Jude's, not an auspicious occasion. She had found her way there in bad weather only because she was conducted by her father, who remembered certain streets he had taken when courting her mother; the concert was badly managed; the audience a 'ragged tough starved set of poor human beings'; and Barnett 'a poor worn looking man, who seems to have buried his health and youth and spirits in the back slums of Whitechapel'.[182] The Positivist leaders ran no such risks: by 1880 all were in comfortable homes in good parts of London. Occasionally they lectured at Toynbee Hall, but usually they had to decline Barnett's invitations because of commitments in Fetter Lane. To Marvin, who had served at Toynbee Hall, Harrison once complained about its hold on promising young men who would not share their talents at Newton Hall: 'though they might not like to call themselves Positivists, they might help in the men's guild where no systematic views are inculcated or required.' It seemed that in order to attract university men 'you must be utterly vague and think "there may be a sort of something after all", and live 4 miles east of Charing Cross.'[183]

There were grounds for Harrison's impatience, for much in Barnett's social and religious philosophy approximated to his own. 'Rational and reverent' hymns were sung in St. Jude's Church, and selections from secular writers were read. Barnett termed the work of his parish and settlement 'practicable socialism', a label close to Harrison's 'moral and religious socialism' for Positivism. At the time of his death in 1913 Barnett was Canon of Westminster Abbey and was eulogized as the greatest practical churchman of his day. Comparing Barnett's influence to his own Harrison pointed out to the widow 'in humility and shame' that he and his colleagues had not had 'time—even if we had the gifts—to shed around our teaching that moral and spiritual inspiration which, in spite of all I have ever said of its shortcomings—I very clearly see is the secret of the gospel of Jesus'. She, in turn, honoured the gospel of Positivism by choosing a hymn for her husband's memorial service in the Abbey from Ethel's collection.[184]

Another community centre Harrison saw attracting impressive support from its inception was the Bishopsgate Institute in the City, founded by William ('Hang Theology') Rogers, Rector of St. Botolph's, Bishopsgate. His mission work in London went back to Harrison's school years, and his advocacy of secular education in board schools had earned him his sobriquet. Harrison, who had probably first met him on the committee to remove religious tests at Oxford, was on the platform at the opening ceremonies for the Institute in 1894, on Rogers's seventy-fifth birthday. Rosebery, then First Lord of the Treasury, presided. The chairman of the Institute following Rogers upon his death two years later was Evan Spicer, a colleague of Harrison's on the LCC and brother of Sir Albert Spicer, Liberal MP and owner, following Harrison's parents, of number 10 Lancaster Gate. Moving in the world of responsible citizenry, it was hard for Harrison to see the success of others in it while his attempts at social service were floundering.[185]

Closest to Newton Hall in aims and programmes were the various groups in the ethical movement, the oldest of which met at South Place Chapel, Finsbury, under Moncure Conway from 1864 to 1884 and from 1892 to 1897. The interim was filled by Dr Stanton Coit, and thereafter regular lecturers were appointed, among them J. A. Hobson, and J. M. Robertson. In Conway's day as many as 1,000 might attend a Sunday morning service. That was easily five times what Newton Hall could expect, yet services at the two places were very similar, with eclectic hymnals, readings, and an address. Conway, however, introduced a transcendental strain from oriental religions that was foreign to the Positivists' Western prejudices; and Coit removed the word 'religious' from the name of the society, substituting 'ethical'.[186] Still, Harrison once defined 'ethicists' as 'simply Positivists *minus* the definite dogmas and formulae of Comte', and when these had clearly proved unappealing to most people, he began envisaging a merger of Positivists and ethicists in London.[187] But when a conference of both groups considered and rejected such a proposal in 1900, he may have felt relieved. Submerging the distinctive features of Positivism would have been painful,[188] and he liked to think his people were 'intellectually and socially' superior to the ethicists, and had higher standards. 'I would not let a tailor without an H lecture on elocution', he told Ethel after visiting the Camberwell Ethical Society to speak.[189] His own talks to Newton Hall and similar centres were often printed, evidence that he was not content to 'twaddle placidly', as Leslie Stephen, president of the London Ethical Society in 1894, once confessed to Harrison he did after 'reflecting on the nature of my congregation'.[190] But how to explain the greater success of these other societies? Harrison once tried: these people have 'one single aim—ethical culture. We have 10—and 9 out of 10 of ours drive off some.'[191]

Judging contemporaries with religious views somewhat like his own, Harrison showed an ability to make distinctions that were useful to the promotion of Positivism. When, for example, Francis Newman died in 1897 he contrasted his personal eccentricities and slight impact to the force of character and enormous fame of his brother, but asserted, too, that while the Cardinal represented only a 'discredited past', the theist had 'done something to bring us nearer to a Greater Future'.[192] Another member of Chapman's old circle, W. M. W. Call, earned his guarded praise in 1893 for having predicted in a critique of natural theology that Humanity would one day be the object of 'dutiful obligation' and the world would stand revealed by 'Positivist Science'.[193] Altogether less charitable was Harrison's response to the philosophic speculation called 'Significs' by Lady Victoria Welby, though she was a

would eventually be abandoned; the conflict between egotism and altruism would have to be confronted each time it arose. (George Eliot's working out of this idea in her fiction may help explain Harrison's reservations about it.) Another thesis of Spencer's, advanced in the *Nineteenth Century* early in 1884, was that primitive religion originated in man's belief in ghosts as the spirits of dead ancestors. He went on to surmise that in the future religious feelings would not find their object in a deity at all, but in the contemplation of nature's 'Infinite and Eternal Energy', which was beyond the ability of science to explain.[199] Harrison denounced this 'agnostic's creed' as the 'ghost of religion', merely a reworking of Mark Pattison's notion of deity gradually being 'defecated to a pure transparency'. Though Spencer was applying 'unction' to his old conception of the Unknown, it would prove about as useful to religion as the Binomial Theorem because—and here Harrison audaciously adapted Cardinal Newman's words—'You may rout a logician by a "pure transparency", but you cannot check vice, crime, and war by it.' What Harrison failed to see was that Spencer did not expect ethical norms to spring from any such 'cosmic emotion', for he believed they would arise out of people's changing needs. Harrison, as Lady Welby would observe, did not trust future generations to constitute their own values but sought to fix them once and for all according to Comtean maxims.[200]

The controversy aroused considerable commentary in the press and was heightened by the entry of a third participant, James Fitzjames Stephen, who wished to say something on the 'comparative blackness of the pot and the kettle'. Finding little to add to Harrison's criticism of agnosticism as a substitute for religion, Stephen reiterated his old objections to a Religion of Humanity. But he also broke new ground. Why need there be any philosophic basis for ethics so long as there was the law? Instead of the angry god he had earlier held indispensable to civilization, he now considered a powerful judge sufficient. In the years following his attack on Mill and Harrison in 1873 he had come to see that men of all religions, and of none, honoured 'temperance, fortitude, benevolence, and justice', and that in this universal understanding lay the possibility of a 'transformed morality'. Privately he said that little remained to divide him from Harrison, except Harrison's 'more enthusiastic view of human nature'.[201]

Writing too soon to consider these arguments in detail, Spencer defended his 'ghost theory' of religion by citing the work of the anthropologist E. B. Tylor, and argued that because the Positivists had adapted religious festivals of primitive peoples, their religion was 'retrogressive'.[202] Meanwhile, Wilfrid Ward had made the duel 'quadrangular'—to use the *Saturday Review's* term. His father, W. G. Ward, had alluded admiringly to Comte in *The Ideal of a Christian Church* in 1844, a Tractarian work so Romish it became an early case in the struggle against religious tests at Oxford. In the Metaphysical Society he had been an affable and witty apologist for Catholicism, ready, he once said, to accept a Papal Bull with his breakfast egg every morning. Now his twenty-eight-year-old son was following in his footsteps by accusing Harrison and Spencer of ignoring the essence of faith—belief in a personal God—and appropriating 'the clothes of religion': Harrison had stolen its moral teaching, Spencer its metaphysical attributes. If they had indeed killed religion, it would 'be more becoming in them to bury it clothes and all'.[203]

Hard pressed, Harrison resorted to his old strategy of defending the Religion of Humanity in Neo-Positivist terms. It was, he said, 'simply morality fused with social devotion, and enlightened by sound philosophy'. But he was not altogether conciliatory. He again contrasted Spencer's 'Unknowable Energy' as an object of worship to Comte's conception of Humanity, and he judged the 'ghost theory' of religion inferior to Comte's account of primitive fetishism. Spencer's sources he derided as 'a pile of clippings from books of travel'. Dealing with his other critics more summarily, he concluded that Stephen was 'something of an unconscious Positivist' and Ward unworthy of attention from serious philosophers because of his Catholicism.[204] Stephen had yielded too much ground to be tempted to reply, but Ward wrote another witty riposte, this one dubbing Harrison a 'Pickwickian Positivist', a term that delighted Cardinal Newman and left Harrison little to say in reply except that he considered his orthodoxy his own affair, which seemed merely peevish.[205] He had by then shifted the ground of debate with Spencer by engaging him in an acrimonious exchange of letters in the press over the degree to which Spencer was indebted to Comte, a subject on which Spencer was always hysterically touchy. Spencer published evidence showing that he was acquainted with Comte's work mainly by hearsay, but this only served Harrison's purpose, for he then argued that so imperfect an acquaintance with Comte made it impossible for Spencer to know 'how truly his own new tune is played on the old instrument.'[206]

Inevitably the four participants in the controversy aroused much speculation about their motives and meaning, none more than Harrison. Charles Bowen detected opportunism in his writing on Positivism: having seen that the age was secular, he and his colleagues had realized that they 'must cut adrift from the ecclesiasticism of Comte, or they will be nowhere'. Why, Bowen wondered, had they made 'such a confounded pother ... if it was not that they wanted to spell Humanity with a big H ... Harrison might have gone into Parliament, Bridges into practice, Congreve still been an Oxford tutor'. Ruskin chided Harrison for persisting in such wrangling instead of helping him 'finish up usury—or smoke—or poison—or dynamite—or some such positive nuisance'.[207]

Such efforts would indeed have been a more useful than Harrison's strategies in his next tangle with Spencer. Their quarrel arose when Spencer allowed his American publisher to issue a volume containing the articles he and Harrison had published in their debate, along with notes by Spencer giving his later views on the issues. There was a preface by his chief American promoter, Dr Edward L. Youmans, and an introduction by another admirer, Goblet d'Alviella, Professor of the History of Religions at the University of Brussels, men about as hostile to Comte as was Spencer. Not consulted in all this, Harrison demanded an explanation from Spencer, who replied coolly that the book was a response to great American interest in his work and that Harrison might wish to issue an English edition with his own notes. Outraged, Harrison published this correspondence in *The Times*, asking who would receive the profits from Spencer's book. It took several more letters, some published, for Spencer to convince Harrison that he had not acted from mercenary motives, and for Harrison to assure Spencer that he had not accused him of such. Spencer stopped the book's publication, absorbing the costs, and Harrison returned the cheque he had received for his share in the profits to date.[208] Meanwhile the articles had been reprinted in *Popular Science Monthly* in America by Youmans, and in the *Revue Occidentale* by Laffitte, and they were soon made widely available by an American admirer of Spencer's, Mary Abigail Dodge, under the appropriate title, *The Insuppressible Book*.[209]

Through all this Harrison insisted privately and in print how he admired Spencer as a philosopher. Their friendship was not one he wished to lose; nor did he. It was to him that Spencer turned in 1889 with an urgent request: would he use the enclosed guinea (went the letter) to have the British Museum's file of *The Pilot* searched for articles by Spencer during the time he had written for it in 1844? Harrison should then read them to determine if, as a recent critic had claimed, Spencer had mentioned 'sociology'. Fulfilling the commission, Harrison was able to assure the anxious Spencer that no such discussion existed, thus enabling Spencer to avow in print, not for the first time, that he had been introduced to Comte's works only in the 1850s, and hence after he had begun elaborating his own social theory. 'Had not this slender thread of evidence been preserved unbroken', Spencer would note in his *Autobiography*, 'my word would thereafter have been held valueless.'[210] Even Harrison was not trusted to judge it fairly. Three years later Spencer sent him a passage embodying a newly-formulated idea: that a secular ethic might be grounded in a 'transfigured sentiment of parenthood' in which man would hold humanity's future as dear as that of his own child or grandchild. Spencer planned to include the passage in *Principles of Ethics*, the conclusion to his *Synthetic Philosophy*, and sought to forestall a charge of plagiarism from Harrison—for, Spencer conceded, this new formulation evinced a 'degree of agreement' between them greater than he had hitherto imagined. The chief difference now seemed 'a matter of names', with himself regarding as part of ethics what Harrison called religion, because Harrison had failed to see that in the modern age ethics and religion had split apart.[211]

Spencer had arrived at this understanding while reading Harrison's part in a controversy with one of Positivism's severest critics, T. H. Huxley. He had coined the term 'agnostic' in the Metaphysical Society to describe his own scepticism in religious matters, and had successfully evaded Harrison's demand that he expound his own philosophic basis for morality. By spelling out the Positivists' case against agnosticism as a comprehensive view of life, Harrison had provoked from Huxley a devastating comparison of the Religion of Humanity and Mormonism which discredited both.[212] When Huxley reprinted the essay in 1892 Harrison returned to the issues dividing them, arguing that if agnosticism was only an attitude of mind, as Huxley seemed to imply, it was implicit in Positivism, but if it was a philosophy or creed, it should deal with the great issues of life, as Positivism did. Still evasive, Huxley in reply asserted only that the evolutionary process in nature offered no guidance of the sort Harrison required of religion, but he again derided Comte's system and interpreted Harrison's willingness to defend only an attenuated version of it as a sign of his defection from the Master.[213] Harrison's flair for finding witty titles did not desert him: he called his next article 'Mr Huxley's Ironicon', indicating that his opponent had not meant to be irenic. Nor did Harrison. Though he depicted himself as 'a man of peace, a poor hand at controversy, and a great admirer of my critic', he quoted from his own works to show his unswerving commitment to Comte's essential teachings, and put words like 'culte', 'supreme being', and 'worship' into a context that removed much of the stigma Huxley had attached to Positivist religion.[214]

Just as Huxley forced Harrison to diminish his claims for the Religion of Humanity,[215] so Harrison forced Huxley to re-evaluate his philosophic position. In his Romanes Lecture in 1893 Huxley finally made explicit an idea he had only adumbrated in his critique of Harrison, declaring in a much-quoted statement that 'social progress means a checking of the cosmic process at every step, and the substitution for it of another, which may be called the ethical process.'[216] Harrison welcomed this 'timely protest from a professed evolutionist against the presumptuous dream of an Absolute Synthesis' and congratulated his old friend.[217] But Huxley's hope, that 'the hatchet may be considered buried',[218] was contradicted by his re-publication, a year later, of his article comparing Positivism and Mormonism, graced with the comment that 'Mr Harrison rejects the greater part of the Positivist Religion.'[219] To Harrison this constituted 'deliberate false witness', but his complaint may never have reached Huxley. The public had wearied of their quarrel, and Harrison's remarks appeared only in the *Positivist Review*.[220] The next year, the man who had been one of the first to congratulate Harrison upon his entry into religious controversy in 1860 passed from the scene. Old claims of friendship were not forgotten when Huxley's son Leonard, married to Mrs Ward's sister and soon to launch a literary career with a biography of his father, asked Harrison to support his candidacy at the Athenaeum. Instantly co-operative, Harrison assured him of a welcome at the club where his father had been 'so well known and so popular'.[221]

FIN DE SIÈCLE

Organized labour added to Harrison's sense of disappointed promise towards the end of the century. He had come to believe that the vast armies of unemployed in London included some who 'would not work'.[222] Moreover, when asked by Gilbert Murray, the young Oxford classicist married to one of Rosalind Howard's daughters, to contribute to a fund for striking engineers in 1897, he declined, arguing that unions were rejecting 'all Middle-Class Liberals' and turning to socialism. Yet at the beginning of the strike he had defended the men's actions, quoting from his own 1865 denunciation of lock-outs; and before it was over he would join the Webbs, Beesly, Crompton, and Ludlow to issue a statement affirming the importance of the trade union movement.[223] His ambivalence toward it stemmed largely from the political aspirations of its leaders. The International Labour Party they founded with socialists in 1893 seemed to him responsible for the 'disorganized politics' of the period: and he told Beatrice Webb that very soon *The History of Trade Unionism* and *Industrial Democracy*, which she had her husband had published in 1894 and 1897, would be the only 'trace' of the benefits won by himself and his friends two decades earlier.[224] More reminiscent of his former radicalism was his defence of John Burns when Admiral Maxse disparaged him in the *Daily Chronicle* for a characteristically extreme statement. So vituperative was Harrison's published letter that Chamberlain called it 'Billingsgate', and Meredith wondered at his resorting to the use of 'street missiles'. Dilke joined them in spirit with a letter explaining away his earlier radical republicanism.[225]

At Blackdown Cottage Harrison at times took on the conservatism of the area. When Lord Egmont's agent evicted a farmer from his humble cottage after a dispute over property rights, Harrison recognized the justice of the man's case but nevertheless advised him to go quietly. Even Frederick Pollock's call for a further examination of the case did not keep Harrison from praising Lord Egmont as a benevolent land-owner. Had he not given public access to Cowdry Castle and provided entertainments for the local horticultural society?[226] Ethel took a similarly complacent view of country ways in several dialogues for the *Nineteenth Century* and fictional sketches for the genteel *Temple Bar*.[227] But espousing the values of the local gentry was easier than affording their style of life. When Gissing visited the Harrisons at Blackdown Cottage in 1896 he noted how high prices were for 'mere pleasure ground', and Harrison decided that year that the terms for renewing his lease were too steep.[228] The family's last extended period in the area was in 1898. They stayed at the new guest accommodation at nearby Blackdown House, a seventeenth-century manor occupied by Sir Frederick Philipson-Stow, a former Kimberley diamond merchant. The Harrisons had grown fond of Lady Philipson-Stow and her many children; but her husband's association with Cecil Rhodes embarrassed Harrison enough to make him assure Morley of his friend's 'sterling honesty'.[229]

In the last years of the century death removed a number of people long important in Harrison's life. In 1895 George and Georgina Hadwen, the parents of Mary Bridges, died within a few days of each other after long illnesses.[230] In 1899, three years after his mother's death and two years after Charles's, his brother Lawrence died in Cairo, leaving twin sons and a daughter.[231] When a young child of the Philipson-Stows died during the Harrison's stay at their guest house, Harrison, reporting the mother's anguish, asked, 'How did that old tent-maker dare to cry out "Death where is thy sting" '[232] But he usually kept his moments of existential uneasiness hidden. After finding him at cricket with his boys at Blackdown Cottage earlier in the decade and discussing with him their disparate philosophies of life, Blunt was led to observe that Harrison could afford his optimism because he 'has never had a pain or ache or sleepless night in his life'.[233]

Blunt had overlooked other sources of Harrison's occasional discontents. He was hardly less frustrated than Blunt about the failure of Irish Home Rule, but he chose to make his contribution to the movement from the sidelines. He never visited the land to which he owed his own Celtic strain, whereas Blunt picked oakum in a Galway gaol for two months for conducting an outlawed meeting there.[234] Predisposition and circumstances made Harrison less of a militant leader than a promoter of militancy in others. His voice did not go unheard. After he argued that 'coercion' and 'intimidation' were really neutral terms in law, though the Government was applying them to Land League tactics that had been declared illegal, Michael Davitt commended Harrison as more a Fenian than even he.[235] Urging Morley to learn 'Dicey on the Constitution' by heart and to have the records of Blunt's trial scrutinized for irregularities, Harrison wanted it made clear to 'Bloody Balfour' that 'we will live to see your lanky fingers picking oakum and your uncle's [Salisbury's] unwieldy belly rolling on his plank bed.'[236] When his appeal to Liberal Unionists to return to the fold provoked an angry reply from the Duke of Argyll, Harrison dismissed it as only a shot meant for Gladstone, since he knew himself to be merely 'a private in the line'.[237] As such, he always had advice for the generals. After the Government began an inquiry into *The Times's* attempt to implicate Parnell in the Phoenix Park murders, Harrison helped Sir Charles Russell prepare his speech on Parnell's behalf. When the forger Pigott eventually broke down under questioning, in effect absolving Parnell, Harrison celebrated the Irish party's vindication in a series of fiery articles. He and Ethel were among the guests in May 1889 at a dinner party given by Sir Charles and Lady Russell to mark the victory, an event made 'remarkable and historical' by the presence together there of Parnell and the Gladstones.[238] And he shared the dismay of Gladstone and the Liberals when all their efforts in behalf of the Irish cause were dashed with Parnell's indictment as co-respondent in O'Shea's divorce suit late the next year. Harrison compared Parnell to Milton's Satan because he refused to withdraw quietly from politics until the scandal was forgotten. Seeking to justify the ways of the G.O.M. to readers of the *Fortnightly*, he declared that the masses, which had become the ultimate political arbiter, would insist on having an Irish leader 'whose hand a decent man can touch'. It was a common argument, but Bernard Shaw, for one, said he expected something better from Harrison.[239]

With Gladstone again in office in 1892, Harrison set about explaining

'How to Drive Home Rule Home'. His suggestions included parading into the House of Lords a contingent of Lifeguardsmen raised to the peerage and pledged to vote for an Irish government, a scheme Lord Salisbury pretended to think represented Gladstone's own attitude, but which merely reminded *The Times* of Harrison's old Communard sympathies.[240] Gladstone's Home Rule measure, providing for some Irish MPs at Westminster with restricted voting rights, seemed worthy of 'loyal acceptance' to Harrison, but he could not resist sketching a few revisions: the great thing, he said, was not to fear changing the Constitution.[241] After the Bill's rejection by the Lords, Harrison heard Gladstone in Scotland declare the issue not yet dead. But the speech, which Ethel thought 'adroit', left her husband puzzling about how the party was to proceed.[242] When Gladstone resigned in March 1894, Harrison conveyed his 'fervent trust' that the aged gladiator would be spared to see the great cause victorious, and noted that his own chances of witnessing the triumph seemed good since longevity ran in his family.[243] Gladstone's funeral four years later was a disappointing climax to Harrison's years of devotion, for Morley could do nothing about providing him with a ticket to the Abbey.[244]

Though too remote from party politics to know the inside story of Rosebery's triumph over Harcourt in the struggle for the Liberal leadership, Harrison was content with the outcome. He attributed Rosebery's defeat at the polls in 1895 to 'false friends', and when Rosebery retired from the leadership he assured him that his critics had all been 'unjust'.[245] Harrison's allegiance to Rosebery was partly due to his belief that Rosebery was inclined to do more than Gladstone to solve the nation's social problems; and he was beguiled by Rosebery's cordiality and the gratifying thought that they had been colleagues on the LCC.

In judging foreign political leaders Harrison was more objective. Visiting Paris in 1888 with a commission from *The Times* to report on General Boulanger's attempt to rally malcontents against the Republic, he observed the General posturing on his white charger, discussed his career with republican friends, and then confidently dismissed him as only the latest of the city's tourist attractions, rising like the Eiffel Tower 'over the Republic, rising no man knows how', and he rightly predicted the General's fall.[246] In Greece with Shaw–Lefevre in 1890 he met Charles Tricoupis, the Prime Minister, who with his sister quickly became effusive and faithful admirers. Yet he did not hesitate to inform Salisbury upon his return that the Greeks were using menacing language about their neighbours.[247] Sometimes, of course, friendship led him to turn a blind eye to political differences. In Cairo in 1895 he spent a pleasant day with Britain's consul, Sir Charles Cookson, who had been injured in the bombardment of Alexandria in 1882, but as they inspected Cairo's new Greco-Roman museum they probably talked less of the politics that kept the British in Egypt than of their days together at King's College School, a preparation for their appreciation of the antiquities before them.[248]

The high point of Harrison's Egyptian trip were three glorious days with the keenest of all critics of Britain's Egyptian policy, Wilfrid Blunt. At Sheikh Obeyd, his 'earthly paradise' of a villa on the edge of the desert north-east of Cairo, Harrison experienced the alien fascination of the Blunts' 'Old Testament' way of life. The flamboyant Arab dress of Blunt and his wife and daughter, the exotic repasts of Arab dishes, the stirring beauty of the desert sunrise, the ways of Bedouins and camels and Arabian horses, filled his letters to Ethel. He would have 'a thousand things' to report to nine-year-old Olive.[249] Among them was no mention of why Blunt insisted on sleeping 'under a sandbank in the open air covered with fur rugs' when they made a two-day excursion into the desert by caravan. It was to enable him to keep an assignation with another guest, Mary Elcho, the daughter of the Earl of Wemyss and March (and probably the mistress of Arthur Balfour). She was also Blunt's cousin and the mother of three children, but none of these facts prevented him from making her a conquest in his long 'pilgrimage of passion'. Of course it is possible that Harrison knew nothing of this. In Blunt's account of the visit Harrison behaved with considerable *naïveté*, 'sliding down sandhills because they reminded him of the Alps'.[250]

There is better evidence that Harrison had not lost his mountaineering enthusiasm. While sightseeing after he left Blunt he amazed his guides by climbing to the top of the Great Pyramid and down again entirely unaided. And without a guide he went exploring Cairo's mosques and museums, back alleys and bazaars on the festive eve of Ramadan. But he had serious interviews in prospect, too. With a dignitary of the El Azhar, the great Muslim university, he proudly spoke of Newton Hall's recent celebration of the thirteenth centenary of the Hegira and of the Positivists' support of Arabi and his cause. A question he asked another scholar about the inferiority of women in Islam was met with shocked indignation by the assertion that they had absolute equality with men, a reply Harrison privately dismissed as 'a dose of Neo-Islamism'. At a luncheon with Lord Cromer, Harrison listened to the great proconsul's 'frank and friendly' account of Egypt's problems, and was impressed enough to admit that Cromer was 'doing his best to make the most of an impossible situation'. Published in *The Times*, this assessment precipitated a rebuke from a 'Twenty-years' Resident', who then declined to discuss the subject further with a mere tourist, 'however justly eminent'.[251]

Harrison had not lost his old aversion to imperialism, but with Europe divided over the scramble for empire he had begun to give higher priority to Britain's prestige and defence. Thus in 1889 he offered the toast to the 'unity of empire' at the National Liberal Federation banquet honouring Dadabhai Naoroji, the Parsee MP who had become an instant celebrity two years earlier when Lord Salisbury had declared that no 'black man' was wanted in a British Parliament. By agreement this lapse in political etiquette was not referred to at the banquet, and Harrison, of course, did not allude to his own misgivings about Naoroji during the early Chapel Street days. Since both he and Naoroji had become well-known critics of imperialism, the *Star* observed that Harrison's role at the banquet was 'rather delicate' and that he had fulfilled it nicely with 'one of his polished, academic little discourses'. His strategy was to present himself as a member of neither the 'bombastic' nor the 'pessimistic' school of empire. He attributed the terms to Sir John Seeley's *Expansion of England* without mentioning that the book represented Seeley's repudiation of one of Positivism's major tenets, though as a friend of Beesly's at University College in the 1860s Seeley had been influenced by Comtean thought. Of Seeley's two goals for the British Empire, its improvement and its expansion, Harrison was prepared to accept the first, and as a meliorist he asserted it was feasible.[252] Yet expansion under some circumstances seemed unavoidable. When Lord Salisbury sanctioned an Anglo-Egyptian invasion of the Sudan under General Kitchener in 1898, Beesly and Blunt were predictably outraged. But Harrison thought the campaign, 'conducted with consummate skill', had been 'forced on Egypt by circumstances' and was justified by the relief it brought the victims of the Khalifa's barbarism, even though it cost the lives of 20,000 Dervishes. Not only was the restoration of order and the maintenance of control on the Upper Nile 'an inevitable condition of the fair administration of Egypt', but it also provided a bulwark against French ambitions in the Sudan. France's 'idiotic and scurvy trick' at Fashoda in laying claim to the Upper Nile region was met, Harrison believed, by British 'good-temper, moderation, and honest peaceableness', and the threat of war averted by the Government's statesmanship.[253]

This degree of accord with the Government's imperial policy and performance was unusual for Harrison, however. His old anti-imperialistic fire flared up brightest when a religious, scientific, or philosophic rationale for colonialism was offered. In 1894 Benjamin

Kidd's *Social Evolution* popularized an amalgam of such ideas in arguing that the white man's superior civilization justified his hegemony over the black man, and that the conflict of races and the inspiration of Christianity were both essential to the progress of Western civilization. Even apart from Kidd's derogatory references to him as an apologist for a non-Christian ethic, the book was obnoxious to Harrison, as was Kidd's later work on the future of civilization, which he dismissed as 'pompous', 'vague', and 'gaseous', an estimate echoed by other critics.[254] He also rejected the evolutionary view of society in *National Life and Character: A Forecast*, published in 1893 by his old school friend Charles Henry Pearson upon his return to England after a career in government in Australia. There Pearson had come to believe that non-white peoples would eventually attain predominance due to their vigorous population growth and adaptability to much of the globe. Ethel deemed Pearson's vision of the decline of Western civilization 'as depressing as a case of influenza', but Harrison dealt with it gently, suggesting that a 'truly human religion' could 'vivify and transfigure anew' all the constituent elements of humanity—an optimistic view that Pearson correctly identified as Positivist in origin.[255]

Harrison, of course, saw that there was no such religious influence at work among contemporary imperialists. When Cecil Rhodes's British South Africa Company sought to extend the rule of law with machine guns in Matabeleland in 1893, he spoke for a delegation of the Aborigines Protection Society that met with Lord Ripon, the Liberal Colonial Secretary, to protest against Rhodes's actions. Arguing as a lawyer, Harrison pointed out that the company lacked the legal right to wage war or exercise sovereignty.[256] Ironically, the delegation's recommendation, that the Cape Colony government assume responsibility for the natives, could be construed as an endorsement of territorial expansion. But normally Harrison resisted any extension of British sovereignty, sometimes linking imperialism abroad with imperialism close at hand. Neatly conjoining Balfour's hostility to Irish Home Rule and his advocacy of aggrandizement abroad, Harrison once prophesied: 'Pharaoh will not let the people go, whilst Pharaoh is resolved to be the king of kings from sea to sea.'[257] Similarly, unable to propose a way out of the economic doldrums of the nineties, he announced: 'Imperial expansion means domestic stagnation.'[258] This echoed what Liberals like J. A. Hobson, Leonard Hobhouse, Sydney Olivier, Charles Trevelyan, and their associates in the Rainbow Circle were saying, and had much in common with the views of young Oxford Liberals like Hilaire Belloc, Francis Hirst, J. L. Hammond, and J. A. Simon. The presence of these men in the Liberal camp was encouraging and helped offset the emergence of the 'Liberal Imperialists'. Since these included political figures he admired, like Rosebery and Asquith, and he wished to avoid aggravating the party's disunity, he reserved his attacks on imperialists for Tories and Unionists or kept his arguments general.

One who provoked him into a reasoned discussion of his principles was Frederick Greenwood, the Tory journalist. His criticism of Morley's Romanes Lecture on Machiavelli in 1897 for failing to appreciate the Florentine's *Realpolitik* rested, said Harrison, on 'sophistries': the belief that the state is above morality, and that a nation could survive only by 'fraud, cruelty, and violence', which thus became acceptable in international policy. To talk of the state as an absolute, said the Positivist, was 'mere fetichism', for it was only an aggregate of parishes, themselves made up of individuals, and it followed that 'Honesty is the best policy for States as for Citizens.'[259] W. F. Farrar, the Dean of Canterbury, affronted him a few years later by calling fighting a 'positive duty' in a just war, a statement Harrison would live to echo but which at the time he termed an 'atrocious blasphemy'. That he published his reaction although Farrar was an old acquaintance and a school friend of Beesly's suggests the degree of his bitterness about the Church's identification with jingoism.[260]

And that bitterness deepened as war in South Africa drew nearer in 1899. After the battle of Majuba Hill eighteen years before, Harrison had romantically depicted the Boers as 'free, quiet, toiling yeomen' who had 'gone out into the desert that they might have such Church and such State as is right and dear in their eyes'.[261] On a visit to Holland in 1895 he had described the Dutch as 'the most industrious, sensible, orderly, and ingenious people on earth'.[262] He was therefore all the more ready to sympathize with their kinsmen in the Transvaal when they denied full political rights to the Uitlanders. A ballot, after all, had never seemed a necessary adjunct to citizenship to him. After Jameson's Raid—the Cape colonists' abortive attempt to foment rebellion in the Transvaal in 1895—he accepted the Boers' military build-up as justified and no *casus belli*. He was convinced that the growing animosity between the Boers and the Cape colonists was due mainly to the British desire to consolidate and extend their influence. Therefore, when war seemed imminent in the summer of 1899, he appealed publicly to Lord Salisbury to employ his diplomatic skills to avert it. By describing those skills fulsomely, he provoked a sharp remonstrance from Blunt. To it Harrison replied: 'It is well to attribute virtue to a powerful man, even if he has it not. It must make him doubt of it.' Ex-diplomat though he was, Blunt remained unimpressed by this logic and condemned the Government in language so violent that Harrison warned him he would be subject to libel if he published his words.[263]

Harrison's own language in the ensuing months was sometimes as fierce as Blunt's, especially in his *Positivist Review* diatribes. Since few people outside Newton Hall saw them, they were mainly therapeutic, allowing him to feel he was doing something to stem the mounting war-fever. One essay he composed on the eve of the war must have caused him pain, however, for by comparing the growing anti-Boer sentiment in South Africa to the hostility towards Dreyfus in France he was abandoning the Positivist conviction that France was in the vanguard of social and political progress. He was not the only Positivist to face the dilemma. Godfrey Lushington in *The Times* and *National Review*, Beesly in the *Positivist Review*, and Swinny at Newton Hall meetings all depicted the imprisoned French officer as a victim of a conspiracy by the military. Harrison argued that just as France was perpetrating an injustice against one man with the cry 'Vive l'Armée!', so Britain, with the same sentiment, was contemplating an unjust war against a whole people. This was one *Positivist Review* article that received wide circulation, for it was published by the Transvaal Committee formed in the early 1880s to promote Boer independence and now revived to meet the new crisis.[264]

In his attempt to prevent the war, and then, after its onset in October 1899, to bring about a negotiated peace that would preserve Boer independence, Harrison was affiliated with a number of individuals and groups besides the Newton Hall Positivists. One was the League of Liberals Against Aggression and Militarism founded by MPs and others opposed to Lord Milner's ambitions for the Cape Colony. When one member, J. A. Hobson, who had been to South Africa as a journalist, published a book on the war, Harrison reviewed it in glowing terms because Hobson traced the war to 'a ring of international financiers, mainly Jewish, and only in part British', a thesis Harrison had long been advancing.[265] Another journalist to whom he became devoted was H. W. Massingham, who had heard his lectures at Newton Hall and whose ouster from the *Daily Chronicle* early in the war signalled that paper's conversion to the Government's side. C. P. Scott, editor of the *Manchester Guardian*, where Massingham found a berth, also gained Harrison's lasting respect by his pro-Boer stand and his employment of Leonard Hobhouse, Bridges's brother-in-law, whose intellectual debt to Positivism was considerable. J. M. Robertson, a lecturer at South Place—like Newton Hall a pro-Boer centre—wrote for the *Morning Leader*; after 1901 the *Daily News* under the editorship of A. G. Gardiner shared Harrison's views; and

J. L. Hammond, at the *Speaker*, found space for some of his hottest anti-war letters. But journalistic sympathizers were few, and to make matters worse, there was difficulty finding places for meetings.[266] Both Newton Hall and South Place provided a forum for S. C. Cronwright-Schreiner, a former Cape Colony minister and husband of the writer Olive Schreiner, when Hobson brought him to England for a speaking tour early in 1900. He later remarked on the Positivists' 'very exceptionally accurate knowledge' of his country and their concern for its black population, forgotten by many on both sides of the controversy.[267] A major anti-war pressure group that Harrison, Leonard Courtney, and others helped to found, the South African Conciliation Committee, had Swinny as its secretary and Quin in Newcastle and Alfred Haggard at Chapel Street among its active members. Harrison gave a private lecture to its leaders on the background of the war, then repeated it at the organization's first public meeting, and it was soon published.[268] Ethel so impressed him when she spoke to the women members that he announced he was almost reconciled to what he had long resisted, feminine politicians; men would have to take a 'back seat altogether when women really come into public life'.[269] Far more politically active than Ethel was Jane Cobden, now married to T. Fisher Unwin, the publisher. Both signed one of the moral protests against the war got up by the Positivists, as did her sister Anne and her husband, Thomas Cobden-Sanderson, the bookbinder whose law career Harrison had sought to foster in the 1860s. Others endorsing the protest included Edward Carpenter, the socialist, sandalmaker, anti-vivisectionist, and sex reformer; Alfred Russel Wallace, the land nationalizer; and Rollo and Agatha Russell, the retired diplomat and his sister, former neighbours of the Harrisons in Hindhead. Commenting on yet another heterogeneous group that had met in the studio of Felix Moscheles, the painter, Harrison told Ethel that 'this war makes all the good people kin.'[270]

It also made the Harrisons anxious and depressed. News that their nephew, one of Robert Harrison's sons, had been wounded at Ladysmith set them wondering if their boys would eventually be involved. The terrible defeats sustained by the British army were alarming despite their belief that Britain was in the wrong, and the decline of the nation's prestige troubled Harrison no less because he had so often pricked its conscience. Austin in Berlin reported that the 'best German military judges' were saying that the British had under-taken a job too great for their resources, and Germany's provocative endorsement of Paul Kruger was worrisome. The arrival in South Africa of General Roberts as Commander-in-Chief was all too reminiscent of the frustrations and recriminations of the Afghan War. In South Africa Britain's forward policy seemed unchecked; by the end of 1900 the Transvaal and Orange Free State had been annexed, and a 'khaki' election had increased the Government's majority. Holding meetings without interference had become almost impossible for the pro-Boers, as Harrison and his colleagues were now being called. With the holiday season approaching, Ethel thought of draping Newton Hall in black instead of the usual decorations; and her husband in his worst moods declared England was no longer fit to live in, and threatened to move the family to Ireland.[271]

But early in the first month of the new century he was contemplating a more realistic, if temporary, change of scene. He had accepted a speaking engagement for late February in Chicago. While he was still making the arrangements, news of the Queen's death led him to speculate about her last hours of consciousness, for it was reported that she had talked with Chamberlain and Roberts about the war. 'Did she say—"Go on to death", *or* "Make some terms"! One or other! Perhaps the latter.'[272] But the time for peace terms had not yet come. Harrison therefore resolved to shun politics when in the New World. He would present himself not as a social critic nor as a religious leader, but as a man of letters and historian, an Englishman who had lived through the longest and most eventful reign in his nation's history and was willing to share his memories of it.

7

The Edwardian Positivist

1901–1914

The decision to visit the United States suggests how vigorous Harrison was as he entered his seventies. He would travel alone, Ethel being again in poor health. For some time he had believed Americans were 'disgusting ... swaggering cads' and that Comte had correctly described their country as 'an appendage' of Britain.[1] But when invited by the American Ambassador, Joseph H. Choate, to be the first Englishman to address the annual George Washington Day celebration of the prestigious Union League Club in Chicago, with expenses paid, he felt too honoured and too curious to decline. Other speaking invitations soon followed, and with a fairly crowded itinerary he sailed on the White Star's *Majestic* on 6 February 1901. His spacious cabin delighted him, as did the ship's electric lighting and elegant public rooms. But he observed that the many Irish emigrants aboard were 'out at elbow' and uncomfortable, and that most passengers in his part of the ship idled away their time drinking and betting on the length of the ship's daily run. He spent his time reading—at least 1,000 pages of print, he estimated—and preparing his lectures, untroubled by the heavy winter swells.[2]

Arriving in New York on 14 February he fared less well. Though dressed in a fur coat, cap, and gloves, he shivered in the cold winds blowing through the customs shed, where he was delayed for hours, and felt 'lumbagoish' for much of his stay in America. His hotel, the Holland House on 30th Street and Fifth Avenue, was alive with messenger boys, telephone operators, lift girls, chambermaids—and besieging journalists. They even waited for him in the corridor when he went to the bath. Feeling like 'the Prince of Wales travelling without servants', he was pleasantly surprised at the attention he received. To greet him on his arrival, Charles Eliot Norton, the Harvard art historian, sent his daughter Sarah, whose kindness reminded Harrison of Mrs Ward's gentler heroines. Abram S. Hewitt, America's foremost iron-master and a friend of the Philipson-Stows, got his daughter to conduct the visitor on a motor tour of the city, which Hewitt had once served as a reforming mayor. The sights included Cooper Union, which Hewitt had helped found with his father-in-law Peter Cooper—a kind of Working Men's College or Newton Hall without the ideology. All this seems to have offset in Harrison's mind Hewitt's anti-labour testimony before the Royal Commission a generation earlier. Another philanthropist with no love of organized labour, Andrew Carnegie, had Harrison to tea at his Fifth Avenue mansion, perhaps telling him about the sale of his steel works, then in progress, which left him with the world's largest negotiable fortune—some $480,000,000. Two other industrialists, General John M. Palmer and George Peabody, dined him at the Millionaires Club. When the time came to depart for Chicago, Palmer ('who goes on royally like the king in a pantomine') made up a party to take Harrison in his private railway car.

Installed in a corner suite on the seventeenth floor of Louis Sullivan's Auditorium Hotel overlooking a frozen Lake Michigan, Harrison had a free day before his address. At the Union League Club he met Vice President Theodore Roosevelt, just returned from hunting in the Rockies and looking 'very like a grisly bear'. Both men addressed the luncheon guests briefly, and then went off together to an art gallery, where some young women seemed about to hug Roosevelt. It was Harrison's turn to be the focus of attention the next morning, Washington's birthday. Ushered into his box in the splendid auditorium that had given the hotel its name, he found an audience of six thousand school children, one thousand of them on the stage. In the course of the patriotic programme they all sang 'The Star-Spangled Banner', and at the words 'long may it wave', a thousand little hands held aloft a thousand little American flags. The English guest of honour was observed covering his face while regaining his composure. Luncheon with prominent citizens followed, and then it was back to the auditorium, where Harrison 'fired off' to five thousand people, probably the largest audience he had ever addressed as principal speaker. Yet he said he felt as if he were at Newton Hall. And his talk would have been appropriate there. Claiming Washington for all humanity, he likened the American rebellion against the British king to the struggles of Cromwell and William the Silent, two of his own favourite heroes. And he defended republicanism with the old formula—opposition not only to a monarch but to all privilege. With this in mind he asked some biting questions: were all public offices in America always filled by the worthiest candidates? Did birth and wealth really carry no weight? Turning to Lincoln, he quoted words of his own written at the time of the Civil War, about the British working class supporting the Union while the upper classes took the side of the Confederacy. Apparently unperturbed at all this radicalism, his hosts, among the most conservative men in Chicago, passed a resolution commending him as a true friend of America during the war—along with John Bright and Queen Victoria![3] In the next few days he visited the local Ethical Culture Society, Hull House ('a female Toynbee Hall'), and the new University of Chicago. Everywhere he 'heard nothing ... but philanthropy, education, social improvement, and art studies'; he saw nothing of the Chicago that was Hog Butcher of the World.

On the East Coast again, Harrison gave a 'harangue' on Alfred the Great at Harvard, in the same hall where Matthew Arnold had been 'quite inaudible'. In Washington D.C. his arrival coincided with the second inauguration of President McKinley, which he viewed from the Presidential platform, later meeting the President and 'half the Senate and most of the Cabinet'. It was Alfred again at Johns Hopkins, followed by an electric train ride to Mount Vernon and an overnight stay in Washington at the British Embassy as guest of the Ambassador, Lord Pauncefote, who lived 'just like a British peer'. Things were more relaxed at Bryn Mawr College, his next scheduled visit. The president was a niece of the Pearsall Smiths in Haslemere, and now he understood why their daughter Alys (married to Bertrand Russell) went about bareheaded all the year round; she had attended the college, where all the girls did. They also entertained their brothers in their rooms and other men in the parlours: it was 'pretty free and easy'. Instead of a formal address, he gave them an account of famous Victorians he had known. From there he made a quick visit to Philadelphia for luncheon with William Jennings Bryan, the defeated presidential candidate, who offered to exchange, copies of *The Commoner*, a paper he was planning, for the *Positivist Review*. Harrison's evening lecture at the University of Pennsylvania was again on Alfred. Back in New York he was made an honorary member of no less than seven men's clubs, his cicerone being Moncure Conway. Saddened by age and loneliness, Conway saw Harrison in the glow of a happier past and always introduced him with ' the most fulsome, outrageous laudation'.[4] His final academic appearances were at Princeton, where he spoke on Cromwell and met Grover Cleveland, and at Columbia, where he traced the rise of the Dutch Republic and was told, not for the first time, that he looked like Dickens. During a last few days spent at Shady Hill, Norton's house near Harvard, he lectured in Boston on the London County Council and Alfred, and renewed an old acquaintance with Oliver Wendell Holmes, who as a young lawyer visiting London in the 1860s had described him as 'a Comte man who is civil'.[5]

Harrison was certainly too civil to press Positivism on his audiences except when it was clear they wanted him to do so, as in Chicago, Philadelphia, and New York, where he spoke to Ethical Culture groups. The New York society met in Carnegie Hall under Dr Felix Adler and was infinitely more prosperous than the local Positivists, a tiny remnant of the group Harrison had optimistically addressed by letter in the early weeks of Newton Hall. Their present leader, Edward King, was a man of no distinction who could not conceal his envy of the energetic and successful Adler.[6] Far more impressive, in Harrison's judgement, was one of King's group, Charles Codman, a seventy-five-year-old enthusiast who had contributed to the Comte memorial statue in Paris and corresponded with Harrison, and whose memories went back to Henry Edger's Modern Times community at Brentwood, Long Island, about which Conway had written with studied irony in the early *Fortnightly*.[7] Since the Positivist movement in America seemed moribund, Harrison had been surprised in Chicago to be asked by a former follower of William Frey's, Dr M. Sahud, a practising physician, to administer the Sacrament of Presentation to his infant son. The Sahuds were probably not true Positivists, but he obliged them anyway in his suite, arranging the furniture and vases of lilies sent up from the auditorium. The father provided the text (Harrison's own) and the mother, an 'eager Russian fanatic', looked on 'open-mouthed' with her Russian and German friends. Afterwards she appeared ready to embrace him. These 'strange medieval creatures' made him feel like a bona fide priest.[8]

Harrison's letters to Ethel showed how much he was enjoying himself, especially in great houses like Hewitt's, with its fine old Italian and French art of all kinds. But American banquet food proved too rich. 'Every meal begins with oysters, and consists of ice cream, oranges, olives, ice-water, champagne, strawberries, turtle-soup, salads, and cigars. Oh, heavens! everything I hate.' And he came near to hating the endless handshaking and talking expected of him: 'no South African mule in the Boer War was drove so hard.' When welcomed at the Authors' Club in New York as if he were 'Carlyle, Ruskin, Gladstone, and John Burns in one', he felt obliged to explain that he 'hardly counted as "An Author" at home, but as a crank who lectured a small lot of fanatics in a dingy hole'. That, at least, is what he told Ethel; at the Club he was no doubt less self-deprecating.[9] He met the ubiquitous Roosevelt again, and the Millionaires Club feted him at a banquet just before his departure. Feeling like a schoolboy going home for the holidays, he boarded the *Teutonic* with £188 left over from his honorariums. But the hob-nobbing with great money was to continue. He carried introductions to several passengers, among them J. P. Morgan, who had just bought out Carnegie. To Ethel he observed that Morgan should be useful in keeping the ship afloat—'if God protects the dollar as they say'.

Harrison was soon making literary use of his experiences. In a review for the *New York Times* he compared socialism to an attempt to divide up the profits of a great transatlantic liner among its officers, crew, and builders—a parallel that John Spargo, the Cornish coalminer turned socialist agitator, found incomplete. Why, he asked, should not the men who made the machinery that produced the ship's plates also be compensated? Harrison, once labour's friend, had become 'a somewhat hopeless degenerate'.[10] In another essay, Harrison described American businessmen as hard-driving but philanthropic, an estimate the *Spectator* found curiously tolerant for one who called British businessmen 'swindlers and braggarts' responsible for the Boer War.[11]

The *Spectator* was quoting one of four vituperative letters Harrison wrote on the war for the *Daily News* after his return. He was inspired by Emily Hobhouse's eye-witness reports of the British 'concentration' camps for Boer civilians in South Africa. Despite the warning of her uncle, Lord Hobhouse, that a 'wordy war' waged on her behalf would do no good, he saw that this 'lady of unimpeachable good faith' had given the protesters new ammunition. Now, he contended, the aim of the British was 'not to defeat an enemy—but to crush a people', and to do so in defiance of 'the recognized laws of civilized war'. This 'new policy of rage and barbarism' had already been used against Afghans, Burmese, Sudanese, and Chinese; now it was being used against people of European origin. He assured the working men of England that they had been 'deceived, hoodwinked, and tricked' into supporting 'crimes' in a war that could only bring them 'reduced wages, dearer food, straitened living, higher taxes'.[12] The *Daily News* termed his language 'Miltonic', and it may have provided inspiration for Campbell-Bannerman's famous 'methods of barbarism' speech, for it came after Harrison's first letter, which use some form of the word four times.[13] When Emily Hobhouse attempted another visit to South Africa, she was denied entry at what Harrison now called the 'Cape of No Hope'. Returning to London she found many houses closed to her, but not the Harrisons'. On one occasion they added lustre to their reception for her by including Blunt and two socially-conscious dramatists, Lady Gregory and Henry Arthur Jones.[14] And Harrison earned the praise of George Meredith by challenging Frederick Pollock's suggestion that legal justification might be found for executing Boer prisoners. Harrison argued that if the executions were thought necessary, the law should be changed, for as it stood they were simply murder.[15]

Angry as he was during the war's last phases, Harrison had some pleasant interludes—the long-awaited King Alfred Millenary celebration in Winchester in September 1901, and a visit to Skibo Castle, Andrew Carnegie's palatial summer home, later in the month.[16] The 'laird', as Harrison was soon calling him, had long been cultivating English intellectuals—Morley, Arnold, and Spencer notably—but with none of them did he seem to have as much in common as with Harrison. Both were energetic, voluble, short and stocky, with ruddy faces and white hair, moustache, and goatee; both had a much-loved younger wife and a daughter born late in the marriage; and neither was ever at a loss to explain how to alleviate the world's ills. Harrison thought Carnegie 'keen as a razor' but as full of fads as Ruskin, possessing an 'insight that amounts to genius' but 'often wrong-headed and ignorant'. Carnegie, he said, treated him as if he were 'a combination of Apostle and Crown Prince'. For that reason alone it is not surprising that Harrison's four visits to Skibo, in 1901, 1902, 1904, and 1908, were gratifying.

'Heaven on Earth', as Carnegie termed the castle he had bought and virtually rebuilt at the turn of the century, was on Dornoch Firth on the North Sea coast of Scotland. Harrison found that it offered guests 'comfort and convenience carried to the highest point', and he attributed these virtues to Carnegie's 'real genius for mechanics' and 'absolutely unlimited purse'. The 'tremendous feudal and sumptuous' chamber assigned to Harrison had twelve electric lights, carved oak panelling on the ceiling and walls, and a marble bathroom. The furniture was all of carved oak, and the wardrobe had fifty brass hooks—a welcome contrast to the horrors of Laffitte's guest room. The castle was more comfortable and luxurious than Sutton Place, but also lacked its historical charm. Everything was new: the gargoyles 'fresh as paint', the colours in the Turkey carpets 'rather too vivid', and the books, selected by Lord Acton and therefore sure to contain no 'nonsense or rubbish', had all been newly leather-bound, and many had uncut pages.[17] But time would mend these faults and make the place 'a dream of beauty about 300 years hence, if castles and parks then exist'.

Meanwhile, there was much to be relished. Skirling bagpipes called the guests to meals and the great pipe organ resounded in the halls every morning. It amused Harrison to see men and women frolicking 'American style' in the glass-enclosed swimming bath, and to know that each day twenty-five horse-drawn carriages waited at the main door to take the guests to their chosen diversion—to golf links, a salmon-stocked stream, shooting grounds, or rambles along the Firth. Sometimes Carnegie's steam yacht was available for short cruises. But Harrison's favourite sport was chaffing the laird. One topic was Carnegie's ignorance of labour history—though Harrison probably refrained from mentioning the infamous Homestead Riots of 1892 that were the climax of Carnegie's vexed relations with his steel workers. Another bone of humorous contention was golf, which Harrison maintained was no game at all; the set of clubs Carnegie gave him ended up in Austin's possession. The best jest of all seems to have been Carnegie's unimaginable wealth. During one picnic at which his nine-year-old daughter helped with the clearing up, Harrison remarked to her father that she could always earn her living as a scullery maid if he were to 'crack up'. Away from Skibo, Harrison allowed himself to criticize Carnegie's reforming interests. When asked by the *Daily Chronicle* to comment on phonetic spelling, which Carnegie endorsed, Harrison scrawled 'vile fad' on the telegram's answer form and then had to make peace with his friend.[18] And when Patrick Geddes submitted to him his first major town-planning scheme before entering it in a competition for a Carnegie grant to redevelop his native Dunfermline, Harrison observed that all the great man's wealth could probably not save 'a generation given over to "sport" and trivialities'.[19]

Harrison was most audacious—and most serious—when it came to religion. Carnegie had first heard of Positivism in the 1860s in Courtlandt Palmer's discussion group in New York, and he was prepared to find virtue in it. He even described his own Hero Fund to Harrison as 'The Worship of Humanity in its highest form'.[20] Encouraged, Harrison sought to nudge him nearer the true faith. Asked to join a group going to church one Sunday at Skibo, Harrison announced that instead he would hold his own worship, using Ethel's hymnal and preaching his own sermon—on the 'vanity of riches'. Carnegie thereupon demanded to hear something from the hymnal, and Harrison obliged with Blake's 'Pity Has a Human Face' and Ethel's 'Faithful Service is the Burden', later handing over the book for inspection. The question of a donation to the Positivists must have arisen at some time, for in 1904 Harrison complained to Ethel that though Carnegie was giving 'two organs to churches and chapels every week', and was 'entirely with us on religion', the Positivists could expect nothing, as Carnegie feared losing his 'usefulness' by openly subsidizing them. Harrison had to be content with purely personal favours, such as braces of grouse and the articles and books that flowed from Carnegie's pen so plentifully that Harrison told him he challenged 'us poor devils ... in the world of letters'.[21] In 1908 Harrison unveiled a bust of his friend in the Carnegie Library in

Keighley, Yorkshire, and made his last trip to Skibo. For some reason, he had begun to feel unwelcome, and when Carnegie tendered another invitation he pleaded age as an excuse for declining, though he was still taking Mediterranean cruises.[22] The truth is probably that the two men had become less tolerant of each other's thoughts on certain issues. In addition to religion, there was the international peace movement, which Carnegie supported enthusiastically but Harrison called only one of 'those half-crown snowballs to save mankind'. There was only one true movement, after all.[23] In June 1914, when Harrison, like many others, was expecting a European war, Carnegie sent him a copy of his own favourite maxim: 'All is well since all grows better.'[24] Even someone as accustomed to vague inspirational generalizations as Harrison could not credit that. Yet at Carnegie's death in 1919 he relied on conventional rhetoric of an equally uncritical sort to recall to the widow his dead friend's 'noble character' and 'splendid gifts to humanity'.[25]

Besides his wealth it was Carnegie's prestige that Harrison coveted for Positivism. By the time of their meeting the movement was sadly reduced in both personal and financial assets. The original nucleus were now old men, with only middle-aged men to assist them, none their equal in education or ability. In 1889 newspaper advertising of their meetings had been curtailed, an economy Harrison later said he regretted, though he was always ambivalent about proselytizing, insisting that numbers alone meant little and scorning the Chapel Street Positivists for holding open-air meetings. In a vain attempt to find an hour when working men could come for meetings on Sundays, Harrison, under protest, agreed that year also to change the hour from 4 to 8 p.m., and the next year to try 7 p.m., though both the new hours interfered with his dinner. He also consented to some desperate juggling of Newton Hall's funds. To cover a deficit of £50 in the General Fund in 1889, money was drawn from the Publishing Fund. By 1895 the total of both, plus the Paris Fund, had fallen to £242, and by 1903 it was down to £162.[26]

By that time, however, expenses had been correspondingly reduced. The lease on Newton Hall expired in 1902, and the Royal Scottish Corporation reclaimed the room. It then stood empty for years, and the Positivists could only conclude that their anti-war views had made them undesirable as tenants.[27] In any case, what they required now was a room seating 50 not 150, and at a cost lower than the £200 annual rent of Newton Hall. The place they found was just down Fetter Lane at number 10 Clifford's Inn. Here they reduced their activities to Sunday meetings, the women's guild, the men's discussion group, and occasional pilgrimages and special programmes. Two years later they moved to Essex Hall, just south of Fleet Street, and in 1906 yet again, to South Place, Finsbury, where they shared the Ethical Society's home. In 1909 they again found a room of their own, number 11 Lincoln's Inn Fields, their address until well into the war years.[28]

Anxious changes in the lives of Harrison's two oldest friends and colleagues coincided with the Society's wanderings. Beesly and Bridges both resigned from his Positivist Committee in 1902 in poor health and financial straits. Beesly, a widower for over a decade, settled in St. Leonard's-on-Sea, leaving Harrison to edit the *Positivist Review*, 'a horrid bore'.[29] Bridges, forced to sell The Brambles, his Wimbledon house, moved first to Ladbroke Gardens, Notting Hill, and then to Park Place Gardens, Paddington, part of the time taking paying guests, among them Godfrey Harrison. Suffering from tuberculosis, a legacy from his ill-paid and frustrating labours among London's sick poor, Bridges sought healthier conditions in Bournemouth early in 1906; but soon a bicycle accident weakened him further and he and his wife then went to Tunbridge Wells. A town of happy honeymoon memories to Harrison, it became a kind of hell for Bridges. He experienced religious hallucinations in which he believed alternately that only a Roman Catholic could be saved, and that he was already damned. When he died on 15 June, leaving no instructions for burial, Mary Bridges, who had never abandoned her Anglicanism, arranged for a service and burial in the local parish cemetery. Dismayed, the London Positivists declined to attend, but in deference to Leonard Hobhouse, her sister's husband, they refrained from adverse comments in their own memorial service. It was held at South Place, with Harrison the principal speaker, for Beesly was too stricken to read his tribute.[30]

In the following six years, death further thinned the ranks of Newton Hall Positivists with any reputation beyond the membership. In 1907 Godfrey Lushington died, twelve years after his retirement from the Home Office. He had been much honoured, serving as an LCC alderman after Harrison and receiving a C.B., a K.C.B., and then the Grand Cross of the Order of St. Michael and St. George. At the time of the Boer War he had quietly dissociated himself from the Positivists, but their eulogies were none the less warm.[31] Vernon, his twin, survived him by five years. Despite his important offices as county court judge, Advocate-General, and Secretary to the Admiralty, he remained faithful to the movement, though after his retirement in 1900 he did little for it but write occasionally in the *Positivist Review* and make his generous annual contribution to the funds. At Newton Hall he had been the acknowledged expert in art and music, and both received less attention from the Positivists after his retirement.[32] Another Positivist link to the London cultural world, Mrs Fanny Hertz, died in 1908. She had never played a leading role in the group, but her interest in everything Harrison did seemed unbounded. He might occasionally dismiss her comments as 'gushing', but he confided in her all the same and no doubt was flattered by her unremitting attention, just as visitors to her Harley Street receptions in the 1870s had been happy to accept her invitations, though many of them—Henry James and James Sully, to name two—spoke of her slightingly as a lion-hunter.[33] The deaths of all three of these old friends closed the door on part of the past that must have seemed all the sadder to contemplate because the hopes of those years had been largely unfulfilled.

But Harrison could observe the decline of organized Positivism with a diminishing sense of personal responsibility. In June 1903 he retired as Chairman of the London Positivist Committee and turned over the editorship of the *Positivist Review* to Swinny. For a time he continued to head the Positivist Society. Conscious of its reduced resources, he vetoed a proposal for a new centre in Gower Street and encouraged co-operative activities with other groups, for example, a conference on the Far East in 1904, the expenses of which he paid. Finally, in the autumn of 1904 he resigned the presidency of the Positivist Society, recalling for its members the unseemly clinging to authority of their 'vanished chief' Pierre Laffitte. Under a new leader, he suggested, they should consider 'concentration with kindred bodies'. Yet by transferring to Swinny 'the entire authority to confer sacraments and to delegate other duties as given me by Pierre Laffitte', he seemed to imply a kind of apostolic succession in their own body that would make any future amalgamation improbable. There was some grumbling about his choice of successor, for Swinny was not married and at the age of forty-seven was unlikely ever to be so, and marriage was a requirement of the Positivist priesthood. Moreover, Swinny had always been less interested in religion than in politics. But since there was no candidate more suitable than Swinny, with his leisure and a private income, he was duly accepted.[34]

One reason Harrison gave up the Positivist leadership was that in 1902 he and Ethel emulated Bridges and Beesly by moving out of London. With all their sons away from home most of the time, 38 Westbourne Terrace had become far too large. After returning from America, Harrison began looking for a country house. A foray into Kent took him to Tunbridge Wells. At the Calverley Hotel he thought of his thirty years of married life that had started there, and momentarily wished to relive it, but then sensibly realized 'how much more precious seem these days than those.'[35] And he meant to enjoy the time left to him in a pastoral setting, away from the noisy bustle of London. But long walks in the Tunbridge Wells area disclosed nothing suitable, and it was not until the spring of 1902 that he found the right place. Elm Hill, west of Hawkhurst, Kent, was a two-storey red-brick house built early in the nineteenth century with an eight-bedroom wing added later. A large ground-floor room at the rear with floor-to-ceiling windows overlooking formal gardens made a fine study for Harrison. The property consisted of thirty-five partly-wooded acres that included a working farm. The region in its way was as conservative as Blackdown. An adjacent estate, Seacox Heath, belonged to an old Oxford friend, George J. Goschen, now Viscount Goschen and recently retired from political life after serving as Chancellor of the Exchequer in Lord Salisbury's government and then as First Lord of the Admiralty. He had encouraged Harrison to become his neighbour, citing the good climate and convenience of Elm Hill to the Hawkhurst station. His recommendation served to offset the prediction of waterless wells from Harrison's former Oxford law colleague, Sir William Anson, who had occupied Elm Hill before becoming the University's Vice-Chancellor and a Member of Parliament.[36]

Not only did the water in this land of Goschen prove plentiful but the life of a country gentleman suited Harrison. He subscribed to Flimwell church, built by Goschen on his estate; purchased a landau formerly owned by a peer; and wrote a historical account of nearby Bodiam Castle. Revelling in his role as a man of the soil he invited Blunt to pasture his horses on a meadow adjacent to Elm Hill and pretended that overseeing his rose beds and adding tulips and hyacinths to his twenty thousand daffodils constituted a new vocation. It was a link with Tennyson's successor, Alfred Austin, who lived at nearby Swinford Old Manor and, according to Blunt, had 'floated to the Laureateship on the success of a prose volume about his garden in Kent'. After a decade's correspondence, Harrison suggested an exchange of visits when their gardens were in full bloom: were they not both 'men of Kent and gardeners'?[37] Henry James wrote from Rye comparing his flight from London and the Harrisons', professing to find it 'charming' that 'literally but one turning in the road' lay between them. James finally took that road, but found to his consternation that either his loquacious host or the witty lawyer E. F. Pember, another guest, pre-empted him whenever he opened his mouth to speak. In 1911 he informed the Harrisons that he was returning to London except for summers, being unable any longer to tolerate Rye's 'solitude and confinement'.[38] These were just the characteristics of Hawkhurst

Harrison most appreciated. 'We know nothing of politics, fashion, or gossip', he wrote to Lady Dorothy Nevill, the veteran Tory hostess whom he always enjoyed calling on in Berkeley Square. To Ethel he contended that he cared little where he lived, for he clung not to 'places but to persons', and with her he could be happy 'even in an ox waggon in the veldt'.[39]

Leaving Westbourne Terrace could not have been quite as painless as this suggests, but with his sturdy good sense Harrison saw that it was necessary. His investments had not been doing as well as he had hoped, and he was not content merely to complain that his returns were declining as an inevitable consequence of the war. For over a decade he had been augmenting his income by his pen, and the relative isolation of Hawkhurst would make preserving time for his writing easier. At an age when most men with sons were no longer financially responsible for them, he found that all but Godfrey still needed his help. Bernard, painting in France and Italy, required over £300 a year, and when his father suggested that he seek employment in London, he protested that he had 'certain ideas' he hoped one day to express. Harrison must have heard an echo in this of his own youthful words, for there was no more talk of a change in Bernard's life, and his parents thereafter sought to further his career by pressing invitations to his annual London shows on their friends.[40] Austin, too, had ideas to express. His first book, *The Pan-Germanic Doctrine*, in 1904, so impressed Sir Alfred Harmsworth by its Germanophobia that he installed Austin as editor of his prestigious Sunday paper, *The Observer*. Harmsworth obtained Austin's European address from his father, writing to request it from Sutton Place, which Harmsworth had purchased when Sidney Harrison's lease expired in 1902. Known as the 'Mad Lord' in Surrey, Harmsworth soon demonstrated his arbitrary power with Austin, replacing him with J. L. Garvin in 1908 but allowing him to stay on to do literary and drama criticism. Harrison was not altogether dismayed, for Austin's editorials had sometimes been very hard on the Liberals, whom Harrison thought 'worthy men trying their best'. In 1910 Sir Alfred Mond engaged Austin to edit the *English Review*, which Ford Madox Ford had founded two years before, and he held the post for thirteen years with considerable success.[41] Godfrey, meanwhile, remained in the solicitors' firm founded by his uncles, displaying dissatisfaction with his staid career in an occasional fling—once, it was reported at Elm Hill, motoring with a typist.[42] René, equally without real vocational or emotional satisfaction, stayed on with Jackson, the architect, long after he hinted that René should strike out on his own. Finally, in a desperate bid for work,

René sailed for Buenos Aires in 1911, where he found little success before the outbreak of the World War.[43]

Olive, on her eighteenth birthday, was said by her father to be competent in French, German, and Italian, and 'something of a historian'. Yet when sent to Allenswood, the expensive girls school Mlle Souvestre opened in Wimbledon after giving up Les Ruches, Olive was desperately unhappy. Part of the trouble was no doubt the intellectuality and dogmatism of her father's old friend. Stimulating to some women— Eleanor Roosevelt among them—these traits may have been too much like her father's to please Olive. In any case, Mlle Souvestre's death in 1905, which evoked published tributes from both her parents, released Olive. Thereafter she was content to ride, play tennis, and visit her friends.[44] She was especially close to Muriel Harris, and their separation during Olive's stay at Allenswood seems to have contributed to her unhappiness there. Later Muriel became a novelist and journalist—a 'new woman'—but she nevertheless pleased Harrison by little attentions and expressions of affection that he missed from his own less demonstrative daughter.[45]

Another young woman whom the Harrisons befriended was Ivy Pretious. Six years older than Olive, she came to their notice about 1895, when her mother, possibly a Positivist, emigrated to South Africa. At Westbourne Terrace Ivy learned enough about dressmaking and journalism to work for *Our Home* magazine and then a Paris dress firm before Harrison got her the post of personal secretary to Emily Hobhouse in 1902. The next year, perhaps again with his help, she became the office secretary of the Free Trade Union. Living on her own in Chelsea, she contributed to the Positivist funds and attended their meetings, but had a private life about which the Harrisons knew nothing. It included a troubled intimacy with the young philosopher Bertrand Russell, who was mired in an unhappy marriage to Alys Pearsall Smith. He protested his innocence, insisting to a friend that he was in fact 'horribly anxious' about Ivy, who was in 'the gravest danger' from the 'great influence' that Reginald McKenna, a Liberal MP and prominent free trader, had gained over her 'by means of his ability and strength of will'.[46] Whatever Ivy's entanglements were, she was clear of them by 1909, when Harrison told Ethel happily of seeing Ivy at a Positivist meeting 'with a sprig of the peerage in tow'. This was Charles Tennyson, grandson of the poet and a rising barrister. Harrison soon learned of their engagement and their desire that he perform the marriage ceremony. They were probably inspired by their friends George Macaulay Trevelyan, the historian, and his wife Janet, whose mother, Mrs Humphry Ward, had devised their unorthodox marriage service. But Harrison objected: the plan would make the Laureate 'turn over in his grave' and embarrass Charles's stepfather, Augustine Birrell, the Secretary for Ireland. 'Had I not better "Give you away" '? he asked, adding, 'Who else will if not I—who knew you when you were 15 in a short frock?' In the end the wedding took place in the Henry VII Chapel of Westminster Abbey, with neither Fred nor Ethel present. But their absence implied no breach of old ties. During a visit of the couple to Elm Hill in June 1912, the Harrisons learned that the baby Ivy was expecting, the first descendant in the third generation from the Laureate, would, if a boy, be named Arthur Hallam.[47] It was a boy; but when they were asked to serve as his 'sponsors' Harrison explained that he was too old, even if Ethel agreed, to carry out the responsibilities as Positivists understood them. Moreover, he disapproved of withholding Anglican rites from the child: there were 'inalienable public interests involved in such a step'.[48]

Still another 'new woman' whose ideas of marriage and family differed from Harrison's was Edith Deverell, who became engaged to Francis Marvin in 1904. Harrison agreed to marry them until he learned that Edith, an advocate of women's suffrage, wished to speak a few words during the ceremony to state her dissent from certain Positivist principles. There would be no such 'evasions', Harrison declared, and declined to conduct the service.[49] Yet cordial relations continued. From Elm Hill came invitations to visit and encouragement of both the Marvins' literary activities, as well as advice on the naming of their first child. Harrison favoured a distinctive name, and Ethel 'scientific nomenclature'—which seemed to mean taking account of the number of syllables in the first and last names. Though birth control was not a subject on which Positivists held official views, Ethel cited her own case to Edith in explaining that young mothers needed to 'lie fallow'; and after the Marvins lost a child some years later Harrison told them he hoped it would be 'long before you have to enlarge your nursery'.[50]

Their own happiness made Fred and Ethel rejoice at every new wedding in their circle. Olive was apparently far from marriage, and her father felt obliged to take her with him on some of his European trips. Their interests understandably differed; he would, for example, rather read a book in his room in the evening than join her in smoke-filled hotel lounges. Uncomfortable without at least one English newspaper a day, he occasionally fired off a letter to the editor in response to some provocative story, and his experiences abroad could prompt remarks. Thus on his Swiss jaunt with Olive in 1906 he took the trouble to praise Zurich's new National Museum in *The Times* and deplore the habits of his countrymen abroad who neglected scenery in their eagerness to break climbing records. But in a few days even he had seen enough of the Alps for that year: a five-hour trek with Olive over the St. Gotthard Pass from Hospenthal to Airolo in a snowstorm left them wet and exhausted. They recovered their spirits at Bellagio, where their hotel was adjacent to the magnificent Villa Serbelloni and shared its gardens and views of Lake Como. The region was sacred to Harrison, who had been there on his wedding journey; but Olive was a less satisfactory travelling companion than Ethel. She was inclined to do things her own way, and was too much attached to her Kodak, which he told her was a 'mechanical invention to enable people to *have* great buildings or views without looking at them'.[51]

Alone in Switzerland the next year at the time of his seventy-sixth birthday, Harrison wrote affectionate letters to his daughter that were obviously intended for publication: they appeared in *My Alpine Jubilee* in 1908. In contrast to such self-conscious reflections, reminiscences, and Ruskinian scenery descriptions, the letters he wrote to Ethel the next year from Montreux, where he had taken Olive for the winter sports, frankly disclose the inevitable differences in the way father and daughter viewed their holiday. She wished to join climbing and bobsledding parties, but he objected on the grounds that the former were dangerous and the latter required the youths of both sexes to wrap their arms and legs around each other as they sped down the slopes. And she was much too willing to spend time at the card table in the evening with the Philipson-Stow girls and their recently widowed mother, who made up his party. Not only did he despise card-playing, but he had hoped the girls might meet marriageable men at the hotel; for since that 'D–d fool Fred' Philipson-Stow had left his capital tied up, Harrison believed the widow had an obligation to marry her daughters well—yet she was forcing them to dress 'like black crows' and take meals isolated from the other guests. When the girls preferred touring a chocolate factory to a scenic ramble through the snow with him one afternoon, he complained of another wasted opportunity: the young were 'as insensible to the beauties of nature as dogs and cats'. But then, a grown man of some note could also be wrongheaded about the great outdoors: he dispatched a postcard to Theodore Roosevelt telling him to 'come here for ice sports instead of shooting lions in the tropics'.[52]

POSITIVISM AND SOCIOLOGY

The decline of organized Positivism in England did not annihilate all interest in Comte. In 1906 A. W. Benn's *History of English Rationalism in the Nineteenth Century* generously assessed his importance by following Lewes and placing him in the English empirical tradition. Benn thought that Harrison's treatment of Anglicanism in 'Neo-Christianity' had been too optimistic: the Church had not yielded to the arguments of critics like Harrison. Rather, an attenuated creed had become the 'faith of the educated classes'. Therefore Harrison's forty-five-year-old essay was still valuable, though, paradoxically, in Benn's judgement, Neo-Christianity seemed 'more likely to absorb the Religion of Humanity than to be absorbed by it'. In spite of this reservation, Harrison embraced Benn in the *Positivist Review* as an 'unconscious Positivist, or a "Positivist on the make" '.[53] Two years later he was equally impressed by Benn's *Modern England*, for though it suggested the author was closer to Mill than to Comte, Harrison thought it made him out to be 'if not a Positivist, a convinced humanitarian Agnostic', and 'for social action these two schools of thought are always found in practical co-operation.'[54]

Like works enhancing Positivism's intellectual reputation, volumes facilitating first-hand study of Comte were always welcome. In 1896 Harrison provided an introduction to a new edition of Harriet Martineau's condensed English version of the *Cours de philosophie positive* and restored its last ten pages, suppressed by Miss Martineau because she feared their sketch of the Religion of Humanity and the Positivist polity would alienate most English readers. Harrison quoted Comte's praise of her work as useful for a popular audience, but added his own long-standing objection to relying on it for systematic study.[55] Within a few years it became evident that, to publishers at least, there seemed no need for any more accurate translations. When Harrison's colleagues H. Gordon Jones and Paul Descours produced a new English version of the first two chapters of the *Cours* in 1904, it was only with difficulty that the Rationalist Press Association, nominally headed by Holyoake, then in his eighties, could be prevailed upon to publish it. The sale of over seven thousand copies in three years, however, proved a pleasant surprise.[56]

Encouraged, the Positivists reissued two other new editions of Comte's works, Bridges's old translation of the first two chapters of the *Système de politique positive*—the *General View of Positivism*—in 1908, and Henry Dix Hutton's translation of Comte's early essays on social philosophy, in 1911. Both were posthumous publications of the translators with introductions by Harrison. He praised Bridges's text as easy to read because 'simpler' than Comte's,[57] whereas he said nothing at all about the achievement of Hutton, who had died in 1907. He had been one of Comte's last living executors and correspondents, and a passionate advocate of his social theory, which he had sought to apply to Ireland, where he was a colleague of John Kells Ingram at Trinity College Library, Dublin. But his association with Chapel Street and the Liverpool Positivists was enough to preclude a personal accolade from Harrison, whose sole comment on the translation was mention of its revision by Descours, Jones, and Swinny.[58]

Not all efforts to make Comte's writing available in England seemed equally desirable to Harrison and his colleagues. They left the editing and translating of his correspondence to the Chapel Street and Paris Positivists. In 1905 Harrison declined an offer from the apparently needy Holyoake to sell him his holograph letters from the Master; and in the same year Beesly confessed that the volumes of correspondence already in print suggested Comte's 'extreme unfitness to be a *pontiff*'.[59] Yet when Harrison reviewed one collection, made by Ingram in 1901, he managed to find evidence to use against the 'idle sneer' that Comte had undervalued women's intellect: he cited Comte's correspondence with the wife of the jurist John Austin, but said nothing about the passages in the *Catechism* and *Polity* relevant to the charge.[60] He and his colleagues were even more embarrassed by the details of Comte's private life, and perhaps for this reason they left the task of producing substantial biographical studies of him to two Positivists with a popular touch. One was F. J. Gould, who wrote *Auguste Comte* in 1920 for the Rationalist Press Association, with which he had been associated since its founding in 1893 even though its suspicion of all ritual troubled him. In 1908 he had left the Leicester secularists to open a Positivist church in a vacant shop in the city with flashing lights in the window illuminating portraits of the Positivist worthies. Later he drifted into moral education work in the schools.[61] The second biographer was Susan Style, artist and a founder of the Temple of Humanity in Liverpool; her *Auguste Comte, Thinker and Lover* in 1928 gave a highly romantic rendering of the facts.[62]

Though Harrison let most French works on Comte go unremarked, and probably unread, in 1899 he welcomed Lucien Lévy-Bruhl's edition of Mill's letters to Comte, and in 1903 wrote an introduction to the English translation of his analysis of Postivism. As a philosopher at the Sorbonne, Lévy-Bruhl could advance that part of Comte's thought Harrison knew to be more apt to attain lasting influence than the religion. He especially valued Lévy-Bruhl's endorsement of the hierarchy of the sciences, which Spencer had so contemptuously rejected, and his belief in the continuity of Comte's scientific and religious thought, a point the English Positivists had always treated as crucial. And Harrison was glad to see that Lévy-Bruhl approved Comte's appropriation of de Vigny's motto: 'What is a great life? A thought of youth fulfilled in the maturity of age.'[63] Old enough to be interested in signs of continuity in his own life, Harrison had already begun to use the motto when asked for his autograph. He never claimed to have added substantially to the body of Positivist thought, only to have devoted his adult life to its promulgation and application. By doing so he liked to think he was fulfilling the youthful aspiration that made his life in this sense analogous to Comte's.

The contemporary whose life more truly paralleled Comte's was Herbert Spencer. Yet Harrison did not compare Spencer to Comte when in America he was called upon to reminisce about 'Great Victorians'. Rather he chose Darwin, explaining to his audiences that both men had earned their reputations for studies which they had undertaken in 'delicate health' and carried out with less emphasis on extensive reading than on 'the right choice of books'. This latter notion probably appealed to Harrison, for he thought Comte had expressed it in his doctrine of 'hygiène cérébrale', according to which one should read only what directly furthered one's work and spiritual life. After returning from America, Harrison got Ethel to copy out for Spencer the passage in his American address likening him to the great biologist. Spencer was pleased,[64] and in a gesture of friendliness early in 1902 subscribed to the *Positivist Review*. But he was far from being converted to its principles. When at Carnegie's behest Harrison sought to cheer him up the following July, he had to report that Spencer was 'still troubling his mind needlessly about the "Infinite and the Unknowable"'.[65] A year and a half later Spencer entered the Infinite and the Unknowable. During the cremation ceremony at Golders Green, which Harrison did not attend, a former Indian government official and Balliol graduate, Shyamaji Krishnavarma, announced his intention of giving £1,000 in stock to endow an annual Herbert Spencer Lecture. Oxford University agreed to sponsor it, and upon Auberon Herbert's recommendation Harrison was chosen to inaugurate the series. The terms did not oblige him to mention Spencer at all, but having the last word in their long debate was too much of a temptation to forgo. On 5 March 1905, speaking at the University on philosophic and religious issues for the first time for over fifty years, Harrison promised he would neither revive old controversies nor eulogize Spencer—but he did both.[66]

The ironies, after all, had to be explored. Oxford was sponsoring the commemoration of a man who had 'curiously misunderstood' its culture, a commemoration by a son of the University whose 'only claim to philosophy' was that for thirty years he had promoted a thinker to whom Spencer had denied greatness. Harrison did not neglect the similarities between Spencer's Synthetic Philosophy and 'Positive systems in the widest sense'—those of Darwin, Littré, Mill, Buckle, Clifford, Huxley, Bain, and Lewes. All recognized the reign of law in every cognitive domain, an evolutionary principle, the relativity of knowledge, and the need to verify hypotheses. All agreed that the goal of philosophy was some synthesis of knowledge. And all were committed to the betterment of human life. For Spencer's labours in constructing his system he deserved to be called the 'most prominent English philosopher of the nineteenth century'. His life had fulfilled de Vigny's maxim. But his life's work was doomed from the start: the kind of objective synthesis of knowledge he sought was an 'impossible Utopia'. His key to all sciences, his universal evolutionary principles, were unprovable, and he offered no general theory of history. Worse, his philosophy included no positive moral teaching, though he had triumphed over his own system in becoming a moral philosopher. The implication of all this, of course, was that as an innovative thinker and social reformer, Spencer was inferior to Comte.[67]

Skilled though he was in making Positivist propaganda out of almost any philosophic position, Harrison found some too uncongenial or too intractable to confront publicly. He disliked late nineteenth-century neo-Hegelianism too much to formulate his objections to it. In the early twentieth century he was similarly alienated by Henri Bergson's Vitalism, but left it to H. Gordon Jones to criticize it in the *Positivist Review*, contenting himself with making marginal notes on his copy of T. E. Hulme's translation of the *Introduction to Metaphysics*. Harrison could commend Bergson's abandonment of traditional metaphysics, but nothing else. The controlling idea of intuition he derided as 'the resort of a simpleton' and 'crude guessing'; and the famous image of reality as a stream passing over the tunnel dug by metaphysics and under the bridge thrown up by science was only an 'unmeaning metaphor'. Beside other parts of the text he thickly sprinkled epithets like 'nonsense', 'wild nonsense', 'roaring nonsense', 'jargon', and 'words! words! words!' The new metaphysics was 'Mystical jabber! worthy of a Hindu Yoghi or Buddhist monk'. His final comment was 'Wordy Humbug!'[68]

Harrison may not have known that Bergson once called the *Cours* 'one of the great works of modern philosophy' and Comte 'a metaphysician at heart'—no pejorative term to Bergson; nor that two of Bergson's disciples sought to appropriate the words 'positive' and 'positivism' for their version of intuitionism. All three philosophers admired Comte's understanding that empirical knowledge could not improve mankind's lot without creative imagination.[69] Harrison gave lip-service to Comte's assertion of that idea, but the great reservations he had about Comte's myth-making attest to his fundamentally literal-minded and commonsensical philosophical temperament. The essay of Harrison's which shows his imaginative impulse at its limit was intended to discredit the metaphysical yearnings of one of his contemporaries. Entitled 'From This World to the Next', the essay is fictional autobiography in a conventional mode. He tells of reading late into the night and then being suddenly paralysed by a stroke. Comatose, he passes over into a condition described by poets, mystics, and drug-takers: the self is absorbed in a cosmic unity of indescribable sublimity, all motion and light and sound. Space becomes time, thought action, and numbers meaningless. Contraries evaporate in harmony, and craving for eternal life seems only a 'sordid lust of the flesh'. But in an instant these wonders vanish, he awakens, and the book he had been reading falls from his hand. It is *Human Personality and its Survival of Bodily Death*, by F. W. H. Myers, the spiritualist. Replacing it on the shelf, Harrison opens his Milton to the speech of the angel Raphael: 'Be lowly wise: think only what concerns thee and thy being.' The next day he turns with renewed ardour to the work he had been studying before Myers: it is Comte's last volume, the *Subjective Synthesis*.[70] Its thesis is the need to subordinate the real to the ideal and science to poetry, to extend the scope of human love to the cosmos and destiny. The new synthesis is humanity, earth, and space, and the new logic is expressed by acrostics: the first letters of sentences within a paragraph spell out the name of some great servant of Humanity or a word rich in Positivist connotations. Though the English Positivists accepted the title of the volume as one of their commonplaces, they never sought to make the work available to English readers, and it is doubtful that many of Harrison's followers knew its contents.

The best extended treatment of Harrison's philosophy and religion is his *Positive Evolution of Religion: Its Moral and Social Reaction*, which appeared in 1913. Besides explicating Comte's religious principles, he considers their value as a substitute for conventional religions. Offering no single definition of Positivism, he argues that it is at once a scheme of education, a religion, a philosophy, and a phase of socialism, and that 'its strength lies in the correspondence of its parts.' Christianity, on the contrary, he describes as undergoing recurring periods of 'shrinkage'. Monotheism represents a shrinkage from Polytheism, Protestantism from Catholicism, Neo-Christianity from Protestantism, Theism from Christianity altogether. At each stage religious sentiment and theology are lost. Yet in an eloquent conclusion Harrison advocates, not for the first time, a considerably shrunken version of the Religion of Humanity, for he denies that Comte invented it—he only gave it 'organic shape'—and asserts that 'there is a mass of Positivism on lines not all identical with Comte's ... The "service" of Humanity ... is a heart full of loving sympathies and a life full of humane acts.'[71] Dean Fremantle rightly observed that Harrison seemed to have hardly moved beyond the position he took in 'Neo-Christianity', so vague were his criteria for Positivism;[72] but Norman Douglas in the *English Review* predicted that the way he spoke of worship would repel the 'finely wrought nature'. Harrison regretted that Austin had assigned his book to 'an utter sceptic', yet he conceded that Douglas had pointed to the real problem of Positivism: its religious spirit revolted the emancipated, while its scientific logic alienated 'every kind of Xian, Deist, and even Mystical Agnostic'.[73]

The break-up of the old leadership of Newton Hall at the turn of the century coincided with uncertainties at Chapel Street, where Congreve's death in 1899 left a vacuum that proved hard to fill. Its satellite groups gradually disappeared except for the Liverpool church under Albert Crompton and the Styles, and Quin's Newcastle congregation. In 1906 a French journalist, Henry Dussauze, assumed control, but his innovations, such as open-air preaching, led to his forced retirement in 1910.[74] He was replaced by Philip Thomas, a fifty-six-year-old railway clerk at the Board of Trade. Loquacious and opinionated, Thomas had lower-middle-class notions of propriety and success that had estranged his son Edward, soon to be recognized as one of England's finest poets. When the father assumed leadership at Chapel Street, the son was barely supporting himself and his young family by writing an occasional commissioned book and regular book reviews, a few of which appeared in Austin's *English Review*. Harrison probably did not know him personally, but what he heard about Chapel Street under Thomas's leadership only made him scoff; the idea of using the name 'Church of Humanity' for 'that dingy hole in Chapel Street' was simply 'pour rire'. The 'silly so-called "services" ', he once said, prevented 'educated and thoughtful men' from taking Comte seriously.[75] Yet Thomas did very little that Congreve had not done there—or that Harrison had not done at Newton Hall.

Harrison was even more unhappy about developments in Paris. Laffitte's death in 1903 left Comte's rooms in the hands of Charles Jeannolle, his chosen successor, who managed to outdo Laffitte in inactivity. Even before Laffitte's death Jeannolle had annoyed Harrison by asking for an increase in the English subsidy. Harrison had rejected the request coldly, warning that after the move from Newton Hall there might be no subsidy at all: 'C'est triste, mais c'est vrai.'[76] But when Laffitte's family from the Gironde claimed possession of the rooms at 10 Rue Monsieur-le-Prince, Harrison felt obliged to join the Occidental Committee formed by Jeannolle to legitimize his occupancy, and he even went so far as to condone Jeannolle's proposal to include women, though after getting Ethel appointed Harrison convinced him that she alone of her sex should serve—temporarily and without a vote. In other ways Harrison made his presence on the committee felt. He took the trouble to attend its meetings in Paris in 1903 and 1904 and insisted he would have nothing to do with an expensive court case, an assertion at odds with his equally vehement declaration that he was not going to be blackmailed by Gironde 'peasants'.[77] When the exasperating Jeannolle delegated his 'spiritual' functions to a colleague, Émile Corra, and then Corra claimed the right to inherit Comte's rooms, Harrison and his English associates backed him, even when Corra was defeated and was forced to set up new quarters at 54 Rue La Seine. Perhaps they recalled an earlier departure of Positivists from their original centre in London. Certainly Harrison was as furious now with Jeannolle ('un coquin') as he had been with Congreve; he resigned from the Occidental Committee and with some financial loss liquidated his investment in the building society Laffitte had formed to purchase the rooms. In the same year, 1908, he resigned from Corra's group, also named the Occidental Committee, and gave his age as the reason, but Ethel remained a member.[78] He had long since stopped writing for Dr Hillemand's *Revue Occidentale*, and had never been interested in Corra's *Revue Positiviste Internationale*, though he allowed both to publish translations of his articles. Altogether he had lost sympathy and patience with the French Positivists. They could not even get his address right, he complained to Hillemand, adding pointedly that his German correspondents always did.[79]

Somewhat compensating for the decay of organized Positivism in the new century was the emergence of sociology as a respected discipline. Harrison viewed this as a consequence of Comte's influence, for had he not coined the term, demonstrated the need for a coherent view of society, and provided the hierarchy of sciences to show how it could be attained? 'Synthesis, synthesis, synthesis—is the first and last word for the modern time man', Harrison once told Marvin. But his criticism of Spencer showed that the synthesis had to come from Comte. Another synthesis, more grandiose even than Spencer's, that seemed to challenge Comte's priority was produced by the American 'father of sociology' Lester Ward. Acknowledging some papers Ward had sent him in 1896, Harrison said that they 'entirely proved' the essential similarity of

Spencer's classification of the sciences to Comte's, and he promised to call attention in England to Ward's work. He never did so, perhaps because Ward's emphasis on the 'scientific', rather than the historical or ethical study of society, was uncongenial, as was Ward's belief that state education was the primary agency of social progress. Moreover, he thought Ward, like Spencer, ignorant of eighteenth-century European intellectual history, the knowledge of which gave Comte his advantage over them.[80] The founding of the American Sociological Society in 1905 confirmed the irrevocable divergence of the discipline in America from Comte's model. On the Continent, too, sociology was undergoing a creative phase not foreshadowed by Comte and largely ignored by the English Positivists.

With the founding of the British Sociological Society in 1904, however, the Positivist view of the discipline was assured of a hearing. Bridges, Swinny, and Geddes were all on the governing council, and they and J. K. Ingram, H. Gordon Jones, and Henry Ellis either gave or commented on papers during the Society's first three years. Even when they did not refer specifically to Comte, it is clear they were guided by him; and there were other members of the Society who acknowledged his influence on their work, notably Émile Durkheim and Leonard Hobhouse. Its aims, as set forth by its first president, James Bryce, were fully consistent with Positivist interests: he called for putting various kinds of social inquiry into 'fruitful relation' and developing their theoretical grounds. As an Oxford professor of jurisprudence, historian, former MP and Cabinet member, Bryce exemplified the varied backgrounds of many of his colleagues, who included Graham Wallas, Francis Galton, Beatrice Webb, and Lady Welby. The meetings were held at the LSE, which in 1907 established the first chair of sociology in England, occupied jointly by Hobhouse and the Finnish anthropologist Edward Westermarck. In the same year, the Sociological Society marked the fiftieth anniversary of Comte's death by discussing his importance to the discipline. And the *Sociological Review*, with Hobhouse as editor, was founded in 1908. All this could not help but gratify Harrison, though his own contributions to the organization came later.[81]

The Positivists welcomed the Sociological Society because Comte had only 'instituted' the discipline he named without 'constituting' it. Ironically, the talent given them by the master had lain buried in a napkin for half a century, and when it was time to show what they had done with it they could produce little more than his generalizations. These demonstrated their overwhelming dependency on historical studies and abstract categories, and their prejudice against factual data and statistical analysis. For Harrison that prejudice had been reinforced by his old quarrel with orthodox political economy; but in any case his Oxford education had ill prepared him for genuine social research. Nor did he find much more of interest in the study of primitive cultures or of psychology than did Comte. Indeed, he candidly conceded that Positivists did not presume to add much to the view of human nature found in ancient literature, the Bible, and the Christian divines.[82] And he warned eugenicists like his good friend and former law colleague Montague Crackanthorpe to be 'very careful indeed' in isolating human traits for study, though he commended the Eugenics Society's interests in the physical determinants of personality, seeing it perhaps as parallel to Comte's emphasis on biology as a preparation for sociology.[83] His opinion of anthropology was dismissive, even hostile. After reading Mill's critique of Maine's *Village Communities* in 1871, which was followed by a defence of Maine by Edward Burnet Tylor, Harrison had trivialized the issues as 'antiquarian moonshine: how did the pair of breeches develop out of the fanciful backside?!!'[84] Whether primitive kinship and legal systems had been patriarchal or matriarchal seemed unimportant, too; discussing a new edition of *Ancient Law* in 1906 he advised the reader simply to ignore the matter [85]

Harrison's own contribution to the Sociological Society came only after Bridges's death. In the *Sociological Review* in 1909 he discussed G. F. C. Masterman's book, *The Condition of England*, finding it an unduly pessimistic portrayal of ordinary humanity as 'a shipwrecked crew' sinking fast. Harrison cited against such gloom the recent reduction in European death rates and, to counter Masterman's use of writers like Shaw, Chesterton, and Belloc, declared that current fiction was no proper source for 'scientific Sociology'; the condition of England had to be seen in its totality, and would not support Masterman's pessimism. This was the familiar demand for synthesis and perspective, and, as usual, Harrison ended with an allusion to a new religion compounded of science, ethics, art, and love, urgently needed and already in sight.[86] In the same year he was elected president of the Sociological Society, and for his inaugural address, delivered at a meeting honouring Bridges, returned to a topic Bridges had chosen for a paper to the Society a few years earlier: the definition and limits of sociology. Harrison restated the Positivist premiss that sociology should not be confused with any of the 'scientific studies' that made up its subdivisions, such as anthropology ('the tattoo marks on a Fijian girl's back'), politics, or the philosophy of history. In the end his strictures left no place in sociology for empirical knowledge; it became philosophical rather than scientific, its task the elaboration of those general laws which had been the grand deliverances of the Master half a century before.[87]

By 1914, events in Europe had changed Harrison's conception of what sociology might legitimately encompass. Elected to serve for that year as president of the International Institute of Sociology, which had been founded in 1893 with Sir John Lubbock as its first president, he betrayed something of the uneasiness about the nature and prospects of the discipline of sociology others had already shown. Leslie Stephen, for example, had declined to join the British society because he feared that the wide range of viewpoints represented would preclude any common action.[88] Now Harrison, in his address to the Institute's members, seemed also to think that mere discussion of theory could not justify the existence of the discipline. He defined sociology as 'the application to social life of the correlated concerns of philosophy, ethics, and religion'. The old emphasis on synthesis was there, but it was the visible result of such interdisciplinary study that Harrison was now seeking. Among the urgent tasks facing sociology he emphasized a solution of the problems posed by the arms race in Europe, competing empires, the loss of executive power in democratic legislatures, and the growth of socialism; in short, sociology had become the dumping ground for his anxieties about modern Europe. By the time his words were translated from the French for the August 1914 issue of the *Positivist Review*, some of the problems he had named had coalesced in an overwhelming crisis that revealed dramatically how far from solution they really were—and how little sociology could do about them.[89]

THE TEMPERING OF LIBERALISM

The sense of political doom that altered Harrison's conception of sociology in 1914 had been with him for at least a decade. During this period his ties with the Liberal Party had become closer. In 1903 he was elected to the National Liberal Club and henceforth slept in its grand new Whitehall Place building when he came to town on short visits, though he continued to use the Athenaeum as headquarters by day. What Irish Home Rule and then the Boer War had been to him in politics, free trade became in the early years of the new century before the Liberals' return to office in December 1905. Though Chamberlain's protectionism and endorsement of the war were equally repugnant to the Positivists, they had for the most part refrained from attacking him personally in their *Review* because Beesly's son Gerald had married Chamberlain's niece; but after Chamberlain's resignation from the Cabinet to agitate openly for protectionism, Harrison could no longer contain his wrath. Commending Jane Cobden Unwin's edition of letters about the horrors of the bread tax in the 'hungry forties', he predicted that, if the protectionists had their way, those hard times would return.[90] Comparing Chamberlain to a Tammany Hall 'boss', he described his political career as 'one long story of mischief, fraud and failure', his popularity as the result of his appealing to all that was 'evil, selfish, braggart and combative' in society. 'Oh! that Joe!', he exclaimed to Lady Dorothy Nevill, 'the most fearful demagogue since Cleon the tanner! If he does win, I shall turn Socialist, and republican, and go for a clean sweep of the governing classes who have so shamefully misled the people.' But his anxiety was relieved by the Liberal victory in the General Election of January 1906. Protectionism seemed quashed; and reading of Chamberlain's absence from public life later in the year because of a reported ankle injury and gout, Harrison guessed the truth and told Ethel, 'one sees that it is paralysis ... What a blessing for our poor dear old country.'[91]

If Chamberlain dismayed Harrison by betraying his youthful radicalism, Balfour outraged him by his consistency. With little change of argument he derided the Religion of Humanity in *A Defence of Philosophic Doubt* in 1879, in an address before the Church Congress in 1888, and in *Foundations of Belief* in 1895. The latter work provoked three *Positivist Review* essays from Harrison, one of which contrasted Balfour's 'absolute' and 'theological' synthesis to Spencer's 'absolute scientific' synthesis and Comte's 'relative scientific' synthesis, and dismissed Balfour's as even less tenable than Spencer's, the embodiment of 'sub-cynical pessimism'.[92] Even worse was Balfour's apparent indifference to working-class suffering and his smooth affability as Prime Minister, a combination that reminded Harrison of Gilbert and Sullivan's Mikado condemning his subjects to death in dulcet tones. Under Balfour's administration, he argued, the Church and the brewers had become twin pillars of government—the Church rewarded by the 1902 Education Act, the brewers by the 1904 licensing legislation.[93]

Aggravating the dismal political scene during these Conservative years was the weakness of the Liberal opposition. But Harrison still blamed much of Parliament's failure to enact social legislation on its own conventions, and once again he advocated the abolition of plural voting, the creation of Life Peers, and more frequent sessions. After unburdening his mind in the *Positivist Review* and *Westminster Gazette*, he summed up his 'Thoughts on the Present Discontents' in the *Fortnightly* early in 1905. His title, from Burke, was meant to recall to the Conservatives their historic concern for the duties accompanying rank and wealth. The text included a French quotation, as had his 1867 essay on Parliamentary reform, but this time his source was not Comte but Voltaire: 'Alors, ce sera un bon tapage. Les jeunes gens ... verront de belles choses.' Mindful of his seventy-four years he added, 'I shall not see them. But I see them coming.'[94]

Yet there was one feature of Balfour's administration Harrison could endorse—its foreign policy. Anxious about Britain's isolation in Europe, he enthusiastically greeted the *Entente Cordiale* with France in 1904, praising it not as an achievement of the Conservative government but, because of the King's role in the negotiations, as a sign that '*personal* direction of affairs' was increasing. Though the accord validated Britain's occupation of Egypt and the Sudan and France's presence in Morocco, he seemed untroubled, so delighted was he at this belated fulfilment of the alliance he had called for in 1866. He must have suspected that some kind of military agreement had been reached, for France, he said, could finally 'meet with an easy smile the heroics of the Kaiser'. In his relief at the thought of England and France together frustrating Germany's threat to European peace, essays proved inadequate. He composed a one-act farce entitled 'Entente Cordiale' in which a young French lieutenant, D'Artagnon, and his sweetheart Fifine, a chanteuse, board an English nobleman's yacht in a spirit of adventure and are mistaken for important French guests; the lord eventually clears up the confusion, producing an Anglo-French accord in personal terms. Harrison's theatre friends were unappreciative of this *jeu d'esprit*, but the kindest of them, like Cyril Maude, gave the high cost of scenery as the reason for not producing it. No one could foresee how high would be the cost to England of the real *Entente Cordiale*.[95] Eager for more alliances, at the end of 1905 Harrison overlooked his long-standing dislike of Russia (expressed the previous year when her navy was defeated by the Japanese) and hoped that an *entente* with the Czar might be forthcoming.[96] Even the knowledge that all such agreements would have undisclosed details did not trouble him now. 'Live Openly' had ceased to be a motto he urged upon his nation's diplomats: the stakes had become too high to forego the advantages of secrecy in treaties.

By clinging to power despite Liberal victories in by-elections, Balfour exasperated Harrison almost beyond endurance, and when the Government finally resigned late in 1905 without dissolving Parliament, he advised the new Liberal ministers to abandon the convention requiring them to seek re-election before taking office: they needed 'practical good sense' to counter 'the scurvy tricks of wriggling shufflers'. But he soon forgot the 'monstrous inconvenience' of new balloting to confirm the Cabinet members in their seats, in his satisfaction with the

overwhelming Liberal victory in January 1906. He especially commended Campbell-Bannerman's appointments of Morley as Secretary
of State for India, Bryce for Ireland, Burns as President of the Local
Government Board, and, apart from these old friends, Birrell as
Minister for Education (who had called the Education Act of 1902 a
'corrupt bargain with the Church'), Asquith at the Exchequer ('one of
the keenest reasoners of our time'), and Lloyd George at the Board of
Trade ('a middle class professional man' replacing an 'obscure peer').[97]
Interpreting the election returns as the nation's repudiation of the
party that had waged an unpopular war—a view that committed the
Liberals to little—he predicted that no social legislation could be
expected until the House of Commons was reformed along the lines he
had long been urging—more committees, shorter breaks, and abolition
of all 'badges of social classification'. Deeming reform of the Lords
even more urgent, he proposed that in the future only Life Peers be
created, drawn from a pool of eminent men, including existing peers,
but that hereditary membership in the House of Lords be abolished.
Privately he was less sanguine about such a reform than his logically
persuasive articles suggested. Where, he asked Rosebery, was the
necessary Caesar or even Chatham to carry out such a Draconian
measure?[98] Rosebery, soon to head a Select Committee studying the
House of Lords, certainly was neither.

Much, but not everything, that the House of Lords did in the first
decade of the century earned Harrison's criticism. Like all friends of
labour he deplored the Lords' Taff Vale Railway decision of 1901,
which denied unions the immunity from court action that, like most
people, he thought had been granted them in the legislation of the
1870s. Predicting the end of trade unions altogether, he warned their
leaders not to take any action that would subject them to the new
ruling. But then, gratuitously undercutting the sympathy he seemed to
express for them in their new predicament, he added that the present
generation of unionists were 'inferior both morally and intellectually
to the men of 1860–1870'.[99] In 1906 he endorsed the Government's
Trades Disputes Bill, which restored the unions' privileged legal status,
though its critics, who included Godfrey Lushington, argued that it
virtually licensed them to commit wrongs. When Lord Lindley
recommended in *The Times* that unions should register under the
Companies Act of 1862, which would eliminate their immunity while
protecting their funds, Harrison, then in Switzerland, dashed off a
letter in language he considered 'unusually violent' even for him. He
believed it would never be accepted by *The Times* and so sent it to the
new Liberal *Tribune*, where it admirably stated the unions' case for

their special status. Every one of them, he wrote, was 'permanently fighting for its very life against a secret, powerful, unscrupulous combination of capitalists who are ready to take an opportunity to destroy or cripple it'. Lord Lindley might be England's greatest lawyer but he was a party 'bigot'. To Ethel, Harrison complained that it was 'disgraceful that a judge—and a paid judge in the Lords all his life, should embitter a violent political and class struggle, which he will have to determine when sitting in Court'.[100] Yet in 1910 Harrison endorsed the Lords' Osborne Judgment, which denied unions the right to levy funds for political purposes, and he called criticism of the Law Lords responsible for the ruling a 'scurvy trick', insisting that they had acted in their capacity as professional lawyers and were not hereditary peers.[101]

Harrison's defence of the Law Lords in the Osborne case is easily explained: he saw them as a bulwark against socialism. Agreeing with a lower court ruling that unions adopting political functions were not within their statutory rights, he said that the decision was in the unions' best interests, for their privileges and even their legal existence would be endangered if they departed from their traditional roles and became 'the tool of the Socialist caucus'.[102] Such reasoning convinced Ramsay MacDonald, secretary of the Labour Party, that Harrison understood neither unionism nor socialism, for according to MacDonald's interpretation of labour history, the alliance of the two had evolved quite naturally out of the activities of the early trade societies, which he thought had always been more political than Harrison realized.[103] Harrison was indeed protesting against an evolution of union functions, for he saw it producing a kind of neo-unionism that blended old-style union concerns and new, socialist, political aims. Having always claimed to be the originator of the plan by which unions had gained 'power and prestige', he believed they were now handing this birthright over to a 'socialist minority' that was 'both craven and dishonest' in its attempt to 'clutch at the savings carefully husbanded to succour the labourer out of work'. As a student of the Constitution he was offended by the 'wild talk' of reversing the Osborne Judgment; if MPs no longer truly represented constituencies but only 'irresponsible unions' who paid their salaries, he warned, 'there is an end put by statute to Parliamentary government.'[104]

The Act of 1911 providing for payment of MPs, and one in 1913 allowing unions to use funds for political purposes if they were voluntarily contributed by the members, removed some of the Osborne Judgment's crushing effects on organized labour and yet met some objections to that ruling. No such compromises emerged in the struggle over women's suffrage in the pre-war years. The campaign for the vote quickened with the return to Parliament of some four hundred MPs committed to some kind of franchise for women, and in response Mrs Ward organized the National Anti-Suffrage League. She had Ethel's help, and Harrison did his part by restating his old demands for improving women's educational opportunities and his case against their obtaining the vote. So as not to jeopardize his influence he forebore to mention the Comtean basis of his arguments, and even reprimanded Ivy Pretious for planning to include a motto from Comte in the first issue of the League's *Anti-Suffrage Review*, which she was helping to edit. He knew that any such association with the League would make Mrs Ward 'furious': even without the motto the first edition of the *Review* seemed to him 'too rather like a Newton Hall address by Dr Bridges'.[105] In 1908 he joined the Men's Committee for Opposing Women's Suffrage, though its prime movers were Lords Cromer and Curzon and the Chamberlain family. When Curzon brought his aggressive self-confidence to his work as the Committee's fund-raiser, Harrison took his 'revenge' by asking him to give £10 to the London Library, noting that 'the true art of public begging was not difficult to acquire if one closely followed the example of a past master.'[106]

Soft-pedalling Positivist theory and hob-nobbing with imperialists were not Harrison's only concessions to the cause. He encouraged Ethel's public activity. She served on the executive board of the Women's National Anti-Suffrage League and even spoke occasionally for it, though her delicate health usually kept her from attending the national meetings in London.[107] In Hawkhurst she organized the League's first branch society at an afternoon tea at Elm Hill, and urged other women to follow her example. She also drew on her experience as a hymnodist to compose songs for the League, and despite the Positivist proscription of statistics she polled her corner of Kent to find out whether its inhabitants wanted women to vote. Her figures showed men opposing women's suffrage 396 to 37 and married women opposing it 357 to 40. Harrison deemed the results 'successful', which suggests that the aim had been opinion-making rather more than fact-finding. Even before the survey Ethel had declared confidently that the 'shrewd country woman is not so easily tempted by the gaudy baits of the suffragists as her sisters in town'.[108] That women as a whole did not seek political rights was the message she drove home in a dialogue in the *Westminster Gazette* (Socrates gets a suffragist to make the point), letters to *The Times*, articles in the *Nineteenth Century and After* (as Knowles's periodical had become), and a fifty-five-page pamphlet, *Freedom of Women*, in 1908 that went into four editions.[109] Just as her husband had slid into journalism despite a theoretical objection to it, so she exercised her considerable literary skills in the service of a campaign to preserve a conception of women in which such activities were anomalies. But in one way her efforts conformed to the traditional expectations of women: in everything she wrote for the cause (except her songs) she emulated her husband's arguments and style. He praised her labours none the less for that.

A letter to an aspiring fiction writer named Miss Waterson in 1906 suggests how sympathetic he could be to individual women forced to support themselves, even while he preached the advantages to society of their more traditional role. After explaining that for every struggling woman there were at least three struggling men, many of whom had landed in their predicament because of women who would work at lower wages, he asked, for good measure, how women could hope to make happy families if they treated men 'as cats treat dogs'; but then he wrote, 'How can I be of use to you? I am very much out of the world of letters and journals, but I might find you some openings.'[110] He was over-modest: as Ivy Pretious and Muriel Harris had cause to know, he could be useful to young women with literary aspirations. Ethel, for her part, took a special interest in women as domestic servants, calling for their better treatment and suggesting sensibly that by keeping a book of their character references they could find better positions.[111] She could be more flexible than her husband on some questions pertaining to women. Called to testify before a Royal Commission on Divorce in 1910, he delivered a sermon about the superiority of a' Positivist wedding to a conventional church ritual—perhaps in the hope of offsetting the effect of Bernard Shaw's play, *Getting Married*, in which a bishop calls his future son-in-law practically illegitimate because his parents had a civil marriage followed by a ceremony at Newton Hall. As for reforming the divorce laws, Harrison warned that it would be the 'thin edge of the wedge' forced by those who 'desired divorce at will'.[112] Ethel more generously argued that divorce, if available at all, should be equally obtainable by women as by men, and by the poor as well as by the rich, though she also noted that working women were not demanding legislative changes affecting marriage— 'all honour to them.'[113]

The Harrisons had been too close to the centres of power in their respective anti-suffrage societies to avoid being involved in the squabbles that followed their amalgamation in 1911. Cromer, the president of the new National League for Opposing Women's Suffrage, antagonized Mrs Ward by insisting upon a male director in the London office, and she regaled the Harrisons with her complaints. She clashed with

Cromer also over the action of a committee she had formed to encourage women to participate in local government. By endorsing a candidate for a local office who challenged one endorsed by the League, she precipitated his resignation. The issue of women in local government was not one on which Ethel and her husband agreed either. He had not swerved from the sentiments that had led him to vote against seating women on the LCC, whereas she joined Mrs Ward's committee. Moreover, Ethel told Curzon, who succeeded Cromer as president of the League, why their campaign must 'in the main depend upon women': it would take women to destroy a women's movement.[114] But the Harrisons were of one mind in disparaging the 'Pankhurst crew', who were stealing the limelight from both the Antis and the proponents of constitutional suffrage reform. At one public meeting Ethel confessed to feeling little sympathy for ladies who 'took rest cures in Holloway', and her husband racked his brain to find a way of circumventing their tactics. One scheme of his (it has not survived) failed to impress Cromer, who said he doubted if anything could prevent the 'she-devils', as Harrison had called them, from making martyrs of themselves if they chose.[115] By 1913 the havoc they were causing, and the alliance of their non-militant sisters with the Labour Party, gave point to Mrs Ward's warning that the 'horrid fight' would have to be kept up for years to come.[116]

One of Harrison's arguments against women's suffrage was that it would make Britain the laughing-stock of Europe.[117] His fear of disturbing the balance of power also underlay his judgements on the prolific pen of his old friend Blunt, eventually producing an estrangement. Harrison could admire Blunt's *Golden Odes of Arabia* in 1903, for they captured 'the whole of the fierce, wild, heroic fire of the beduin, without European manners or Christian mawkishness'.[118] But Blunt's memoirs of Gladstone's Egyptian policy of the early 1880s were something else. When in 1905 Blunt asked his opinion of them, already set up in type, Harrison pronounced the book 'impossible to publish at present'. With a General Election expected, he thought it was no time to be raking over the sins of a past Liberal ministry.[119] Blunt accepted the advice temporarily, but within a year of the Liberals' return to power, and without consulting Harrison, published an inflammatory pamphlet entitled *The Atrocities of Justice Under British Rule in Egypt*. The deed done, Harrison could only urge that the work should not be translated into French and Arabic, which would make it useful to foreign critics, though, of course, that was just what Blunt desired.[120] Worse followed. After Cromer resigned his position in Egypt and returned to England in 1907, Blunt reissued his 1895 volume, *The Secret*

History of the British Occupation in Egypt. In it he inserted letters written during the 1882 crisis by associates of Gladstone who, the letters seemed to show, had made some private comments that belied the official accounts of the Egyptian adventure. Attacked by the *Athenaeum* for this unauthorized use of correspondence, Blunt defended himself, but like a good many other people, Harrison was not conciliated. He itemized for Blunt seventeen objections, of which two stood out: Blunt had imputed motives to men still living, who '*must* take some notice', and he had not provided evidence for his assertions, which would not be believed. Harrison especially challenged Blunt's claims that Gladstone, Granville, and Morley had 'knowingly conspired' to have Arabi '*murdered in cold blood*' and that Morley had been personally responsible for everything appearing in the *Pall Mall Gazette* at that time.[121]

Reiterating his charges and giving his rationale for publishing them, Blunt warned Harrison that a controversy, 'possibly of a public kind', might be in the offing. It was, for Blunt added this and a later exchange of letters with Harrison to a second edition of the *Secret History*, thus provoking yet another remonstrance from Harrison.[122] Published in *The Times*, it led Blunt to call for a burial of their 'private hatchets'.[123] Harrison, however, brandished his again in the *Positivist Review*, first in another discussion of Blunt's sins,[124] and then in an account of Cromer's virtues. Of course he said nothing of his recent association with the former Proconsul in anti-suffrage work; it was Cromer's *Modern Egypt*, containing the 'mature views of a great Proconsul at the close of a memorable career', that Harrison was recommending. He found no evidence in it that Cromer had been responsible for the British occupation of Egypt, and indeed thought Cromer appeared to disapprove of it. Recalling their conversation in Cairo in 1895, Harrison said he had caught then a 'glimpse of the energy, honesty, and success of the British administration so far as it went'. He also remembered the 'inextricable antagonism of race, creed, and life between Europeans and Moslems', and observed that occupation forces were likely to commit the kind of 'atrocities' Blunt denounced. But such incidents had nothing to do with the cause of the occupation, which he still attributed to British economic interests, not to Gladstone, who had only 'misunderstood' the situation in 1882, not truly created it.[125]

Though their views on Egypt's immediate past were irreconcilable, Harrison and Blunt were both optimistic about the future of another Muslim state—Turkey. When the successful *coup d'état* of the Young Turks in July 1908 eroded the Sultan's autonomy, Harrison tried to forget the Turks' brutal suppression of their Armenian subjects a

12. Frederic Harrison, about 1885

14. Ethel Bertha Harrison, 1889

13. Frederic Harrison, 1889

15. Newton Hall

16. The Harrison family at Elm Hill, Hawkhurst, Kent. Foreground, Godfrey; seated, Olive, FH, Ethel Bertha; standing, René, Austin, Bernard. Probably taken on 17 August 1907, the Harrisons' thirty-seventh wedding anniversary.

17. Frederic Harrison with portrait of Ethel Bertha by Sir William Blake Richmond

18. Frederic Harrison at Elm Hill, December 1907

19. Elm Hill, Hawkhurst, Kent, Harrison's residence, 1902–1912

20. Frederic Harrison at 10 Royal Crescent, Bath, April 1919, Harrison's residence, 1912–1923

21. Royal Crescent, Bath

22. Frederic Harrison

decade earlier and hoped the new regime would frustrate the ambitions of Russia and Austria–Hungary in the Balkans. Blunt blithely expected that a constitutional government in Constantinople would improve the chances of one in Cairo. In September, three months after the *coup*, Ethel noted in letter to her husband, then with Carnegie at Skibo, that the Young Turks seemed to take a 'somewhat different view', for they had announced that editors inciting unrest in Egypt would be punished. 'Poor old Blunt!', she exclaimed; a letter of his showed 'many sad things: that he is very ill and feels himself a wreck—and has few friends left—and a misspent life'.[126] Blunt was in fact in poor health, and his philandering had alienated his wife and daughter. But he would live to receive homage from a new generation of poets and inspire struggles for independence throughout the Muslim world, partly through his monthly, *Egypt*, which was edited by a young friend of Swinny's, Frederick Ryan, who also wrote for the Positivists.[127] Blunt sometimes had misgivings about his own political pronouncements, but Harrison hardly ever, and like Blunt he was expert in putting the most sanguine construction on events that pleased him. He told the members of the Byzantine Research and Publication Fund that their problems of scholarship in the Levant would be greatly mitigated by the 'men of culture' among the Young Turks.[128] To the Positivists he offered another reason for rejoicing in the *coup*. The president of the Chamber of Deputies in Constantinople set up under the new constitution, Ahmed Riza, had become a Positivist during his exile in Paris (his use of Comte's dating and motto, 'Order and Progress', for his party's newspaper irritated some of his colleagues). Visiting the Harrisons shortly before he returned to Turkey for the *coup d'état*, he greatly impressed them by his modest demeanour and sensible talk. He gave no hint of an imminent revolution, but spoke of decades being required for any real change in his country. Still, he led Ethel to believe that 'perhaps the regeneration of the world will come again from the East.'[129]

Despite a counter-*coup* in April 1909 that limited the Young Turks' power, Harrison continued to think their success 'quite the most important of all European questions', and later that year he agreed to succeed Bryce as President of the Eastern Questions Association.[130] Hours before Harrison's inaugural address the following February, Blunt, who had resigned from the organization because he thought it embraced imperialists, sent a message to Harrison at the National Liberal Club threatening to 'attack' him; but the speech went off without incident.[131] In it Harrison recalled Comte's explaining the Crimean War to him as the attempt of England and France to defend the principle of nationalism, an interpretation Harrison wisely did not discuss. And in tracing the origins of the EQA to the Bulgarian atrocities agitation, he avoided dwelling on the anti-Turk sentiment he had found so excessive at the time. What surprised Ethel when she read the speech in *The Times* the next day was that he used it to announce that his term of office would be short. She guessed, probably correctly, that the organization's 'slippery' permanent secretary, Edward Atkin, had somehow offended him, and that his meeting with some Bulgarians concerned about the Christians under Turkish rule had given him a disquieting new glimpse into the complexities of 'Eastern Questions'.[132]

When Harrison left office at the end of 1910 he gave his advanced age as the reason, but his seventy-nine years had not prevented his sailing on the *S. S. Vectis* the previous March with Bernard to investigate the consequences of the revolution in Constantinople, much as he toured Italy in 1859 and France in 1877 to study their politics in transition. Ahmed Riza took him to the Chamber of Deputies, where his interpreter was Professor Edward Granville Browne, a Cambridge Orientalist who had addressed the EQA on the night of Harrison's inauguration. In *The Times* Harrison later compared the Chamber's efficiency to that of his beloved LCC, though to Ethel he complained of its terrible noise and called Ahmed Riza a 'not very adequate chairman'. More satisfying was the non-political side of the trip: the splendour of the British Embassy ('pour épater les Turques'); a banquet at which Ahmed Riza kissed him French fashion and talked Positivism all evening; an excursion to the resort town of Brusa; and meetings with two resident English authors whose books on Turkey he had reviewed: Professor Alexander van Millingen, of Robert College, and Sir Edward Pears, a barrister.[133] During his stay he found himself repeatedly wondering if the new regime could 'regenerate the composite and effete Ottoman Empire'.[134] He soon came to doubt it. Its infamous treatment of subject peoples caused him to tell Turkish leaders in 1911 that if the British had not shown more respect for local traditions in their empire they would long ago have reduced it to chaos.[135] In other days he might have likened the oppressive features of the two empires, but as European tensions mounted, so too did his patriotism; and his dismay at Turkey's Balkan policies was tempered by his fear that without Turkey's hegemony the Balkan states would involve Europe in their quarrels. When Ahmed Riza protested to him about Italy's occupation of Tripoli in 1911, Harrison transmitted the message to the Positivists,[136] and when the Balkan Wars of 1912 and 1913 deprived Turkey of most of her European lands, he feared that the West had entered upon a 'new era' in which Britain would find her role more precarious.[137]

More precarious, too, did the British position in India become in the pre-war years, though Harrison took less interest in it than in the heightening tensions in Europe. The demand of educated Indians for greater responsibility in their government had his whole-hearted approval, partly, he told a London meeting of the Indian National Congress in 1905, because of the Congress's twenty-five-year history, and partly because of what he had learned from his Indian law students and the books and letters coming to him 'constantly' from India.[138] He might have mentioned the Positivists' ties with that country. Chapel Street displayed the names of its Indian affiliates on its walls, and one of its most distinguished members was Henry Cotton, who after thirty-five years in the Bengal Civil Service was, as he put it, 'flung to the wolves' by the Conservatives' Viceroy, Lord Curzon. Forced into retirement, Cotton returned to England in 1902 and was knighted. More important, he was also 'unmuzzled', and became a spokesman for Indian nationalist aspirations.[139] Among the Newton Hall Positivists, Swinny, a good friend of Cotton's, took a special interest in India, visiting the sub-continent and serving on the National Congress's committee for the replacement of British by native officials in Indian government.[140] Morley's appointment as Secretary of State for India in December 1905, and the return of a hundred and fifty MPs in January pledged to the Congress's demand, seemed grounds for optimism; yet by 1908 nothing had been achieved. In a statement to an Anglo-Indian conference that year Harrison blamed 'one from whom we hoped so much' and a Government that had offered 'little but phrases, promises, and trivial reforms'.[141] The Morley–Minto reforms announced the next year, which provided for Indian members on the councils of both the Viceroy and the Indian Secretary, additional elected members on provincial councils, and separate Muslim electorates, seemed 'more satisfactory, as far as they go', but he noted that if enacted earlier, along with redress of grievances like Curzon's partition of Bengal, they might have given 'confidence in the good intentions of the British government'.[142]

Far worse than what Morley failed to do was what he was willing to do in order to win acceptance of his reforms by the House of Lords: condone repressive measures against extremist nationalists. The assassination of his aide-de-camp in 1909 by a young Punjabi student had brought home to him the danger of their unrestrained actions. Ironically, the assailant was thought to have been inspired by Shyamaji Krishnavarma, editor of the *Indian Sociologist*, who had established the Herbert Spencer Lectures that Harrison had inaugurated. Knowing the Positivists' consistent opposition to government interference with political expression, Morley assured Harrison that the Indians themselves were making 'no serious clamour about Deportation, etc.'.[143] Harrison kept his own views to himself, for he did not wish to embarrass the Liberal Government or his old friend. Two years earlier, when Morley's stepson John Ayling had pleaded guilty to forgery in an Edinburgh court, Harrison had told Morley that he and Ethel felt the blow 'as if it had happened to our own kin'.[144] Even before Morley accepted a Viscountcy in 1908, Harrison had urged him to retreat from party politics to the Lords so as to save time for literature; after all, Morley was just the kind of elder statesman, full of years and experience, that Harrison wanted in the Upper House. When Morley continued to sign himself plain 'John Morley', Harrison could not contain his exasperation. 'Is not this a piece of his foolish conduct about himself— undecided?', he asked Ethel.[145] But he probably agreed with the summary of Morley's career at the India Office she formulated upon his retirement in 1910. The Indians, she said, knew that he had been their friend and he had 'earned his rest'.[146] The Harrisons were not unfamiliar with the difficulties of balancing the claims of order and progress, and in their loyalty to their friend they declined to assess publicly his attempt to do so.

ALARUMS AND HONOURS

Almost everything Harrison wrote on international policy during the pre-war years was coloured by his Germanophobia. Its roots lay in his early and unchanging hostility to Bismarck and Bismarckism. When Austin went to Berlin for *The Times* in 1898 Harrison told Morley it was too bad old 'Blood and Iron' was already dead; he would have liked Austin to be on the desk when the news of that event came in.[147] Austin wrote two books about Germany's designs on Europe: *The Pan-Germanic Doctrine*, in 1904, and *England and Germany*, in 1907. They gave his father new confidence in formulating his own apprehensions. Though he lacked first-hand knowledge, he never lacked reasons why Britain should increase her defences. Her obligations to the Empire constituted one argument. When Goschen, as first Lord of the Admiralty, asked his views on enlarging the navy in 1895 he had replied: 'If you are to go on with all these transmarine and imperial adventures, I should advise you to double the fleet *and to treble the army at home.*' Two years later he showed his concern by asking permission of the War Office to view colonial troops assembled for the

Jubilee. The revelations of Britain's military weakness during and after the Boer War were very much on his mind; and during the important Parliamentary debate on Reginald McKenna's naval estimates in 1909 he brought to a climax his frequent warnings by thundering in *The Times*: 'How hollow is all talk about industrial reorganization until we have secured our country against a catastrophe that would involve untold destitution and misery in the people in the mass.' The German navy was being expanded to serve as a 'spearhead of a magnificent army' that had been trained to invade the British Isles, on which 'every road, well, bridge, and smithy' on the East coast was 'docketed in the German War Office'.[148] There were many Cassandras by this time, but Harrison's eloquence, and his reputation as an opponent of all British military adventures overseas, lent such authority to his letter that Lord Roberts's National Service League, which agitated for compulsory military training, reprinted it as a pamphlet, and the National Union of Conservative and Constitutional Associations circulated an excerpt as a flyer. *The Times's* highly respected military correspondent, Charles à Court Repington (whose brother was married to Lawrence Harrison's daughter) gave his *imprimatur* to the letter by declaring that it left little to say about military security.[149]

Though uncompromising in his demand for a larger army and navy, Harrison declined to say whether he favoured compulsory military training, even when Lord Roberts overlooked their old antagonisms and personally solicited his endorsement of the idea in 1913.[150] His warning of what would follow any breakdown of Britain's sea defences naturally appealed to navy enthusiasts, but the extremists—the Blue Water School—were impatient with his concern about land forces. His repudiation of the peace movement and advocacy of the Liberals' armament programme convinced Blunt that they had finally come to the parting of the ways, but gratified others as politically diverse as the Socialist Hyndman and the Conservative Leopold Maxse. Once again Harrison found himself with some unlikely allies and facing unlikely critics. In any case, many old political alliances were undergoing revisions. Suggestive, perhaps, of his state of anxiety in these years was the curiously un-Positivist, even 'metaphysical' language he fell into occasionally, as, for example, in describing the rising antagonism between Britain and Germany as 'independent of persons, even of the will of peoples' and 'borne on by the elemental springs of national destinies'.[151]

Whereas Conservatives welcomed the military provisions in Lloyd George's 1909 Budget but not his social legislation, and radicals and socialists approved the welfare reforms but not the armaments, Harrison wanted both. He dismissed as 'mere verbiage' the 'obsolete maxims of Gladstone, Bright, and Cobden about economy, peace, and brotherhood of nations', for in the face of the German menace any hope of continued peace in Europe seemed delusory and dangerous. Not only did the graduated income tax 'so perversely resisted by Gladstone' appear moderate when compared to Carnegie's recent suggestion of death duties up to half a millionaire's estate, but new land taxes promised to reform a system that as a conveyancer he confessed, 'to my sorrow and shame', to have helped perpetuate. Warning that if the Lords repudiated the 'People's Budget' there would be a constitutional crisis and fiscal chaos, he precipitated a spate of letters in *The Times* in September on the technical issues.[152] 'An Old Tory' questioned his credentials for discussing them and quoted Lecky's derisory account of Harrison's 1892 proposal to create five hundred new peers to push Home Rule through. Not yet ready to be associated with so drastic a solution in the present situation, Harrison pointed out that he had written only of the Government's 'technical right' without actually advocating its exercise.[153] The Parliamentary crisis developed as he predicted when the Budget reached the Lords. To observe events and assess the reaction to his letters, he went up to London at the end of the month. At first he decided that the Lords would give way; but very soon he became convinced that the creation of new peers would in fact be necessary. Would *The Times* publish an open letter to the King recommending that step? he wondered on the 1st of October.[154] But within a few days the Cabinet would decide against taking any immediate action, and the king would suggest a General Election in January. Before Harrison had time to speculate further, a fall incapacitated him. Since Ethel was at Blackdown House, where the rough terrain would make walking difficult, he took the train to Boscombe, near Bournemouth, there to breathe sea air and enjoy the luxuries of the Hotel Burlington. But he did not altogether forget the 'People's Budget'. A visit to the nearby Shelley estate provided an 'object lesson' in the proposed land clauses, for he learned that the value of the estate had much increased since the poet's lifetime. It was just such wealth Lloyd George wanted to tax.[155]

When the Lords rejected the finance bill at the end of the year, as they had much of the earlier social legislation sent up by the Liberals, Asquith dissolved Parliament. To Harrison this defiance of the peerage made the Prime Minister appear a noble defender of 'popular government' pitted against 'great proconsuls' who were seeking to apply at home the 'outlandish doctrines of domination they had sought to impose on distant subjects of Empire'.[156] Despite his frequent protests that he played no role in party politics, he became so eager for a Liberal victory in his home constituency in January that he circulated a hard-hitting flyer posing 'Forty Plain Questions for Candidates' and reprints of his *Positivist Review* denunciation of Chamberlain, whose tariff reform scheme was still an issue. He even lectured in Hawkhurst on fiscal policy and arranged two outdoor meetings in support of the local Liberal candidate. Although painfully aware that there were probably few Liberals in the area besides himself and his household servants, Harrison was shocked by the hostility shown him at these meetings. Deciding that 'organised toughs' had been brought in by the Conservatives, he refused to let any but local men speak, and sought to ingratiate himself with one crowd by saying he wished the proposed new tax on incomes above £5,000 applied to him.[157]

Even before polling began in mid-January, Harrison sent Asquith two proposals, his 1886 Home Rule scheme and a plan to transfer the powers of the House of Lords to a three hundred-member senate, one-sixth chosen by the existing Lords, one-sixth by the Crown, and two-thirds by public bodies like the LCC.[158] Asquith did nothing more than acknowledge receipt of these documents, but Harrison did not give up. When the constitutional conference following the King's death was unable to settle the conflict between the two houses of Parliament, and another election, in December 1910, confirmed the Liberals in office, he devised a 'Parliamentary Irenicon' calling for a provisional committee of Privy Council members to function as a national legislature until the relation of the houses was decided upon.[159] This scheme he sent not to the Prime Minister but to *The Times*, which was, he saw, within his sphere of possible influence, though Whitehall did not appear to be. Two months later he followed this communication by a lyrical letter interpreting the exceptional profusion of spring flowers in Kent as a token that 'every growing thing promises well' and signed himself 'E Laurentino Meo' to suggest a delight in his country life like Pliny's.[160] As if this contradiction between trying to undermine the prerogatives of the Lords on the one hand and celebrating the gratifications traditionally enjoyed by them on the other were not enough, in June he accepted an invitation from *The Times* to reflect for its readers on King George V's coronation, which he, Ethel, Olive, and Bernard witnessed from seats in Whitehall they owed to the Secretary for Scotland. Recalling Queen Victoria's coronation seventy-three years earlier, he concluded that the intervening changes in material things had not greatly altered the 'essentials of our national life'. That they still included a monarch seemed not to disturb him, and in the foreign representatives attending the coronation he found hope for 'the continued peace of the Civilised World.[161]

If Asquith had chosen to settle the constitutional crisis by swamping the House of Lords with new peers, Harrison might have found his own republicanism, such as it was by now, put to the test: his name, bracketed with his brother Robert's, was on the list of two hundred and thirty-eight men the Prime Minister had at hand for such a contingency. How Harrison would have responded to the call is uncertain. Having often urged others to accept a peerage in order to create a more enlightened Upper House, he may have welcomed the chance to play elder statesman himself. For titles he cared nothing, once saying he would not be made a duke for £10,000, and would regard the offer of even a knighthood as 'an impertinence'. Hollow honours he rejected out of hand, such as a decoration the Grand Vizier of Constantinople was prepared to confer upon him after his presidency of the EQA.[162] Recognition of his legal experience, on the contrary, pleased him. Unfortunately, the efforts of Lord Russell of Killowen to obtain his election to the governing body of Lincoln's Inn were frustrated by one bencher, Lord Grimthorpe. A self-appointed watchdog of Lincoln's Inn and of Anglican Church discipline, and notorious for his spiteful behaviour in controversies, Grimthorpe objected to Harrison on theological grounds.[163] Working through Shaw–Lefevre and other Liberals after the 1906 election, Harrison secured an appontment as Justice of the Peace for Kent, an unsalaried but not undemanding post normally given to men of some social standing. Though he later rejected the charge of radicals that the upper-class make-up of the benches precluded even-handed justice, he conceded that a selection aiming at a wider social representation would be beneficial, and argued, too, for more magistrates like himself who had experience in law.[164]

Honours from academia came relatively late in life to Harrison. He happily agreed to be made Doctor of Letters by Cambridge University in 1905 and Doctor of Laws by Aberdeen University in 1909.[165] Finally, and 'long overdue', as Ethel rightly said, came the invitation to be made Doctor of Civil Law by Oxford University in 1910. He had not been entirely pleased with the University since leaving it. Its growth, the introduction of new subjects, the tendency towards specialization, the presence of 'hermaphrodite girl scholars', and even Thorley's successor as Warden of Wadham—P. A. Wright-Henderson, not a Wadham man and a woman suffragist—had all been disquieting. Yet Harrison kept his name on the Foundation, returned occasionally for functions, and had been proud to show Olive his old haunts. There was no question about his satisfaction in contemplating Oxford's recognition.[166]

That recognition had an enhanced significance because it coincided with the celebration of Wadham College's Tercentenary. On 22 June Harrison went up to Oxford for the events, unaccountably alone, fortified for the train journey by a book and sandwiches. Once in the familiar streets, all the old complaints were forgotten. The Warden's garden seemed a 'paradise' and he easily imagined himself as a student, so little had anything in the appearance of the College changed. The ceremony in the Sheldonian Theatre the next morning was appropriately solemn. His was the only doctorate conferred, and there was mild cheering when he advanced to hear himself described as a 'learned and subtle thinker', a lover of good literature, and *dux positive societatis*—an acknowledgement of his life's mission that rather surprised him. That evening the Wadham chapel service was crowded, the hymns 'really grand', and at the College dinner in his honour afterwards there were speeches by two prominent Conservatives, Lord Curzon, Chancellor of the University, and F. E. Smith (later Lord Birkenhead), just then working to resolve the Parliamentary crisis, and by Lord Rosebery, whose words seemed to Harrison meant for him alone. When his own turn came, Harrison discussed the College's religious climate in his student days in general terms, without mention of Positivism, and said he trusted that the same chapel service would be heard when his ashes reposed in their urn in the Wadham College ante-chapel. This was an allusion to an arrangement made by him earlier in the day whereby after their deaths he and Ethel would be cremated and their ashes mingled in an urn placed in the spot he had described in his dialogue on Mark Pattison as just the place for listening to the choir 'as if ... studying a noble dead religion'.[167] Nothing better illustrates Harrison's anomalous position at Oxford—his desire to be considered one of her honoured sons although he had rejected her religion—than this choice of a final resting-place.

Taking all this in stride, when he left Oxford, Harrison went on to Fawsley Park, in Daventry, Northamptonshire, the home of Lady Knightley, the sixty-eight-year-old widow of a Tory MP and a founder of the Girls Friendly Society and the Working Ladies Guild. Her philanthropic interests and vast experience of political and royal life—she had been intimate with the Royal Family in her youth—offset her Primrose League and suffragist affiliations in his eyes, and he had found her 'decidedly agreeable' when they met on his Mediterranean cruise to Turkey three months before. Now his account of her country friends convinced Ethel that Lady Knightley inhabited a 'centre of reaction'.[168] The social climate was rather different when Harrison broke his journey again on his way home to see cousins in Leicester. It was his first visit, and by arrangement a genealogically knowledgeable member of the family was on hand to show him Harrison gravestones dating to the time of Queen Anne and a family-tree with their line traced to the seventeenth century. He was somewhat embarrassed to find 'Harrison and Sons' on signs around the city—like 'Oxo' or 'Carter's Pills'—but after touring a seed shop established by an ancestor in 1776 and an associated factory that employed a hundred and sixty people, and noting the prosperity of both firms, still in the family, he asked Ethel, 'Why did we not make our boys businessmen?' Learning that the women in the family were 'churchy', however, he felt better; the London Harrisons had gone beyond that. Outside Leicester he was taken to Stocking Farm, the family seat from whence his grandfather had set out for London as a youth and to which he had returned to die. Now it was owned by Lord Dysart, whose seat was the magnificent Ham House, Richmond. Harrison's description of the area's rich soil, locally attributed to the blood of soldiers slain there during the Civil War, prompted Ethel to deplore the condescension with which some of their London family talked about their country forebears, who she told Fred were 'worthy beef-growing men who made you body and soul'. 'What a strange thing is descent, and race inheritance', she mused.[169].

Later in the year Ethel had reason to dwell again on those great issues. She was staying at Newbiggin Hall, Westmorland, with old London friends, Montague and Blanche Crackanthorpe. It was their boys the Harrison boys had met at Lake Ullswater in 1884, before the Cookson family had changed its name, a requirement for inheriting their ancient family hall. Since then, the sad fate of the eldest Crack-anthorpe son, Hubert, had cast an ironic light on his father's promotion of Eugenics and the articles both his parents had written on the ideals of married life. Hubert's modestly successful decadent fiction had explored unhappy lives and marital discord, and he himself had drifted into a bohemian life that led to the breakdown of his marriage in 1896. During a visit from his anxious mother to him in Paris, he had disappeared, and weeks later his body was found in the Seine, the circumstances of his death unknown. Ethel attended the memorial service in London; and no doubt both she and Fred, who had visited Newbiggin Hall subsequently, were shown the urn bearing Hubert's ashes in the family chapel. All this, the fact that the other sons were living in remote parts, and that Montague was in poor health, created a melancholy atmosphere in the great house.[170]

By contrast, at Elm Hill the Harrisons had Olive with them and frequently entertained her friends; and on holidays they could expect one or more of her brothers. Their own retreat to the Kentish country did not preclude refreshing visits to town together. They both occasionally felt what Ethel called 'the stirring in one's bones for London, for the life of it and the work of it and the sorrow of it, which is indescribable but very real'.[171] She stayed at the Ladies' Athenaeum in Dover Street, communicating with Fred at the National Liberal Club by letter if necessary. Her health continued to be troublesome at times, but his was a source of pride to them both, and he freely recommended his regimen when asked, as he was by Stead for the *Review of Reviews* in 1908: a modest diet—little meat and only light wine—several hours of walking almost daily, and an afternoon and evening nap. So proud was he of having always read without spectacles that when an opthal-mologist pointed out in *The Times* that anyone over fifty who could do so must have been near-sighted in youth, he wrote to dismiss such 'nonsense'.[172]

Harrison took his last cruise in August 1911, leaving behind a nation torn by labour strife, suffragette militancy, and a Parliamentary crisis, all of which made civil war seem possible. Far from providing total escape from political anxieties, the cruise intensified his fear of Germany and dislike of Russia, sentiments he no doubt communicated to his travelling companions, Olive, Godfrey, and three Philipson-Stow girls. The dock strike delayed their departure and the heat was so great that Ethel, at home, felt 'like a dried pea'. But at last the *S. S. Mantua* was off. At Oslo Lady Constance Battersea entertained him and urged him to accompany her luncheon party to meet the King and Queen of Norway; but Harrison preferred to spend his time inspecting Viking relics and the monument to Ibsen, and to relax back on ship with 'the most poetic, tragic, and Shakespearean drama in modern literature'— *The Bride of Lammermoor*. The ship's wireless reports on the Parlia-mentary crisis at home were even more exciting, and a fellow passenger, Spencer Lyttleton, formerly Gladstone's private secretary, had 'all the latest news'. At Copenhagen Harrison made out as best he could from the Danish papers what was happening in the House of Lords, then debating the Parliament Bill that would limit its power to block legis-lation. He predicted a comfortable margin for the Bill, and was delighted to learn from the wireless when the ship was at sea again that the majority exceeded his expectation. But at Stockholm the British Min-ister, Cecil Spring-Rice, gave him something new to worry about: the 'awful' suggestion that in the much-discussed Agadir incident in June the Germans had sent their gunboat *Panther* to Moroccan waters in part to lure elements of the British North Sea Fleet to the Mediter-ranean, thus leaving Britain more vulnerable to attack. Hearing this was enough to convince Harrison that the strikes in England were the work of 'German Jew financiers, *who want war*, as they are hungering to handle the £1,000,000 that Germany is to have as an indemnity for retiring from London, Chatham, and Portsmouth'. Ethel, the recipient of this astounding opinion, added to his anxieties by reporting that the record heat continued and there was now a food-shortage scare.

At Kronstadt the young people left by train for six days in Moscow while Harrison went on to St. Petersburg. There the British Ambassador, Sir George Buchanan, entertained him at a dinner for twelve in his villa and talked privately with him about European and English politics with a surprising openness. St. Petersburg turned out to be one great city that disappointed Harrison. Except for two wonderful churches, St. Isaac's and Kazan, its buildings were 'monuments of human vulgarity, ostentation, and insolent pride in mere material size and waste', and the people 'lousy savages', a 'race of underfed mongrels'. The indifferent hotel servants tried his patience, and he was repelled by the icon-kissing penitents in the churches, some 'even slobbering the pavement'. Because of a religious holiday unknown in the West the Hermitage was closed during the first two of his three days, but its pictures and pre-Christian gold work proved 'quite A-1'. Still, 'there never was, and never will be, any pure art in the slough of such obstinate superstition and ignorant pride.' In the end he deemed the cruise worth the thirty guineas it cost him, if only because he had found out what Russia really was—'a whale that has gone ashore and is flapping about to get out to sea'.[173]

On his eightieth birthday that October Harrison felt 'wonderfully well', but an afternoon in St. Leonard's with Beesly, now lame with arthritis, made him look ahead; he hoped to 'go quietly off' when his time came, as had his parents. Meanwhile, there were new worries. Ethel had an attack of phlebitis in the spring of 1912 necessitating a nurse during most of their stay at Blackdown House, and the family's financial picture was darkening. His gilt-edged railway stocks had fallen thirty per cent, 'for the men are now in a position to force higher wages', and a £1,000 American investment had to be written off completely. His sons, 'with all their industry, my means of bringing them on, and their admitted capabilities', were still not financially independent. The moral was that 'the day of the middle-class and professional man of £1,000 p. an. is ended.'[174] His four indoor and four outdoor servants, plus Ethel's medical expenses, were a drain that he felt even more when the new insurance payments required by the Liberals' legislation began in 1912. Yet after consulting friends he decided that 'decent employers' would buy not only the stamps representing their contribution to their servants' insurance but their servants' stamps as well: 'We shall have to lick', he said resignedly, adding 'It is shameful how the vulgar and selfish rich will abuse and rebel against this Act—one of the most beneficent of our age. Stupefied by their indolent luxury and [made] selfish by their anti-social prejudices, they will bring the whole social system to collapse and ruin this country in its fall.'[175]

A more immediate threat to the social system was the Irish crisis, for Ulster refused to consider any Home Rule scheme that linked it to the Catholic counties, and the Irish Nationalists rejected any plan not including Ulster. Asquith's Home Rule Bill in the spring of 1912 won Harrison's support because like his own proposal of 1886 it provided for Irish MPs at Westminster and limited the proposed Irish Parliament's autonomy.[176] But after the Bill had been twice passed through the Commons, twice defeated by the Lords, and finally returned to the Commons late in 1913 for the last round prescribed by the recent Parliament Act, the problem of Ulster still remained. In a personal letter and a communication in *The Times*, Harrison advised Asquith to postpone any decision on the vexed matter until six months following the next General Election and meanwhile to form a 'grand committee' of all MPs elected by Ulster to the new Irish Parliament mandated by the Bill and let it handle Ulster's internal affairs. Morley, now in the Cabinet as Lord President, warned his ever-inventive friend that there might well be 'cards in the play of which you are not aware'. One was probably the refusal of the Irish Nationalists to negotiate; another, the report of Birrell, the Irish Secretary, of a shipment of arms to Ulster.[177] In February 1914 Harrison called for a national referendum on the Irish problem, and by invoking the memory of his Ulster grandfather he exasperated Morley, who commented: 'What would *he* think of him? Comtist, atheist philosopher, and lay head of the Positivist Church?'[178] When men as differently schooled as Thomas Hardy and the historian A. F. Pollard judged the idea of a referendum to be more revolutionary than Home Rule itself, Harrison was provoked into calling the Constitution 'a venerable relic that might be put in the British Museum'.[179] He could not now approve the Government's provisions for a Parliament in Dublin because they denied Ulster any autonomy and thus embodied a 'fatal mistake'. Having proposed a series of solutions, all to no avail, he fell back on the metaphysical rhetoric that was a sure sign of his frustration and despair: 'It all looks as if we were spectators in some Greek tragedy, where the contending persons seem bound in honour, in duty, by religion, to work out their predestined purpose to a foreseen catastrophe from which fate will not suffer them to shrink.'[180]

If Ireland suggested a Greek tragedy, European politics had become almost a melodrama for Harrison, with Germany the villain menacing an England caught in the grip of 'fossil Radicalism and Labour Socialism' that foolishly resisted military readiness and expected German workers to restrain the Kaiser.[181] He now viewed the *Entente* with France as ineffectual, and at a luncheon given by Morley in March 1911 he found that Sir Alfred Lyall, retired from the Indian service, and Valentine Chirol, foreign correspondent of *The Times*, agreed with him, though Morley did not.[182] Harrison's Germanophobia was even damaging his relations with Swinny, who complained that Harrison considered him 'cowardly and unpatriotic' because he did not 'tremble at the Kaiser's name, nor dream of German invasion'.[183] When ratification of the Declaration of London, which would establish principles governing maritime trade in time of war, was being publicly debated, Harrison at first hesitated to endorse it. Critics argued that it would restrict Britain's freedom of action on the seas; but he came to believe that any disadvantages to Britain would be balanced out by restraints upon the other nations adhering to the document. In any case, he preferred order and arbitration in international legal matters to the existing confusion.[184] When international tensions kept some of his countrymen from supporting the scheduled 1916 Olympic Games, Harrison gave his guinea but called the spirit of international competition they fostered 'dismal ... as the race in armaments'.[185] By 1913 he was so alarmed over the international scene as to find the number thirteen in the date ominous, however 'fanciful'; and he wrote of the dismemberment of Turkey's European empire, which he had so long feared, as apparently 'a decree of providence', so powerless had Britain been to halt it. Since Slav states now blocked Germany's access to the Aegean and Black Sea, where, he asked, could she go but westward? A German invasion of Holland, Belgium, and northern France seemed so inevitable by 1912 that he called for a war loan of at least 150 million pounds to prepare to fight off 'Goths, Vandals, Teutons, and Huns'.[186]

Harrison's New Year's Day Address to the Positivists in 1913, reflecting his deep apprehensions, was the last he would deliver. The previous summer he and Ethel had decided to look for a less expensive house, for having recently had to sell some stocks, it seemed unwise to continue to pay £300 annual rent and taxes on Elm Hill, plus the £400 for the garden and stables and the wages of eight servants. They considered living in Oxford, but decided that the climate there was bad, the streets would be too crowded for Ethel, and 'the old dons and young tutors are queer creatures—all of them.' Surrey villas such as Sidney had built in Mayford and Charles's widow occupied during the

the summers near Dorking were 'banal in the extreme'. They would have to go further from London.[187] At last they found just the right place, in Bath. Number 10 Royal Crescent was a nine-bedroomed house in the great semi-ellipse of thirty attached Georgian houses that was a showplace of the ancient resort and spa. The Crescent overlooked a spacious park beyond which the Mendip Hills could be seen; and behind the house was a one hundred and sixty-foot-long walled garden, complete with a grape-vine and greenhouse, which provided a lovely vista for Harrison's library. Recently renovated, the house had the Morris paper so dear to the Harrisons' generation, two baths, electricity, and even a telephone. They took a fourteen-year lease at £125 a year, which Godfrey, the family financial expert, declared a bargain, and by the end of the year Bernard, the family art expert, had arranged the pictures and furniture. Ethel was soon benefiting from treatments in the city's famous hospital, and Fred learned all about the restorations being carried out in Bath Abbey by René's mentor, Thomas Graham Jackson. Olive had the Philipson-Stow girls and Alex Pringle, a Hawkhurst girl-friend, as guests to help ease the awkwardness of finding new companions, and the family renewed acquaintance with Mildred Davey, daughter of their Fernhurst neighbours, now living outside Bath with her husband, Richard Strachey, a relation of the Lancaster Gate family.[188] By the spring of 1914 Harrison had attained an appointment as Justice of the Peace and was circulating a typescript description of his new library and a *Cornhill Magazine* essay on Bath as 'An Old Garden City'.[189]

Yet, other places, familiar and new, still called. Harrison spent five days in London in the spring of 1913 attending meetings of the Royal Society and the Historical Congress, the latter a confusing affair 'run by that ass Gollancz', the publisher. Twice he had tea at the House of Lords with the Earl of Wemyss and March, who was 'full of go' despite his ninety-five years and eager for Harrison's opinion of his unpublished memoirs, which mentioned their co-operation on the Royal Commission on Trade Unions, and his views on art. With Morley Harrison talked 'about everything'; at the Athenaeum he read Charles Tennyson's autobiography, *Cambridge from Within*; and he enjoyed two plays, Lengyel's *Typhoon*, about Japanese agents in Paris, and Jerome K. Jerome's *Passing of the Third Floor Back*, about Jesus in Bloomsbury. 'The great thing', he liked to say, 'was to vary your impressions.'[190] In May he climbed the hill behind Blackdown Cottage and was so encouraged by his low pulse after the exertion that on Dartmoor with Ethel in July he climbed Hay Tor.[191] That holiday was cut short by the sudden death of his brother Sidney. His estate, which included his inheritance from Charles, subject to the life interest of Charles's widow, proved to be in such a jumble that Godfrey had heavy work for a time. Harrison decided that by giving his children his half of Charles's estate—the other heir was Robert—they could each hope to receive about £5,000 if he lived three years longer and thus cleared the money of death duties. But his figures were far from certain, and there was no telling when Sidney's estate would pass to them. He estimated his own income as £2,000 a year, enough to live on but not to help his sons as much as he wished were possible.[192]

In June 1914 the Harrisons made a sentimental journey that roughly followed the route of their wedding trip forty-three years earlier. The past was recalled in disturbing ways. Émile Corra held a reception for them in Paris, but most of the assembled guests in the Positivists' rooms in Rue de Seine were strangers to them. Harrison recounted the story of his interview with Comte and spoke bravely of his own faith in the movement. Far different were the words he set down in a diary upon reaching Switzerland. Reflecting on the whole Positivist scene he deplored the 'miserable divisions' among the French and the personal jealousies dividing the English, Brazilian, and Hungarian Positivists as well. 'The whole work will have to be begun anew', he concluded; but first socialism would have to be tried and seen to fail. As for peace in Europe, he wrote, 'I cannot hope for it.'[193] The assassination of the Archduke Franz Ferdinand at Sarajevo had occurred during the Harrisons' stay in Paris, but its meaning was hidden. They continued their journey and stayed quietly in Switzerland while desperate diplomacy preoccupied the last month of old Europe. Towards the end of July they hurried back to England with a deep sense of foreboding, passing through Paris, which was in a state of extreme agitation. Within a few days of their arrival home, Austria–Hungary, Serbia, Germany, and Russia were at war. As in 1870, their immediate thoughts were of France; but now they knew that in the coming conflict England could not remain a spectator.

The Positivist as Man of Letters
1870–1914

THE GREAT ASSIZE OF LETTERS

Harrison eased into his vocation as literary critic only after he had become well known as a writer on politics, law, and religion. But even in his school-days he had literary opinions, and as a young man in London enjoyed sharing them with the Shore and Hall sisters and directing the reading of his future bride. Among family and such friends, of course, he had the authority of an Oxford man, and, by the mid-sixties, one acquainted with some prominent writers. In the seventies his intimacy with Morley gave him insights into the world of journalism, and its sycophancy, backbiting, and avarice reinforced Comte's strictures against professional writing. With his father's wealth behind him he could afford to take a stand against the urgings of Morley and others that he move deeper into that world himself. The anonymity of most reviewing especially repelled him, not only because it contradicted Comte's teaching to 'live openly' but because, as one who had become inured to controversy, he did not like to see others escape the consequences of their unpopular opinions. Thus when Robert Buchanan, a minor poet and critic, used a *nom de plume* in attacking Rossetti, Swinburne, and Morris as 'fleshly' poets in 1872, Harrison protested to Knowles, who had published the article in his *Contemporary Review*, and told Morley that in the Positivist republic a publisher guilty of Knowles's offence would have to 'stand on a pillory and chew his publications ten hours a day'. Yet Harrison and Morley were far from enthusiastic about Buchanan's victims. Morley had been savage about Swinburne's 'libidinous' verse in an anonymous review in 1866 and Harrison spoke contemptuously of their having formed a 'joint stock mutual puff and admiration co. (unlimited)'. Log-rolling seemed to him as bad as anonymity.[1]

Harrison could accept a good deal of sensuality in poetry if mixed with more congenial qualities. In this respect he was only following Comte. They were alike, for example, in their admiration of Byron; he was in Comte's Calendar and his 'selected works' (barring *Don Juan*) were listed in the Positivist Library. In one of Harrison's earliest published statements on literature, in *The Times* correspondence columns in 1873, he defended the poet against charges of faulty grammar, endorsing Beesly's estimate of him as the greatest poet since Milton 'by virtue of his massiveness, his pathos, his versatility, and, in spite of coarseness both in soul and brain, his indomitable heroic fire'. 'Coarseness' was as close as Harrison would come to acknowledging Byron's moral flaws. In *The New Calendar of Great Men* he associated him with Shelley and Goethe because he 'put into immortal words the consciousness of man's moral force as the arbiter of his own destiny', and in another essay valued his prose even higher than his verse because it more completely revealed his greatness of character. In 1906 Harrison endorsed a privately circulating book by E. H. Pember and R. E. Prothero repudiating the revived charge of Byron's incest, and he shared the anxiety of its printer, John Murray, grandson of Byron's publisher, about the book's reaching the public and opening up the subject anew.[2]

Though in Harrison's judgement Byron's themes could compensate for certain lapses of style, form rather than content usually determined his evaluation of writers. He held fast to traditional literary modes. Meredith's 'uncouth conundrums' and 'jerky and cryptic' diction made his novels unreadable; and no doubt he also held against Meredith his comic treatment of eternal widowhood in *The Egoist* and his un-Positivist attitudes toward women. Swinburne's verse advanced ideas of humanity and republicanism, but Harrison dismissed it as 'bombastic', 'cloying', and 'monotonous'. And his appreciation of Browning's poetry fell a good way beneath that of fellow Positivists like Cotter Morison and Charles Herford, members of the Browning Society, and of Fanny Hertz, who often entertained the poet. Though Harrison admired Browning personally as 'the most original and sane spirit' of all the writers he knew, he found his verse unmusical, a common enough criticism. Altogether the poets of the seventies seemed so unappealing that in a fit of pique he exploded to Morley: 'Why do they exist—who wants their yelling [?]' For a social critic, he reasoned, 'form is a trifle', but with a poet, 'one offence against reason, art, taste, and harmony puts him out of the pale of the Elysian fields where the select few discourse with calm and courtly grace.'[3]

This emphasis on form stemmed partly from Harrison's unwillingness to regard poets primarily, or even importantly, as prophets. Having warned against Neo-Christianity in theology, he was not prepared to tolerate its counterpart in literature. Mill, Arnold, Pater, Myers, and Leslie Stephen argued that poetry such as Wordsworth's could do some of the work of religion; and Clifford and Symonds even imagined poetry and science fusing to produce 'cosmic emotion'. Neither view was Harrison's. With his customary audacity he chose to develop his objections to poetic pantheism at South Place, where Moncure Conway often used Oriental and Western pantheistic and ethical texts in his services. Poetry, Harrison declared firmly, 'is one thing, Science, Action, Life, Religion are far other—all much wider and more continuous. Poetry is but one mode of Art, and Art is but *one* side of *one* of the elements of Human Nature.' A passing shot at Arnold made his meaning plain: 'poets are not (for all some people say) the guides of life: their business is to beautify life.' Here was an echo of John Henry Newman's denial that poetry could inculcate morality. Harrison even used an image recalling Newman's comparison of the attempt to 'quell the passion and pride of man' with mere knowledge and reason to the attempt to 'moor a vessel with a thread of silk'. Harrison called literary formulations about as useful as 'packthread' in anchoring a soul 'tossed and buffeted in a storm of passion'.[4] But if pantheism was thus banished from Positivist theology, it crept into Newton Hall's liturgy: Ethel's hymnal included George Herbert's 'Great World-Mother', a selection from Shelley's *Prometheus Unbound*, and eight fragments from Wordsworth (though she had to delete Newman's 'Lead Kindly Light' because it offended the anti-religious).

Literature might be no substitute for Positivist dogma, but the great books were the foundation of Positivist education, and Harrison pressed their claims even before becoming head of the Positivist Society. Lecturing on reading at the London Institute and at the Working Men's College in the 1870s he did not refer to the Positivist Library but took its categories of science, history, literature, and a combination of philosophy and religion as a guide, and he recommended many of its titles. These lectures fulfilled a hope he had expressed early in his marriage to make some use of the lists he had drawn up to direct Ethel's reading before their engagement. Since then the Education Act of 1870 had been increasing the size of the reading public, and to meet its demands the number of new books and periodicals had proliferated. Against their attractions, Harrison set the great works of the past, those that had gained their status in a 'great assize of letters' presided over by Humanity itself. It could be, he solemnly judged, that the 'gates which lead to the Elysian fields may slowly wheel back on their adamantine hinges to admit now and then some new and chosen modern', but for the most part, the 'company of the masters of those who know ... is a roll long closed.' Making the right choice of books, then, was no light matter, for it implied a desire to place oneself under the tutelage of Humanity's greatest servants, and a 'view of man's duty and powers as a moral and social being—a religion'.[5] Such formulations gave a Positivist turn to a lesson already taught by Carlyle, Ruskin, and Arnold. It was not its originality but its currency that Alexander Macmillan recognized when Harrison offered the publisher his lecture on reading as the title piece in a collection of essays. Macmillan, a close friend of leading Christian Socialists, put aside his earlier judgement of the Positivists as 'hardly at the centre of truth', and offered half-profits and £ 50 for the American and colonial rights. Eventually there was a de luxe edition as well.[6]

In February 1886, shortly before *The Choice of Books* appeared, Sir John Lubbock addressed the Working Men's College on the 'One Hundred Best Books'. Since he was speaking only of reading for pleasure, he noted that Comte's list was not 'suitable for us', and he omitted scientific works altogether (though he, more than Harrison, found pleasure in them).[7] Inevitably, too, Lubbock did not include most of the French works that made Comte's list so unpalatable for English readers. Published in the *Pall Mall Gazette*, Lubbock's list instantly became the talk of the literary world. It was soon annotated by the 'hundred best judges' in a journalistic gambit of Charles Morley, who had joined the *Pall Mall* staff during his uncle John Morley's editorship. Variants such as 'Books for Girls', 'Books for Boys', 'Books for Holidays', and 'Highland Books' were soon appearing. The brash literary entrepreneur Frank Harris, now editing the *Fortnightly Review*, published 'Fine Passages in Verse and Prose Selected by Living Men of Letters'. They included Harrison, who ranged widely over Western literature for his choices but named only one Victorian work, *Vanity Fair*. 'As you see', he admitted, 'I am for the accepted judgment of the world.'[8] Profiting from these offshoots of Lubbock's list, *The Choice of Books* went into many editions and became Harrison's best-known volume, its sales helping to induce Macmillan to take other works by Harrison over the next quarter-century though none did nearly as well. And Macmillan used the book's format for Lubbock's even more popular volume, *The Pleasures of Life*, containing his address and list of the one hundred best books. Both men thus paved the way for the innumerable inexpensive editions of the classics that became a phenomenon of the following decades.

But no such success awaited the pamphlet on Comte's *Positivist Library* that Harrison published the same year as *The Choice of Books*. He was often asked to speak on books and reading in later years, but it was to the man of letters and critic, not to the Positivist, that the invitations were tendered, and he had to be content to accept them in that spirit. He also had to accept defeat at the polls by Lubbock in July 1886, just when their book-lists were being compared, usually to Lubbock's advantage. But their cordial relations remained unimpaired. Acknowledging Lubbock's presentation copy of *The Pleasures of Life*, Harrison commented on 'how much more enduring and real are the resources of science, art, and literature, than the stormy joys of the political field.'[9] The grapes may have been a trifle sour, but Lubbock probably agreed.

That Harrison and Lubbock valued many of the same books is evident from their lists. Lubbock's, in one version, even included Comte's *Catechism*. Both offered to audiences without university education a choice of books that seems formidable indeed today. Yet there is no doubt that each had acted out of unfeigned delight which he sincerely desired to share. Harrison went farther than Lubbock in making his list educationally useful, for he gave some information about editions and translations. Homer he called the indispensable author because he had depicted a life that was 'wholly beautiful, complete, and happy', one in which 'care, doubt, decay are as yet unborn'. It was a world Harrison thought he had briefly entered on his visit to Greece in 1881, when his brother Charles had moored his yacht and the party had gone ashore to ramble on the hillsides among the shepherds, Harrison using his classical Greek as best he could to communicate with them. Later poets, he believed, had to imagine the ideal images that the Greeks found in reality; and only if they made that imaginative leap could he truly enjoy their work.[10] Dante, for example, he praised for presenting human life as a whole, but especially for seeing it as it might be, and for conveying his paradisial vision in language that deserved immortality. (Harrison forbore to mention that Comte deemed Italian the language of the future, something he probably remembered in 1891 when he joined Gladstone in protesting against the India Office's deletion of Italian from its examination requirements.)[11]

Two essays in *The Choice of Books* show how uncongenial Harrison found literature that brought the reader face to face with psychological realities which threatened ideal images. They were his reprinted reviews of two controversial biographies, Froude's life of Carlyle and Cross's life of George Eliot. Biography was a crucial genre for Positivists because only the biographer's right choice of facts and interpretation of them could enhance his subject's subjective immortality. Both books disappointed Harrison, Froude's because of what it included, Cross's because of what it left out.

Few Victorians escaped Carlyle's influence, and the Positivists were no exception. Harrison had once thought Morison and the Lushingtons too much imbued with it to appreciate Comte fully, and in *Order and Progress* he had felt obliged to compare Comte's political thought to Carlyle's at some length. Guilt about his own relative affluence in the seventies had caused him to admire the simplicity of Carlyle's way of life, which he glimpsed on a few visits to Cheyne Walk, and he thought it a useful lesson in hero-worship for his boys to take them to Carlyle's door to inquire about his condition the day before he died.[12] Yet Froude's biography, completed in 1884, interested him partly because it revealed that Carlyle had come to enjoy the comforts of fine houses and the attentions of wealthy friends. Carlyle's relentless pessimism, despite these sources of solace and the improvement in his own financial circumstances, seemed a clear sign that his philosophy of life was inadequate. Harrison would later make a similar observation about Gissing, and Froude's revelations about the marital discord in the Carlyle household distressed him just as he did Gissing's stories of marital problems. In his review, Harrison characterized Froude's Carlyles as 'Brobdingnagian'; they 'railed at each other like giant and giantess in a fairy tale'. What right or duty, he asked, 'have we to be called in so long after death to sit in judgment on these full hearts?' Yet he wondered whether it was possible ever to 'hear enough as to the sources of happiness and misery, of love and despair?'[13] To Morley he expressed a more personal concern. Thinking of 'all the garrulous things we drop out in hasty scrawls being given to mankind the moment we are dead', he considered what use might one day be made of his correspondence with Morley: 'I have nothing to fear—thank humanity—but you—oh you—Bernard will have to decide which of all the hasty things you write are to be burnt and which added to your collected works in 30 octavo volumes.'[14]

When Alexander Carlyle, the writer's nephew, commissioned Charles Eliot Norton to make a new edition of Carlyle's early letters in order to correct Froude's transcription errors, Harrison gave Norton's work a good review, but he was clearly less interested in Norton's greater verbal accuracy than in his softer image of Carlyle. What Harrison wanted was an inspiring portrait.[15] He withheld comment when criticism of Froude's work continuing after his death led his heirs in 1903 to publish his account of material he had suppressed, the most damaging of which showed that Carlyle had probably been impotent and at times cruel to his wife. The next year Harrison edited a collection of Carlyle's early essays that he noted in his introduction contained 'hardly a sentence which could provoke controversy or indignation'.[16] And, less than four years before his own death, in thanking Lady Airlie for letting him see some unpublished letters of the Carlyles in her possession, he said that Froude, for all his 'literary keenness', had produced in the end an 'unfair and distorted' portrait of the couple. But Harrison saw no point in reviving the old controversy by bringing the new evidence before the public.[17]

In both content and form, Cross's biography had more for Harrison to admire than Froude's. By telling his story mostly through excerpts from George Eliot's journals and letters, including some lent by Harrison, Cross gave his work a specious air of objectivity. Harrison spent hours over the proofs with Cross. Then, without hiding his identification with the project, he convinced T. H. S. Escott at the *Fortnightly* that Cross wished him to review the work; and he also told Cross that Escott had pressed him to take the assignment.[18] His eagerness was not motivated by the desire for the reviewer's fee, though he called it 'handsome'. (Escott had probably inflated the amount because Harrison had only recently declined payment for the text of his Annual Address at Newton Hall, pointing out that there was an 'old and inflexible rule' there against taking money for sermons.)[19] He was no doubt savouring an opportunity for Positivist proselytizing, and he accomplished a fair amount in his review.

Though Cross passed over episodes in George Eliot's life that he apparently thought might undercut her reputation as a sage—her attachments to Chapman and Spencer, for example—Harrison pronounced the portrait 'truly faithful', at least where her literary life was concerned, and he said that the public need have no concern with anything else. He welcomed the evidence that her writing rested on a basis of wide and systematic reading, for this reinforced his own teaching against over-indulgence in peripheral, contemporary literature, and he noted that she had found inspiration in the works of one the 'higher criticism' (Arnold) had vilified as a 'grotesque French pedant', and that she had never supported women's political rights. Had Harrison known of the many transcriptions from Comte's works in her journal entries not published by Cross, he might have searched her novels more diligently than he ever did for evidences of Positivism. Instead, he acquiesced in Cross's view of her appreciation of Comte's teaching as 'thoroughly selective', and even introduced a negative note understandably absent in Cross: he regretted that she and Lewes had not chosen to honour Comte's teaching on marriage, which would make it 'indissoluble by law, and indissoluble even by death'.[20] To Morley, Harrison revealed an even harsher judgement of her marriage to Cross than of her liaison with Lewes. Having accepted that liaison as a marriage, he considered her union with Cross a betrayal of Lewes as well as disloyalty to Comte. 'If I ever wrote a life', he declared, 'it would be to say a few words of poor dear old Lewes, in some ways the finest mind, and the best heart of the lot, poor dear old boy how ill he has been used by men not fit to black his boots and by that epicene woman whom he so loved and who got to loathe the very memory of him.'[21] It may be that Harrison knew of the rumour about George Eliot's having discovered in Lewes's papers after his death some evidence of infidelity to her, which made her feel free to marry Cross.[22] But it is equally likely that her intellectuality and the adoration she inspired in women like Edith Simcox and Mrs Congreve seemed to Harrison symptomatic of an aversion to heterosexuality. According to Lord Carlingford's journal, Harrison confidently asserted that the Leweses had never lived together as man and wife.[23]

The miscellaneous character of *The Choice of Books* justified one critic's complaint that Harrison warned against peripheral writing but reprinted his own. Besides the two reviews, the book contained an essay on Morison's *St. Bernard of Clairvaux* rejected by the *Westminster Gazette* in 1863; essays from the *Fortnightly* and *Nineteenth Century* on the eighteenth and nineteenth centuries in England, the historiography of the French Revolution, and old London; his replies to Ruskin and Arnold; and articles from the *Pall Mall Gazette* on art and from *The Times* on the Courts of Justice and the Tower of London. Much in all this was highly critical of modern life; yet in his London Institute lecture Harrison defined his age as one of 'great expectation and unwearied striving after better things'. His essay on eighteenth-century England appreciated that era's dynamic qualities, too, and contributed to the late Victorian revival of interest in its culture; and his essay on books about the French Revolution anticipated the studies that its centennial would soon inspire. The variety of Harrison's subjects and the felicity of his prose impressed many who would have hesitated to say a good word for anything political or philosophical from his pen; and altogether it seemed that the book marked a welcome new stage in his life. Ethel told the boys that their father had met with professional difficulties because of his endorsement of the trade unions, but was now 'free to devote himself to the true business of his life, which was art and religion'.[24] The break was not as sharp as this reminiscence of Austin's implies, but it is perhaps significant that Harrison finally gave up his long-neglected chambers at Lincoln's Inn the very year he became a literary figure. His new reputation was undeniably a relief to his family. Austin, thirteen at the time and tired of being chided at Harrow for having an atheist father, overheard with satisfaction one of the masters order *The Choice of Books* for the school library; and his grandmother, then seventy-nine, received her copy proudly, saying she thought it contained much that would benefit her in her remaining years.[25]

Not only the right choice of books but their useful circulation interested Harrison. He had therefore helped to fill the shelves of the little library corner at both Chapel Street and Newton Hall, and had sent books to Laffitte's centre in Paris. In 1891 he joined Chief Justice Coleridge and Lord Randolph Churchill in support of the local library in Paddington when voters denied it public funds.[26] A life member of the London Library since his marriage, he served on its executive committee. Taking a paternal interest in its librarian, C. T. Hagberg Wright, he tried first to get his salary raised and, when that failed, supported his candidacy for librarian of the House of Lords, again to no avail. Wright, a student of Russian literature, alarmed him by his enthusiasm for Tolstoy, a 'dangerous anarch' whom Harrison declared did 'more harm than some very evil men'. Instead of going to Russia as head of an English committee to celebrate Tolstoy's eightieth birthday in 1908, Wright should 'see the sun and watch spring' with his sovereign in Biarritz.[27] When a vacancy on the Library's executive committee occurred in 1904, Harrison sought to enlist Goschen, Morley, and George Trevelyan: 'We want senior men well before the world.'[28] His friendship with Leslie Stephen stemmed largely from their joint work on the committee. Stephen's successor, Arthur Balfour, was far less congenial, for in addition to their philosophical and political antagonisms, Balfour had offended by flippantly advising a St. Andrews University audience to ignore Harrison's praise of the great books and to 'read everything you find interesting and nothing you don't.'[29]

To facilitate the proper choice of books at the London Library, Harrison helped the staff with its Author Index in 1903 and headed the committee for the Subject Index in 1909, explaining the merits of the latter in *The Times Literary Supplement* and at the Library's annual meeting. An interruption at that gathering by suffragettes no doubt outraged him, though he was not above digressing from literary business himself: at one meeting he inveighed against 'these motors, these week-ends, this tearing about' as distractions from reading.[30] Partly to honour the Library's history, in 1907 he saw through the press an edition of letters exchanged by Carlyle and William Dougal Christie about the founding of the institution. Christie's daughter Mary, who had drifted away from the Positivists in the eighties and attained some success as a journalist and novelist, had almost completed the edition when she succumbed to cancer, and at her sisters' request, Harrison finished the task, assigning the profits to them. In his preface he quoted

Carlyle's famous description of a collection of books as 'more than a university ... a Church also ... but with no quarrelling, no Church rates'. The quotation might not have entirely pleased Mary, who had returned to the Anglican fold.[31]

Since *The Times* Book Club in 1905 promised to aid the circulation of books by allowing the paper's subscribers to borrow volumes without charge and purchase them at reduced prices, Harrison endorsed the plan. Frederick Macmillan led the fight against it by withholding the usual trade discount on the club's book purchases, and John Murray complained to Harrison personally about *The Times*'s retaliatory action— its refusal to advertise or review books of the rebellious firms. When a book of Harrison's was boycotted, he decided that the scheme had become 'suicidal', and he was relieved when *The Times* arrived at the same conclusion and abandoned it. Fortunately for him, Macmillan overlooked his original endorsement and *The Times* continued to publish his letters to the editor and occasionally even to report his movements in 'Court News'.[32]

Harrison's reputation as a man of letters was furthered by his work on committees formed to honour writers. 'One *ought* to do *something*', he told Morley in 1892, announcing that he would participate in the centenary celebration of Shelley's birth even if it meant listening to Gosse as a speaker. Nor did the irony of placing a tablet to an atheist in the Horsham church deter him, though it and the speeches making light of the poet's radicalism amused Richard le Gallienne, John Lane, and Grant Richards, who were soon to be styled Decadents, and irked Bernard Shaw, who thought Harrison's 'bogus Shelleyism' was in the service of a plan for a free public library at Horsham.[33] When unveiling portraits of Lamb and Keats in Edmonton's library in 1899 Harrison said less of them than of libraries, and eulogized the building's donor, J. Passmore Edwards, who had been so parsimonious towards Newton Hall.[34] If tablets and portraits enhanced subjective immortality, how much more could the residence of a writer, preserved and open to the public? Harrison was on the committee that bought Carlyle's house in 1895, and he compared its acquisition to the Positivists' purchase of 10 Rue Monsieur-le-Prince.[35] Eulogies on writers always interested him, the more auspicious the occasion the better. He attended the Westminster Abbey burials of Browning and Tennyson and compared the latter to Renan's burial in the Pantheon in Paris, which in his view had considerable advantages over Christian ritual.[36] When Ruskin's family declined the offer of an Abbey burial for him in 1900, Harrison, who had helped to promote the idea, headed the committee that engaged Onslow Ford to design a memorial medallion for the Poets' Corner.

After groping in semi-darkness there, Harrison decided that the spot over Scott's bust chosen by his colleagues was 'intolerable', but, ever the good committee man, he defended it when Lady Burne-Jones and Octavia Hill objected on the ground that Ruskin would not have wanted *any* addition to those hallowed walls. Harrison maintained that the plaque would neither disfigure the Abbey nor wrong Ruskin's memory, though he seized the occasion to press for some new national place of burial in which to honour the eminent.[37]

Leslie Stephen, as a biographer and founding editor of the *Dictionary of National Biography*, seemed especially deserving of a memorial when he died in 1904. Harrison signed the appeal for funds to present an engraving of Watts's portrait of Stephen to the institutions with which he had been associated. He also published his reminiscences of Stephen in Stephen's own *Cornhill*, and reviewed the *Life and Letters* by F. W. Maitland. The parallels in their two careers were, as Harrison noted, striking. In the 1860s they had been reformers and freethinkers in the same circles, and as fellow Alpinists had once met at the top of Mont Blanc. Later they had both led ethical societies, written on philosophy, ethics, religion, and literature, served the London Library, and edited a biographical dictionary. Harrison passed over in silence Stephen's published criticism of Positivism, but also a recent letter to him in which Stephen said that had he gone to Oxford instead of Cambridge he might have become a Positivist since he had been impressed by Comte's theories at the time and lacked only like-minded companions to effect a conversion. Harrison rightly saw that Stephen's rationalism and common sense left no room for 'the enthusiasm for humanity', and in the *Cornhill* essay alluded to this difference between them. But having visited Stephen in his last illness, Harrison could also testify to the fortitude Stephen had shown during those painful days, working on lectures he would never live to deliver and showing at times evidence of the old 'irrepressible humour'.[38]

Though loyalty to friends and favoured writers past and present was, as Austin observed, a cardinal trait of his father's, Harrison warned against excessive memorializing. He called 1909 an 'annus mirabilis' because it brought commemorations of Johnson, Paine, Calvin, Tennyson, Darwin, and Gladstone—too many, he thought, since aviation records, rival budgets, and Halley's comet had also been stirring the imagination. And to mark anniversaries of births seemed unscientific; to Positivists only the date of death was sacred, for it completed one's contributions to Humanity. 'Did heaven ring and earth shake when a rather shiftless tradesman at Stratford, in April 1564, had a third child?', Harrison asked. But he helped mark both births and deaths of so many that he once compared himself to Scott's Old Mortality.[39]

Positivist saints were most systematically honoured in *The New Calendar of Great Men*, conceived by Harrison in Newton Hall's early days as a way of reaching the non-Positivist community. He said little of Comte in his brief preface and thought of the work as complementing his own essay on the choice of books. To Lubbock he spoke of it as the 'hundred and fifty best lives' (though there were over five hundred and fifty). He also called it a handbook of history (and as such Victor Branford assigned it to his sociology students) and said its selectivity gave it an advantage over the *DNB*, an 'interminable snake', though at the banquet marking the completion of that work in 1900 he gracefully toasted its staff.[40] His own editorial labours, infinitely painful, earned no public plaudits and were often ignored by his contributors. They disregarded his instructions, fell behind schedule, and submitted entries he could not use. The delinquent Marvin, assigned to the category of Ancient Poets, enlisted aid from his Oxford friend Gilbert Murray, then at the start of his career; but despite a generally benevolent attitude towards Positivism engendered by Marvin and an aunt who had taken him to Chapel Street, Murray failed to sense what Harrison wanted and produced over-scholarly essays. So did Marvin, who dwelt so largely on the authorship of the *Iliad* and *Odyssey* that in exasperation Harrison declared: 'It is not the *germ* we want to know but the fruit.' And when Marvin and Murray together finally provided entries on four names in the month of Homer—Aeschylus, Aristophanes, Phidias, and Virgil—Harrison found them less useful than lectures of his own, which he blithely substituted for their essays.[41] The later, non-Positivist publications of both men pleased him more, for they furthered the reading he advocated, Marvin by simplifying Homer for children, and Murray by his highly readable translations of Greek drama and studies of Greek literature. So impressed was Harrison by Murray's scholarship that when the Regius Professorship of Greek at Oxford fell vacant he said he hoped the gods would see to Murray's election. They did; and Murray introduced some 'good Positivism' in his inaugural address.[42]

ORDER AND PROGRESS IN THE ARTS

During the debate over Tennyson's successor as Poet Laureate in 1893, Harrison advanced a paradox that expressed his own literary values. He declared that Tennyson's technical proficiency had created a standard that other poets strove to meet, and in so doing neglected their own talents.[54] At the same time he argued that the fiction of the late nineteenth century was inferior to that which had delighted his generation. Both assertions rest on standards that he would not have advanced in the seventies, when the formal features of literature seemed to determine his judgements. Now he required of the greatest literature that it possess 'curious passion and picturesque incident', and 'variety, contrast, individuality, the eccentric', all of which in his critical lexicon constituted 'romance'. The decline in these character-istics in the fiction of the nineties he termed the 'Decadence of Romance', using 'decadence' without the connotations it was just then acquiring from Arthur Symons, and 'romance' without the meaning given it by Richard le Gallienne for works by himself, Lionel Johnson, John Davidson, Oscar Wilde, Stephen Phillips, and some of the Yellow Book contributors, all of whom were seeking to escape from the materialism and conventions of modern life and letters. Harrison, on the contrary, wrote as if no escape were possible. He disliked the 'topsy-turvy straining after new effects' that had led Stevenson to Samoa and Kipling to the Sudan; and since by his own admission he was insensible to the mystical, he could not appreciate the devotion to fantasy of the Celtic Renaissance. Prose writers, he believed, depended upon reality for inspiration more than did poets, and since modern life was 'against the romance of colour, movement, passion, and jollity', the subjects of modern fiction were less captivating than they once had been. The irony of his argument is patent, for the social progress he blamed for the 'decadence of romance' was the main goal of the Positivist movement. Recognizing this, he conceded that the 'march of democratic equality and of decorous social uniformity is too certain a thing, in one sense too blessed a thing, to be denied or to be denounced'. A romantic age would come again, 'but not to-day nor to-morrow'.[44]

Also attesting to the romanticism of Harrison's views on literature were his warnings that 'the artist should never preach' and should be wary of formal education: he advised aspiring writers in the Palmerston Club at Oxford to flee the University lest it clip their literary wings.[45] He had long insisted that art was impervious to laws and commands: in 1855, lines from his 'penal poem' (exacted for an 'irregularity' by the Oxford Essay Society) proclaimed:

> All song must flow unbidden from the heart,
> The caged bird forgets his wonted strain;
> Song listens not to cunning nor to art,
> It is no smooth work of the 'prentice brain.[46]

Harrison's 'prentice brain had learned much from the prosody, rhyme, imagery, and critical theory of the English Romantics.

The debate over literary realism and idealism had been going on for at least a decade in both England and France when Harrison wrote 'The Decadence of Romance' in 1893. And there was nothing new in his dividing realism into two modes—'Zolaesque bestiality' and the 'Kodak' depiction of ordinary life. In his very first letter to Gissing, in 1880, he had avowed his intolerance of the French naturalist; and he became increasingly unhappy with Gissing's devotion to the second mode of realism. Harrison illustrated its inanities in a dialogue in his 1893 essay that might have come straight from a Gissing novel, but he forebore ever to try his hand at a typical Zola scene. His dislike of Zola's work ironically entailed rejecting a canon today hailed as the first to raise sociology 'to the dignity of art'. It was a dislike not unique to Harrison among the Positivists. Alfred Cock, QC, co-signer of the lease on Newton Hall with Harrison, served as counsel for Zola's English translator and publisher, Henry Vizetelly, on both occasions when Vizetelly appeared in Old Bailey on charges of publishing indecent literature in translation. And on both occasions Cock advised him to plead guilty. In the first trial, in 1888, Vizetelly escaped with only a fine, but the next year he received a prison sentence of three months, and Patrick Geddes was apparently the sole Positivist among the writers who urged his release on the grounds of his advanced age and infirmities.[47] The absence of Newton Hall Positivists on the list of petitioners is striking because freedom of publication—the independence of the spiritual realm, to use Comte's term—was always a high priority with them. Early in 1881, for example, they had 'stigmatized' the Government's prosecution of the anarchist paper *Freiheit*, though it so little interested them for its own sake that at the discussion the only member of the Positivist Society capable of translating from it freely was the young Gissing.[48] Several years later they issued two manifestos on related themes, one deploring Bradlaugh's repeated expulsion from his Parliamentary seat, and the other denouncing the sentences handed out to the secularist G. M. Foote and his associates for publishing material judged blasphemous. Writing independently as a Lincoln's Inn barrister, Harrison called the law invoked in the Foote case unfair since it afforded Positivists no protection when their religion was ridiculed.[49] To the Positivists, political and religious unorthodoxy clearly seemed more defensible than offences against standards of literary propriety.

By the time Harrison wrote 'The Decadence of Romance' those standards had changed enough in England for Zola to be given a warm reception at two of Harrison's preserves, the Athenaeum and Lincoln's Inn. He was not in the welcoming party at either; nor did he soften upon learning three years later from Dr Hillemand that Zola was about to declare himself a Positivist. Any such profession would only damage their cause, replied Harrison.[50] And he did not refer to any sympathetic interest in Positivism on Zola's part, which in any case Hillemand had exaggerated, when he reviewed *Lourdes*, the first of Zola's trilogy about a priest who loses his faith. Harrison, who had recently visited the shrine himself (which is probably why he deigned to write on the novel for the *Positivist Review*) said Zola had failed to do justice to the holiday atmosphere of the place or to its role in the revival of the Church in France, which, like Zola, Harrison deplored.[51] In the last of the trilogy, *Paris*, it was not the realism but the 'dogmatism' Harrison faulted, for Zola's sceptical priest remains unsatisfied with any of the philosophies he considers, including Comte's. Recommending the book to Morley nevertheless, Harrison exclaimed: 'Fancy Zola being a Positivist—though he does us no credit. Every sensible man is a Positivist now—except you.'[52] In his notice of Zola's death in 1902 Harrison ignored altogether his last work, *Les Quatre Evangiles*, yet the three completed novels dealt with categories familiar to Positivists— family, in *Fecondité*; city, in *Travail*; and state, in *Verité*—and Harrison knew that the fourth was to consider an ideal humanity. Like Comte, Zola had abandoned his analytic, objective treatment of reality for a synthetic, idealistic fiction, having been influenced by Comte's theories. Yet Harrison warned the Positivists against considering Zola one of them in any strict sense, and he even dismissed Zola's celebrated profession of humanitarianism in the defence of Dreyfus as mere 'literary effusion'.[53]

Another French writer who rather surprisingly failed to appeal to Harrison was Victor Hugo. Besides damning his work as 'rank stage balderdash', Harrison was disappointed by his appearance when they were introduced in Paris. Always interested in physiognomy, Harrison thought Hugo resembled a seafarer and was a 'poseur' as well.[54] George Sand, about whom he exchanged hyperboles with Morley in the seventies but never met, eventually offended by her 'unwomanly proneness to lust'. The popularity in England of Paul Bourget's fiction convinced him that 'one has only to be Parisian, write one or two horrid stories, and then one has a world-wide reputation.' To Harrison the attraction French fiction had for cultivated Englishmen was comparable to an addiction to absinthe, and its 'manufacture' was a 'crime', for its world of 'adultery without love, sentiment or excuse' was not the world of France he knew.[55] When Mlle Souvestre brought Edouard Rod, a Swiss novelist and former Professor of Comparative Literature at Geneva, to lecture at Stafford House in a similar vein, Harrison helped to arrange the affair—and was observed by Shaw to be furious upon discovering that the seats were not reserved.[56] Some modern French fiction did not come under Harrison's censure: *L'Orme du Mail*, by Anatole France, whom the Harrisons thought had put his friend Laffitte in the novel and who at Laffitte's funeral declared that no thinking person could remain a stranger to Positivism; *L'Ombre de l'Amour*, by Madame Marcelle Tinayre, a member of Laffitte's circle known to the Harrisons; and Octave Feuillet's *Roman d'un Jeune Homme Pauvre*, which Harrison admired for the same reason Pater praised the author, because Feuillet understood that fiction should provide 'a refuge into a world slightly better—better conceived, or better finished—than the real one'.[57]

In 'The Decadence of Romance' Harrison sought to give intellectual rigour to his critical judgements by expounding a theory that is reminiscent of Hippolyte Taine's notion of literature reflecting the author's *race*, cultural *milieu* and *moment*, a sociological explanation that probably owed something to writers also drawn upon by Comte. Without mentioning Taine, Harrison relied on a combination of *milieu* and *moment* in dividing the nineteenth century in Britain into three periods. The first, which ended in the 1830s, he left nameless, 'romantic' not yet being in general usage; the second, ending in the mid-sixties, he termed 'early Victorian' (a usage for which he gets credit in the *Oxford English Dictionary*); the third, like the first unnamed, extended to the date of his writing. His thesis was that by the end of the first period the great authors of 1800 were all dead or like Wordsworth no longer creative, in the second the early Victorians whose reputations he was seeking to advance had emerged, and in the third there began the falling off he was lamenting. Not only is this interpretation at odds with the idea of cultural progress he elsewhere expounded, but to explain the decline of literature he pointed to a 'scientific and sociological interest' that began to 'overshadow, if not to oust, the literary, poetic, and romantic interest' in the mid-sixties. He even named Comte among the writers who had proved 'not the best foster-mothers of Poetry and Romance'. But there is a Positivist explanation for this apparently anti-Positivist theorizing. Just as Comte thought his philosophy had established the true, and his polity the good, so he thought art should represent the beautiful, and, by transcending realities, inspire men to amend them. Art was an agent of the transition to the Positivist era but no substitute for Positivist philosophy or religion.[58] In aesthetics as in so much else, Positivism accorded well with Harrison's proclivities. In late middle age, when he began to formulate his critical theories, he looked back to a time when life seemed more exciting and beautiful than at the present, and the literature of that earlier time inevitably took on a nostalgic glow. Moreover, just as he refused to let Neo-Christianity or poetry take over the work of religion, so he would not yield up fiction to a vulgarized sociology not his own. Hence there is the irony of Harrison, the advocate of trade unions and land taxes, complaining that 'Sam Weller today has joined a union and reads Henry George.'

A similar bias against modernity informs Harrison's art criticism. Though never offered as more than passing commentary, it found its way into leading organs of public opinion and contributed to his reputation as a champion of what had once been new. He first undertook to decry the misuse of art by the fashionable and the choice of ugly and obscure subjects by painters. In two pieces for the *Pall Mall Gazette* in 1882 written partly to oblige Morley and partly to divert himself after his father's death, Harrison sailed into this new critical sea with his usual self-confidence.[59] His belief that an imperfect society inevitably produces tasteless or degraded art had roots in both Comte and Ruskin; but more idiosyncratic was his complaint that by choosing obscure events as subjects, artists were requiring galleries to produce detailed catalogue descriptions. In them Harrison detected the smell of pedantry, and perhaps feared that interest in subject-matter would displace aesthetic appreciation and elevate the second-rate. In the galleries as in the schools he saw an unhealthy competitiveness—but he never shrank from playing the school examiner at art exhibitions. At first he called the British penchant for the trivial and vulgar in art only a mild version of the 'lewdness and bombast' of French art, but in 1893, the year he published 'The Decadence of Romance', he devoted an essay to the 'decadence' of English art.[60] Then, encouraged by praise from the Slade Professor of Art at Oxford, Sir Hubert von Herkomer, and stimulated by Bernard's choice of vocation, he paid increasing attention to London's annual art exhibitions. He seldom liked much that he saw. In 1905 he cast his complaints in a dialogue for which he consulted his old friend the Earl of Wemyss and March, a life-long connoisseur of art and now, at eighty-seven, exhibiting a statue of Venus and Cupid by his own hand. Harrison used it as a touchstone to condemn much in modern art, praising the piece so immoderately that Wemyss pointed out in surprise that he had tried to reproduce all his model's physical features, even faults, such as a bunion on one toe and an arch so flat no bug could crawl under it. Recalling that after their Royal Commission days Harrison had commended him for having 'the genius of compromise', he wondered if there was too little of that virtue in Harrison's strictures on realism in modern art.[61]

In art as in literature, the kind of realism Harrison most deplored was that which called attention to sexuality. He conceded that the community should set the standards for decency, and that they changed with time, but he thought total nudity in painting not yet tolerable. It was a judgement Havelock Ellis cited to illustrate the 'perverse relation to nature' that it was his mission to correct.[62] In 'The Cult of the Foul' in 1912 Harrison assigned to Rodin the role in art Zola had played for him in literature, accusing the sculptor of distorting reality and glorifying brutality. In reply, a champion of the new impressionism, D. S. McColl, challenged his belief that Rodin was still in the avant-garde, and named instead Maillot, Mestrovic, and Epstein, arguing that in any case it was not the reality depicted by the artist that mattered but his attitude towards it. Against this public correction Harrison could set the private endorsement of his views by Philip Burne-Jones, the painter's son, and Sir William Blake Richmond, whose portrait of Ethel had once graced the Grosvenor Gallery. It was not long before Burne-Jones and Richmond were doing battle against a more formidable critic than McColl, the young Roger Fry, for his denigration of Sir Lawrence Alma–Tadema. But not even 'Alma–Tad of the Royal Acad' was entirely acceptable to Harrison, who once complained that his 'archaeological eccentricities' jeopardized his high calling, which was not to show the 'tricks and tomfooleries' of the ancient world but its 'splendour' and 'beauty'.[63]

Harrison's second collection of essays offering a choice of books, *Studies in Early Victorian Literature*, appeared in 1895. It could be said to illustrate Comte's maxim 'Destroy Only What You Replace', for having decried the decay of fiction Harrison argued that there was much that was preferable to late Victorian writing in the best works of Carlyle, Macaulay, Disraeli, Thackeray, Dickens, Charlotte Brontë, Kingsley, Trollope, and George Eliot. Their reputations had been inflated in their own day, had since suffered a decline, and deserved rehabilitation. Keeping in sight his literary watershed of the mid-sixties, he preferred the early to the later works of Dickens, George Eliot, and Trollope, which meant throwing into the shade all of Dickens after *David Copperfield*, all of George Eliot after *Adam Bede*, and Trollope's *The Way We Live Now*. Yet despite their early dates, the religious and political themes of Disraeli's *Tancred* and Carlyle's *Sartor Resartus* made them less attractive to Harrison than other works by those writers. His insistence on idealism in matters of sex and marriage caused him to regret the paucity of good women in Thackeray's canon, to wonder how the coarse Trollope could have depicted so many 'pure … delicate, brave women' ('it does one good to be admitted to the sacred confessional of their hearts'), and to sniff out Kingsley's 'most unclerical interest in physical torture and physical voluptuousness'. There were other surprisingly negative judgements in a book designed to enhance literary reputations, and even Harrison's praise is sometimes curiously qualified. He valued Macaulay and Carlyle more as stylists than as pundits, and found George Eliot 'more the artist when ... least the thinker'. But there are apt formulas, too, usually comparisons, an approach Comte in his tendentious way had said sociology appropriated from biology. Charlotte Brontë's cloud descriptions make her a 'prose Shelley'; *Wuthering Heights* is a 'kind of prose Kubla Khan'; Trollope's conversations resemble Mr Woodhouse's gruel, being 'thin but not so very thin'; and George Eliot's novels are like some 'enfant de miracle', late arrivals that cost the mother much pain and provoked in her friends 'wondering trepidation'.[64]

Studies in Early Victorian Literature allowed Harrison to be the Rhadamanthus in literature that he never became in law. Calling the literary critic a 'judge in the supreme court of equity', he handed down decisions that inevitably provoked comment outside his courtroom. A. V. Dicey and Leslie Stephen delighted in the book, but for different reasons, Dicey because so many of Harrison's judgements coincided with his own, Stephen because they so differed. Sidney Colvin, about to publish his friend Robert Louis Stevenson's posthumous *Vailima Letters*, urged Harrison to write a 'Studies in Later Victorian Literature' in order to soften the picture of Stevenson, whom Harrison had called a man 'looking on at life in kid gloves from an opera box'—a re-working of his depiction of Arnold. Grant Duff noted that even if his own eyesight had not been seriously impaired, he doubted that he could have read and remembered as much as Harrison seemed to.[65]

Several reviewers compared Harrison's book to George Saintsbury's *Corrected Impressions*, which covered many of the same authors and also came out in 1895. The *Westminster Review* preferred its more relaxed approach to Harrison's 'terrible dogmatism', but the Liberal *Speaker* was put off by Saintsbury's Tory opinions and found his 'familiarity posing as charm' less congenial than Harrison's seriousness and care for style. It was a feather in Harrison's fairly new literary cap even to be compared with Saintsbury, who, after taking his degree at Merton in 1867 and failing to obtain an Oxford fellowship (Harrison supported his candidacy at Wadham but perhaps only because he was a King's College School 'Old Boy'), rapidly rose to prominence as a prolific and versatile critic and was appointed Regius Professor of Rhetoric and English Literature at Edinburgh University within the year his book and Harrison's appeared. Saintsbury did as much as anyone to promote modern French literature and to revive the reputations of certain minor writers. But neither of these lapses in his choice of books, nor his Tory and High Church views, prevented cordial relations from developing between him and Harrison when they became neighbours in the Royal Crescent in Bath.[66]

The publication of *Studies in Early Victorian Literature* marked a new stage in Harrison's vocation as a literary critic. For *The Choice of Books* he had collected disparate essays and reviews, but he wrote all of the 1895 volume, except part of the introduction, as a series for the New York *Forum* after being offered £ 30 an essay.[67] Such payment seemed generous for writing that required no scholarship beyond re-reading works with which he had long been familiar, and he had none of the reviewer's anxiety about offending his subjects, since they were all dead. But his agreement with the *Forum* entailed publication of the volume by Edward Arnold, which caused Macmillan some consternation. Harrison, by then experienced in handling publishers, replied with a diatribe on the American copyright system, 'a scandal and a nuisance', and spoke slightingly of his American 'child'. Nor did he mention it when negotiating with Macmillan about a sequel, *Tennyson, Ruskin, Mill, and Other Literary Estimates*, which in 1899 brought together his essays from the *Nineteenth Century*. Besides the writers named in the title there were estimates of Arnold, Symonds, Froude, and Freeman; and once again, none of his subjects was living, except Ruskin, who had long been out of touch with the world. Harrison assured Macmillan that the book would enjoy a good sale, since 'people who will not read me on any controversial matter seem to be willing to read what I say of books and writers.'[68] 'Controversial' clearly had a political and religious meaning, for his two previous books on literature had shown how contentious he could be in that sphere. And he had not laid down his literary lance. In the new collection his aim was to settle some old scores.

The book's *pièce de résistance*, Harrison told Macmillan, was the essay on Tennyson. The poet was ripe for re-evaluation, he thought, because of Hallam Tennyson's recent *Memoir* of his father and the inexpensive reprints of the poetry that had followed the expiration of copyrights.[69] Since Macmillan had long been Tennyson's publisher, it was bold of Harrison to call attention to his own less than laudatory estimate, which was that the Laureate's powers of expression had greatly exceeded his powers of thought. This was not original, but coming from Harrison it was inconsistent: having previously denied that poetry should be seen in a religious context, he now charged Tennyson with failing to provide religious direction. 'We have but faith;

we cannot know', he quotes from *In Memoriam*, and adds, 'Well, we need to know a little more, and Tennyson ... re-echoes most musically our sense of ignorance.' He finds the poet guilty of blending F. D. Maurice's 'illogical piety' and Jowett's 'philosophy of mysticism'—in short, of poetical Neo-Christianity.[70]

If Tennyson's reputation seemed inflated because he expressed ideas that had become religious commonplaces, Ruskin's seemed undervalued because he challenged conventional opinion. In this respect Harrison clearly identified himself with his old friend; Austin recalled that his father 'rarely got through a meal without referring to that important personage'.[71] One of three Ruskin pieces in *Tennyson, Ruskin, Mill* is a dialogue set on Blackdown between a professor who lives there and a young painter like Bernard home from his studio in Paris. The sunset glow reminds them of Turner's sunset painting, the *Fighting Téméraire*, and Ruskin's praise of its colours. But Ruskin's aesthetic values are passé, says the younger man, and so are his other teachings: 'art is its own religion.' This gives the Professor the opportunity to discourse on Ruskin's greatness as an influence on both art and social thought, placing him in the 'romantic, historical, catholic, and poetical revival' along with Scott, Carlyle, Coleridge, Freeman, Newman, and Tennyson. When he concedes that Ruskin, like all poets and reformers, had 'extravagances' that 'nobody but a critic remembers', and names Carlyle, Shelley, and Hugo among those who also 'flung out some wild stuff', the younger man with a smile suggests adding Comte to the list, a sally the professor ignores, maintaining that 'we all of us have the defects of our qualities.' Later, however, he agrees that in their 'moral and religious socialism' Ruskin and Comte were 'constantly saying the same thing'; and he argues that even though the Guild of St. George came to little, it was worth the writing of many beautiful books. Indeed, he predicts that those Ruskin did write would one day be read the way Plato's *Republic*, the book of Ezekiel, and Dante's *New Life* are read—solely for 'the melody of the language, the inspiring poetry, and their apocalyptic visions'. In 'Neo-Christianity' he had predicted a similar future for the Bible.[72]

The same strategy, of praising literary achievement at the expense of thought, served Harrison in assessing the canon of Matthew Arnold. His death in 1888 had removed from the Victorian scene the literary critic even Harrison acknowledged to be the greatest of the age. He reiterates this judgement in his essay, but with considerable attention to Arnold's lapses. Fresh from his own less than generous assessment of Tennyson, he finds Arnold too little influenced by the Laureate. Though he considers Arnold's poems a successful blending of classic and romantic impulses, he turns Arnold's touchstone method against them, calling attention to their unmusical lines. His harshest judgement is directed at Arnold's philosophy and theology. Writing to Morley, who was to read the essay before it went to the printer's, Harrison recalled that it was 'on your knees that I sat and you held the bottle in my final bloody round with that anything but light weight—the Pet of Culture.' The essay is a return match. Harrison declares that Arnold has taken the secret of Culture with him to the grave, and he imagines Arnold in the Elysian Fields greeting Comte 'in that inimitable genial way', saying, 'Ah, well! I see now that we are not so far apart, but I have not had patience to read your rather dry French you know.' This, of course, acknowledged that Arnold's notion of Culture was not entirely unintelligible, else how could Harrison have found parallels to it in Positivism? But he does not face that issue. With a self-assurance worthy of Arnold himself, he says, 'Let us think no more of his philosophy—the philosophy of an ardent reader of Plato, Spinoza, and Goethe; [nor] of his politics—the politics of an Oxford don who lived much at the Athenaeum Club; nor of his theology—the theology of an English clergyman who had resigned his orders on conscientious grounds.' Arnold's fame must rest on his poetry and literary criticism.[73]

Like Ruskin and Arnold, John Addington Symonds appears as something of a Positivist *manqué*. Originally the essay was a review of Horatio Brown's biography of Symonds, which included Symonds's letters and autobiographical fragment. Harrison's judgements differed from those of most contemporary critics. They ignored or disliked Symonds's posthumously published *Essays, Speculative and Suggestive*, but he admires its 'frank and courageous handling of the eternal problems of Man and the Universe, Humanity and its Destiny'. Symonds's evolutionary view of culture, and his belief that religion had to lead to social action, were congenial themes, and Symonds's favourite maxim, 'im Ganze, Guten, Schonen, resolut zu leben' was 'essentially Positivist'. Symonds, Harrison notes, had reflected upon Comte's conception of humanity as the supreme power, but, forced to live in Switzerland for his health, he was 'not likely to accept a practical religion of life for others', especially since Comte's teaching had 'been early presented to him in its pontifical, not its rational form'. This was an allusion to the references in Symonds's letters and autobiography to his discussions with Congreve, who on one occasion left him with the feeling that he had asked for bread but been given a stone. Symonds had never been a close friend of Harrison's but he had been a contemporary of Morley's at Oxford and a friend of Oscar Browning, Albert Rutson, F. W. H. Myers, and Edmund Gosse, all of whom could have

told Harrison something of the man's religious doubts and homo-
sexuality, which, as much as his health, accounted for his long exile
from England. To explain it, however, Harrison mentions only a
'delicacy of constitution', and begins his essay on an elegiac note by
describing Symonds's grave in Rome.[74]

The chapter on Mill also begins with a reference to the subject's
distant grave; the remoteness of Avignon seems to Harrison symbolic
of the distance between what Mill's reputation in his lifetime had been
and what it had become since his death in 1873. He does not entirely
regret the decline in influence of the man he had called 'teacher,
master, and friend' in his letter of condolence to Mill's stepdaughter.
To the extent that Mill's empiricism had yielded to the neo-Hegelianism
of the later decades of the century, Harrison wanted to encourage
appreciation of Mill. He had pressed Morley to produce the long-
awaited assessment, disclaiming his own ability to do so because he
and Mill had never been intimates. Harrison confessed that they had
been separated by 'education, habits, tastes, and temperament', and
that he had been unable to accept many of Mill's doctrines, especially
after Mill had 'attacked my own master with unsparing, and I hold,
unjust, criticism'. In his essay Harrison inevitably pits Comte's principles against Mill's, but also falls back upon 'the greatest of religious
teachers' to offset Mill's political individualism: 'We are all members
one of another.' The worst thing about Utilitarianism is the word itself,
associated as it is with utility, expediency, and self-interest, though
Mill meant by it essentially the 'highest welfare of mankind'. That
conception, Harrison observes, others more appropriately called 'The
Service of Man'. Indeed, he finds Mill's ethical theory substantially
coinciding with Comte's, but in the end less useful. In *The Subjection
of Women* Harrison admires much, but he likens its exposure of male
arrogance to eighteenth-century satires on women; both distort the
truth. Even worse in his judgement is that Mill calls for changes
implying a social revolution, not the gradual progress that Comte said
should spring from order. Tracing the most objectionable features of
Mill's treatise to Harriet Taylor, Harrison fails to remember that
Comte's critics were harshest when they dwelt on the parts of the
system inspired by his infatuation with Clotilde de Vaux. Yet turning
to Mill's posthumously published essays, he finds that Mill's religion
was not 'after Comte's model' but it 'virtually amounted to the same
result', a comment that suggests how much of Comte's ritualism Harrison
was willing to overlook in order to take so prestigious a thinker as Mill
into the periphery, at least, of the Positivist fold.[75]

If Harrison judged the thought of Victorian writers by reference to

Comte, he judged style by the standards of the Romantics. He finds Tennyson's influence unfortunate because it overshadowed that of Byron, Wordsworth, and Shelley, who 'shook men's minds' as Tennyson never did. In European influence Tennyson never matched Byron, in originality he fell below Wordsworth and Shelley, and in prophetic power he was inferior to all three. Only as a poet of nature could he rival the Romantics; Harrison liked to think that, because he knew Freshwater and Blackdown, he had a special appreciation of the nature imagery Tennyson drew from those places. Since he also made great claims for Tennyson's technical skill in poetry, he devoted considerable space to its analysis, and told Gosse he hoped that part of the essay would offset what he said about the poet's 'religious and epical weaknesses'.[76] His discussion of sound and metre in Tennyson, like that of the poet's religion, is not without contradictions. He writes of the verse of *In Memoriam* flowing 'as if from some native well-spring of poetic speech' and calls Tennyson an Andrea del Sarto whose work sometimes cloys because of its 'serene perfection'. Yet he thinks his rhymes are sometimes imperfect or require mispronunciation: only yokels say 'hundred' to match 'blunder'd'. Comte in his arbitrary way had depicted the language of poetry as 'nothing but the language of common men more perfectly expressed', and thought skill in prosody was 'easily acquired by a few days' practice'. Harrison, having written rhymed verse, knew better. He valued Tennyson's achievement, but using classical metre as a somewhat dubious guide, criticized his love of Alexandrines and heavy use of monosyllables.[77]

His discussion of the Laureate's technique attests to Harrison's close attention to verse. But when Gosse praised this part of the essay he declared that it had taken him 'quite out of my element'. This was false modesty. When poets sent him their work he often made suggestions about metre and sound patterns. Reviewing Morton Luce's verse in 1908 he compared it to *In Memoriam* because of its elegiac theme, 'unsurpassed melody', and 'purity of language'; and when Luce's Royal Literary Fund pension lapsed he did not hesitate to urge Hallam Tennyson to act on his behalf—if only because Luce had produced a useful Tennyson handbook.[78] Yet it was not Tennyson's verse but the Italian language he told young 'versifiers' to study when he contributed to a correspondence on prosody in the *Westminster Gazette* in 1910. After a reader warned that Harrison's advice might result in a dangerous 'cult of the vowel', he reiterated his old objections to poets like Browning, Meredith, and Kipling, who had a 'horrid crack in their singing voices'. With all his faults, Tennysons's notes were essentially true.[79]

Since Ruskin's prose style seemed worthy of more attention than he could give to it in the dialogue set at Blackdown, Harrison wrote a separate essay on the subject for the 1899 volume. His thesis is that good poetry and prose are informed by the same qualities of language, euphony above all. The Romantics had made the idea a commonplace and more recently it had received attention in Hallam Tennyson's *Memoir* of his father, where the Laureate calls De Quincey's prose 'fine as any verse' and ranks it and Ruskin's among the 'stateliest' written by Englishmen. Harrison no doubt took a special interest in the quotation for he had been present on the occasion, the poet's eighty-third birthday at Aldworth.[80] Pride in his own prose had once led Harrison to copy out a passage from his 1876 *Fortnightly* essay on Ruskin, linking the letters that made for alliteration and assonance,[81] an exercise that disproved his assertion in that very essay about having only the 'flat monotone of prose' to use against Ruskin. He made a similar 'vivisection' of Ruskin's prose in the 1899 volume, using a passage from *Modern Painters*. But Ruskin's syntax fares less well than his sound patterns. Judging *The Harbours of England* the 'high water mark of Ruskin's prose method'—an unconscious pun—he notes that Ruskin imagines not only the past and future joy and beauty and danger of the little fishing boats he spied on the beach one day but also the 'Almighty Hand' at each helm. A 'noble vision', Harrison grants, but one presented in '*impossible*' prose, a 255-word sentence with 26 intermediate marks of punctuation, a passage exemplifying the author's 'ungovernable flux of ideas', his 'wilful megalomania and plethoric habit'. The less mannered prose of *Unto This Last* would better serve to plead his case 'before the Supreme Court of the Republic of Letters'.[82]

Harrison's preference for Ruskin's plainer style was in accord with what he told the Bodley Literary Society at Oxford in 1898, when René was president. Beginning diffidently enough, he referred to his own youthful aspiration to nothing more elegant in prose than legal forms—hardly the truth—and went on to caution neophyte writers against accepting uncritically the recent pronouncements of well-known writers, especially those of the 'ingenious professor of literature' who had 'propounded everything that can usefully be said about his art in a style which illustrates things you should avoid'. This was Walter Pater, whose criteria of style were in fact close to Harrison's own—'simplicity, ease, charm, precision and serenity of tone', and an 'inimitable felicity which stamps the individual writer'.[83] The two men had become acquainted at Mrs Hertz's by the late 1870s, some years after Pater's admiring comment about Harrison's 1873 essay on Fitzjames Stephen—'so stirring and so really conciliatory'—had been passed on to Harrison by Morley. He explained that he was publishing Pater's work in the *Fortnightly* because it would 'quicken public interest in the higher sort of literature'. Morley seems to have recognized in the young Oxford tutor something akin to his own diluted form of Positivism. Harrison, however, was less willing than they to allow literature, whether of the Neo-Positivist sort or not, to undercut the role of religion, for with religion superseded by literature, what hope was there that Christianity might evolve into the Religion of Humanity? Thus, what Harrison especially liked in Pater's essay on Wordsworth, the poet to whom many now looked for the consolation traditionally offered by religion, was Pater's recognition that Wordsworth's poetry mingled 'genius and porridge'. Pater was less acceptable to Harrison as the prophet of a new dispensation than as a mere man of letters, and that is no doubt how he viewed Pater when they were fellow literary lions at Mrs Hertz's salon in the late 1870s.[84]

Harrison's criticism of Pater for not practising what he preached could easily have been turned against himself, for had not another Victorian man of letters warned Harrison against 'Carlylese'? The very lecture in which Harrison insisted on the merits of a plain style contains passages of verbal excess. Moreover, his pronouncements on fellow writers often disclosed a bias towards self-conscious prose. Austin recalled his father's 'infatuation' with the work of Maurice Hewlett, for example. His first novel, *The Forest Lovers*, seemed to Morley, who read it for Macmillan in 1898, to be as affected in style as Meredith's work. Harrison, unaware of this pre-publication judgement, exclaimed to Morley about the novel's 'rare, pure graceful English' and said it was like what 'G. Meredith would have written if he had not chosen to play the fool and concoct conundrums'. Hewlett, a nephew of Knowles, soon had cause to think of Harrison as a mentor, as Gissing had once done, for Harrison enjoyed introducing him to his literary friends as he had Gissing. This time, however, there was no resistance to the idea of a writer's prospering by meeting the public's taste. In a few years Hewlett was able to give up his civil service post, pay £25,000 for a house in St. John's Wood (close to where Harrison first attended Mr King's school), and note in his diary that critics were classing him among the 'elect' and Harrison even 'above them'. Despite Hewlett's prodding, however, Harrison declined to publish his praise until 1901, when he named *Richard Yea-and-Nay* his favourite work for 1900 and reviewed it as evidence that England at last had 'a fine writer of romance'. But by 1906 he was having second thoughts about the violence, 'spasmodic love', and mannered prose in Hewlett's fiction. And when Hewlett began expounding advanced views on women and marriage—his own marriage having fallen apart—Harrison had nothing further to say of him in print.[85]

Harrison's views on drama at the turn of the century were as conservative as his views on art and fiction, though he conceded more progress in the theatre than in literature. It was clear that both acting and stage sets had improved since his youth, yet the theatre was still not serving civilization as it had in past times. In 1893 he argued that the long runs fostered by the actor-manager system limited the growth of an educated audience and jeopardized the quality and variety of productions, and he called on public-spirited citizens to support a repertory company.[86] In 1904 he signed an appeal for a national company but was still pessimistic about the theatre's prospects: too many people objected to a curtain time that interfered with late dining, to the custom of wearing evening dress, to the prohibition of smoking during performances, and to the innovation of the darkened theatre intended to heighten the effect of the new electric stage lighting.[87] No such considerations kept Harrison away, especially when Ethel was in the country and he felt lonely. He might take Ivy Pretious or Lady Dorothy Nevill, or accompany one of his sons. Since drama, like fiction, appealed to him mainly as a diversion, he did not want it to be too serious. Revivals of Gilbert and Sullivan and of Shakespeare probably pleased him best. When Cookson was in poor spirits in the spring of 1898 after his recent retirement from the consular service, Harrison took him to Beerbohm Tree's *Julius Caesar*, just half a century after Cookson had played Cassius to Harrison's Brutus at King's College School.[88] Harrison had recently been a guest of Tree's at the production's opening in Tree's new theatre, Her Majesty's, built with profits from *Trilby*. The occasion was marked by a souvenir booklet (written with the help of the Positivist Charles H. Herford) and supper on stage after the performance. Such invitations delighted Harrison; seeing Tree backstage in his Caliban or Mephistopheles costume brought Harrison closer to the living theatre than he had been since his schooldays. And Tree's blend of stage realism and pageantry touched the same chord in Harrison as that which led him to prefer romance to fiction about ordinary life. At the same time, Tree's productions did not strain credulity as did, for example, James Barrie's *Peter Pan*, which Harrison never appreciated. To him Barrie, whom he met at Gosse's, seemed a 'little dry dog' and 'quite ignorant'. Ethel, more generous, wished the anti-suffragists could find a playwright as telling as the author of *What Every Woman Knows*—and she thought Tree a 'mountebank'. Others shared her opinion, but her husband remained enthusiastic, ranking his Hamlet above Macready's, Booth's, Sarah Bernhardt's, and a dozen others: 'I go for Tree!'[89]

He also went for Stephen Phillips, whose extravagantly romantic verse drama *Herod* was staged by Tree in 1900. Soon after he met the author at Gosse's, Harrison began receiving copies of Phillips's plays, sent in the hope that he would write something about their 'new departure' in drama. He did not feel confident enough to comply; and before seeing Phillips's *Ulysses*, he even speculated about the chances that the audience would laugh.[90] Phillips's costume dramas were more congenial to Harrison than most plays with modern settings and controversial themes, against which Phillips was revolting, but he took pains not to offend the authors of the new problem plays. To Henry Arthur Jones, for example, he seemed to imply that his own objections were to particulars: the finances of the heroine in *Mrs Dane's Defence* and the denouement of *Joseph*.[91] References to sex on the stage troubled him most, but not enough to overcome his old abhorrence of official censorship. He signed protests against the Lord Chamberlain's denial of a stage licence to Maurice Maeterlinck's *Monna Vanna* in 1902 and to Eden Phillpotts's *The Secret Woman* in 1912, but he warned Phillpotts that foreign 'men of genius'—probably an allusion to Maeterlinck and Ibsen—were corrupting English taste.[92]

A leading man of genius just then changing English taste to something not wholly acceptable to Harrison was Bernard Shaw. His condescending references to Positivism in several plays, and his paradoxical treatment of social evils and their remedy, would have irritated Harrison no end.[93] Ironically, Shaw set the opening scene of *Mrs Warren's Profession*, which he wrote in 1893 to lift the moral stigma from prostitution, incest, and the New Woman, in the garden of Blackdown Cottage. He had not been there himself (though he would occupy the house in 1900, after it became too expensive for the Harrisons), but he obtained details of the setting from a friend, perhaps Beatrice Webb, who had visited the Harrisons there. And to compound the irony, it was she who inspired Shaw's heroine by urging him to depict a 'real modern young lady of the governing classes'. Well might she and Shaw have chuckled at his situating his wealthy prostitute and her liberated daughter in the summer home of a leading anti-suffragist and moral teacher. But Harrison probably knew nothing of such matters and perhaps not even of the play itself. It was not granted a performing licence in England until after his death and first appeared in a collection in 1898 whose title alone would have been enough to put him off—'Plays Unpleasant'.[94]

THE CRITIC AS FRIEND

Writing to Gosse about his *Short History of Modern English Literature* in 1897, Harrison confessed that 'grumpy fogeydom' kept him from sharing Gosse's high estimate of authors 'whose first book I can remember'.[95] But fogeydom proved marketable; the new century brought many requests for Harrison's further thoughts on writers he had known. In the case of Trollope, he aimed to carry further the effort he had made in 1895 to reverse the decline in Trollope's reputation. In his introductions to inexpensive reprints of the Barsetshire novels in 1906 and to the Phineas Finn novels in 1911 he praised Trollope's accurate depiction of mid-Victorian life, citing his own familiarity with the comfortable homes they described, and with the law courts, politics, and clubs that figure in them. He denied that they contained 'positive portraits of well-known persons', though he thought some characters possessed traits of real people. That judgement has been debated, but his belief that readers would find pleasure in contemplating a disappearing era through Trollope's eyes was borne out by the popularity of the novels during the hardships of two world wars.[96]

Of all his literary friends except Morley, George Eliot left Harrison with the richest store of letters, and he apparently planned to make some use of them when he withheld the most interesting from the batch he lent Cross for the *Life*. While in America, he obtained a commission to refer to them in an essay for *Harper's*, 'Reminiscences of George Eliot', which appeared late in 1901. He was not coming before the public as her unqualified admirer. His 1895 essay had praised the early fiction as romances that lifted the genre to a higher plane but had judged *Romola* 'too erudite', *Middlemarch* 'tedious and disagreeable', and *Daniel Deronda* 'preposterous and wearisome'. It had also found her poetry deficient in inspiration and *Theophrastus Such* merely the embodiment of the 'sour affectations' of an exhausted woman (though it was he who had urged her to compose those 'pensées' in the first place). In his *Harper's* essay he partly redeems himself, providing an account of their friendship that exaggerates neither it nor her Positivism, and offering fresh evidence of her love of 'good-natured gossip', pride in her household management, and kindness to friends and servants— all traits he hoped would offset any view of her as a narrow intellectual.[97] In a discussion of Leslie Stephen's *George Eliot* a year later he dealt with her relations to the Positivists, correcting Stephen's inference that she had contributed to the funds of the Paris as well as those of both London Positivist centres, and challenging Stephen's belief, traced to a remark of Congreve's, that *The Spanish Gypsy* was 'a mass of Positivism'. Fedalma's ideal was not humanity at all, Harrison argues, but a 'mere tribal craze', and, as Stephen himself had seen, Zarca, her father, 'behaves like a lunatic'.[98] In other accounts of George Eliot in 1907 and 1911 Harrison concentrates not on her womanly traits or her Positivism but on the influence of her translations of Strauss and

Feuerbach on his own religious development and that of his generation. Ranking her as a moralist alongside Mill and Ruskin, but inferior in some ways to Lewes, he finds her mind greater than her art, her life 'more than her books'.[99] In the end it is not easy to pin down Harrison's judgement of his most famous friend. Perhaps this reflects his desire on the one hand not to underestimate her lest that friendship seem less important than he wished it to seem, and on the other hand not to give the highest accolades to a writer who studied Comte but declined to become a true Positivist or even conform to the code of personal morality Comte shared with the mid-Victorians.

A mingling of admiration and censure had also characterized Harrison's essay on Tennyson in *Tennyson, Ruskin, Mill* in 1889; the *Spectator* complained he was building the tomb and then slaying the prophet. Harrison repeated the formula in at least one lecture on Tennyson, at Bristol University in 1913, and in reviews of two books whose authors he knew and which he promoted in hyperbolic terms. Andrew Lang's study was all a Tennyson-lover could 'reasonably want to know about his favourite poet', and Sir Alfred Lyall's offered 'the final and authoritative judgment of the twentieth century'—this in 1903. When the centenary of Tennyson's birth rolled round in 1909 Harrison ranked him with the best poets of his age, but not much above them.[100] Meanwhile, he dined out on stories about his one-time neighbour at Blackdown although he had already got into trouble in 1890 by circulating Francis Palgrave's humorous suggestion that the Pilot in 'Crossing the Bar' was really the poet's dead son Lionel. Harrison repeated the notion to his old family friend Andrew Hichens, and was dismayed to learn later that Hichens had passed it on to Hallam Tennyson. Notoriously sensitive about his father's dignity, he chided Harrison, and he in turn chided Hichens (whose widow would marry the widowed Hallam Tennyson in 1918), but in the end Harrison was not remorseful. He told Hichens that the *contretemps* had enriched 'Tennysoniana'.[101]

Harrison's three chapters on Ruskin in the 1899 volume had been much appreciated at Brantwood, on Lake Coniston, where Ruskin's niece, Joan Severn, cared for the long-silent prophet. In October 1898 she had allowed Harrison to pay him a last visit.[102] After Ruskin's death in January 1900 Harrison inevitably contributed to the flood of reminiscences about him.[103] On that occasion he naturally muted his reservations about Ruskin's achievements, and he did so again when presiding over a public meeting the following year to announce the formation of a Ruskin Union.[104] That organization was soon lost in the welter of other Ruskin societies, but by then Harrison had found a good use for his knowledge of Ruskin: a volume on his life and work for Morley's new English Men of Letters series. He was in a good position to undertake the assignment. At Brantwood he had seen something of Ruskin's manuscripts, books, and art works and had talked with W. G. Collingwood, whose biography of Ruskin provided the basic facts. Sidney Lee, editor of the *Dictionary of National Biography*, sent him proofs of the Ruskin entry by E. T. Cook.[105] For Ruskin's economic and social thought he had studies by J. A. Hobson and Patrick Geddes. The work of the two leading French scholars, Robert de la Sizeranne and Jacques Bardoux, was familiar to him. When George Allen, Ruskin's publisher and watchdog of his reputation, objected to passages in Lady Galloway's translation of Sizeranne's *Ruskin et la religion de la beauté* in 1899, Harrison interceded for her by appealing to Mrs Severn, and eventually Allen published an edited version of the work.[106] Bardoux had been an acquaintance of René's at Oxford and had published his memories of university life before turning his Sorbonne thesis on Ruskin into a book.[107] Harrison, not content with all these printed sources, sought personal reminiscences from Lord Wemyss, who had been at Christ Church with Ruskin, and from Charles Eliot Norton.[108]

On the subject of Ruskin's marriage and annulment Harrison told Ethel he could 'only guess at the facts' and he naïvely thought he would be enlightened by Norton. But the man who had criticized Froude's attempt to tell part of the truth about Carlyle's marriage, and had helped Mrs Severn destroy some of Ruskin's papers after his death, was not prepared to divulge any private information. The formulation Harrison fell back on was that the marriage had 'brought no happiness ... and was but marriage in name, though no suggestion of rupture or dispute has ever been made known', and he added characteristically that it 'is not the duty of a biographer to pass judgment on this miserable episode in a chequered life'.[109] Norton was, however, willing to say he had tried to prevent Ruskin from letting his passion for the young Rose La Touche exceed 'the limits of a manly and restrained sentiment'. Harrison acknowledges the disastrous consequences of that passion, but softens his account of its manifestation in Ruskin's obsession with St. Ursula by comparing it to Dante's devotion to Beatrice. In the end he faults the world for having no room for Ruskin's 'saintly ecstasies'. Such views were perhaps themselves manifestations in the Positivist mind of Comte's obsession with Clotilde, and an impatience with the world's indifference to the religion it inspired.

Elsewhere in his *John Ruskin* Harrison brings Comte in more obviously. When Morley tried unsuccessfully to persuade him to write the Shakespeare volume in an earlier English Men of Letters series he had promised to let him 'smuggle the whole religion of Humanity in upon the English public'.[110] Now Harrison took at least modest advantage of his new opportunity. He compares Ruskin to Comte in their reading lists (Ruskin's only a 'meagre exchequer' next to Comte's), in their criticisms of orthodox political economy, and in their insistence that only religion could provide a basis for morality. In lauding Ruskin's personal philanthropy he advances Comte's notion of altruism as the religion of the modern man. And there is perhaps the thought of Comte's meticulously articulated synthesis behind his dismissal of Ruskin's Oxford Lectures as 'stray jottings for a vast unfinished encyclopedic scheme'. Not all Harrison's readers could judge the extent of his reliance on Positivism. One reviewer was relieved at finding that Harrison had not indulged his 'amiable weakness' for it; others thought it obtrusive. *Saint George*, the journal of true Ruskinians, predicted that the book would not entirely satisfy its readers but called it 'deeply sympathetic'. In 1909 a Paris Positivist, Louis Baraduc, translated it into French.[111]

Regarded as a Ruskin expert, Harrison wrote entries on his life for the *Encyclopaedia Britannica* in 1902 and Bryan's *Dictionary of Painters and Engravers* in 1906. He also reviewed volumes of the great Library Edition of Ruskin's works published between 1903 and 1912 and Ruskin's biography by one of the editors, E. T. Cook, in 1911.[112] He had lent Cook his letters for the Library Edition and approved his decisions to omit 'wild and foolish' stuff and to include passages revealing Ruskin's regard for Harrison and Harrison's courtesy towards Ruskin 'under considerable provocation'.[113] In his own account of Ruskin's parents Harrison had not overlooked the repressive side of their religion, but neither had he traced Ruskin's troubled mental history to it. Rather, he called Ruskin's morbid excitability a 'kind of literary *oestrus*', and the discrepancy between Ruskin's public aggressiveness and private gentleness a 'psychological puzzle'—descriptions but not explanations. Ruskin's outward submissiveness to his parents he deemed 'amongst the most beautiful things that dwell in my memory', a formula that perhaps reflected both his desire to please the Ruskinians and his unwillingness to deal frankly with yet another painful issue. Having long since made peace with his own parents, Harrison had no heart to scrutinize the far less successful *modus vivendi* attained by his old friend.

Sometimes Harrison responded more frankly to what he perceived as failures in the work of giants like Ruskin than to the inadequacies of lesser writers, especially if they happened to be women. Like Comte he believed that women could never hope to excel as writers of epic or drama, and that their proper *métier* was fiction. Comte had also predicted that they and working-class men would one day produce a higher type of verse than existed in the transition period, and Harrison professed to find intimations of that in the work of some women poets of his acquaintance, even while he dismissed George Eliot's verse as unsuccessful and told Gosse that Mrs Browning was 'only a beautiful soul, who once or twice wrote some lines'. As for homosexuals, they were outside the pale; Walt Whitman had 'poured his poetic gift on the ground like Onan—and instead of poetry he left some spermatozoa and a stink'. Apologizing to Gosse for his language, he quoted Dr Johnson: 'Who criticizes brutes should himself be brutal.'[114]

It followed, apparently, that in criticizing the literary efforts of the gentle sex one should himself be gentle. Harrison was indeed so when asked by Arabella Shore, a figure out of his past, to write a memoir of Louisa Shore for a volume of her poems in 1896, a year after her death at the age of seventy-one. Since his marriage he had seen little of the sisters, who had left Beckenham and become articulate defenders of women's rights. Encouraged by Mrs Hertz and kind words from Meredith and Browning, they had published several volumes of poetry by the time he agreed to honour Arabella's request. He managed to praise the 'ideality' and 'nobility of soul' of Louisa's poems and to observe that the lyric 'O perfect race that is to be! O perfect time!' was inspired by the same thought as George Eliot's poem on the Choir Invisible, which appears next to it in the Positivist hymnal.[115]

Early in his career as a literary critic Harrison used his influence with James Knowles to give a boost to the poetry and prose of a woman destined to have far more success than the Shore ladies. This was Margaret L. Woods, daughter of Dean Bradley of Westminster Abbey and wife of the President of Trinity College, Oxford. Writing for the *Nineteenth Century*'s 'Noticeable Books' section while on a winter holiday at Westgate-on-Sea in January 1889 'far from the madding crowd of yelping journalists', he commended the 'faultless art' and deep pathos of *A Village Tragedy*, her tale of a London girl's suffering when forced to live with boorish country folk and separated from the father of her illegitimate child. To the author he remarked that every page made the flesh creep, and he urged friends to read it. One who did, Cardinal Manning, found in it useful evidence of how 'Calvinism crushes religion out of the soul'. Having already let Harrison see her verses, Mrs Woods allowed him to discuss them in his notice and was encouraged by it to publish them—without, he noted happily, the 'niggling' kind of revision that so often spoiled the work of Tennyson. Her lyric to the unknown dead found its way into Ethel's hymnal but the author resisted Harrison's suggestion that she study Comte. Instead, she went on to a successful literary career without discernible ideology but an interest in psychological complexities Harrison could not share. Nor did he approve of her innovations in prosody. Nevertheless he greeted almost her every work with a letter of congratulation and was especially generous about her novel rehearsing Jonathan Swift's love for Esther Vanhomrigh, calling it superior to *Romola*. Comparison to George Eliot had become his favourite form of flattery; after seeing Mrs Woods's play *The Invader* performed at Oxford he reported that the dons all deemed her George Eliot's successor.[116]

Matilda Betham-Edwards, another minor novelist, was well established when she and Harrison met in 1890, but it was years before he gave her fiction his endorsement. They became acquainted as a result of his two reviews of her edition of Arthur Young's *Travels in France*. Thereafter they corresponded, but not until 1907 did Harrison comment on her fiction. In that year he picked up one of her novels by chance in Bernard's rooms in Paris when he went over to keep him company during an attack of scarlet fever; and later in the year he read more of her stories when Olive left him to his own devices in Montreux. Belatedly he pronounced himself an ardent admirer. He especially liked *The Lord of the Harvest*, based on her youth in East Anglia, a region he said must be more charming than his corner of Kent, where the harvesters were all 'dirty hoppers'. Miss Betham-Edwards had retired to Hastings after living many years in France, and had been honoured by that country for her literary services to its cultural life. It was therefore only natural that she should become acquainted with the most Francophile of the Positivists, Beesly, at nearby St. Leonard's-on-Sea. She thereafter kept Harrison informed about his declining health, for the two old friends had begun to differ so much on politics that they apparently saw each other infrequently after leaving London. Harrison also imagined that Beesly disapproved of his literary activity because most of it was no longer concerned with Positivism and some was even at odds with their creed's promise of social progress. For example, when Harrison consented to write an introduction to the World's Classics edition of *The Lord of the Harvest* in 1912, he asked a question symptomatic of his increasing nostalgia: was not life early in the nineteenth century generally happier and more truly religious and humane than it had since become? There were times, he confessed, when he thought so.[117]

Nostalgia and regard for an old acquaintance figured in Harrison's appreciation of *Trilby*, George Du Maurier's novel in 1894 of a self-sacrificing Paris model and the British art students who befriend her, the 'three Musketeers of the Brush'. Besides having belonged to a youthful trio who took their nicknames from Dumas's story, and having a 'little Billee' of his own in a Paris studio, Harrison had fond memories of Du Maurier's comic French songs on rather dull afternoons at the Priory. Du Maurier's *Punch* cartoons of the aesthetic Cimabue Browns and their friends probably inspired his own humorous types in his *Pall Mall Gazette* dialogue, 'The Aesthete', in 1882. *Trilby*, however, presented an entirely idealistic view of artists, and Harrison was only one of many who begged the author for a sequel.[118] But what Du Maurier chose to repeat in later works was the one theme in *Trilby* Harrison would not have relished—the supernaturalism adumbrated in Svengali.

One of Harrison's longest literary friendships was with Thomas Hardy. They seem to have met a few years after the opening of Newton Hall, by which time Hardy's intense interest in Comte had abated. In the seventies he had copied out passages from Comte's works—more, in one of his notebooks, than from the work of any other writer.[119] Though George Eliot was similarly immersed in Positivist literature, their relations to the movement differed: she wished it well, out of friendship with its leaders but never attended its meetings, while Hardy dropped into Newton Hall from time to time on his own initiative before he became acquainted with them. On Sunday, 14 July 1889, he heard Harrison deliver an address on the centenary of the fall of the Bastille, and Ethel's choir sang 'La Marseillaise' in French; he was impressed, perhaps even influenced in some way, for just then *The Dynasts* was taking shape in his mind.[120] Harrison seems not to have read Hardy's fiction until some years after they met. When Hardy sent him his *Wessex Tales* in 1888 Harrison judged their rural scenes 'beautiful work of a kind I like best', and he always preferred them to the later more philosophical novels, much as he preferred George Eliot's earlier, sunnier fiction.[121] In 1891 he warned Hardy that *Tess of the D'Urbervilles* would prove 'too much ... for our Pharisaical Philistines' and said it read 'like a Positivist allegory or sermon'. But he had completed only the first of three volumes, and seems to have been alluding only to its anti-Christian theme, for he wondered that the 'orthodox public' did not 'take alarm' and found it 'very remarkable' but 'most natural' that the three writers of the day he ranked highest—George Eliot, Margaret L. Woods, and Hardy—were all 'saturated with human and anti-theological morality'. He promised to look out for an opportunity to 'justify' the tale as 'an essentially pure, most

moral, and socially instructive work', but he warned that his endorsement would do 'harm—not good'.[122] He had been unsuccessful in
recruiting Hardy for Newton Hall pilgrimages, but managed to elicit a
word of praise for the *New Calendar of Great Men*. Privately, Hardy
observed that in it Comte had made a great mistake by omitting Christ
and thus alienating Christians who might otherwise have been led to
'modulate gently into the new religion'.[123] Hardy himself never really
'modulated' into the Religion of Humanity, and his other friends in the
Positivist circle, Judge Fossett Lock and Charles Kegan Paul, were
close to him because of their Dorset origins and not their ideology.

Yet critics as early as Mrs Sutherland Orr, in an essay commissioned
by Kegan Paul in 1879, have detected Positivism in Hardy's writing: his
interest in the evolution of religion, in the survival of fetishism in
modern life, and in the collective consciousness of humanity and
subjective immortality. Harrison did not mention specifically these or
other themes when writing to Hardy, and he was no more an unqualified
admirer of Hardy's work than he was of George Eliot's, similarly
labelled Positivist by some. Not only did he never find the chance to
praise *Tess* in print as he promised to do, but he said nothing of the
later novels, *The Mayor of Casterbridge* and *Jude the Obscure*. Their
treatment of sex and marriage probably made him feel like asking the
question he had told Ethel in 1913 he felt like asking Hall Caine about
The Woman Thou Gavest Me: 'What arrangement of the sexes he
proposes to substitute for marriage?'[124] After reading Hardy's early
novel *Far From the Madding Crowd* in 1901, he assured the author it
was 'more interesting' than anything by George Eliot, about whom, he
added, 'we have all said and thought too much'.[125] This brought an
invitation to Max Gate, but Harrison acted upon it only in September
1913, during a solitary sight-seeing tour of Dorset and the West. He
found the widower accompanied by Florence Dugdale, and was not
surprised the following year to learn of their marriage. Instead of
holding Hardy to the Positivist standard of eternal widowhood, Harrison
expressed satisfaction over his friend's 'restored home life'.[126]

Acknowledging the author's gift of volume two of *The Dynasts* in
1906, Harrison pointed to certain important differences between its
cosmic pessimism and his own philosophy. '*Everything is relative*', he
said, quoting Comte; 'this earth is no paradise. Pain, want, and suffering
are inscrutable facts ... Death, even slaughter, are ... proportionately
minor evils in the Universe.' In any case, man had to face all evil
squarely, 'as the Japs do without pondering on the *dark* side, nor
hysterically longing for any Heaven here or hereafter'. He returned to
the differences between them when sending him *The Positive Evolution*

of Religion in 1913. After remarking that Hardy was one of the few people 'with mind sufficiently open ... to accept it', Harrison added sadly that poets always 'come back to crave at the end, the unfathomable, the mystical, the indescribable'. Would he not say 'in plain words' what he believed 'about Creation—God, Immortality, Worship, and Duty'? But Hardy, no more than George Eliot, was willing to recount why he had come so close to Positivism and then withdrawn.[127]

Nor, apparently, did Gissing confront Harrison fully with their philosophic differences, though there were heated luncheon-table discussions during the years Gissing tutored at 38 Westbourne Terrace, and in 1883 a 'very *vive*' session over 'Mrs Grundy's Enemies', a novel he was reluctantly revising at Harrison's urging because the publisher, George Bentley, a King's College School contemporary of Harrison's, thought it 'unwholesome' and 'almost beyond enduring'. Eventually both he and the author abandoned it, but Gissing published increasingly angry novels of working-class life in the following years, as well as stories of the demoralizing effects of poverty on educated and ambitious members of the middle class. He depicted marriage as an anachronism and women as the chief cause of marital unhappiness. The compassion for the poor that had made *Workers in the Dawn* so appealing to Harrison yielded to scepticism about their regeneration and distrust of any system of thought aimed at their improvement. Art and literature emerged as Gissing's only refuge from the unhappiness of life—an attitude no Positivist could condone.[128]

There was little occasion for Harrison and Gissing to meet after Bernard and Austin entered St. Paul's School in 1884, but sometimes the boys would visit their former tutor in his flat off Marylebone Road or accompany him on London walks. For coaching Bernard for some ten hours in 1887 Gissing received £15, a sum he deemed generous since he was commanding only £50 for a three-volume novel that took months to write. But his trust in the Harrisons' good will was not strong enough to permit his introducing them to the uneducated woman he married in 1891, three years after the wretched death of his first wife. Nor did he accept their invitation to 'settle' in Westbourne Terrace when he came to town from Exeter, where he had taken his second wife to live.[129] Sending an 'account of myself' in 1895 he recalled his debt to them, and in reply Harrison congratulated him upon attaining 'the first line of the higher order of living romancers'. But perhaps thinking of George Eliot's fiction, which he had always maintained suffered because of the isolation her liaison with Lewes had forced upon her, he warned Gissing against neglecting society, arguing that the writer of fiction depended upon direct observation of it more than did the poet, whose inspiration came from within.[130] The statement suggests that Harrison was unaware of how far Gissing had come socially. For a number of years he had been enjoying the occasional company of authors like Meredith, Gosse, Grant Allen, and Edward Clodd, and when he and Harrison attended an Omar Khayyam Club dinner in 1896 Harrison came only as a guest and Gissing as a regular member.[131] At the *Cosmopolis* dinner a few months earlier Gissing had found Harrison's speech 'sadly dull',[132] and when he accepted the Harrisons' invitation to stay overnight at Blackdown Cottage in August he found their friends the Horace Daveys at nearby Fernhurst 'very dull' also. According to Austin, Gissing sat in the Daveys' garden looking 'mute and dejected' like a 'wet bird'.[133]

Neither Austin nor Bernard, who happened to be home at the time of Gissing's visit, seemed 'particularly intelligent' to him, making it all the harder for him to bear the thought of the privileges enjoyed by members of their class. Bernard had just sold a 'not very striking' canvas to the Daveys, and Austin had been studying languages in France and Germany to prepare for the Foreign Service examination. As he and Gissing walked over the wooded slopes of Blackdown to see Aldworth, Gissing learned that the Crackanthorpes had paid George Moore £200 to teach prose style to their eldest son, the ill-fated Hubert, once Gissing's pupil. And on the journey home in the train Gissing encountered another former pupil, Kitty Lushington, now a charming society hostess married to Leo Maxse, whose father, Admiral Maxse, had bought the *National Review* for him. What would Gissing not have given for such parental indulgence?[134]

A presentation copy of *The Private Papers of Henry Ryecroft* in the spring of 1903 prompted Gissing's last exchange of letters with the Harrisons. In his story of a writer's peaceful country retirement on a legacy—one of many such fantasies in Gissing's fiction—Ryecroft's bitter memory of his life as a tutor casts a faint shadow. Perhaps anticipating the effect of this theme on his own former employer, Gissing told Harrison he hoped not too much would be made of the book's autobiographical character.[135] The comment was partly justified, for Gissing had not attained the serenity of his hero. Having left his second wife and two children behind in England, he had settled in a tiny village in the foothills of the Pyrenees with a French common-law wife, and was in failing health. The thought that he might not live to complete what he called his first 'really honest piece of work', a novel about the sixth-century Gothic war in Italy, preyed on his mind. In reply to Austin's congratulations on *Ryecroft*'s success and objections to its harsh references to the poor, Gissing distinguished between the 'human sweepings' for whom he felt no kindness and the 'decent, hard driven' masses with whom he sympathized 'profoundly'.[136] This selective regard for Humanity helps explain Gissing's choice of a historical subject for his last work: it offered some relief from the contemplation of the social injustices, miseries, and intolerable mode of life of modern England's lower classes. It also enabled him to feel that he was at last fulfilling the promise of his youthful academic success in the classics. Sadly he told Harrison that his bad lungs were keeping him in France, and to Austin he wrote bravely of hoping to see Italy once more before he died.

It was not to be. On 28 December 1903 Gissing succumbed to a heart ailment and pneumonia at the age of forty-six. Reading of the death in a London paper, Harrison sent condolences to his French address and in reply received a mourning card in French signed 'Madame Gissing'. Puzzled, he inquired of H. G. Wells—known to have been at Gissing's bedside shortly before the end—whether she was the same ill-educated woman Gissing had told Ethel in 1891 he had taken for his second wife, and because of whom he could no longer mingle in polite society.[137] Wells must have explained something of the circumstances of Gissing's past few years, for Harrison promised to be 'discreet' about this 'mere trifle' in the 'irregular and melancholy life of our friend'. He also sought to dispel the 'myths' of Gissing's ' "grinding poverty", "solitude", "hunger", "neglect", etc.' by assuring Wells that real deprivation began only in Gissing's eighteenth year and virtually ended after he met the Harrisons.[138] Since Harrison seemed to think that he alone knew the details of Gissing's early years, Wells pointed out that he was aware of the Owens College incident and had 'an easy charity in my heart for that crime [illicit sex]'.[139] Wells had already warned Gosse, who was trying to obtain a Civil List pension for Gissing's two sons, that the youthful scandal should be kept from the press, though he thought the Prime Minister, Balfour, would have to be told. Wells also asked Harrison to help in the matter of the pensions, and, in reference to possible gossip about Gissing, declared that since journalists wrote such 'careless and slovenly nonsense' it seemed 'better for them to slop about with legends than with facts'.[140] Harrison offered to do what he could for the boys, and with Ethel suggested that Fettes College, Edinburgh, where her brother Crawford had taught until his death in 1900, was prepared to handle such cases.[141] This came to nothing, but the boys were granted an annual pension of £37 each. Balfour's good deed, Harrison remarked, would be remembered on judgement day, when he would need all he could find of 'extenuating circumstances'.[142]

The common purpose that seemed to prevail among Gissing's friends during the first weeks after his death faded quickly after Wells, at the request of Gissing's executors, wrote an eighteen-page biographical preface to *Veranilda*, the novel of sixth-century Rome that Gissing had left almost completed and they wished to publish. True to his distrust of journalists, Wells glossed over the Owens College episode and Gissing's marital history. He judged the main body of Gissing's work a misguided effort to emulate Balzac when he had neither the requisite talent nor human feelings, and he praised *Veranilda* at the expense of the earlier works.[143] Harrison read the preface in manuscript before seeing *Veranilda*, and somehow believing the novel was probably autobiographical, he approved in principle of Wells's biographical approach, but not of misleading the public as to the 'true acts'. When Gissing's brother Algernon, one of the excutors, asked Harrison's opinion of the preface, he had by then read proofs of the book and was convinced that Wells's account of Gissing's life was unnecessary and would have pained him. Since Algernon and the family agreed, Harrison accepted their invitation to write a new preface.[144] In less than three pages he covered Gissing's death, their early association, and his own unwillingness to assess the fiction before *Veranilda*, confessing that he had not read it all and had not felt in tune with all he had read. Yet like Wells, he called *Veranilda* by far Gissing's best work because it at last offered proper scope for his classical learning and familiarity with Italy.[145]

Perhaps Harrison thought his praise would carry more weight than Wells's because of his credentials as a historian (he had published his Rede Lecture at Cambridge on Byzantine history four years earlier) and as a student of Roman literature. By coincidence, his 'romantic monograph', *Theophano*, a story of the Byzantine world of the tenth century, was just then running in the *Fortnightly Review*. But the critic Clement Shorter did not even wait to read Wells's unused preface when it appeared as an article in the *Monthly Review* in August before complaining that it had been passed over for 'the very tame substitute of a historical essay by Mr Frederic Harrison'. Others objected to Harrison's high estimate of *Veranilda* and his slighting of Gissing's other works.[146] Annoyed at having his efforts unappreciated, and chagrined to find himself involved in a quarrel between the executors and Wells over the rejection of the preface, Harrison wrote to Wells, Shorter, and Algernon Gissing to justify himself.[147] In the *Positivist Review* he decried 'lightning critics' who disliked the formal dialogue by which Gissing had sought to create the ambience of the classical world in *Veranilda*, a common device Harrison himself had utilized in

Theophano. To the slaves of modernity, he protested, Hamlet's lines would become, 'Is life worth living, Horry? you bet your bottom dollar it isn't.'[148]

Regarding his vexed role in the publication of *Veranilda* as a thankless interruption of his own work—he had just undertaken a study of Chatham—Harrison published nothing further of importance about Gissing. In 1913 he left it to C. H. Herford, the Manchester Positivist, to overcome moralistic objections to a fund that Herford, Wells, and others sponsored for a memorial plaque by Eric Gill and a lecture series to honour Gissing at his old college, where Herford had become Professor of English Literature.[149] Austin published several influential essays about his former tutor overstating, as had his father, the family's 'unbroken' relations with Gissing, and, like his father, diagnosing Gissing's troubles as caused largely by a lack of practical good sense. Austin also recalled Gissing as more fond of poetizing and botanizing, and more subject to outbursts of hearty laughter, than was generally appreciated, and as an innovative 'feminist' author.[150] The writing of both Harrisons influenced Frank Swinnerton when, without unpublished material, he wrote the first book on Gissing, which appeared in 1912. Their view was consistent, too, with the portrait of Gissing by his school friend Morley Roberts in the *roman à clef*, *The Private Life of Henry Maitland*, published the same year. But these works differed in their treatment of Harrison: Swinnerton referred to him deferentially and echoed his judgement of *Veranilda*, while Roberts made his narrator refer to him as Maitland's wealthy and kind employer who only 'to some extent appreciated him', and Maitland speaks of him with 'implied scorn'. Maitland's attitude is said to be justified by the cold preface that 'Harold Edgworth' (Harrison) wrote for Maitland's posthumously published classical novel, *Basil*, which the narrator thinks belied Maitland's true talents. Most critics of *Veranilda* have agreed, but with two notable exceptions: Wells and—years later—Gissing's younger son Alfred.[151]

Though Harrison and Wells approved of Gissing's choice of late Rome for a subject in his last years, their views of the education that had made it possible were poles apart. To Wells, Gissing's 'pompous grammatical training' seemed largely responsible for his personal difficulties in life; it had destroyed his relish for modern urban existence by giving him standards which could never be met.[152] Wells's own early years had been even harsher than Gissing's in some ways, and he believed that he had risen above deprivation because his education had not been primarily classical but scientific. Born in 1866, he had spent his first years in a poor, shopkeeping family in Bromley, Kent, not far from Eden Park, Beckenham, where each summer the Harrisons were enjoying so different a life. Like Gissing, he became fiercely ambitious at school, but his promising academic career at Huxley's Normal School of Science was, like Gissing's at Owens College, blighted by his sexuality, though in Wells's case this meant only failed examinations. While teaching in 1888 he became ill and, again like Gissing, in his misery thought of appealing to Harrison, for his physician, Dr William Job Collins, had been on Harrison's election committee at London University two years earlier (and would mishandle his resignation from the LCC in 1893) and could, so young Wells thought, persuade Harrison—or Huxley or Shaw—to engage him as a 'literary fag'. When that notion came to nothing, Wells returned to teaching, soon supplemented by journalism, and without Gissing's distaste for both, prospered. He later recalled that his earliest readers included the kind of people who read the *Positivist Review*—that is, those who shared his faith in the application of science to modern life.[153] When *Mankind in the Making* appeared in 1903, the publisher, possibly at Wells's direction, sent Harrison a copy, thus initiating their correspondence shortly before Gissing's death. Harrison found the book unduly pessimistic, but passed it on to Swinny, who gave a good account of it in the *Positivist Review*. When Wells thanked Harrison in a letter sent to his old Westbourne Terrace address, Harrison wondered how so forward-looking a writer could use an outdated directory.[154] Wells got his revenge in his next book, *The Food of the Gods*, by lampooning Harrison as one who was likely to reject the miraculous comestible because it was out of harmony with Comte's teaching. Acknowledging a presentation copy, Harrison assured the author that even at seventy-three he was not too old to enjoy the 'brilliant fun of those who have the world before them'.[155] A similar mixture of irony and admiration informs his comment to Wells about *A Modern Utopia* in 1905: 'Dream, young man, dream boldly: and the dreams shall be prophecies.'[156] But Wells was not content only to dream. In a Sociological Society paper the next year titled 'The So-Called Science of Society', he denied that Comte and Spencer were 'to be exalted as the founders of a new and fruitful system of inquiry', urging instead that an understanding of society was best rendered in imaginative literature (such as he was producing). Swinny responded by accusing Wells of hiding his debt to Comte, a charge Wells admitted only years later, attributing his reluctance to acknowledge Comte's 'sort of priority' in 'sketching the modern outlook' to his dislike of Comte's 'deification'.[157]

THE BUSINESSMAN OF LETTERS

Just as Harrison had published *Order and Progress* to gain authority for his political convictions in the 1870s, so he expected *The Choice of Books* to establish his literary credentials in the next decade; and he was not disappointed. He never acted as a paid publisher's reader, as did Stephen, Morley, and Meredith, but for a few years beginning in 1889 George Bentley sent him advance copies of his firm's books, hoping, perhaps, for quotable comments. Harrison always found something positive to say without hiding his prejudices. He objected to the obtrusive scholarship in Mary Marks's *Masters of the World*, and to the Irish dialogue in her *Thorough*, but praised both novels; and he criticized legal inaccuracies in Mary Cholmondeley's *Diana Tempest* but welcomed its 'womanly' refinement 'in these days of Zola'.[158] Bentley no doubt agreed. There was nothing controversial to worry about in Ethel Harrison's three fictional sketches of country life near Blackdown published by Bentley in *Temple Bar* between 1895 and 1898; their slightly condescending, if largely sympathetic, point of view perfectly suited his middle-class readers.[159]

When urging Bentley to consider three stories, Harrison did not refer to Ethel's previous writing for the Positivists as evidence of her literary experience—her hymns, entries in *The New Calendar of Great Men*, and *Positivist Review* articles. Rather, he cited her two *Nineteenth Century* essays recently accepted by Knowles: a contribution to a symposium on 'The Revolt of the Daughters' inaugurated by her friend Blanche Crackanthorpe, and her denunciation of smoking. Her arguments against the New Woman were cast in dialogue form, which Harrison pointed out was 'the most difficult of all literary types'.[160] She had learned it from him, of course, and in content as well as form she followed his direction in these and later contributions to the *Nineteenth Century*, the *Fortnightly*, the *Cornhill*, and the *Nation*. His essays on political economy were matched by hers on mistresses and servants; his 'Emancipation of Women' by her anti-suffrage pieces; his defence of the Paris Commune by her memories of Communard refugees in London; his 'Choice of Books' by her 'Christmas Books for Children'; his 'Decadence of Romance' by her 'Thoughts about the Novel'; his translation of Comte by hers of an address on Ruskin in Venice by Sizeranne. Only in fiction did she depart significantly from his standards, praising Tolstoy and other writers he had slighted and calling the novel an instrument of social reform. Moreover, while he wrote of sociology only in the abstract, she published sketches of the life of

London's poor in the *Westminster Gazette*, in these columns and in her dialogues showing a talent for rendering modern speech and devising plots that might have led to a novel had she possessed the requisite ambition and health.[161]

While Ethel was emerging as a writer for periodicals, Harrison kept his own name before the reading public in part by reprinting old work. She had frankly told Marvin that she had been motivated to write for Knowles in the first place by thinking of the pin money she could earn.[162] Her husband, on the contrary, never acknowledged outside the family how heavily he had come to rely on his pen to supplement the income from his investments. His correspondence with Macmillan, however, leaves no doubt that it was Harrison and not the publisher who proposed the five volumes of his articles that Macmillan published between 1906 and 1908. Harrison expressed the most sanguine opinions about their sale, and called attention to favourable reviews while brushing aside unfavourable judgements as the work of suffragettes turned journalists or of otherwise biased or inexperienced types. When the firm suggested that he accept royalties instead of a single payment, his reply was that his advanced age made such an arrangement injudicious. In 1906 he received £300 for *Memories and Thoughts* (a book he told Ethel would probably strike reviewers as a 'ragbag of old newspaper clippings') and in 1907 and 1908 £250 for each of four volumes: *The Creed of a Layman*, *The Philosophy of Common Sense*, *National and Social Problems*, *Realities and Ideals*. The first two reprinted religious essays introduced by the story of his conversion to Positivism; entitled 'Apologia Pro Fide Mea', it was, he unabashedly told Macmillan, 'more manly, more rational, and much better English than that mawkish meandering' of Cardinal Newman's similarly titled work. The third brought together social and political pieces, and the fourth contained articles from the *Positivist Review*, which makes the book something of a retreat from his old objection to taking payment for Positivist teaching.[163]

Inspired by the fiftieth anniversary of the Alpine Club in 1907, Harrison also prepared a collection on mountaineering. When Macmillan's declined to add it to their list, he placed it with Smith Elder, an appropriate choice since three chapters had already appeared in the *Cornhill*, the firm's monthly. These included his reminiscences of its long-time editor Leslie Stephen, whose walking club Harrison had entertained in the country at least once, providing fare that Stephen called too rich for his 'Sunday Tramps'.[164] But if Harrison's more vigorous expeditions were behind him, his delight in country rambles was not, and *My Alpine Jubilee* has Olive's photograph of him posed on his lawn at Elm Hill dressed in plus-fours, spats, a brimmed hat, and leather gloves, and holding a cane jauntily behind his back. The book itself was something of a literary *tour de force*, containing every major kind of prose about mountaineering: climbing anecdotes; cautionary tales about foolish Alpinists; testimonies to great ones; descriptions of mountain scenery; arguments for climbing as a sport; and reflections on the Alps as a source of awe, delight, and psychic health. Positivism is only marginally present: 'to know, to feel, to understand the Alps is to know, to feel, to understand Humanity.'[165]

Having reprinted most of the writing in his files that seemed to be of general interest, at the end of 1908 Harrison began negotiating with Macmillan about an autobiography. He had had such a work in mind for decades, and there was a rich harvest of correspondence to prod his memory: letters between him and his parents from as far back as his Oxford days, from Morley and the Positivists (and some of his returned by the recipients), and from a large number of famous contemporaries. He had at hand the family history he had written at St. Adresse in 1882 when grieving over his father's death and meditating about the pattern of his own first fifty years. There was also now a privately printed bibliography of his published books and articles up to mid-1908, compiled by him at the request of a 'Frederic Harrison Club' in Rochester, New York. And he had masses of newspaper articles by and about himself from a cutting service going back to the eighties. Considering his many resources he confidently promised a book that would be 'at once history, criticism, and memoir ... artistic and studied'. If for nothing else, he hoped to be 'remembered at least as an artist in language'.[166]

By alluding to the interest of other publishers in his memoirs, Harrison obtained acceptable terms from Macmillan: £500 to be paid upon completion of the first of the two projected volumes and £1,000 upon publication of both, with the firm retaining the serial rights. Serial publication proved impossible, however, and the firm's request that he take £500 less caused him to threaten to bring the case before the Society of Authors. But when Sir Frederick Macmillan (as he had become in 1909) pointed out that his only hope of a profit was in selling the serial rights, and then mercilessly listed the periodicals that had declined to buy them, Harrison backed down. He even agreed to provide an index (for 'lightning reviewers'), and let further attempts at serialization proceed, thus delaying publication. Putting the best possible face on the matter, he declared that interest in the work could only grow with time and it would be a 'classic someday in this century'.[167]

Autobiographic Memoirs was bound in the maroon cloth used for the four volumes in 1907 and 1908 and appeared on Harrison's eightieth birthday in 1911. Despite the Positivist motto on the title page—'Vivre au grand jour', which the English Positivists always translated 'Live Openly'—and the dedication to Ethel on the fortieth anniversary of their marriage, there is little in the text about her or the rest of the family. And there is less on Positivism than might be expected. After the first section, written in 1882, it becomes clear that Harrison was overwhelmed by his material and pieced together a narrative out of letters, diaries, and excerpts from his published articles. The omissions and repetitions are glaring, and though the prose binding the disparate parts is usually graceful, it lacks the vigour and wit of his best writing. While engaged in his formidable task he read Gosse's *Father and Son* and declared to the author that he feared his own story in comparison was 'unworthy to be told or remembered'; what would Gosse advise? The reply was that Harrison should limit his portraits to persons 'vividly seen and felt' and produce a work 'like a splendid monument in sculpture, realistic and classical in one'.[168] Such advice was hardly helpful, and Gosse himself admitted the difficulties when in his review of the two volumes he confessed that doing justice to Harrison's life would require a reviewer who was 'equally at home in political economy, in history, in jurisprudence, in religion; he should have travelled widely and observed keenly; he should have been a moving figure in the sociology, the criticism, the poetry, the psychology, the revolutions of eighty years'. In deference to the achievement of that life, Gosse and many other reviewers concentrated on it and not the book, though its deficiencies did not escape notice. Even Harrison saw that he had not produced the 'artistic' narrative he had promised; though he still predicted that it would one day become a 'classic', he began speaking of it as a historical document.[169]

The literary inadequacies of the work stem in part from Harrison's failure to take Gosse's suggestion to present vivid portraits of contemporaries he had known. Too often a phrase or two had to suffice for persons no longer living, and friends and acquaintances still alive were for the most part passed over altogether. This meant that even his most intimate friendships were illuminated hardly at all. Moreover, his previously published accounts of his French and American visits, and of controversies of many kinds over two generations in England, robbed his later renderings of interest, for in recapitulating this mass of autobiographical material he brought few new perceptions or judgements to bear on the past. Still, enough of the old enthusiasms, prejudices, complaints, and aspirations shine through to lend individuality to the retelling, and recollections encompassing four reigns by so self-confident a writer could not help but command attention. Reviewers naturally did not agree in their estimates, but most judged *Autobiographic Memoirs*, despite its disappointments, a valuable record of a useful life. Harrison pronounced himself content, and as usual was absurdly optimistic about sales. When Macmillan reported that the 1,000 copies printed were not selling well, Harrison countered with Bernard's news of 'eulogistic' reviews in Paris, and he predicted good sales abroad. He even proposed that Macmillan pay him in advance for a one-volume edition to appear posthumously; but with little likelihood of profit from the existing volumes, the publisher showed no interest.[170]

The firm did not, however, close the door to other proposals. Early the next year it contracted for another volume of Harrison's essays for £250, half the sum he originally demanded. The collection would be called 'Among My Books' and incorporate the six-part series then appearing under that title in Austin's *English Review*. In an unsuccessful attempt to raise Macmillan's offering figure, Harrison had reported that Austin was investigating other publishers. But when Harrison accepted Macmillan's terms he implied that it was out of loyalty to the house that had published *The Choice of Books*, to which the new book would be a companion piece.[171] In fact, the essays were less suited to book publication than Harrison's earlier collections. Rambling discourses on his favourite authors and on the vagaries of an old book-lover, they contradicted the lesson of the title essay in *The Choice of Books*. In one passage Harrison imagines himself in his new library in Bath crying out as his hand falls upon a presentation copy of a book he had received long ago: 'Great Heavens! it is still uncut, or but cut in parts, though full of what I want to know. I seize my paper-knife. I will read it now!' Yet many of the old judgements are here: Dante as his Bible; Milton his 'lifeboat in the storms of modern literature'; Aeschylus the greatest of Greek tragedians because he teaches the sanctity of oaths, of family, and of marriage, and gives 'the sense of a just providence'. He joins in the current speculation about Homer's identity, suggesting that there might have been one author of the *Iliad*, another of the *Odyssey*; yet elsewhere he refers to Homer as one individual and calls him truly religious because he teaches man to be at peace in his homeland—earth.[172]

As such a comment suggests, Harrison's Positivism was veiled in much of the book. It appears most obviously in the reprinted 1886 account of Comte's Library, or book list, but the essays making up the rest of the volume—on historical and literary figures, the coronation of

George V, Westminster Abbey, and the London Library—could have been written by any man of letters of Harrison's generation. Still, he was not forsaking his Positivist colleagues. Even before the book was out he had in hand a collection of his Newton Hall lectures that, he explained to Macmillan, they had 'commandeered' and Heinemann would publish as *The Positive Evolution of Religion.*[173]

Harrison's thoughts turned to his books in 1912 because he was occupied at the time with organizing his library at number 10, Royal Crescent, Bath. There, as spring blossoms were appearing outside his study window, and he and Ethel and Olive were beginning to feel settled, he received a disconcerting letter from Austin. His editorship of the *English Review* for the past two years had not been an unmixed blessing to his father. Austin published pieces by him that might not have found a berth elsewhere, but he also published articles and fiction dealing more openly with sexuality than his father could condone— especially by the notorious Frank Harris. In 1911 Harris asserted in an essay for Austin that he had heard the story of Carlyle's marital difficulties and impotence from his own lips. Hardly had the resulting furore died down than the incorrigible Harris demanded greater freedom for all writers handling such sensitive subjects. When in consequence the *Spectator* banned references to the *English Review*, Austin initiated a protest signed by Thomas Hardy, George Moore, Anatole France, D. H. Lawrence, H. M. Hyndman, and others, including his father. But to the family Harrison complained about this endorsement of the 'scurvey and disgusting' Harris, and he feared that the *Spectator*'s clerical readers would soon be gloating, 'See what comes of a Positivist home.'[174] Austin would later characterize the teachings of that home by recalling his attempt to sound out his father on a question that had just begun to interest him: 'what is a fellow to do who cannot marry and falls in love?' 'Do!' Harrison cried, 'Do what every gentleman does in such circumstances. Do what your religion teaches you. Do what morality prescribes as right.' When Austin insisted on pursuing the matter, his father declined to discuss it, and Austin had to be content that at least his father had listened without being 'fussy' or insincere. It was in reaction to such old-fashioned views that Austin determined to publish advanced writers and even a story of his own treating illicit love sympathetically. His letter to his parents revealed that for some time he had been acting on his own principles and not his father's.[175]

Austin confided that he was soon to marry an American woman he had met nine years earlier in Berlin, where she had been a student of the violin. Her husband, preoccupied with his own musical career, had neglected her and their son and even encouraged her attachment to

Austin. Two daughters were born to them, but only recently had the husband consented to a divorce. Marriage would mean that Austin required an income larger than his editor's salary. Could the family help? In reply to a 'most human letter' from his father, Austin explained that he would probably not be named in the divorce proceedings, that his future wife would gain custody of all three children, and that he would legally adopt them. He was, therefore, not breaking up a family but rescuing one. Was that not better than turning against marriage altogether because a perfect one was impossible?[176]

With Olive at twenty-five so self-willed she seemed unlikely to find a husband, and Bernard, Godfrey, and René apparently without plans to marry, Harrison could not for long resist knowing that the family name would be carried into another generation. After the divorce, which, as Austin had predicted, went off without notice in the press, Harrison invited him to take whatever furniture and silver he wanted from his uncle Sidney's estate to set up house, and gave him £500. The money was borrowed, for Harrison's investments and savings were yielding only enough for normal expenditures, and he had recently sold his only profitable copyright, on *The Choice of Books*, to Macmillan for £50.[177] Yet the move to Bath promised a more economical style of life, and in his continuing good health he felt confident about finding lucrative literary themes. It would not be long, however, before concerns of family and finances were overwhelmed by events that provided awesome new texts for his still active pen.

9

The Positivist as Historian
1880–1914

One of the earliest papers in Harrison's hand is a parody of Barthold Niebuhr dated 1849. It shows that even as a schoolboy Harrison was impatient with endless historiographic analysis and revision. He makes Niebuhr argue that the Corn Law agitation was in fact an early episode in a civil war of which no account survives, the evidence for it being Lord Derby's admonition to his followers, 'Up guards and at them', and the report of Cobden (spelled 'Coabdeen' according to French authorities) attending a peace congress. And he makes Niebuhr take credit for demonstrating that the Battle of Waterloo was an invention of English vanity.[1] Though young Fred enjoyed such fun at the great historian's expense, Niebuhr's *History of Rome* may have inspired a bold image from the new railways in another school essay, on classical Greece. It compares Greek culture to steam, both products of 'the most divine acting on the most beautiful of the elements', and asserts that the influence of Greece would have 'evaporated' without the Roman Empire, through whose 'iron symmetry' it 'has never ceased to drive forward the wheel of civilization'.[2] The analogy is interesting as a foreshadowing of an idea Harrison would later find in Comte and other historians, the continuity and unity of history.

At Oxford Harrison learned more respect for the modern historians like Niebuhr but he would always speak disdainfully of undigested historical facts on narrow subjects offered as history. His own bent from childhood was for far-ranging study of the past. He must have been delighted to learn from Charles Eliot Norton just after Theodore Roosevelt became President of the United States that Roosevelt's first words upon meeting him were about Harrison: 'the only man who could talk intelligently with him of the invasion of the Mongols'.[3] But it was Western European history that really engaged Harrison's attention; he left the study of India and China, for example, to other Positivists. As a student, teacher, and practitioner of English law he kept his investigations into the origins of English jurisprudence running in tandem with his reading in English political and social history, seeking to work out the idea he had from Comte and Maine that social progress was the consequence of intellectual progress. Since he believed that law embodies a people's ideas of justice, he felt that his own work in raising the ethical sights of his fellow Englishmen made him a kind of Shelleyan 'unacknowledged legislator'. But he was no more willing to let it go at that than were his Positivist colleagues. All were keen political agitators. Harrison once declared that 'there has never been a great historian who has not made politics his first business.' He thought experience in politics fostered discrimination in the selection and use of historical documents, and political interests seemed to him even more important for the historian than a 'strongly literary mind'.[4]

It was the importance of history in Comte's system that first attracted Harrison to it at Oxford. Science, which shared honours with history in the system, never deeply interested Harrison, though his youthful analogy of steam and Greek influence shows how early he was ready to invoke scientific ideas in argument. Nor did the history of science engage him, as it did Bridges. The dominant scientific image of their day was, of course, that of the organism growing to maturity, and Harrison showed the popular predilection for using it as a model for history, insisting on the interrelatedness of social and political events and on the continuity of institutions and ideas through time. With such convictions, he felt able to do without a clear position on free will and law in history, which proved so troublesome in his controversy with Goldwin Smith in 1861. He was quite ready to set aside such philosophic considerations, just as he had given up preoccupation with biblical criticism after 'Neo-Christianity' in favour of more tractable issues and more pressing interests.

From his Working Men's College days onward, Harrison's lectures to many groups forced him to organize and synthesize his knowledge of the past. Arresting formulations were called for, not research. Inevitably he spoke as much about the importance, meaning, and sources of history as about particular events or personages. His message, as in his lectures and essays on reading, was that works of history should be chosen carefully and the judgement of the world trusted. And just as the right choice of literature meant a selection defined by Comte's categories, so in history there were definite periods to be covered: the Theocratic Age, Greek and Roman Civilizations, the Middle Ages, and the Modern Period, its decisive event the French Revolution. Getting sidetracked into minutiae was the great sin.[5] He noted impatiently that if Macaulay's *History of England* had ever been completed on the scale of its existing eight volumes it would occupy fifty, and take a hundred and fifty years in the writing; and he even thought J. R. Green's *Short History of England* could stand shortening.[6]

The epochs most studied by Harrison in his early years as a historian were the Middle Ages and the French Revolution. Having lectured on medieval history to the Christian Socialists and on St. Bernard to the secularists, for an address to the Oxford Summer School in 1891 he took the thirteenth century as his subject. Dante was the period's representative figure, one of the last writers who could still co-ordinate all of human knowledge, and also one who treated the Church with the 'audacious intellectual freedom' of an 'Oxford doctor'. The period itself he called the last one inspired by a single creed, which gave it a 'confidence such as we never again find'. The survey was so suggestive that years later Sir Frederick Pollock still thought it the best illustration of Harrison's talents in print, and Sir Almeric Fitzroy called it the 'most impressive vindication of the Catholic Church ... ever wrung from ... an antagonist'. Harrison himself valued it enough to plan a full-scale work on the Middle Ages. But like his projected studies on political economy and on the Paris Commune, it remained unwritten.[7] Apparently he never seriously considered writing an extensive treatment of the French Revolution: its significance interested him more than its events. His delight in visiting sites of the Revolution in Paris with Laffitte or Dr Robinet was little more than that of the informed tourist; and his discussions of existing studies show that he was more confident about what he disliked in them than about what he deemed needed. Many narratives were dull, he warned, the recollections of the period were scrappy, the great books by Michelet and Carlyle were highly readable but obscure in spots, and the works of Lamartine, Blanc, and Sybel were unreliable. Harrison's comments on the Revolution and its historians occasioned by the centenary in 1889 show that he had fully assimilated Comte's view of it as the watershed of modern history.[8] Today that centenary celebration can be seen to have coincided roughly with a watershed in the fortunes of the English Positivist movement. One reason that Harrison was able to pursue his major historical and literary studies after the mid-eighties is that Newton Hall had begun to lose its momentum and its claims upon his time.

According to Austin it was the 'cloistered life' at Sutton Place that induced Harrison to spend more time at his desk; the 'strangely mellow beauty' of the place 'lit him up and inspired him'.[9] One consequence was *Annals of An Old Manor House*, a book that evolved from his musings about the 'evanescence' of the generations that had occupied the Tudor mansion and from his investigations into its architectural details for his father's renovations. With the help of local genealogists and the owner, Francis Henry Salvin, Harrison produced an essay for the Surrey Archaeological Society in 1885 and, in 1893, an opulent quarto volume for Macmillan. It took considerable time to work out the publishing arrangements: shared profits, with the firm retaining the copyright and Sidney Harrison, who lived at Sutton Place with his mother, supplying photographs, architect's drawings, sketches he had commissioned of the building as it might have appeared in earlier days, and coloured plates and woodcuts of the glass and terra-cotta ornamentation.[10] In his eloquent preface Harrison recalled a well-known historian's suggestion: that by sinking a shaft in any spot of England's annals one could bring up much rich material not found in history books. Lytton Strachey would later use a similar image in his preface to *Eminent Victorians*, a work of calculated historical impiety. Harrison on the contrary treats with fascination and reverence every detail, and dredges up so many oddities and paradoxes, and offers so many suppositions, that at times his narrative almost grinds to a halt. But taken as a whole, especially with its illustrations, *Annals of An Old Manor House* is one of his most accomplished and fascinating works. It demonstrates that the narrow focus and extreme detail he usually dismissed as barren pedantry could be put to good effect if the historian had style and imagination.

Harrison speculates that the builder of Sutton Place, Sir Richard Weston, was influenced in his conception by the chateaux he had seen on the Loire when acting as emissary for Henry VIII to Francis I. Weston's son, Francis, probably named after the French King, was executed when the friends of Queen Anne Boleyn fell from grace with her, and he left a son who married a cousin of Queen Elizabeth's who like her husband had lost a father on the scaffold. The fourth in descent from the builder was another Sir Richard Weston. Forsaking political and military life for agricultural and industrial interests, he nicely anticipated what Comte said would happen generally in the Positivist era (though Harrison does not make the point). He introduced clover, grasses, and turnips into England as crops, and on the River Wey meandering through his land built one of the first English canals with locks. In the amalgamation of architectural styles in Sutton Place Harrison professed to find a defiance of precedent typical of the Tudors, and he dwelt in detail on the structural changes made by succeeding generations. Altogether the care he expended on the text, typography, paper, illustrations, and binding—on which the Weston crest is embossed in gold—did justice to the aristocratic and royal associations of the early owners—though perhaps at the expense of Harrison's reputation as a critic of the monarchy and landed interests.

As for the unbroken Roman Catholic associations of the house, he assured Macmillan that they would prove an asset: the book would be desired by 'every Catholic family of distinction'.

In his preface Harrison pictures himself as fulfilling a 'sort of social duty' for all those who had the good fortune to be able to rescue a relic found 'mouldering in the flotsam and jetsam of time'. Besides this graceful allusion to his family, he wrote specifically of paying a debt to his father, and to the house itself, a place 'endeared ... by the recollection of hours of perfect peace'. At the end of the century, after the deaths of Harrison's mother and his brother Lawrence, Sidney, the sole lessee, decided to give up Sutton Place. (Meanwhile, Harrison persuaded Macmillan to publish an abridged edition of *Annals of An Old Manor House.*) The property passed to Sir Alfred Harmsworth, later Lord Northcliffe, and, after the First World War, to the Duke of Sutherland, who opened it to the public in the 1950s with Harrison's history providing excerpts for the guidebook. From 1959 until his death in 1976, J. Paul Getty owned and occupied Sutton Place. Another American multi-millionaire, Stanley J. Seeger, Jr., acquired the property in 1980 and began its transformation into an ambitious arts centre, that has, in old Mr Harrison's words, 'astonished the natives'.

Having discovered historical riches through assiduous research, Harrison had the ingenious and, at the time, novel idea of intentionally preparing treasure troves for easy access by future historians. He proposed that underground repositories be constructed for experts to stock with representative samples of the art, artifacts, literature, and miscellaneous records of modern life. They would be opened and studied a century or more hence, each century preparing collections for the next century's analysis. It seemed the duty of every age to preserve evidence of its contributions to the 'progress of mankind'. In Positivist fashion Harrison did not mention the inclusion of any evidences of man's inhumanity to man, though his time-capsule would hold specimens of animals threatened with extinction because of man's 'vile thirst for sport'.[12]

'A Pompeii for the Thirtieth Century' appeared in the *Nineteenth Century* in September 1890. Three months later Harrison published another essay there which sought to put tangible history on an altruistic basis. He was promoting an idea perhaps picked up in Athens earlier that year when he spoke to the Greek Prime Minister, Charles Tricoupis, a man long familiar with London, and other Greek patriots who were still hoping for the restoration of the Elgin Marbles sold to the British Museum in 1816. Byron had vigorously protested at their loss, and Harrison now took up the cause, arguing that the sculpture was endangered by London's sooty air and that students must see it at the original site.[13] Unimpressed, Knowles assured the philhellene Gladstone that Harrison, as a mere 'rhetorician about Art—not a *lover* of it', could not see that 'Providence has made England the world's trustee for these most priceless gems.' Then in an article of his own he called Harrison's a joke designed to parody modern political demagoguery.[14] An angry Harrison demanded space to reply and was further incensed by Knowles's refusal to promise it. When Harrison complained that his long affiliation with the *Nineteenth Century* had earned him more consideration, the editor noted with heavy irony that·it had been his 'great pleasure' to have paid for twenty-nine of Harrison's articles, but he also owed something to 'Art' and 'common sense', both of which Harrison jeopardized by his 'neo-radical sentimentalism'.[15] Feeling betrayed, and knowing nothing of Knowles's notes to Huxley as well as to Gladstone, Harrison carried the dispute to the pages of the *Fortnightly*, speculating that Knowles's attack might really have been the work of some opponent of Home Rule, most likely Huxley. And in the *Pall Mall Gazette* he complained further that the *Nineteenth Century* had been given over to 'pigs, monkeys, protozoa, and their bearing on the Gospels'—an allusion to its recent debates between Gladstone and Huxley about the Gadarene Swine.[16] Harrison's anger was widely noted in the press, and Huxley protested to him about being accused of fighting from under cover.[17] But Harrison could take heart from the responses of two younger men: George Nathaniel Curzon, who partly supported his views in the *Fortnightly*, and Sidney Cockerell, who asked him to 'prick the nation's conscience' about the stained glass from Sainte Chapelle held by the South Kensington Museum. Tricoupis and John Gennadius, the Greek Minister in London, were grateful to Harrison, and he had a new topic for public lectures.[18]

'Where would it stop?' was asked by many who objected to the return of the Elgin Marbles to Greece. Harrison posed the same question in 1886 about the use of old forms of names by historians seeking authenticity. He derided as 'palaeographic purism' and 'a pedantic nuisance' Grote's use of 'Kleopatra', Carlyle's of 'Friedrich', and Freeman's of 'Aelfred', and attributed the practice to the bias of those historians in favour of the peoples associated with the names. He noted that Freeman, a major offender and an ardent admirer of the Anglo-Saxons, was not troubled by 'William' for the Conqueror, though old French forms were available, but as a passionate philhellene he insisted on 'Sokrates'. With complete consistency, Harrison indulged his own love of neologisms and scorned the listing of Voltaire as 'Arouet' and of George Eliot as 'Marian Evans' as the result of a 'baptismal-certificate theory', coined 'anarchaism' for the use of older terminology, and denounced inordinate interest in England's Teutonic origins as 'Neo-Saxonism'.[19] In reply Freeman pointed out that he always used conventional spelling in his 'less scientific' writing and deplored the levity of Harrison's 'reckless raid into regions where he does not know the road'.[20] Since Harrison's views were by no means unique, he could cite support for them from 'men of widest learning', and he asked if one could not be 'merry as well as wise' in this 'age of Teutonic Grundlichkeit'.[21]

In 1893, about a year after Freeman was succeeded as Regius Professor of Modern History at Oxford by his old rival James Anthony Froude, Harrison sought to be both merry and wise by comparing them in a dialogue set in an Oxford college garden. The Reverend Aethelbald Wessex, a history tutor who has been labouring on the Old English period for a decade without reaching the time of 'Eadweard', defends the previous Regius Professor from the criticism of a brash student who is thought to be 'shaky in his pre-Ecgberght chronicles' but has learned to value the study of the French Revolution, its antecedents and aftermath, from Oscar Browning at Eton and the writing of John Morley. Wessex calls Browning a 'radical' and Morley a 'terrorist'—a caricature of Freeman's worship of things Anglo-Saxon and political conservatism—and advises the student to choose his period of study (he hopes it will be Old English), stake out his claim like a California miner, then wash, sift, and crush his lumps of evidence, but not cry 'Gold!' without testing. Unpersuaded, the younger man declares his allegiance to the blood-stirring narratives of Michelet, Macaulay, Carlyle, and Froude, the new Regius Professor. A visitor, Jack Middleman, QC, MP, and examiner in the Law School, arrives to mediate by repudiating both extremes in history, 'microscopic analysis' and 'pictorial bravura'. He calls Freeman a 'consummate historical scholar' and Froude an 'elegant' writer but thinks neither fulfils every requirement for great history: 'indefatigable research into all the accessible materials', a 'sound philosophy of human evolution', a 'genius for seizing on the typical movements and the great men', and literary artistry in describing them.[22]

Within a year of this dialogue the real Jack Middleman was aspiring to the Regius Professorship of Modern History at Oxford. Learning of Froude's serious illness in the autumn of 1894, Harrison asked Morley to recommend him for the chair if, as seemed likely, it became vacant. He acknowledged that he had no 'strictly original research' behind him, but deemed that less important than his ability to arouse interest in the study of the past, demonstrated, he thought, in his lectures and publications over thirty years. And knowing that Morley, then Chief Secretary for Ireland, had the ear of Rosebery, the Prime Minister, he reminded him of his support of the Liberals. Morley sought to check his hopes by noting that their friend had much to consider besides the 'd—d nonsense about merit' but promised to press Harrison's claims during a forthcoming visit to Dalmeny.[23] Instead, he sent Harrison's letter to Rosebery with the comment that it was unfortunate that there were 'drawbacks' to him as to another candidate, Lord Acton. Rosebery in turn thought it 'strange that our party choice would lie between a Papist and a Comtist'.[24] Harrison meanwhile conceded to Morley that there were 'strong bars' to his candidacy, but did not think they included his Positivism, since Oxford professors were all 'heretics'. Later he listed the 'enemy' as Churchmen, Unionists, and jingo professors, and said 'nothing that you can do can either conciliate them or add to their hostility.'[25]

When in the end Frederick York Powell was appointed to the chair, Harrison concluded that Rosebery had been unable to 'resist the pressure of the old Oxford gang'.[26] But its choice was in some ways inexplicable. Powell was even less an establishment figure than Harrison; atheist, socialist, friend of the working man, he even looked like a sailor on shore leave. He took his degree at Oxford only after Harrison had begun to examine there, and then had read history at his father's house near the elder Harrisons in Lancaster Gate. He obtained his lectureship at Oxford through Harrison's old school contemporary, Henry Liddon. His scholarship showed no evidence of breadth and was chiefly in the peripheral field of Icelandic literature. As if all this were not enough to rankle in Harrison's mind, as Regius Professor Powell ridiculed Comte and advocated a 'scientific' history unconcerned with ethics. Harrison's bitterness must have been understood by Morley, for years later he told him his appointment would have made a great difference to a generation of historians, and called Powell's a 'complete failure', the 'worst mistake of that unhappy ministry'.[27]

Denied the chair of history he coveted, Harrison consoled himself shortly after the disappointment by judging the merits and faults of the two predecessors of Powell with greater seriousness than he had in his Oxford dialogue. In essays on Freeman and Froude for Knowles he faced the problem of how to provide engaging narrative without sacrificing the solid matrix of fact history required. Freeman, good at fact-finding and with a 'truly historical mind', had nevertheless done scant justice to the crucial idea of the unity of history, though he espoused the conception. Froude's work suffered from his Protestant bias and from inaccuracies. (Using some of Froude's sources in his own research on Sutton Place had convinced Harrison that both these common charges were true.) But Freeman's failure to undertake research in manuscripts did not in Harrison's opinion disqualify him as a 'scientific' historian because it was not the historian's business to undertake such work: that was for the palaeographer or editor. As for Froude's criticism of Comte, it stemmed from his mistaken belief that Comte wrote about a science of history, whereas his goal was a science of society. Differentiating between the two, Harrison rejected the possibility of the former and assigned the latter to the sociologist. The historian's task was to 'narrate events and to describe the acts of those who cause or suffer them'. Out of such narratives the sociologist could construct his theories. What the historian needed was the lawyer's ability to sift the evidence and the statesman's understanding of men and events. In a review of Herbert Paul's biography of Froude in 1906 Harrison put it another way: the historian (like the literary critic) needed the qualities of a judge; he held a 'kind of mimic rehearsal of the Last Judgment, only he had no Recording Angel to tell him the facts truly'.[28]

Harrison's view of the historian's vocation brought an impassioned rejoinder from Horace Round, a member of the Oxford History School whom William Stubbs had introduced to more exacting methods of scholarship than Freeman's or Froude's. Round, a critic of both, suggested that while a cynic might attribute Harrison's scorn of original research to the 'galling contrast between the towering splendours of the Public Record Office and the Positivist meeting-house in Fetter Lane', his 'caricature' of the professional historian was actually a misguided product of his 'very pretty satiric gift'. Not less but more research was wanted, Round insisted, but he knew the demands on the historian to be daunting. He needed considerable wealth, indefatigable energy devoted to narrowly restricted topics, a willingness to have his work ignored or criticized by men who would then use it, and a readiness to create enemies by correcting others' errors.[29] To Round these circumstances explained why historical knowledge advanced so slowly. They may also suggest why Harrison's contribution to that progress was relatively slight.

Harrison's aversion to exhaustive research (despite his occasional practice and admiration of it) had not only personal but ideological grounds. It was Comte's own aversion to serious research in the natural and the social sciences that fixed the prejudices of his followers in this respect; and so it was with history too. Originality and revisionism could only threaten established theory; what was needed was illustration, not testing. For Comte history was the use of accepted authorities to provide examples and generalizations consistent with the patterns of theory: the law of the three stages, progress from order, and their ramifications. Historians were essentially philosophers of the past, and the 'true historical spirit' was 'naturally universal'.[30] Deep new research was likely to be unhelpful: it would be either irrelevant to grand truths or subversive of them.

Moreover, Harrison associated some of the more disagreeable influences in historical writing with Germany, a nation he always distrusted. The German scientific school had emphasized sources and evidence and was now identified with sterile philology and epigraphy; German romanticism and metaphysics in history had left a legacy of obscurantism that he no more than Comte was prepared to set right in the name of Positivism; and the dominant Prussian School was aggressively nationalist and so anathema to him. He was as suspicious of the folk-lore and folk-poetry that German-inspired historians considered a valid component of history as he was of myth and poetry as the basis of modern religion. Most important, perhaps, German-inspired research on English history that strengthened claims for its Teutonic origins and institutions seemed to enhance modern Germany's kinship with England, and this Harrison was increasingly unwilling to credit as their political rivalry grew. If his 'Little Englandism' lay behind some of his reservations about Froude, so his Germanophobia contributed to his distrust of Freeman.

HISTORICAL CELEBRATIONS

Since the only English historian given unqualified praise by Jack Middleman in the Oxford dialogue is Gibbon, it is not surprising that at his centenary in 1894 Harrison felt 'keenly impelled' to see it properly celebrated. For support he turned to the Royal Historical Society. Some historians, including Bryce, thought its standards of membership slack, but its President, Grant Duff, shared Harrison's desire to popularize history and was instantly enthusiastic.[31] To state the case for the celebration, Harrison returned to the *Nineteenth Century* in July, after four years of sulking in his tent. He said nothing of the *Decline and Fall* being in the Positivist Library, or Gibbon in the Positivist Calendar, but he echoed the account of his merits and limitations in Cotter Morison's English Men of Letters *Gibbon*: the historian had done enormous original research, written on the largest scale, and was an unequalled stylist; but he was not philosophic, the philosophy of history being 'in mere germ' in his time. (York Powell, in later calling Gibbon deficient 'precisely in the quality Mr Harrison is always calling for, the consciousness of human evolution', was forgetting that the Positivists were historical relativists.) Harrison argued that Gibbon especially deserved honouring because his 'unbroken' and growing reputation was not yet recognized by any memorial in England, his house in Bentinck Street was not marked, there was no portrait of him in any public collection, and, worst of all, the manuscripts he left were unavailable to scholars. John Holroyd, the first Earl of Sheffield, his patron and literary executor, had pieced together Gibbon's memoirs from six manuscript versions and fragments, publishing them in the *Miscellaneous Works* in 1796. Eighteen years later he brought out an enlarged edition and then forbade in his will any further publication of the manuscripts. Sir Horace (now Lord) Davey had assured Harrison that the restriction was no longer binding, and it was Harrison's hope that the British Museum would acquire them and permit their publication.[32]

The Royal Historical Society under Grant Duff in November opened an exhibition at the British Museum of manuscripts, books, portraits, and memorabilia of Gibbon, mostly lent by the third Earl of Sheffield. In making the arrangements Harrison had visited his 'neighbour' at Sheffield Park, Sussex, and found him cordial and even willing to act as chairman of the Centenary Committee, though he later proved exasperatingly dilatory. As the exhibition was about to open he told Harrison by telegram of his discovery in his housekeeper's room of a long-lost portrait of Gibbon (and eventually he would turn up more manuscripts and a missing diary).[33] Harrison addressed the Gibbon Centenary meeting of the Royal Historical Society three days later, repeating his belief that the manuscripts on exhibit should remain in the British Museum. A cursory examination had disclosed to him something he thought not widely known but which would excite scholars—that the first Earl had considerably altered the wording of the manuscripts of Gibbon's memoirs, and the handwriting on them showed that he had been aided in his work by his eldest daughter Maria Josepha Holroyd. (Her daughter, the now elderly second Lady Stanley of Alderley, mother of Lyulph Stanley, Rosalind Howard, Kate Amberley, and Blanche, Countess of Airlie, was in the audience and privately remonstrated with Harrison for praising her mother, under whom she had greatly suffered.) Harrison also hinted that despite Gibbon's avowed dislike of Magdalen College, Oxford, where he had spent a few miserable terms, his coffin should be moved there from the Sheffield family's private mausoleum, and he urged that Gibbon's house be marked.[34]

Organizing the Centenary gratified Harrison in much the same way as did his aldermanic functions, so recently ended, and Lady Gregory observed that his appearance seemed recently to have improved; the grey in his hair and beard she thought becoming, though she found him an unsympathetic speaker.[35] Behind the scenes, there was still more to do. Six days after his address, Patrick Dove, one of the Committee's secretaries, shot himself dead in his Lincoln's Inn rooms, leaving tangled records revealing £74 of the Committee's funds missing, as well as £1,000 he handled for the Selden Society. Harrison was non-plussed by the copy of *The Logic of Christian Faith* written by Dove's father and sent to him in a parcel of other books and papers prepared for him by Dove on the fatal day; but he sent it on to the British Museum where it joined other works by Dove senior—including a treatise on the revolver. The scandal caused the erratic Lord Sheffield to retrieve his Gibbon materials summarily, thus ending the exhibition.[36] Magdalen ignored the hint about honouring its recalcitrant ex-student's remains. But after Sir Frederick Leighton's intervention, a medallion was duly mounted on the Bentinck Street house; and after months of negotiations engineered by Harrison, Lord Sheffield sold most of the exhibition items to the British Museum. Its authorities and John Murray, who wished to publish an amended version of the memoirs and some of the other manuscripts, had found his price too high. Needing money for cricket, yachting, and travel, the 'sporting Earl', as Harrison now dubbed him, held out until Harrison devised a scheme whereby Sheffield received his price, shared by both interested parties.[37] Still not finished, Harrison monitored Murray's editing of the memoirs. His comments would have suprised those who thought him indifferent to scholarly detail, for he warned and worried about inaccuracies in the transcriptions, urged the hiring of a palaeographer, and regretted that all the versions would not be printed verbatim. For the final product, *The Autobiographies of Edward Gibbon*, Harrison wrote an introduction, and, as a guest on the Earl's yacht, persuaded him to put his name to it in order to improve sales.[38] Reading the proofs enabled him to review the book in the New York *Forum* at the time of publication; and later Murray's two new volumes of Gibbon letters gave him yet another occasion for praising 'our greatest historian'.[39]

As a consequence of enlisting the Royal Historical Society for the Gibbon celebration Harrison was made a Vice-President and life member. In 1897 he proposed for it an even more enterprising undertaking. While sitting out the Queen's Diamond Jubilee at Rutland Lodge, Petersham, and at Sutton Place that summer, he decided to turn his forthcoming Presidential Address to the Birmingham and Midlands Institute into a plea for a 'real jubilee' to mark the one-thousandth anniversary of Alfred the Great's death. In the 1860s he had lectured on Alfred, 'the most romantic of any hero in history' (though at the same time he warned Louisa Shore against making Alfred a lover in her drama); and in his biographical sketch for the *New Calendar of Great Men* he had endorsed Comte's view of him as the purest of the chiefs who had effected the incorporation of the Polytheists into the European system. It was on a Newton Hall pilgrimage to Winchester, Alfred's capital, that he had conceived of the millenary celebration, and his Birmingham address, delivered on his sixty-sixth birthday, abounded in ideas for it. Why not a mausoleum in Alfred's honour to hold relics of his time and receive the bones of future British heroes? Why not a new edition of his writings? A new biography? He even thought the Holy See might consider claims for Alfred's sainthood. By contrast, the Mayor of Winchester, appropriately named Alfred Bowker, soon proposed a more provincial tribute, some kind of public building in his city. To outwit the 'self chosen knot of busy bodies and functionaries' in Winchester who wanted to keep the occasion local required Harrison's protest in *The Times* and untold letters to eminent men of his acquaintance.[40] Eventually, the Mayor agreed to invite the Royal Historical Society to conduct a commemorative meeting in Winchester in 1901 in co-operation with municipal and Church officials. Passing on news of this triumph to Grant Duff, Harrison urged that other learned societies and the universities be invited to participate, though he knew it would not be easy to stage-manage such a gathering.[41]

At a Mansion House meeting the next spring, Harrison got Mandell Creighton, now Bishop of London, to move the proposal for a national celebration of King Alfred to be held in Winchester, which Bryce seconded, and the Archbishop of Canterbury and Frederick Pollock carried another motion for a permanent memorial there.[42] A statue of Alfred by Hamo Thornycroft was decided upon and the sculptor was soon explaining to Harrison that the fifteen-foot figure on a thirty-foot pedestal proposed by his committee was larger than appropriate and would cost at least £5,000, far more than it could raise.[43] A compromise was reached, and when Harrison left for America early in 1901 Thorny-croft was at work on a smaller but no less heroic figure in a belted tunic and flowing cape, one hand holding a sword before him like a cross, the other resting on his shield. This image of Alfred, the strong but pious peacemaker, seemed a happy one; in proposing the com-memoration Harrison had even said that the Wessex king served to unite Little Englanders and imperialists and both with Americans. Untroubled by the absence of historical evidence for the statue's physical features—the beard, for example—or by the question of whether Alfred really died in 901, he dismissed 'dryasdust' scholars who were 'raising clouds'; nothing they produced had tarnished the image of the historical Alfred: giver of laws; builder of churches, abbeys, and schools; teacher, historian, man of letters; restorer of London; and saviour of his people by wisdom not conquest. Others might question the facts in Asser's *Life*, but he assured the audience at the opening of a King Alfred exhibition at the British Museum that the manuscript of the work it held was in the main true. And just to touch Alfred's Jewel, bearing the legend 'Alfred made me', gave him a thrill like that felt by men of old kissing a fragment of the true Cross.[44]

Myth and history were at times at odds at Winchester in the three days beginning on 18 September 1901. The Mayor led off by conducting a tour of the city, during which he spoke disdainfully of those who thought Alfred's bones lay within its precincts; but Harrison in his talk in the Guildhall admitted he for one had not abandoned that hope. (Freeman, he had said elsewhere, was 'needlessly angry' in dismissing the story of the burned cakes.) There was danger of losing sight of Alfred because Saxon remains were so few compared with those of the Normans. In proposing the vote of thanks, Shaw–Lefevre compared the proceedings to a canonization, which must have pleased Harrison, as, no doubt, did Alfred's own words in the printed programme, about desiring to preserve his memory in good works. Eminent scholars and public figures lent dignity and authority to the events, the most important of which was Lord Rosebery's unveiling of the heroic bronze statue on its twelve-foot-high stone pedestal (resting on a layer of sugar donated by a local merchant to allow for level settling). Oxen were roasted for the poor and there were fireworks.[45] Harrison was widely acknowledged as the inspirer of the occasion and given a candlestick of oak from the ancient roof of Winchester Cathedral. In the Mayor's edition of commemorative essays, Harrison's came first. The only disappointment was his failure to extract yet one more honour for the Wessex hero: a poem by Hardy.[46]

As Vice-President of the Royal Historical Society Harrison sought to increase its professionalism by proposing in 1896 that it should sponsor a 'scientific' bibliography of printed works on English history—a more scholarly version of the choice of books on history he had been urging for decades. He thought the project feasible for the Society because of its imminent merger with the Camden Society, which had some 160 titles to its credit. His rationale for the scheme was published, but despite the support of Grant Duff and George Prothero, who became President of the Society and was co-editor of the Cambridge Modern History, no action was taken until 1910. Then Prothero was named editor of the bibliography, and the American Historical Association agreed to co-operate. Prothero had by then retired as President. He had been persuaded to serve in the first place only when told that by repeatedly urging the election of Harrison to the office he was jeopardizing harmony. Apparently Harrison's Positivism and lack of credentials as a historian disqualified him in the minds of certain members. He may not have been aware of the low regard they had of his work; his aspiration to the Regius Professorship suggests a certain naïveté on his part. What he did see was that more historical projects came his way than he could handle. In history, as in law studies and literary criticism, there was always need for the popularizer and teacher. They were roles he consciously sought and never despised, and by not looking too intently at those ranged on either side of him, the very learned and the uninformed, he managed to maintain a remarkable equipoise for a very long time.[47]

Whatever some historians may have thought of Harrison, his stature was sufficient by 1896 for one of the greatest of historians to take him seriously. Lord Acton, appointed Regius Professor at Cambridge the previous year, had just projected the scheme of the Cambridge Modern History and invited Harrison to contribute. He tentatively agreed to write on one of the topics suggested to him, the 1830 Revolution in France.[48] Before a firm decision was reached, however, he was seeking Acton's support for another scheme of his own, a Congress of Diplomatic Historians to promote the publication of selected European diplomatic documents before 1815. The Foreign Office and the Italian government were interested, he said, and the Russians were only waiting for the English to decide before coming in.[49] But this attempt to get the nations of Europe to 'Live Openly' came to nothing. In 1900 Harrison asked Acton to be excused from the roster of the Cambridge Modern History, for he was by then busy with Byzantine studies, and in any case felt that 'the more I meditate on the French history of this century, the more incapable do I find myself to grasp it.'[50] But Acton, too, troubled Harrison. He depicted him in the *Positivist Review* as 'the most learned historical student of our time' but also as a Roman Catholic of that nondescript variety, 'a "new Catholic" ... utterly alien to Comte and to Positivist Sociology'.[51] For this reason he may have feared Acton's editorial pen; indeed, from the beginning he was concerned about whether a 'uniform theory of politics' was to be maintained throughout the history.[52] Acton, in his famous letter to prospective contributors, had expressed the hope that readers would be unable to tell without a list of authors 'where the Bishop of Oxford laid down the pen, and whether Fairbairn or Gasquet, Liebermann or Harrison took it up'. But Harrison always insisted that a historical synthesis (like the Positivist synthesis) had to be subjective in the sense that it had to represent a philosophic perspective. In the end, Acton's dream of objectivity was bound to fail, even if he had not died in 1902 with the project barely under way. As one modern historian suggests, each contributor saw himself as a pontiff in his own domain and gave Acton only the 'courtesy title of Pope'.[53] Ironically, by scrupulously trying to protect his right to express his own point of view, Harrison sacrificed a chance to place it before a wide audience in the company of the world's most respected historians.

THE CITY IN HISTORY

Like the hero, the city seemed to the Positivists able to sum up a civilization. In an address at Toynbee Hall in 1886 Harrison considered the European city's ancient, medieval, modern, and ideal characteristics and speculated that the race had only survived because healthy people from the countryside continually streamed into the cities to take the place of those who had fallen victim to insanitary urban conditions. Municipal hygiene for him was a fundamental application of scientific principles to life. Yet there was a certain irony in asserting that the city was at once the most progressive part of a culture and at the same time an unhealthy environment, and that the modern city had failed to maintain the religious, political, and artistic unity that characterized the historic city.[54] When he turned to specific places he naturally chose the great capitals for subjects. In their eminence and complex riches they were analogous to the great books of the past. But his ambivalence about cities was undeniable. The Haussmannization of Paris troubled him because so many quaint vistas and historical buildings he loved had been destroyed to make way for the grand new avenues.[55] His desire to increase the efficiency of London's government meant undermining traditional local authorities, and, as the creation of Kingsway would show, the sacrifice of beloved perspectives to progress. He never presumed to have an answer to the question of how to improve the salubriousness and convenience of city life without loss of history and charm. On his first visit to Athens in 1890 he found the intermingling of the ancient and modern so compelling that he said actually seeing the city was 'worthy the study of a hundred books'.[56] Rome, by contrast, seemed bent on 'destructive municipalism' that was making it 'vulgar, overgrown, Frenchified'.[57]

Another of the future's 'insoluble problems' was that of Constantinople. Of all the capitals he visited and studied, none engaged both

Harrison's historical and political interests so fully and so fruitfully. Oxford had ignored Byzantine studies in his day; and Congreve's *Roman Empire of the West* in 1855 was written as if the fall of the West were the end of the Empire. Admittedly, Comte's concentration on the Roman rather than the Greek heritage, and on Western Europe almost exclusively, would hardly have prompted his followers to undertake Byzantine studies. But Harrison appreciated that the survival and influence of the Eastern Roman Empire exemplified Comte's teaching about the unity and continuity of history. He had read much on Constantinople by the time of his first visit, in 1890, and he found it as familiar as if he had known it from childhood. So, at least, he told Ethel. In 1894 he published two lengthy essays on Constantinople in the *Fortnightly*, arguing that the still unappreciated achievements of the Eastern Empire were of decisive importance for European civilization. And he was equally concerned with its modern problems. The Turkish occupation of Constantinople remained permanently unsatisfactory, especially since Muslims were a minority, but each of the other minorities would tolerate no rule but its own. And the spectre of Russian control, with its implications for the balance of power in Europe, was deeply disquieting to him.[58] In *The Meaning of History* in 1894 he reprinted the 1862 essay of the title together with subsequent studies, mostly on great capital cities. Though some critics noted the Positivist bias and lack of depth of the book as a whole, J. B. Bury, already an eminence in Byzantine studies, praised the two reprinted articles on Constantinople as useful stimulants to historical re-evaluation.[59]

Harrison's Byzantine passion came to fruition in June 1900 when he gave the Rede Lecture at Cambridge, the first Oxford man so honoured since Matthew Arnold. 'Byzantine History in the Early Middle Ages' (the eighth to the early eleventh centuries) was an elegant summary of Byzantine culture that drew heavily upon his *Fortnightly* essays. Removing the incubus of Gibbon's disdain was the great achievement of modern Byzantinists—all of them Continental except for Bury. It was no longer possible to see Byzantine history as a depressing chronicle of intrigue and decay: its variety and creativity were full of incident and of lessons for the West. The Imperial administration and law code won his highest praise as unsurpassed models of practical rationality; and he rehearsed the splendours of Constantinople's buildings and art and scholarship with admiration. Far more research still was needed, he believed, to encompass the grandeur and relevance of the civilization of the New Rome.[60]

Instead of taking his own advice, Harrison was soon at work on a novel set in the Byzantine world, *Theophano: The Crusade of the Tenth Century*, subtitled 'A Romantic Monograph' to indicate his dual aim, literary and scholarly. It took four years to complete, for other literary tasks, pro-Boer activities, and the move to Hawkhurst were distractions, and he wished to spare no effort to produce a work of art, not a mere antiquarian novel like *Romola*. He decided not to follow Scott and most other historical novelists who put fictional characters at centre stage while using real historical persons for background only. His heroine was the tenth-century empress of the title. She gave him the most trouble but the most pleasure too, for he indulged his fantasies freely. From a shy Greek maiden she rapidly becomes a ruthlessly ambitious empress, hastens her weak husband's death, marries his general, Nicephorus, who has become Emperor, then has him murdered in a conspiracy with another general who takes the throne but finally repudiates her intrigues. 'I am determined to finish the bitch even if she finish me!', wrote Harrison to Gosse in 1901. 'We will go down together and fight it out in hell.'[61] He depended for his sources on exhaustive recent German scholarship and on such books as *The Medieval Empire*, by H. A. L. Fisher, who had reviewed the Rede Lecture favourably. Karl Krumbacher, one of the greatest of Byzantinists, gave him tips about using the Vatican Library when they met at a historical congress in Rome in 1903. Just to look at specific paintings and manuscripts of interest to him there took considerable brashness, but the librarian who finally acceded to his insistent requests got a copy of the Rede Lecture for his trouble. In the end, still anxious about accuracy, he had the manuscript read by Bury, to whom he dedicated the book.[62]

At the time of the almost simultaneous publication of *Veranilda* and *Theophano*, Harrison told Algernon Gissing that in his brother's work 'history, excellent as it is, is distinctly subordinate to romance', whereas in *Theophano* romance is 'subordinate to *history*'.[63] But Harrison's amalgam had as little success as Gissing's. Three publishers including Macmillan refused it before Chapman and Hall brought it out after its serialization in the *Fortnightly*. Friends were evasive or selective in their comments. Meredith thought it 'swollen' by its history. Blunt said only its history kept him from pitching it overboard while *en route* from Trieste to Cairo. Hewlett, always verbally complex, described it as 'figuring nations "as men walking"'. Hardy wished he had Harrison's reason for studying Byzantine history. Bryce wished he had seen the book before revising his *Holy Roman Empire*. Morley, in a long review, noted that by endowing his characters with ideas, Harrison had provided 'many deep things to ruminate upon', although the canvas seemed too crowded. ('But Gibbon is crowded!', spluttered Harrison.) Friends in Greece ran it serially in two Greek-language newspapers. But no one urged him to write another novel.[64]

The most obvious flaw in *Theophano* is its stilted dialogue. *The Times Literary Supplement* blamed it on the traditional practice of historical novelists, but Blunt and Morley held stage conventions responsible.[65] Harrison was indeed caught up in the London theatre just then, and in the hope of tempting Beerbohm Tree he hurriedly composed *Nicephorus*, a blank verse drama that Chapman and Hall published in 1906. Based on *Theophano*, its models were Stephen Phillips's *Herod* and similar heroic dramas, Gilbert Murray's translations of Greek tragedies, and even the New Testament (before his assassination, Nicephorus cries, 'My God! Why am I forsaken and betrayed? ... Thy will be done—Thy kingdom come!'). Friends were encouraging, but theatre people resorted to the same excuse he was hearing in his attempt to find a producer for his one-act play, *Entente Cordiale*: the sets would be too expensive.[66] After allowing a German to write a libretto for an opera of *Nicephorus* (which failed to interest composers), Harrison eventually secured the acting rights by presenting a public reading. Given in Bath shortly after his move there, it featured him in the title role, a platform appearance he knew would make Beesly snort in contempt.[67] As his hopes of ever seeing a production diminished, there was consolation in thinking that *The Times Literary Supplement* had been right when it observed in its rather generous review that the age had 'set its face against heroic tragedy'. Playwrights and producers were not to blame if poetic drama had no chance, Harrison told one aspiring dramatist; the crowd wanted only 'pretty girls, fun, farce, or nasty intrigues ... the tragic, the terrible, the ideal, bores and frightens them.'[68]

BIOGRAPHY AS HISTORY

Writing for and editing the *New Calendar of Great Men* was Harrison's most onerous and misunderstood historical enterprise. In his plan for the 1892 volume he followed Comte's scheme and arranged the 558 biographical entries in a roughly chronological order within each of the thirteen months, which comprised epochs and themes combined, as in 'Ancient Philosophy', 'Feudal Civilization', and 'Modern Statesmanship'. Though he admitted it would be 'grossly absurd' to think of any list as incapable of amendment, he described Comte's Calendar as a 'very careful and balanced whole' and made neither deletions nor additions. He offered the work as a 'biographical Manual of the general course of civilisation', its subjects not necessarily saints or heroes, but individuals 'remembered for effective work in the development of human society'. A somewhat similar compilation in 1878, *Portraits of the One Hundred Greatest Men of History*, had an advantage over the Positivists' volume: its sections were introduced by such luminaries as Arnold, Froude, Taine, Renan, Max Müller, and A. P. Stanley. By contrast, most of Harrison's contributors were little known outside Positivist circles and few were fully prepared for their assignments. The bulk of the writing was done by the three leading Positivists, Harrison concentrating on ancient and modern literature and the Middle Ages generally, Beesly on ancient and modern statesmen, and Bridges, who did more than anyone else, on ancient religion and Catholicism, ancient and modern science, technology, and philosophy. Their four hundred entries were supplemented by seventy-five from the Lushingtons, Marvin, and Swinny; and among the other contributors was Ethel, with five biographies. When writing his hundred and thirty-six entries, Harrison was not alone in finding his knowledge stretched to its limits, and he fell back upon speculation and general history when faced with the need to say something about Fo-Hi, Manco-Capac, Berosus, Sosigenes, or the 'Theocrats' of Japan and Tibet. He had to ask Laffitte, author of another Comtist compilation, *Les Grands Types de l'Humanité*, what Thilorier had done. Characteristically, there was no reply, so he pressed Dr Hillemand. His own researches meanwhile turned up two Thiloriers, the father, who had tried to interest Napoleon in invading England by balloon, and the son, who had liquefied gases and solidified liquids. The chemist appears in the *New Calendar*, illustrating 'man's mastery over Nature'.[69]

For Comte, and therefore for Harrison, the periods and realms of activity requiring representation in the *Calendar* largely determined the list of biographical subjects, all of whom had to be fitted into the scheme. Months with a limited supply of notables to fill their ranks required the mustering of unknowns, and populous categories (six of the thirteen months covered 'modern' times) necessitated arguable omissions. Not only did 'types' of an epoch sometimes edge out greater but less representative figures, but Comte's peculiar biases, arbitrariness, and limited knowledge defined the contents. Hence, in addition to a plethora of obscure personalities and an excessive proportion of Frenchmen, there were such omissions from the roll of Humanity's Great Men as Jesus, Epicurus, Plotinus, Justinian, Luther, Calvin, Johnson, Napoleon, Keats, Wordsworth, Coleridge, Gauss, Faraday, and Humboldt; and there were no representatives of Byzantium or of the French Revolution. Of course Comte was not without a rationale for some of the exclusions: promotion of mankind's progress (irrespective of private morality) was the test, and merely vainglorious power or revolutionary destructiveness, which included Protestantism, failed it. Harrison agreed, or at least tolerated much of this (though he regretted the lack of space for Bach, Haydn, Schubert, and Mendelssohn), and in his preface provided only minimal explanation for the selectivity he must have known the reviewers would seize upon with glee.[70]

For the most part they predictably ignored the stated criteria and positive values of the *New Calendar* to complain about who was and was not in it. There were exceptions to this among friends—Hardy called it a 'terrible reminder of one's ignorance', and Grant Allen a unique and 'unpretentious' volume—but even Morley could not refrain from rehearsing its lacunae. And with reason: he had written books on two of the most eminent of the missing, Burke and Rousseau, and had occupied the rooms of another, Wesley, at Lincoln College, Oxford. Yet he found in the *New Calendar* a 'rationalized scientific hagiography' illustrating a scheme of history that, like all such schemes, was better than none at all.[71] The Positivists made up a few of its deficiencies without calling attention to them: Beesly in his biography of the omitted Queen Elizabeth, Harrison in his of Chatham and in the Rede Lecture. One use of the *New Calendar* he never dwelt on was as a précis of the history of science, a subject that never much interested him and was, indeed, not yet a scholarly discipline in his day. Yet he would have been gratified to know that a founder of the modern history of science, George Sarton, was once taken to Chapel Street by Marvin and thought enough of the *Calendar* to analyse the way in which it anticipated his own concerns (even though he thought Comte himself 'crazy').[72] Understandably, no critic outside the Positivist circle ever quite matched Vernon Lushington's paean in a sonnet sequence on the *Calendar*: he called it the 'record wise and true/ of that immortal Progress no one knew/ Until the Master came'.[73]

Being early in a new field of research may present pitfalls to the unwary. Bridges, who had written much on scientists and philosophers for the *New Calendar*, became deeply interested in Roger Bacon while doing the research for his entry and resolved to spend the first years of his retirement in preparing a new edition of the *Opus Majus*, which had not been printed since the eighteenth century. He diligently studied Bacon manuscripts in London, Oxford, Dublin, Paris, and the Vatican Library, and in 1897 Oxford University Press published his edition with an introduction. But almost simultaneously a leading Catholic historian, Fr. Francis Gasquet, wrote in the *English Historical Review* about his recent discovery of a hitherto unknown manuscript part of the *Opus Majus* in the Vatican Library, and published the Latin text. As if that were not enough, reviewers began to point out errors in Bridges's interpretation of his sources. Gasquet and Robert Steele, a Bacon scholar, then asked Oxford to withdraw Bridges's edition and let them prepare a new one.[74] Harrison, meanwhile, had said nothing of these complications in his laudatory account of the book for the *Positivist Review*, and to friends he fulminated about the 'infamous pack attack' by a 'gang of Romans'.[75] Incapable of such verbal 'sword play' himself, Bridges resolutely set about revising his work, which Oxford had stopped advertising. He obtained palaeographic help, returned to Rome, and with much labour had a revised version ready by 1900. But broken in spirit by the ordeal, and with his health deteriorating and finances in ruins, he never produced the *opus majus* of his own that his friends had hoped would crown his life.[76]

Harrison's two full-length biographies of Positivist worthies in the *Calendar* proved altogether more satisfying than Bridges's editorial labours. *Cromwell* in Morley's Twelve English Statesmen series in 1888 and *William the Silent* in Bury's Foreign Statesmen series in 1897 both enjoyed the success of those publishing ventures. Forced to be comprehensive while limited to 250 pages, and not expected to do extensive research nor offer original interpretations, he had helpful limits and yet considerable freedom. Undertaking the *Cromwell*, he told Morley, would satisfy his desire to have some study in hand besides his law courses, for he felt time passing and 'the night cometh when no man can work.'[77] *Order and Progress* and *The Choice of Books* grew out of his belief that a man needed a substantial publication in a field to which he hoped to contribute. *Cromwell* was his bid for consideration as a historian. It is perhaps no coincidence that his subject was the very one Comte had unsuccessfully urged upon Congreve, with whom Harrison was by now in deadly rivalry.[78] Money was a consideration, too: Macmillan paid £100 for the copyright. But Harrison's personal involvement in his subject is shown by the middle name he gave Bernard (Beesly, who wrote on Cromwell for the *New Calendar*, had named his second son Oliver) and by the name of the daughter born just as his work on the book was most intense.

As a schoolboy Harrison had taken King Charles's side in debates on Cromwell, but at Oxford Carlyle's rehabilitation of the Protector prepared him for Comte's equally strong admiration. Having agreed with Morley that no research was necessary, he nevertheless followed Cromwell's trail to Cambridge, Ely, and Huntingdon, and delved so deeply into issues of genealogy and heraldry that he eventually needed four appendices for his findings. Cromwell, long a favourite with liberals and freethinkers, had recently been treated at length in books by Goldwin Smith, David Masson, and J. Allanson Picton; Harrison's was not in any important way revisionist. By applying relativist principles he exonerated Cromwell of some of the onus attached by most scholars to his authoritarianism in England and cruelties in Ireland, and he simply did not dwell on policies—the Dutch maritime war, the seizure of Jamaica, the Western Design for empire—which to a Positivist might have needed justification. He clearly regarded Cromwell's religious zeal as pathological by modern standards, but suggested that in good men like him it gave 'solemnity and power'. Cromwell's devotion to family and country, his religious tolerance (Ireland is treated as a political problem), and his institution of the Commonwealth were admirable. Altogether he is said to deserve the praise of a 'philosopher of another country'—obviously Comte—who called him 'the most enlightened statesman who ever adorned the Protestant world'.[79]

Morley declared himself 'entirely delighted' with the book, but queried some passages in his own copy.[80] Gladstone annotated his copy even more assiduously, bracketing references to Cromwell's religion and the author's evident distance from it, his granting of religious liberty, his commanding personality, and his belief that the massacres in Ireland were ordained by God ('so the Turks', Gladstone wrote). Where Harrison sought to excuse Cromwell's sacrifice of Parliament to expediency Gladstone asked 'Why not call a new one?', and with a question mark he disagreed with Harrison's claim that Cromwell had no taste for 'arbitrary or martial rule'. Harrison's speculation that the Protectorate might have lasted longer if Cromwell had lived seventy-five years, 'now almost the normal limit for modern statesmen', received two question marks from the seventy-nine-year-old former Prime Minister.[81] Two years before the book appeared, Gladstone had told Harrison at a party in the most vehement manner, and to the consternation of others at the table, that he did not think Cromwell was as great a man as the late Lord Althorp.[82]

Harrison's book received good reviews, even from the leading Cromwell scholar, S. R. Gardiner.[83] It became a text in India, went through many reprintings, and brought prestigious assignments. Between 1891 and 1902 the *English Historical Review*, edited by Gardiner for most of that period, published four reviews by Harrison of Camden Society volumes edited by Sir Charles Firth, who in 1903 succeeded York Powell as Regius Professor of Modern History at Oxford. That year in the same journal Harrison assessed Firth's lectures on Cromwell's army, and in 1910 Firth's two volumes bringing Gardiner's history to the end of the Protectorate. And he welcomed Firth's biography of Cromwell in the *Cornhill* in 1900 and a new edition of Gardiner's history in the *Speaker* the next year.[84] In all this he deferentially credited Firth with supremacy in dealing with manuscript sources and Gardiner in presenting biographical detail; but privately he complained to George Trevelyan that Gardiner had made Cromwell out to be 'as powerless as Lord Salisbury to control a difficult situation'. And when Morley was starting work on his own biography of Cromwell in 1898, Harrison expostulated with him: 'Research be d—d! Remember that Gardiner and Firth have now absolutely sucked dry every scrap of MSS available.' He thought Firth's 'fussy prosing' about in his documents came to little. 'My housemaid has reams of MSS never before printed … and here is one of them.' Gardiner's lack of sympathy for Cromwell was easy to explain: 'No man can be a hero to his valet—or to a pedant.' But he added in closing, '"For Gaud's sake" as Kipling says, don't print this or I am undone.'[85]

His enthusiasm for Cromwell involved Harrison in several controversies. One concerned the statue of Cromwell now outside Westminster Hall. Just before leaving office in 1895 the Liberals asked for Parliament's approval of a statue but had to scrap the idea when Irish MPs howled in outrage. Rosebery thereupon decided to pay for it himself. This seemed a good solution to Harrison, who always liked to see the wealthy act as public benefactors. The sculptor would be Thornycroft, whose work he admired. But anxious about the location to be chosen (he favoured Charing Cross), he wrote to Rosebery for information and received only a non-committal reply.[86] The announcement of the site, adjacent to the hall where Charles I had been condemned and Cromwell made Lord Protector, revived the outcry. Harrison, however, welcomed Rosebery's gift and blithely announced that hatred of Cromwell's memory had 'fizzled out in the whining of a handful of Ritualists, Jew financiers, and Jacobites'.[87] Yet the unveiling in 1899 was not wholly satisfactory, for Rosebery, who that year published his own biography of Cromwell, failed to invite the established Cromwell scholars: Gardiner, Firth, Morley, and Harrison.[88]

No mere replica of Cromwell was the subject of another controversy. In his book Harrison suggested re-interment in Westminster Abbey of bones in the possession of Sir George Wombwell, who claimed that after the exhumation of Cromwell's body in 1660 it had been brought to the house he now occupied in Yorkshire.[89] Unable to make progress in this cause, Harrison took up the claim of the Revd Horace Wilkinson, who said he possessed Cromwell's mummified head, exhibited on a pinnacle of Westminster Hall after the exhumation. Beclouded by uncertainties, the macabre discussion carried on by Harrison and others in the newspapers for over a decade was eventually deemed 'unedifying' by *The Times*.[90] Meanwhile, the manipulation of Cromwell's subjective immortality troubled him even more. Neither Morley's biography nor Theodore Roosevelt's, both of which appeared in 1900, was adulatory enough. Two years later, criticism of Cromwell's Irish policy by General Sir William Butler, a prominent Catholic, seemed to him 'mendacious fanaticism'. Harrison's letter to the *Speaker* brought an acrimonious reply from Mary Marks, whose Irish historical novel *Thorough* he had found too elaborate in its detail when Bentley asked him about it in 1894.[91] In the end John Drinkwater probably came closest to meeting Harrison's requirements in his long poem, a cycle of shorter poems (written at Harrison's suggestion and dedicated to him), a drama, and a character study—all on Cromwell.[92]

For *William the Silent*, as for Cromwell, Harrison had ample printed sources. The most important were books by Americans: Motley's *Rise of the Dutch Republic* and Ruth Putnam's recent biography. The primary documents were all in print, an 'endless' literature in six languages. Harrison's visit to Holland in October 1895 was, therefore, more self-indulgent than necessary. His command of Dutch proved sufficient, even in an altercation with officials of a temporarily closed museum that held a portrait of William he was determined to see, and during his fruitless search 'all over Holland' for the garment William wore when he was assassinated, thought to be somewhere preserved. He loved the quaintness of the country and thought the girls as 'wholesome' as English girls—'not so coquettish and smart as the French, not so bony as the German, not so brusque and tasteless as the Swiss'. But stopping in Belgium on the way home he was relieved to 'get into a Catholic country and see fine churches, open, and with good music'. The girls were prettier, too. At home he worked intermittently, about two years all told, and lectured on William in several cities, in Glasgow staying with Gilbert Murray.[93] Upon completing his manuscript he told Morley he had tried to write a 'sort of Walter Scott historical romance based on original documents—in fact to combine the brilliance of Macaulay, the romance of Froude, and the rigid accuracy of a Freeman in one tableau!!!'[94]

Not even Harrison could claim that he had done so. But Ruth Putnam and most reviewers praised his graceful condensation of the vast materials he had consulted.[95] As with Cromwell, he had been able to stress his subject's private virtues, and he was forbearing about William's four marriages. His successive profession of Lutheranism, Catholicism, and Calvinism Harrison explained as his enlightened subjection of theological to political values. His heroic struggle against the Spanish is depicted as a precursor of the Puritan revolution in England, the American Revolution, and, less directly, the French Revolution. Ultimately, William's claim to honour is made to rest on his having left Holland 'indestructible and great'. After consulting the Dutch wife of the historian W. E. H. Lecky, Harrison requested permission of Queen Regent Emma of Holland to dedicate the biography to her, pointing out that it was the first by an Englishman. Publication had to wait until the request was granted. On its appearance in October 1897 Professor P. J. Blok of Leyden University, the author of the standard history of Holland, deemed the book worthy of translation into Dutch; but he disliked the epithet 'The Silent' and changed it to 'Prince of Orange' in the translation he supervised.[96]

Soon Lord Salisbury, at the instigation of Sir Henry Howard, the British Minister at the Hague, asked Harrison to represent the Foreign Office at the Congress of Historians to be held there in the autumn of 1898. Harrison travelled with Oscar Browning, and they planned to share lodgings. When that proved impossible, Browning went off by himself and wound up with three lawsuits brought by his landladies.[97] Harrison, by contrast, found a comfortable hotel (enough hooks) from which he sallied out to find himself 'persona grata' at the Congress. He read a paper for an absent delegate and managed to quash some 'silly resolutions'.[98] But he thought the meetings amounted to little, and was quite willing to depart early when asked to take Lord Salisbury's place at the enthronement of Princess Wilhelmina as Queen. He went to Amsterdam in a special railway carriage with the French president of the Congress, who might have been surprised to know that in a letter home Harrison called the French delegates 'helpless asses'. At the ceremony in the Westerkerk, he and two Americans were the only 'blackbeetles amongst about 80 blazing creatures covered with gold lace, diamonds, crosses and stars', but he, at least, sported an orange emblem. Noticing him bowing low to the new Queen as she passed them upon leaving the church, the Dutch Foreign Minister, de Beaufort, paused to shake his hand.[99] But Harrison had not really lost his republican beliefs. In his account of the proceedings for *The Times* he termed Wilhelmina, as he had Victoria, the hereditary head of an essentially republican nation. In the *Positivist Review* he argued that her people should command the allegiance of Britain as a vital buffer between Germany and France. The Dutch seem to have replaced the French as his model for Europe. Still considering himself 'persona grata' in Holland, the next September he sent an urgent letter to de Beaufort proposing the 'one thing' that might prevent the war now imminent between the British and the

Boers in South Africa: a 'personal private autograph letter from Q[ueen] W[ilhelmina] to Q[ueen] V[ictoria], written spontaneously in her words and very strong as Queen to Queen and granddaughter to grandmother etc.'.[100]

Harrison agreed to write his third political biography early in 1904, on Chatham. It would complete the Twelve English Statesmen series, relieve Morley of an undesired assignment he had inherited at Froude's death, and earn £250 for Harrison—£50 more than Macmillan had paid for *Ruskin*, because he claimed travel and research expenses.[101] At first he worried about what friends would say of his 'taking up the founder of the British Empire', but he was soon calling Chatham 'the greatest man we ever had' and revelling in the eighteenth century, its 'powder—rats—scandal and eloquence'.[102] But he had not lost touch with the twentieth century. Preoccupied with Balfour's iniquities, he exclaimed, 'Oh! if there were only a "Chatham" now!' Falling under the sway of the great orator's speeches, he was reminded of his disappointment with the performance of Morley, who had depicted Gladstone's eloquence in his biography but did not emulate it in Parliament.[103] If Chatham's style was admirable, some of his turns of policy gave trouble. But Harrison usually had an explanation that preserved his hero's stature. Chatham's surprising support of Prussia, for example, he saw as part of a necessary strategic plan and evidence that he 'cared little for rigid consistency'. There were uncongenial sides to Chatham that Harrison could not ignore—his 'despotic' politics, devotion to commercial interests, love of luxury, and acceptance of a title—but they were far outweighed by his endorsement of an independent Irish Parliament, reforms in India, removal of Dissenters' disabilities, and a more representative House of Commons. Especially important were Chatham's contribution to Britain's maritime supremacy and his support of the rights of the American colonists against tyrannous British policies. At the beginning of his chapter on Chatham's 'Defence of America' he quoted from George Trevelyan's recently published *American Revolution*, which he had reviewed early in 1904. It confirmed his judgement that Chatham's great relevance was his strong sense of the rights of Englishmen on whichever side of the Atlantic they found themselves. Though Chatham extended Britain's domains further than had any other statesman, he was a 'real, and not a pinchbeck, Imperialist', not one to whom 'Empire' meant 'small colonies of white settlers, holding in serfdom vast masses of some inferior race'.[104] When Harrison had almost finished his labours, he embodied his ever recurring antipathies for Balfour's government in a *Fortnightly* essay whose title came from Burke, 'Thoughts on the Present Discontents'. Writing about the inspirational leadership and bold achievement of Burke's greatest contemporary was one way he sublimated his sense of frustration and impotence in a climate of political adversity.

The reception of *Chatham* in the spring of 1905 was satisfying to Harrison but hardly spectacular; one displeasing review he blamed on 'party animosity'.[105] Though the book had nothing like the success of his previous political biographies, he did not let his third subject fall into oblivion any more than he had Cromwell or William. He assessed the next biography of Chatham, a massive Germanic one by Albert von Ruville, finding it a 'degradation of the biographer's art', and delivered two addresses on Chatham, one to the Royal Historical Society on the bicentenary in 1908, and another, the next year, to the American Circle, on Chatham and the colonies. He delighted in reading aloud his account of the famous last speech and collapse of Chatham.[106] In 1910 Lord Rosebery, who had written a biography of Pitt the Younger, and was his great, great grand-nephew, published *Chatham, His Early Life and Connections*, using new manuscript sources. Harrison reviewed it favourably and urged Rosebery to go on and write a full-scale life, which in his preface Rosebery had said could not be done because the facts were not fully known. But what should that matter in dealing with 'an essentially public man'? asked Harrison, and he once again discouraged delving too deeply into any such figure's personal life.[107]

In 1917 Harrison found a reason to be interested in Chatham's private life. On 5 December Godfrey, his third son, married a great, great, great granddaughter of Chatham. Alexandra Blanche Hester Pringle was the only daughter of the late Reginald Pringle and his wife, and a friend of Olive's at Hawkhurst.[108] Harrison gave her two privately printed books about her eminent ancestors that had been given to him by Rosebery. One contained letters of Chatham's younger daughter, Lady Harriot Eliot, whose daughter, Harriot Hester Eliot, had married Reginald Pringle's grandfather, General William Henry Pringle, one of a distinguished military family. The other book contained the letters Pitt the Younger wrote to William Eden, Lord Auckland, some about his daughter Eleanor, to whom Pitt was once engaged but had 'begged off'. She was living at the time with her parents at their house at Eden Farm, Beckenham, the very place where, as Eden Park, Harrison spent his bachelor summers two generations later.[109] Thus towards the close of his vocation as a historian did he see strands of his own family history interwoven with the nation's.

10

The Positivist as Prophet

1914–1923

THE GERMAN PERIL

The Great War of 1914 to 1918 vindicated Harrison's warnings about Germany but also exposed his error in basing hope for European peace on a balance of power. He would often remind his readers of that prescience but say little of the treaty system's failure to prevent aggression. Hints of the imminent diplomatic breakdown in July 1914 led the Harrisons to cut short their Swiss holiday; returning to Bath on the 25th of the month he devoured the English newspapers, seeking some clue to the meaning of the confused diplomacy that had begun to unfold with the assassinations at Sarajevo. He must have regretted that early in the year he had banned all political talk with Morley because they differed so on the Government's policies. At the time Morley, who had remained in the Cabinet as Lord President of the Council after resigning the India Office in 1910, had contemptuously commented: 'One might suppose without arrogance that you might pick up a crumb or two from a member of the government, even after the wisdom of the half-pay colonels and generals of the Bath Club.' Morley's resignation from the Cabinet when it decided to stand by Belgium and France on 4 August was in Harrison's judgement a 'gran rifiuto' like Gladstone's refusal to aid France in the Franco-Prussian War.[1]

To Harrison, the war was a crusade as holy as any undertaken by the Church. Austin would later declare that his father's 'unflinching war determinism in 1914 caused him to be more popularly known and appreciated in extreme old age than had been the case during the Victorian epoch'.[2] The fervour with which he had once supported the cause of the Paris Commune, the Afghans, the Egyptians, and the Boers was matched if not exceeded by his hatred of the Germans. At last his views were shared by the majority of the nation. He lacked the useful connections of earlier days, but he made the most of every opportunity to communicate his sense of urgency. On 13 August the Mayor of Bath called on him to move the principal resolution at a

Guildhall meeting to inaugurate a relief fund drive, and he used the occasion to predict that the war would not be a short one, as many were expecting, and to insist that it ought not to end until the 'curse of imperial aggression' was crushed.[3] In September he was back at the Guildhall telling the Workers' Educational Association that the 'real German attack had been upon England', and that no peace overtures should be considered until German sea power had been broken and the German 'creed of Blood and Iron destroyed.'[4] By mid-October the Victory League had sold almost 13,000 copies of his pamphlet calling the war a fight for 'our honour, for our homes, for the future of civilization, freedom, and peace'.[5] In a collection of essays by 'Representative Men and Women' honouring the King of Belgium, he invoked the Athenians' heroic struggle against the Persians; and when Italy joined the Allies in 1916 he recalled that nation's 'ancient valour' in a parallel volume.[6]

Before the first wartime Christmas, both Harrisons were expressing fierce thoughts about the Kaiser. Ethel confessed that she was not sure if she wished his death or not but thought it would have 'great moral effect' and felt 'no mercy or pity'. Her husband's demand in *The Times* for 'condign reprobation' included the proposal that the Kaiser—'if, indeed, he choose to survive'—be subjected to the degradation inflicted on 'poor Dreyfus': 'let his bloodstained sword be broken on his craven back and the uniform and orders of which he is so childishly proud be stamped in the mire.' St. Helena or Devil's Island might be his 'prison and his grave'.[7] Brutal as this was, it was not too harsh for many. Henry James assured Mrs W. K. Clifford that Harrison's letter would be 'as much a relief to my nerves and yours, and to those millions of others, as to his own splendidly fine old inflamed ones; meaning by nerves everything that shall most formidably clamour within us for the recorded execration of history'.[8] Harrison may have thundered on like an Old Testament prophet—or a *Times* leader—but he also had juridical conceptions in mind. Though he dismissed critics of his letter as 'sanctimonious purists and hypocritical pretenders to the "higher morality" ', his words were not merely a 'futile menace by way of Retaliation'; he had suggested a 'formal method of showing the Neutrals and our own people that we hold the German chiefs as degraded outlaws and not as honourable foes'. Behind this lay the same belief that had fired his denunciation of British military adventures in Afghanistan and South Africa—namely, that certain humanitarian principles governed the conduct of soldiers of civilized nations in peace and war alike. By their offences against their enemies the Germans had abandoned that code of honour.[9] When a German submarine crew was captured in the spring of 1915 he argued, as 'an old lawyer' who could remember the trial and hanging of foreign pirates in London in 1861 and 1876, that since the Germans were pursuing civilian as well as military shipping, the men should be tried in a civilian court. To the response that they had acted under orders he replied that such logic would make the Kaiser alone culpable. And when it was further argued that all existing English law on piracy was made for peacetime conditions, he declared that unless the crew's responsibility was established by trial, after the war 'some new German Grotius will arise to prove that all these modern atrocities have been incorporated into an amended Law of Nations.'[10] It was an argument that would be heard again after a second World War, at Nuremburg.

Convinced that nine-tenths of the Germans whole-heartedly supported the war, Harrison made no distinction between the liability of the people and their leaders. When some prominent German scholars issued a statement denying that their nation was guilty of starting the war, violating neutral territory, or committing atrocities, a number of equally impressive British scholars and men of letters, including some Positivists, signed a rejoinder. Harrison was not asked, perhaps through oversight, but he published a statement saying he did not 'care to bandy recriminations with these German defenders of the attack on civilisation'. Giving vent to his old animus against the pretensions of Culture, which he now wrote *Kultur*, he accused the German scholars of believing that 'to have put the critics right about a few lines in Sophocles, or to have discovered a new chemical dye, dispenses the German Super-man from being bound to humanity, truthfulness, and honour.'[11] This reasoning inevitably ended his forty-five-year-old friendship with one of the German signatories, Lujo Brentano. Their correspondence had already demonstrated that their common preference for the old over the new-style trade unions did not offset their disagreement on the German naval construction programme. In one letter Harrison had attributed it to 'mere monomania' and declared that a British attack on Germany was a logical impossibility, though if Germany fell on France, his people would be 'forced in honour and to save our own existence to do what little we could to stop such an act of piracy'. Germany was out to obtain colonies, 'by bullying if possible— if not, by war'; it was a patent case of 'wolf and lamb'.[12] During the war he returned to the animal imagery in an open letter to Brentano explaining that Englishmen did not hate Germans because 'one does not hate a mad dog or a hungry wolf', but he predicted that after the war the British would not restore Germany's colonies or their trade with the fatherland. How then would Germans survive? he asked: 'you are a great economist. Perhaps you can tell them.'[13]

Harrison's virulent Germanophobia, and the nation's, stemmed in great measure from atrocity stories confirmed early in 1915 by the report of an investigating committee. Headed by Sir James Bryce (as Harrison's old friend had become in 1914), and numbering among its members Sir Edward Clarke, Sir Kenelm Digby, and Frederick Pollock, all lawyers he knew and respected, it could not fail to carry weight with him.[14] And like so many others he was pained by the realization that many of the nation's best young men would be lost in fighting the inhumane foe. His own sons were all beyond normal military age, but almost immediately two were serving. Bernard, in France, joined the Red Cross early in the war to help organize military hospitals. Later he obtained an army commission and served as a censor and translator; and in this capacity in 1917 he produced an English version of a propaganda pamphlet by the French literary scholar Joseph Bédier, *German Atrocities from German Evidence*. René, who had returned from Argentina early in 1914, was commissioned in the Third Leicester Regiment and by his thirty-eighth birthday in April 1915 had been at the front for a month as a lieutenant. Austin remained a civilian and in the *English Review* criticized the meagre allowances given the volunteer army; his own dependents were the main reason he did not enlist. Godfrey, in the family law firm, eventually wore the khaki armband signifying willingness to go if needed.

Late in 1914 Austin had a literary success with *The Kaiser's War*, a collection of his pre-war warnings about Germany with an introduction by his father. And Harrison the following July published a similar collection, *The German Peril: Forecasts 1864–1914, Realities 1915, Hopes 191-*. Though some of his wartime pieces echoed Austin's complaints about government inefficiency and civilian injustices caused by war measures, he more often dealt with abstract issues. He was, after all, further from sources of information and gossip than Austin, and by age, experience, education, and temperament was more prone to feel that events had outstripped his ability to understand them. His commentary on the war resembled that of a Greek chorus which sees the tragic pattern of the drama unfolding but cannot alter it. In place of his ready suggestions and ingenious political plans of a past day, he now usually dwelt on the need to support the nation's leadership and accept the necessary sacrifices. Some of his letters to *The Times* contained passages from Virgil and Livy, which placed the immediate events in a more universal context and somehow for him made them more tolerable. And in the *English Review* he gave his choice of 'The Old Books in Wartime', especially recommending translations of classical texts by old acquaintances like Lord Bowen, W. J. Courthope, and Professor Conington. It was as if he were saying that while men of the older generation had brought the nation to its agony, others of it had provided a means of enduring the travail. But there was no avoiding the painful fact that it was a younger generation that was being decimated. He dedicated the book to 'Our Dead'.

For Harrison the phrase had a terrible personal meaning. On the night of 15 May 1915 René was wounded while leading his company in a large-scale attack on the enemy near Festubert. When word reached Royal Crescent, Harrison acted with characteristic resolution. Unmindful of his eighty-four years, he insisted upon accompanying Godfrey to the base hospital at Boulogne, where René had been taken. Arriving on the 19th they remained at his bedside until he died on Sunday the 23rd. According to Austin his father refused to let the chaplain approach the bed, telling him brusquely that 'if he thought his prayer could help the dead, he could pray outside.' But there was no question of forgoing the traditional ritual of military burial. Harrison and Godfrey, joined by Bernard, followed the coffin by foot up the hill to the Cimetière de l'Est, some four miles, despite inclement weather. Then, while still on French soil for what would be the last time, Harrison informed his Positivist colleagues in Paris of his loss, closing his letter with the litany 'Vive la France, Vive la civilisation des Allies, Vive l'Humanité triomphante.'[15]

Upon his return home, Harrison had Ethel and Olive to comfort and letters of condolence to answer. For advice on how to respond to a telegram from the King and Queen, he consulted Rosebery, whose visit to Bath at the end of May for three weeks provided a welcome diversion. Motoring was still permitted, and Harrison, despite his old fulminations about its offences to quiet country living, enjoyed being driven around the area with Rosebery, exchanging political opinions with one who, like himself, had long been outside political circles and had grown distrustful of the Liberal party. Rosebery, now a widower and in poor health, welcomed Harrison's frank, sometimes alarmingly unrestrained political commentary in an extended correspondence after the visit, which marked a new stage in their friendship.[16] To Rosebery and others Harrison could report that René's superior had written of his great popularity and competence in military affairs and of his gallant leadership of his company, though only a junior officer, on the night he fell. The odds against the British had been overwhelming. A shortage of artillery shells had reduced the effectiveness of their advance bombardment. The Germans floodlit them with flares and raked them with artillery fire from high ground, and replacements were inadequate because of the Germans' recent introduction of poison gas and the diversion of British troops to the Dardanelles. In the end, little ground was gained, and *The Times* could find comfort only in the valour shown by the young officers. 'He did all that a brave man and a competent soldier can do', Harrison said of his son.[17]

Having 'paid his toll in blood', as one friend put it, Harrison was more than ever prone to predictions of doom. In reply to Henry James's 'stammer of sympathy and fidelity' he foresaw ruin for all Europe no matter which side was victorious; America would be left to carry on civilization, 'at least in all things material and practical'. Where the faith to carry on would come from he could no longer say with confidence.[18] In *The Times* he contrasted the suffering he had seen in France to evidences of 'business as usual' at home, and was ready to follow Austin in calling for 'universal discipline for all workers, whether in labour or under arms'. He pointed out that he had always opposed conscription but had called for a thoroughly trained expeditionary force of at least a million men, which, had it existed, he thought might have prevented the war. But he did not say how such an army could have been created without conscription, much less equipped. Nor did he spell out what 'universal discipline' meant in 1915.[19] During his absence in France, Asquith had been forced to form a coalition Government with Lloyd George as the newly-created Minister of Munitions. The cabinet upheaval had been precipitated by the resignation of the Admiral of the Fleet, Lord Fisher, in opposition to Winston Churchill's Dardanelles campaign, and was affected, too, by the disclosure of a serious shortage of shells on the Western Front by *The Times*'s military correspondent, Charles à Court Repington. That alarming report had appeared in *The Times* the day before Harrison left for Boulogne and must have started angry thoughts in his mind: would René have fallen if the British had had sufficient shells? Harrison had every reason to trust the account of his relative by marriage who had commended his call for armaments before the war.[20] Upon his return Harrison did not refer to Repington's inflammatory charge directly, but his own demand for 'universal discipline' was an indirect response, as was his written message in September to the Trades Union Congress meeting in Bristol. He must have called for increased sacrifices from labour, for he told a friend he was thinking 'on the lines of Lloyd George' who, according to *The Times*, had put the TUC into a 'chastened mood' by his 'plain words' about its obligations.[21] As the war went on Harrison became increasingly devoted to the Welsh Wizard because of his willingness to accept personal responsibility in government; he attained for Harrison something of the stature of the Positivist dictator. (Harrison may never have known that his hero's secretary was also his mistress and had first caught his eye while teaching at Allenswood, Mlle Souvestre's school—or, on the credit side, that his own Newton Hall addresses had been read by Lloyd George with interest during his student years at Lincoln's Inn.) The Munition Minister's ability to overcome labour's recalcitrance was attractive to Harrison, who in dark moments regretted having helped the unions to attain their position of strength.

But in Harrison's worst moods no individual's efforts seemed to count: whether England survived or not was a matter of fate, and he felt like a 'fly on the wheel of destiny'.[23] Yet to the family he remained a pillar of strength. In June he took Ethel and Olive to Stroud for the summer. They occupied Rose Cottage, where Mrs Craik, wife of Macmillan's partner, had written the popular novel *John Halifax, Gentleman*, about the kind of early Victorian industriousness Harrison was now urging on the nation for patriotic reasons. Ethel did her part, too; having observed apples rotting on their garden trees she sent *The Times* a Normandy housewife's recipe for drying pippins.[24] While the Harrisons were enjoying this idyllic retreat, *The German Peril* was published, containing, among other bold utterances, Harrison's account of having told a neighbour who had asked at the outset of the war what England should do: 'Send for Kitchener, and make him a dictator!' He now feared that any such public appeal to abrogate traditional political procedures would be viewed as a 'sign of madness'. Yet he did not stay his pen, and the extremity of his opinions would soon cause C. P. Scott of the *Manchester Guardian* to refer to him privately as a 'wild man'.[25]

The debate over conscription in 1916 revealed how enormous was the gap between Harrison and the orthodox Liberals like Scott. 'Perish "Principle" ... and save us by any change in old habits which is necessary for Victory' was Harrison's theme. He termed anyone who defended conscientious objectors on grounds of 'constitutional principles' a 'humbug and a sneak—in plain words, an ass and a traitor'. He was hardly less demanding of those unqualified to serve in the army. Improving upon the Bishop of Oxford's 'happy thought' of linking Lenten abstinence to the war effort, he admonished believers and unbelievers alike to give up all pleasures save those leading to 'increased energy of mind or of muscle—such as forms a more resolute soul, a more enduring patience of pain and loss'.[26] He welcomed the resignation of Asquith and the formation of the War Cabinet under Lloyd George at the end of 1916 because he thought the change promised more efficiency, and he even suggested giving the new Government an electoral mandate, perhaps strengthened by a petition to the King.[27] His support of Lloyd George remained unshaken by Major General

George Frederick Maurice's charge in May 1918 that the Prime Minister had been deceiving Parliament about England's military strength in France. The Commons division on the issue fatally split the Liberal Party, but that no more troubled Harrison than had the division in the Church caused by Maurice's grandfather when he challenged orthodox doctrines of eternal punishment. The Liberal Party in 1918, like the Church sixty years earlier, seemed to him moribund. The previous year he had told Rosebery that he was 'coming to think [of] the G. O. M. legend as a sinister myth, and the G. O. M. lot—especially the L. O. M. (Lesser Old Man) as bad as the crew of Lord North in [the] 18th century'.[28] Accountability to the people was, for Harrison as for Comte, a sufficient check on a strong executive, and he answered complaints about Lloyd George's tyrannous ways by pointing out that an English Prime Minister was ever 'at the mercy of a hostile division'. But this reference to Parliamentary conventions was only a rhetorical strategy. It did not mitigate his frustration at seeing the 'old humdrum Parliamentary machine ... rumbling along, though our men die and food-ships sink'. Past wars, he recalled, had been won only when 'men like Cromwell, Chatham, and Wellington broke away from Parliamentary fetters'.[29]

The stalemate in the trenches was not the only cause of Harrison's unguarded authoritarianism. The 'malevolent neutrality' of the Irish had drained much of his former good will. Home Rule had come to seem a 'pre-war shibboleth'. In the execution of the leaders of the Easter Uprising in 1916 he saw the 'grave of H. H. A. liberalism'—and was unmoved. A proposal for temporary Irish Provincial Councils struck him as promising, and to govern Ireland's national affairs he suggested a triumvirate of John Redmond, head of the Irish Nationalist Party, Sir Edward Carson, Ulster's spokesman, and Lord Dunraven, supposedly impartial on Irish politics. But this was armchair diplomacy; more realistically, and sadly, he asked in response to Redmond's death towards the end of the war, 'Are all Irish reformers to die without seeing the fruition of their hopes?'[30]

Socialism was still another wartime 'curse'. When its leaders in England joined labour officials to congratulate the Russian revolutionaries in the spring of 1917, and there was talk of forming Russian-style workmen's and soldiers' councils in England after the war, Harrison's disenchantment with labour was complete. He approved of the Government's denial of passports to socialist and labour leaders wishing to attend an International Socialist Congress in Stockholm that August. 'Mr Ramsay MacDonald, Mr Sidney Webb have no more right to be taken as representatives of Labour than I have myself', he wrote in he wrote in *The Times*.[31] Convinced that 'passionate groups of revolutionists' were attempting to 'divert the national war of Free Peoples against military Absolutism into a civil war of Labour against Capital', he could have no faith in labour's professed internationalism. At best it was only a 'grand ideal' that would require a spiritual reform which was not yet a practical possibility. In October the new Russian Bolshevik regime confirmed his belief that nothing good could come of 'Democratic Government—when without education, ethic, or religion'. And now the task of providing such enlightenment had become urgent, for the immediate question was how to make the English people aware of their patriotic responsibilities.[32]

The war years tested the relevance of Positivism in spiritual as well as temporal matters. Less than two months after René's death word came to Rose Cottage, Stroud, that Beesly had died at his house in St. Leonard's-on-Sea on 7 July. Just hours before Britain's entry into the war he had written to *The Times* to say that the nation's failure to aid France would be a repetition of the 'blunder of 1870, with less excuse and tenfold shame'.[33] Beesly had probably retained more of his old love of France than had Harrison, but his declining health had precluded further comments on the war. There were two Positivist memorial services in London, the first at Chapel Street—for Beesly had friends among the older members—and another at the South Place Ethical Society held by the Newton Hall remnants. Harrison attended neither, but sent a eulogy to be read at the second. He also contributed accounts of Beesly's life to the *Positivist Review* and the *Wadham College Gazette*, but, curiously, he left unchallenged the strangely misleading obituary in *The Times*. It denied that Beesly had ever adopted Comte's religion, criticized his use of historical evidence, accused him of sharing the antipathies rather than the hopes and beliefs of democratic leaders, and affirmed as 'fact' his descent from the Byzantine Empress Theophano (a bizarre notion perhaps derived from a preposterous genealogical sketch among his papers).[35] Nor was Harrison able to be helpful when Beesly's son Alfred undertook to edit his father's letters for publication. The project fell through, leaving Beesly, the most consistent political radical of the three Wadham friends, without any memorial volume or collection of writings.[35]

Far different was Harrison's response to the most profound break with the past, the death of his wife. Ethel had rejoiced with the family over the birth of a grandchild, Austin's son, born 28 April 1916, and named after René. Then, just days short of the first anniversary of René's mortal wound, she suffered a cerebral embolism. For three weeks she was only intermittently conscious. Bernard obtained emergency leave from France and Austin and Godfrey came from London. Olive was distraught. It was a terrible time for them all.[36] After Ethel's death on 6 June there was the cremation and service at Woking, and on 25 June a memorial service at Chapel Street, a place Harrison had vowed never to visit again. It had become the sole London Positivist centre a few months earlier, when the depleted Newton Hall group gave up its old scruples and rejoined the parent society. Harrison had opposed but did not interfere with the merger, and his presence at Chapel Street for the service did nothing to reconcile him to it. He complained afterwards to Marvin about the term 'Church of Humanity' applied to such a 'dingy hole' and called the music 'excruciating'. Yet he sent copies of the service to friends and took care to list the hymns. Returning with Olive to Rose Cottage, where they had found consolation after René's death, he began compiling a list of Ethel's works for the *Positivist Review*.[37]

By this time Harrison was far from happy with the movement it represented, and the unwanted reunion was only one reason. Under Swinny and Philip Thomas, assisted by Marvin and eventually F. J. Gould, London Positivism was fading into a colourless humanism which, if it did not arouse the same degree of ridicule that once greeted the orthodox teachings at Newton Hall and the old Chapel Street centre, also failed to win followers remotely comparable in number or quality. One change must especially have annoyed Harrison, if he knew of it: the admission of women into the Positivist Society. Meanwhile, Émile Corra in Paris managed to maintain the *Revue Positiviste Internationale* through the war, whereas the rival *Revue Occidentale* ceased at its onset; but he had to resort to reprinting old essays and was careless about sending copies.[38] Organized Positivism on both sides of the Channel no longer greatly interested Harrison, and he believed it could amount to little in the post-war world. But the alliance of England and France during the war, if nothing else, precluded any break with Paris. And in England there was no denying that his colleagues measured up even to his high standards of patriotic sacrifice. Their war dead testified to that. The Styles in Liverpool, Professor Herford in Manchester, Patrick Geddes, Carey Hall, and F. J. Gould all lost a son; Philip Thomas two sons, including the poet Edward Thomas; Thomas Sulman a grandson; and T. S. Lascelles a brother. In families once associated with Positivism, the losses included Gissing's son Walter; a son of Judge Fosset Lock; a brother of Ivy Pretious Tennyson; a grandson of Edward Pember and the Horace Daveys (the Daveys' daughter had married the Pembers' son); and Henry Crompton's son, who with his wife and six children went down with the *Lusitania*.[39]

'MOST UNNECESSARY VITALITY'

For relief from personal grief, the ceaseless war news, and his loneliness at 10 Royal Crescent, Harrison turned to the past. In 1917 he contributed a graceful foreword to *Sketches in Verse*, nostalgic lines on pre-war travel by Lady Davey's daughter, Mrs Richard Strachey, whose home at Ashwick Grove outside Bath had become as familiar to him as her widowed mother's, Blackdown House.[40] The next year he edited sixteen of his Newton Hall addresses originally planned for posthumous publication, pointing out to Macmillan that he might as well see them through the press himself, though by appearing before his death the book, which he titled *On Society*, might lack a 'certain interest' it would gain from that 'imminent event'.[41] In dedicating the work to Ethel he was conscious of emulating Mill's tribute to his wife in *On Liberty*, to which *On Society* was, in Harrison's mind, a rejoinder. But by appearing in the month between the Armistice and the General Election, Harrison's contribution to the ongoing debate at the heart of Mill's text was overshadowed by events. In 1918 he brought together the monthly letters he had published the previous year in the *Fortnightly Review* and called the collection *Obiter Scripta, 1918*. It contained the sort of commentary on people, books, and events that in past times he poured out to Ethel, and which still filled his letters. Leslie Stephen's daughter Virginia observed in her review that he wrote as if talking to someone in the next room, or to a 'world that has ceased to exist', one in which there was agreement on life's 'moral and spiritual purposes'.[42] He still aimed, as often in the past, to settle old scores or puff old friends. Morley's *Recollections*, for example, he called a 'rare combination of high politics and great literature', and then asked Rosebery if he had not done 'the handsome thing—in what I said and in what I did not say?' Alluding to Morley's responsibility, along with the 'whole Gladstonian lot', for failing to perceive the German threat, he told Gosse that they 'ought to be interned as dangerous aliens'. In Dilke's posthumous *Life and Letters* he found a record of industry and judgement that might have helped England in time of need if Dilke had not fallen into a 'moral disaster' and forgotten that public men 'have no *private* life'. *A Writer's Recollections* by Mrs Humphry Ward had too much praise of her Uncle Matt, of the Master of Balliol, and of 'Old Pat'; their work had been more critical than constructive, whereas hers, especially for women, had furthered 'social innovation'. L. P. Jacks was too reverential and gossipy in editing the *Life and Letters* of his father-in-law Stopford Brooke, whose literary judgement was better than his understanding of Comte. Benjamin Kidd's *Science of Power* offered merely 'disguised Positivism' in unpalatable form, but Mallock's *Limits of Pure Democracy* showed the author not altogether hostile to 'a true and nobler Socialism'. James Sully's *Life and Friends* was so 'truthful and vivid' that readers would want to learn more. And *Old Saws and Modern Instances*, by the *Fortnightly*'s editor, Leonard Courtney, though generally excellent, especially on Beerbohm Tree, made some preposterous comparisons, as between Aeschylus and Hardy.[43]

On one of the great issues of the day, a possible League of Nations, Harrison expressed what one critic called the 'arrogance of a judge'. He dismissed proposals for an international peace-keeping organization as altogether premature and wholly unrealistic. The Allied Powers were already such a League, struggling to save civilization. Which nations in the incalculable flux of war would survive to comprise some future world union? Could the present enemies of civilization be any part of it? Would the Allies be likely 'to submit their very existence to the intrigues of a miscellaneous Areopagus of foreigners?' How could power be apportioned? What sanctions could a future League impose? If it had no arms it would be as impotent as the Hague Convention, and to preach peace without force was like preaching 'vegetarianism to a man-eating tiger'. If armed it would require huge budgets. A cycle of imponderable problems daunted the imagination. To one set of problems, however, Harrison had given much theoretical attention years earlier: the sanction and limits of national authority, the conflict of laws among nations, and the issue of viable international law. It was by coincidence that his lectures to the Inns of Court in the late 1870s on these and related themes were republished in 1919. A Toronto law professor, A. H. F. Lefroy, who had been using them in his classes, and was about to publish them with annotations, died before the project could be completed, so Harrison himself saw the book through the Oxford University Press. *On Jurisprudence and the Conflict of Laws* revealed that his Austinian assumptions about sovereignty had a long-term consistency. The search for an independent ethical sanction for a community or nation's exercise of sovereignty was misguided; the right was inherent and traditional. It was a 'fantastic sophism' to argue that some supranational law or world authority could ever be 'imposed by reason of its logical consistency on the various tribunals of Europe'. A balance of power remained the only realistic basis for peace. But Harrison was bound to be suspicious of any international organization for entirely different reasons as well: its backing by pacifists and socialists. They seemed all too willing to let the 'sacred name of Country ... pale before that of Class'. And they had been too willing to settle for less than the 'Knock-Out Blow' and the utter degradation of the enemy after the war. Just before the Armistice, Harrison had revealed an extremity of punitive sentiment in *The Times* by demanding that when victory was won enemy officers should be subject to public humiliation and the major cities of the Central Powers militarily occupied for at least a year.[44]

The Armistice came in time to allow Harrison to close his *Fortnightly* series on a triumphant note which he sought to turn to political advantage. Having already called upon the Government to strengthen its position by obtaining a new mandate, he asked the nation to trust 'the greatest War Minister in our history' to lead the way to 'Peace at home and abroad'. When Lloyd George set the election for mid-December, Harrison made his support plain in a pamphlet entitled *Save the Coalition*. Lloyd George might not be all they wanted, he told Rosebery, but asked, 'whom else have we?' As for the Liberal Party, in *The Times* he asked if it was to 'come back—having forgotten nothing, having learned nothing?', and answered, 'Never! Never again.'[45] But then a surprising circumstance silenced further public pronouncements. Austin Harrison decided to challenge the lion himself in his very den—to stand against the Coalition as an Independent Liberal for Lloyd George's own seat, Caernarvon Boroughs. Like his father's Parliamentary candidacy in 1886 it was a foredoomed gesture arising from principle. One of the earliest and most imaginative promoters of a League of Nations, Austin, like many others, feared that the cause of international peace would not be well served by Lloyd George, who was allowing himself to be identified with such sentiments as 'Hang the Kaiser!' Audaciously Austin took his wife and his agent, the dramatic producer Lewis Casson, who had family connections in Caernarvonshire, to barnstorm the constituency in an open car. Of course, the returns surprised no one: almost 14,000 votes for the famous incumbent, less than 1,100 for Austin. (In Clapham the Positivist Philip Thomas, standing in the Liberal interest, lost to a Conservative; but in contrast, the Positivist John Frederick Green, a supporter of both the Coalition and the League, heavily defeated the Labour member for East Leicester—Ramsay MacDonald.)[46]

Harrison was delighted with the Coalition's landslide victory, which guaranteed that Lloyd George would head Britain's delegation to the Treaty talks at Versailles early in 1919. They at first won Harrison's endorsement as bringing 'peace with justice' and exacting from the defeated 'only a fraction of what stern justice might claim'. Altogether they were a great improvement over 'the ways of Metternich and Bismarck'.[47] But soon the implications for Britain seemed less happy.

He debated the issues in a dialogue set in a London club. 'Pessimist', his spokesman, is a retired colonel, ex-diplomat, and MP—for after Lujo Brentano's shameless chauvinism, Woodrow Wilson's prolonged neutralism, and Gilbert Murray's impractical idealism, Harrison would no longer present himself as a professor. 'Pessimist' fears that politically naïve voters, especially newly enfranchised women, will induce the Government to keep Britain's soldiers at home, thus endangering the Treaty's guarantees to small nations. He is also suspicious of a similarity between Russian revolutionaries and English workers who hope to live in state-paid houses and manage industry. 'Optimist', a north-country industrialist and a Liberal, thinks these notions foolish but cannot counter them.[48] Six months later, in January 1920, Harrison was ready to substitute dogma for dialogue. Resuming his monthly essays in the *Fortnightly*, collected the next year as *Novissima Verba: Last Words, 1920*, he found that Lloyd George was the 'only real statesman' at Versailles; Clemenceau had had to learn that 'soldiers must not override political necessities', and Wilson had risked a renewal of the war by insisting on the Covenant of the League. By February the Treaty had come to seem economically disastrous for Britain since it would require her to reconstruct Europe without American help, and by the end of that month his reading of John Maynard Keynes's *Economic Consequences of the Peace* had convinced him that Germany would sink beneath the financial obligations imposed by the Treaty, bringing all Europe to ruin. Forgetting his own prophecies and threats about what the Germans should expect in defeat, he now called attempts to bar her from international trade 'little more than a grim joke'. To complement Keynes's economic analysis he recommended a political assessment of the Treaty by Charles Sarolea, a Belgian whose journalistic and academic careers in England he had fostered before the war. By 1920 the problems discussed by both writers had become the 'Tragedy of Nations'.[49]

On other post-war issues he proved equally confused and desperate. Reluctant to blame Lloyd George or the Government for disappointments in foreign and domestic politics, he faulted, as so often in the past, the English Constitution. It should be revised to accommodate the requirements of a new era. Among the profound departures he entertained at times was a complete new 'Act of Settlement' that would draw upon the ideas of Bagehot, Bryce, and Dicey, among others, and on the written constitutions of France and America, and perhaps take the form of a republic, with the monarch as the 'Hereditary Chief'. But meanwhile he was deploring to Rosebery the possibility that Parliament as they knew it might be 'swept away like the Tsar and

Duma by strikes, riots and mutiny in the army'.[50] The emergence of the Irish Republican Army made the Irish situation more desperate than ever, and he was equally unsure about any remedies there. When a Dubliner sent him a scheme for Home Rule through devolution, he provided a preface to it and sent it, along with another Irishman's constitutional proposals, to the acting Foreign Secretary, Lord Curzon, asking him to forward both to the Prime Minister. To Rosebery, however, he said that 'the only thing left is to clear out—let the natives murder each other—and if they then touch British interests, conquer the island over again—and start fresh—if it cannot be sunk in the Atlantic.'[51] The stalemate between the IRA and the Royal Irish Constabulary led him to predict—as his former political enemies the Unionists had always done—that a rebellious Ireland meant the break-up of the Empire. The act of Parliament that partitioned Ireland late in 1920 between Ulster and the South did nothing to dispel his apprehensions. Morley, frail and gaunt at the age of eighty-three, supported by his nephew Guy, moved its ratification in the Lords in barely audible tones, pronouncing himself 'sanguine' that Ulster would co-operate. Bryce, also making his last appearance in the Upper Chamber, thought it represented a 'surrender' by the Government but accepted the 'inevitable'. Harrison, on the contrary, termed it only an 'inevitable experiment' and predicted failure, for he thought it would simply exacerbate the prevailing 'spirit of anarchy'.[52]

He saw the same spirit in the working class of England, for he magnified both its socialism and its solidarity. 'Laborare est orare' was his anachronistic Carlylean reply to labour's post-war demands for shorter hours and better pay. His message was made no more congenial to that class by his assertion that the miners little appreciated 'what long hours, wasting capital, and half incomes meant to the middle class and so-called luxurious orders whom their strikes are pinching to the bone'. He urged the wealthy to 'forbear to divert the labour of millions in catering for their idiotic love of frivolities'. Fearing an 'early and violent explosion' on the labour scene, he inquired of friends which investments would be safest if property were confiscated. Having lost £2,000 in ill-fated Mexican mine and railway investments just before the war, he needed to be cautious. But his concern was not exclusively for his own class. 'I TELL YOU STARVATION STARES YOU IN THE FACE', he warned labour in a 'Veteran's Appeal'.[53] In May 1920 he accepted the presidency of a Liberal Anti-Nationalization Committee and opened its conference next door to the National Liberal Club.[54] From his study in Bath flowed a stream of protests against strikes and wage demands. One letter, calling the miners' strike of 1921 'suicidal folly' of

Communist inspiration, provoked the aged H. M. Hyndman to insist that it was not Communism but Social Democracy that was on the horizon for England.[55] What the General Election of November 1922 showed, however, was that the nation was to be governed by a Conservative Party freed of the Liberal members who figured in the Coalition, with the Labour Party acting as the official opposition. A more complete defeat of Harrison's political hopes could hardly have been imagined.

Despite his dismay over the peace, Ireland, and labour, Harrison declined to extrapolate from events any theory of cultural decline. For doing just that, in *Novissima Verba* he taxed two writers whose company he had occasionally enjoyed in recent years, the 'gloomy' Dean Inge of St. Paul's and Thomas Hardy. The 'monotony' of pessimism in Hardy's latest volume of poetry he thought especially unjustifiable in one who had 'everything that man can wish—long and easy life, perfect domestic happiness, warm friends, the highest honour his Sovereign can give [the Order of Merit], the pride of a wide countryside'. Stung by this 'stern pronouncement', Hardy appended an 'Apology' to his next collection, early in 1922: he denied that he had ever tried to 'co-ordinate' a view of life from the 'fugitive impressions' that inspired his verse, and he cited Comte as his authority for believing that the pattern of human advancement might at times be a 'looped orbit', with mankind occasionally 'drawing back for a spring'.[56] Since Harrison, unlike Hardy, did not let his own dark view of the post-war years unduly interfere with his customary pleasures and duties, he had a full budget of news when he wrote to congratulate Hardy on his eighty-second birthday shortly after the 'Apology' appeared but before he had read it. He had been a week in London seeing his sons and grandchildren, including Godfrey's infant son, and meeting with Positivists and other old friends. He hoped Hardy would one day join the band of those like himself who strove 'to be happy and useful at 90'. In reply Hardy said he rather shrank from reaching that age, which Harrison had 'quite coolly done', for Hardy feared he would not be vigorous enough to make it 'worth while'. Thus this last exchange of letters revealed again that difference in temperament which had always underlain their unreconciled world views.[57]

Why Harrison's philosophic optimism survived the war and its aftermath is perhaps explained by a passage in J. B. Bury's *The Idea of Progress*, published in 1920. It placed the belief in progress in the same category as the beliefs in providence and immortality—unprovable and requiring an 'act of faith'. In his *Fortnightly* series, Harrison said the book inevitably raised the issue whether Bury himself believed in progress and was therefore one of the school of optimists (including

Comte) to whom he had dedicated his work. Bury had termed his inquiry 'purely historical', but had also made plain his conviction that the idea of progress possessed a religious force and had helped to reform the ethical code of Western civilization.[58] To Harrison this made the book 'really crypto-Positivist'. He may not have been surprised by its thesis. His correspondence with Bury had turned mostly on Byzantine studies and the Young Turks' alarming proposal to demolish Constantinople's historic walls. But in 1912 Bury, then writing his *History of the Freedom of Thought*, asked if in Harrison's opinion the liberty to speak out on religious issues had increased in England over the past forty years. The book soon showed that he, for one, thought that such progress could be demonstrated and he mentioned Harrison as an 'indefatigable' worker in that cause. But *The Idea of Progress* seven years later contained a view of Positivism that Harrison felt obliged to correct—that it was indifferent to ongoing technological change. Not so, said Harrison, pointing to two figures in the Calendar: Joseph Montgolfier, who pioneered aerial flight, and Charles Wheatstone, who advanced telegraphy (and was the last of the Calendar worthies to survive, a man Harrison had met).[59]

In contemporary thinkers Harrison was just as sure he could detect something of Comte's prescience. Popular accounts of Einstein's theory of relativity led him to observe that Positivists had always rejected absolutes; and Freud's 'mind healing' reminded him of Comte's awareness that physicians failed to recognize the mental element in disease (the corollary of Comte's notion that spiritual leaders should be physicians).[60] The new Hegelianism seemed now in some ways compatible with Positivism: Bosanquet's 'Be a whole, or join a whole' he thought a beautiful though not religious admonition; and he told Lord Haldane that from almost 'opposed philosophic bases' they seemed to 'coincide in the real end in view'.[61] Even the League of Nations came to resemble Comte's 'Republic of the West', a good in itself but as yet only a dream.[62] The full-fledged Positivist system still seemed best. Therefore, when H. G. Wells, in a passing religious phase induced by the war, published *God the Invisible King* in 1919 without rendering unto Comte what was properly his, Harrison responded with another dialogue set in an Oxford college garden. A Dean in Holy Orders and an elderly London barrister greet with equal disapproval, but different reasoning, a junior Fellow's account of his instant conversion in the trenches to the 'Personal and intimate God' of 'our premier novelist'. The Dean points out that since the new religion lacks Bible, Church or moral teaching, no one could know if it made for virtue or vice, and the barrister concludes that what is rational and religious in it—its humanism—is obviously from Comte, 'the Invisible prompter'.[63] It was Harrison's old complaint about Culture as a religion, and formulated with something of his old wit. But the intervening half-century had made a difference: Philip Thomas considered it appropriate to read parts of this *jeu d'esprit* to the Kingston Humanitarian Society, which the Positivists had just accepted as an affiliate, an ecumenical move Harrison would have once repudiated. Even now, when its necessity was apparent, he was still wary of people making off with the honey without entering the hive. Swinny was rather too 'kind to miscellaneous rebels', though he partly redeemed himself by doing the lion's share of work on the second edition of the *New Calendar of Great Men*, published in 1920.[64] H. G. Wells's immensely popular *Outline of History* seemed so 'curiously on the lines of Comte' that Harrison chided him in 1922 for neither acknowledging his Positivist predecessors in general history nor advancing the conception of Humanity. To have done so would risk 'social taboo', Harrison admitted, but 'we have lived through it.'[65]

Since Positivism as he had preached it was clearly not going to be the religion of the future, Harrison did not devote much of his 'most unnecessary vitality' in his last years to fighting its battles.[66] Long mocked for his distinctive views, he now found himself ignored as just another obsolete Victorian. The most famous of the generational critics was the son of his old friend Lady Strachey. But somehow thinking that Lytton's *Eminent Victorians* was a kind of Shavianism, he failed to read it when it first appeared. When its fame persuaded him to obtain a copy, its satire delighted him. And why not, since its subjects were two zealous churchmen, a Bible-crazed imperialist, and an aggressive spinster? Publicly he recommended as a surer guide the sober *Freethinkers of the Nineteenth Century* by Janet Courtney, wife of the *Fortnightly* editor.[67] His own frequent letters to *The Times* usually turned not on religious or philosophic issues of the past but on the details of ordinary Victorian life—cricket, travel, and the men and conventions of the Oxford of his youth.[68]

Now nearly the oldest Fellow of his College, Harrison was indulged at Wadham as a teller of anecdotes, or so Maurice Bowra, who came up in 1919 and eventually became Warden, would recall.[69] To Harrison Oxford had long seemed a backwater, but Paris still had its old interests, and only an injured Achilles' tendon in the summer before his ninetieth birthday prevented him from going there to address the Positivists, meet politicians, and with Bernard, who had resumed his old life in the city, travel on to Switzerland.[70] Almost to the end, London remained accessible. In 1919 he stifled his objections to Chapel Street enough to deliver a farewell address there and that year and the next lectured at the Royal Institution in Albemarle Street on Constantinople and on Comte.[71] Having resigned his Athenaeum and National Liberal Club memberships after moving to Bath, he sometimes stayed with Sir Edward Boyle or with Godfrey, sometimes at a hotel in Albemarle Street convenient to the art exhibitions. One stroll through the National Portrait Gallery led him to inveigh in *The Times* against the practice of putting paintings under glass—some newer ones hardly deserved preservation.[72] London's latest landmark was the Cenotaph in Whitehall by Sir Edwin Lutyens, which starkly memorialized the fallen in a war Harrison had whole-heartedly endorsed—unlike the wars of empire, such as the late father of the architect's wife, Harrison's old antagonist Lord Lytton, had presided over in Afghanistan. Harrison sought to make the monument's meaning explicit with an epitaph, 'We lie dead in many lands so that you may live here in Peace'—which would have been unintelligible to most passers-by because he proposed it be inscribed in Latin or Greek.[73] The memorials and monuments that had always moved him took on ever greater significance. Once, after a service in Westminster Abbey, he mused awhile among the effigies of the mighty dead, where, he later told Rosebery, 'one is in the past—in Heaven.'[74]

SUBJECTIVE IMMORTALITY

Moving more than ever between the present and the past, Harrison still greatly enjoyed life in his 'urbs in rure', as he liked to call Bath, the 'Garden City'. His age kept him from undertaking to write its history, but probably also enhanced some of its features for him. Remembering Ethel's treatments at the Royal Mineral Waters Hospital, he appealed for funds to maintain it after the war, played Beau Nash to friends and acquaintances come to visit (including, in 1919, the enfeebled Morley), and gossiped with elderly local ladies in the Pump Room. His life-long disdain for card-playing was a disadvantage he easily made up for with his endless stories. With the men of Bath he found much more to do. One who welcomed him in 1912 was Sir Francis Younghusband, the Asiatic explorer. He had just published a book of meditations and wanted Harrison's views; he had not read Comte but thought their ideas compatible.[75] In 1916 George Saintsbury came to live at number 1A Royal Crescent, and thereafter Harrison, as he trudged almost daily into town, would see the bearded scholar in his black skullcap in his study window, or meet him for exchange of literary opinion. In 1920 Harrison joined some half-dozen retired clergymen and professors to form a Socratic Society for monthly discussions of philosophic and literary topics. Soon doubled in size, the group included Edward Sonnenschein, a classicist from Birmingham University, and Henry Wace, retired Dean of Canterbury and Chaplain of Lincoln's Inn. Harrison occasionally took the chair and presented a paper on English translations of the classics. When the theme permitted, he held forth on Positivist ideas. Once he brought Bernard and Sir Frederick Macmillan as guests; the paper that afternoon was on 'Modernism in Poetry' and Harrison commented in 'a negative vein'. After tea Bernard discoursed on 'Modernism in Art', assuring the Socratics that cubism was 'largely out'.[76]

Other Bath and Somerset societies found Harrison a willing lecturer, and he cultivated the head of the city library, Reginald Wright, as he once had another Mr Wright, at the London Library. But for most of his needs his own library and memory sufficed. In a Keats centenary volume he rejoiced at the post-war revival of literary pilgrimages; and he chronicled Somerset's literary celebrations. Major anniversaries could not be neglected: he wrote tributes for Dante's sexcentenary, Molière's tercentenary, Smollett's bicentenary, and centenaries of Kingsley and George Eliot.[77] For the latter occasion, in 1919, he lent her letters to him for an exhibition in Coventry but declined to go himself, or to a celebration at Chapel Street.[78] At home he encouraged a local poet, one Henry Chappell, a railway porter at Bath station whom Kipling had met there by chance and advised to 'make the platform speak'. Harrison vetted Chappell's poems, got Austin to publish one, and was repaid by extra attention when settling into the train for the run to London. On his ninetieth birthday Chappell implored him in verse to 'Count midst the voices fraught with accents dear/ The humblest mine, but not the least sincere.'[79]

His was no doubt the humblest on that occasion. Harold Spender, the veteran Liberal journalist, brother to J. A. Spender of the *Westminster Gazette* and a native of Bath, delivered to Harrison a birthday greeting signed by ninety prominent men and women, including the Prime Minister, one for each of his years.[80] A month later he was enrolled as a Freeman of Bath in a splendid public ceremony that began with a procession into the Guildhall to the sound of trumpets in which he and many dignitaries followed officials bearing the city sword and mace. On the platform he pronounced the formula, 'Health, Wealth, and Prosperity to the City of Bath' before sipping from the civic loving cup and passing it to the Mayor, who ended the ceremony with the cry 'God save the King!' A year before, Harrison had declined the King's offer to make him a Companion of Honour, but civic, like academic honours, were different and welcome.[81]

The war had considerably softened Harrison's old animus against the Empire, which he now preferred to call a 'confederation of commonwealths'. But new foreign commitments, such as were implied in the British mandate over Palestine, worried him for the same reason he had always thought colonies a hazard: the nation's forces simply were not strong enough, especially after drastic military cuts in 1921, to police far-flung territories. In any case, the claims for a Jewish state displeased him all the more because promoted by his *bête noire*, Arthur Balfour. In his 1920 *Fortnightly* series Harrison termed the idea a 'Sinn Fein kind of dream', or 'Zangwillism'. Israel Zangwill, having just challenged Austin's alarmist views of Jewish economic and political influence, wrote in the *Fortnightly* to set Austin's father straight on Jewish history. To Harrison this only illustrated 'how vengeful these Jews are!'[82] The French proved vengeful in a more serious way; Harrison bitterly conceded that they preferred the humiliation of Germany 'far more than either peace or commerce—or even indemnities or money'.[83]

The most immediately critical consequence of vengefulness emerged in the prostrate Ottoman Empire. The Allies, outraged by the Turks' alliance with Germany (ironically for Harrison at the behest of some opportunistic Young Turks), by the débâcle at Gallipoli, and by the Armenian massacres, sought to solve the Eastern Question once and for all in 1920 with the Treaty of Sèvres. Its punitive provisions precipitated Mustafa Kemal's militant nationalist revival, war with Greece, and the Smyrna massacres. In a letter to *The Times* in September 1922 Harrison opposed the Treaty, just as he had resisted driving the Turks out of Europe 'bag and baggage' in 1876; deplorable as were their acts, the modern Turks, like the Byzantine Empire of old, had 'unsuspected powers of recuperation' and could be dangerous.[84] Events were indeed bearing him out: a week later, when Kemal's army threatened the British garrison at Chanak on the Dardanelles, Lloyd George made an abortive attempt to back up the Treaty with force. Harrison tried to get Lord Eversley (Shaw–Lefevre), who shared his views, to endorse them publicly; but Eversley, exactly his age, pleaded infirmity.[85] Lord Bryce, who had preceded Harrison as president of the Eastern Questions Association and would have seen the problems of the Treaty, had died earlier in the year. And Blunt, Islam's most outspoken friend, had just been laid to his final rest in his Sussex garden wrapped in his Turkish travelling carpet. Feeling isolated in Bath, Harrison could only watch the downfall of the Coalition Government after Chanak and the growing symptoms of an 'agonizing dilemma' for Britain in the Near East.[86]

At home, changes in public and private life disturbed him. Six million women voted in 1918, marking the final defeat of the cause to which he and Ethel had been so long devoted. Though women's work outside the family during the war set a precedent he deplored, he privately conceded their great contribution to the victory. In his own circle, Olive had made artificial limbs, Muriel Harris had written inspiringly on the war effort, and Ivy Pretious Tennyson had earned an OBE for heading a staff of nine thousand women in the Ministry of Munitions.[87] Another innovation, in the world of letters, posed a new 'terror' for old Victorians like himself: their private letters and conversations were being revealed to the world by memoir writers, journalists, and reviewers. He protested when Matilda Betham-Edwards's posthumous *Mid-Victorian Memories* appeared with excerpts from his letters that made him seem boastful instead of merely lively, which had been his aim, and when Morton Luce quoted invidiously from his conversation in reviewing his books. Worst of all was Sir Algernon West's *Diaries*, published late in 1922, which garbled the truth about Gladstone's associates and undermined confidence in government. As a veteran journalist Harrison hated such distortions and despised the book's 'tittle-tattle'. In what proved to be the last of more than two hundred letters to the editor published by *The Times*, he sought to set the record straight—and added some tittle-tattle of his own.[88]

His correspondence continued to be as frank as ever, and as full of his literary activities. He revised *William the Silent* in 1922, finding no judgement in it he would wish to change; obtained permission for an Indian professor to publish a collection of his essays; and, failing to interest Macmillan in a new collection, got Fisher Unwin to publish it.[89] *De Senectute* began with an essay in his favourite form, the dialogue. Set at Oxford, it makes the Reverend Onesimus Senior, former Rector of Felix-in-the-Weald, announce that the proper choice of books has been the chief solace of his long life. Death holds no terrors for him, and he is content to think that in his small parish he has done as much as he was capable of and more than he had thought possible. Thus in a college garden, the symbolic realm where Christianity and the Religion of Humanity merged in his own life, did Harrison profess the fulfilment of his religious vocation. At the end of the dialogue, his *alter ego* recalls Alfred Rethel's etching, 'Der Tod als Freund', depicting an aged bellringer asleep in his armchair at the close of a radiant day, an open book of psalms beside him, a crucifix above. It is his last sleep, and before him shrouded in the robes of a monk stands Death, come as a friend to toll the bells for him as he had so often done for others.[90]

Harrison's own final peace was attained without loss of his characteristic enjoyments. Austin vividly recalled dining with him at a London club late in 1922,

and after a good meal, in which he drank half a bottle of claret, he strolled out with me on the Embankment, 'to have a look at the weather'. He was full of vigour and enthusiasms, and his voice rang out, like a bell, exactly as I had first heard it when a child.[91]

Early in January Harrison took Sir Frederick Pollock to a meeting of the Socratic Society, leaving with him an impression of 'perpetual youth'.[92] But about this time he began having arm and chest pain, and got his doctor to visit daily. Olive was away for a few days, and on Thursday the 11th Marvin came to spend two nights on his return from a Historical Association meeting in Exeter. Since he hoped to found a chapter in Bath, Harrison introduced him to the mayor, Cedric Chivers, publisher and bookbinder, and agreed to be its first president. He talked animatedly about reading Reinach on the origins of Christianity and an Indian philosopher who failed to appreciate Comte. The next afternoon he visited the family of Harold Spender; and on Saturday morning, Marvin, before leaving, found him sitting up in bed correcting proofs of *De Senectute*. They discussed its contents, and Marvin was impressed by Harrison's undiminished mental power and vivacity; advising Marvin on a personal matter he showed all the old 'confidence in the capacity of his friends'. Alone after that except for the servants, Harrison dispatched eightieth-birthday greetings to Sir William Treloar, a King's College School Old Boy and former Mayor of London, and worked on his proofs. Early on Sunday, 14 January, before he rose, and perhaps while he was still asleep, his heart failed and he received his last, long-awaited visitor, come as a friend.[93]

*

In reviewing the long life, most writers hit upon what particularly interested them. *The Times* mentioned his frequent contributions; the *Manchester Guardian*, his early endorsement of trades unions; T. P. O'Connor, the radical journalist and Father of the House of Commons, his early advocacy of Home Rule and the deference paid him when he appeared in the inner lobby of the Commons just before his ninetieth birthday; Irish papers, his mother's Belfast origins; *Country Life*, his love of Bath; Gould, his work for the Sociological Society. Pollock traced his intellectual 'solidarity' to his legal and historical studies, and Saintsbury thought *The Choice of Books* contained criticism as sound as any he knew. Eversley wrote of their sixty-two-year friendship, but Morley, with nearly as long an association, was now mentally 'hors de combat' according to Augustine Birrell, and, indeed, he survived Harrison by only eight months. Younger writers, Birrell observed, knew 'nothing whatever' of Harrison: 'This is what comes of living to be 90!'[94]

A series of memorial services produced further recapitulations. Swinny presided at the cremation at Golders Green on 19 January in the presence of the family, a few Positivists, and representatives of Oxford University, the London Library, the National Liberal Club, and the City of Bath.[95] The Positivists held their own service at South Place two months later: Swinny spoke on Harrison 'the man', Marvin on his 'public action', Pollock on his historical and legal achievements, and Sir Edward Boyle on his later years. A message was read from Émile Corra in Paris, and one from Lord Haldane, the senior bencher of Lincoln's Inn and author of a recent book on humanism.[96] In Bath the flags were lowered when the death was announced, the Abbey bells tolled, and there was an Abbey service on 23 January.[97] In June an urn containing the mingled ashes of husband and wife was placed in a niche prominent in the ante-chapel of Wadham College. The eloquent Latin inscription beneath, composed by Maurice Bowra and H. T. Wade-Gery, proclaimed Harrison an authority on the law, a man of letters, and an indefatigable champion ('propugnator indefessus') of all that was wisest and best in humanity. F. E. Smith, recently created Earl of Birkenhead, one of the College's most distinguished graduates, lent the dignity of a former Lord Chancellor to the dedication ceremony—though not without a *faux pas*. To the audience, which included Harrison's old friend, Sir Thomas Graham Jackson, who had designed the urn setting, Birkenhead announced, 'We are met today on a solemn and memorable occasion to welcome to their last resting-place the ashes of a very distinguished Englishman, of a very distinguished Oxford man, of a very distinguished Wadham man, the ashes of no less a person that Mr Jackson.' At this, the eighty-seven-year old Jackson looked up perplexed; but the Warden boomed 'Harrison!' and the unruffled Birkenhead corrected himself and went on to depicit Harrison's attainments and the 'loveableness' observed by Birkenhead only a few months before at a College dinner. Gilbert Murray, in the principal address, asked whether Harrison's life had been a failure and declared that it had not, since 'A good life serves always something greater than it knows.' Such an allusion to Humanity, vague as it was, might have gratified Harrison, who had always remonstrated with

Murray for trying to fashion a religion out of the classics. The Warden deemed the memorial appropriate since Harrison had embodied 'the spirit of an Oxford "greats" education'. And finally Godfrey, in unveiling the urn, expressed the family's appreciation that his father's dearest wish had been realized: to have his ashes within the precincts of his University.[98]

There was a fifth and final memorial service in June 1923. In Bath a tablet was unveiled above the door at 10 Royal Crescent, and the principal speaker in the Concert Hall afterwards, at Godfrey's request, was Lord Haldane. Seeking to minimize the differences between Positivism and Christianity, he affirmed Harrison's belief that (in Haldane's words) 'it was only in injustice and face to face with sin that the highest could be reached and the spirit of Christ attained.' When Godfrey wrote to thank him for his remarks a few days later, he noted how odd it was that only in this last ceremony had there been any considered mention of his father's religious convictions. But he said nothing of the ironic fact that Haldane, in language alien to his father, had associated him with a religion he had worked all his life to supplant. Haldane, like most others over the years, had never been much moved by the Religion of Humanity and thought the best he could do for Harrison was to assimilate it into a vaguely aspiring humanism.[99]

None of the many eulogists did justice to the larger pattern of Harrison's life. He had never expressed regrets about having consciously turned aside from the upward path in the law which might have led him to that place of eminence held in his youth by Westbury and in his old age by Birkenhead and Haldane: before leaving Oxford, and before meeting Comte, he had told his father he did not see the 'glory of becoming Lord Chancellor'. Instead, he would devote himself to being a 'witness and narrator' of social evils, with the law only one way of serving that purpose. His many vocations had all, by his standards, furthered morality and enlightenment. Like Comte, he took for himself de Vigny's motto, 'What is a great life? A thought of youth fulfilled in the maturity of age.' In those terms his life had been a success. Though he conceded towards the end that his efforts had been 'far too dispersive', he was not contrite.[100] The institutional aspect of Positivism may have preoccupied him at the expense of more creative use of his education and powers; but without the direction provided by Positivism, that education might have served only a narrow professionalism and those powers only personal ends. Though Positivism imposed constraints on his imagination and promoted dogmatism in his opinions, he proved able to ignore many of its unpalatable features, and his native good will reinforced its altruistic principles. The movement manifestly failed to influence policy or win popularity, and verged on extinction within his lifetime, but his own vital power of happiness shielded him from despair. 'Live for Others' had its foolish side; 'Live Openly' its unrealistic aspect; and 'Humanity' its metaphysical and sentimental dimensions. Yet Harrison's career demonstrates that Comte's formulas, taken together, could prove worthy of a life's devotion.

BIBLIOGRAPHICAL NOTE

Though Frederic Harrison has waited long for a biography, he has not been neglected. In 1926 his son Austin published *Frederic Harrison: Thoughts and Memories*, a vivid impressionistic study which emphasizes temperament rather than thought and does not claim to be a life. The next year F. W. Hirst's two-volume *Early Life and Letters of John Morley* printed both sides of a correspondence which is now in the Harrison Collection at the London School of Economics. Hirst's volumes lie behind Edwin M. Everett's *The Party of Humanity: 'The Fortnightly Review' and Its Contributors, 1865–1874* (1939) and Frances K. Knickerbocker's *Free Minds: John Morley and His Friends* (1943). Within two decades of his death there were three American dissertations on Harrison—Garetta H. Busey, 'The Reflection of Positivism in English Literature to 1880: The Positivism of Frederic Harrison' (U. of Illinois, 1924); Louis C. Zucker, 'Frederic Harrison: Positivist Victorian' (U. of Wisconsin, 1928); and Walter Maneikis, 'Frederic Harrison: Positivist Critic of Society and Literature' (Northwestern U., 1943)—and an MA thesis by Mary Kelly, 'Frederic Harrison: A Study of His Legal and Historical Work and His Service to Trade Unions up to 1870' (Columbia U., 1928). Zucker had interviewed Thomas Spooner Lascelles, a London Positivist, and it was to Lascelles that John Edwin McGee dedicated the first comprehensive study based on interviews and Positivist records, *A Crusade for Humanity: The History of Organized Positivism in England* (1931).

There were few London Positivists still living when I began my research, but I was able to meet Mrs Margaret Lascelles, Frank Ellis, and Donald Fincham. My early work on Harrison coincided with a revival of interest in him, but I completed my dissertation in 1959 without access to two other dissertations from which I subsequently learned much: H. W. McCready's 'Frederic Harrison and the British Working Class Movement, 1860–1875' (Harvard, 1952) and Sydney Eisen's 'Frederic Harrison: The Life and Thought of an English Positivist' (Johns Hopkins, 1957). D. G. Charlton's *Positivist Thought in France during the Second Empire 1852–1870* (1959) and W. M. Simon's *European Positivism in the Nineteenth Century* (1963) helped me to find my way through the tangle of thought often loosely termed 'Positivist', and Simon's 'Comte's Orthodox Disciples: The Rise and Fall of a Cénacle' in *French Historical Studies* iv (1965) clarified Harrison's relations with his French co-religionists. Richmond L. Hawkins's *Auguste Comte and the United States (1816–1853)* (1936) and *Positivism in the United States (1853–1861)* (1938), Geraldine Hancock Forbes's *Positivism in Bengal* (1975), Georg Regozini's *Auguste Comtes 'Religion der Menschheit' und ihre Ausprägung in Brasilien* (1977), and Leopold Zea's *Positivism in Mexico*, translated by J. H. Schulte (1968), depict four Positivist movements in which Harrison showed little interest.

While my research was progressing, the Shaw scholar Warren Sylvester Smith included the Positivists in *The London Heretics, 1870–1914* (1967); a political scientist, James Maurice Murphy, examined their impact in 'Positivism in England: The Reception of Comte's Doctrine, 1840–1870' (Ph.D. diss., Columbia U., 1968); and a sociologist, Susan Budd, analysed their assumptions and strategies in *Varieties of Unbelief: Atheists and Agnostics in English Society 1850–1960* (1977). After my biography was completed, Harry R. Sullivan's volume on Harrison in Twayne's English Authors Series appeared (1983), but in a format incapable of accommodating so versatile and prolific a writer and without reference to any unpublished material. The major manuscript and pamphlet collections on the English Positivists are at the London School of Economics, the British Library, the Bodleian Library, the Harry Cohen Library at the University of Liverpool, and in Le Musée d'Auguste Comte.

To some scholars Harrison's contributions to radical politics have been central. His friends Beatrice and Sidney Webb provided an early account of his efforts on behalf of labour in their *History of Trade Unionism* (1894, 1920). The first book based on the Harrison Collection after its acquisition by the London School of Economics was *Before the Socialists: Studies in Labour and Politics, 1861–1881* (1965) by Royden Harrison (not a relative), who treats Harrison and even more prominently Beesly as 'labour's intellectuals'. Also based on that collection are Paul Adelman's Ph.D. thesis, 'The Social and Political Ideas of Frederic Harrison in Relation to English Thought and Politics, 1855–1886' (U. of London, 1967) and his essay in *History of Political Economy* III (1971). Two useful studies relating the Positivists to other political radicals are Christopher Harvie's *The Lights of Liberalism: University Liberals and the Challenge of Democracy 1860–86* (1976) and Christopher Kent's *'Brains and Numbers': Elitism, Comtism, and Democracy in Mid-Victorian England* (1978). There is a long entry on Harrison by John Saville in Vol. ii of the *Dictionary of Labour Biography*, edited by Saville and J. M. Bellamy (1974), and another by Kent in a forthcoming volume of the *Dictionary of Modern British Radicals*, edited by J. O. Baylen and N. J. Gossman.

Harrison has been less well served by students of Victorian law (apart from trade union law), literary criticism, and historiography. Zucker, Maneikis, and Sullivan discuss his published (but not unpublished) views on literature, and John Gross considers him sympathetically in *The Rise and Fall of the English Man of Letters* (1969). As a historian he is treated judiciously if briefly by Eisen. Of course, many memoirs, biographies, and collections of letters provide glimpses of Harrison, as do modern studies of such contemporaries of his as George Eliot, John Morley, George Gissing, Matthew Arnold, John Ruskin, and Thomas Hardy. There is a very useful bibliographical essay on Harrison by John W. Bicknell in *Victorian Prose: A Guide to Research*, edited for the Modern Language Association of America by David J. DeLaura (1973).

Frederic Harrison's first name is commonly misspelt, with a final 'k'. He should not be confused with four Frederick Harrisons: his father; the actor-manager of the Haymarket Theatre; the medieval historian and Canon of York Minster; or the Victorian railway magnate.

NOTES

(The ampersand in MS letters has been changed to 'and')

Chapter 1. The Early Years 1831–1855

1. On family, see *AM* i, ch. 1 and appendices; EBH, 'Family History', FC.
2. Taylor, *Home Education*, 1st American from 22nd Eng. edn. (New York, 1838).
3. *AM* i, 16; H. Naylor to [FH], n.d. (writing 'after so many years'), HC.
4. *AM* i, 3.
5. *AM* i, 2, 10; see F. W. M. Draper, *Muswell Hill Past and Present* (1936; rpt. Hornsey Public Libraries Committee, 1962).
6. F. J. Harvey Darton, *Children's Books in England: Five Centuries of Social Life* (Cambridge, Eng., 1932), 227–8.
7. *AM* i, 6–7.
8. Ibid.
9. *AM* i, 26–7; *CL* 10–11.
10. *WG*, 4 Nov. 1908, 5a; letter signed 'F.H.' possibly FH, denouncing corporal punishment for children and recalling having his ears boxed by his mother at the age of 16.
11. *AM* ii, 72–6; FH, *The Times*, 5 June 1922, 11e (quoted); Thomas Arthur Nash, *The Life of Richard Lord Westbury …*, 2 vols. (London, 1888).
12. Mr King to Mr Harrison (1835), HC, in *AM* i, 32n; copies of FH's verse, HC, some in *AM* i, 74–5.
13. *AM* i, 32–4, 58–62; Frank Miles, *King's College School: A Register of Pupils in the School under the Headmaster, Dr. J. R. Major, 1831–1866* (London, 1974); Frank Miles and Graeme Cranch, *King's College School: The First 150 Years* (London, 1979).
14. KCS Reports, 114–15; *AM* i, 32–3; *AMB* 24–5; *Samuel Butler, Author of 'Erewhon'. A Memoir*, ed. Henry Festing Jones, 2 vols. (London, 1919), ii, 371–2.
15. (A. H. Kennard) 'Recollections of Lord Chancellor Westbury', *Macmillan's Magazine* xlvii (1833), 469–81.
16. *AM* i, 37–8; FH, 'Sir Charles Cookson', *RI* 402–5, from *PR* xv (1906); *The Times*, 5 Feb. 1906, 10d, 6 Feb. 1906, 9f.
17. *AM* i, 36, 55; FH, 'Canon Liddon', *RI* 397–401, from *PMG* 13 Sept. 1890, quoted in J. O. Johnston, *Life and Letters of Henry Parry Liddon* (London, 1904), 6–7.
18. *RI* 403; cp. *AM* i, 38, 55, mistakenly calling the church St. Andrew's.
19. *CL* 8–9.
20. *AM* i, 44–5 (quoted), 67; *CL* 7–8.
21. *AM* i, 78, holograph copy, FC.

22. Letters to FH, HC, one in *The Letters of Lewis Carroll*, ed. Morton N. Cohen, 2 vols. (Oxford, 1979), i, 507.
23. *AM*, i, 81–3; 'Memorandum of College Expenses' and Mr Harrison to FH (7 Nov. 1849), FC.
24. ESB correspondence with FH, 1852–71, HC; ESB papers, UC; obits. in *Wadham College Gazette* (1915), 382–3 (by FH), *Reynolds's Newspaper*, rpt. *PR* xxiii (1915), 177 (by T. P. O'Connor); see also *AO*.
25. No JHB papers survive, but see M. A. Bridges, ed., *Recollections of John Henry Bridges* (London, 1908), quotations on 58, 71; Susan Liveing, *A Nineteenth-Century Teacher: John Henry Bridges* (London, 1926); *AO*.
26. Canon Barnett to FH, 4 June 1888, HC, about Thorley's portrait for Wadham.
27. *AM* i, 106–7, 116, 121–2 (FH to 'Porthos' (ESB), 20 Sept. 1852); *Recollections of Thomas Graham Jackson, 1835–1924*, ed. Basil H. Jackson (London, 1950), 25.
28. *AM* i, 163–4.
29. Ibid., 114–15, letter to ESB, July (1852), HC.
30. Ibid., 118, letter 20 Sept. 1852, HC.
31. Ibid., 119.
32. Ibid., 122–5, letter dated 'Tues.' (Oct. 1853), HC.
33. Ibid., 95.
34. RC's papers at the Bod. and BL; see esp. autobiographical records, BL, Add. MS 45261; biographical information compiled by wife, Bod. MS Eng. misc. c. 349; 'Richard Congreve', *Encylopaedia Britannica*, 11th edn; obit. *Wadham College Gazette* (1899), 127–9 (by FH, in *AM* i, 85–7).
35. *AM* i, 83–8, 91, 107–9, 113–14.
36. Ibid., 91.
37. Ibid., 92; cp. fragment of letter by FH (1852), FC, about Wall's great reputation.
38. Ibid., i, 88.
39. FH to Mr Harrison, Fri. (1852), FC.
40. *AM* i, 132–9.
41. Ibid., 106, 138 (quoted); *CL* 14 (quoted).
42. *AM* i, 97–105; *CL* 13, 17; J. Wells, *Wadham College* (London, 1898), 180; W. R. Ward, *Victorian Oxford* (London, 1965), 119–22; C. M. Bowra, *Memories, 1898–1939* (London, 1966), 129–30 (on Symons's 'harm to the college, out of which he made nearly £ 200,000').
43. *CL* 16–17; *AM* i, 96–7, 150–1.
44. *AM* i, 94–7; Guiseppi Mazzini, *Life and Writings*, 6 vols. (London, 1891), iv; Harry W. Rudman, *Italian Nationalism and English Letters* (New York, 1940).
45. *AM* i, 121 (letter 20 Sept. 1852); *PCS* xxiv; Michael St. John Packe, *The Life of John Stuart Mill* (New York, 1954), 272; Geoffrey Faber, *Jowett, A Portrait with Background* (London, 1957), 177–83.
46. See Frank E. Manuel, *The Prophets of Paris* (1962; rpt. New York, 1965).
47. Frank E. Manuel, *The New World of Henri Saint-Simon* (Cambridge, Mass., 1962).

48. *The Ideal of a Christian Church* (London, 1844), 46–8; Ward, *Victorian Oxford*, 119–21.

49. *AM* i, 87; *CL* 18–19; *RI* 403–4; obit. *The Academy*, 11 June 1887, 433 (by George Saintsbury).

50. *A Biographical History of Philosophy*, 2nd edn., 4 vols. (London, 1852–3), iv, 245–63; Hock Guan Tjoa, *George Henry Lewes: A Victorian Mind* (Cambridge, Mass., 1977), 12–13; Alice P. Kaminsky, 'George Henry Lewes', *Encyclopedia of Philosophy*, ed. Paul Edwards, 6 vols. (New York, 1967).

51. *AM* i, 87.

52. *Lettres d'Auguste Comte à Richard Congreve* (London, 1899); *Lettres à des positivistes anglais* (London, 1889); 'Retrospective Account by Richard Congreve of his Relations with Auguste Comte', BL, Add. MS 45259, fols. 1–87.

53. Herbert Arthur Morrah, *The Oxford Union, 1823–1923* (London, 1923), 118.

54. *AM* i, 89–90; *MAJ* 30, 40.

55. *AM* i, 91.

56. FH to Mrs Harrison (Apr. 1853), FC; Codrington obit. *The Times*, 13 Sept. 1922, 13f, and FH's comments, 15 Sept. 1922, 13c.

57. FH to Mrs Harrison (Apr. 1853), FC.

58. *AM* i, 92; *The Life and Letters of Benjamin Jowett*, ed. Evelyn Abbott and Lewis Campbell, 2 vols. (London, 1897), i, 184n (Jowett's refusal to serve as examiner if RC was passed over, and RC's refusal to serve).

59. *AM* i, 92; telegram in FC.

60. FH to Mrs A. Austin, 10 May 1912, YUL; *AMB* 63, from 'Poets that I Love', *ER* x (1912), 425–41; cp. FH to Mr Harrison (Dec. 1853), FC, complaining that in his 'selfish cunning' Symons reduced the prize from £10 to £4.

61. *AM* i, 92, 125–6; 2 letters from FH to Mr Harrison (Dec. 1853), FC.

62. *AM* i, 93–4; ii, 106.

63. Mr Harrison to FH, fragment, FC.

64. Charles Harrison to the Earl of Aberdeen, 13 Mar. 1854; Ashby Blair Haslewood to same, 16 Mar. 1854, with note by C. J. London, 18 Mar. 1854; Clinton Dawkins to Charles Harrison, 2 Aug. 1854, all BL, Add. MS 43256, fols. 60–65b.

65. Information from the late R. A. Harrison.

66. FH to Mr Harrison (Nov. 1853), FC, quoted in *AM* i, 128–30.

67. Ibid.

68. FH to Mr Harrison, 2 letters, Sunday and undated (1854), FC; RC to future wife, 18, 20, 21 Mar. 1854, Bod. Eng. lett. c. 181, fols. 85–6.

69. Mr Harrison to FH, 20 Mar. 1854, FC, reporting Bethell's comments.

70. FH to Mrs Harrison (envelope dated 25 Apr. 1854), FC; *AM* i, 93–5; 'Memorandum of College Expenses', FC.

71. FH to Mr Harrison, Friday (1852), FC.

72. *AM* i, 95.

73. Ibid., 93; Sir Henry Steward Cunningham, *Lord Bowen: A Biographical Sketch, with a Selection from his Verses* (London, 1897), 46–7, cited by FH, *The Times*, 4 Oct. 1920, 13d; Charles Henry Pearson, *Memorials by Himself, His Wife, and His Friends*, ed. William Stebbing (London, 1900), 72–7; Arthur D. Elliott, *The Life of George Joachim Goschen, First Viscount Goschen, 1831–1907*, 2 vols. (London, 1911), i, 24.

74. Minutes of the Oxford Union Society, viii, 27 Feb., 20 Mar., and 30 Jan. 1854, 21 May 1855; Morrah, *The Oxford Union*, 171.

75. Minutes of the Oxford Union Society, viii, 14 Nov. and 5 Dec. 1853 (ESB) and 20 Feb. 1854 (FH).

76. ESB, 'Sir Godfrey Lushington', *PR* xv (1907), 70–1; obit. *The Times*, 6 Feb. 1907, 9f; Thomas W. Jex-Blake, 'Rugby Memories of Three Eminent Rugbeians', *National Review* xlix (1907), 232–6; *DNB*; *AO*; 'In Memoriam: Vernon Lushington', *PR* xx (1912), 65–6 and FH, memorial address, 92–4.

77. FH to ESB (1854), HC; Ward, *Victorian Oxford*, 186–7.

78. *AM* i, 98 (quoted); *CL* 19; *MT* 14.

79. *AM* ii, 253.

80. *AM* i, 99; cp. Sir Thomas Erskine Perry, 'A Morning with Auguste Comte', *NC* ii (Nov. 1877), 621–31.

Chapter 2. Neo-Positivism 1855–1861

1. FH, fragment, HC.

2. FH, fragment and letter to ESB (1856), HC, part in *AM* i, 170–2.

3. *AM* i, 149, 155; (Frederick Harrison), 'Memorandum of College Expenses', FC.

4. *AM* i, 152, 157–8, ii, 76–7; 'Maine's *Ancient Law* Revised', *MT* 110–14; 'Memorandum of College Expenses', FC, recording payment of £52-10-0 in 1857 to 'Mr Baine, Barrister, to read with him', name corrected to 'Maine'; George Feaver, *From Status to Contract, a Biography of Sir Henry Maine, 1822–1888* (London, 1969), ch. 3.

5. *AM* i, 152, 157–8, ii, 77.

6. Ibid., i, 152.

7. FH to ESB (1858), HC.

8. FH to Mr Harrison (16 Dec. 1857), Fri. night (18 Dec. 1857), FC; *Records of the Honourable Society of Lincoln's Inn, Vol. II, Admissions from 1800–1893* ... (London, 1896), entry 26 Jan. 1858; *AM* i, 152–3.

9. *AM* ii, 253–5; *CL* 21–2. Liveing, a friend of JHB, became Registrar of the Royal College of Physicians, and his brother George a distinguished chemist.

10. *Polity*, i, 550–7; vocations corresponded to these faculties: active=soldiers, industrialists; speculative=priests, scientists, philosophers; affective=workers.

11. Ibid., i, 498, 509; *AM* ii, 255, 112 (about meeting Darwin and observing his 'extraordinary nervous delicacy').

12. FH to ESB, 29 Aug. (1865, but marked '1866'), HC.

13. *CL* 22.

14. FH to JM, Monday (7 Mar. 1871), HC.

15. FH to ESB, Sun. Wadham (1854), HC; *Some Recollections of John Henry Bridges*, 77; Liveing, *A Nineteenth-Century Teacher*, 58.

16. *AM* i, 167–8; FH in *Some Recollections of John Henry Bridges*, 77–9; JHB in *Oxford Essays*, iii (Oxford, 1857).

17. BL, Add. MS 45259, fols. 25–6.

18. FH to ESB, Fri. (1857), HC.

19. FH to ESB (1856), HC, in *AM* i, 168–9.

20. FH to ESB (1856), HC; (vl), 'Carlyle', *The Oxford and Cambridge Magazine* ... (London, 1856), 193–211, 292–310, 336–52, 697–712, 743–7; see also (vl), 'Two Pictures', 479–88.

21. (FH), 'A Dream of the Past, Sir Isumbras', FC.

22. 'Dates in the Life of Richard Congreve', BL, Add. MS 45261.

23. FH to ESB (1856), HC.

24. RC to Miss Bury, 11 Mar. 1854, Bod. MS Eng. lett. c. 181, fol. 85, about FH and Thorley thinking it an honour to 'put right' his MS.

25. FH to ESB, Monday, marked 'Gibraltar' (1856), HC; RC, '*Gibraltar*, rpt. in *EPSR* i.

26. FH to ESB (1858), HC, part in *AM* i, 181; *India*, rpt. in *EPSR* i.

27. FH to ESB (1858), HC.

28. *Saturday Review* v (29 May 1858), 563–4.

29. Mrs Harrison to FH, Wed. (1857), FC, saying 'a mother's love supplies the place of the higher mental and better cultivated powers of your sex.'

30. FH to ESB (1858), HC; *AM* i, 282–3, from a diary that has not survived.

31. FH to ESB (1857), HC, in *AM* i, 183–4; FH to Mrs Harrison, (1856), FC, part in *AM* i, 142–3.

32. FH to Mrs Harrison (1857), FC, part in *AM* i, 142–7, with changes.

33. *AM* i, 158–9.

34. FH to ESB, 2 June, n.y., HC.

35. FH to ESB, undated letters, HC; *AM* i, 265, ii, 30; 'Early Documents Relating to the Formation and Activities of the College 1854–1880', no. 12, Working Men's College Archives; J. F. C. Harrison, *A History of the Working Men's College 1854–1954* (London, 1954); F. J. Furnivall, 'Social Life of the College', *The Working Men's College*, ed. Revd J. L. Davies (London, 1904), 58–9.

36. FH to ESB (1860), HC.

37. FH to Maurice, undated, Working Men's College Correspondence, AE 198b, 198c, Working Men's College Archives; *AM* i, 151, 159; *CL* 46.

38. Maurice to FH, 24 Dec. (1860), HC; Maurice to Furnivall, 11 and 16 Aug. 1858, FU 574, 576, 29 Oct. 1858, FU 578, 14 June (1859), FU 582, 28 Feb. (1859), FU 579; 'Copy for Rejected Programme, F.J. Furnivall', FU 298, all HEH.

39. FH to ESB, undated, HC, part in *AM* i, 177–80.

40. *Polity*, iii, 51–4.

41. Letters of intro. from Campanella and Saffi, (1855), HC; FH, 'Poets That I Love', *AMB*, ch. 3, from *ER* x (1912).

42. Harold Spender, 'Frederic Harrison', *The Reader*, 26 Jan. 1907, 357.
43. FH to ESB (1859), HC; *AM* i, 186–7.
44. FH to ESB, 3 letters (1859), HC, part in *AM* i, 187–8; see Bright to Congreve, 12 Nov. 1858, BL, Add. MS 45241, fols. 13–14, saying people expected too much of him.
45. *AM* i, 188–9.
46. Ibid., 190.
47. *Daily News*, 10 June 1859, letter signed 'E.S.B.'.
48. Ibid., 18 July 1859, letter signed 'F.H.'; FH to ESB (20 July 1859), HC, in *AM* i, 192–5.
49. *England and the Italian Question*, rpt. Arnold, *CPW* i, 90–1; F. W. Newman, *Reminiscences of Two Exiles* ... (London, 1888), 125; Denis Mack Smith, *Victor Emanuel, Cavour, and the Risorgimento* (London, 1971), 102–5.
50. *AM* i, 195–7; Count Francis Pulszky to FH, 8 Aug. 1859, HC.
51. *AM* i, 192–200; *AMB* 47; *NSP* 116–17; Spender, *The Reader*, 26 Jan. 1907, 357; letters of intro., including one from Baron Poerio, HC.
52. *AM* i, 197–201, with excerpts from letters signed 'H' in *Daily News*, 30 Sept. and 10 Oct. 1859; see also letters 'from our special correspondent', probably FH, 5, 7, 8, 11, 14, 17, 18, 19 Oct. 1859 and in *Morning Post*, 11 and 18 Oct. 1859.
53. *Daily News*, 20, 24, 26, Oct. 1859, signed 'Liber'; 21 Oct. 1859, editorial.
54. 'Cavour and Garibaldi', *NSP* 116–62, from *WR* lxxv (1861); FH to Mrs Hadwen (19 June 1860), HC.
55. *AM* i, 201–12; FH to Mrs Hadwen, 29 Jan. 1861, HC.
56. FH to ESB, 3 Sept. (1862), HC.
57. Ibid.
58. *AM* i, 206; *Recollections of John Henry Bridges*, 79–80.
59. Gordon S. Haight, *George Eliot and John Chapman, with Chapman's Diaries*, 2nd edn. (Hamden, Conn., 1969).
60. Reviewed in *WR* liv (1851), 353–68, by George Eliot, sub-editor.
61. Ibid., lxix (1858), 305–24; Chapman's part of the review, 324–50, was more critical; RC to JHB, 6 Oct. 1858, Bod. MS Eng. lett. c. 185, fols. 4–12 (copy), naming also JHB.
62. *Diary, Reminiscences, and Correspondence of Henry Crabb Robinson*, 2nd edn., 3 vols. (London, 1869), iii, 480.
63. FH to ESB, 2 undated letters (1859) and letter marked 4:30 p.m. (1860), HC; University Hall Minute Books, v, 202–3; Negley Harte and John North, *The World of University College London 1828–1978* (London, 1978), 60, noting that F. W. Newman and A. H. Clough had preceded ESB in the post.
64. Lieving, *A Nineteenth-Century Teacher*, 66–8 (quoted); *Recollections of John Henry Bridges*, 80–1.
65. FH to ESB, 3 letters, Fri., Wed., and undated (1860), HC; *Polity*, iv, 481; Thomas à Kempis, *The Imitation of Christ*, iii, ch. 5, verse 82.
66. *ESPS* i, 278–303; BL, Add. MS 45261, 19 Jan. 1858 ('first sermon as Positivist apostle in London').

67. RC to wife (6 Nov. 1858), Bod. Eng. lett. e. 51, fols. 303–4, calling FH 'very good company'.

68. *WR* lxxiv (1860), 225–8; see my 'More Light on *Essays and Reviews*: The Role of Frederic Harrison', *Victorian Periodicals Review* xii (1979), 105–16.

69. *AM* i, 205–6; *CL* 26–8.

70. FH to ESB, 7 Aug. 1860, HC; *AM* i, 208.

71. *AM* i, 208.

72. *CL* 92–151, rpt. essay from *WR* lxxiv (1860).

73. *AM* i, 207–9, 219–28, part from letters in FC.

74. Huxley to Chapman, 18 Oct. 1860 and John Tyndall to Chapman, Tues. (1860), HC; 'Memorandum as to Herbert Spencer by Frederic Harrison', Herbert Spencer MS 791/355/9, ULL.

75. *Quarterly Review* cix (1861), 248–305.

76. *Edinburgh Review* cxiii (1861), 461–500, quotation 464; *AM* ii, 100, calling the article 'bitter', and FH to ESB, Wed. (1861), HC, calling it 'vicious'.

77. *The Life and Correspondence of A. P. Stanley*, ed. Rowland E. Prothero, 3rd edn., 2 vols. (London, 1894), ii, 41; *Essays Chiefly on Questions of Church and State from 1850–1870* (London, 1870), 50, n.

78. *AM* i, 206–8 (diary); *CL* 28, 33; FH to ESB (1860), HC, calling the essay 'certainly not exactly what I should make it if I wrote it again'; Haight, *George Eliot and John Chapman*, 250, Chapman's diary, 19 Aug. 1860, on his visit and decision to let FH's 'excellent' essay 'stand as no. 1'.

79. (Stanley) to FH, 7 May 1861, HC, signature missing.

80. Jowett to FH, 23 Apr. 1861, HC, part in *Letters of Benjamin Jowett*, ed. Evelyn Abbott and Lewis Campbell (London, 1899), 14–15; in *AM* i, 207, FH says Campbell's book tells the 'story ... fairly (but not exactly)'.

81. Jowett to FH, 30 Apr. 1861, HC, part in *Letters of Benjamin Jowett*, 15–16; for harsher words on Positivism see *The Life and Letters of Benjamin Jowett*, i, 261.

82. *AM* i, 207 (quoted); *CL* 29–30.

83. Ibid., 208–9.

84. *CL* 29; FH to (Mrs Hadwen), Thurs. 9 Jan. 1861 (error for 1862) (quoted), HC; Faber, *Jowett*, 282, 339–42.

85. Hon. Stephen Lushington, *The Foundation Stone: A Hymn* (Newcastle-upon-Tyne, 1850); F. S. Wiswall, *The Development of Admiralty Jurisdiction and Practice Since 1800* (Cambridge, Eng., 1970), 32–73; obit. in *The Times*, 21 Jan. 1873, 9f; *DNB*.

86. Geoffrey Rowell, *Hell and the Victorians* (Oxford 1974), 118–19, on Dr Lushington's unhappiness over the judgement.

87. *AM* i, 355–6, citing letter to Miss Shore, 25 Feb. 1864, FC; copy of epitaph in FH's hand, marked 'by E.H.P. and F.H.', HC.

88. Owen Chadwick, *The Victorian Church*, Part II (London, 1970), 83–4; Standish Meacham, *Lord Bishop: The Life of Samuel Wilberforce 1805–1873* (Cambridge, Mass., 1970), 248–51.

89. Nash, *The Life of Richard Lord Westbury*, i, 82; *CL* 30–1.

90. *AM* i, 211–18, citing letter JHB to FH, 12 Dec. 1860, and FH to Mrs Hadwen, 10 Mar. 1861, HC.

91. Ibid., 208, 260–1; FH to Mrs Hadwen, 29 Oct. (1860); 29 Sept. (1861), 14 Nov. (1862), HC; *CL* 25.

92. J. M. Ludlow, *Tracts for Priests and People, no. 7: Two Lay Dialogues* (London, 1861); for RC's objections see *EPSR* i, 258–61; F. D. Maurice, *The Mote and the Beam: A Clergyman's Lessons from the Present Panic* (Cambridge, 1861).

93. *The Life of Frederick Denison Maurice Chiefly Told in his Own Letters* ed. Frederick Maurice, 2 vols. (New York, 1884), ii, 59 (on Comte), 380 (letter to Hughes, 3 Jan. 1861 noting 'with much satisfaction' the absence of FH's name on the new programme); Maurice to FH, 27 Feb. (1861), HC.

94. FH to ESB (1860), and to Mrs Hadwen, 10 Dec. 1861, HC; *AM* i, 255, 265–6.

95. *AM* i, 267–8; G. J. Holyoake, *Sixty Years of an Agitator's Life*, 2 vols. in one (London, 1906), ii, 63–8; 290–4; Lee E. Grugel, *George Jacob Holyoake: A Study in the Evolution of a Victorian Radical* (Philadelphia, 1976), ch. 4; Holyoake to FH, 25 Nov. 1905, HC.

96. *The Meaning of History* (London, 1862), rpt, *MH* with changes.

97. *The Speedy Extinction of Evil and Misery, Selected Prose of James Thomson*, ed. William David Schaefer (Berkeley, 1976), 235–6, article 3 Jan. 1863; FH's green account book, FC; FH to Holyoake, Thurs., 9 Feb. (1863), Co-operative Union, Manchester (acknowledging another review, in the *Secularist World*, 'more than such a trifle deserves').

98. FH to Mrs Hadwen, Wed. (Apr. 1862) and 24 Mar. (1863), HC, in *AM* i, 267–9.

99. *The Reader*, reviews signed 'F.H.', 17 Jan. 1863, 63–4, of *The Life and Times of St. Bernard, Abbot of Clairvaux* (London, 1863) and 28 Mar. 1863, 303–4, of H. Castille, *Histoire de la Revolution* (Paris, 1863).

100. FH, *In Memoriam, James Cotter Morison* (London, 1888); *Lincoln's Inn Admission Register 1420–1893*, Vol. ii, entry 23 Dec. 1857; see anon., *A Biographical Sketch of James Morison: The Hygeist ...* (London, 1873).

101. *The Reader*, 22 July 1865, 88–9.

102. 'Maine on Ancient Law', *WR* lxxv (1861), 457–77; *MT* 111.

103. Feaver, *From Status to Contract*, 44.

104. Goldwin Smith, *Lectures on the Study of History delivered in Oxford, 1859–61* (Oxford, 1861) and *Oxford Essays*, ii (Oxford, 1856), 295–311, his criticism of RC's lectures, *The Roman Empire of the West*.

105. 'The Limits of Exact Science as Applied to History', lecture 12 Nov. 1860, in *The Roman and the Teuton* (London, 1901), 307–43.

106. See Duncan Forbes, *The Liberal Anglican Idea of History* (Cambridge, Eng., 1952).

107. 'Mr Kingsley on the Study of History', *WR* lxxv (1861), 305–36; FH to ESB, 2 Sept. and Tues. (1861), HC.

108. 'Mr Goldwin Smith, *The Study of History*', *WR* lxxvi (1861), 293–334.

109. FH to ESB, 2 Sept. (1861), HC.

110. *Daily News*, 16 Oct. 1861.

111. Ibid., 28 Oct. 1861; see also Smith's letters, 29 Oct. and 20 Nov. 1861; cp. *AM* i, 262–5, implying he had not answered Smith.

112. FH to Mrs Hadwen, 30 Oct. 1861, HC, in *AM* i, 264–5; Chapman to FH, 22 Oct. 1861, HC, urging him to write.
113. FH to Mrs Hadwen, 30 Oct. 1861, 2 Feb. (1862), and to ESB (1861), HC.
114. *AM* i, 281–2, undated diary entry.

Chapter 3. Alliances with the Working Class 1861–1870

1. *AM* i, 247–8, 254–5; *The Working Men's College Magazine* ii (1860), 24–8, 48–52; FH to Mrs Hadwen, 29 Oct. (1860), HC.
2. RC *EPSR* i, 108–10; *Polity*, iv, 365.
3. *AM* i, 250–4; *The Times*, 15 July 1861, 6f, 22 July 1861, 10b; in *Spectator* and *Daily News* on same date; R. W. Postgate, *The Builders' History* (London, 1923); Sidney and Beatrice Webb, *The History of Trade Unionism*, rev. edn. (London, 1920), 245–6; *Dictionary of Labour Biography*, ed. Joyce Bellamy and John Saville, 2+ vols. (London, 1972–) (hereafter cited as *DLB*), entries on W. R. Cremer, George Howell, J. M. Ludlow, T. H. Hughes, FH.
4. FH to ESB, 11 July, Mon., and undated (1861), and to Mrs Hadwen, 23 July, 2 Aug. and (3 Sept.) 1861, HC; FH to Chapman, 1 Aug. (1861) and Mill to Chapman, 4 Aug. 1861, YUL; *AM* i, 251, ii, 217; *Daily News*, 1 and 5 Aug. 1861.
5. FH to Mrs Hadwen, 23 July (1861, marked '1862'), HC, in *AM* i, 254; *Spectator*, 13 Apr. 1861, 387–8.
6. FH, 'The Strike of the Stonemasons in London, 1861–1862', *Trans. NAPSS, London Meeting, 1862* (1863), 710–22; FH to Mrs Hadwen, 2 letters (1862), HC; *Polity*, iv, 56; F. M. Leventhal, *Respectable Radical: George Howell and Victorian Working-Class Politics* (Cambridge, Mass., 1971), 27–32.
7. *AM* i, 251; Webb, *History of Trade Unionism*, ch. 5; Philip S. Bagwell, *Industrial Relations* (London, 1974), 21–6, on more recent scholarship.
8. FH to Mrs Hadwen (30 Oct. 1861), HC; *AM* i, 255–60; FH, *In Memory of William D. Hertz, born June 16, 1825, died ... February 16, 1890* (London, 1890); *PR* xvi (1908), 115–20; Fanny Hertz, 'Mechanics Institutes for Working Women ...', *NAPSS, 1859* (1860), 347–54.
9. *Letters of Mrs Gaskell*, ed. J. A. V. Chapple and Arthur Pollard (Manchester, 1966), 680–82; *AM* i, 257.
10. Holyoake to FH, 31 Mar. 1863 and FH's MS diary of trip, HC; FH to Holyoake, undated and 13 Apr. (1863), Co-operative Union, Manchester; *AM* i, 275–8; H. W. McCready, 'The Cotton Famine in Lancashire, 1863', *Trans. Hist. Society of Lancashire and Cheshire*, cvi (1954), 127–33.
11. FH, 'The Political Action of Working Men', *BH*, 30 Jan. 1864; see Royden Harrison, *Before the Socialists: Studies in Labour and Politics 1861 to 1881* (London, 1965), ch. 2; E. D. Adams, *Great Britain and the American Civil War* (New York, 1925), 290–5.
12. *The Times*, 23 Apr. 1863, 7ef, 27 Apr. 1863, 5de.

13. 'Lancashire', *WR* lxxx (1863), 191–219; FH to Mrs Hadwen, 27 Apr. (1863), HC; *AM* i, 277–8; JHB in *The Times*, 14 Mar. 1863, 14b, 20 Mar. 1863, 5ef; Liveing, *A Nineteenth-Century Teacher*, 95–103; *Polity*, iv, 275, 332, 406, 415; Mary Ellison, *Support for Secession: Lancashire and the American Civil War* (Chicago, 1973).

14. FH to ESB, Thurs. (1861), Wed. (1861), 19 Jan. (1864), Wed. (4 May 1864), and FH to Mrs Hadwen, 26 Nov. (1863, marked '1864'), HC; FH, 'The *Bee-Hive*', *Bee-Hive*, 16 Jan. 1864; see Stephen Coltham, 'The *Bee-Hive* Newspaper; its Origin and Early Struggles', *Essays in Labour History in Memory of G. D. H. Cole*, ed. Asa Briggs and John Saville (London, 1967), 174–204.

15. *Bee-Hive*, 13 May, 24 June 1865. The arbiters, who included Beales, Hughes, and GL, decided against probing into the paper's war policy.

16. FH, 'The Iron-Masters' Trade Union', *FR* i (1865), 96–116.

17. *Bee-Hive*, 9, 16, 30 Jan. and 6 Feb. 1864; 3 and 10 Nov. 1866; FH to ESB, Tues., 15 Jan. (1865), HC.

18. FH to ESB, 8 Dec. (1865), HC.

19. FH to ESB (1855), HC; *Leader*, 3 Apr. to 14 Aug. 1852 (on Comte) and 14 Apr., 8 May, 3 July, 31 July 1852 (on Comte subsidy).

20. *AM* i, 204; *MT* 135–6.

21. Gordon S. Haight, *George Eliot* (Oxford, 1968), 298–300; RC to wife, 14 Mar. 1859, Bod. Eng. lett. e. 51, fols. 307–8.

22. JHB to GE, 11 Sept. (1859), *GEL*, viii, 243–4; Haight, *George Eliot* 269–70, 283–5.

23. FH to ESB (1865), HC; see also letter 'Tues' (1865), calling ESB's 'Catiline as a Party Leader', *FR* i (1865), 167–84, an 'immensely funny jibe' at received historical opinion.

24. FH to ESB, Tues. (1865) (about refusing to alter his essay 'to please triflers'), Thurs. and (May 1865), HC.; *Bee-Hive*, 20 May 1865 (objecting to the essay's brevity); *GEL* iv, 192 (George Eliot's hope that the disadvantage of the small type would be overcome by the subject's 'importance' and the 'excellence' of its treatment).

25. 'The Limits of Political Economy', *FR* i (1865), in *NSP* 272–306; on Smith, see *NSP* 274, 301; *AM* i, 271–3; and 'The Iron-Masters' Trade Union', *FR* i (1865), 96.

26. *NSP* 273–4, 287–90, 297–8, 301; Mill's *Auguste Comte and Positivism* appeared first in *WR* lxxxiii and lxxxiv (1865), 339–405, 1–42; FH to ESB (May 1865), HC, calling his own essay a reply, and to Mrs Hadwen, n.d. HC, praising JHB's reply, *The Unity of Comte's Life and Doctrine* (London, 1866).

27. *NSP* 271; cp. *AM* i, 230, acknowledging the influence of Ruskin, Carlyle, and the Christian Socialists.

28. (Ruskin) to Furnivall and (Ruskin) to FH, n.d., HC; *AM* i, 230, dating the first visit late 1860 and 204–5 dating it 'Sun. 22 Dec.', which makes it 1861.

29. *AM* i, 231–2, quoting letters in HC; see FH, *JR* 94; *The Works of John Ruskin*, ed. E.T. Cook and A. Wedderburn, 39 vols. (London, 1903–12), 551–2 (hereafter '*Works*').

30. William R. Hopper, 'An Iron-Master's View of Strikes', *FR* i (1865), 742–56; FH, 'The Good and Evil of Trade Unions', *FR* iii (1865), 33–54, part in *NSP* 307–32.

31. Ruskin to FH (12 Dec. 1865), HC, part in *AM* i, 233.

32. 'Industrial Co-operation', *FR* iii (1866), 477–503, in *NSP* 333–76, and see FH in *Bee-Hive*, 23 May 1868, 12 Oct., 9 Nov. 1872.

33. *GEL* iv, 214–15 (5 Jan. 1866) and 176–7 (saying Comte's house was one of the most interesting sights she had seen in Paris); Lewes, 'Auguste Comte', *FR* iii (1866), 385–410; FH to ESB, 4 Jan. (1866), HC (quoted).

34. FH to GE (11 Jan. 1866), *GEL* iv, 216–19, see also 215, n.7; *MT* 137–9; Fred C. Thomson, 'The Legal Plot in *Felix Holt*', *SEL* vii (1967), 691–704.

35. FH to GE, 27, 29, 30 Jan. (1866) and GE to FH, 31 Jan. 1866, *GEL* iv, 222–32.

36. FH to GE, 19 July (1866), *GEL* iv, 284–9; W. F. T. Myers, 'Politics and Personality in *Felix Holt*', *Renaissance and Modern Studies* x (1966), 5–33, treats Holt as a Positivist; no one has noted the contrast between her hero's high-minded rejection of an inheritance from patent medicine and Cotter Morison's acceptance of a similar bequest.

37. FH to GE, 5 Feb. (1867), *GEL* iv, 342–3; 'A Mouldy Conveyancer' (Alfred Bailey), in *PMG*, 11 Feb. 1867, identified by FH in 'Reminiscences of George Eliot', *Harper's Magazine* ciii (1901), 579 n., not in reprinted essay, *MT* 134–49.

38. FH to GE, 1 June (1866), *GEL* iv, 265.

39. FH to GE, 19 July (1866), *GEL* iv, 284–9 (quoted); on *Deronda*, see 100, 105, 110–11, 126, 147–53; *MT* 139–40.

40. *Polity*, i, 227, iv, 266; GE to FH, 15 Aug. (1866), iv, 300–2.

41. FH to GE, 11 Nov. (1868), *GEL* iv, 483–5; *MT* 141.

42. FH to EBS (May 1868), H.C.

43. 'George Eliot', *PR* x (1902), 160.

44. FH to GE, 25 May (1868) and GE to FH, 25 May (1868), *GEL* iv, 448.

45. Stephen, 'Trade Unions', 'Masters and Men', *PMG*, 21 Nov. and 8 Dec. 1865; FH's letters, 7 and 12 Dec. 1865; Leslie Stephen, *The Life of Sir James Fitzjames Stephen* (New York, 1895), 213.

46. FH to ESB (11 Jan. 1868), HC, about 'Stray Chapters from a Forthcoming Work on Labour, ...' *FR* ix (1868), 77–88; see also Thornton on FH, 'What Determines the Price of Labour or Rate of Wages?' *FR* vii (May 1867), 565–6.

47. Cairnes, 'M. Comte and Political Economy', *FR* xiii (May, 1870), 579–602; FH, 'Professor Cairnes on M. Comte and Political Economy', xiv (July, 1870), 39–58; Cairnes, 'A Note', (Aug., 1870), 246–8; see Robert B. Ekelund, Jr. and Emilie S. Olsen, 'Comte, Mill, and Cairnes: the Positivist-Empiricist Interlude in Late Classical Economics', *Journal of Economic Issues* vii (1973), 383–416.

48. FH to ESB, Thurs. (23 Jan. 1868) and see Leslie to FH, 8 June 1873, 19 June 1878 (blaming criticism of his work by Cairnes and others on his endorsement of FH's economic views), HC; see Leslie, *Essays in Political Economy*, 2nd edn. (Dublin 1888) and *Land Systems* (London, 1870).

49. Ingram (1823–1907), visited Comte the same year as Harrison and entered Lincoln's Inn 11 days after him; see *Essays in Economic Method*, ed. R. L. Smyth (New York, 1963), reprinting 'The Present Position and Prospects of Political Economy'; obit. *The Times*, 2 May 1907, 9f.

50. The invitation came from the leading critic of his paper on the Stonemasons' strike in 1862, William Newmarch, who wrote, 6 Nov. 1875, HC; on FH, see *Political Economy Club ... 1899–1920 ... Questions Discussed* vi (London, 1921), xv–xvii, 100, 107, 110, 111, 363; *AM* ii, 92–3; *NSP* 271.

51. *NSP* 271; Mill, *CW* v, 680–700; Howell, *The Conflicts of Capital and Labour Historically and Economically Considered* (London, 1878), 22; H. Sidgwick, 'The Wages-Fund Theory', *FR* xxxii (Sept. 1879), 401–13; see William Breit, 'The Wages Fund Controversy Revisited', *Canadian Journal of Economic History* xxxiii (1967), 509–28 also neglecting FH.

52. 'The Illegality of Unionism: The Case of Hornby v. Close', *Bee-Hive*, 26 Jan. 1867; see also FH in *PMG*, 5 Jan. 1867.

53. *The Times*, 12 Feb. 1867, 8d, 9ef; *Bee-Hive*, 16 Feb. 1867; ESB to Howell, 26 Jan. and 8 Feb. 1867, Bishopsgate Institute.

54. *AM* i, 315–16; *Hansard*, 3rd ser. clxxxv HC, 190 (8 Feb. 1867) and 522–6 (18 Feb. 1867); H. W. McCready, 'British Labour and the Royal Commission on Trade Unions, 1867–9', *University of Toronto Quarterly* xxiv (1955), 393–5; Maurice Cowling, *1867: Disraeli, Gladstone, and Revolution* (Cambridge, Eng., 1967), 378, fn. 2, citing Derby MSS, Box 153/4, Walpole to Derby, 11 Feb. 1867, about FH.

55. *AM* i, 316, 328–9; FH to ESB, 22 Feb., Mon., and 2 undated letters (May 1867), HC; FH to Miss Shore, Sat. and 22 Apr. (1867), FC; on the Bovill case, *The Times*, 4 Sept. 1867, 4d; on the Railway Companies Bill, 2 Aug., 5ab, 9 Aug. 10c, 13 Aug. 8d, 28 Aug., 5d, and *Hansard*, 3rd ser. clxxxviii, HC (26 July 1867), 156–64.

56. *AM* i, 322, 358–9 (FH to 'Miss Shore', 10 Jan. (1868) quoted, slightly changed from MS in FC).

57. *AM* i, 322–3 (source of FH's judgements unless noted); *The Times*, 25 Jan. 1869, 4a, review of Erle, *The Law Relating to Trade Unions* (London, 1869).

58. Christopher J. Kauffman, 'Lord Elcho, Trade Unionism and Democracy', *Essays in Anti-Labour History: Responses to the Rise of Labour in Britain* (Hamden, Conn, 1974), 182–207; Daphne Simon, 'Master and Servant,' *Democracy and the Labour Movement: Essays in Honour of Dona Torr*, ed. John Saville (London, 1954), 160–201, esp. 180–9 on Elcho; *Hansard*, 3rd ser. clxxxv, HC (1 Mar. 1867), 1257–60.

59. *Bee-Hive*, 12 Aug. 1865 (Lichfield's quarrel with Potter); *The Times*, 10 Aug. 1867, 11a; B. C. Roberts, *The Trades Union Congress, 1868–1921* (London, 1958), 25, 37.

60. *Hansard*, 3rd ser. clxxxv, HC (8 Feb. 1867), 180–2, 190 (Walpole's account), 518–22 (Roebuck's account).

61. *Diaries of Sir Daniel Gooch, Baronet*, intro. by Sir Theodore Martin (London, 1892), esp. 231 (on miners' high wages).

62. *Parl. Papers: Report from the Select Committee on the Master and Servant Law, 1866*, xiii, 118–23, Qs. 2418–2533 (Mathew's testimony).

63. FH to ESB (?14 or 21 May 1867), HC; Mault testified on 7, 14, 21, 28 May and 5, 18 June 1867, *Parl. Papers*, xxxiii (C. 3873) *First Report ... 1867*, Qs. 2951–3462, 3679–3731; (C. 3893) *Second Report ... 1867*, Qs. 3969–4082; (C. 3910) *Third Report ... 1867*, Qs. 4083–4325, 4728–4731.

64. *Parl. Papers*, xxxix (C. 3981–VI) *Tenth Report ... 1868*, Qs. 19,095–19,340; FH to ESB, 20 July (1868) and Nasymth to Charles Harrison, 4 Jan. 1880, HC, sending sketches of the Tay Bridge disaster; Samuel Smiles, *Lives of the Engineers*, 3 vols. (London, 1861–2) and Smiles's edn. of Nasymth's *Autobiography* (1883; popular edn., London, 1912), 209, 214, 297 on unions.

65. *Parl. Papers*, xxxii (C. 3893) *Second Report ... 1867*, Qs. 3732–3968; (C. 3952) *Fourth Report ... 1867*, Qs. 6895–6984; xxxix (C. 3980–I) *Fifth Report ... 1868*, Qs. 9269–9390.

66. FH to ESB, 24 June (1867), HC; *Parl. Papers*, xxxii (C. 3952–I) *Trade Unions: Sheffield Outrages ... 3 June 1867–8 July 1867*.

67. *Bee-Hive*, 6 July 1867; *PMG*, 3, 8 July 1867 (summarizing comments); *Punch*, 13 July 1867, 14; ESB to FH, 6 July 1867, HC, and to Henry Crompton, 14 July 1867, UC; ESB, *The Sheffield Outrages ...* (1867), from *Daily News*, 9 and 10 July 1867; FH to ESB, 5 July (1867), HC; FH, *PMG*, 12 July 1867, in *AM* i, 317–21.

68. FH to ESB (2 July 1867), HC; T. Wemyss Reid, *The Life, Letters, and Friendships of Richard Monckton Milnes, First Lord Houghton*, 3rd edn., 2 vols. (London, 1891), ii, 176; *The Diaries of John Bright*, ed. R. A. J. Walling (London 1931), 309; University of London Council Minutes, 23 July 1867; Mill, *CW* xvi, 1297, letter thanking Grote for his vote; Minute Books, University Hall, 20, 26 July, 16 Oct., 16 Nov., 13 Dec. 1867.

69. RC, *Mr Broadhead and the Anonymous Press* (17 July 1867), in *ESPR* i, 165–75; FH to ESB (Aug. 1867), Stephen to FH, ?18 Aug. 1867, and ESB to FH, 10 Aug. 1867, all HC.

70. *Bee-Hive*, 6, 13, 20, 27 July, 3 Aug. 1867; *Hansard*, 3rd ser. clxxxviii HC 1438–9 (12 July 1867); FH to Miss Shore (29 July 1867), FC; RC, *ESRP* i, 176–8; ESB to Marx, 13 June 1871, International Institute of Social History, Amsterdam (hereafter IISH), D 258.

71. *GEL* iv, 483–4; see also FH to Miss Shore, 17 Feb. 1869, FC, in *AM* i, 359, and to ESB, 31 Oct. and (15 Dec. 1868), HC.

72. *AM* i, 322–3; McCready, 'British Labour ...', *University of Toronto Quarterly* xxiv (1955), 400–5, citing copy of FH's Memorandum in the Lushington Papers; see also FH to Elcho, 31 Dec. (1868) and Elcho to FH, 3 Jan. (1869), Wemyss Collection.

73. *Parl. Papers*, xxxi (C. 4123, 4123–I) *Eleventh and Final Report ... 1868–9*, dated 9 Mar. 1869 and including Booth's 'Draft Report' and Earle's 'Memorandum on the Law Relating to Trade Unions' (enlarged in *The Law Relating to Trade Unions, 1868* (London, 1868); *Polity*, iv, 365.

74. *AM* ii, 35–6.

75. Brentano to FH, 2 Mar. 1873, HC; Brentano, 'The Growth of a Trade Union', *North British Review* liii (1870), 59–114 and *Mein Leben* (Jena, 1931), 45–56; James J. Sheehan, *The Career of Lujo Brentano* (Chicago, 1966), 33.

76. 'Trade Unions in the City and in Mayfair', *Fraser's Magazine* lxxviii (1868), 159–74, 443–60; see also his 'The Modern Spirit', ibid., lxxv (1867), 626–39 and 'The Politics of Young England', ibid., lxxvi (1868), 71–9; W. Robertson Nicoll, *James Macdonell Journalist* (London, 1890).

77. Wayne Burns, *Charles Reade: A Study of Victorian Authorship* (New York, 1961), 272–4.

78. Edward C. Mack and W. H. G. Armytage, *Thomas Hughes ...* (London, 1952), 158, 164 fn. 42; ESB to H. Crompton, 12, 26 Sept. and 5 Oct. 1867, UC; R. Harrison, *Before*, 283.

79. FH to ESB, 25 July, 15 Dec. 1868, (16 Apr. 1869), HC; Mr Harrison to FH, 11 Mar. 1869, FC (discounting Hughes's 'generosity' towards FH); W. H. G. Armytage, *A. J. Mundella: The Liberal Background of the Labour Movement* (London, 1951), 68; Mack and Armytage, *Thomas Hughes*, 160.

80. *The Times*, 22 Apr. 1869, 5c, 29 Apr. 1869, 12e, 24 June 1869, 12f; *Bee-Hive*, 24 Apr. 1 May, 26 June 1869; FH to ESB, 24 June 1869, HC.

81. 'The Trades-Union Bill', *FR* xii (1869), 30–45.

82. Webbs, *History of Trade Unionism*, 274–6; Armytage, *A. J. Mundella*, 71; *The Times*, 12 July 1869, 11b.

83. Holyoake to FH, 25 Nov. 1905, HC.

84. See Christopher Kent, *Brains and Numbers: Elitism, Comtism, and Democracy in Mid-Victorian England* (Toronto, 1978) and Christopher Harvie, *The Lights of Liberalism: University Liberals and the Challenge of Democracy 1860–86* (London, 1976).

85. *AM* i, 158–9, 208–9; FH to ESB, Mon. (dated 1862 later), HC; Lewis Campbell, *On The Nationalisation of the Old English Universities* (London, 1901) 30, 136; Harvie, *The Lights*, 79–88; Ward, *Victorian Oxford*, 243.

86. *AM* i, 355; Campbell, *On the Nationalisation*, 284–93, Appendix C.

87. Campbell, *On the Nationalisation*, 130; Ward, *Victorian Oxford*, 235, 246–8; G. G. Bradley, *Recollections of A. P. Stanley* (London, 1883), 91–3; Elliott, *The Life of Lord Goschen*, i, 64.

88. FH to ESB, Fri. (15 Apr. 1864), HC; G. P. Gooch, *Life of Leonard Courtney* (London, 1920), 67–8; Sir Edward Clarke, *The Story of My Life* (London, 1918), 61, 68; *AM* i, 83; *RI* 372–3.

89. *AM* i, 168, ii, 82–3; *RI* 369–77 (quoted), from *Cornhill Magazine* n.s. xiv (1903); FH to T. Huxley, 21 Apr. (1866), Huxley Papers, xviii, fols. 44–5, Imperial College of Science and Technology (hereafter Imperial College); Spender, 'Frederic Harrison', *The Reader*, 26 Jan. 1907, 357; FH to ESB, (1865) and undated, HC; ESB to HC, 21 Nov. 1864 and 25 Mar. 1865, UC.

90. FH to EBH, 20 Mar. 1871, FC; FH to ESB, 10 Oct. 1862, HC.

91. FH to Mrs Hadwen, 3 Mar. (1866), and fragment of letter to ESB, HC; *AM* i, 68; FH, Memorial Address, *Lady John Russell, A Memoir*, 3rd edn., ed. Desmond MacCarthy and Agatha Russell (London, 1926), 306–8.

92. FH to ESB, undated, HC.
93. *Polity*, i, 114–16, 158, iv, 277, 333.
94. FH, 'Clubs and Unions', *Bee-Hive*, 14 July 1866.
95. FH to ESB, Tues., Thurs. and 28 Aug. (1864), and Mr Harrison to FH, 21 Aug. (1864), HC; *AM* ii, 80–1.
96. Lawrence Harrison to FH, 10 Sept. (1864), FC.
97. FH to ESB, n.d., HC (quoted); see his 'Foreign Policy', *Questions for a Reformed Parliament* (London, 1867), partly quoted in his 'Abraham Lincoln', *GW* 34–6.
98. FH in *Bee-Hive* in 1863: 2 May (on the meeting), 21 Mar., 27 June, 1 Aug., 21 Nov.; *AM* i, 288; see John F. Kutolowski, 'English Radicals and the Polish Insurrection of 1863–4', *Polish Review* ii (1966), 3–27.
99. 'The Destruction of Kagosima', *NR* xviii (1864), 270–93, part in *AM* i, 293–4; *Bee-Hive*, 14 Nov. 1863, 13 Feb. 1864.
100. FH to ESB, Thurs. (7 Apr. 1864), HC.
101. FH to ESB, Fri. (15 Apr. 1864) and undated but marked '11:30', HC; *The Times*, 22 Apr. 1864, 7c (letter from Saffi); Jasper Ridley, *Garibaldi* (London, 1974), ch. 36.
102. FH to ESB (15, 22 Apr. 1864), HC; FH to Russell, 15 Dec. 1906, BL, Lord Charnwood MS, Add. MS 10742 (about advising Cremer against challenging the police after the meeting).
103. FH to ESB, Mon. '11 a.m.' (9 May, 1864) (quoted), Sat. (14 May, 1864), HC; *The Times*, 1864, 25 Apr., 7ab, 9 May, 8de; *Bee-Hive*, 30 Apr., 7 and 14 May, 1864.
104. *The Times*, 11 May, 1864, 7e, 12 May, 14e; FH to ESB, Mon. (16 May, 1864), HC; *AM* i, 356–7.
105. FH to Mrs Hadwen (11 June 1864), HC; *AM* i, 356–7; FH, 'The Departure of Garibaldi', *Bee-Hive*, 21 May 1864.
106. FH to ESB, 10 Nov. (1865), HC.
107. FH to ESB, 14 Aug. (1867), HC; see Saffi to FH, 15 Feb. 1867, HC, offering to tutor him in Dante and mentioning Italy's troubles.
108. FH to ESB (24 Sept. 1867), HC; Spender, 'Frederic Harrison', *The Reader*, 26 Jan. 1907, 357; Ridley, *Garibaldi*, 576–8.
109. 'Napoleon and Italy', *Bee-Hive*, 9 Nov. 1867.
110. ESB, 'The International Working Men's Association', *FR* xiv (1870), 517–35; FH to ESB, 3 Nov. (1870), HC; R. Harrison, 'E. S. Beesly and Karl Marx', *International Review of Social History* iv (1959), 22–58, 208–38.
111. *Bee-Hive*, 21 Sept. 1867; FH to ESB (24 Sept. 1867), HC.
112. FH, 'The European Crisis', *Commonwealth*, 16 June 1866; *AM* i, 294–5.
113. 'Governor Eyre to be Tried at Home', *Bee-Hive*, 9 Dec. 1865.
114. 'Jamaica', *Commonwealth*, 21 July 1866; *Martial Law: Six Letters to the 'Daily News'* (London, 1867), 8 (Letter 27 Nov. 1866).
115. Mr Harrison to FH, 27 Nov. (1866), FC.
116. *Martial Law*, 39, 41, letter 12 Dec. 1866; 'tiger in our race' provides a chapter title in Geoffrey Dutton, *The Hero as Murderer: The Life of*

Edward John Eyre (London, 1967), and is quoted in Bernard Semmel, *The Governor Eyre Controversy* (London, 1962), 131–2.

117. Dutton, *The Hero*, 266–8; *The Times*, 8 Feb. 1867, 8b, 2 Apr. 1867, 12f; L. Stephen, *Sir James Fitzjames Stephen*, 227–31.

118. *AM* i, 302.

119. FH to Miss Shore, 20 Feb. (1866), FC; FH in *Bee-Hive*, 10 Nov. 1866 and in *Commonwealth*, 14 Apr., 24 Nov., 1 Dec. 1866, 5 Jan. 1867.

120. FH to ESB, 3 letters (29 Apr., 6 May, 13 June 1867) and Bright to FH, 30 Apr. 1867, HC; ESB to FH, 4 May 1867, UC; Bright to RC, 11, 20 Apr. 1867, BL, Add. MS 45241, fols. 21–4; RC, *ESPR* i, 213–15; *Hansard*, 3rd. ser. clxxxvi (3 May 1867), 1929–33, clxxxvii (14 June 1867), 1886–1906; *The Times*, 4 May 1867, 9de.

121. FH to ESB, various undated letters, HC; FH to Miss Shore, 20 Feb. (1866), FC; *AM* i, 358.

122. R. B. McDowell, 'Henry Dix Hutton: Positivist and Cataloguer', *Friends of the Library of Trinity College Dublin: Annual Bulletin* (1952); S. H. Swinny, 'In Memoriam: Henry Dix Hutton', *PR* xvi (1908), 21; FH to ESB, 20 Nov. (1865), 17 Apr., 12 June (1866), and undated, HC.

123. FH to ESB, Thurs. (1866), HC.

124. *The Troublemakers: Dissent over Foreign Policy, (1792–1939)* (Bloomington, Ind., 1958), 67.

125. *International Policy: Essays on the Foreign Relations of England* (London, 1866); FH, 'England and France' is in *RI*; FH to ESB, Nov. (1866), HC.

126. Fremantle, 'M. Comte and His Disciples on International Policy', *CR* iii (1866), 477–98; Maurice, *Life*, ii, 553–4; L. Stanley, 'Critical Notice', *FR* v (1866), 636–40; *GEL* iv, 301; FH to Laffitte, 30 May (1866), MAC; FH to ESB, Sat. (May 1866), HC.

127. FH, 'Foreign Policy', *Questions for a Reformed Parliament* (London, 1867), 233–58; *AM* i, 295; FH to ESB, 22 Feb. (1867) and (Apr. 1867), HC; see Harvie, *The Lights* and Kent, *Brains*.

128. 'Reform Essays', *Quarterly Review* cxxiii (1867), 244–77.

129. *Hansard*, 3rd ser. clxxxii (26 Apr. 1866), 2078–9.

130. *Commonwealth*, 12 and 26 May 1866 (Kell), 19 May, 2 June 1866 (FH).

131. A. P. Martin, *Life and Letters of Robert Lowe*, 2 vols. (London, 1893), ii, 280; Lowe, who had coached RC at Oxford, seemed to FH an 'inimitable table companion' when they met at Zermatt in 1851, and an admirable political speaker in 1852 (*AM* i, 90, 119).

132. FH to ESB, 22 Feb (1867), HC; FH to Henry Parkes, 22 Oct. 1875, Mitchell Library, Sydney, N. S. Wales, saying Lowe had learned 'home truths' in Australia.

133. *FR* vi (Mar. 1867), 261–83, in *OP* as 'Parliament before Reform, 1867'.

134. On Bagehot and FH's changes in his text for *OP* see my introduction, *OP* (1975).

135. JM, *Recollections* 2 vols. (London, 1917), i, 5–7, 31–2, 85.

136. *OP* 148, 150–2; *Hansard*, 3rd ser. clxxxii (13 Mar. 1866), 147–8.

137. Arnold, *CPW* v, 87–114.

138. Ibid., 75–6, from *PMG*, 22 Apr. 1867.
139. 'Culture: A Dialogue', *FR* viii (Nov. 1867), 603–14, in *CB* 97–118.
140. *Letters of Matthew Arnold, 1848–1888*, ed. G. W. E. Russell, 2 vols. (London, 1895), i, 432–3.
141. FH to JM, 4 June (1869), HC.
142. Arnold, *CPW* v, 314 (from *PMG*, 8 June 1869, 539), fn. 315; in *Culture and Anarchy*, Arnold satirizes three other members of the Royal Commission: Gooch, Elcho, and Roebuck.
143. *OP* 181–5, from 'The Transit of Power', *FR* ix (Apr. 1868), 374–96 (quoted passage added in 1875); Arnold, *CPW* v, 119, 122, 132–3, 158, 186, 223–4, 385; Packe, *John Stuart Mill*, 458–61.
144. FH to ESB, Thurs. (Dec. 1865), HC; cp. *Polity*, iv, 325, proscribing violence.
145. FH to Howell, 5 Sept. (1866), Bishopsgate Institute; cp. FH, 'The Programme of the League', *Bee-Hive*, 20 Oct. 1866.
146. FH to ESB, Fri. (22 Apr. 1864), undated (6 May 1867) (saying he had 'put a stopper on one of the dirtiest tricks that d—d Jew ever tried on about Hyde Park'), Wed. (8 May 1867), HC; ESB to FH, 4 May 1867, UC.
147. *OP* 184–5, from 'The Transit of Power'.
148. 'Workmen's Representatives', *Bee-Hive*, 2 Nov. 1867.
149. FH to Howell, 7 Aug. 1867, Bishopsgate Institute; FH to ESB, 27 Sept. and 2 Oct. 1867, HC; *Bee Hive*, 7 Sept. 1867; *PMG*, 1 Oct. 1867.
150. *The Political Function of the Working Classes* ... (London, 1868), in *OP* 207–41.
151. 'The Transit of Power', *FR* ix (Apr. 1868), 374–96, rpt. *OP* 162–206, with change in passage quoted.
152. A. O. Rutson to FH, 4 Feb. (1868), enclosing letter from F. J. Walthan, HC.
153. FH to ESB, 25 July and 21 Nov. (1868), HC; see A. F. Thompson, 'Gladstone's Whips and the General Election of 1868', *English Historical Review* lxiii (1948), 189–200; R. Harrison, *Before*, ch. 4; Leventhal, *George Howell*, 93, 103–14.
154. FH to ESB, 2 June, 20, 25 July 1868, HC.
155. *AM* i, 27–8; FH to Mrs Hadwen, 28 Dec. (1863) and to ESB, 16 Nov. (1869), HC; *Lytton Strachey by Himself: A Self-Portrait*, ed. Michael Holroyd (London, 1971).
156. FH to Mrs Hadwen, 22 June 1861, HC.
157. Lawrence Harrison to FH, 10 Sept. (1864), FC; fragment of letter, and FH to Mrs Hadwen (22 June 1861), HC; *The Times*, 11 Nov. 1865, 1a.
158. FH to Mrs Hadwen (22 June 1861); Thurs. 24 July (1862), in *AM* i, 279–80.
159. FH to Mrs Hadwen, 6 May 1861; undated (May 1866), 18 and 22 June 1861, and Jane Harrison to Mrs Hadwen, 30 May (1861), HC.
160. FH to Mrs Hadwen, 31 Dec. 1860, HC; FH to Miss Louisa Shore, 29 Feb. 1864, FC, in *AM* i, 359–61.

161. FH to Mrs Hadwen, 3 Apr. (1862), 22 Oct. (1863), 18 Apr. (1867, marked 1865), HC; her son Frederic, aged 17, entered KCS on 24 Apr. 1867.

162. Arnold, *CPW* v, 347, *PMG*, letter xii, 29 Nov. 1870.

163. FH to ESB, undated, HC; (FH, using pseudonym of 'Historiomastic'), 'The Stage and its Critics', *The Reader*, v (1865), 427–8, in *AM* i, 337–42, Part II, 711–12; ESB, using initials, 544, 712.

164. FH to Miss Shore, 1 Mar. 1866, FC.

165. FH to ESB, 13 Aug. (1863), HC; (FH), 'London to Rome, Notes ESB', FC.

166. *The Times*, 15 Oct. 1868, 4e (in *MAJ* 88–103), 21 Oct. 1868, 10f; FH to Mrs Harrison, 12 Sept. 1865, FC; FH to GE, 11 Nov. 1868, *GEL* iv, 483–4.

167. FH to Lawrence, 22 Sept. (1865), FC; 'Memoranda', 5 Dec. 1865 and FH to JHB, 30 Nov. 1865, HC; Ronald Clark, *The Day the Rope Broke* (New York, 1965).

168. *MAJ* 104–41, from *WR* lxxxii (1864), 276–90; FH to ESB, 6 Oct. (1864), HC; *AM* ii, 84; 'Sir Leslie Stephen', *MAJ* 80–7, from *Cornhill Magazine* xvi (1904), 433–43; Ronald Clark, *Victorian Mountaineers* (London, 1953).

169. Mr Shore to FH, 14 Apr. (1862) and FH to Miss Shore, 25 Feb. (1864), FC; *AM* i, 270; The Revd T. Shore, *The Churchman and the Free Thinker* ... (London, 1862); A. O. Sherrard, *Two Victorian Girls, with Extracts from the Hall Diaries*, ed. A. R. Mills (London, 1966), esp. 280–7, 296, 301, 307–9; A. R. Mills, ed., *The Halls of Ravenswood, More Pages from the Journals of Emily and Ellen Hall* (London, 1967); A. R. Mills, ed., *Two Victorian Ladies, More Pages from the Journals of Emily and Ellen Hall* (London, 1969), esp. 53–4, 59–60.

170. *AM* i, 246.

171. FH, *Memoir and Essays of Ethelbertha Harrison* (Bath, 1917); Anne Harrison to FH, 17 July (1865) (quoted) and 24 Apr. (1868), FC.

172. FH to ESB, 4 Jan. (1866), HC; FH, 'Anthony Trollope', *SEVL* 202, from *Forum* xix (May 1895), 324–37.

173. Mr Harrison to FH, 11 Mar. 1869, FC.

174. FH to Lady Amberley, 19 May (1869), Russell Archives, McMaster U.

175. FH to ESB, 11 June (1869), HC; JHB to RC, 30 June, 9 July, 26 Aug. 1868, BL, Add. MS 45227, fols. 109–28; RC to JHB (copy), 3 July 1868, Bod. MS Eng. lett. c. 185, fols. 14–20; *Recollections of John Henry Bridges*, 105–8.

176. ESB to GE, 20 May 1869, *GEL* v, 40; ESB to Marx, 21 May 1869, IISH; FH to ESB, 11 June, 20 July, no date, and 13 Dec. (quoted) 1869, HC.

177. *AM* i, 301–2, quoting a letter that does not survive; FH to ESB, 18 June (1869), HC, quoting EBH.

178. *Working Women's College Annual Reports for 1867 and 1868* (London 1868), 2, 12–13, 16; FH to Lady Amberley (9 Aug. 1866), Russell Archives, McMaster U.; Hester Burton, *Barbara Bodichon 1827–1891* (London, 1949), 169.

179. Liveing, *A Nineteenth-Century Teacher*, 141–4; *Recollections of John Henry Bridges*, 130.

180. VL to Francis Galton, 30 Dec. 1874, Galton MS, UC, 122/1E (on similarities between the brothers); VL's wife Jane was a daughter of Francis Mowatt, MP.

181. FH to ESB, 16 Nov. (1869) (quoted), HC; *AM* i, 332–4; *The Times*, 6 May 1870, 11f, 25 May 1870, 6b; William O'Connor Morris, 'The Digest of Law Commission', *FR* ix (1868), 698–708.

182. *AM* i, 328; *The New Reports Containing Cases Decided in the Courts of Equity and Common Law* (London, 1863).

183. FH to Mrs Hadwen, 30 June (1865), HC; see also FH, *The Times*, 5 June 1922, 11e; Nash, *Life of Westbury*, ii, 123–45.

184. *AM* i, 328–9; The Chairman of the Council was Sir Spencer Walpole, who had appointed FH to the Royal Commission on Trade Unions.

185. FH to ESB, 25 July (1870), HC; FH might have noted that Lord Romilly, as member of the Judicial Committee and Master of the Rolls, had found twice for Bishop Colenso, and that his father had been a reformer of the criminal law; H. Crompton's brother Charles, a barrister, married a daughter of Mrs Gaskell, one sister married George Croom Robertson and another the Revd John Llewelyn Davies.

186. JM to H. Crompton, 1 Aug. 1870, quoted in Stanley A. Wolpert, *Morley and India 1906–1910* (Berkeley 1967), 14; FH to JM, 1, 2 Aug. (1870), HC; John W. Bicknell and C. L. Cline, 'Who was Lady Morley?', *Victorian Newsletter* xl (1973), 28–31.

187. FH to ESB, n.d. (in FH's hand, '£200 was subscribed by 4'), HC.

188. FH to ESB, Easter (21 Apr. 1867), and undated, HC; 'Selections from Congreve's Journal', BL, Add. MS 45261; *GEL* iv, 360, 363.

189. FH to ESB, Fri. (Jan. 1868), HC.

190. RC, 'Memorandum on the Sacerdotal Fund', BL, Add. MS 45258, listing FH's admission, 14 May 1867; *CL* 47; FH to Howell (1868), Bishopsgate Institute; FH to C. E. Norton, 13 Nov. (1868), Harvard U.; *AMB* 316, from 'Charles Eliot Norton', *Cornhill Magazine* xxvi (1909).

191. FH to JM, 29 May (1869), HC; FH, *Sundays and Festivals* (London, 1867).

192. Huxley, 'On the Physical Basis of Life', *FR* xi (1869), 129–45; RC, 'Mr Huxley on M. Comte', ibid., 407–18; FH, 'The Positivist Problem', ibid., xii (Nov. 1869), 469–93; FH to ESB, Tues. (1866), RC to FH, 11 Oct. and 9 Nov. 1869, HC; *AM* i, 352, n. (quoted).

193. *GEL* v, 75–6.

194. Ruskin to FH, 9 July 1869, HC, part in *AM* i, 234.

195. Ruskin to FH, 3 Feb. 1870, Cornell U.; FH to Ruskin, 4 Feb. (1870), Morgan Library; *PMG*, 5 Jan. 1870, article signed 'Patriae Quis Exul'.

196. *PMG*, 11 Jan. 1870; see FH to JM (11 Jan. 1870), HC (about Frederick Greenwood, editor of *PMG*, deleting 'bits which really hit Stephen').

Chapter 4. Shaping a Positivist Policy 1870–1880

1. *AM* ii, 2.
2. Studied at London U. and Middle Temple; called to the Bar 1871; joined S. E. Circuit with chambers in London.
3. (1832–95); studied at Rugby under Congreve; BA, 1854, Corpus Christi, Oxford; Fellow, 1859.
4. FH to ESB, various letters, 1870, HC; McGee, *Crusade*, 47, 61; *AM* ii, 256–8.
5. Jones, *Samuel Butler*, i, 197-8.
6. FH to JM, 7 Sept. (1876), HC.
7. FH to ESB, Tues. and 6 July (1870), HC; R. P. Masani, *Dadabhai Naoroji: The Grand Old Man of India* (London, 1939).
8. RC Journal, BL, Add. MS 45261, 13 June, 10 July 1871; FH to ESB (June 1870), FH to JM, 14 Apr. (1871), HC; FH, 'Necrologie, James C. Geddes', *RO* iv (1888), 462–6.
9. Alan Willard Brown, *The Metaphysical Society: Victorian Minds in Crisis, 1869–1880* (1947; rpt. New York, 1973).
10. FH to JM (16 June) 1870, HC; cp. *MT* 39, from 'Tennyson: A New Estimate', *North American Review* clxxvi (1903); Richard Le Gallienne, *The Romantic '90's* (London, 1951), 36–7, placing the confrontation at one of Lewes's breakfasts.
11. FH to JM, 26 July (1870), HC; 'The Subjective Synthesis', *FR* xiv (1870), 184–97, in *PCS*.
12. 'The Romance of the Peerage', *FR* xiii (1870), 655–67, in *CB*; Robert Blake, *Disraeli* (New York, 1967), 518, opposes treating the novel as a 'gaudy romance of the peerage'.
13. FH to ESB, 27 May (1870) and to JM, 11, 17, 20 May (1870), HC.
14. FH to ESB, 27 May (1870), HC (quoted); *The Times*, 4 Nov. 1870, 4d (on the epidemic, which left 1076 dead in London for the quarter ending 30 June); on Bridges see Ruth G. Hodgkinson, *The Origins of the National Health Service* ... (London, 1967), 516–19, 588, 668–9; Liveing, *A Nineteenth-Century Teacher*, chs. 13, 14.
15. FH to ESB, 10 Aug. (1870), HC; *The Times*, 19 Aug. 1870, 1a; *AM* i, 348.
16. *Recollections of Dean Fremantle Chiefly by Himself*, ed. the Master of the Temple (London, 1921), esp. 51–3; with George C. Brodrick he edited *A Collection of the Judgments of the Judicial Committee of the Privy Council* (London, 1865), including the judgement on *Essays and Reviews*.
17. Anne Harrison to EBH, 18, 25 Aug. (1870), FC.
18. Ibid.; *AM* ii, 2–3; FH to ESB, 25 July (1870) and to JM, 27 Oct. (1870), HC.
19. ESB, *A Word for France* (London, 1870), reissued with *Why We Should Stand by France* (London, 1870) by JHB, in *Papers on the War between France and Germany* (London, 1870); *The Times*, 16 Sept, 1870, 7cd (quoted); R. Harrison, *Before*, 229; RC's Journal, BL. Add. MS 45261.
20. FH to JM, 27 Oct. (1870), HC; JM, 'France and Germany', *FR* xiv (1870), 367–76 and 'England and the War', ibid., 479–88; Hirst, i, 172–5.

21. *GEL* v, 124–5; *FR* xiv (1870), 631–49, in *NSP*.

22. Dora Neill Raymond, *British Policy and Opinion during the Franco-Prussian War* (New York, 1921), 261; Hirst, i, 173–4.

23. *PMG*, 6, 7, 8, 9 Dec. 1870, part in *AM* ii, 4–12; *The Times*, 18 Nov. 1870, 6d (Carlyle), 18 Feb. 1871, 4f (Freeman); Nirad C. Chaudhuri, *Scholar Extraordinary: The Life of Professor the Rt. Honourable Friedrich Max Müller* (London, 1974), 247–52; Raymond, *British Policy*, 262.

24. 'The War', *Bee-Hive*, 7 Jan. 1871.

25. *AM* ii, 15; FH to JM, 11 Jan. 1871, HC (quoted); Hirst, I, 176; FH to Isa Blagden, 7 Feb. (1871), Michelet MS IX, A4739, fols. 20–1, Bibliothèque historique de la ville de Paris; *Bee-Hive*, 7 Jan. 1871.

26. 'The Effacement of England', *FR* xv (1871), 145–66, in *NSP* called 'The Duty of England'; Richard Millman, *British Foreign Policy and the Coming of the Franco-Prussian War* (Oxford, 1965), 218, 222, 225 (3 times calling Britain's policy 'effacement').

27. *Later Letters of Lady Augusta Stanley 1864–1876*, ed. Dean of Windsor and Hector Bolitho (New York, 1929), 118; *AM* ii, 45–6; Father Hyacinthe, *Orations, with a Sketch of his Life*, trans. Leonard Woolsey Bacon (London, 1871); *The Times*, 18 Aug. 1870, 5d.

28. Ruskin, *Works*, xxviii, 26–9, from *Daily Telegraph*, 14 Jan. 1871; Mill to JM, 6 Jan. 1871, in *CW* xvii, 1794–6; R. Harrison, *The English Defence of the Commune 1871* (London, 1971), 43 (on Marx); *The Amberley Papers*, ed. Bertrand and Patricia Russell, 2 vols. (1937; rpt. London, 1966), ii, 456–68.

29. FH to Amberley, 29 Dec. 1870, Bertrand Russell Archives, McGill U.

30. *The Amberley Papers*, ii, 462–9, 473–81.

31. *AM* ii, 13; Houghton to FH, 3 March (1871), HC.

32. Michelet, *Journal*, iv, ed. Claude Digeon (Paris, 1976), 245–8, 257, 274; Isa Blagden to Michelet (4 Jan. 1871), Michelet MS xxxiii, A4893, fols. 198–9, Bibliothèque historique de la ville de Paris; Michelet to FH, (12 Jan.), 24 Jan. (1872), HC.

33. FH to Blagden, 7 Feb. (1871) and to Michelet, 7, 15 Feb. (1871), Michelet MS IX, A4739, fols. 18–23, Bibliothèque historique de la ville de Paris; Michelet to Souvestre, 19 Feb. 1871 (copy) ibid., fols. 77–8, holograph in HC, quoted in *AM* ii, 41.

34. Michelet, *Journal*, iv, 279, 506; FH to EBH, 10 Mar. (1871), FC; *AM* ii, 41; Michelet, 'To My Translator', *France Before Europe* (Boston, 1871), mentioning proof correction by 'one whom I value and esteem'.

35. *AM* ii, 42–3 (quoted), citing letters from Michelet and wife, HC; *The Times*, 25 June 1877, 10b.

36. Guizot to FH, 19 Feb. 1871, in *AM* ii, 39–40.

37. Mr Harrison to FH, 25 Feb. (1871), FC.

38. FH to Norton, 26 Jan. 1871, HU.

39. Hypatia Bradlaugh Bonner, *Charles Bradlaugh: A Record of His Life and Work by His Daughter*, 2 vols. (London, 1894), i, 319.

40. *AM* ii, 15; cp. Taylor, *The Troublemakers*, 13–14.
41. FH to JM, 22 Mar. (1871), HC.
42. FH to JM, Easter Sunday (13 Apr. 1871), HC; 'The Revolution of the Commune, Lecture, Chapel St., May 1871', in FH's hand, Bristol U.
43. FH to JM, 22 Mar. (1871), HC.
44. FH to JM, 20 Feb. (1871), HC.
45. FH to JM, Easter (13 Apr. 1871), HC.
46. FH to JM, 20 Apr., 4 May (1871), HC.
47. FH to JM, 20, 24 Apr. (1871), HC.
48. FH to JM, 18 Apr. (1871), HC.
49. 'The Revolution of the Commune', *FR* xv (1871), 556–79; *Polity*, iv, 365–6; Louis M. Greenberg, *Sister of Liberty: Marseilles, Paris, and the Reaction to a Centralized State, 1868–1871* (Cambridge, Mass., 1971).
50. FH to Maxse, 30 May (1871), WSRO; FH to E. Oswald, 30 May (1871), Bod. MS polyglot d. 1 (15).
51. FH to JM, 9 June, 1 July (1871), ESB to JM, 17 July 1871 (on Marx's address and FH's forthcoming essay), HC; *AM* ii, 18–19, 22–4; 'The Fall of the Commune', *FR* xvi (1871), 129–55, in R. Harrison, *The English Defence*, with essays by JHB and ESB.
52. *PMG*, 15 Apr. 1871; Storr, *BH*, 3 June 1871; Bradlaugh, *National Review*, 24 Dec. 1871, cited in Fergus A. D'Arcy, 'Charles Bradlaugh and the English Republican Movement, 1868–1878', *The Historical Journal* xxv (1982), 375; R. Harrison, 'E. S. Beesly and Karl Marx, II', *International Review of Social History* iv (1959), 212; Salisbury, 'The Commune and the Internationale', *Quarterly Review* cxxxi (1871), 549–80; Taine, *Sa vie et sa correspondance*, 3 vols. (Paris, 1905), iii, 143; Leon Edel, *Henry James Letters, ii, 1875–1883* (Cambridge, Mass., 1975), 157, letter 17 Feb. (1878).
53. *The Times*, 1 June 1871, 6c; see Mill, *CW* xvii, 1821–2.
54. FH to Maxse, 24 Feb. (1871), WSRO (quoted); Yvonne Kapp, *Eleanor Marx*, i, *Family Life, 1855–1883* (London, 1972), 137; FH, *AM* ii, 19.
55. *AM* ii, 30–2; FH, *The Times*, 1872: 2 Feb., 6c, 26 Feb., 12b, 18 Mar., 12e.
56. *AM* ii, 32–3; EBH, 'French Refugees to England in 1871–2', *Cornhill Magazine*, 3rd ser. xci (1905), 612.
57. FH to JM, 13 Feb. (1872), HC; FH to Cowan, 8 Jan. 1872, Newcastle-upon-Tyne Libraries; FH to Maxse, 24 Feb. (1872), WSRO; *AM* ii, 31.
58. Blanc to FH, 25 Nov. 1871, HC; FH to Oswald, 15 Dec. (1871), Bod. MS, polyglot, d. (10); FH to JM, 28 Jan. (1872), HC; Oswald, *Reminiscences of a Busy Life* (London, 1911), 428.
59. EBH, 'French Refugees', op. cit., 611; 'Selections from Congreve's Journal', 2 Feb. 1871, BL, Add. MS 45261; Humphry Sandwith, 'Earl Russell, the Commune, and Christianity', *FR* xvi (1871), 35–41; EBH to Lady Amberley, 31 May (1872?), Bertrand Russell Archives, McGill U.
60. *AM* ii, 19; FH to Dilke, 6 July (1871), BL, Add. MS 43898, fols. 151–2; FH to W. Toynbee, 17 Jan. 1912, Osborn Collection, YUL; FH to EBH, 7 Apr. 1903, FC; Leon Noël, *Camille Barrère, Ambassadeur de France* (Paris, 1948).

61. FH to Maxse, 8 Nov. (1871), WSRO; FH to Stanley, 18 Nov. (1871), JRL; Greenberg, *Sisters of Liberty*, 142, 158–63.
62. *AM* ii, 33–4, cited in David McLellan, *Karl Marx, His Life and Thought* (New York, 1973), 413–14; on Le Moussu see Alfred Vizetelly, *My Adventures in the Commune of Paris 1871* (London, 1914), 138, 233–4, 238, 261, 286; FH to JM, Wed. (1871), HC, suggesting he get Marx to write on Germany for the *FR*.
63. FH to JM, 11 Jan. (1872), HC.
64. FH to JM, 9 June (1871), HC; FH to EBH, 10 Mar. (1871), FC.
65. *AM* ii, 36–7.
66. FH to EBH, 10 Mar. (1871), FC.
67. FH to JM, 22 Mar., 8 Feb. (1871), HC.
68. *AM* i, 37; FH to EBH, 14, 15, 16, 17, 20 Mar. (1871), FC; Ruskin to FH, 15 Apr. 1871 and FH, 'Review of Relations with Ruskin 1860–1895', HC.
69. FH to JM, 24 Apr., 21 June, 18 Nov. (1871), HC.
70. EBH to FH, 17 Mar. (1871), FC; W. H. Mallock, *Memoirs of Life and Literature* (London, 1920).
71. JM to FH, 6 Apr. 1873 (on Mill), Hirst, i, 193–4, and 17 Nov. 1872, HC; on the Cosmopolitan Club, *AM* ii, 85, Sir Algernon West, *Cornhill Magazine* lxxxviii (1903), 63–73, and T. H. S. Escott, *Club Makers and Club Manners* (London, 1914), 167–9.
72. FH to EBH, 17 Mar. (1871), FC (quoted); on the Radical Club, FH to Dilke, 8 Feb. (1872), BL, Add. MS 43898, fols. 153–4; Harvie, *Lights*, 187–8.
73. FH to EBH, 15 Mar. (1871), FC.
74. FH to JM, 30 Sept., 13, 14 Oct. (1873), and Anne Harrison to FH, 14 Oct. (1873), HC.
75. *Polity*, ii, 170.
76. *GEL* v, 331–2, 341.
77. FH to JM, 13 Jan. (1873), HC.
78. FH to JM, 1 Mar. (1870), HC; JM, 'A Short Letter to Some Ladies', *FR* xiii (1870), 372–6; VL as Under Sec. to the Admiralty testified in 1871 about the Act's satisfactory execution but not on the policy itself.
79. FH to JM, 13 Jan. (1873), HC; Feaver, *Sir Henry Maine*, 113; FH to JM, 4 Jan. (1873), HC, about lawyers' cliques.
80. FH to JM, 13 Jan. (1873), HC.
81. FH to JM, 12 Jan. 1874, HC.
82. Mr Harrison to FH, 25 Dec. 1872, 22 Dec. 1873 (quoted), FC.
83. Mr Harrison to FH, 6 Nov. 1875, FC.
84. FH to JM, 28 July (1873), HC.
85. *AM* i, 195.
86. FH to JM, 25 Aug. (1873), HC.
87. *AM* i, 303; Mill to FH, 13 Apr. 1873, Cornell U.; FH to JM, 19 Apr. (1873), HC (giving other reasons).
88. JM to FH, 6 Apr. (on Mill), 26 June (on Lytton), 28 Aug. (on Pater), all 1873, FH to JM, 2 May 1871, HC.

89. FH to JM, 27 June (1871), JM to FH, 8 Oct. (1872), HC; see John W. Bicknell, 'John Morley', *Victorian Prose, A Guide to Research*, ed. David J. de Laura (New York, 1973), 513–14 (quoted).
90. Mr Harrison to FH (25 Feb. 1871), FC; R. Harrison, *Before*, 288–90; Harcourt to FH, undated, with note by FH dating 1871, HC, about the bill 'on your lines'.
91. *Bee-Hive*, 29 July 1871 (ESB), 5 Aug. 1871 (report of FH, Cromptons, and 5 TUC members); 31 May, 14, 21 June 1872 (FH), 25 Jan. 1873 (FH Leeds address); FH to JM, 21 Jan. 1873, HC; Leventhal, *Respectable Radical*, chs. 7–8; R. Harrison, *Before*, 290–300; Hirst, i, 231–2.
92. *Tracts for Trade Unionists*: *no. 1, Imprisonment for Breach of Contract, or the Master and Servant Act, 1867*; *Tracts … no. 2, Workmen and the Law of Conspiracy*; *Tracts … no. 3, The Criminal Law Amendment Act*, all 1873; FH *The Times*, 24 Mar., 7 Apr., 7 July 1873, also in *Bee-Hive*; H. W. McCready, 'British Labour's Lobby, 1867–75', *Canadian Journal of Economic and Political Science* xxii (1956), 141–60; FH to JM, 'Fri.' (Mar. 1873), HC; Hirst, i, 230–2.
93. FH, *Bee-Hive*, 17 Aug., 19 Oct. 1872; 'Mr Brassey on Work and Wages', *FR* xviii (1872), 268–86.
94. *The Times*, 1874: 15 Jan. 12a-e, 16 Jan. 12a-d; FH to EBH, (13 Jan. 1874), HC.
95. McCready, 'Frederic Harrison' (Ph.D. Harvard 1952), 300.
96. FH to EBH, 'Friday' (15 Jan. 1874), HC; cp. FH, *Bee-Hive*, 5, 12 Dec. 1874, on an employers' paper.
97. FH, *The Times*, 3 Nov. 1870, 4e, 4 Dec. 1875, 6f; FH to ESB, 3 Nov. 1870, HC; *RI* 233–5; S. Hutchinson Harris, *Auberon Herbert* (London, 1943), 133, 185.
98. FH to JM, 4, 21 Aug., 8 Dec. 1873 (quoted), HC; Hirst, i, 266–302, ii, 5; D. A. Hamer, *John Morley: Liberal Intellectual in Politics* (Oxford, 1968), 96–107.
99. FH to JM, 'Mar.' (1874), HC; Hamer, *Morley*, 106–11.
100. FH to JM, various letters Feb.–Apr. 1875, Mar. 1876, HC; *Manchester Examiner and Times*, 23 Mar. 1875, 6; *The Times*, 20 Mar. 1878, 13b; 'Church and State', *FR* xxvii (1877), 653–75, in *OS* as 'A State Church'; *Practical Modes of Disestablishment and Disendowment* (London, 1878).
101. FH, 'Church and State', *FR* xxvii (1877), 668; 'Church Endowments', *PMG*, 2 Apr. 1875; FH to JM, 11 Feb., 31 Mar., 8 Apr. 1875, HC; W. R. W. Stephens, *The Life and Letters of Edward A. Freeman*, 2 vols. (London, 1895), ii, 33.
102. Mr Harrison to FH, 5 Jan., 7 Feb., 12 Apr. (error for 13), 1878, FC.
103. John Tulloch, 'The Dogmatism of Dissent', *CR* xxxiii (1878), 570–87; FH, 'Principal Tulloch's "Dogmatism of Dissent" ', ibid., 825–32.
104. JM to FH, 28 Mar. 1876, HC.
105. *AM* ii, 294–5; FH to JM, 9 May 1874, HC.
106. JM to FH, 28 Aug., 6 Sept. 1873, FH to JM, 27 Aug., 3 Dec. 1873, HC; FH to Knowles (copy) 31 Mar., 1, 31 May (1873), collection of Mgr. Alphonse Chapeau.

107. Manning to FH, 23 Nov. 1873, HC; *AM* ii, 90.
108. *FR* xx (1873), 548–56, 549 (quoted).
109. Ibid., xxi (1874), 286–94 (287 quoted); note by JM 293–4; FH to JM, 30 Jan., 10 Feb. 1874 (quoted); JM to FH, 1, 11 Feb. 1874 (quoted); EBH to JM, 25 Dec. (1873), all HC.
110. *AM* i, 183–4.
111. Ibid., 304; Frank Hardie, *The Political Influence of Queen Victoria 1861–1901* (London, 1935), 206; see also 283, her comment on the Positivists: 'How very curious, and how very sad! What a pity somebody does not explain to them what a mistake they are making. But do tell me more about this strange M. Comte' (from Sidney Lee, 'Queen Victoria', *Quarterly Review* cxciii (1901), 321).
112. FH to JM, 20 Feb. (1871), HC; Harris, *Auberon Herbert*, 134–6.
113. FH to EBH, 2 May 1872, FC.
114. 'The Monarchy', *FR* xvii (1872), 613–41, in *OP*.
115. JM to FH, 14 June, 1872, HC; Kingsley Martin, *The Magic of the British Monarchy* (Boston, 1962), 48–9.
116. James, *English Hours*, ed. Alma Louise Lowe, 2nd edn. (New York, 1960), 84–7.
117. R. Harrison, *Before*, 324; Henry Ellis, 'Some Reminiscences: Edward Spencer Beesly', *PR* xxiii (1915), 175; Joseph Arch to FH, 15 Mar. 1877, HC.
118. FH to JM, 22 Oct., 4 Nov. (1873), HC; A. Beesly, *The Times*, 3 Nov. 1873, 5f and in *FR* xix (1873), 352–72, 732–53, xxi (1874), 385–406.
119. FH to Dilke, 5, 12, 15 May 1874, BL, Add. MS 43898, fols. 165–72; Dilke to FH (1874), FH to JM, 12, 15, 16 May (1874), and fragment, HC; Dilke, 'Memoirs', BL, Add. MS 43932, fols. 46–68; Roy Jenkins, *Victorian Scandal: A Biography of the Right Honourable Gentleman, Sir Charles Dilke* (New York, 1965), 83–5.
120. FH to Mrs Webb (1 Nov. 1893), Passfield Papers, ii, 4-a-17; ESB to FH, 11 Mar. 1872, HC; FH, *Report on the So-Called 'New Social Movement'* ... (London, 1872), and in *Bee-Hive*, 11 May 1872 and *PR* ii (1894), 1–18.
121. FH to Dilke, 24 July, 1 Aug., 5, 13, 28 Nov. 1872, BL, Add. MS 43898, fols. 155–64; *The Times*, 13 Nov. 1872, 10d-f.
122. FH to JM, 1, 8, 9 Feb., 8, 9 Apr., 2 July (1873), JM to FH, 6 Apr. (1873), HC.
123. FH to JM, 12 May (1873), HC.
124. FH to JM, 28 July (1873), HC.
125. FH to JM, 8 Apr., 6 May (1873), HC.
126. FH to JM, 19 Apr., 3, 5, 6, 14, 19 May (1873), HC.
127. 'The Religion of Inhumanity', *FR* xix (1873), 677–99, in *PER*; FH to JM, 14 May (1873), HC.
128. JM to FH, 4 June 1873, HC, advising FH against treating Stephen to a 'wrangle'; Stephen, *Liberty, Equality, Fraternity*, 2nd edn. (1874), ed. R. J. White (Cambridge, Eng., 1967); JM, 'Mr Mill's Doctrine of Liberty', *FR* xx (1873), 234–56.

129. 'His Relation to Positivism', *John Stuart Mill: His Life and Works, Twelve Sketches* ... (New York, 1873), 88–90, from *The Examiner*, printing part of Chapel Street address, 11 May 1873.
130. FH to JM, 13 July (1874), HC.
131. FH, 'The General Elections', *Bee-Hive*, 8 Mar. 1873; see also FH in *Bee-Hive*, 31 Jan. 1874 and *FR* xxi (1874), 279–309, in *OP*; FH to JM, 10 Feb. (1874), HC.
132. Mr Harrison to FH, 15 Mar. (1874), FC.
133. FH to JM, 13, 15 Feb., JM to FH, 17 Feb. 1873, HC.
134. See my Intro. to *OP* (1875; rpt. 1975).
135. FH to Carlyle, 4 July 1871, National Library of Scotland, Edinburgh; FH to JM, 11 Jan. (1872), 21 Jan. (1873), HC; *AM* ii, 103.
136. Stephen, *FR* xxiii (1875), 820–34; *PMG*, 3 Apr. 1875; *Saturday Review* 10 Apr. 1875, 489; *WR* civ (1875), 240–1; Mr Harrison to FH, 6 Nov. 1875, FC.
137. Parkes to FH, 31 July 1875, FH to Parkes, 22 Oct. 1875, 23 Dec. 1876, Mitchell Library, Sydney, NSW.
138. FH to JM, 10 Apr. (1875), HC.
139. FH to JM, 1 June (1874), HC.
140. FH to JM, 12, 27 Feb., 23 June (1874), HC; 'Mr Lewes's *Problems of Life and Mind*', *FR* xxii (1874), 89–101, in *PCS*.
141. RC thanked FH and Thorley for help, Preface, *The Politics of Aristotle with English Notes*, 2nd edn. (London, 1874).
142. *Catalogue of a Series of Photographs from the Collections of the British Museum taken by S. Thompson*, 1st ser. (London (1872)), intro. by Charles Harrison; *The Times*, 8 Aug. 1872, 4df; C. Harrison to Layard, 21 July, 3 Nov. 1872, BL, Add. MS 39001, fols. 96–9, 208, and to Trustees, BM, with their 'Minutes ... Jan. 1866 to Dec. 1872', BL. Original Papers, xx.
143. FH to JM, 19 Aug. (1873), HC.
144. Mr Harrison to FH, 6 Nov. 1875, FC.
145. Arnold to FH, 8 Nov. (1875), Cornell U.
146. JM to FH, 27 Oct. 1875, 15, 18 Sept. 1876, HC.
147. FH to JM, 17 Sept. (1876), HC; Mrs Harrison to FH, 25 Sept. (1874), FC; FH to Manning, 3 Aug. 1875, collection of Mgr. A. Chapeau; FH, *Annals of an Old Manor House*.
148. FH to JM, 17 Sept. (1876), HC.
149. Mr Harrison to FH, 28 Oct. 1874, 6 Nov. (1875), HC; Andrew Saint, *Richard Norman Shaw* (New Haven, 1976), 221, 224, 241.
150. FH to W. Stebbing, 19 July 1874, UT; FH to [E. W. B.] Nicholson, 24 Sept. 1880 (quoted), Bod. MS Eng. lett. e. 121, fols. 82–3; Mr and Mrs Harrison to FH, 16 Aug., 5, 10, 17, 25 Sept. 1874, FC.
151. FH to Myers, 16, 21 Sept. (1875), Trinity College Library, Cambridge.
152. EBH, 'In Memoriam: Marie Souvestre', *PR* xiii (1905), 115–16; FH, *The Times*, 1 Apr. 1905, 6b; J. M. Strachey to FH, 1 Apr. 1905, FH to JM, 19, 28 May 1873, HC; B. Webb, *My Apprenticeship* (London, 1926), 275–6,

Our Partnership, ed. B. Drake and M. I. Cole (London, 1948), 302 (quoted).

153. *AM* i, 234–7, quoting Ruskin's letter, 27 June 1875, HC; *The Times* 24 May 1875, 8f, giving sale price of 'The Pig-Killers', 24,000 fr.

154. Receipt from Mrs Cameron, 5 Oct. 1878, for £43, HC; *AM* ii, 104.

155. Geraldine Hancock Forbes, *Positivism in Bengal* (Calcutta, 1975), 32, 42–8; Cotton to RC, 14 Oct. 1878, BL, Add. MS 45228, fols. 5–7, and to H. Crompton, 16 Oct. 1878, fols. 8–9 (copy); Cotton, *Indian and Home Memories* (London, 1911), 57; Henry Taylor, *Autobiography*, 2 vols. (New York, 1885), ii, 153–6 (another version of the meeting).

156. *Illustrated London News*, 8 Oct. 1842, 351; letters from Frederick and William Harrison to FH and EBH, FC.

157. W. Crane, *An Artist's Reminiscences* (New York, 1907), 80, 133–4, 164.

158. *Punch*, lxxxii (24 June 1882), 300.

159. AH, *Frederic Harrison*, ch. 4; FH to (E. W. B. Nicholson), 24 Sept. 1880; Bod. MS Eng. lett. e. 121, fols. 82–3.

160. FH, *The Times*, 1874: 14 Mar., 7e, 19 Mar., 10d, 23 Mar., 9d, and 21 Jan. 1875, 12a; FH to Howell, 26 Apr. 1874, Bishopsgate Institute; Hughes, *Bee-Hive*, 21 Mar. 1874.

161. FH to unnamed, 13 Jan. 1875, YUL; Mundella to Howell, 18 Feb. 1875, Bishopsgate Institute; *The Times*, 1875: 19 Jan., 7f, 20 Jan., 10ab, 21 Jan., 12bc; Roberts, *The Trades Union Congress*, 86.

162. Masterman, *Ludlow*, 220–4; FH, *The Times*, 1 July 1875, 12f; *Citrine's Trade Union Law*, 3rd edn. by M. A. Hickling (London, 1967).

163. FH to H. Crompton, 2 Sept. [1875], YUL; H. Crompton to Howell, 29 Aug., 6, 9, 19 Sept. 1875, FH to Howell, 5 Aug. 1877, Bishopsgate Institute; 'The French Workmen's Congress', *FR* xxix (1878), 662–77.

164. FH, *Diminished Production ...* (London, 1879); *Scotsman*, 25 Nov. 1879, HC (Bramwell).

165. Webbs, *History of Trade Unionism*, 362–3; R. Harrison, *Before*, 313, 326–7; Spender, 'Frederic Harrison', *The Reader*, 26 Jan. 1907.

166. Henry Broadhurst, Preface, Sir James Fitzjames Stephen, *A Lecture on the Codification of the Criminal Laws* (1877); H. Crompton, *Our Criminal Justice* (1877; rpt. London, 1905) and various *FR* articles.

167. Mr Harrison to FH, 21 Dec. (1877), 12 Apr. (1878), FC; JM to FH, 1 Sept. 1879, HC.

168. 'The English School of Jurisprudence, I: Austin and Maine on Sovereignty', *FR* xxx (1878), 475–92; II, 'Bentham's and Austin's Analysis of Law', 682–803, both in *Jurisprudence and the Conflict of Laws*.

169. 'The English School of Jurisprudence, III: The Historical Method', *FR* xxi (1879), 114–30, in *Jurisprudence ... .*

170. 'The Historical Side of the Conflict of Laws', *FR* xxxii (1879), 559–76; 'The Conflict of Laws Analytically Considered', 716–31, both in *Jurisprudence ... .*

171. FH to JM, 13 Apr. (1874), Gambetta to FH, 19 Apr. 1874, HC; FH, *FR* xx (1873), 685, 679 and 'France After the War', xxi (1874), 841–56, in *NSP*.

172. Ibid., xxi (1874), 287.
173. Ibid., 284–6.
174. Ibid., 286; xx (1873), 551.
175. FH to JM, 13 Apr. (1874), HC.
176. *NSP* 82–4.
177. JM to FH, 9 Nov. 1875, HC; John Eros, 'The Positivist Generation of French Republicanism', *Sociological Review*, n.s. iii (1955), 265–77.
178. Morison, 'The Abortiveness of French Revolutions', *FR* xx (1873), 41–53; 'Is a Republic Possible in France?' xxii (1874), 1–26; cp. ESB, 'The History of Republicanism in France', ibid., 471–94; FH to JM, 13 Apr. (1873), HC, calling Morison 'not at all Positivist'.
179. FH to EBH, 28 Oct. (1877), FC; FH to Stebbing, 13, 17 July, 5 Oct. 1877, UT; Stebbing, *The Times*, 17 Jan. 1923, 12d; *AM* ii, 49–51.
180. Mr Harrison to FH, 29 Sept. (1877), FC.
181. Philip Gilbert Hamerton, *An Autobiography 1834–1858* ... (London, 1897), 622 (FH's visit in 1894); Hamerton, 'The Chief Influences on My Career', *Forum* xviii (1894–5), 423–4; Hamerton to FH, 16 Sept. 1892, HC.
182. 'The Republicans and M. Thiers', *The Times*, 12 Sept. 1877, 6bc, part in *AM* ii, 51–2; (FH), *The Times*, 1877: 14 Sept., 11ab, 28 Sept., 4c-e, both signed 'From an Englishman in the French Provinces'.
183. *The Times*, 9 Oct. 1877, 6ab.
184. FH to EBH, 21 Oct. (1877), FC.
185. Ibid., 10 letters Oct.–5 Nov. 1877, FC; *AM* ii, 50–3.
186. FH to EBH, 28 Oct. (1877) and other letters, FC; *Le Temps*, 18, 20, 24, 25 Oct., 1, 28 Nov. 1877; Schérer to FH, 15 Jan. 1878, HC; *AM* ii, 48–51.
187. *The Times*, 5 Nov. 1877, 6b-d; Blowitz to FH, 10 Oct. 1877, HC; FH to EBH, 29, 30 Oct. (1877), FC.
188. FH to EBH, 20, (29 Oct. 1877), FC; Stebbing, *The Times*, 17 Jan. 1923, 12d.
189. FH to EBH, (29) (30 Oct. 1877), FC; FH to Stebbing, 31 Oct. 1877, UT; *The Times*, 10 Nov. 1877, 10d-f, part in *AM* ii, 53–5.
190. 'The Republic and the Marshal', *FR* xxviii (1877), 742–72; Mr Harrison to FH, 21 Dec. (1877), FC.
191. 'The French Workmen's Congress', *FR* xxix (1878), 662.
192. FH to EBH (11, 12, 13 Feb. 1879), FC.
193. 'First Impressions of the New Republic', *FR* xxi (1879), 353–72.
194. FH to Mr Marshall, 6 Sept. 1879, Library of Congress; cp. JM, *FR* xxxi (1879), 647–66; J. P. T. Bury, *Gambetta and the Making of the Third Republic* (London, 1973), 5, 71; Simon, *European Positivism*, 63, 83–5, 154–6, 169; Theodore Zeldin, *France 1848–1945*, ii: *Intellect, Taste, and Anxiety* (Oxford, 1977), 156–7, 595–600; Louis Legrand, *L'Influence de positivisme dans l'oeuvre scolaire de Jules Ferry* (Paris, 1961).
195. FH to JM, 5, 30 May 1876, HC; FH to Maxse, 10 June (1876), WSRO; *Fors Clavigera*, letters 66, 67; FH, 'Past and Present', *FR* xx (1876), 93–105, in *CB* 121–44.

196. FH to JM, 9 July (1876), HC; *The Order of the Burial ... Anne Tonge Harrison, died July 8th, 1876, aged 57 years ...* (1876), FC.
197. FH to JM (2 Aug. 1876), HC.
198. FH to JM (20 Aug. 1876), HC.
199. Ibid.; *The Collected Letters of George Meredith*, 3 vols., ed. C. L. Cline (Oxford, 1970), i, 519–20, 524–5.
200. FH to JM, 17 Sept. (1876), HC.
201. FH to JM, 16 Feb., (early June), 20 June 1876, HC; Gladstone, *Gleanings of Past Years 1844–78*, iii, *Historical and Speculative* (New York, (1878)), 134, from *CR* xxviii (1876).
202. *AM* ii, 69; *SEVL* 92.
203. FH to JM, 17 Sept. (1876), HC.
204. *Polity*, i, 315; iii, xli-xliv, 477–8; iv, 410, 442–4.
205. RC, 'England and Turkey', *FR* xxvi (1876), 517–36, in *ESPR* ii, 7–30; FH to JM, 6 Oct. 1876, HC.
206. FH to JM, (Oct. 1876), JM to FH, 13 Oct. (1876), HC.
207. FH to JM, 20 Nov. (1876), HC.
208. 'Cross and Crescent', *FR* xxvi (1876), 709–30.
209. JM to FH, 23 Nov. 1876, HC; Mr Harrison to FH, 29 Sept. (1877), FC.
210. FH to JM, 24 Nov., 9 Dec. (1876), JM to FH, 3 Dec. 1876, HC; *Report ... National Conference at St. James's Hall, London, Dec. 8, 1876* (London, 1876).
211. FH to JM, (Aug. 1877) (typed copy), 25 Dec. 1877, HC; cp. RC, 'England's Policy', 1 Feb. 1878, *ESPR* ii, 31.
212. ESB to RC, 10, 12, 19 July 1878, BL, Add. MS 45227, fols. 76–81.
213. 'The Anglo-Turkish Convention (1878)', *Positivist Comments on Public Affairs: Occasional Papers Issued by the London Positivist Society, 1878–1892* (London, 1892), hereafter cited as *Positivist Comments*.
214. *AM* ii, 101–2; *The Times*, 16 July 1880, 10f; MS of Pember's poem, HC; RC, 'The Prince Imperial', *ESPR* ii, 32; Hirst, ii, 79–80.
215. FH to JM (15 Sept. 1873) (9 Oct. 1873), JM to FH, 12 Oct. 1873, HC; *FR* xx (1873), 689.
216. *FR* xxi (1874), 703–4.
217. 'The Afghan War (27 Nov. 1878)', *Positivist Comments*; *RO* iii (1878), 645–9.
218. *The Times*, 1878: 22 Oct. (Lawrence), 16, 20, 22, 23, 26, 28 Oct. and 12, 15 Nov. (Stephen); L. Stephen, *Sir James Fitzjames Stephen*, 395–7; R. W. Seton–Watson, *Disraeli, Gladstone and the Eastern Question* (London, 1935), 540.
219. FH to Bryce, 13 Dec. 1879, Bod. Uncat. MS; *The Times*, 16 Dec. 1879, 10e.
220. L. T. Hobhouse and J. L. Hammond, *Lord Hobhouse: A Memoir* (London, 1905), 69–74, 125–7; *The Times*, 16 Dec. 1879, 10e.
221. FH to Bryce, 13 Dec. 1879, Bod. Uncat. MS.
222. FH, 'Martial Law in Kabul', *FR* xxxii (1879), 784.
223. JM to FH, 26 June, 23 Aug. 1873, FH to JM, 25 Aug. 1873, Forster to

EBH, 22 Sept. 1873, HC; FH to Lytton, 27 Aug., 7 Sept. 1873, Hertford-shire County Record Office (hereafter cited as HCRO), D/EK, C36.

224. FH to JM, 5 Mar. (1873), HC.

225. *Personal and Literary Letters of Robert, First Earl of Lytton*, ed. Lady Betty Balfour, 2 vols. (New York, 1906), i, 325.

226. FH to JM, 8 Feb. 1876, Lytton to FH, 5 Mar. 1876, HC.

227. Lytton to FH, 2 Apr. 1878, HC, in Balfour, *Personal*, ii, 97–9.

228. *The Times*, 31 May, 2 June, 13 Oct., 27 Dec. 1877, 4 Jan. 1878, IOL, MSS Eur. E. 218/521/7, note from Stephen's son to Lytton's daughter, Lady Betty Balfour, saying her father got his father his KCSI in 1877.

229. Strachey to Lytton, 28 Sept., 31 Oct. 1878, IOL, MSS Eur. E. 218/517/6, fols. 73, 98; Hyndman, 'The Bankruptcy of India', *NC* iv (1878), 585–608; Rosalind Travers Hyndman, *The Last Years of H. M. Hyndman* (New York, 1924), 312; H. M. Hyndman, *The Record of an Adventurous Life* (London, 1911), 167, 173–6; (JM), 'The Impoverishment of India Not Proven', *FR* xxx (1878), 867–81.

230. 'Martial Law in Kabul', *FR* xxxii (1879), 767–84, part in *NSP* 164–83.

231. FH to Bryce, 13 Dec. 1879, Bod. Uncat. MS.

232. *The Present and the Future: A Positivist Address* (London, 1880), part in 'Empire and Humanity', *FR* xxxiii (1880), 288–308, and in *RO* iv (1880), 372–425 and *NSP*.

233. *Martial Law in Kabul* (London, 1880), preface dated 10 Jan. 1880; *AM* ii, 121.

234. *The Times*, 3 Feb. 1880, 4f; *Lord Hobhouse*, 125–9; *AM* ii, 121; *Hansard*, 3rd ser. ccl (5 Feb. 1880), cols. 116, 147 (Commons), 36, 44–5 (Lords).

235. *The Times*, 1880: 11 Feb., 10e (Hobhouse), 17 Feb., 10f (FH).

236. Lytton to Roberts, 5, 24, 25 Jan. 1880, Roberts Papers, National Army Museum, AC 7101–23–37, R 37/66, 69, 72; Roberts to Lytton, 16 Jan. 1880, Printed Correspondence, XIII, 294, ibid.; Hansard, 3rd ser. ccl (13 Feb. 1880), cols. 597–82 (Lords), 592 (Commons); *The Times*, 14 Feb. 1880, 9ab.

237. Hobhouse to FH, 9, 10, 12, 15 Feb. 1880, HC; 'Martial Law in Kabul, II', *FR* xxxiii (1880), 439–50, see esp. 441, 443–5, 447, 452–4, 445–7, quoting *Pioneer Mail*, passages not in Howard Hensman, *The Afghan War of 1879–80*, 2nd edn. (London, 1882); on Hensman and FH see Colonel H. B. Hanna, *The Second Afghan War 1878–79–80* ..., 3 vols. (London, 1910), iii, 264–74.

238. Hobhouse to FH, 10, 24 Feb. 1880, Northbrook to Hobhouse, 23 Feb. 1880, HC; Norman, 'The Scientific Frontier', *FR* xxx (1879), 1–14; Norman to Northbrook, 15 Oct. 1879, Northbrook Papers, IOL, Eur. C. 144/7, fols. 394–6; Mary Lutyens, *The Lyttons in India* (London, 1979), 125.

239. Roberts to Stanhope, 31 Mar. 1880, Roberts Papers, Printed Corres-pondence, National Army Museum, xiii, 389–90; Roberts to Lytton, 5 June 1880, ibid., 474–7, saying the article 'annoys, amuses', and 503–4, Memo replying; D. P. James, *Lord Roberts* (London, 1954), 164–5,

suggesting that anxiety over such criticism caused Robert's gastric distress on the march to Kandahar.

240. Lytton to FH, 22 Feb., 9 May 1880, HC; FH to Lytton, 6 Apr. 1880, HCRO, D/EK, C 36, on Lytton's 'generous spirit'.

241. FH to Lytton, 30 Aug. 1879, IOL, Eur. E. 218/517/8, fol. 55; Morley to Lytton, 5 Nov. 1879, ibid., fol. 97; Hobhouse to FH, 23 March 1880, HC, asking him not to write on Afghanistan until after the election.

242. W. E. Gladstone, *Midlothian Speeches 1879* (1879; rpt. New York, 1971), 91–4 (speech 26 Nov. 1879); 'Martial Law in Kabul, II,' *FR* xxxiii (1880), 458–9.

243. Lytton to FH, 9 May 1880, HC; FH to Lytton, 6 Apr. 1880, HCRO, D/EK, C36.

244. Argyll to FH, 20 Feb. 1880, HC; *Hansard*, 3rd ser. ccl (5, 20 Feb. 1880), cols. 48–50, 1021–97.

245. 'A Modern Symposium: The Influence upon Morality of a Decline in Religious Belief', *NC* i (1877), 351–3 (Argyll), 345–9 (FH), 331–3 (Stephen); Argyll, *The Afghan Question from 1841 to 1878* (London, 1879), 2–3; Ripon Diary, CLII, BL, Add. MS 43642, fol. 74.

246. (Jane) Strachey to Lytton, 12 Dec. 1879, Lewes to Lytton, 5 Jan. 1878, IOL, Eur. E. 218/517/8, fol. 112 and Eur. E. 218/521/3, fols. 26–8; *William Allingham's Diary* (Carbondale, Ill., 1967), 288; *GEL* ix, 282; Greg to FH, 4 Feb. (1880), Freeman to JM, March 1880, George Pyecroft to FH, 28 Feb. 1880 and undated, Norman to FH, 17 Apr. 1880, all HC.

247. FH to Norton, 1 Dec. 1878, HU; FH to Lytton, 6 Apr. 1880, HCRO, D/EK, C 36.

Chapter 5. Shaping a Positivist Religion 1875–1901

1. Mortimer Collins, *The British Birds: a Communication from the Ghost of Aristophanes*, 2nd edn. (London, 1878), 48.

2. *Bee-Hive*, 16 Jan. 1864.

3. GE to Mrs Congreve, 3 Jan., 1865, *GEL* iv, 174; Thomas Pinney, 'More Leaves from George Eliot's Notebook', *Huntington Library Quarterly* xxix (1966), 356; FH to RC, 21 Mar. (1872), BL, Add. MS 45228, fols. 239–45.

4. FH to RC, 21 Mar. (1872), BL, Add. MS 45228, fols. 239–45; JM to FH, 13 Nov. 1872, HC.

5. Simon, *European Positivism*, 17–19; *The Times*, 4 May 1870, 9e.

6. RC to Maria Congreve, 22, 27 Nov. 1872, Bod. MS Eng. lett. e. 54, fols. 54–60; BL, Add. MS 45242, fols. 1–8 (RC's accounts), 9–14 (Pradeau's correspondence), 15–20 (protest by ESB and associates).

7. Overton to EBH, 26 Sept., 19, 23 Oct. 1874, 7, 20, 25 Jan. 1875; EBH to Overton, 29 Jan., 2 Feb. 1875, and n.d.; fragment, Mary Christie to unknown, 29 Jan. 1879, all HC; Overton, *Harry Hartley: or, Social Science for the Workers* (1859).

8. F. J. Gould, 'The Imitation of Christ', *PR* xxxii (1924), 224–5.

9. Sir Mountstuart E. Grant Duff, *Notes from a Diary 1873–1881*, 2 vols. (London, 1898), ii, 102–3; AH, *Frederic Harrison*, 169; J. K. Ingram edited the work for the Early English Text Society in 1893, Charles Kegan Paul translated it at Cardinal Newman's behest, and Rayner Storr published a Latin concordance in 1910 that won papal praise; Morley, Commonplace Book, U. of Manchester library.

10. Brown, *Metaphysical Society*; Priscilla Metcalf, *James Knowles: Victorian Editor and Architect* (Oxford, 1980).

11. FH to JM, 4, 8 July (1870), HC; 'The Subjective Synthesis', *PCS* 22–43, from paper 13 July 1870, in *FR* xiv (1870), 184–97.

12. FH to EBH, 15 Mar. 1871, FC; 'The Absolute', *PCS* 131–41.

13. 'On the Supposed Necessity of Certain Metaphysical Problems', *PCS* 1–21, from paper 9 July 1872, in *FR* xviii (1872), 517–29.

14. Brown, *Metaphysical Society* cites papers on 9 March (Clifford) and 13 Apr. 1875 (Magee) published as 'The Scientific Basis of Morals', *CR* xxvi (1875), 650–9; FH's contribution, 'The Basis of Morals: A Symposium at the Metaphysical Society', is in *PCS* 142–50, from *CR* xxvi (1875), 670–5.

15. JM to FH, 9 Nov. 1875; FH to JM, undated, HC.

16. 'The Religious and Conservative Aspects of Positivism', *CR* xxvi (1875), 992–1012, xxvii (1875), 140–95.

17. Arnold, *CPW* viii, 134, from *CR* xxviii (1876), and note, *CPW* 412.

18. FH to JM, 3 Dec. 1877, HC; *The Book of the Spiritual Life by the Late Lady Dilke, with a Memoir ... by the R. Hon. Sir Charles Dilke* (1905; rpt. London, 1973), 10; see also Lady Dilke, 'The Idealist Movement and Positive Science: An Experience', *Cosmopolis* vii (1897), 643–56; Betty Askwith, *Lady Dilke, A Biography* (London, 1969).

19. FH to Pattison, 23, 24 Jan. (1876), Bod. Pattison MS 57, fols. 193–4, 210–11; Pattison to FH, 25 Jan. 1876, HC and to EBH, 22 Feb. 1876 (saying 'Neo-Christianity' justified his replying).

20. 'The Religion of Positivism; by a "Theosophist" ', *CR* xxvii (1876), 593–614.

21. FH to Pattison, 6 Mar. (1876), Bod. Pattison MS, fols. 224–5.

22. 'Humanity: A Dialogue', *CR* xxcii (1876), 862–85, in *CL* 152–87.

23. FH to Pattison, 26 Apr. 1876, Bod. Pattison MS 57, fols. 245–6; see John Cotter MacDonnell, *The Life and Correspondence of William Connor Magee*, ... 2 vols. (London, 1896), ii, 89–90, about a meeting 14 Feb. 1878 in which FH 'argued stoutly for *dogma* against Pattison'.

24. Pattison to FH, 18 Feb. 1868, 9 Jan. 1885, HC; but see Pattison's note, *FR* xxviii (1877), 285–6, on JHB, 'Evolution and Positivism', *FR* xvii (1877), 853–74, xviii (1877), 89–114.

25. JR, *Works*, xxviii, 614, 618–25, letter 66, June 1876; see also xxix, 565–6 (draft) and xxviii, 13–14, letter 37.

26. FH to JM, 20 June, n.d. (1876), HC; *AM* i, 237–42.

27. JR, *Works*, xxviii, 662–3, letter 67, July 1876; FH, 'Past and Present', *FR* xxvi (1876), 93–105, in *CB*.

28. JM to FH, 18 Sept. (1876), Chamberlain to FH, 3 July 1876, HC.

29. Ruskin's MS letters in HC are in JR, *Works*, xxix, 566–9, except for letter quoted, 14 July 1876, in *AM* i, 239.
30. FH to JR, 22 July (1876), HC; *AM* i, 240; JR, *Works*, xxix, 567–8.
31. JR to FH, 30 July, 9 Aug. 1876, 4 Sept., 1877, HC; *Fors* in *Works*, xxviii, 669–73, 701, 718.
32. JR to FH, 21 Sept., 10 Oct. 1880, HC; *AM* i, 243.
33. FH to JM, 20 June (1876), HC.
34. *AM* ii, 90–1; Metcalf, *James Knowles*, 283–4.
35. *NC* i (1877), 331–58, 531–46, and in *A Modern Symposium* (1879); FH's part in *PCS* 150–6.
36. FH, *The Soul Before and After Death* (9 Jan. 1877), Metaphysical Society Papers, Bodleian; in *NC* i (1877), 623–36, 832–42 (and in *PCS* 189–200, 832–42), commentaries, 329–54, 497–521; FH's replies, 521–36 (in *PCS* 231–54); the Revd Charles Voysey preached a sermon on FH's paper (copy in Dr William's Library) and the symposium is said to have influenced Browning's poem, 'La Saisiaz'.
37. Mr Harrison to FH, 29 Sept. (1877), FC.
38. *The New Paul* ... (1877: rpt. with intro. by John D. Margolis, Lincoln, Nebraska, 1978); Mallock, *Memoirs of Life and Literature*, 2nd edn. (London, 1920), 67.
39. MacDonnell, *Life ... William Connor Magee*, ii, 263.
40. Mallock, *Is Life Worth Living?* (London, 1879) and *Atheism or the Value of Life* (London, 1884); FH, 'Apologia Pro Fide Nostra', *FR* l (1888), 680 and 'Theological Pessimism' *NC* xxxviii (1895), 214–26; Mallock's reply, 661–72; FH's rejoinder, *PR* iii (1895), 189–92.
41. *NC* iii (1878), 797–822 (FH 814–22); iv (1878), 174–92.
42. 'Mr Lewes's *Problems of Life and Mind*', *FR* xxii (1874), 89–101, in *PCS* 102–21; FH to JM, 12, 27, 28 Feb. (1874), HC.
43. Haight, *George Eliot*, 515–16, quoting Frederick Locker; Grant Duff, *Notes from a Diary 1873–1881*, ii, 88; FH, 'George Henry Lewes', *Academy* xiv (7 Dec. 1878), 543–4, quoted extensively by Trollope in *FR* xxxi (1879), 15–24; FH, 'George Henry Lewes', *RO* ii (1879), 277–80, quoted by Acton, Cambridge MS 5019, fol. 836.
44. FH, *The Social Factor in Psychology* (10 June 1879), Metaphysical Society Papers, BL, in *PCS* 122–30.
45. *AM* ii, 86; Brown, *Metaphysical Society*, 34; Metcalf, *James Knowles*, 224; MacDonnell, *The Life ... Magee*, i, 284; Waldo Hilary Dunn, *James Anthony Froude; A Biography*, ii, *1857–94* (Oxford, 1963), 316–17; Grant Duff, *Notes from a Diary, 1873–1881*, ii, 217, quoting Sir Arthur Russell; *William Allingham's Diary*, 353, citing Martineau; A. S. and E. M. S. Sidgwick, *Henry Sidgwick, a Memoir* (London, 1906), 222–3.
46. *AM* ii, 86–7; FH to JM, 16 Feb. (1876), HC.
47. FH to JM, frag. HC.
48. FH to JM, 18 Dec. 1875, HC.
49. FH to JM, 16 Feb. (1876), HC; *AM* ii, 86.
50. Brown, *Metaphysical Society*, 248.

51. FH to JM, 18 Dec. (1875), HC; FH's scepticism is vindicated in Trevor H. Hall, *The Strange Case of Edmund Gurney* (1964; rpt. London, 1980).
52. 'Mystery in Religion', *PR* xvi (1908), 10–13.
53. FH to Manning, 14 July 1889, collection of Mgr. A. Chapeau; Manning to FH, 20 July 1889, HC; FH, *The Times*, 13 Apr. 1916, 9d; *AM* ii, 91.
54. 'The Comtist Utopia', *Fraser's Magazine* lxxx (1869), 1–21; 'The Scepticism of Believers', *FR* xxviii (1877), 355–76, trans. for Littré's organ, *Philosophie positive* xx (1878), 18–39.
55. Caird to FH, 16 Apr. 1885, HC; FH to unnamed, 15 Sept. n.d., YUL.
56. Grant Duff, *Notes from a Diary, 1892–1895*, 2 vols. (London, 1904), ii, 230; see FH to Laffitte, 12 March. 1879, MAC, introducing Grant Duff and Sir John Lubbock, with Laffitte's annotation about the visit.
57. FH to RC, 15 May (1876), BL, Add. MS 45228, fols. 246–7; JHB to RC, 15 May (1876) and ESB to RC, 14 May 1876, BL, Add. MS 45227, fols. 142–4, 55.
58. FH to JM, 9 Oct. (1873), HC.
59. BL, Add. MS 43844 (Register of Sacraments, 10 Feb. 1874), fol. 9; RC to wife, 14 Feb. 1873, Bod. MS Eng. lett. e. 54, fol. 81.
60. FH to RC, 15 May 1876, BL, Add. MS 45228, fols. 246–7.
61. FH to RC, 19, 20, 30 May, 8, 25 Oct. (1876), BL, Add. MS 45228, fols. 248-59.
62. BL, Add. MS 43844, fol. 13; FH to GE, 12 June 1877, *GEL* ix, 194–5.
63. *AM* ii, 258; RC, 'Personal Recollection ...', BL, Add. MS 45259, fol. 86.
64. McGee, *A Crusade*, 58; JBH to RC, 5 Nov. 1877, BL, Add. MS 45227, fols. 150–1 (praising the prayers); cp. RC, *ESPR* ii, 80 (on JHB's 'sneer' at them), 81 (denying ESB's claim to have suggested them).
65. RC, 'Personal Recollection ...', BL, Add. MS 45259, fols. 52–9; 'Selections from Congreve's Journal', BL, Add. MS 45261, 8 Sept. 1877; Sémérie to RC (1 Sept. 1877), BL, Add. MS 45239, fols. 230–51.
66. See W. M. Simon, 'Auguste Comte's English Disciples', *Victorian Studies* viii (1964), 164–7.
67. FH to Laffitte, 15 Oct. 1877 (from Bordeaux, asking for a meeting) and 19 Nov. 1877 (discouraging him from resigning), MAC; BL, Add. MS 43844 (Register of Sacraments, 8 Feb. 1878), fol. 14; RC to wife, 18 Jan. 1878, Bod. MS Eng. lett. e. 55, fol. 117, about FH's 'quite smooth' letter.
68. BL, Add. MS 45227, fols. 72–3, 45242, fols. 90–165, including letters from FH to Sulman and Kaines.
69. JHB, *Appeal to English Positivists*, 12 Oct. 1878, BL, Add. MS 45242, fols. 168–72; ESB, *Remarks on Dr Congreve's Circular* (n.d.), fols. 173–6; VL, untitled paper, 9 Oct. 1878, fols. 177–8.
70. FH to RC, 9 Oct. 1878 and RC to FH, 10 Oct. 1878, BL, Add. MS 45228, fols. 260–2.
71. Cotton to H. Crompton, 16 Oct. 1878, with FH's comments, BL, Add. MS 45242, fols. 183–93.
72. Minutes, meeting 3 Nov. 1878, BL, Add. MS 45242, fols. 194–205; H. Crompton to JHB, 17 Nov. 1879, fol. 206; circular of new committee, 24 Nov. 1878, fol. 211.

73. *AM* ii, 258; RC, 'Personal Recollection ...', BL, Add. MS 45259, fol. 86.
74. Geddes, Intro., Liveing, *A Nineteenth-Century Teacher*, 7.
75. FH to Gosse, 8 Dec. 1908, BLL.
76. FH to Laffitte, 19 Nov. 1877, 4 Jan., 17 Feb., 1878, 7 Feb. 1880 (quoted), MAC.
77. FH, *The Present and the Future* (London, 1880) (quoted); LPS, *Report for the Year 1879* and *Report for the Year 1881*; FH, *Science and Humanity* (London, 1879); FH to Laffitte, 28 Dec. 1880, MAC.
78. Dubuisson to FH (30 May 1880), FC.
79. FH to EBH (1 June 1880), FC; FH to EBH, 18 Apr., n.d., HC.
80. *AM* ii, 257–69; FH, 'The Positivists' Mecca', *The Sphere* viii (1902), 274.
81. 'Indenture' signed by FH and Cock, and designs of the hall made just before its demolition in 1928, shown to me by Mr Robert Cook, Secretary, The Royal Scottish Corporation; FH to Laffitte, 23 Apr. (1881), MAC; Lorenza Rodd, 'Newton Hall and After', *PR* xxxi (1924), 211–13.
82. FH to Dr Robinet, 25 Feb. 1879, MAC; AH, *Frederic Harrison*, 172.
83. FH to Laffitte, (15), 22, 23 Apr. 1881, MAC; Grant Duff, *Notes from a Diary, 1873–1881* ii, 320; Gwynn and Tuckwell, *The Life ... Dilke*, i, 381; AH, *Frederic Harrison*, 165.
84. Morris to FH, 30 Apr. (1881), Cornell U.
85. *OS* 315; FH, *PMG*, 29 Nov. 1883, in *AM* ii, 260; *Service of Man*, new edn. (London, 1908), 144; McGee, *A Crusade*, 157.
86. Marcella M. Carver, *A Positivist Life: A Personal Memoir of My Father, William Knight (1845–1901)* (London, 1976).
87. Herbert E. Crabbe to FH, 4 Dec. 1911, G. E. Littleworth to FH, 20 Oct. 1912, HC.
88. Arthur Porritt, *The Best I Remember* (London, 1922), 164–5.
89. E. Scott King, 'A Visit to the "Temple of Humanity" ', *Great Thoughts* xxxiii (1900), 215–16; AH, *Frederic Harrison*, 176; Sir Chihchen Lofengluh to FH, 7 Nov. 1898, with FH's note, HC; *The Morning Leader*, 2 Jan. 1900, 5b.
90. James Sully, *My Life and Friends* (London, 1918), 222.
91. EBH to FSM, 5 May 1893, Bod. MS Eng. lett. e. 108, fols. 98–101.
92. Overton to EBH, 8 Oct. 1890, HC; Paul Descours, 'Necrologie: John William Overton', *RO* 2 ser. iv (1891), 116–17, reporting FH's graveside eulogy.
93. RC correspondence, BL, Add. MS 45231, fols. 18–19 (to wife); MS 45233, fol. 113 (to J. K. Ingram).
94. Moncure Conway, *Autobiography, Memories and Experiences*, 2 vols. (London, 1904), ii, 383–4.
95. FH to EBH, 21 Feb. 1881, FC; cp. 'A Positivist Sermon', *Daily Chronicle*, 9 Dec. 1895, calling FH 'above all things the superior literary man'.
96. LPS, Minutes of the Committee, May 1883–April 1905, LSE; LPS, *Report for the Year 1881*, and ibid. for years to 1889.
97. LPS, *Reports for the Years 1881–1883*; JHB, *Essays and Addresses*, intro. FH (London, 1907), 235–63; *CL* 50–1.

98. FH to Laffitte, 25 Nov. 1881, MAC.
99. *The Times*, 23 Dec. 1881, 6d; Somerset House records.
100. FH to JM, 19 May 1882, HC.
101. FH to EBH (11 May 1882), FC.
102. FH to Laffitte, 31 Dec. 1881, MAC.
103. Programme in FC; see my essay, 'The Choir Invisible: The Poetics of Humanist Piety', *George Eliot: A Centenary Tribute*, ed. Gordon S. Haight and Rosemary T. VanArsdel (London, 1982).
104. FH to Laffitte, 21 Mar. 1882, MAC.
105. VL to FH, 29 Jan. 1884, HC; VL, *The Day of All the Dead* (1883); see Derek Hudson, *Munby: Man of Two Worlds: The Life and Diaries of Arthur J. Munby 1828–1910* (London, 1972), 348, 375 (on the Lushingtons' experiment in simple country living before returning to London in 1877 and VL as one of 3 confidants told by Munby of his marriage to his servant); *Emma Darwin, A Century of Family Letters*, by her daughter, H. E. Litchfield, 2 vols. (London, 1904), ii, 304.
106. FH to Laffitte, 20 Dec. 1889, MAC; see also FH to JM (13 Dec. 1889), HC; Emily Beesly was not a Positivist (see her diary, ESB Collection, UC) and was buried with Anglican rites by Llewelyn Davies.
107. FH to Conway, 3 Sept. 1884, Conway Collection, Columbia U.
108. Jane Harrison to FH, 4 Jan. (1884), FC.
109. S. H. Swinny, 'In Memoriam: Judge Fossett Lock', *PR* xxx (1922), 175–7.
110. LPS, *Report for the Year 1881* and ibid. to 1889.
111. *DNB*; *King's College School: A Register*; E. K. Chambers, 'The Disintegration of Shakespeare', *Proceedings of the British Academy* (1924); Fleay, *Three Lectures on Education*, with Preface by FH (London, 1883); FH to JHB, (14 May 1880), HC; *AM* i, 36.
112. *AM* ii, 288–90; LPS, *Report for the Year 1884*, ibid. to 1889, and for 1893; Dean Bradley to FH, 28 May 1886, 1 June 1887, HC; FH to Laffitte, 7, 15 June 1886 and printed circulars, MAC; (Bockett), *PMG*, 15 June 1886.
113. *Le Figaro*, 14 June 1886; FH to EBH (15 June 1886), FC.
114. EBH, 'In Memoriam: Lady Macfarren', *PR* xxiv (1916), 138–9; Macfarren to FH, 13 May 1883, HC.
115. LPS, Positivist Society, 1878–91, LSE (list, in ESB hand, of members); Percy Marshall Young, *George Grove, 1820–1904* (London, 1980), 238; see obit. in *San Francisco Chronicle*, 12 Dec. 1905.
116. EBH to FSM, 21 Apr. (1890), Bod. MS Eng. lett. d. 249, fols. 101–2; letters of permission to EBH, EBH to LPS Committee (1897), and memoranda by JHB and VL, 1897, all HC.
117. EBH to FSM, 10 Oct. (1889), Eng. lett. e. 105, fols. 41–2; 'A Women's Guild: A Chat with Mrs Frederic Harrison' (1887), cutting HC; EBH, *PR* i (1893), 175–8.
118. Obit., *PR* xxv (1917), 212–13, and FH on, 257–8.
119. Obit., *PR* xxxi (1923), 181–9.
120. Cecil H. Desch, 'Francis Sidney Marvin, 1863–1943', *Isis* xxxvi (1945–6), 7–9; FH to FSM, 25 Sept. 1887, Eng. lett. e. 248, fols. 25–6.

121. ESB to FSM, 23 Oct. 1889, 10 Feb. 1891, Bod. MS Eng. lett. e. 105, fols. 49–50, d. 251, fols. 45–6; FH to FSM, 18 Sept., 29 Oct., 16 Dec. 1889, e. 105, fols. 27–8, 51–2, 76–81; LPS, Minutes of the Positivist Committee, 14 Oct., 9 Dec. 1889, LSE.

122. *PR* xi (1903), 21–4; ESB to FSM, 7 Aug. 1893, Bod. MS Eng. lett. c. 108, fols. 103–4.

123. FH to JM, 3 July 1891 and (27 Apr. 1891), HC.

124. JHB to FH, 1886, HC; Liveing, *A Nineteenth-Century Teacher*, 218; LPS, Minutes of the Committee, 20 Jan. 1890.

125. Morison to FH, 18 Sept. 1886, HC; FH to EBH (12 Feb. 1881), EBH to FH, 30 Jan. 1884, FC; FH to Theodore Morison, 10, 28 Nov. 1888, U. of Newcastle-Upon-Tyne Library, MS Album; Morison letters to Gosse, BLL (on his last illness); Gissing on his having been 'ruined by luxury', *Letters of George Gissing to Eduard Bertz* ed. Arthur C. Young (London, 1961), 205.

126. Letters in William Frey Collection, New York Public Library; LPS, Minutes for 1887–8; ESB, *The Life and Death of William Frey* (London, 1888); Avrahm Yarmolinsky, *A Russian's American Dream: A Memoir on William Frey* (Lawrence, Kansas, 1965).

127. LPS, Minutes for 17 May, 11 July, 12 Dec. 1887, 23 Jan. 1888, LSE; Swinny, 'In Memoriam: Judge Fossett Lock', *PR* xxx (1922), 175–7.

128. FH to FSM, 24 June, 2, 22 July 1889, 1 Dec. 1896, Bod. MS Eng. lett. d. 248, fols. 119–20, 131–2, 152–3; EBH to FSM, 21 Jan. 1896, Bod. MS Eng. lett. e. 110, fols. 7–10.

129. *Lady John Russell: A Memoir, with Selections from Her Diaries and Correspondence*, ed. Desmond MacCarthy and Agatha Russell (London, 1910), appendix.

130. FH, *In Memory of William D. Hertz* (1890); *G. Paul Macdonell: In Memoriam*, ed. Grant Allen (London, 1895), 56–64.

131. FH, *Grant Allen, 1848–1899* (London, 1899); FH to JM, 13 July 1896, HC; FH to E. Clodd, 22 June 1900, BLL.

132. Sulman to RC, 30 Nov. 1884, BL, Add. 48229, fols. 272–3 (suggesting candles left on the altar for ladies to light).

133. FH to Laffitte, 21 Jan. 1881, MAC; RC to H. Crompton, 16 July 1886, BL, Add. MS 45231, fols. 22–4.

134. FH to Laffitte, 13 Dec. 1883, MAC.

135. LPS, Minutes of the Committee, 15 Feb. 1884; Kaines was Secretary to the Commercial Travellers' Benevolent Association and a member of the British Association for the Advancement of Science; *PR* viii (1900), 61–2 (obit.).

136. FH to Laffitte, 9 Nov. 1885, MAC; cutting, *Manchester Guardian*, letter signed C. H. H. 24 Nov. n.y. HC (replying to FH's critics); *The Times*, 27 Apr. 1931, 12d (obit).

137. FH to Laffitte, 29 Dec. 1886, 3 June, 5 July 1889, MAC; FH, *A New Era* (1889), an address to Higginson's group; LPS, Minutes of the Committee, 21 Jan. 1889; Manchester Positivist Society's Book of Sacraments, *Reports*,

and *President's Annual Circular, Sixth Session, 1889–90*, in Manchester Central Library.

138. FH to Laffitte, 7 July 1894, MAC; FH to EBH, 18 Feb. 1907, FC; LPS, Minutes of the Committee, 30 Apr. 1900.

139. McGee, *A Crusade*, 129–38; Papers in the Fraser Collection, Harold Cohen Library, U. of Liverpool.

140. Malcolm Quin, *Memoirs of a Positivist* (London, 1924), esp. 115 (FH's visit); FH, review of Quin's *Catholicism and the Modern Mind*, *ER* xi (1912), 167–8; McGee, *A Crusade*, 139–51.

141. ESB to Mrs Congreve, 6 July 1899, Bod. MS Eng. lett. c. 186, fols. 2–3; *AM* i, 85–7, from *Wadham College Gazette* i, no. 7 (1899), 127–9.

142. EBH to FH, 23 Oct. 1901, FC; FH to Jeannolle, 5 Nov. 1901, MAC.

143. FH to Hillemand, 10 Dec. 1891, MAC; Simon, *European Positivism*, 63.

144. FH to Laffitte (13 May 1886), FH to Jeannolle, various letters, 1888, 1896–1900, and FH to Hillemand, 1894–5, MAC; FH, 'The Statutes of the Positivist Society of Paris, 11 March 1894', *PR* ii (1894), 138–41.

145. FH to Laffitte, 21 Apr. 1897, MAC: FH, 'Nomination of his Successor by M. Laffitte', *PR* v (1897), 109–11; FH to *The Times*, 13 May 1897, 5f.

146. FH to EBH, 10, 12 Sept. (1896), FC.

147. FH, 'Pierre Laffitte', *Cosmopolis* ii (1898), 334–5.

148. FH, 'Statue of Auguste Comte', *PR* iv (1896), 153–6; 'The Monument of Auguste Comte', viii (1900), 85–7; 'Paragraphs', x (1902), 130, 'The Commemoration of Auguste Comte', 165; Goldwin Smith to FH, 9 May 1900, GL to FH, 27 Sept. 1898, Charles A. Codman to FH, undated and 13 Aug. 1901 (quoted), HC; RC, *The Statue of Auguste Comte: Some Remarks* (London, 1898).

Chapter 6. Positivism, Politics, and Philosophy 1880–1901

1. FH to Dilke, 3, 5 Apr. 1880, BL, Add. MS 43898, fols. 177–87.

2. FH to Dilke, 1 May 1880, ibid., fols. 189–90.

3. Chamberlain to FH, 2 May 1880, HC (saying he had hoped Dilke would be in the Cabinet).

4. FH to Mundella, 1 May 1880, U. of Sheffield.

5. *The Times*, 15 Dec. 1880, 8b (about Roberts, by now Baron Roberts of Kandahar) and Lytton being honoured at the Merchant Taylors' School on Prize Day, where F. S. Marvin, future Positivist, was top student).

6. 'The War in the Transvaal' (10 Feb. 1881), *Positivist Comments*; *Pall Mall Gazette*, 16 Feb. 1881; FH to EBH, 10, 12, 14, 15, 17, 18 Feb. 1881, FC; *Echo* 17, 18 Feb. 1881, part in *AM* ii, 126–7; ESB to FH, 17 Feb. 1881, FC.

7. FH to EBH (7, 12 Feb. 1881), FC; 'The Irish Coercion Bill' (10 Feb. 1881), *Positivist Comments*; ESB, 'Our Foreign and Irish Policy', *FR* xxxv (1881), 229–43; ESB, *Some Aspects of Positivism* (London, 1881), 26–7 (on boycotting); FH, *RO* vii (1881), 285.

8. *RO* vii (1881), 284–5; FH to Dilke, 12 Aug. 1881, BL, Add. MS 43898, fols. 195–6.

9. FH, 'Deadlock in the House of Commons', *NC* x (1881), 317–40; 'The Crisis of Parliamentary Government', xi (1882), 9–28.

10. JM, *The Life of William Ewart Gladstone*, 3 vols. (New York, 1903), iii, 51; *The Diary of Sir Edward Walter Hamilton 1880–1885*, 2 vols., i, *1880–1882* (Oxford, 1972), 165; Gladstone to unknown correspondent (copy), 2 Sept. (1881), HC.

11. FH to EBH (18 Feb. 1881), FC.

12. *AM* ii, 81–2.

13. GG to FH, 9 July 1880 (copy), FH to GG, 22 July 1880 (copy), GG to his brother Algernon, 23 July 1880 (about the promise of 'glorious help' from FH), 20 Aug. 1880 (about dining twice with FH), all CPL; Jacob Korg uses this episode to begin *George Gissing, A Critical Biography* (Seattle, 1963), a source of biographical information following unless otherwise specified.

14. GG to Algernon Gissing, 29 July 1880, CPL, and 20 Aug. 1880, in *Letters of George Gissing to Members of his Family*, collected and arranged by Algernon and Ellen Gissing (Boston and New York, 1927), 79–80 (hereafter cited as *GG Letters*).

15. *GG Letters*, 80; the essays are in *Notes on Social Democracy*, ed. by Jacob Korg (London, 1968); see also GG, 'On Battersea Bridge', *PMG*, 30 Nov. 1883.

16. GG to Algernon Gissing, 18 Nov. 1880, YUL; Pierre Coustillas, *George Gissing and Ivan Turgenev* (London, 1982).

17. EBH to FH, 9, 10, 14 Dec. 1880, FC; GG to Algernon Gissing, 21, 23 Dec. 1880, YUL; AH, *Frederic Harrison*, 80–3 and 'George Gissing', *NC and After* lx (Sept. 1906), 453–63.

18. FH to EBH, 2, 3, 4, 5, 7 (Feb. 1881), FC.

19. FH to EBH, 8, 9, 21 Feb. 1881, FC; GG to Algernon Gissing, 25 Feb. 1881, YUL (about moving from Islington to Westbourne Park West to save shoeleather), 4 May 1881 (quoted), 8 Mar. 1882, Berg; 2 Sept. 1883, YUL (on the food's good effects).

20. FH to EBH, 7, 8, 21 Feb. 1881, FC; *GG Letters*, 88 (13 Jan. 1881).

21. FH to H. G. Wells, 27 Jan. 1904, in *George Gissing and H. G. Wells, Their Friendship and Correspondence*, ed. Royal A. Gettmann (Urbana, 1961), 230 (quoted); AH, *Frederic Harrison*, 84; *Manchester Facts and Places* (Manchester, 1896–7), viii, 108–9 (on Higginson's entry, Owens College 1874, his BA and MA (1878), London U., and his father, a Unitarian minister who once had a church at Wakefield, where Gissing grew up).

22. GG to Algernon Gissing, 9 Apr. 1881, YUL; P. Coustillas, 'George Gissing à Manchester', *Études Anglaises* xvi (1963), 255–61.

23. GG to Algernon Gissing, 24, 29 Sept. 1883, YUL; GG to Algernon Gissing, 2 Nov. 1882, the Tracy W. MacGregor Library, U. of Va.

24. FH to Cross, 6 May 1880, *GEL* vii, 271–2.

25. FH to (William Henry) Hall (Cross's brother-in-law), 23 Dec. 1880, YUL (citing EBH's illness and his examining at Oxford; he had apparently not yet heard of his uncle Charles Harrison's death that day).

26. FH to JM, 23 Oct. (1885), HC.

27. Spencer to FH, 26 Dec. 1880, HC; Haight, *George Eliot*, 549.
28. *The Times*, 30 Dec. 1880, 6c; Haight, *George Eliot*, 488, 549.
29. FH to Laffitte, 29 Dec. 1880, MAC; ESB, *Some Public Aspects of Positivism* (London, 1881), 7–8.
30. MSS at Folger Library, Berg, YUL, CPL, variously published.
31. GG to Algernon Gissing, 3 Nov. 1880, YUL; 11 Nov. 1880, in *GG Letters*, 85; 24 Apr., 4 May 1881, Berg.
32. GG to Algernon, 6 Oct. 1882, YUL; MS 'The Hope of Pessimism', CPL, in *George Gissing, Essays and Fiction*, ed. Pierre Coustillas (Baltimore, 1970), 75–97; cp. GG to Algernon, 15 May 1884, YUL (recommending the study of Comte).
33. GG to Algernon Gissing, 25 June 1884, YUL (quoting FH).
34. GG to FH, 24 June 1884, CPL; GG to EBH, Fri. 6 July (error for 4 July), 1884, CPL.
35. AH, 'George Gissing', op. cit., 453–63; GG to Algernon, 12, 14 Aug. 1884, YUL; GG to FH, 17 Aug. 1884, CPL; BH to EBH, Fri. (8 Aug. 1884), FC.
36. On the family of Montague Cookson, Lincoln's Inn barrister who took the name of Crackanthorpe in 1888, see David Crackanthorpe, *Hubert Crackanthorpe and English Realism in the 1890s* (Columbia, Mo., 1977).
37. GG to Algernon, 14 Aug. 1884, *GG Letters*, 145–6; GG to FH, 17 Aug. 1884, CPL.
38. GG's place at Bonscale was taken by EBH's brother George Crawford Harrison, who had just earned his BA at Oriel, Oxford, and became a housemaster at Fettes College, Edinburgh, where he died in 1900.
39. J. R. de S. Honey, *Tom Brown's Universe* (New York, 1977), 318 (quoted); Walker to ESB, 3 letters in 1867 and ESB to H. Crompton, 14, 19 July 1867, UC; Walker to Mrs Congreve, 14 July 1899, Bod. MS Eng. lett. c. 187, fols. 110–115; J. W. Shepard to FH, 13 Sept. 1884, FC.
40. GG to FH, 17 Aug. 1884, CPL; GG to Algernon Gissing, Sat., 31 Jan. 1885 (misdated 30), YUL (quoted).
41. GG to Algernon Gissing, 25 Aug. 1884 (quoted), 28 Dec. 1886, Berg.
42. GG to Madge Gissing, 12 July 1882 (quoted), GG to Algernon Gissing, 13, 22 June 1883, Berg; AH, 'George Gissing', op. cit., 461–2.
43. GG to Ellen Gissing, 24 Aug. 1885, in *GG Letters*, 167–8.
44. Pierre Coustillas makes this point in a note to his intro. to the novel, rpt., 2 vols. (Brighton, 1969).
45. GG to Algernon Gissing, 26 June 1883, Berg; *The Times*, 23 Apr. 1883, 4bc; John Halperin, *Gissing: A Life in Books* (Oxford, 1982), 57, and Coustillas suggest as Isabel's prototype the Harrisons' friend Mrs Gaussen, on whom see Anthony Curtis, 'Gissing and the Gaussens: Some Unpublished Documents', *Gissing Newsletter* xii (1976), 1–5, and M. S. and A. R. Vogeler, 'Gissing's Friends: More Light on the Gaussens', 6–14.
46. First published in *George Gissing, Essays and Fiction*, 227–30, the story is dated autumn 1882 by P. Coustillas.
47. GG to Algernon, 18 Aug. 1881, YUL; FH to Wells, 4 Feb. 1904, U. of Illinois.

48. AH, *Frederic Harrison*, 82.
49. GG, 'The Death of the Children', *ER* xvii (Apr. 1914), 1; *The Times*, 28 Apr. 1884, 10a, and 17, 23 Dec. 1884, 12a and 6b; FH to Bentley, 22 Dec. (1884), U. of Illinois; FH to Brassey, 22 Dec. 1885, Bod. MS Autographs, b. 9, fols. 204–6; FH to Sir William Henry and Lady Gregory, 25, 27 Dec. 1884, Berg; GH and RH to EBH, (1884), FC.
50. FH to EBH, 7, 8, 9 May 1882, FC.
51. *NSP* 184–5, from Anti-Aggression League Pamphlets, no. 1, speeches of meeting reported in *The Times*, 23 Feb. 1882, 5e; *AM* ii, 121–2; *Life and Letters of Herbert Spencer*, 2 vols. (New York, 1908), i, 294–6; Herbert Spencer, *An Autobiography*, 2 vols. (New York, 1904), i, 443–51; Spencer, *The New York Evening Post*, 26 Mar. 1896.
52. *PMG*, 7 June 1882; Taylor, *The Troublemakers*, 90, *PMG*, 2 May 1882; FH, *The Times*, 19 June 1882, 8d, quoted in *AM* ii, 124–6.
53. *PMG*, 8 June 1882 (editorial); FH, ibid., 12 June 1882; FH to JM, 3 June (1882), and fragment, HC.
54. *NSP* 210–24, rpt. *The Crisis in Egypt: A Letter to Mr Gladstone* (London, 1882); FH to Gladstone, 5 July 1882, BL, Add. MS 44476, fol. 10.
55. Gladstone to FH, 7 July 1882, HC.
56. FH, *The Times*, 13 Jan. 1873, 7b, agreeing with ESB's estimate, 11 Jan., 5e.
57. Wilfred Scawen Blunt, *Secret History of the English Occupation of Egypt* (London, 1907), 321–22; see Elizabeth Longford, *A Pilgrimage of Passion: The Life of Wilfrid Scawen Blunt* (London, 1979).
58. FH to JM, 3 June 1882, HC; Lady Anne Blunt's Diary, 20 June (1882), BL, Add. MS 53917; Blunt, *Secret History*, 321–2, 341–9, 358; *The Times*, 23 June 1882, 4ab.
59. 'The Aggression in Egypt' (14 July 1882), *Positivist Comments*; Newman to FH, 31 July, 1 Sept. 1882, HC.
60. AH, *Frederic Harrison*, 94–5; FH to EBH (10 May 1882), FC.
61. FH to EBH (18 Oct. 1882), FC; FH to Blunt, 28 Nov. 1882, Berg.
62. Blunt, *Secret History*, 543–44; *AM* ii, 126; 'The Trial of Arabi Pasha, an Address to … Gladstone' (11 Oct. 1882), *Positivist Comments;* Bright to FH, 30 Apr. 1883, HC; *Seventy Years: Being the Autobiography of Lady Gregory*, ed. Colin Smythe (Gerrards Cross, 1974), 50, 54–5.
63. *The Times*, 6 June 1884, 3f (Blunt), 9 June, 10a (FH); Blunt to FH, 9 June (1884), Cornell U.
64. FH to JM, 6 Nov. 1884, HC.
65. 'Review of the Year (Newton Hall, 1 January 1885)', *FR* xliii (Feb. 1885), 189–91.
66. FH to EBH (15 Feb. 1881), FC.
67. JM to FH, 24 Feb. 1884, in Hirst, ii, 220, see also 214–19.
68. FH to JM, 12 Feb. (1885), HC.
69. *The Times*, 5 Mar. 1885, 6a, c; Lady Anne's Diary, BL, Add. MS 53950, 4 Mar. 1885, calling it a 'very good' speech before about 150 people.
70. *The Times*, 3 Apr. 1885, 5ef; see also 'Retirement from the Sudan' (13 Feb. 1885), *Positivist Comments*.

71. FH to EBH (27, 30 Nov. 1882), FC; *CB* 259–72, rpt. 'The Royal Courts of Justice', *The Times*, 2 Dec. 1882, 6a–e.
72. Sir Frederick Pollock, 'Frederic Harrison, Jurist and Historian', *ER* xxxvi (May 1923), 412.
73. 'Curiosities of the Law of Treason', *FR* xxxvii (1882), 587–601; 'History of the Law of Treason, Part II', 698–710.
74. *AM* ii, 244; *The Times*, 11 Mar. 1886, 10c; FH to Stephen, Midsummer Day (24 June 1885), Add. 7349/15, CUL; K. Muir Mackenzie for the Lord Chancellor to FH, 18 June 1885, Lord Coleridge to FH, 1891, HC.
75. Sir Henry Sumner Maine, *International Law: The Whewell Lectures*, ed. by Frederick Pollock and FH (London, 1888); Maine's widow to FH (after 1910), HC (recalling him looking 'altogether smart' years earlier); FH's appreciation of Grant Duff's *Memoir* of Maine is quoted in Grant Duff's *Notes ... Diary, 1892–5*, i, 137.
76. *RI* 236–8; *The Times*, 19 Mar. 1884, 12a; Duncan, *Life and Letters of Herbert Spencer*, ii, 319–22; Holyoake, *Sixty Years*, ii, 255–7.
77. *PMG*, 5 Oct. 1885.
78. F. W. Lawson, *The Oxford Law School 1850–1965* (Oxford, 1968), 213; FH, *RO* iv (1880), 143–50.
79. *OS* 392–8, Annual Address, 1 Jan. 1882.
80. George to FH, 23 May 1881, HC; FH to Bramwell, 16 May 1883, quoted in Charles Fairchild, *Some Account of George William Wilshire, Baron Bramwell of Hover and his Opinions* (London, 1898), 241–4; Bramwell to FH, 21 May 1883, HC.
81. FH, 'The Progress of Labour', *CR* lxiv (1883), 477–89; FH to EBH, 13, 14 Sept. (1883), FC; 'Impressions of the Trade Union Congress', *PMG*, 19 Sept. 1883.
82. 'The Nationalization of Land', *PMG*, 28 Sept., 3 Nov. 1883.
83. Charles Albro Barker, *Henry George* (New York, 1955), 397–8, quoting George, 'At last, at last I am famous'; Henry Fawcett to FH, 19 Jan. 1884, HC, encouraging him to publish on the land question.
84. FH to EBH, 26, 28, 30, 31 Jan., 1, 3 Feb. 1884, FC; FH to Geddes, 3 Jan. 1883, National Library of Scotland, Edinburgh.
85. FH to EBH (3 Feb. 1884), FC; Norman Saul to RC (26 Jan. 1884), BL, Add. MS 45240, fols. 252–3; Watson, *The National Liberal Federation from its Commencement to the General Election of 1906* (London, 1907); Morley, *Recollections*, i, 184; *Newcastle Daily Chronicle*, 4 Feb. 1884; Quin, *Memoirs*, 103.
86. FH, 'A New Industrial Inquiry', *PMG*, 8 Sept. 1884, in *Industrial Remuneration Conference: The Report of Proceedings and Papers* (1885; rpt. New York, 1968); FH to JM, 27 Nov. 1884, HC; Hirst, ii, 205–6; Brassey to FH, 27 Mar. 1884, HC; FH to Dilke, 2, 4, 11 Dec. 1884, BL, Add. MS 43898, fols. 198–203; *The Times*, 28 Jan. 1885, 6a, e, 29 Jan., 10a–e; *NSP* 377–420 (FH's speech).
87. John Saville, intro. *Industrial Remuneration Conference* (New York, 1968).

88. *The Times*, 3 Feb. 1885, 6cd (Wallace), 4 Feb. 6c (FH); FH to Wallace, 11, 15 June 1885, BL, Add. MS 46440, fols. 94–5; Wallace to FH, 11 June 1885, HC; James Oliphant, Preface, *The Claims of Labour* (Edinburgh, 1886).

89. EBH to Miller, 2 Nov. 1885, FC; Miller to EBH, 29 Oct., 3 Nov. 1885, HC.

90. FH to JM, 14 Oct. 1885, HC, part in Hirst, ii, 258.

91. FH to JM, 26 Aug. 1885, in Hirst, ii, 246; see D. A. Hamer, intro. to *The Radical Programme* (1885; rpt. Brighton, 1971).

92. Unless noted, sources of this episode are Jenkins, *Victorian Scandal*, Askwith, *Lady Dilke*, and *The Times*, indexed articles, Feb., July 1886.

93. EBH to FH, 14 Mar. (1871), FH to EBH, Mon. (27 Nov. 1882), FC; Cline, ed. George Meredith, *Letters*, ii, 614n. 1; *The Times*, 3 Jan. 1919, 9e (Crawford's obit.).

94. FH to EBH (26 Jan. 1884), Mr Harrison to FH, 4 Aug. (1876), FC; FH to JM (Oct. 1876), HC.

95. FH to Laffitte, (21 Mar. 1882), MAC.

96. FH to JM, 26 Aug. 1885, HC.

97. Chamberlain to JM, 22 Oct. 1885, in J. L. Garvin, *The Life of Joseph Chamberlain*, ii, *1885–1895* (London, 1933), 45; FH to JM, 24 Oct. 1885, HC.

98. FH to JM, 24 July 1886, HC.

99. FH to EBH, Tues. (15 Feb. 1881), FC.

100. *PMG*, 2 Jan. 1886; Stead to FH, 9 Jan. 1885 (error for 1886), HC.

101. EBH to FH, Thurs. (2 Sept. 1885), FC; Ann Stafford, *The Age of Consent* (London, 1964).

102. *PMG*, 17, 20 Dec. 1883 (Liddon), 2 Jan. 1884 (FH's comments in his Annual Address); Stead to FH, 9 Jan. 1884, HC; FH to Antoine, 19 Dec. (1884) MAC.

103. Shane Leslie, 'Virginia Crawford, Sir Charles Dilke, and Cardinal Manning', *The Dublin Review* ccxli (1967), 177–205; see her 'Journalism as a Profession for Women', *CR* lxiv (1893), 362–71.

104. *The Athenaeum*, 12 June 1886, 786.

105. *Memoirs of Lady Ottoline Morrell: A Study in Friendships, 1873–1915*, ed. Robert Gathorne Hardy (New York, 1964), 83–4.

106. *AM* ii, 63–4; 'Leon Gambetta', *NSP* 97–115, from *CR* xliii (1883), 311–24; criticized by R. W. Dale, 'M. Gambetta: Positivism and Christianity', 476–97, and by Arnold, *CPW* ix, 129.

107. *The Times*, 2 Jan. 1886, 7e; 'The Radical Programme', *CR* xlix (1886), 264–79.

108. FH to JM, 1 Feb. 1886, HC; *PMG*, 8 Feb. 1886; *The Times*, 16 Feb. 1886, 12cd (in *AM* ii, 223–34) and editorial, 9.

109. *Mr Gladstone or Anarchy!* (London, 1886).

110. Lubbock to FH, 30 June, 3 July 1886, HC; Horace G. Hutchinson, *Life of Sir John Lubbock, Lord Avebury*, 2 vols. (London, 1914), i, 226; *AM* ii, 219–23; C. Harrison to FH, 13, 14, 19 July 1886, FC; W. J. Collins to FH, 27, 29 June 1886, HC.

111. FH to JM, 7 July 1886, HC.
112. Obit. notices of Mrs Beesly in ESB Collection, UC.
113. FH to JM, 24 July 1886, HC.
114. Muriel Harris, 'Frederic Harrison at Ninety', *New York Times Book Review*, 1 Jan. 1922, sec. 3, 8.
115. Letters from boys to parents, FC; cf. Rosalind Howard to EBH, 26 Apr. 1888, HC (about being unreconciled to her husband's 'unholy alliance' with the Tories).
116. Rosalind Howard to EBH, 11 May 1887, HC; FH to EBH, 4 Sept. (1896), FC; Dorothy Henley, *Rosalind Howard: Countess of Carlisle* (London, 1958); Charles Roberts, *The Radical Countess* ... (Carlisle, 1962).
117. AH, *Frederic Harrison*, 150.
118. M. S. Wilkins, 'The Non-Socialist Origins of England's First Important Socialist Organization', *IRSH* iv (1959), 199–207; S. H. Swinny, *PR*, xxvi (1918), 206–9, review of Belfort Bax, *Reminiscences* ... (London, 1918); Norman and Jeanne MacKenzie, *The First Fabians* (London, 1977), 27, 36, 60–2, 109–112, 250.
119. FH, 'The Emperor's Industrial Project', *Speaker*, 15 Feb. 1890, 171; *NSP* 440–62; 'Police Interference with Socialist Meetings' (25 Sept. 1885), *Positivist Comments*; Donald C. Richter, *Riotous Victorians* (Athens, 1981), 101, citing ESB to Cross, 25 Sept. 1885, HO 45/X 7215; Longford, *Pilgrimage*, 241–2.
120. Webb, *My Apprenticeship*, 186–220; Swinny, 'Charles Booth', *PR* xxvii (1919), 63–7; T. S. and M. B. Simey, *Charles Booth, Social Scientist* (Oxford, 1960); FH to Mrs Booth, 11 Dec. 1916, ULL.
121. *The Letters of Sidney and Beatrice Webb*, ed. Norman MacKenzie, 3 vols. (Cambridge and London, 1978), i, 57; Webb, *My Apprenticeship*, 112, 275–6.
122. Webb, *My Apprenticeship*, 129, 275–6.
123. 'Diary of Beatrice Webb Typewritten Transcript', xiii, 1023, LSE.
124. Webb, *My Apprenticeship*, 124–5.
125. *NSP* 421–39, from 'The New Trades-Unionism', *NC* xxvi (1889), 721–32.
126. *AM* ii, 104, 241; Grant Duff, *Notes from a Diary ... 1892–1895*, ii, 253–4 (quoted); EBH to FSM, 17 Aug. 1891, Bod. MS Eng. lett. e. 106, fols. 3–4; FH to JM, 1 May 1889, HC.
127. 'A Plea for the Tower of London', *CB* 275–90, from *The Times*, 27 June 1883, 4de; 'The Sacredness of Ancient Buildings', *MH* 459–78, from *CR* lii (1887).
128. FH speeches at Toynbee Hall, reported in *The Spectator* lx (20 Nov. 1886), 1554–5; *The Times*, 19 Dec. 1887, 10c, rpt. *PMG*, 22 Dec. 1887; ibid., 19 Dec. 1887 (quoted).
129. 'Charles Harrison', *People of the Period*, ed. A. T. Cambden Pratt, i (London, 1897), 449–50 (quoted).
130. *AM* ii, 240–1; FH to JM, 29 Dec. (1888), HC; Sir Gwilym Gibbon and Reginald W. Bell, *History of the London County Council 1889–1939* (London, 1939), 83–6; William Saunders, *History of the First London*

County Council 1889–1890–1891 (London, 1892), 1–8; *London County Council, Minutes of the Proceedings of the Council 1889*, 5 (hereafter cited as *LCC Minutes* with year).

131. 'London's Municipal Government' (March 1883), *Positivist Comments*.

132. FH to JM, 13 Apr. 1889, HC; Saunders, *History*, 69–73, 262; *AM* ii, 241; FH, 'The Amalgamation of London', *CR* lxvi (1894), 743.

133. *LCC Minutes 1890*, 20 May, 421–22, 11 Feb., 100–3; FH, 'The Veto on Drink', *RI* 196–201; FH, 'Home Rule for London', *PR* i (1893), 1–5.

134. FH to JM, 17 Feb. 1891, HC; FH to Burns, 4 Mar. 1892, BL, Add. MS 46290, fol. 63; FH, 'London Improvements', *New Review* vii (1892), 518; Burns to FH, 6 Oct. 1892 and to EBH, n.d., HC.

135. FH to EBH, 10 Mar. (1892), FC; FH to B. Webb, All Saints (1 Nov.), 1893, Passfield Papers, II-4-a-17, LSE.

136. Saunders, *History*, Index: Personal; *LCC Minutes 1889*, 31 May, 384–5; 'The Use of Sunday', *RI* 189–95, from *PR* ii (1895); Lord Coleridge to FH, 13 Feb. 1891, HC; *LCC Minutes 1892*, 8 Nov., 1014–5; FH, 'London Improvements', op. cit., 415 (quoted) *AM* ii, 242–3.

137. FH to J. W. Collins, 5, 20 Sept. 16, 18 (2 letters), 19 Oct. 1893, Collins to FH, 18 Oct. 1893, ULL.

138. *The Star*, 1, 20 Feb. 1889; Lubbock to FH, 14 Mar. 1892, HC; Hutchinson, *Lubbock*, i, 319–24.

139. FH to Rosebery, 9 Feb. (1889), Rosebery to FH, 10 Feb. 1889, National Library of Scotland, Edinburgh; FH to JM, 19 July, 8 Oct. 1889, HC (quoted).

140. FH to JM, 13 Apr., 17 May 1889, HC; FH to EBH, Fri. (11 Mar. 1892), FC.

141. FH to JM, Thurs. n.d., 30 Mar. 1892, HC; Webb, *Our Partnership*, 72; *The Times*, 27, 31 Dec. 1897, 7f, 4d.

142. 'Cremation', *RI* 169–73, from *PR* v (1897); Sir Henry Thompson to FH, 30 July 1897, 4 Jan., 18 Feb. 1898, HC.

143. 'Ideal London', *MT* 278–98, from *CR* lxxiv (1898), 139–52; *Spectator* lxxxi (10 Dec. 1898), 855; M. Ward to FH, 26 Dec. 1898, HC.

144. *Spectator* lxxxviii (7 Dec. 1901), 902–3; FH, 'Sir John Lubbock and the London County Council', *New Review* v (Nov. 1890), 401.

145. Lubbock to FH, 2 June 1906, Burns to FH, 8 Oct., 1906., HC; Gibbon and Bell, *History* (the painting reproduced).

146. Crane to FH, 3 Mar. 1890, HC; Crane, *An Artist's Reminiscences*, 332–3.

147. 'London Improvements', op. cit., 414–21; 'Municipal Museums of Paris', *RI* 399, 413, from *FR* lxii (1894).

148. FH, *The Times*, 16 Nov. 1900, 8f; *AM* ii, 242–3; FH to Gosse, 15 Oct. 1905, BLL; *Daily Chronicle*, 18 Oct. 1905.

149. *LCC Minutes 1889*, 18 June, 443; *LCC Minutes 1890*, 11 Mar. 201; Gibbon and Bell, *History*, 79–80 (noting that a 1907 act empowered women to sit on borough and county councils).

150. *Daily News*, 12 Mar. 1889, 5; Andrew Rosen, *Rise Up, Women! The Militant Campaign of the Women's Social and Political Union 1903–1914* (London and Boston, 1974), 12–15.

151. Janet Penrose Trevelyan, *The Life of Mrs Humphry Ward* (London, 1923), 221 (quoted), 230–1.

152. Mrs Humphry Ward, *A Writer's Recollections*, 2 vols. (New York, 1918), ii, 74.

153. *Robert Elsmere* (1888; rpt. Lincoln, Nebr., 1967), with intro. by Clyde de L. Ryals, esp. chs. 37–41; Enid Huws Jones, *Mrs Humphry Ward* (London, 1973), 44, 77; William S. Peterson, *Victorian Heretic: Mrs Humphry Ward's 'Robert Elsmere'* (Leicester, 1976), esp. 168, citing Gladstone to Lord Acton, 13 May 1888, on FH's advice and her essay, *NC* xxv (1889), 454–80, replying to Gladstone's, ibid., xxiii (1888), 766–88; Morley, *Gladstone*, iii, 358, on his letter to Acton saying his 'kindness to the Positivists' was due to their keeping in view 'the great human tradition; *plus* a very high appreciation of the personal qualities of our friend ...' (which I take to refer to FH).

154. EBH to FSM, 18 May 1889, Bod. MS Eng. lett. d. 248, fols. 98–9.

155. J. Stephen to EBH, 19 May (1889), EBH to JM, 31 May 1889, Emily Beesly to EBH, 20 May (1889), FH to JM, 27 May 1889, HC; Webb, *Our Partnership*, 360–3; Trevelyan, *Mrs Humphry Ward*, 229; Mrs Ward, 'The Women's Anti-Suffrage Movement', *NC and After* lxiv (1908), 343–52.

156. FH to JM, 1, 5 May 1889, HC; *NC* xxv (1889), 781–8.

157. FH to B. Potter, 7 July 1889, in 'Diary of Beatrice Webb Typewritten Transcript', xiii, 138–9, and her reply, 139–40, LSE.

158. EBH to Bryce, 26 June 1890, Bod. Uncat. MS.

159. See Jill Conway, 'Stereotypes of Femininity in a Theory of Sexual Evolution', *Suffer and Be Still*, ed. Martha Vicinus (Bloomington and London, 1973), ch. 8.

160. *RI* 65–84, from *FR* lvi (1891).

161. FH to Hillemand, 23 Sept. 1891, MAC.

162. *FR* lvi (1891), 673–85.

163. EBH to FSM, 5 Aug. 1893, Bod. MS Eng. lett. c. 108, fols. 90–100.

164. GG to Ellen Gissing, 4, 13 Nov. 1887, Berg; *London and the Life of Literature in Late Victorian England: The Diary of George Gissing, Novelist*, ed. Pierre Coustillas (Hassocks, Sussex, 1978), 17–18 (hereafter cited as *London Diary*); *The Pauline*, Nov. 1888.

165. Burne-Jones to FH, n.d., (William) Parsons to EBH, 26 Mar. (1890), J. E. Millais to FH, 25, 30 Mar. 1890, FH to JM, 5 Apr. 1890, Lytton to FH, 12 Dec., 1890, HC; FH to Millais, 30, 31 Mar. 1890, Pierpont Morgan Library.

166. FH to Laffitte, 1 Apr. 1890, MAC; Hamerton to FH, 16 Sept. 1892, Lytton to FH, 12 Dec. 1890, HC; Hamerton, 'Chief Influences on My Career', *Forum* xviii (1894), 423–4, cited by EBH, *PR* ii (1895), 59.

167. AH, *Frederic Harrison*, 101.

168. EBH to FSM, 22 June 1891, Bod. MS Eng. lett. d. 251, fols. 144–5; Schomberg K. McDonnell to FH, 3 July 1895, Eric Barrington to FH, 5 July 1895, FH to JM, 10 Mar. 1898, HC.

169. FH to JM, 29 July 1898, HC; FH to EBH, 14, 16, 17, 18 (2 letters) Sept. 1898, FC.

170. FH to EBH, 24, 25, 27 Jan. 1899, FC; FH to JM, 14 Apr. (1898), HC.

171. 'The Sacrifice of Education to Examination', *NC* xxiv (1888), 617–52 (FH, 645–52, rpt. *RI* 346–58); Müller to FH, 1 Nov. 1888, HC.

172. (C. B. Adderley), 'Two Conflicting "reports" on Education', *NC* xxiv (1888), 863–78; William A. Knight, Harold Arthur Perry, H. Temple Humphreys, 'The Protest ...', ibid., 919–32; Knowles, Pollock, Joseph Fayrer, F. Galton, W. O. Priestly, Goodwin, 'The Sacrifice ...', ibid., xxv, (1889), 284–322.

173. *Hansard*, 3rd ser. cccxli (28 Feb. 1890), 1445–83.

174. John Roach, *Public Examinations in England, 1850–1900* (Cambridge, Eng., 1971), 278 and *passim*.

175. *Speaker* ii (26 July 1890), 91–3; *MH* 146–79 from *FR* lvi (1891).

176. *Politics and Education: An Address at the Annual Meeting of the Social and Political Education League ... 2 Mar. 1887* (London, 1887).

177. JHB, *PR* iii (1895), 17–22; FH, ibid., ii (1894), 193–5.

178. FH, 'Primary Education', *RI* 226–32, from *PR* v (1897), 29–33.

179. FH to B. Webb, 20 Mar. 1896, Passfield Papers, ii, 4-a-47, LSE.

180. Webb, *Our Partnership*, 93; Edwards to FH, 2 May 1898, 29 Apr. 1907 (another 'small subscription'), HC; Trevelyan, *The Life of Mrs Humphry Ward*, 79–92, 120.

181. Henrietta O. Barnett, *Canon Barnett, His Life, Work and Friends*, 2 vols. (Boston, 1919), i, 44.

182. EBH to FH, 10 Feb. (1879), FC.

183. FH to FSM, 10 Apr. 1890, Bod. MS Eng. lett. d. 249, fols. 109–112.

184. S. A. Barnett to FH, 13 Feb. 1900, HC; Barnett, *Canon Barnett*, i, 277–81, 343, 373, ii, 381, 383; *The Toynbee Record* i (13 Oct. 1888).

185. R. H. Hadden, *Reminiscences of William Rogers, Rector of St Botolph, Bishopsgate* (London, 1888); *The Times*, 26 Nov. 1894, 10a-d; *Albert Spicer 1847–1934, ...* (London, 1939); Philip Unwin, *The Publishing Unwins* (London, 1972), 19–20.

186. S. K. Ratcliffe, *The Story of South Place* (London, 1955); John d'Entremont, *Moncure Conway, 1832–1907* (London, 1977).

187. FH to FSM, 11 Nov. (1893), Bod. MS Eng. lett. e. 108, fols. 125–6.

188. EBH to FSM (1891), Bod. MS Eng. lett. e. 106, fols. 181–2; FSM, 'Positivism and the Ethical Societies', *PR* ix (1901), 29–30.

189. FH to EBH, 30 Jan. (1899), FC.

190. L. Stephen to FH, n.d., HC; *Ethical Society: Ninth Annual Report, 1894–1895*.

191. FH to EBH, 30 Jan. (1899), FC.

192. 'Francis W. Newman', *RI* 390–6, from *PR* v (1897).

193. 'Natural Theology', *PCS* 164–74, from *PR* i (1893).

194. Their correspondence is in York University Library, and is referred to in *Echoes of a Larger Life: ... Welby* (London, 1929), 165–6, 168, and in *Other Directions: ... Welby* (London, 1931), 69, both works ed. by

Mrs Henry Cust; see also S. Hardwick, intro., *Semiotic and Significs; The Correspondence Between Charles S. Pierce and Victoria Lady Welby* (Bloomington and London, 1977), and her pejoratively annotated copy of *PCS* in ULL.

195. EBH to FSM, 13 Dec. 1897, Bod. MS Eng. lett. d. 253, fols. 161–2; *AM* i, 136.
196. *AM* ii, 109; FH to EBH (10 Dec. 1880), FC.
197. Spencer to FH, 7 May 1883, 10 Apr. 1889, HC; AH, *Frederic Harrison*, 166; James Howard Bridge, *Millionaires and Grub Street* (1931; rpt. Freeport, New York, 1968), 12–13.
198. *The New York Evening Post*, 26 Mar. 1896.
199. 'Religion: A Retrospect and Prospect', *NC* xv (1884), 1–12.
200. 'The Ghost of Religion', *PCS* 344–63, from *NC* xv (1884); Lady Welby to FH, 15 July 1892, typed copy, York U.
201. 'The Unknowable and the Unknown', *NC* xv (1884), 905–19; L. Stephen, *The Life of Sir James Fitzjames Stephen*, 454.
202. 'Retrogressive Religion', *NC* xvi (1884), 3–26.
203. 'The Clothes of Religion', *National Review* iii (1884), 554–73; Duncan, *Life ... Spencer*, i, 340.
204. 'Agnostic Metaphysics', *PCS* 364–405; rpt. from *NC* xvi (1884).
205. 'A Pickwickian Positivist' *National Review* iv (1884), 222–37, rpt. with Newman's letter in *The Clothes of Religion* (London, 1886); *PMG*, 18 Nov. 1884 (FH), 24 Nov. (Ward).
206. *The Times*, 1884: 6 Sept., 10c, 12 Sept., 8f, 17 Sept. 10d (FH); 9 Sept., 5f, 15 Sept. 7c (Spencer); Duncan, *Life ... Spencer*, i, 341–3; Spencer, 'Last Words about Agnosticism and the Religion of Humanity', *NC* xvi (1884), 826–38; FH, *PMG*, 18 Nov. 1884 (quoted); Spencer, *An Autobiography*, i, 517–8.
207. Bowen quoted in *Life and Correspondence of John Duke Lord Coleridge ...* ed. E. H. Coleridge, 2 vols. (New York, 1904), 343–4; Ruskin, *Works* xxxvii, 479–80.
208. Duncan, *Life ... Spencer*, ii, 346–55.
209. Sydney Eisen, 'Frederic Harrison and Herbert Spencer: Embattled Unbelievers', *Victorian Studies* xii (1968), 33–56, esp. 49, 52.
210. Spencer to FH, 5, 6, 8, 10 Apr., 16 July 1889, HC; Spencer, *Autobiography*, i, 292–3.
211. Spencer to FH, 4 Dec. 1892, HC, 23 Dec. 1892, Cornell U.
212. FH, 'The Future of Agnosticism', *PCS* 255–74, from *FR* li (1889); Huxley, 'Agnosticism', *NC* xxv (1889), 169–94.
213. FH, Mr Huxley's Controversies', *PCS* 275–307, from *FR* lviii (1892); Huxley, 'An Apologetic Irenicon', ibid., 557–71.
214. 'Mr Huxley's Ironicon', *PCS* 308–22, from *FR* lviii (1892), 713–21.
215. cp. FH to Mrs Hertz, 7 Jan. 1893, HC.
216. 'Evolution and Ethics', *Evolution and Ethics and Other Essays* (New York, 1897), 81.
217. FH to Huxley, 5 June 1893, Huxley Collection, Imperial College.

218. Huxley to FH, 8 June 1893, HC.
219. *Science and the Christian Tradition* (London, 1894), 262.
220. *PR* ii (1894), 77–8.
221. FH to Leonard Huxley, 13 Mar. 1896, Huxley Collection, Imperial College.
222. Sir Mountstuart E. Grant Duff, *Notes from a Diary, 1886–88*, 2 vols. (London, 1900), i, 139 (23 June 1887).
223. FH to Murray, 23 Oct. 1897, Bod. Gilbert Murray MS 24; FH 'The Lock-out on the Clyde', *Daily Chronicle*, 9 Nov. 1895; *Ludlow Pamphlets* xiii, no. 6, Appendix 148–9, ULL.
224. FH to Murray, 23 Oct. 1897, Bod. Gilbert Murray MS 24; FH to B. Webb, Christmas Eve (1897), Passfield Papers, II, 4–2–63, LSE.
225. Maxse, *The Times*, 14 Feb. 1894, 8c; cuttings from *Daily Chronicle*, 1894: 15, 21 Feb. (FH), 17, 20, 23 Feb. (Maxse), 21 Feb. (Dilke); Maxse to FH, 15 Feb. 1894, HC; *The Collected Letters of George Meredith*, ii, 1155.
226. Cuttings from *Daily Chronicle*, Oct. 1894, FH, MS letter marked 'no. 6, unpublished', HC.
227. 'Mothers and Daughters', *NC* xxxv (1894), 313–22; 'Smoke', ibid., 389–96; 'An Educational Interlude', *FR* lxv (1896), 359–69; 'Our Village', *Temple Bar* cv (1895), 98–106, cxiv (1898), 417–28, 'The Woodman', ibid., cix (1896), 91–8.
228. GG to Algernon Gissing, 27 Aug. 1896, Berg Collection; EBH to FH, 11 Apr. 1910, FC.
229. FH to JM, 20 Aug. 1896, HC; *The Times*, 18 May 1908, 10e, obit. of Sir Frederick Samuel Philipson Philipson-Stow.
230. EBH to FSM, 24 Mar. 1895, Bod. MS Eng. lett. e. 109, fols. 47–8.
231. Lawrence, who died 18 Feb. 1899, and his son Lawrence Frederick, both served on the Stock Exchange Committee.
232. FH to JM, 18 Aug. (1898), HC.
233. W. S. Blunt, *My Diaries, Being a Personal Narrative of Events 1888–1914* (New York, 1932), 233 (18 July 1896).
234. Longford, *A Pilgrimage*, 241–2, ch. 13; FH to JM, 14 Dec. 1888, HC.
235. 'The Report of the Special Commission', *New Review* ii (1890), 199–211; Davitt to FH, 1 Mar. 1890, HC.
236. FH to JM, 13, 14 Feb., 7 Nov. 1888, HC; see 'Protest against the Irish Coercion Bill' (6 May 1887), *Positivist Comments*.
237. *An Appeal to Liberal Unionists* (London, 1889), from *CR* liv (1888); Argyll, 'A Reply to Our Appellant', *CR* lv (1889), 1–23; FH, 'A Rejoinder ...', ibid., 301–16.
238. *AM* i, 308–10; Russell (later first Baron Russell of Killowen) to FH, 16 Apr. 1889, and n.d., HC; FH, 'Are We Making Way?' *NC* xxv (1889), 753–62; 'The Forger Party', *Journal of the Home Rule Union*, no. 13 (1889), 193–8; 'The Report of the Special Commission', *New Review* ii (1890), 199–224; Lady Anne Blunt's Diary, BL, Add. MS 53972 (transcription), 28 May 1889.

239. EBH to FSM, 28 Nov. 1890, Bod. MS Eng. lett. d. 250, fols. 107–8; *AM* i, 309; FH, 'The Irish Leadership', *FR* lv (1891), 125 (quoted); G. B. Shaw, *The Star*, 27 Nov. 1890.

240. FH, 'How to Drive …', *FR* lviii (1892), 273–87; Salisbury, 'Constitutional Revision', *National Review* xx (1892), 289–300; *The Times*, 27 Oct. 1892, 9ab.

241. FH to Gladstone, 23 Feb. 1893, BL, Add. MS 44517, fols. 52–3; Gladstone to FH, 25 Feb. 1893, HC; FH, 'Notes on the Home Rule Bill, i: Clause Nine', *CR* lxiii (1893), 305–10 (a 3rd article was by Donald Crawford).

242. FH to JM, 19 Apr., 24 Oct. 1893, HC; EBH to FSM, 1 Oct. (1893), Bod. MS Eng. lett. e. 108, fols. 119–20.

243. FH to Gladstone, 7 Mar. 1894, BL, Add. MS 44518, fol. 92, 31 Dec. 1894, Add. MS 44519, fol. 318; Spencer Lyttleton (for Gladstone), to FH, 9 Mar. 1894, and Gladstone to FH, 2 Jan. 1895, HC.

244. JM to FH, 24 May 1898, HC.

245. FH to JM, 3 Mar. 1894, HC; EBH to FSM, 19 Mar. 1894, Bod. MS Eng. lett. c. 258, fols. 58–9; FH to 'Dear Rector', 14 Aug. 1895, YUL; FH to Rosebery, 12 Oct. 1896, National Library of Scotland, Edinburgh.

246. *AM* ii, 60–62; *The Times*, 1888: 23 May, 10a-c, 29 May, 8a-c; John C. MacDonald (*The Times*) to FH, 5 June 1888, HC (sending £25); Naquet to FH, 8 May 1888, HC; FH to Laffitte, 8, 11 May 1888, MAC; FH to Maxse, 26 May 1888, WSRO.

247. S. K. McDonnell to Lord Salisbury, 20 Nov. 1890, Christ Church Library, Oxford; FH to EBH, 10 Oct. (1890) (2 letters), Tricoupi to FH, 4 Oct. 1891, HC.

248. FH to EBH, 15 Feb. 1895, FC; *AM* ii, 165–6; 'Sir Charles Cookson', *RI* 402–5, from *PR* xiv (1906).

249. FH to EBH, 17, 21 Feb. 1895, FC; *AM* ii, 173–81.

250. Longford, *A Pilgrimage*, 312–13.

251. FH to EBH and Olive, 21 Feb. to 1 Mar. 1895, FC and in *AM* ii, 181–6; FH to Blunt, 'Eve of Ramadan 1313' (1895), WSRO; *The Times*, 1896: 24 Nov., 4f, 27 Nov., 5e, 30 Nov., 12b, 3 Dec., 12b, 8 Dec., 4e (FH), 26, 28 Nov., and 1, 5 Dec. ('A Twenty-Years' Resident'), cuttings HC.

252. *The Star*, 22 Jan. 1889; *The Times*, 22 Jan. 1889, 7f; cutting, undated, HC; Masani, *Dadabhai Naoroji*, 263–5; Lady Gregory, *Seventy Years*, 235; M. E. Chamberlain, *Britain and India* (London, 1924), 106, 172–3; Deborah Wormell, *Sir John Seeley and the Uses of History* (Cambridge, Eng., 1980).

253. 'Peace or War', *PR* x (1898), 202–3.

254. 'Mr Benjamin Kidd's Philosophy', ibid., xiv (1902), 90–2.

255. EBH to FSM, 25 May 1893, Bod. MS Eng. lett. e. 108, fols. 69–72; FH, 'The Evolution of Our Race: A Reply', *FR* lx (1893), 28–41; Pearson, 'An Answer to Some Critics', ibid., 149–70; Pearson to FH, 5 Sept. 1893, HC; FH to Pearson, 4 Oct. 1893, Bod. MS Eng. lett. d. 188, fols. 87–8; John Tregenza, *Professor of Democracy; The Life of Charles Henry Pearson …* (London, 1968).

256. *The Times*, 15 Dec. 1893, 3de; FH, *PR* ii (1894), 13–14.
257. 'The Situation at Home and Abroad', *FR* lix (1893), 202.
258. 'Imperial Expansion', op. cit.
259. 'The Modern Machiavelli', *NC* xlii (1897), 462–71, FH's reply to Greenwood, 'Machiavelli in Modern Politics', *Cosmopolis* x (1897), 307–22; Greenwood judged FH's argument 'clumsy, wild, and rather injurious', in *NC* xlii (1897), 532–48; FH to JM, 11 Sept. 1897, HC, praising ESB's reply, *PR* v (1897), 157.
260. 'Christianity at the Grave of the Nineteenth Century', *North American Review* clxxi (1900), 817–28, referring to the Revd F. W. Farrar, 'Imperialism and Christianity', ibid., 289–95.
261. *AM* ii, 127.
262. FH to EBH (7 Oct. 1895), FC.
263. *AM* ii, 129, quoting from *Daily Chronicle*, 30 Aug. 1899 and *Two Open Letters to Lord Salisbury* ... (London, 1899); Blunt, *My Diaries*, 327–9; Blunt to FH, 2 Sept. 1899 (copy), MS 965–1977, Fitzwilliam Museum.
264. 'Justice—English and French', *PR* vii (1899), 169–73, 'Honour:—True or False', ibid., 126–30; on Dreyfus see GL, *The Times*, 13 Oct. 1898, 5a-f, 6ab and *National Review* xx (1899), 4 issues and special supp.
265. 'Mr J. A. Hobson on the Transvaal', *PR* viii (1900), 69–73.
266. Stephen Collini, *Liberalism and Socialism: L. T. Hobhouse* ... (Cambridge, Eng., 1979); Koss, *The Pro-Boers* (Chicago, 1973) and *The Rise and Fall of the Political Press in Britain*, i, *The Nineteenth Century* (London, 1981); Arthur Davey, *The British Pro-Boers 1877–1902* (Capetown, 1978).
267. S. C. Cronwright-Schreiner, *Land of Free Speech* (London, 1906), 385–6.
268. *The Boer Republics, a Lecture ... 7 Dec. 1899 ... and 31 Jan. 1900 ...* (London (1900)); *AM* ii, 129–30; Gooch, *Life of Lord Courtney*, 393; letters to P. A. Molteno Oct. 1899–Dec. 1900 from FH, Swinny, Haggard, South African Public Library, Capetown.
269. FH to EBH, 21 Feb. (1900), HC.
270. 'The Purpose of Conquest, An Appeal', in Koss, *The Pro-Boers*, 130–1; FH to EBH, 22 Feb. (1900), HC.
271. Lord Davey to FH, 16 Jan. 1900, HC; Ralph Nevill, *The Life and Letters of Lady Dorothy Nevill* (New York, n.d.), 235–7; EBH to FSM, 20 Dec. (1900), Bod. MS Eng. lett. d. 255, fols. 100–1; Ralph Nevill, ed., *The Reminiscences of Lady Dorothy Nevill* (London, 1906), 276–7.
272. FH to EBH, 21 (Jan. 1901), FC.

Chapter 7. The Edwardian Positivist 1901–1914

1. FH to EBH, Tues. (8 Oct.), 1895, FC.
2. *AM* ii, 187–216, letters in FC (source of details about the trip).
3. *Union League Club, Chicago: Exercises in Commemoration of the Birthday of Washington, February 22, 1901* (Chicago (1901)); *The Chicago Daily Tribune*, 23 Feb, 1901, 2cd.

4. FH, *PR* xv (1907), 284–5, obit. of Conway.
5. Mark de Wolfe Howe, *Justice Oliver Wendell Holmes: The Shaping Years, 1841–1870* (Cambridge, Mass., 1957), 226.
6. King to FH, Tues. (1 Apr. 1901), FC; FH, *New Year's Address*... (London (1886)); *The Religion of Duty* (Philadelphia, 1901), in *OS* 3–31.
7. FH to EBH, 31 Mar. (1901), FC; Conway, *FR* i (1865), 421–34.
8. FH to Hember, 16 Mar. 1901, Dr M. Sahud to FH, 24 Mar. 1901, HC.
9. FH to EBH, 13, 19 Mar. 1901, FC, in *AM* ii, 206, 209; cp. *PR* ix (1901), 113–18 (text of his speech).
10. FH, *New York Times Saturday Review of Books and Art*, 25 May 1901, 361–2, on *La Question Sociale* by Auguste Brasseur; Spargo, *Social Democrat* v (15 Jan. 1901), 197–9.
11. *MT* 173–201, from *NC* xlix (1901); *Spectator* lxxxvi (1 June 1901), 791.
12. Hobhouse to FH, 12 Jan. 1901, HC; *The Boer War: Letters by Frederic Harrison ... May 30–June 29* (London, 1901), 1–3.
13. *Daily News*, 31 May 1901; Davitt to FH, 31 May 1901, HC.
14. D. L. Hobman, *Olive Schreiner* (London, 1955), 119–22; Blunt, *My Diaries*, i, 433 (2 Mar. 1902); A. Ruth Fry, *Emily Hobhouse, A Memoir* (London, 1929), 87–147; FH, 'Martial Law Again', *PR* ix (1901), 209–12 and 'Materialism and Irreligion', x (1902), 33–48.
15. Frederick Pollock, *The Times*, 10 Mar. 1902, 14b-d; FH, *Speaker*, n.s. v/vi (22 Feb., 15 Mar. 1902), 588–9, 673–4; *AM* ii, 314; *NSP* 229–43, rpt. *The State of Seige*, SACC pamphlet no. 92; *The Collected Letters of George Meredith*, iii, 1424–5.
16. FH's impressions of Skibo from FC; Joseph Frazier Wall, *Andrew Carnegie* (New York, 1970).
17. Carnegie's copy (with bookplate) of *AM*, pages uncut, is in the author's possession.
18. FH to Carnegie, 8 Sept. (1906), Library of Congress; FH, *PR* xiv (1906), 238–9.
19. FH to Geddes, 21 Oct. 1903, National Library of Scotland; Abbie Ziffren, 'Part One, Biography of Patrick Geddes', *Patrick Geddes ...*, ed. Marshall Stalley (New Brunswick, 1972), 47–9.
20. Carnegie to FH, 8 June 1904, HC.
21. FH to Carnegie, 24 Oct. 1902, Library of Congress; FH, *PR* xvii (1909), 5–10.
22. *The Times*, 16 Mar. 1908, 10b; FH to Carnegie, 6 Aug. 1913, Library of Congress.
23. *GP*, ch. 5.
24. Carnegie to FH, 25 June 1914, FC.
25. FH to Mrs Carnegie, 16 Aug. 1919, Library of Congress.
26. LPS Minutes, 11 Feb. 1889 and 8 May 1897; FH to FSM, 8 Feb. 1899, Bod. MS Eng. lett. d. 254, fols. 86–7; FH to Mrs Hertz (9 May 1892), HC.
27. McGee, *A Crusade*, 207.
28. Lorenza Rodd, 'Newton Hall and After', *PR* xxxi (1924), 232–4.
29. FH to EBH, 16 Apr. (1903), FC; FH to Jeannolle, 30 Oct. 1901, MAC.

30. JHB to FH, 29 Mar. (1906), Mary Bridges to FH, 11, 17, 19 Apr., 16, 18 June 1906; Fanny Hertz to FH, 14 Apr. 1906, Swinny to FH, 25 June 1906, Hobhouse to FH, 20, 22 June 1906, HC; *PR* xiv (1906), 178–80; Mary Bridges, *Recollections of John Henry Bridges*, 210–11; Hobhouse edited JHB's *Essays and Addresses* (London, 1907), with an intro. by FH; ESB edited JHB's *Illustrations of Positivism* (London, 1907).

31. ESB, *PR* xv (1907), 70–7 (obit.); VL to Swinny, 8 Feb. (1907), VL to FH, 8 Feb. (1907), HC.

32. *PR* xx (1912), 65, 92–4, tributes by ESB, FH; Susan Lushington to FH, 24 Jan. 1912, HC.

33. *PR* xvi (1908), 115–17, tributes by ESB, Swinny.

34. LPS Minutes, 16 June 1903, 28 Oct., 25 Nov. 1904.

35. FH to EBH, 22, 23 Oct. (1901), FC.

36. Goschen to FH, 26 Dec. (1901), Anson to FH, 6 Aug. 1903, HC.

37. Goschen to FH, 13 Sept. 1902, 'Assistant Curate Fund, Flimwell, 1911', HC; FH to EBH, (5 Sept, 1902), FC; FH to Blunt, 28 Sept. 1902, 14 June 1903, WSRO; FH to Austin, 30 Oct., 5 Nov. 1908, YUL; 'Address to Souvenir Normand on "Bodiam Castle," by Frederic Harrison, 22nd August, 1903', proof, HC.

38. James to FH, 16 Oct. 1902, HC; James to EBH, 19 Oct. 1911, in *Letters of Henry James*, ed. P. Lubbock, 2 vols. (New York, 1920), ii, 202–4; Muriel Harris, *N.Y. Times Book Review*, 1 Jan. 1922, sec. 3, 8.

39. *The Life and Letters of Lady Dorothy Nevill*, 237; FH to EBH, 14 Sept. (1902), FC.

40. BH to FH (18 Dec. 1901), FH to EBH, 10 Feb. (1910), EBH's list of BH's sales, FC.

41. AH to FH, 9 Mar. (1900), FH to EBH, 12 June 1907, FC; Harmsworth to FH, 10 July 1905, HC; AH, 'Lord Northcliffe', *ER* xxxv (1922), 26; Alfred M. Gollin, *The Observer and J.L. Garvin, 1908–1914* (London, 1960), 1–2, 7, 16–22, 137–8; Reginald Pound and Geoffrey Harmsworth, *Northcliffe* (London, 1959), 261, 401–6; AH, 'The Old "English" ' *ER* xxxvi (1923), 512–15.

42. FH to EBH, 4 Oct. (1909), FC.

43. Jackson to FH, 28 July, 1903, 9 Dec. 1911, HC; FH to RH, 14 Sept. 1905, Canon Egerton Leigh Collection, BBL; FH to EBH, 2 Jan. 1909, RH to EBH, 10 June (1911), FC.

44. FH to Carnegie, 11 June 1904, Library of Congress; Mlle Souvestre to FH, undated and 22 Sept. 1904, Olive to EBH, 21, 23 Sept. 1904, FH to EBH, 24 Sept. 1904, FC.

45. Muriel Harris to FH, 17 Oct. 1906, HC.

46. Sir Charles Tennyson, 'Ivy Gladys Tennyson', and FH to Ivy Pretious, 30 Nov. 1901, 2, 4, 6, 20 Dec. 1903, collection in the possession of the late Sir Charles Tennyson; B. Russell to Lucy Donnelly, 19 Sept. 1904, Russell Archives, McMaster U. (quoted); Ronald W. Clark, *The Life of Bertrand Russell* (New York, 1967), 102–4, 116, 121–2, 153; Barbara Strachey, *Remarkable Relations* (London, 1981), 221.

47. FH to EBH, 2 Jan. (1909), FC; FH to Ivy Pretious, 26 Apr. (1909), Sir Charles Tennyson Collection; *The Times*, 30 July 1909, 13 b; Janet E. Courtney, 'Frederic Harrison: 1831–1923', *North American Review* ccxvii (1923), 520.

48. FH to Charles Tennyson, 4 Feb. 1913, Sir Charles Tennyson Collection.

49. FH to FSM, 3 June 1904, FH to Edith Deverell, 20 June 1904, Edith Deverell to FH, 18 June 1904, U. of Keele; FH to Edith Deverell, 21 June 1904, Bod. MS Eng. lett. c. 257, fols. 28–9.

50. FH to FSM, 13 May 1906, 12 Oct. 1911, Bod. MS Eng. lett. d. 257, fols. 70–1 and c. 260, fols. 112–13; EBH to FSM, 10 May (1906), d. 257, fols. 50–3; EBH to E. Marvin, 17 Feb. 1909, c. 257, fols. 172–3.

51. FH to EBH, letters Sept. 1906, FC; FH, *Tribune*, 12 Sept. 1906, 8b; *The Times*, 17 Sept. 1906, 4c, in *MAJ*; see also FH, *The Times*, 1909: 15 Jan., 8c; 21 Jan., 8b; 28 Jan., 4d; 2 Feb., 4c.

52. FH to EBH, 7, 9, 11 Jan. 1909, FC; obit. and funeral of Philipson-Stow, *The Times*, 18 May 1908, 10e, 20 May, 12c.

53. A. W. Benn, *History of English Rationalism in the Nineteenth Century*, 2 vols. (London, 1906), ii, 128–9; FH, 'The Progress of Religion', *PR* xiv (1906), 250–4, 269–72.

54. FH, *PR* xvi (1908), 186–8; Benn to FH, 7 Aug. 1908. HC.

55. FH, 'Introduction', *The Positive Philosophy of Auguste Comte*, trans. and condensed by Harriet Martineau, 3 vols. (London, 1896); FH to Dr Hillemand, Easter Monday 1896, MAC; *PCS* 335–43, from *PR* iv (1896).

56. LPS Minutes, 28 Oct., 12 Dec., 1904, 27 Jan. 1905; Swinny to FSM, 4 Mar. 1907, Bod. MS Eng. lett. d. 258, fol. 33.

57. FH, 'Introduction', *A General View of Positivism* (London, 1908).

58. FH, 'Introduction', *Early Essays on Social Philosophy, translated ... Hutton* (London, 1911); see A. Comte, *Lettres ... à Henry Dix Hutton* (Dublin, 1890); Swinny, 'In Memoriam—Henry Dix Hutton', *PR* xvi (1908), 21.

59. FH to Holyoake, 18 Nov. 1905, Co-operative Union; ESB to FSM, 2 Jan. 1905, Bod. MS Eng. lett. d. 256, fols. 36–7.

60. FH, *Speaker*, n.s. v (1 June 1901), 251–2, review of *Passages from the Letters of Auguste Comte*, selected and trans. John Kells Ingram (London, 1901); Ingram to FH, 22, 30 Oct. 1896, 28 Nov. 1898, HC; Swinny, 'The Death of Dr Ingram', *PR* xv (1907), 128–31.

61. FH, *PR* xviii (1920), 199–200, review of Gould, *Life Stories of Famous Men—II, Auguste Comte*; Gould, *The Life-Story of a Humanist* (London, 1923); McGee, *A Crusade*, 206–7.

62. Jane M. Style, *Auguste Comte, Thinker and Lover* (London, 1928); *The Celebration of the Golden Wedding of Sydney and Jane M. Style in the Temple of Humanity, Parliament Place ...* (Liverpool, 1928).

63. FH, *Daily Chronicle*, undated cutting, HC; 'Introduction', Lucien Lévy-Bruhl, *The Philosophy of Auguste Comte*, trans. Kathleen de Beaumont-Klein (London, 1903); see my 'Comte and Mill: The Early Publishing History of their Correspondence', *The Mill News Letter* xi (1976), 17–22.

64. FH to Spencer, 20 Nov. 1901, enclosing transcription, Spencer MS 791/287 and 791/355/2, ULL; Spencer to FH, 21 Nov. 1901, HC.

65. Spencer to FH, 31 Jan. 1902, HC; FH to Carnegie, 7 July 1902, Library of Congress.
66. Krishnavarma to FH, 20, 23, Feb. 1905, W. W. Merry (Vice-Chancellor of Oxford) to FH, 24 June 1905, Edward Caird to FH, 12 Feb. 1905, printed terms of lectureship, HC; Harris, *Auberon Herbert*, 358–9.
67. FH, *The Herbert Spencer Lecture* ... (Oxford and London, 1905); *RI* 413–18, from *PR* xvi (1908), review of Duncan, *Life and Letters of Herbert Spencer*.
68. FH's annotated copy of T. E. Hulme's translation generously given to me by Christopher Ricks, who has discussed it in *Notes and Queries* vi (1959), 175–8.
69. Simon, *European Positivism*, 106–10.
70. *NC and After* liii (1903), 645–50.
71. *The Positive Evolution of Religion: Its Moral and Social Reaction* (London, 1913), xix, 230, 266–7 (all but chs. 1–4 had appeared in *PR*, 1911–12.
72. Fremantle to FH, 24 Feb., 5 Mar. 1912, HC.
73. FH to EBH, 1 Apr. 1913, FC, about unsigned review by Norman Douglas, *ER* xi (Apr. 1913), 165–6, rpt. revised, in *Experiments* (privately printed, USA, 1925) and in *Late Harvest* (London, 1946).
74. McGee, *A Crusade*, 188–92, 202–3.
75. Ibid., 204–5, citing Swinny, 'In Memoriam, Philip Thomas', *PR* xxix (1921), 43–5; E. Thomas, 'July', *ER* v (1910), 608–16; FH to FSM, 28 Oct. 1916, 11 Dec. 1921, Bod. MS Eng. lett. c. 263, fols. 221–2, c. 260, fols. 155–6 (misfiled with 1911 letters).
76. FH to Jeannolle, 30 Oct. 1901, MAC; W. M. Simon, 'Comte's Orthodox Disciples: The Rise and Fall of a Cénacle', *French Historical Studies* iv (1965), 42–62.
77. FH to Jeannolle, 9 Mar., 29 Apr., 19 Oct. 1903, EBH to Jeannolle, 24 Apr. 1904, MAC.
78. FH to Jeannolle, 20, 25 July, 24 Nov. 1908, MAC; FH to (Corra), 24 Nov. 1908, Archives Nationales, 17 AS 3.
79. FH to (Hillemand), (24 Aug. 1912), MAC.
80. FH to FSM, 5 Feb. 1890, Bod. MS Eng. lett. d. 249, fols. 48–50; FH to Ward, 15 Dec. 1896, Brown U.
81. Bryce, 'Introductory Address', *Sociological Papers, 1904* (London, 1905), xiii–xvii; see vols. published 1906–7 for Positivists' contributions; Philip Abrams, *The Origins of British Sociology, 1834–1914: An Essay with Selected Papers* (Chicago and New York, 1968), 54–5; J. M. Burrow, *Evolution and Society* (Cambridge, Eng., 1966), 83–4, 207; FH, *PR* xii (1904), 283–5, xiv (1906), 284–5, on Hobhouse's books.
82. FH, 'The Jubilee of Auguste Comte', *PR* xv (1907), 217–29; 'The Positivist View of Character', *The Times*, 8 Mar. 1906, 10e.
83. 'Mr Frederic Harrison on Eugenics', *The Times*, 9 Mar. 1909, 9c; 'The Eugenics Education Society', ibid., 10 Mar., 12b.
84. FH to JM, 5 May 1871, HC, cited in Feaver, *From Status to Contract*, 122, on the controversy.

85. 'Maine's *Ancient Law* Revised', *MT* 110–14.

86. *Sociological Review*, ii (1909), 396–400.

87. 'Sociology: its Definition and its Limits', ibid., iii (1910), 97–104; FH, substituting for JHB, addressed the Institut International de Sociologie, 7 July 1906, at U. of London, on 'Social Strife in England', in *PR* xiv (1906), 175–9.

88. L. Stephen to (Victor Branford), 22 June 1903, U. of Keele.

89. René Worms to FH, 29 Dec. 1899, 1 Jan. 1915, HC; FH, *La Tache du Nouveau Siècle, extrait de la Revue International de Sociologie* (Paris, 1914); trans. in *PR* xxii (1914), 169–77, and in *GP* 196–213.

90. FH to T. Fisher Unwin, 7 Nov. 1904, Cobden MS 154, WSRO; FH, *PR* xii (1904), 284.

91. FH in *PR* x (1902), 114–15; xi (1903), 270–5; xii (1904) 9–14, 27–8; Nevill, *Life and Letters of Lady Dorothy Nevill*, 238; FH to EBH, 28 Sept. 1906, FC.

92. *PR* ii (1895), in *PCS* 323–3, 53–9.

93. FH in *PR* xi (1903), 36–7; xii (1904), 26–7, 193–8; xv (1905), 1–4.

94. FH in *PR* xiii (1905), 58–61, 198–201, 250–3, 285–6; FH, *WG*, 10, 25 July 1905; FH, 'Thoughts on the Present Discontents', *FR* xxxciii (1905), 1–15.

95. 'Thoughts on the Present Discontents', op. cit., 1; *PR* xii (1904), 99–103, 127–9; xiii (1905), 265–8; 'The Entente Cordiale', typescript, and Cyril Maude to FH, 13 Jan. 1908, HC.

96. *PR* xii (1904), 87–91, 145–8; xiii (1905), 222–5.

97. *WG*, 4 Dec. 1905; FH to Goldwin Smith, 15 Dec. 1905, HC; FH, *PR* xiv (1906), 12–14.

98. Barnett, *Canon Barnett*, ii, 194–5; FH, 'Parliamentary Procedure', *RI* 254–72, from *NC and After*, lix (1906), and *RI* 239–53, from *PR* xiv (1906), 150–3, 197–200, 217–18; FH to Rosebery, 2 Apr. 1907, U. of Edinburgh.

99. FH, *PR* ix (1901), 177–81.

100. FH, *PR* xiv (1906), 73–6; *The Times*, 1906; 6 Sept., 6ab (Lord Lindley), 7 Apr., 2b, 4 Dec., 4bc (GL); *Tribune*, 12 Sept. 1906: 8b; FH to EBH, 9, 10, 11 Sept. 1906, FC.

101. FH, *The Times*, 10 Nov. 1910, 6d, 26 Oct. 1910, 8ab (quoted).

102. FH, *The Times*, 4 Dec. 1908, 4d; 29 Dec. 1908, 8f; 2 Jan. 1909, 8d.

103. MacDonald, ibid., 7 Dec. 1908, 10c; see also 11 Nov. 1910, 7d.

104. FH, ibid., 1910: 26 Oct., 8ab, 27 Oct., 10e; 10 Nov., 6d; see also 6 June 1911, 7d; cp. Swinny, *PR* xviii (1910), 234–7, W. E. Singleton, 252–5.

105. *RI* 85–141; FH to EBH, 3 Oct. (1908) (2 letters), FC; see Brian Harrison, *Separate Spheres: The Opposition to Women's Suffrage in Britain* (London, 1978).

106. FH to EBH, 30 May 1913, FC; Curzon to FH to EBH, 5 letters, HC.

107. 'Mrs Frederick [*sic*] Harrison', *Anti-Suffrage Review* (Sept. 1910), signed L. V. M., probably Violet Markham, praised by FH to Mrs Ward, 1 Mar. 1912, UT.

108. *Kent and Sussex Post*, 3 Oct. 1903, cutting HC; E. H. Pember to EBH, 3 Oct. 1908, FC; EBH *The Times*, 15 Aug. 1908, 14c; EBH, *Anti-Suffrage Review* (Feb. 1911), 28 and (Dec. 1908), 7 (quoted); FH to Bryce, 11 Jan. 1911, Bod. uncat. MS.

109. EBH, *The Times*, 15 Aug. 1908, 14c; 2 Apr. 1909, 12d; 22 Mar. 1912, 6b; *WG*, 4 May 1907; *The Nation*, 16 Mar. 1907, 114, 25 Jan. 1908, 605–6, 8 Feb. 1908, 698, and other articles listed in *PR* xxiv (Aug. 1916), 178–9.

110. FH to Miss Waterson, 12 Dec. 1906, CPL.

111. EBH, 'Mistress and Maid', *NC and After*, liii (1903), 284–9.

112. 'The Divorce Commission: Mr Frederic Harrison's Evidence', *PR* xx (1912), 279–81; *The Times*, 1 Dec. 1910, 4d.

113. 'A Woman's View of Divorce', *NC and After*, lxix (1911), 329–34.

114. Mrs Ward to FH, 13, 26 Jan. 1912, HC; see Harrison, *Separate Spheres*, 130–5.

115. EBH, *The Times*, 2 Apr. 1909, 12d (quoted), 22 Mar. 1912, 6b; Curzon to FH, 17 Mar. 1914, (quoting FH), Herbert Gladstone to FH, 4 Jan. 1910, HC.

116. Mrs Ward to FH, 26 Jan. 1913, HC.

117. *The Times*, 15 July 1910, 9a, letter to be read at the League's London meeting.

118. Longford, *A Pilgrimage*, 425.

119. Blunt, *My Diaries*, 534 (8 July 1905); FH to EBH, 12 Sept. 1905, HC; FH to Blunt, 24 Oct. 1905, WSRO.

120. FH to Blunt, 11 Sept., 14, 21 Oct. 1906, WSRO; FH to EBH, 12 Sept. 1906, FC; Blunt, *My Diaries*, 567 (13 Sept. 1906).

121. *The Secret History of the British Occupation of Egypt*, 2nd edn. (London, 1907), 630–5, printing the *Athenaeum* article, Blunt's reply, and FH's letter, 9 July 1907, in WSRO.

122. *The Secret History*, 636–44.

123. FH, *The Times*, 13 Dec. 1907, 17a; FH to Blunt, 13, 21 Dec. 1907, WSRO; Blunt to FH, 24 Dec. 1907, in the Earl of Lytton, *W. S. Blunt: A Memoir by His Grandson* (London, 1961), 117–18.

124. FH, 'Mr W. S. Blunt's *Secret History*', *PR* xvi (1908), 22.

125. FH, 'The Occupation of Egypt', *PR* xvi (1908), 96–103; *AM* ii, 146, and *NSP* xii.

126. EBH to FH, 5 Sept. (1908), FC; FH, 'The Turkish Reform', *PR* xvii (1909), 42–3; Blunt, *My Diaries*, 621–2, 626–7.

127. Blunt, *My Diaries* (on Ryan), 657, 819, 821, 824–5; Longford, ch. 19; Frederick Ryan, 'Michael Davitt', *PR* xvi (1908), 175–81; 'An Open Letter to the Young Turks', ibid., vii (1909), 13–16; ibid., xxi (1913), 138–9, obit. by Swinny.

128. *The Times*, 19 Nov. 1908, 13d; Rennell Rodd, 8 July 1908, HC; FH to Carnegie, 14 Nov. 1908, Library of Congress.

129. FH, 'Turkish Reform', *PR* xvii (1909), 42–3; FH and EBH to Blunt, 27 Aug., 3 Nov. 1908, WSRO; FH to FSM, 28 Aug. 1908, Bod. MS Eng. lett. d. 260, fol. 13; Feroz Ahmad, *The Young Turks* (Oxford, 1969), 177;

Ernest Edmondson Ramsaur, *The Young Turks* (Beirut, 1965), 22–6, 29–30, 35–40, 50, 52, 57–8, 68–75, 90–1.

130. FH, *The Times*, 29 July 1909, 8f (quoted); FH, *PR* xvii (1909), 235–7, xviii (1910), 43–4 (translation of Ahmed Riza's address to the Deputies from a paper dated 16 Nov. 1908); Ahmad, *The Young Turks*, 15–17, 41–6, 50–6, 102; Edward Aiken to Blunt, 13 Sept. 1909, WSRO.

131. FH to EBH, 2 Feb. 1910, FC.

132. *The Times*, 3 Feb. 1910, 6c, in *PR* xviii (1910), 60–4, and *AM* ii, 131–3; Atkin to FH, 19 Feb. 1910 and memo. 17 March 1910, HC; Atkin, *PR* xvii (1909), 208–10, 235–7.

133. Ahmed Riza to FH, 10 Feb., 29 Mar., 22 Dec. 1910, HC; FH, *The Times*, 4 July 1910, 6c; *AM* ii, 144–5; FH to EBH, various letters 22 Mar. to 5 Apr. 1910, FC; FH reviews in *Speaker*, n.s. i (11 Nov. 1899), 144–5, *PR* xi (1903), 138–40.

134. *AM* ii, 136–7, 142–4 (quoted); *The Times*, 4 July 1910, 6c; 'Turkey under its New Rulers', *PR* xviii (1910), 181–2.

135. Letter, 27 Sept. 1911, in *GP* 144–5.

136. Ahmed Riza to FH, 9 Oct., 10 Dec. 1911, HC; *PR* xix (1911), 359–61, 381–4.

137. *GP* 151–83, rpt. '1913', from *ER* xiii (1913).

138. FH, 'The Indian National Congress', *PR* xiii (1905), 31–3.

139. Sir Henry Cotton, *Indian and Home Memories* (London, 1911), 276–80; see his *New India*, rev. edn. (London, 1907).

140. S. K. Ratcliffe, 'Commemoration of Mr S. H. Swinny', *PR* xxxi (1923), 225.

141. FH, 'The Future of India', *PR* xvi (1908), 58–60; *The Times*, 15 Feb. 1908, 2e; see also EBH, 'The Englishwoman in India', *PR* xv (1907), 134–6.

142. FH, 'The Reform Proposals: A Symposium', *Indian Review* x (1909), 3–4.

143. JM to FH, 14 Mar. 1909, HC, quoted in Stephen Koss, *John Morley at the India Office, 1905–1910* (New Haven and London, 1969), 167; on Krishnavarma see his intro. to a new edn. of RC, *India* (London, 1907), and Stanley A. Wolpert, *Morley and India, 1906–1910* (Berkeley, 1967), 124–5.

144. FH to JM, 19 Nov. 1907, MSS Eur. D. 573/51, fol. 19, IOL; *WG*, 18 Nov. 1907, 9c; *The Times*, 26 Nov. 1907, 11d.

145. FH to EBH, 8 Sept. 1908, FC.

146. EBH to FH, 2 Nov. (probable error for 3), 1910, FC; cp. Koss, *John Morley*, Wolpert, *Morley and India*, and R. J. Moore, 'John Morley's Acid Test: India 1906–10', *Pacific Affairs*, lx (1968), 333–40.

147. FH to JM, 29 July 1898, HC.

148. *GP* 15; Alfred Lyttleton to FH, 15 June 1897, HC; FH, *The Times*, 18 Mar. 1909, 9a–c (quoted) and 24 Mar., 9a; see also *GP* 109–11, from *PR* xiv (1906).

149. *The Times*, 25 Mar. 1909, 9c; see Repington, *Essays and Criticism by the Military Correspondent of 'The Times'* (London, 1911).

150. Roberts to FH, 19 Dec. 1913, HC.
151. Henry Arthur Jones to FH, 27 Mar. 1909, HC; David Hannay, *The Times*, 19 Mar. 1909, 9c; Blunt, *My Diaries*, 654 (18 Mar. 1909); *GP* 148–50 and ch. v; Maxse, *National Review* xl (1906), 5–6.
152. FH, *PR* xvii (1909), 57–62, 145–8, 193–7; FH, *The Times*, 1909: 7 Sept. 10e, 10 Sept. 8c, 24 Sept. 8a.
153. 'An Old Tory', in *The Times*, 25 Sept. 1909, 10a; Lecky, *Democracy and Liberty*, cabinet edn. 2 vols. (1896; London, 1906), i, 435; FH, *The Times*, 27 Sept. 1909, 7a.
154. FH to EBH, letters 28 Sept. to 6 Oct. 1909, FC.
155. FH to EBH, letters 30 Sept. to 9 Oct. 1909, FC.
156. 'Peers Versus People', *PR* xxi (1910), 1–4.
157. FH to Goldwin Smith, 25 Jan. 1910, HC, cuttings from *Kent and Sussex Post*, 25 Jan., 5 Feb. 1910, copy of flyer, HC.
158. FH to Asquith, Jan. 1910, Bod. MS Asquith Papers 12, fols. 81–2, referring to *A Real Upper House* (London, 1910) from *ER* iv (1910), and proofs of *AM* ii, 217–39; Asquith to FH, 6 Jan. 1910, HC.
159. *The Times*, 13 Mar. 1911, 7a.
160. *The Times*, 10 May 1911, 12b; see Pliny's letter to Gallus beginning 'Miraris, cur me Laurentinum'.
161. 'The Two Coronations', *AM* i, 376–80, from *The Times*, 23 June 1911, 10d; FH to RH, 21 June 1911, HC.
162. Roy Jenkins, *Asquith* (London, 1964), Appendix A; FH to John Drinkwater, (Apr. 1913), YUL (quoted); Atkin to FH, 18 Sept. 1911, HC.
163. Lord Russell to FH, 1 Apr. 1896, 13 Jan. 1897, with FH note, HC.
164. Letters to FH from Shaw-Lefevre, Charles M. Reith (?) for the Lord Chancellor, and E. H. Pember, all 1906, HC; FH to Sir Frederick Macmillan, 12 Mar. 1911, BL, Add. MS 55037, fol. 32; *AM* ii, 244–50.
165. Edward A. Beck to FH, 24 Mar. 1905, A. W. Ward to FH, 19, 24 May 1905, HC.
166. P. A. Wright-Henderson to FH, 24 May 1910, HC; EBH to FH, 24 June 1910, FC; FH to Mrs Woods, 30 June 1907, Bod. MS don. d. 120.
167. FH to EBH, 22 June 1910, FC; FH to EBH, 23, 24 June (1910), HC; *The Times*, 24 June 1910, 4d; MS and typed copy of speech, 23 June 1910, HC; FH, 'A Socratic Dialogue', *CL* 174.
168. FH to EBH, 20 Mar., 25, 26, 27 June (1910), EBH to FH, 28 June 1910, FC; *The Journals of Lady Knightley of Fawsley*, ed. Julia Cartwright (London, 1915).
169. FH to EBH, 25, 27, 28 June 1910 and EBH to FH, 25, 26, 29 June 1910, FC.
170. ESB to FSM, 6 Apr. 1894, Bod. MS Eng. lett. c. 258, fols. 70–2; *The Times*, 2 Jan. 1897, 6c; Crackanthorpe, *Hubert Crackanthorpe*.
171. EBH to FH, 23 Sept. (1910), FC.
172. Letter signed, 'F. H.' in *The Times*, 9 June 1914, 10a, replying to 'F.R.C.S.' on 5 June 1915, 14e; for his rejoinder, see 11 June 1914, 9d-e; FH, *Review of Reviews* xxxv (1908), 143–4, xxxviii (1908), 525, 528; FH, 'Health', *PR* xvi (1908), 272–4.

173. FH to EBH and EBH to FH, 8 to 23 Aug. 1911, FC; FH, 'My Reisebilder—Old and New', *AMB* 357–59, from *NC and After*, lxx (1911); FH, *WG* 12 Oct. 1911; D. Mackenzie Wallace to FH, 17 Dec. 1911, HC (endorsing his account of the churches); Constance Battersea, *Reminiscences* (London, 1922), 320; *Letters and Friendships of Sir Cecil Spring-Rice: A Record*, ed. S. Gwynn, 2 vols. (London, 1929), ii, 144, 164–5.
174. FH to RH, 7, 19 Sept., 4 Oct. 1911, FC.
175. FH to EBH, 19, 24 June (1912), FC.
176. FH, *WG*, 15 Apr. 1912, 1c, 2a.
177. FH to Asquith, 28 Oct. 1913, Bod. MS Asquith Papers, 38, fols. 249–50; Asquith to FH, 30 Oct. 1913, HC; FH, *The Times*, 18 Nov. 1913, 5b; JM to FH, 28 Nov. 1913, HC; Edward David, ed., *Inside Asquith's Cabinet: from the Diaries of Charles Hobhouse* (New York, 1977), 151–2.
178. FH, *The Times*, 18 Feb. 1914, 9f; JM quoted in Sir Almeric Fitzroy, *Memoirs*, 2 vols. (New York, n.d.), ii, 536; see criticism *WG*, 18 Feb., 8a; FH's reply, 20 Feb., 3c, 21 Feb., 3a.
179. Pollard, *The Times*, 23 Mar. 1914, 5b; Hardy to FH, 23 Mar. 1914, UT; FH, *The Times*, 23 Mar. 1914, 5a, 27 Mar., 10d.
180. FH to Bryce, 22 Jan. 1914, Bod. Uncat. MS; Bryce to FH, 24 Jan. 1914, HC (agreeing); FH, *The Times*, 4 May 1914, 10b; see *The Political Diaries of C. P. Scott 1911–1928* (Ithaca, 1970), 85.
181. FH, '1913', op. cit.
182. Blunt, *My Diaries*, 755–6 (2 Mar. 1911) citing EBH on the luncheon.
183. Swinny to FSM, 25 Feb. 1911, Bod. MS Eng. lett. d. 261, fols. 38–41.
184. FH, 'The Declaration of London', *ER* vii (1911), 709–11, and in *The Times*, 14 Feb. 1911, 7a, 18 Feb., 6b; 25 Feb., 24c; and 'International Arbitration', *PR* xix (1911), 73–77.
185. FH, *The Times*, 1913; 26 Aug., 9de, 1 Oct., 13c, 14 Oct., 7f; FH, *WG*, 2 Oct. 1913, 3b.
186. FH, '1913', op. cit.
187. FH to RH, 31 July 1912, FH to EBH, 5, 6 July 1912, EBH to FH, 31 July (1913), FC.
188. FH to RH, 12, 26 Sept., 10, 31 Oct. 1912, 30 Jan., 27 Mar. 1913, 4 Jan. 1914, EBH to FH, undated and 1 Apr. (1913), FC; Jackson to FH, 5, 12 Aug. 1913, HC.
189. Letters to FH from Hugh Butler for the Lord Chancellor, 10, 16 Oct. 1912, 6 Feb. 1913, and from Lord Haversham, 24 Dec. 1912, HC; FH to RH, 27 Mar., 10 Apr. 1913, FC; FH, typescript, 'A Library', and Gosse to FH, 27 Dec. 1913, HC; 'An Old Garden City: In Praise of Bath', *Cornhill Magazine* cix (1914), 460–5.
190. FH to EBH, 31 Mar., 1, 2, 3, 4 Apr. (2 letters) (1913), FC.
191. FH to EBH, 27, 29 May, 30 July, 1, 2 Aug. 1913, and FH to RH, 27 Aug. 1913, FC; FH to Hardy, 20 Aug. 1913, Dorset County Museum.
192. FH to RH, 5 Sept., 9 Oct., 6 Nov. 1913, 12 Feb. 1914, EBH to FH, 5 Sept. 1913, FC.
193. FH, 'A Positivist Reception in Paris', *PR* xxii (1914), 186–7; *GP*, ch. xi, quoting diary, typed copy in HC.

Chapter 8. The Positivist as Man of Letters 1870–1914

1. FH to JM, 11 Jan. (1872), 4 Jan. (1873), Buchanan's flattering letters to FH, 16 Nov. 1871, 9 Mar., 4 Dec. 1893, 10 Feb., n.y., HC; Buchanan, 'Mr Morley's Essays', *CR* xvii (1871), 319–37; rpt. as 'A Young English Positivist', *Master-Spirits* (London, 1873), and 'The Fleshly School …', *CR* xviii (1871), 334–50.

2. *The Times*, 1873: 11 Jan, 5e, 13 Jan, 7b (FH); 11 Jan, 5e (ESB); 10 Jan, 5b (John Murray); Murray to FH, 27 Dec. 1906, HC; *AMB* 82, rpt. 'Great Biographies', *ER* x (1912).

3. *AM* ii, 106–7 (Browning), 115 (Meredith); FH to JM, 14 Jan. n.d., 27 Feb. 1874, HC; FH to A. Austin, 4 May 1909, YUL (Swinburne).

4. FH, *Pantheism and Cosmic Emotion: A Discourse …* (London, 1881), in *NC* x (1881), 284–95 and *CL*; FH to Conway, 26 May, 16 June 1881, Columbia U.

5. *CB*, ch. 1, from *FR* xxxi (1879); *The Times*, 20 Dec. 1878, 6c (on his London Institute lecture, MS in Bristol U.) and 7 Feb. 1879, 6b (WMC lecture, MS in HC); see also FH to JM, 18 Mar. 1871, HC.

6. *Letters of Alexander Macmillan*, ed. George A. Macmillan (Glasgow, 1908), 217 (quoted); agreement and FH letters, BL, Add. MS 55035, fols. 7–20.

7. *The Times*, 11 Jan. 1886, 8a, quoted passage not in *The Pleasures of Life*, reprinting 'On the Pleasure of Reading' from *CR* xl (1886).

8. FH, *FR* xlviii (1887), 591–3; see Martha S. Vogeler, 'The Victorians and the Hundred Best', *Texas Quarterly* xi (1968), 184–98.

9. *The Positivist Library of Auguste Comte*, trans. and ed. by FH (London, 1886), rpt. in *AMB*; FH to Lubbock, 16 July 1887, BL, Add. MS 49686, fol. 44.

10. *AM* ii, 138–42; *CB* 26–7; cp. *Polity*, i, 239.

11. *CB* 48–50; see also *AMB* 45–6; *DS* 121–5; typed copy, FH's letter to Gladstone and Gladstone to FH, 19 Jan. 1891, HC.

12. FH to EBH, 3 Feb. (1881), FC.

13. 'Froude's Life of Carlyle', *CB* 175–99, from *North American Review* cxl (1885).

14. FH to JM, 23 Oct. (1885), HC.

15. FH, 'Letters of Thomas Carlyle from 1826 to 1836', *NC* xxv (1889), 625–8; 'Charles Eliot Norton, 1827–1908', *AMB* 321–22, from *Cornhill Magazine* XXVI (1909).

16. FH, Introduction, *Essays by Thomas Carlyle*, Red Letter Library (London, 1904); see also his introduction to Carlyle's *Past and Present*, Shorter's 19th Century Classics (London, 1897).

17. FH to Lady Airlie, 23 June 1920, National Library of Scotland.

18. FH to Escott, 21 Dec. 1884, 11 Jan. 1885, BL, Add. MS 58781, fols. 64–5, 68; FH to Cross, 26 Dec. (1884), YUL.

19. FH to Escott, 1 Feb., 2 Mar. 1885, BL, Add. MS 58781, fols. 70–2; FH, 'Review of the Year: Newton Hall, 1 January 1885', *FR* xliii (1885), 177–96.

20. *CB* 203–30, from *FR* xliii (1885).
21. FH to JM, 23 Oct. (1885), HC.
22. Marghanita Laski, *George Eliot and Her World* (London, 1973), 112; *Henry James Letters*, ii, 337.
23. *Lord Carlingford's Journal: Reflections of a Cabinet Minister, 1885*, ed. A. B. Cooke and J. R. Vincent (Oxford, 1971), 145.
24. *PMG*, 2 Mar. 1886; *WR* cxxv (1886), 588; *Athenaeum* lxxxviii (20 Mar. 1886), 383–4; *The Critic* viii (10 Apr. 1886), 180; *Dial* vi (1886), 330; AH, *Frederic Harrison*, 122.
25. AH to EBH, (20 Nov. 1887), Jane Harrison to FH, 1 Mar. 1886, FC.
26. Paul Dubuisson to FH (30 May 1880), FC; *The Times*, 1891: 13 Apr., 7d; 22 Apr., 9e; 8 May, 11f.
27. *AM* ii, 84; FH to Gosse, 5 Jan. 1903, BLL; FH to Rosebery, 20 Jan. 1904, National Library of Scotland; FH to Graham Wallas, 30 Dec. 1902, LSE; Goschen to FH, 24 Jan. [1904], HC; FH to Wright, 29 Mar., 23 May (1908), London Library.
28. FH to Sir Robert Giffen, 1 Jan. 1904, Giffen Collection, ii, 63, LSE (quoted); Trevelyan to FH, 27 Feb. 1904, HC; FH to Gosse, 6 Jan. 1904, BLL.
29. Blanche E. C. Dugdale, *Arthur James Balfour*, 2 vols. (London, 1936), i, 189–90.
30. FH to Gosse, 5 Jan. 1903, BLL; *AMB* 385–94, from *The Times Lit. Supp.*, 18 Nov. 1909, 434–5; *The Times*, 21 June 1912, 4d.
31. Catherine Christie to FH, 2, 23 July, 29 Oct. 1906, 1 Feb. 1907, HC; FH to Miss Christie, 8 letters from 26 June 1906 to 18 Feb. 1907, and FH to Wright, 7 Nov. 1906, London Library; Maud Withers's memoir in *A Tardiness in Nature and Other Papers* by Mary E. Christie (Manchester 1907).
32. FH, *The Times*, 9 Oct. 1906, 10b, 26 Nov. 1907, 15e; J. Murray to FH, 27 Dec. 1906, and C. Moberly Bell to FH, 15 Sept. 1905, HC; FH to Macmillan, 14 Oct. 1906, 30 Apr. 1908, BL, Add. MS 55036, fols. 56, 135.
33. FH to JM, 3 Aug. 1892, HC; *The Times*, 5 Aug. 1892, 11ab; Richard Whittington-Egan and Geoffrey Smerdon, *The Quest of the Golden Boy* (London 1960), 192–4; *Pen Portraits and Reviews by Bernard Shaw* (London, 1931), 236–46.
34. *TRM* 186–98, from *CR* lxxvi (1899).
35. 'The Carlyle House', *MT* 90–5, from *Daily Chronicle*, 7 Dec. 1895, 5; Alexander Carlyle to FH, 2 Aug. 1906, HC, commenting on proofs.
36. *MT* 20–30, rpt. 'Literary and Municipal Problems in England', *Forum* xiv (1893).
37. FH to (E. T. Cook), 28 Apr. 1900, Ruskin Galleries, Bembridge School; G. Burne-Jones, printed letter, 8 Aug. 1900, HC; *The Times*, 23 Aug. 1900, 6e (G. Burne-Jones and O. Hill), 30 Aug. 1900, 4a (FH); Ruskin, *Works* xxxv, xlv–xlviii; James S. Dearden, ed., *The Professor, Arthur Severn's Memoir of John Ruskin* (London, 1967), 136–7.
38. *The Times*, 4 May 1904, 9f; FH, 'Sir Leslie Stephen', *RI* 378–89, partly in *MAJ*, from *Cornhill Magazine* lxxxix (1904); FH, review of F. W. Maitland's *Life* in *The Tribune*, 9 Nov. 1906; L. Stephen to FH, 31 May 1902, HC.

39. *AMB* 339–43; from *The Times*, 23 Nov. 1909, 14a; *AM* ii, 290.
40. FH to JM, 16, 31 Jan. 1891, HC; FH to Lubbock, 26 June 1891, BL, Add. MS 49651 (640B), fol. 112; Victor V. Branford, Introduction, *University of London (University Extension Lectures) Syllabus ... Sociology* (London, 1909); *The Daily News*, 30 June 1900.
41. FH to FSM, 10 Apr. 1890, 15, 17 Feb., 3 Apr. 1891, Bod. MS Eng. lett. d. 249, fols. 109–12, d. 251, fols. 49–57, 90–1; Murray to FSM (16 July 1885), e. 104, fols. 57–58; FH to Lady Mary Murray, 14 Jan. 1890, Bod. G. Murray MS 24; Gilbert Murray, *An Unfinished Autobiography ...* (London, 1960), 83, 86–7.
42. FH to JM, 30 June 1897, HC; FH to Murray, 23 Apr., 6 May 1896, Easter Sunday 1897, 18 Apr. 1908, Bod. G. Murray MS unclassified; Murray to FH, 24 Apr. 1897, HC; Murray typed letters to FSM, 4 Feb. 1909, Bod. MS Eng. lett. c. 259, fol. 16 (quoted).
43. *MT* 24–5, from 'Literary and Municipal Problems in England', op. cit.
44. *SEVL* 27–42, from 'The Decadence of Romance', *Forum* xv (1893).
45. *MT* 16 (quoted) from 'Formative Influences', *Forum* x (1890); typescript of address, 31 May 1890, HC.
46. MS in FC.
47. *The Times*, 31 May 1889, 12d; Ernest Vizetelly, *Emile Zola, Novelist and Reformer* (London, 1904), 256–98; F. W. J. Hemmings, *Emile Zola*, 2nd edn. (Oxford, 1966), 306.
48. GG to Algernon Gissing, 4 May 1881, Berg.
49. 'Parliamentary Affirmative Bill' and 'Punishment for Blasphemous Libel' (1 Mar., 27 July 1883), *Positivist Comments*; FH, *PMG*, 12, 14, 15 Mar. 1883.
50. FH to Hillemand, 14, 16 June 1896, MAC; *AM* ii, 49.
51. *MT* 253–8, from *PR* iii (1896); on Zola and Comte see René Ternois, *Zola et sa temps: Lourdes—Rome—Paris* (Paris 1961), 641–2; Vizetelly, *Emile Zola*, 502–3.
52. 'Zola's Paris', *PR* v (1898), 81–4; FH to JM, (12, 14 Apr. 1898), HC.
53. FH, *PR* x (1902), 247–8; *AM* ii, 49; Henri Mitterand, Introduction, Zola, *(Œuvres Completes*, 15 vols. (Paris, 1967–70), xiv; M. Le Bond, 'Les projets littéraires d'Emile Zola au moment de sa morte', *Mercure de France*, cxix (1927), 5–25.
54. *AM* ii, 45; FH to JM, 27 Feb. (1874), HC; FH to EBH, 26 Sept. (1896), FC.
55. FH to JM, 6 Feb. (1873), HC; Hirst, i, 214, 220–1; FH to EBH, Tues. (8 Oct., 1895), FC; *CB* 69.
56. FH to Grant Duff, 21 Mar. 1898, GD Papers, xix; Bernard Shaw, *Collected Letters 1898–1910*, ed. Dan H. Laurence (New York, 1972), 21.
57. EBH, 'Visits to Paris after the Great War', *Cornhill Magazine* xc (1904), 599–600; Tinayre to FH, 22 Oct. 1910, HC; FH to EBH, 22 Mar. 1910, FC; A. Keufer, 'M. Tinayre', *RO*, 2nd ser. xi (1895), 263–6; *CB* 69–70 and FH to EBH, 20 Sept. (1906) (on Feuillet), FC; Pater, *Appreciations ...* (London, 1910), 219.
58. *Polity*, i, ch. v; *SEVL* 1–42, from 'English Literature of the Victorian Age', *Forum* xvi (1894) and 'The Decadence of Romance', op. cit.

59. *CB* 291–300, rpt. 'The Aesthete', *PMG*, 3 May 1882, 301–8, rpt. 'At Burlington House', *PMG*, 23 May 1882; FH to JM, 19 May 1882, HC.
60. *MT* 325–47, rpt. 'A Few Words about Picture Exhibitions', *NC* xxiv (July 1888); *RI* 306–33, rpt. 'Decadence in Modern Art', and 'Art and Shoddy: A Reply to Criticisms', *Forum* xv (1893).
61. Herkomer to FH, 13 June 1893, HC; FH to Herkomer, 16 June 1893, in J. Saxon Mills, *Life of Herkomer* (London, 1923), 209–10; *MT* 355–68, rpt. 'A Morning at the Galleries', *FR* xxxv (1905) and 369–73, rpt. 'At Burlington House, Ancient Masters', *Observer*, 7 Jan. 1906, 4e; FH to Wemyss, 11, 16, 18, 26 May, 9 June 1905, Wemyss Collection; Wemyss to FH, 12, 20, 27 May 1905, HC.
62. *MT* 348–54, rpt. 'Nude Studies' (1885), *The Times*, 25 May 1885, 10de; RI 435–52, rpt. 'Paris in 1851 and 1907', *NC* lxii (1907); H. Ellis, *Studies in the Psychology of Sex*, 2 vols. (New York, 1936), ii, pt. iv, 94.
63. *AMB* 325–8, rpt. 'Aischro-Latreia: The Cult of the Foul', *NC* lxxi (1912); D. S. MacColl, ' "Ugliness", "Beauty", and Mr Frederic Harrison', *NC* lxxi (1912), 546–56; P. Burne-Jones to FH, 2 Apr. 1912 and W. B. Richmond to FH, n.d., HC; *The Nation*, 18 Jan., 1, 8, 15 Feb. 1913 (last two letters by L. Strachey and G. B. Shaw); FH, *MT* 337.
64. *SEVL* 196, 181–2, 222, 155, 150, 191, 210 quoted.
65. Dicey to FH, 29 July 1896, L. Stephen to FH, 22 Nov. (1895), Colvin to FH, 15 Nov. 1895, HC; Grant Duff, *Notes from a Diary, 1892–1895*, ii, 298.
66. *WR* cxlv (1896), 519–25; *Speaker* xiii (22 Aug. 1896), 201–2; Saintsbury's obit. of FH, *FR* cxix (1923), 374.
67. L. J. (?) Metcalf to FH, 7 Nov. 1889, HC; on the editor, Walter Hines Page, see FH, 'A Great American Ambassador', *PR* xxx (1922), 165–7.
68. FH to Macmillan, 13 Dec. 1894, 25, 28 Jan., 29 Dec. 1895, 4 Oct. 1899, BL, Add. MS 55035, fols. 95–104, 167–8; F. Macmillan to FH, 17 Dec. 1894 (letter press), MS 55446, fols. 738–9.
69. FH to Macmillan, 4 Oct. 1899, 12 Dec. 1897, 28 Oct. 1899, BL, Add. MS 55035, fols. 167–8, 141–4, 175.
70. *TRM* 11–12, 21–5.
71. AH, *Frederic Harrison*, 71.
72. *TRM* 77–104, rpt. 'Unto This Last: The Influence of John Ruskin', *NC* xxxviii (1895).
73. FH to JM, 22 Jan. 1896, HC; *TRM* 111–34, rpt. 'Matthew Arnold', *NC* xxxviii (1895).
74. *TRM* 135–58, rpt. 'J. A. Symonds', *NC* xxxix (1896); *AM* ii, 112; Brown, *John Addington Symonds, A Biography*, 2nd edn. (London, 1903), i, 296–7.
75. FH to H. Taylor, 13 June 1873, Mill-Taylor Collection, Vol. iii, item, no. 71, LSE; FH to JM, (2) June 1896, HC; *TRM* 285–322, rpt. 'John Stuart Mill', *NC* xl (1896).
76. FH to Gosse, Christmas Day, 1899, BLL.
77. *Polity*, i, 235; *TRM* 1–50.

78. FH, to Gosse, Christmas Day, 1899, BLL; FH, 'An Unknown Poet', *NC and After* lxiv (1908), 803–10; Luce to FH, 15, 20 Aug. 1908, 18 Mar. 1909, HC; FH to Lord Tennyson, 7 Feb. 1911, City of Lincoln Public Library.

79. *WG*, 30 Sept. 1910; *Saturday Westminster Gazette*, 12 Nov. 1910 (cutting in HC); cuttings of letters by others, HC.

80. Hallam Tennyson, *Alfred Lord Tennyson, A Memoir by his Son*, 2 vols. in one (London, 1905), ii, 414.

81. 'Musical Assonance: Analysis of a sentence in Letter to Mr Ruskin by F. H. Fortnightly Review', undated MS, HC.

82. *TRM* 61–6, rpt. 'Ruskin as Master of Prose', *NC* xxxviii (1895).

83. *TRM* 159–77, rpt. 'On English Prose', *NC* xliii (1898).

84. JM to FH, 21 June 1873, HC, and Apr. 1873, in Hirst, i, 240; FH to JM, 2 Apr. 1874, HC; *Henry James Letters*, ii, 212, on Mrs Hertz's salon.

85. AH, *Frederic Harrison*, 153; Morgan, *The House of Macmillan*, 148–50; FH to JM, 18 Aug. (1898), HC; Metcalf, *James Knowles*, ch. 2; Hewlett to FH, 14 letters beginning 24 Aug. 1898, many undated, HC; 3 letters, 1899, to FH in *The Letters of Maurice Hewlett…*, ed. Laurence Binyon (London, 1926), 46, 53–4; Hewlett's Diary, typed, BL, Add. MS 41075, fol. 57; FH, *Academy* lx (5 Jan. 1901), 60; 'Maurice Hewlett', *FR* lxxv (1901), 61–71; *MT* 245–52, rpt. 'Ecco La Toscana!', *Speaker* xi (31 Dec. 1904) and 164–72, rpt. 'Maurice Hewlett', *Tribune*, 27 Feb. 1906, 2de.

86. *RI* 290–4, rpt. 'The Revival of the Drama', *Forum* xvi (1893).

87. *FR* lxxv (1904), 191–2.

88. Lillah McCarthy to FH, n.d., HC; FH to EBH, Tues. (12 Apr.) 1898, FC; *AM* i, 58.

89. Tree to FH, 7 letters, Jan. 1898–30 Sept. 1908, HC; FH to EBH, 2 Oct. 1894 (on *Hamlet*), EBH to FH, 24 Jan. 1899 (on Barrie), 12 Sept. 1908 (on Tree), FC.

90. FH to Gosse, 2 Jan. 1900, BLL; Colvin to FH, 30 Dec. 1899, Phillips to FH, n.d., HC; FH to Sidney Lee, 31 Jan. 1902, Bod. MS Eng. misc. d. 177, fol. 328.

91. FH to Jones, 10 Oct. 1900, 24 Jan. 1904, BBL.

92. *The Times*, 20 June 1902, 7d, Lawrence Alma-Tadema to FH, 16 June 1902, HC; *The Times*, 14 Feb. 1912, 10c; Phillpotts to FH, 15, 20 Feb., 1 Apr. 1912, HC; FH to Phillpotts, 18 Feb., 30 Mar. 1912, UT.

93. *The Bodley Head Bernard Shaw Collected Plays with their Prefaces*, 7 vols., ed. Dan H. Laurence (London, 1970–74), ii, 776, iii, 598, iv, 135, v, 395; FH, *MT* 360.

94. GBS to J. G. Links, 20 July 1943, ANS privately owned, Bernard Shaw Text 1984 The Trustees of the British Museum, The Governors and Guardians of the National Gallery of Ireland and Royal Academy of Dramatic Art; *Mrs Warren's Profession*, ed. Margot Peters, Bernard Shaw Early Texts: Play Manuscripts in Facsimile, General Ed. Dan H. Laurence (New York, 1981); *The Letters of Sidney and Beatrice Webb*, i, 14 Sept. 1891, B. Potter, on such a visit.

95. FH to Gosse, 7 Nov. 1897, BLL.

96. FH, Introduction to *The Warden* (London, 1906) and to *Phineas Finn and Phineas Redux*, 2 vols. in one (London, 1911).

97. *MT* 134–49, from *Harper's Monthly Magazine* ciii (1901); Cross to FH, 18 Apr. 1901, Gertrude Lewes to FH, 26 Apr. 1901, HC.

98. *PR* x (1902), 159–62; Stephen to FH, 31 May, 29 Nov. 1902, HC.

99. *CL* 16–17; *AM* i, 204, ii, 108–10.

100. *Spectator* lxxxiv (13 Jan. 1900), 54–5; FH, *Speaker*, n.s. v/vi (30 Nov. 1901), 256–7; *MT* 31–46, from *North American Review* clxxvi (1903); *AMB* 284–96, from 'The Centenary of Tennyson', *NC and After* lxvi (1909).

101. *A Victorian Diarist; Later Extracts from the Journals of Lady Monkswell*, ed. E. C. F. Collier (London, 1946), 162–3; FH to Hichens, 20 Sept., 6, 9 Nov. 1890, and note by H[allam] T[ennyson] saying 'F. H. has invented. In fact it is a d–d lie—"why is the pilot spelt with a big P" is always my answer to these fools', YUL.

102. FH to Mrs Severn, 25, 29 Sept., 11 Oct. 1898, JRL; FH to EBH 6, 7 Oct. 1898.

103. *Literature* vi (3 Feb. 1900), 105.

104. *The Times*, 9 Feb. 1900, 15f.

105. FH to Lee, 9 Aug. 1901, Bod. MS Eng. misc. d. 177, fols. 326–7.

106. FH to Mrs Severn, 21 Jan. 1899, Viljoen Collection; George Allen to FH, 11 Oct., 20 Dec. 1895, 26 Jan. 1899, and to Lady Galloway, 14 letters, 1899, George Allen Archives, microfilm (Chadwyck-Healey/Somerset House) reels, 2, 4.

107. FH, *JR* 61, 153, 155, citing Bardoux, *Le Mouvement idéaliste et social dans la littérature anglaise au XIXe siècle: John Ruskin* (Paris 1901); FH, 'A French Study of British Jingoism', *The Tribune*, 20 June 1906, on Bardoux, *Essai d'une psychologie de l'Angleterre contemporaine: Les crises belliqueuses* (Paris, 1906); Bardoux, *Memories of Oxford*, trans. W. R. Barker, preface by Margaret L. Woods (London, 1899); Bardoux to FH, 30 Mar. n.d., 12 July 1902, HC.

108. FH to Wemyss, 29 July 1901, Wemyss Collection.

109. FH to EBH, 24 Jan. 1899, FC; Norton to FH, 12 Aug. 1901, HC; *JR* 55–7.

110. Hirst, ii, 82.

111. William Morton Payne, *Dial* xxxiv (L Mar. 1903), 145–7, quoted; *The Athenaeum* mdcccii (4 Oct. 1902), 443–4; *Spectator* xxix (25 Oct. 1902), 609–10; *St. George* v (1902), 311–12; Louis Baraduc to FH, 6 letters, 4 May 1903 to 31 Mar. 1912, HC.

112. *Tribune*, 15 Jan. 1906 (rpt. in *MT* 150–63), 27 Mar., 7 May, 11 June 1906; *AMB* 308–13, review of E. T. Cook, *The Life of John Ruskin*, from *ER* x (1911).

113. Cook to FH, 30 Jan. 1907, HC.

114. FH to Gosse, 18 Apr. 1896, BL, Add. Ashley MS 5739, fols. 195–6.

115. *Poems by A. and L.* (London, 1897), containing extracts from comments by Meredith and Browning and from FH's 'Appreciation' in Louisa Shore's *Poems* (London, 1897); Grant Richards's Archives, microfilm

(Chadwyck-Healey/Somerset House), showing that Arabella Shore paid for the publication of this and later volumes.

116. *NC* xxv (1889), 215–21; FH to Mrs Woods, letters from 25 Dec. 1888 to 30 June 1907, Bod. MS don. 120, fols. 48–53, 56–9, 60–3, 71; Mrs Woods to FH, 27 Dec. (1888), 10, 23 Jan., 12 July and n.d. (1889), HC.

117. FH, *Daily Graphic*, 8 Jan. 1890; 'France in 1789 and 1889', *MH* 217–18, from *Forum* x (1890); Betham-Edwards to FH, 16 Feb., 2 Mar. 1890, 2 Oct. (1911), HC; FH to Betham-Edwards, 30 May, 28 Sept. 1907, 6 Apr. 1914, BLL; FH, 'Introduction', *Mid-Victorian Memories of Matilda Betham-Edwards* (New York, 1919), and *PR* xxvii (1919), 39–41, obit. by FH.

118. George Du Maurier to FH, 9 Aug. 1894, HC; *AM* ii, 109.

119. FH to Hardy, 12, 15 June 1885, Dorset County Museum (hereafter cited as 'DCM'); Hardy to FH, 17 June 1885, *The Collected Letters of Thomas Hardy*, Vol. i (1840–1892), ed. Richard Little Purdy and Michael Millgate (Oxford, 1978), 134–5; Florence Emily Hardy, *The Life of Thomas Hardy, 1840–1928* (1962; rpt. New York, 1965), 220, 416; Lennart A. Björk, 'Hardy's Reading', in *Thomas Hardy the Writer and His Background*, ed. Norman Page (New York, 1980), 103–27, summarizing evidence in *The Literary Notes of Thomas Hardy*, 2 vols. ed. Björk, vol. i (Göteborg, 1974).

120. Walter F. Wright, *The Shaping of The 'Dynasts'* (Lincoln, Neb., 1967), 29–30.

121. FH to Hardy, 1 June 1888, DCM.

122. FH to Hardy, 29 Dec. 1891, DCM.

123. FH to Hardy, 15 June 1885, DCM; Hardy to FH, 1 Jan. 1892, *The Collected Letters of Thomas Hardy*, i, 251; Florence Emily Hardy, *The Life*, 146.

124. FH to EBH, 2 Aug. 1913, FC.

125. FH to Hardy, 27 July 1901, DCM.

126. FH to Hardy, 20 Sept. 1913, 13 Feb. 1914, DCM.

127. FH to Hardy, 21 Oct. 1906, 10 Nov. 1913, DCM.

128. AH, *Frederic Harrison*, 82–3; GG, *Family Letters*, 121–3; Royal A. Gettmann, *A Study of the Bentley Papers* (Cambridge, 1960), 215–20.

129. AH, 'Memories of Gissing: London Rambles with my Unconventional Tutor', *T.P.'s and Cassell's Weekly*, 24 Apr. 1926, 23; AH, 'George Gissing', op. cit., GG, *London Diary*, 17; GG to EBH, 21 Apr. 1891, CPL; GG to Algernon, 22 Nov. 1892, Berg.

130. GG to FH, 7 Nov. 1895, CPL; FH to GG, 10 Nov. 1895, C. C. Kohler Collection.

131. GG, *London Diary*, 427.

132. Ibid., 414.

133. Ibid., 420; GG to Algernon Gissing, 27 Aug., 1896, Berg; AH, 'George Gissing', op. cit., 462.

134. GG, *London Diary*, 420; AH, 'George Gissing', op. cit., 456.

135. GG to FH, 11 Feb. 1903, CPL.

136. GG to AH, 3 June 1903, CPL.
137. FH to Wells, 27 Jan. 1904, in Gettmann, *George Gissing and H. G. Wells*, 229–30.
138. FH to Wells, 4 Feb. 1904, in Gettmann, *George Gissing and H. G. Wells*, 231–3.
139. Wells to FH, 20 Mar. 1904, HC.
140. Wells to FH, 6 Feb. 1904, HC; Paul F. Mattheisen and Arthur C. Young, 'Gissing, Gosse, and the Civil List', *Victorian Newsletter*, xxxii (1967), 11–16.
141. FH to Gosse, Mar. 1904, BBL; EBH to Wells, 12 Feb. 1904, U. of Illinois.
142. Gosse to FH, 28 Mar. 1904, HC; FH to Gosse, 2 Apr. 1904, BLL.
143. Wells, 'George Gissing: An Impression', Gettmann, *George Gissing and H. G. Wells*, Appendix D.
144. FH to Wells, 8 May (p.c.), 9 Aug. 1904, U. of Illinois; FH to Shorter, 9 Aug. 1904, BLL.
145. FH, untitled preface to *Veranilda* (London, 1904).
146. Shorter in *The Sphere*, 6, 13 Aug. 1904, 134, 156; Pierre Coustillas, 'The Stormy Publication of Gissing's *Veranilda*', *Bulletin of the New York Public Library* lxxii (1968), 588–610.
147. FH to Wells, 9 Aug. 1904, U. of Illinois; FH to Shorter, 9 Aug. 1904, BLL, and in *The Sphere*, 20 Aug. 1904, 178; FH to Algernon Gissing, 13 Oct. 1904, P. Coustillas Collection.
148. FH, 'George Gissing's *Veranilda*', *PR* xi (1904), 261–2.
149. Percy Withers to FH, 10 Apr. 1912, HC; *WG*, 7 Mar. 1913, 3b (appeal signed by Withers, Wells, Herford, and others, but not FH); Francis Noel Lees, *TLS*, 3 Dec. 1971, 296–7.
150. AH, 'George Gissing', op. cit., 'Signposts of Fiction', *CR* cxxviii (1925), 82–9, 'Memories of Gissing …', op. cit., *Frederic Harrison*, 80–4, 89, 110–12.
151. Swinnerton, *George Gissing: A Critical Study*, 3rd edn. (Port Washington, 1966), Preface, 30–5; Wells's article in Gettmann, *George Gissing and H. G. Wells*, Appendix D; A. C. Gissing, 'Gissing's Unfinished Romance', *National Review* cviii (1937), 82–91 and 'Frederic Harrison and George Gissing', typescript, 1938, CPL.
152. H. G. Wells, *Experiment in Autobiography* (New York, 1934), 484; see also 477, 481–93.
153. Ibid., chs. 1–6 (calling Collins a second-generation Positivist); Geoffrey West, *H. G. Wells: A Sketch for a Portrait* (London, 1930), 74–6; Patrick Parrinder, ed., *H. G. Wells: The Critical Heritage* (London and Boston, 1972), 2.
154. FH to Wells, 19 Nov., 15 Dec. 1903, U. of Illinois; Swinny in *PR* x (1903), 275ff.
155. FH to Wells, 5 Oct. 1904, U. of Illinois.
156. FH to Wells, 15 Apr. 1905, U. of Illinois.
157. Wells, 'The So-Called Science of Sociology', and 'Discussion', 26 Feb. 1906, *Sociological Papers*, iii, 357–77; *Experiment in Autobiography*, 561–2.

158. FH to Bentley, 29 Apr. 1889, 16 Nov. 1893, U. of Illinois.
159. EBH, 'Our Village: Poor Neighbours', *Temple Bar*, cv, 98–106; 'The Woodman', cix (1896), 91–9; 'Our Village: The Stranger', xxiv (1898), 417–28.
160. FH to Bentley, 14 Aug., 3 Sept. 1894, U. of Illinois.
161. See FH's bibliography of her publications, *PR* xxiv (1916), 178–9.
162. EBH to FSM, 6 Apr. 1894, Bod. MS Eng. lett. c. 258, fols. 70–2.
163. FH to Macmillan, letters 1906–8 and 1911, BL, Add. MS 55036–7; FH to EBH, 25 Sept. 1906, FC.
164. FH to Macmillan, 19 Sept. 1907, 15 Jan. 1908, BL, Add. MS 55036, fols. 117, 128; F. W. Maitland, *The Life and Letters of Leslie Stephen* (London, 1906), 360.
165. *MAJ* 5 (quoted).
166. FH to Macmillan, Dec. 1908, BL, Add. MS 55036, fols. 150–1; 24 Sept. 1909, Add. MS 55037, fol. 9.
167. FH to Macmillan, letters, Sept. 1909–Aug. 1911, BL, Add. MS 55037, letter of 18 Jan. 1911, fol. 30 quoted; Macmillan letter book, letters to FH, MS 55497, fols. 986, 1050; MS 55498, fols. 1133, 1279, 1318, 1999; MS 55499, fols. 640–1, 697.
168. FH to Gosse, 8 Dec. 1907, 28 June 1909, BLL; Gosse to FH, 30 June 1909, HC.
169. Gosse in *ER* x (1911), 708–11; FH to Gosse, 2 July 1909, 17, 21 Nov. 1910, BLL; FH to Macmillan, 17 Nov. 1911, BL, Add. MS 55037, fol. 43.
170. FH to Macmillan, 22 Nov. 1911, BL, Add. MS 55037, fol. 44; see also *Times Lit. Supp.*, 19 Oct. 1911, 393, and cuttings of reviews, HC.
171. FH to Macmillan, 2, 6, 7, 9 Feb., 13 Apr. 1912, BL, Add. MS 55037, fols. 46–52.
172. *AMB* 5, 46, 63, 166 (quotations).
173. FH to Macmillan, 14 July 1912, BL, Add. MS 55037, fol. 62.
174. Harris, 'Talks with Carlyle', *ER* vii (1911), 419–34; 'Thoughts on Morals', viii (1911), 434–43; *Spectator* cvi (19 June 1911), 875–6; '*The Spectator*: A Reply', *ER* viii (1911), 666–70; FH to RH, 21 June 1911, FC.
175. AH, *Frederic Harrison*, 126–9; AH, 'The Puntilla', *ER* iv (1910), 208–22.
176. AH to FH, 7, 8, 25 Apr. 1912, FC.
177. FH to RH, Christmas Eve, 1913, FC.

Chapter 9. The Positivist as Historian 1880–1914

1. MS in HC.
2. *AM* i, 79.
3. *Letters of Charles Eliot Norton*, ed. S. Norton and M. A. De Wolfe Howe, 2 vols. (Boston, 1913), ii, 313.
4. Raymond Blathwayt, 'The Writing and Teaching of History: A Talk with Mr Frederic Harrison', *Great Thoughts* x (10 July 1897), 232–3.

5. e.g., 'The Place of History in Education', lecture, Working Men's College, 18 Dec. 1880, MS Bristol U.; *The Times*, 17 Jan. 1880, 12b, lecture at the London Institution, and 15 Oct. 1888, 6c, at Toynbee Hall.

6. *SEVL* 84.

7. *MH* 146–79, rpt. 'A Survey of the Thirteenth Century', *FR* lvi (1891); Pollock, 'Frederic Harrison, Jurist and Historian', *ER* xxxvi (1923), 411; Fitzroy, *Memoirs*, 2 vols. (London, n.d.), ii, 792; FH to Hillemand, 10 Dec. 1891, MAC.

8. *CB* 391–414, from a London Institution address, in *North American Review* cxxxviii (1883); *MH* 180–216, rpt. 'What the Revolution of 1789 Did', *FR* xlv (1889) and 217–32, rpt. 'France in 1789 and 1889', *Forum* ix (1890); 'The Centenary of the Bastille', *CR* lvi (1889), 194–206; *The Times*, 2 Jan. 1889, 6a, a Newton Hall address.

9. AH, *Frederic Harrison*, 199.

10. FH to George L. Craik or 'Dear Sir', 20 Dec. 1888 to 10 Feb. 1893, BL, Add. MS 55035, fols. 29–67.

11. FH to Macmillan, letters 12 Apr. to 26 June 1899, BL, Add. MS 55035, fols. 153–65.

12. *RI* 467–83, from *NC* xxviii (1890).

13. *RI* 453–66, rpt. 'Give Back the Elgin Marbles', *NC* xxviii (1890); Sophie Tricoupis to FH, 14 letters 1890 to 1909, HC.

14. 'The Joke about the Elgin Marbles', *NC* xxix (1891), 495–506; Knowles to Gladstone, 1 Jan. 1891, cited in Metcalf, *James Knowles*, 345.

15. FH to Knowles, 4, 7 Mar. 1891 (copies), Knowles to FH, 7, 9 Mar. 1891, FC.

16. Knowles to Huxley, 26 Mar. 1891, Imperial College; FH, 'Editorial Horseplay', *FR* lv (1891), 642–55; *PMG*, 2 Apr. 1891.

17. Press cuttings and Huxley to FH, 28 Mar. 1891, HC; FH to Huxley, 2 Apr. 1891, Imperial College.

18. Curzon 'A Suggestion on the Elgin Marbles', *FR* lv (1891), 833–5; Cockerell to FH, 20 Apr. 1891 and Gennadius to FH, 14 Dec. 1890, 10 Jan. 1891, HC.

19. *MH* 478–507, rpt. 'A Pedantic Nuisance', *NC* xix (1886).

20. 'Things, Names and Letters', *CR* xlix (1886), 546–59.

21. 'A Few More Words about Names', *NC* xix (1886), 664–72; Sir William Smith (ed. of the *Quarterly Review* and a neighbour in Westbourne Terrace) to FH, 5 June 1886, HC (commending the article); *MT* 260–71, part from *PR* vi (1898) (on 'England' in preference to 'Britain') and *The Times*, 7 June 1910, 13d (FH on 'bust').

22. *MH* 124–45, rpt. 'The Royal Road to History, an Oxford Dialogue', *FR* lx (1893).

23. FH to JM, 11 Sept. 1894, Rosebery Papers, National Library of Scotland, Edinburgh; JM to FH, 15 Sept. 1894, HC.

24. JM to Rosebery, 17 Sept. 1894 (with 'You need not return F.H.' written on the top) and Rosebery to JM, 29 Sept. 1894, Rosebery Papers, National Library of Scotland, Edinburgh.

25. FH to JM, 20 Sept., 3 Oct. 1894, HC.

26. FH to JM, 9 Jan. 1895, HC.
27. JM to FH, 7 Aug. 1905, 30 Dec. 1913, HC; *Frederick York Powell; A Life and a Selection from his Letters and Occasional Writings*, ed. Oliver Elton, 2 vols. (Oxford, 1906), i, 189.
28. *TRM* 235–56, rpt. 'The Historical Method of J. A. Froude', *NC* xliv (1898), and 257–84, rpt. 'The Historical Method of Professor Freeman', *NC* xliv (1898); *MT* 96–102, rpt. 'Scientific History' from *The Tribune*, 27 Jan. 1906.
29. J. H. Round, 'Historical Research', *NC* xliv (1898), 1004–14.
30. *Polity*, iii, 1, 261–2, 335.
31. *AM* ii, 93; Bryce to FH, 4 July 1894, HC.
32. FH to JM, 1 July 1894, HC (on returning to the *NC*); *MT* 77–89, rpt. 'The Centenary of Edward Gibbon', *NC* xxxvi (1894); *Frederick York Powell*, ii, 25–6; *AM* ii, 94–5.
33. FH to Grant Duff, 31 Oct. 1894, Grant Duff Papers, i; FH to John Murray, 9 Apr., 21 May 1895, Murray Archives; FH to (Clement Shorter), 12 Nov. 1894, BBL; Lord Sheffield to FH, 5, 8, 12, 17 Jan. 1907 and Murray to FH, 27 Dec. 1906, 8 Jan. 1907, HC.
34. *Royal Historical Society, Proceedings of the Gibbon Commemoration, 1794–1894* (London, 1895); *AM* ii, 94.
35. *Seventy Years … Lady Gregory*, 274–5.
36. *The Times*, 24 Nov. 1894, 12a; R. A. Humphreys, *The Royal Historical Society, 1868–1968* (London, 1969), 25; *Gibbon Commemoration*, 8–9; FH to (C. Shorter), 1 Dec. 1894, BBL; Richard Garnett to FH, 11 Dec. 1894, Grant Duff to FH, 23 Jan. 1895, HC.
37. Leighton to FH, 17 Nov. 1894, HC; FH to unnamed, 13 Dec. 1894, UT; FH to Canon Farrar, 9 Oct. 1894, NYPL; FH to Guy Le Strange, 21 Mar. 1895, Fitzwilliam Museum; FH to Murray, 5 letters, 14 Nov. 1894 to 12 June 1895, John Murray Archives; *AM* ii, 93–5.
38. FH to Murray, 15 letters, 12 June to 25 Sept. 1895, Murray Archives, *AM* ii, 93.
39. FH to Murray, 12 letters, 17 Oct. 1895 to 11 June 1898, Murray Archives; Murray to FH, 21 Dec. 1896, HC; *TRM* 199–216, from *Forum* xxii (1897) and 217–34, from *Forum* xxiii (1897); FH, *Literature*, 11 June 1898, 672–3.
40. *AM* i, 269–70, ii, 291; *MT* 47–54, rpt. 'Millenary of King Alfred', *PR* vi (1898); *The Times*, 1897: 20 Nov., 10a, 25 Nov., 8d; FH to Mrs Severn (n.d.) 1898 (quoted), JRL; FH to JM, 24 Nov. 1897, HC; FH to Acton, 24 Nov. 1897, 8 Jan. 1898, CUL; FH to Lord Tennyson, 12 Dec. 1897, YUL; FH to Bryce, 18 Jan., 29 Mar. (1898), Bod. Uncat. MS, and letters to FH from Lords Russell and Brassey, Dean Bradley, Burne-Jones, York Powell, M. Creighton, Bryce, HC.
41. FH to Grant Duff, 28 Nov., 6 Dec. 1897, 2 Jan. 1898, Grant Duff Papers xix; Grant Duff to FH, 4 Dec. 1897, HC.
42. *The Times*, 1898: 19 Feb., 13cd, 19 Mar., 10ab.
43. Thornycroft to FH, 6 Nov. 1898, 2, 24, 28 Jan. 1899, HC.

44. *The Times*, 15 July 1901, 7e; *George Washington and Other American Addresses*, chs. 3–4.
45. *The Hampshire Chronicle*, 21 Sept. 1901; *The Times*, 1901: 19 Sept. 8ab, 20 Sept., 4cd, 21 Sept., 10ad; FH, 'The Historical Alfred', *PR* x (1902), 220–2 (quoted); papers in the Hampshire Record Office and City Archives, Winchester, and in BL.
46. *Alfred the Great Containing Chapters on his Life and Times*, ed. Alfred Bowker (London, 1899); FH to Hardy, 6 Dec. 1898, DCM; candlestick owned by FH's descendants.
47. FH, 'A Proposal for a New Historical Bibliography', *Trans. Royal Hist. Soc.*, n.s. xi (London, 1897), 19–30; C. W. Crawley, 'Sir George Prothero and His Circle', ibid., 5th ser. xx (London, 1920), 110–12; Humphreys, *The Royal Historical Society*, 27–33, 66; H. E. Wortham, *Oscar Browning* (London, 1927), 131.
48. Acton to FH, 21, 27 Nov., 3 Dec. 1896, HC; FH to Acton, 25 Nov., 4 Dec. 1896, CUL.
49. FH to Acton, 22, 28 Dec. 1898, 27 Apr., 1 May 1899, CUL; Acton to FH, 23 Jan. 1898, 21, 28 Mar. 1899, HC.
50. FH to Acton, 14 July 1900, CUL.
51. FH, 'Law of Three Stages', *PR* xxi (1913), 145–51.
52. FH to Acton, 25 Nov. 1896, CUL.
53. Gertrude Himmelfarb, *Lord Acton: A Study in Conscience and Politics* (Chicago, 1952), 224 (Acton's letter), 227 (the contributors).
54. *MH* 233–64; *The Times*, 15 Nov. 1886, 6e (reporting the address).
55. *MH* 387–414, 'Paris as an Historic City', a lecture; 415–32, rpt. 'The Transformation of Paris', *North American Review* cxlix (1889); *RI* 419–34, rpt. 'The Municipal Museums of Paris', *FR* lxii (1894).
56. *MH* 298–323, lectures mentioned by FH to John Gennadius, 9 Jan. 1891, Gennadius Library, American School of Classical Studies, Athens; FH to A. Hichens, 6 Nov. 1890, YUL.
57. *MH* 265–97, rpt. 'Rome Revisited', *FR* lix (1893).
58. *MH* 324–57, rpt. 'Constantinople as an Historic City', *FR* lxi (1894); 358–86 rpt. 'The Problem of Constantinople', *FR* lxi (1894); FH to EBH, 10 Oct. (1890), FC.
59. *Athenaeum* civ (8 Dec. 1894), 785; *Spectator* lxxiv (26 Jan. 1895), 108–9; *Academy* xlvi (1 Dec. 1894), 441–2; *WR* cxliii (1895), 107–9; J. B. Bury to FH, 6 May 1894, HC.
60. W. Chawnet, 25 Jan. 1900, HC; *AM* ii, 292–3; *AMB* 180–231, rpt. *Byzantine History in the Early Middle Ages. The Rede Lecture ... 12 June 1900* (London, 1900); Bury to FH, 11 July (1900), HC.
61. FH to Gosse, 23 Apr. 1901, BLL; see also FH to Gilder, 1 Apr. 1902, CM 710, Huntington Library; *SEVL* 215–16.
62. 'Notes' in *Theophano: A Crusade of the Tenth Century* (London, 1904); FH to EBH, 4, 7 Apr. 1903, FC; Fisher, *Speaker*, n.s. ii (30 June 1900), 360–1; Bury to FH, 3, 7 Apr. 1904, HC.
63. FH to (Algernon) Gissing, 13 Oct. 1904, transcript from P. Coustillas.

64. Meredith, *Collected Letters*, iii, 1665; *Friends of a Lifetime: Letters to Sydney Carlyle Cockerell*, ed. Viola Meynell (London, 1940), 170–1; *The Letters of Maurice Hewlett*, 76–8; Hardy to FH, 24 Jan. 1904, UT; Bryce to FH, 5 Oct. 1903, HC; JM, *NC* lvi (1904), 571–90; FH to EBH (15 Sept. 1904) and Sophie Tricoupis to FH, 2 pc, 9, 15 Aug. 1905 about publication in *Neon Asty*, from Athens, and copies of *Patris*, from Bucharest, containing instalments, FC.

65. *Times Lit. Supp.*, 7 Oct. 1904, 302.

66. FH to Murray, 18 Aug. 1908, Bod. G.M. MS 24; FH to Austin, 4 May 1909, YUL; Hardy to FH, 30 Dec. 1905, UT; letters to FH in HC from EBH, 19 Apr. (1905), Henry Arthur Jones, 7 Dec. 1905, Galsworthy, 18 Mar. 1911, Lillah Granville Barker, 16 Mar. 1911, C. Vaughan, 8 Dec. 1914, Sir John Martin Harvey, 4 Feb., 6 Mar. 1912; Blunt, *My Diaries*, ii, 130.

67. Richard Raubusch to FH, 8, 19 Dec. 1911, 30 Oct. 1912, HC; typescript of libretto in English and of reading text used at the Royal Theatre, Bath, HC; Betham-Edwards, *Mid-Victorian Memories*, 24–5.

68. *Times Lit. Supp.* 13 July 1906, 248; *Tribune*, 6 Apr. 1906, 2b (review by W. Archer); FH to [?] Stuart, 20 Feb. 1906, UT.

69. FH, Preface, *New Calendar ...* (London, 1892); FH to Laffitte (1 Sept. 1891) and to Dr Hillemand, 23 Sept. 1891, MAC.

70. *WG* cxxxvii (1892), 338; *Nation* liv (21 Jan. 1892), 54–5; *Times Lit. Supp.* 25 Nov. 1920, 769ab.

71. Hardy to FH, New Year's Day 1892, UT; *PMG*, 5 Feb. 1892; EBH to FSM, 13 Jan. 1892, Bod. MS Eng. lett. d. 252, fols. 13–14 (identifying Allen as author); JM, *NC* xxxi (1892), 312–28; JM's annotated copy in Manchester U. Library.

72. Sarton, 'Auguste Comte, Historian of Science', *Osiris* x (1952), 328–57.

73. *PR* x (1901), 159.

74. Correspondence from JHB, Gasquet, Steele, and others, Oxford University Press archives; Fr. F. A. Gasquet, 'An Unpublished Fragment of a Work by Roger Bacon', *English Historical Review* xii (1897), 494–517.

75. *PR* v (1897), 178–92; FH to Dr Hillemand, 27 May 1898, MAC; FH to JM (Oct. 1897), HC.

76. Liveing, *A Nineteenth-Century Teacher*, 238–40 (quoted); JHB letters, Oxford University Press archives.

77. FH to JM, 23 Oct. 1885, HC.

78. FH to Laffitte, 31 Dec. 1889, MAC (denying he meant his book to fulfil Comte's request to Congreve).

79. *OC* 30, 222; *AM* i, 54; FH to JM, 23 Oct. 1885, HC; receipt from FH, BL, Add. MS 55035, fol. 26; FH, 'Cromwell's Toleration', *The Jewish Historical Society of England, Trans.* iii, sessions 1896–8 (Edinburgh and London, 1899), 101.

80. JM to FH, 9 Apr. 1888, HC; JM's copy is in U. of Manchester Library.

81. Gladstone's copy is at St. Deiniol's Library, Hawarden.

82. Grant Duff, *Notes from a Diary, 1889–1891*, 2 vols. (London, 1901), ii, 76; *The Private Diaries of the Rt. Hon. Sir Algernon West*, ed. Horace G. Hutchinson (London, 1922), 348–9; FH, *The Times*, 6 Dec. 1922, 10c.

83. Gardiner, *Academy* xxxiv (28 July 1888), 48–9; cp. *Spectator* lxi (16 June 1888), 882–3, attributed by FH to Ludlow, 'furious enemy of "Comtism" ' and 'sort of Ironsides himself' (FH to JM, (June), 1888, HC); W. E. Hoare, *Notes* ... (Madras, 1890); B. Sen and S. C. Maulik, *A Key to* ... (Calcutta, 1894).

84. *English Historical Review* vi (1891), 781–5, x (1895), 374–8, xv (1900), 377–9, xvii (1902), 584–6, xviii (1903), 169–71, xxv (1910), 177–81; *AMB* 361–75, rpt. 'Mr Firth's Cromwell', *Cornhill Magazine* lxxxiii (1900), 169–78; *Speaker*, n.s. iv (20 July 1901), 443–4; Firth to FH, 7, 15 Nov. 1909, 20 Oct. 1912, HC.

85. FH to Trevelyan, 30 May 1897, Trevelyan Papers 123, U. of Newcastle-upon-Tyne; FH to JM, 26 Apr. 1898, and 2 undated, HC.

86. *Hansard*, 4th ser. xxxiv (17 June 1895), cols. 1341–62; N. Waterfield (for Rosebery) to FH, 13 Nov. 1895, HC.

87. *MT* 64–70, rpt. 'Oliver Cromwell', *Speaker*, n.s. i (18 Nov. 1899), 167–9; *Daily Chronicle*, 4 July 1895.

88. FH to Mrs Hertz (16 Nov. 1899), HC; *The Times*, 15 Nov. 1899, 9cd.

89. *OC* 36–7; *MT* 71–6, rpt. 'The Remains of Oliver Cromwell', *Daily Chronicle*, 26 Oct. 1895; *AM* ii, 101, n. 1.

90. *The Times*, 1911: 18, 24 Apr., 6b, 7d (FH), 7, 14 Apr., 14c, 9d (Henry A. Howorth), 20 Apr., 7e (quoted); letters to FH from J. E. C. Welldon, 22, 25 Aug. 1905, Howorth, undated, and Marquis of Ripon, 28 Apr. 1909, HC; Welldon, *NC* lviii (1905), 928–47.

91. *AMB* 363 (on Morley's); *Speaker*, n.s. iii (6 Oct. 1900), 22–3 (on Roosevelt's), vi (12 Apr. 1902), 48–9 (on Butler), (19 Apr., 3 May 1902), 73, 142 (Mrs Marks), (26 Apr., 1902), 112 (FH on Mrs Marks); FH to Bentley, 28 Apr. 1894, U. of Illinois.

92. Drinkwater to FH, 3 Feb. 1912, 2 Jan., 9 Dec. 1913, HC; FH to Drinkwater, 9 letters, 29 Jan. 1912 to 13 May 1914, YUL; Drinkwater, *Oliver Cromwell and Other Poems* (1913) and *Cromwell: A Character Study* (1927).

93. FH to Macmillan, 3 June 1896, BL, Add. MS 55035, fol. 109; Horace Rumbold to FH, 8 Oct. 1895, HC; FH to EBH, 7, 8, 12, 13 Oct. (1895), FC; FH to FSM, 26 Apr. 1896, Bod. MS Eng. lett. e. 110, fols. 82–3; *AM* ii, 292.

94. FH to JM, 29 July 1897, HC.

95. Putnam to FH, 7 June, 18 Sept. (?1898), HC.

96. FH to Macmillan, 20, 25 Sept., 2 Oct., 1 Nov., 12 Dec. 1897, BL, Add. MS 55035, fols. 125–7, 132–3, 140–4; P. J. Blok, *Willem I, Prins van Oranje* (s'Gravenhage (1898)); FH to Dutch Ambassador in London, 17, 25, 28 Sept. 1897, Government Archives, the Hague.

97. Oscar Browning, *Memories of Later Years* (London, 1923), 47–9.

98. FH to EBH, 31 Aug., 1, 2, 5 Sept. 1898, HC, in *AM* ii, 149–53 (with changes).

99. FH to EBH, 6, 7, 8, 10 Sept. 1898, HC, part in *AM* ii, 152–3.
100. *AM* ii, 154–9, rpt. *The Times*, 13 Sept. 1898, 11ef, and 161–4, rpt. 'Netherland and Orange', *PR* vi (1898); FH to Blunt, 22 Sept. (1899), WSRO.
101. FH to Macmillan, 15 Mar. 1904, BL, Add. MS 55036, fol. 25.
102. Ibid., 24 Aug. 1904, fols. 30–1; *Life and Letters of Lady Dorothy Nevill*, 242 (letter dated 18 Oct. 1904).
103. *Life and Letters of Lady Dorothy Nevill*, 243 (letter dated 7 Dec. 1904); FH to Norton, 4 June 1904, Harvard U.
104. *Chatham*, 87–8, 141, 79, 209–10; FH, 'The American Revolution, part II', *Independent Review* ii (1904), 162–8; G. M. Trevelyan to FH, 31 Jan. 1904, HC (saying FH had understood the book's 'main motive').
105. FH to Macmillan, 6 Apr. 1905, BL, Add. MS 66036, fol. 42.
106. *Trans. Royal Hist. Soc.*, 3rd ser. iii (London, 1909), 33–49; *AMB* 251–62; FH to EBH, 24 Apr. (1905), FC.
107. *AMB* 263–75, rpt. review from *Daily Chronicle*, 22 Nov. 1910.
108. *The Times*, 6 Dec. 1917, 1a, on the marriage, at St. Stephen's, Gloucester Road.
109. FH to 'My dear daughter', June 1918, FC; *The Letters of Lady Harriot Eliot, 1766–1786*, ed. Cuthbert Headlam (Edinburgh 1914), copy in FC; *Letters Relating to the Love Episode of William Pitt ...* (London, 1900), copy in FC and rpt. in Rosebery's *Miscellanies Literary and Historical*, 2 vols. (London (1921)), 7–15, from correspondence now in BL, Add. MS 59704.

Chapter 10. The Positivist as Prophet 1914–1923

1. *FH to Hardy, 22 Aug. 1914, DCM; JM to FH, 18 Jan. 1914, HC.*
2. *AH, 'Frederic Harrison', Encyclopaedia Britannica, 13th edn. (1927).*
3. *PR* xxiii (1914), 199–200.
4. *GP* 256–62.
5. *The Meaning of the War: For Labour—Freedom—Country* (London, 1914); Macmillan MS, BL, Add. MS 55037, fol. 73.
6. *King Albert's Book: A Tribute to the Belgian King and People from Representative Men and Women Throughout the World* (London, 1914), 28; *The Book of Italy*, ed. Raffaello Piccoli (London (1916)), 25.
7. EBH to FH, Thurs. (10 Dec. 1914), FC; *GP* 237–8, rpt. with changes, *The Times*, 31 Aug. 1914, 9d.
8. *Letters of Henry James*, ed. Lubbock, ii, 398.
9. *GP* 238.
10. *The Times*, 1915: 10 Mar., 11e, 16 Mar., 7e (FH), 11 Mar., 9e (Herbert Stephen); 12 Mar., 9d, 18 Mar., 8b (FH, excerpts in *GP* 240–2).
11. *GP* 245–52, letter in the *Morning Post*, rpt. in *King's College School Magazine*, n.s. xvi (1914), 28–9; L. T. Hobhouse, *The Nation*, 14 Nov. 1914, 202 adding names of FSM and Raynor Storr to the list; *The New York Times, Current History of the European War*, i, *What Men of Letters Say* (New York, 1914), 82–6.

12. FH to Brentano, 3, 18 Jan. 1912, Brentano Papers, Bundesarchiv, Coblenz, lxxii, fols. 45–8; Brentano to FH, 7 Jan. 1912, HC.
13. *King's College School Magazine*, n.s. x (1918), 15–16.
14. Arthur Marwick, *The Deluge: British Society and the First World War* (Boston and Toronto, 1965), 131–2, on the great influence of the report.
15. *The Times*, 27 May 1915, 4a; S. H. Swinny, 'In Memoriam: Lieut. C. R. Harrison', *PR* xxiii (1915), 165; *Journal of the Royal Institute of British Architects* xxii, 3rd ser. (1915), 396, 404; AH, *Frederic Harrison*, 41; FH to Dr Hillemand, 24 May 1915, MAC.
16. FH to Rosebery, 29 May, 4 June 1915, and transcription of the telegram, National Library of Scotland, Edinburgh; the Marquess of Crewe, *Lord Rosebery*, 2 vols. (London, 1931), ii, 654–5.
17. FH to Bryce, 3 June 1915, Bod. Uncat. MS (quoted); FH to Sidney Lee, 12 June 1915, Bod. MS Eng. Misc. d. 177, fols. 337–8; *The Times*, 1915: 18 May, 8e, 29 May 6cd.
18. Lyulph Stanley (now Lord Sheffield) to FH, 20 July 1915, ESB Collection, item 31, UC; James to FH, 3 June 1915, UT; FH to James, 23 June 1915, Harvard U.
19. *The Times*, 29 May 1915, 7de.
20. *The Times*, 14 May 1915, 8cd; Lt. Col. Charles à Court Repington, *The First World War 1914–1918*, 2 vols. (London, 1920), i, 34–41; FH to Rosebery, 31 Aug. 1916, National Library of Scotland, Edinburgh (saying he trusted Repington).
21. *The Times*, 1915: 10 Sept. 9f, 11 Sept., 9ab; FH to G. Prothero, 12 Sept. 1915, PP. 3/4/1, Royal Historical Society.
22. FH to Rosebery, 5 Aug. 1915, National Library of Scotland, Edinburgh.
23. FH to Rosebery, 29 Apr. 1916, National Library of Scotland, Edinburgh.
24. FH to Prothero, 12 Sept. 1915, PP3/4/1, Royal Historical Society; EBH, *The Times*, 20 Aug. 1915, 9c.
25. *GP* 16; *The Political Journals of C. P. Scott, 1911–1928*, ed. Trevor Wilson (New York, 1970), 358 (Scott to Hobhouse, 13 Oct. 1918).
26. *The Times*, 1916: 24 Jan., 9c, 3 Mar., 9c.
27. 'The War of Liberation: Do it Now', *ER* xxiv (1917), 132–8.
28. FH to Rosebery, 24 Jan. 1917, National Library of Scotland, Edinburgh.
29. *ObS* 89–92, rpt. 'Obiter Scripta', *FR* cix (1918).
30. FH to Rosebery, 17 July 1916, National Library of Scotland, Edinburgh; *The Times*, 27 Oct. 1916, 7d; *The New York Times*, 18 May 1917, 6ef; *ObS*, 59, rpt. *FR* cix (1918).
31. *The Times*, 18 Aug. 1917, 9d.
32. *The Times*, 1917: 9 Oct., 3b, 19 Oct. 5d; FH to Bryce, 30 Oct. 1917, Bod. Uncat. MS.
33. ESB, *The Times*, 5 Aug. 1914, in *PR* xxiii (1914), 215.
34. *PR* xxiii (1915), 169–78, 208–14, 242–8; *Wadham College Gazette* (1915), 382–3; *The Times*, 9 July 1915, 11d.
35. FH to Alfred Beesly, 22 July 1915, ESB Collection, UC.
36. EBH to Marie Harrison, 7 May (1916), R. A. Harrison Collection; FH to Ivy Tennyson, 15 June 1916, Sir Charles Tennyson Collection.

37. *The Times*, 7 June 1916, ia; FH to Prothero, 21 June 1916, PP 1/8/10, Royal Historical Society; *PR* xxiv (1916), 162–77, 210–11; FH to FSM, 10, 28 Oct. 1916, Bod. MS Eng. lett. c. 263, fols. 209–10, 221–2; *Ethelbertha Harrison, 1851–1916* (privately printed, 1917) and in *PR* xxiv (1916).
38. FH to Corra, 27 Mar. 1914, Archives Nationales 17 AS 1, dossier 3, BN; FH to FSM, 10 Oct. 1916, Bod. MS Eng. lett. c. 263, fols. 209–210.
39. *PR* xxviii (1920), 148–52; FH to Lady Davey, 7 Oct. 1917, HC.
40. FH to Mrs Daffarn, 20 June 1917, UT, about visiting Lady Davey.
41. FH to Macmillan, 26 June 1918, BL, Add. MS 55037, fol. 83.
42. (Virginia Woolf), *Times Lit. Supp.*, 17 July 1919, 386.
43. *ObS* 5–8, 178–82, 11–14, 70, 53–5, 183–7; FH to Rosebery, 27 Jan. 1918, National Library of Scotland, Edinburgh; FH to Gosse, 21 Jan. 1917, BLL.
44. *The Times*, 1918: 7 Sept., 4f, 12 Oct., 8e, 15 Oct., 8e.
45. *OS* 190; FH to Rosebery, 26 Sept. 1918, National Library of Scotland, Edinburgh; *The Times* 5 Nov. 1918, 8d; FH, *Support the Coalition*, in FSM Collection, MS Eng. lett. c. 265, fol. 212.
46. FH to Blunt, 9 Dec. 1918, WSRO; Henry R. Winkler, *The League of Nations Movement in Great Britain 1914–1919* (1952; rpt. Metuchen, N.J., 1967), 152–4; John Casson, *Lewis and Sybil: A Memoir* (London, 1972), 78; *The Times*, 1918: 6 Dec., 10f; 7 Dec., 10e; 10 Dec., 9e; 30 Dec. election supp., iiie; Swinny, 'In Memoriam: Philip Thomas', *PR* xxix (1921), 43–5; L. Macneill Weir, *The Tragedy of Ramsay MacDonald* (London, 1938), 32.
47. 'Peace with Justice', *PR* xxvii (1919), 127–9, rpt. *Daily Chronicle*, 8 May 1919.
48. 'Pessimist and Optimist: A Conversation at a London Club', *NC and After* lxxxv (1919), 1077–87.
49. *NV* 11–14, 22–3, 40–9, 56–8.
50. *NV* 189–203; FH to Rosebery, 15 July 1920, National Library of Scotland, Edinburgh; FH, *The Times*, 12 Mar. 1921, 6b (on reforming the House of Lords).
51. FH to Curzon, 21 Sept. 1919, Beaverbrook Library; FH to Prothero, 29 Oct. 1919, PP 1/11/9, Royal Historical Society, about *Home Rule Through Devolution*, by Frederic W. Pim (London, 1919); Curzon to FH, 20 [?error for 21] Sept. 1919, HC; FH to Rosebery, 16 Dec. 1919, National Library of Scotland, Edinburgh.
52. *The Times*, 1921: 15 Dec., 5b–d; 16 Dec., 6c; FH, 14 Jan. 1922, 11e–12f.
53. *DS* 162–5, from the *Manchester Guardian*; FH to Gooch, 19 Oct. 1919, Courtney Collection, item 34, fol. 55, LSE; FH to Prothero, 29 Oct. 1919, PP 1/11/9, Royal Historical Society; *A Veteran's Appeal to Labour Leaders ... from the 'Daily Chronicle'* (London, 1920).
54. *The Times*, 1920, 2 Mar., 13f, 9 Mar., 13d, 1 May, 9d.
55. *The Times*, 1921: 1 Apr., 4e (FH), 4 Apr., 6f (Hyndman).
56. *NV* 109 (Inge), 27–34 (Hardy); W. R. Inge, *Diary of a Dean* (New York, 1950), 57 (on FH); Hardy, 'Apology', dated Feb. 1922, *Collected Poems*, ed. James Gibson (London, 1976), 556–62.

57. FH to Hardy, 23 May 1922, DCM; Hardy to FH, 24 May 1922, UT.
58. *NV* 71–7.
59. FH to FSM, 22 Apr. 1920, Bod. MS Eng. lett. c. 267, fol. 23 (quoted); Bury to FH, 29 Oct., [?] Nov. 1909, 16 June, 12 Oct. 1912, HC; FH, 'The Idea of Progress', *PR* xxviii (1920), 121–4; J. B. Bury, *A History of the Freedom of Thought* (New York and London, 1913), 186.
60. *PR* xxviii (1920), 9–11; *The Times*, 28 July 1921, 12a; *NV* 166–8.
61. *NV* 163–4; FH to Haldane, 4 Jan. 1919, National Library of Scotland.
62. *PR* xxvi (1918), 223–5.
63. 'A Very Invisible God', *NC and After* lxxxii (1917), 771–81.
64. P. Thomas, 'Kingston Church of Humanity', *PR* xxv (1917), 273; FH to FSM, Easter Mon. 1919, Bod. MS Eng. lett. c. 266, fols. 68–9.
65. FH to Wells, 25 Jan. 1922, U. of Illinois.
66. FH to Gosse (20 June), 1920, BLL.
67. FH to Rosebery, fragment (12 Oct. 1920?), National Library of Scotland, Edinburgh; Muriel Harris, 'Frederic Harrison at Ninety', op. cit.; *NV* 95–8.
68. *DeS* 23–54, from *The Times*, 5 July, 1921 (Oxford), 24, 26 Sept. 1921 (travel), 7 Apr. 1922 (Victorian types); *The Times* 20 May, 1919, 8f (cricket), 4 Oct. 1920, 13d (Henry Cunningham), 6 Feb. 1922, 6a (Bryce), 1 June, 1922, 8b (links with the past), 15 Sept. 1922, 13c (Robert H. Codrington).
69. C. M. Bowra, *Memories, 1898–1939* (Cambridge, Mass., 1967), 137–8.
70. FH to Macmillan, 8 Nov. 1921, BL, Add. MS 55037, fol. 117.
71. *PR* xxvii (1919), 92; *DeS*, 55–78, rpt. 'The City of Constantinople', *FR* cxi (1919), MS in Bristol U. Library, 166–201, rpt. 'A Philosophic Synthesis', *PR* xxviii (1920).
72. *The Times*, 1922: 7 June, 15f, 21 June, 10b, 29 Aug., 13f.
73. *The Times*, 21 Aug. 1919, 6a; see also 23 Aug. 1922, 11b, proposing a Latin motto for Britain's airmen.
74. FH to Rosebery, 2 May 1920, National Library of Scotland, Edinburgh; see also *The Times*, 1920: 7 July, 10b, 13 July, 8d, 15 July, 10c, on Abbey restoration.
75. Francis Younghusband to FH, 30 Nov. 1912, 29 Jan. 1913, HC.
76. Minutes of the Socratic Society, Bath Public Reference Library.
77. *DeS* 121–61; *NV* 15–16; FH, *PR*, xvii (1919), 280–1.
78. FH letters, 23 May, 23, 24, 27 Oct. 1919, City of Coventry Libraries.
79. FH letters to Henry Chappell and copies of Chappell's works, Bath Public Reference Library; holograph of poem quoted, HC.
80. *The Times*, 1921: 18 Oct., 13e, 19 Oct., 12c, 26 Oct. 15e; *Bath and Wilts. Chronicle*, 18 Oct. 1921; *PR* xxix (1921), 257–8; Harold Spender, *The Fire of Life* (London (1926)), 299.
81. *Bath and Wilts. Chronicle*, 23 Nov. 1921; scroll and FH's reply, *The City of Bath, An Appreciation* (pamphlet), Guildhall archives, Bath; Lloyd George to FH, 22 Dec. 1920, FH to Lloyd George, 26 Dec. 1920 (copy), FC.
82. *NV* 87–90; Zangwill, 'The World and the Jews', *ER* xxx (1920), 64–7 and in *FR* cxiii (1920), 176 (on FH); FH to Gosse (June 1920), BLL.

83. FH to Eversley, 5 Jan. 1923, R. Austin Harrison Collection.
84. *The Times*, 22 Sept. 1922, 11e.
85. Eversley to FH, 11 Oct. 1922, HC.
86. FH to Eversley, 5 Jan. 1923, R. Austin Harrison Collection.
87. FH, *The Times*, 21 Oct. 1918, 9c; FH to Ivy Tennyson, 4 Nov. 1918, Sir Charles Tennyson Collection; Muriel Harris, *Living Age* cclxxxxviii (1918), 682–4, 809–10, cclxxxxix (1919), 755–7; Sir Charles Tennyson, *Stars and Markets* (London, 1957), 122–3.
88. FH, *Times Lit. Supp.*, 30 Oct. 1919, 611 (quoted); *The Times*, 6 Dec. 1922, 10c (on West); FH to 'Dear Sir', 21 Oct. 1919, Lilly Library, Indiana U.; *Mid-Victorian Memories … Betham-Edwards*, vi; *Times Lit. Supp.*, 1919: 6 Nov., 631 (Luce), 13 Nov., 65 (FH); see also Walter Crane to FH, 28 Oct. 1907, HC.
89. FH to Sir Frederick Macmillan, 2 Feb., 4 Oct. 1922, BL, Add. MS 55037, fols. 121–7; FH to Prof. Amaranatha Jha, 17 May, 1922, ibid., fol. 124; Jha published *Selected Essays, Literary and Historical* (London, 1925).
90. *DeS* 1–22, rpt. 'A Dialogue in a College Garden', *NC and After* xc (1921).
91. AH, *Frederic Harrison*, 202–3.
92. *The Pollock-Holmes Letters*, ii, 109–11; Minutes, Socratic Society, 5 Jan. 1923.
93. Spender, *The Fire of Life*, 299; FSM, *PR* xxxi (1923), 30–1 and intro. to *DeS*; *The Times*, 15 Jan. 1923, 7c (on Treloar), 10f (FH); AH, *Frederic Harrison*, 221; AH to Hardy, 30 Jan. 1923, DCM.
94. *The Times*, 1923: 15 Jan., 11c, 12cd, 16 Jan., 16c (unsigned letter) and 17 Jan., 12d (William Stebbing); *Manchester Guardian*, 19 Jan. 1923; T. P. O'Connor, *Daily Telegraph*, 15 Jan. 1923; *Country Life*, liii (20 Jan. 1923), 69; Gould, *Sociological Review* xv (1923), 158; Pollock, *ER* xxxvi (1923), 410–13 (his South Place Address); Saintsbury, *FR* cxix (1923), 374–81; Birrell to Ivy Tennyson, 21 Jan. 1923, U. of Liverpool.
95. *The Times*, 20 Jan. 1923, 11b.
96. Ibid., 19 Mar., 1923, 9d; *PR* xxxi (1923), 75–7, 88–9.
97. *The Times*, 24 Jan. 1923, 13c; Minutes of the Socratic Society, Bath Reference Library; see also *The Times*, 23 May 1923, 9g; Chivers to GH and Olive Harrison, undated, 1923, HC (about a portrait of FH painted from a photograph by Margaret Deborah Cookesley, now at the Guildhall, Bath).
98. *The Times*, 7 June 1923, 17c; correspondence about urn and typed copy of addresses, HC; Bowra, *Memories, 1898–1939*, 147.
99. *The Times*, 11 June 1923, 15d; GH to Haldane, 12 June 1923, National Library of Scotland, Edinburgh; GH to BH, 30 Apr. 1923, HC; FH to Murray, 31 Aug. 1918, Bod. MS G.M. 24.
100. FH, *PR* xxix (1921), 258.

INDEX

The following entries are selective only: Edward Spencer Beesly, John Henry Bridges, Auguste Comte, Ethel Bertha Harrison, Frederic Harrison, John Morley, and the 559 'Worthies' of Comte's Calendar.

DATE DUE
